Roadfood

BROADWAY BOOKS ✳ New York

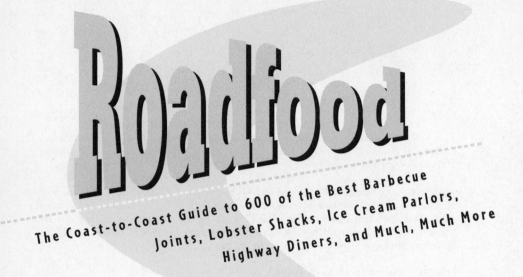

Roadfood

The Coast-to-Coast Guide to 600 of the Best Barbecue
Joints, Lobster Shacks, Ice Cream Parlors,
Highway Diners, and Much, Much More

Jane and Michael Stern

This book was originally published by Random House in 1978 and 1980, and a subsequent edition was published in 1992 by HarperCollins, and a revised edition was published in 2002 by Broadway Books.

PRINTED IN THE UNITED STATES OF AMERICA

BROADWAY BOOKS and its logo, a letter B bisected on the diagonal, are trademarks of Broadway Books, a division of Random House, Inc.

Visit our website at www.broadwaybooks.com

First Broadway Books trade paperback edition published 2002

Designed by Caroline Cunningham
Maps designed by Jeffrey L. Ward

Library of Congress Cataloging-in-Publication Data

Stern, Jane.
    Roadfood : the coast-to-coast guide to 600 of the best barbecue joints, lobster shacks, ice cream parlors, highway diners, and much, much more / Jane and Michael Stern.
        p. cm.
Includes index.
        1. Restaurants—United States—Guidebooks.   I. Stern, Michael, 1946–   II. Title.

    TX901.2.S839 2005
    647.9573—dc22

                                                                    2004057149

ISBN 0-7679-2264-6

10   9   8   7   6   5   4   3   2   1

Acknowledgments

We personally eat in every Roadfood restaurant we recommend, but we never would have found them all without tips, suggestions, exhortations, and directions from other travelers devoted to the pursuit of good food. To all who have helped us in our pursuit, we raise a glass of cool, pre-sweetened ice tea in thanks.

We are deeply grateful to the Rushmore family—Steve Sr., Stephen, Kristin Little, and Cindy—as well as Marc Bruno for inviting us to come along on what has proven to be the excellent adventure of creating *www.roadfood.com* in cyberspace. Roadfood never had such good and devoted advocates, and such enthusiastic appetites!

To our colleagues and constructive critics at *Gourmet* magazine we are especially grateful for providing such a stimulating environment for our "Roadfood" column every month, and for encouraging us to go farther, eat more, and write better. Our own life on the road is deeply enriched by our knowing that we are writing stories to be read and edited by visionaries who include Ruth Reichl, Doc Willoughby, Bill Sertl, and James Rodewald.

Our editor, Jennifer Josephy, and literary agent, Doe Coover, have enabled us to spend the vast majority of our time eating and writing rather than worrying about the intricacies of publishing.

Finally, we thank those people who take care of our animals at home when we are away: Jean Wagner and Marybeth Gruber for watching over Lewis, Elmer, and Clementine, and Mary Ann Rudolph and Ned Schankman for keeping our equine pals KT and Piegan fat and happy.

Contents

Southwest   431

West Coast   511

Introduction to Roadfood 2005

When we wrote the first edition of *Roadfood* nearly thirty years ago, we believed we were documenting the end of an era. Good, inexpensive food served in colorful places along the road seemed to be a thing of the past, and we saw a bleak future of soulless franchised restaurants from coast to coast. While there is no denying the awful ubiquity of national chains and their depredations against good eating (not to mention their uglification of the landscape), we are happy to report that delicious regional food is alive and thriving.

We know this because our *Roadfood* files keep growing, and we have enough enticing tips to keep us hunting good meals for a couple of lifetimes. One-third of the six hundred restaurants in this new edition were not in the previous one, published in 2002. Eating around the USA in the last three years, we have found more opportunities to eat well than time and appetite allow. (And we have eaten in every *Roadfood* restaurant ourselves.)

While this book is bigger than previous editions, we had to drop nearly one hundred listings to make room for new discoveries. Some needed to be removed because they're gone, at least as we knew them. RIP, Aunt Eunice of Huntsville and your glorious Country Kitchen, M&J

of Albuquerque, and The Tuba City Truck Stop! Some others were eliminated because they're not as good as they used to be, and some we've cut just because we haven't visited them recently enough to remain confident our review still holds true.

The criteria for inclusion in *Roadfood* are simple. We want to direct readers to restaurants that express the soul of their region or neighborhood, primarily by serving wonderful food you won't find elsewhere. We love places where locals come to eat, whether that's Pastrami Queen of New York City, Mamie's Biscuits outside Atlanta, Gnaw Bone Food and Fuel in Southern Indiana, or a tiny chili parlor called El Farolito in El Rito, New Mexico. Restaurants earn high marks on the Roadfood scale if they serve their good food in a location or manner that's unique to the area—a wharfside lobster pound in Maine (page 30) or an Oyster market along Highway 101 on the Oregon coast (page 546), a drive-in custard stand in Milwaukee (page 393) or a meat-market barbecue in Texas Hill Country where butcher paper is used in lieu of plates and the brisket's tenderness makes utensils superfluous (page 481).

With few exceptions, Roadfood is cheap. That's because it is the people's food. As much as we might appreciate a dress-up dinner cooked by a master chef who should rightfully be called a gastronomic artist, *Roadfood* is based on the proposition that America's truly great meals are sleeves-up fare, no reservations required. We have come to believe that this nation's culinary gift is like our other contributions to world culture—jazz, blues, movies: a democratic experience enjoyed every bit as much by ordinary folks as by connoisseurs. At its best Roadfood is an edible folk art.

Aside from America's newfound appreciation of its regional specialties, one of the other advances in civilization, at least as we've known it over the last few decades, is the ability to amplify that appreciation on the Internet. Please join us at Roadfood.com, where you can read reviews of our latest finds—as well as post your own reviews, pictures, and opinions—in a community of passionate eaters. Or write us at Broadway Books, 1745 Broadway, New York, NY 10019. We welcome suggestions for new places to eat, as well as comments, critiques, and kudos on the restaurants in this book.

We hope to see you on down the road one morning over biscuits, donuts, muffins, cinnamon rolls, sticky buns, or beignets. Please pass the gravy!

—Jane and Michael Stern

Notes About Using This Book

✴ If you are planning a special trip to any restaurant in this book, *please* call ahead to make certain it is open and is serving what you want to eat. Hours of operation change over the course of the year and proprietors sometimes go fishing. Our notation of BLD, meaning breakfast, lunch, and dinner, can mean different times in different places. For instance, many Heartland restaurants do serve dinner, but the dinner hour can end as early as seven o'clock. Also, some specialties are seasonal. (When calling, be aware that telephone area codes are changing all the time.)

✴ The vast majority of Roadfood restaurants require no reservations and are come-as-you-are. Some pricier ones do have a dress code and a few require a reservation. We've made note of which ones get insanely crowded, and what you can do about it. But again, if in doubt, please call ahead.

✴ Our approximate cost guide for one full meal is as follows:
    ✴ $ = under $10
    ✴ $$ = between $10 and $25
    ✴ $$$ = over $25

New England

Connecticut * Maine * Massachusetts *

New Hampshire * Rhode Island * Vermont

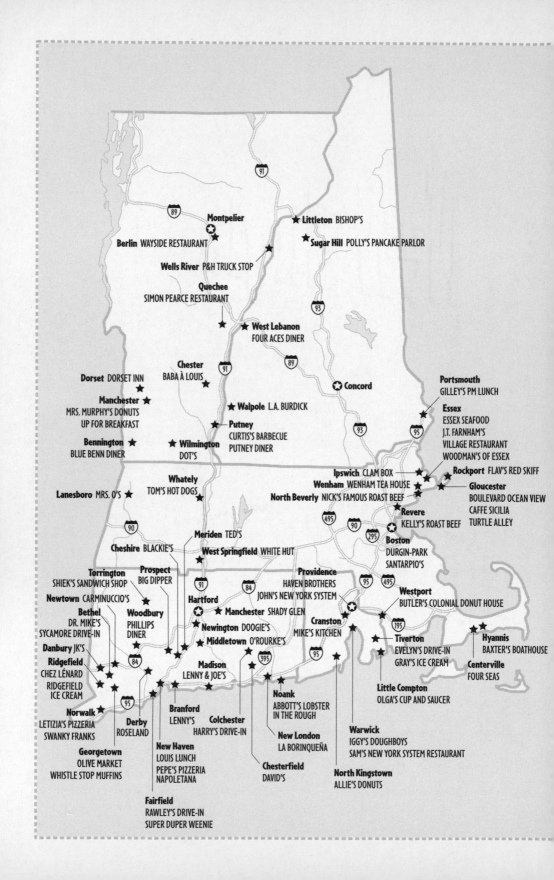

Montpelier

Berlin WAYSIDE RESTAURANT

Littleton BISHOP'S

Sugar Hill POLLY'S PANCAKE PARLOR

Wells River P&H TRUCK STOP

Quechee
SIMON PEARCE RESTAURANT

West Lebanon
FOUR ACES DINER

Chester
BABA À LOUIS

Concord

Portsmouth
GILLEY'S PM LUNCH

Dorset DORSET INN

Manchester
MRS. MURPHY'S DONUTS
UP FOR BREAKFAST

Walpole L.A. BURDICK

Essex
ESSEX SEAFOOD
J.T. FARNHAM'S
VILLAGE RESTAURANT
WOODMAN'S OF ESSEX

Putney
CURTIS'S BARBECUE
PUTNEY DINER

Bennington
BLUE BENN DINER

Wilmington
DOT'S

Ipswich CLAM BOX   **Rockport** FLAV'S RED SKIFF
Wenham WENHAM TEA HOUSE
North Beverly NICK'S FAMOUS ROAST BEEF   **Gloucester**
Whately   BOULEVARD OCEAN VIEW
TOM'S HOT DOGS   CAFFE SICILIA
Lanesboro MRS. O'S   TURTLE ALLEY

Revere
KELLY'S ROAST BEEF

Meriden TED'S

Cheshire BLACKIE'S   **West Springfield** WHITE HUT   **Boston**
                                                                DURGIN-PARK
                                                                SANTARPIO'S

Torrington   **Prospect**   **Providence**
SHIEK'S SANDWICH SHOP   BIG DIPPER   HAVEN BROTHERS   **Westport**
                                              JOHN'S NEW YORK SYSTEM   BUTLER'S COLONIAL DONUT HOUSE
Newtown CARMINUCCIO'S

Bethel   **Hartford**
DR. MIKE'S   **Manchester** SHADY GLEN
SYCAMORE DRIVE-IN
                Woodbury   **Cranston**   **Hyannis**
Danbury JK'S PHILLIPS   **Newington** DOOGIE'S   MIKE'S KITCHEN   BAXTER'S BOATHOUSE
                  DINER   **Middletown** O'ROURKE'S   **Tiverton**
Ridgefield   EVELYN'S DRIVE-IN   **Centerville**
CHEZ LÉNARD   GRAY'S ICE CREAM   FOUR SEAS
RIDGEFIELD   **Madison**
ICE CREAM   LENNY & JOE'S   **Little Compton**
                                                            OLGA'S CUP AND SAUCER
Norwalk
LETIZIA'S PIZZERIA   **Branford**
SWANKY FRANKS   LENNY'S   **Noank**
                                      ABBOTT'S LOBSTER
         Derby   **Colchester**   IN THE ROUGH   **Warwick**
         ROSELAND   HARRY'S DRIVE-IN   IGGY'S DOUGHBOYS
                                      New London   SAM'S NEW YORK SYSTEM RESTAURANT
Georgetown   **New Haven**   LA BORINQUEÑA
OLIVE MARKET   LOUIS LUNCH
WHISTLE STOP MUFFINS PEPE'S PIZZERIA
                      NAPOLETANA   **Chesterfield**   **North Kingstown**
                                      DAVID'S   ALLIE'S DONUTS

Fairfield
RAWLEY'S DRIVE-IN
SUPER DUPER WEENIE

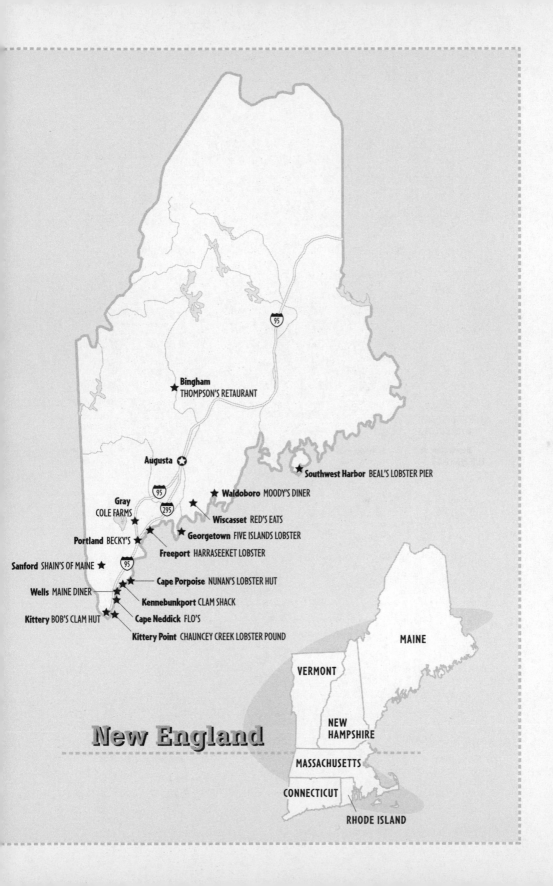

Bingham
THOMPSON'S RETAURANT

Augusta

Southwest Harbor BEAL'S LOBSTER PIER

Waldoboro MOODY'S DINER

Gray
COLE FARMS

Wiscasset RED'S EATS

Portland BECKY'S

Georgetown FIVE ISLANDS LOBSTER

Freeport HARRASEEKET LOBSTER

Sanford SHAIN'S OF MAINE

Cape Porpoise NUNAN'S LOBSTER HUT

Wells MAINE DINER

Kennebunkport CLAM SHACK

Kittery BOB'S CLAM HUT

Cape Neddick FLO'S

Kittery Point CHAUNCEY CREEK LOBSTER POUND

New England

MAINE

VERMONT

NEW
HAMPSHIRE

MASSACHUSETTS

CONNECTICUT

RHODE ISLAND

Connecticut

Abbott's Lobster In the Rough

117 Pearl St.   860-536-7719
Noank, CT   LD May-Labor Day, then weekends
                                through mid-October | $$

Abbott's is renowned for chowder and lobsters, both of which have defined seafood excellence in eastern Connecticut for decades. The chowder is a style unique to southern New England shores: steel-gray, briny, full of clam flavor, plenty of clam meat, and a handful of potatoes; and the lobsters are steamed to perfection. But beyond these glories, Abbott's posted menu suggests a whole range of other fine seafood items: steamers, mussels, clams and/or oysters on the half shell, hot lobster rolls that are nothing but buttered pink meat on a bun, lobster salad rolls (cool, bound with mayonnaise), crab rolls (hot or cold), and shrimp salad rolls. There is even broiled chicken for the lost soul who finds himself at this great seafood restaurant craving poultry.

Abbott's is a very pretty place to dine al fresco. Seating is at bare wooden tables (although civilized sorts bring their own tablecloths as well as their own wine); the air is filled with the salt smell of shore breezes, and background music is provided by gulls screeching in the sky (but kept away from the tables by invisible netting).

Big Dipper Ice Cream Factory

91 Waterbury Rd.   203-758-3200
Prospect, CT $

Here is irrefutable evidence that ice cream makes you happy. The girls behind the counter, no matter how fast they scoop on a busy summer night when the line for cones and cups goes clear out the door, are delighted to be Big Dipper folk. Many of them are high school girls, some are older women who started here in high school but enjoy coming back during vacations because they consider themselves part of the Big Dipper family. You will understand their bliss when first you taste the amazing toasted almond ice cream, which the boss says was originally inspired by a vintage Good Humor bar, but which we say transcends it.

If this particular flavor is not your idea of heaven on earth, don't worry. The Big Dipper has a few dozen others, ranging from silly (cotton candy) to swank (café Vienna, which is coffee and cinnamon) to serious (espresso). All are rich in butterfat (16 percent), but not so rich that they cloy. These are ice creams we can easily eat double and triple dips of, several times a week. The repertoire changes daily, but you always can count on toasted almond.

Blackie's

2200 Waterbury Rd.   203-699-1819
Cheshire, CT   LD (closed Fridays) | $

Blackie's just may serve the best hot dog in Connecticut, a state with some of the highest hot dog consciousness in the nation. While there are a couple of other items on the menu (hamburgers, cheeseburgers), hot dogs are so entirely the specialty of the house that most regular customers sit down at the counter and simply call out a number, indicating how many they want.

The dogs are pink Hummel-brand plumpies that are boiled in oil to the point that they literally blossom with flavor as their outside surface bursts apart. They are served plain in basic buns, and it is up to each customer to spoon out mustard and relish from condiment trays that are set out all along the counter. That's the really good part about dining at

Blackie's: dressing the dogs. The mustard is excellent, and we recommend a modest bed of it applied to the top of each wiener, all the better for the relish to cling to. The relish is transcendent: thick, luxurious, dark green, and pepper-hot enough that your lips will glow after lunch. Blackie's—and its customers—are so devoted to this formula for frankfurter perfection that the kitchen doesn't even bother to offer sauerkraut or chili.

Blackie's is a charming destination dog house, especially in good weather when the long counter offers semi–al fresco seating. Service is nearly instantaneous, so if your preference is *hot* hot dogs, it is entirely practical to order them one by one until you can't eat any more.

La Borinqueña

992 Bank St.   860-437-0408
New London, CT   LD | $

"La Borinqueña" is the title of the anthem of the Commonwealth of Puerto Rico, but a lot of regular customers know this cute little eat-shop by the name on the sign outside: Roast Pork Café.

It's an apt name when you consider the magnificent pork sandwich that is the signature dish. It is made of pork shoulder, roasted all night until the skin is as crisp as bacon and the inside is velvet soft. The meat is cut with a scissors into variegated shreds, chunks, and strips that are piled inside a long hero roll, preferably with a layer of Swiss cheese and some mayonnaise, then toasted in a sandwich press that converts the potentially fall-apart sandwich into a tidy tube. The pork packs an amazing flavor punch; it is salty, redolent of spice, and dripping juice. While it is possible to have a "Cuban" sandwich, to which ham is added, and even a *tripletas* (pork, ham, and steak), we love the simplicity and intensity of pork, cheese, and bread.

In addition to magnificent sandwiches, the Colón family offers fried chicken, roasted chicken, and such fascinating side dishes as yucca patties, green banana patties, and meat-stuffed potato balls. There is a lunch special every day, including fried pork chops and breaded steak on Monday, with a choice of white or yellow rice on the side.

The restaurant's interior isn't much more than a tiny kitchen and order counter. Seating is outdoors at picnic tables, and all meals are available to go.

Carminuccio's

76 South Main St. (Route 25)   203-364-1133
Newtown, CT   LD | $

One of the lesser-known culinary gold mines in Connecticut is Route 25 between Monroe and Newtown. A garish, congested patch of two-lane with more than its fair share of *un*interesting places of business, it happens to be home of at least two superb hot dogs (at the Botsford Drive-In and Mr. Mac's Canteen), nice Italian sandwiches (at Panino's), plus a number of promising diners and cafés we have yet to try. One of the reasons we haven't done a whole lot of homework on this stretch of road is that we are so often drawn to Carminuccio's. Here in Connecticut, home of America's most delicious pizzas, this house by the side of the highway serves some of the best.

When you walk in, it isn't much to look at. The interior consists of an order counter and a small array of bare-topped tables with a glass case in back holding cannoli, stuffed breads, and a few pasta dishes. If you look to the right as you enter, you will see a most appealing sight: pizzas being made to order. Available toppings range from basic cheese to escarole and beans, barbecued chicken, sautéed spinach, and a knock-out BLT combo of pesto sauce, bacon, sautéed escarole, and roasted tomatoes. Pepperoni and sausage are generously applied; we especially recommend roasted peppers. These meaty little squiggles are radiant with flavor, and just wonderful on a pizza with nothing other than cheese. As for the crust, it's Neapolitan style, meaning it is fairly thin with a chewy rim of crust all around the circumference and a brittle undercrust with enough grit from the oven to give it real character.

Beyond the pizza, do pay attention to the stuffed breads. These are fat savory loaves wrapped around such ingredients as ham or capicola, pepperoni and cheese, broccoli and sausage. Served steaming hot, one of these breads is a soulful meal every bit as satisfying as a pizza.

David's

1647 Route 85   860-442-7120
Chesterfield, CT   LD (summer only) | $

One of our favorite sunny summer day drives is along Route 85 just west of the Thames. There, in Chesterfield, we pay a visit to our favorite rock 'n' fossil store—Nature's Art—and go across the road for thick cardboard plates piled high with excellent whole-bellied fried clams (strips are also available).

The menu at this cheerful drive-in is eat-in-the-rough fare with a Greek twist. The twist can be tasted in the form of spinach pie—a plate of savory, well-spiced spinach-and-feta-and-phyllo served with French fries and cole slaw—but the list of non-Greek items are such Yankee shore standbys as shrimp, scallops, and calamari—each fried to golden goodness, as well as top-drawer fish 'n' chips.

While the fried food is exemplary, the sleepers on David's menu are grinders. These are some mighty hero sandwiches; their fillings ranging from demure tuna salad to a spectacular *steak bomb,* which means the sliced beef is topped with sautéed onions, peppers, mushrooms, and cheese. And, this being a Greek-run kitchen, we recommend paying close attention to the gyro and chicken gyro grinders. They're immensely satisfying versions of the street-food sandwich, particularly good with a pile of David's fresh-cut French fries. For dessert: homemade rice pudding.

Chez Lénard

Main St.   No phone
Ridgefield, CT   LD | $

Chez Lénard of Ridgefield has no address and no phone number. It is a sidewalk cart on Main Street with no tables or chairs. Accommodations for dining include sidewalk standing room and Ballard Park across the street. Some car customers pull to the curb, toot their horn, and get their meal delivered to the window without ever leaving the driver's seat.

Despite the lack of amenities, Chez Lénard is indubitably high tone. When the original "Lénard," a Manhattan rat-race refugee, parked his cart here in 1978, he established an urbane ambience with a French accent that has thrived under subsequent proprietors' incumbency. Citizens of Ridgefield have come to treasure the happy incongruity of a man in a billowy chef's toque exclaiming "oo-la-la!" as he slathers on hot relish, or *"merci beaucoup"* when making change. The blackboard menu lists such exotic-sounding delights as "Le Hot Dog Choucroute Alsacienne" (with sauerkraut and mustard), "Le Hot Dog Excelsior Veneziano" (with Italian peppers and sautéed onions), and "Le Hot Dog Façon Mexicaine" (a chili dog).

The dogs themselves, plucked with tongs from a hot water bath in the cart, are *magnifiques:* kosher all-beef franks with a taut casing and firm insides, long enough to stick out from both ends of the bun, and buxom enough that a pair of "Supremes" (with mustard, relish, ketchup, and chopped onions) with a can of Dr. Brown's soda make an immensely satisfying meal.

Chez Lénard is open year-round, every day except Easter, Thanksgiving, and Christmas or when the weather is extremely awful. "I am pitied in the winter," says proprietor Chad Cohen. "But I am envied in the summer. For me, this is always a great job because everyone I meet is happy. Who isn't happy when they eat a hot dog?"

Doogie's

2525 Berlin Turnpike	860-666-1944
Newington, CT	LD | $

A second Doogie's is located at 560 Chase Ave., Waterbury.

Doogie's boasts that it is "home of the 2-foot hot dog," but in our experience the hot dogs are significantly longer than that. Closer to thirty inches. While one of them, in its yard-long bun, looks like a party sandwich for a table of eaters, especially if it is loaded with sauerkraut, chili, onions, bacon, cheese, etc., you will see some big boys walking into Doogie's at lunchtime and ingesting a pair of them (that's about six feet of frankfurter!) with a large soda and an order of jumbo French fries with cheese sauce on the side.

If only for its size, Doogie's hot dog would be worth noting in the annals of amazing Roadfood; but the more important fact is that this extra-long sausage is delicious. Firm-fleshed and with a chewy skin that gets slightly charred on the grill, it has a vigorously spicy flavor that holds up well not only under any and all extra-cost toppings but also when spread with Doogie's superb homemade hot relish or just ordinary mustard. The brand name of the dog is Grote & Weigal, and for those of meek appetites, it is available in mere ten-inch configuration, too. Mention must also be made of the bun, which of necessity is significantly sturdier than your ordinary cotton-soft hot dog roll. More like a grinder roll, but somewhat slimmer, Doogie's bun is actual, good-quality bread! We have never seen anyone actually pick up a whole hot dog and bun, though. Etiquette for eating one of these fellas is to grasp one end eight to ten inches from the tip and tear off a section that would be about the size of a normal frankfurter anywhere else. You'll get about four of these per dog.

Beyond hot dogs, Doogie's sells all sorts of other sandwiches, New England–style clam chowder, a real hot lobster roll, and that junkiest of junk foods, so beloved hereabouts—fried dough. Doogie's version, a plate-size disc of deep-fried dough, is available veiled in cinnamon sugar or under a blanket of red tomato sauce. Either way, it is a mouthful!

Hamburgers, cooked on the same charcoal grill where the hot dogs are made, have a delicious smoky flavor. The top-of-the-line hamburger is described on the menu as "the ultimate"; and while not as awesome as the elongated hot dog, it is quite a sight: two five-ounce patties with bacon, cheese, grilled onions, and sautéed mushrooms. Its formal name on the menu is the Murder Burger.

Casual in the extreme, Doogie's is a serve-yourself joint (adjacent to Ruth's Chris Steak House, which might be a good fallback if you arrive after 8 P.M. when Doogie's closes). Step up to the counter, place your order, pay your money, and wait for your name to be called. When your order is ready, tote your tray to the condiment bar, heap on what you like, find a molded plastic seat in the square little dining room, and prepare to feast on the king of all weenies.

Dr. Mike's

158 Greenwood Ave.   203-792-4388
Bethel, CT   LD | $

Forget psychotherapy and medication! The best antidepressant we know is a visit to Dr. Mike's. We didn't know about Dr. Mike's ice cream shop when we moved to a neighboring town, but it wasn't too long before chowhounds in the neighborhood clued us in. We found the out-of-the-way place off Bethel's main street and, at first lick, we became converts. As ice cream lovers, we must tell you that there is nothing quite like Dr. Mike's, and there are occasions—rare occasions—when its ultra-richness is actually too, too much.

Most of the time, the cones and cardboard cups dished out year-round by this little shop are just what the doctor ordered. Several proprietary flavors set standards unequaled by any other brand. The longtime standard-bearer, "rich chocolate," for example, is stunningly flavored, cocoa brown, and more deliriously chocolaty than a pure melted Hershey bar, but has the added luxury of all that high-butterfat cream. We must warn you, however, that sometimes it gets scooped from the tub cold and hard; and the flavor does not blossom until it is on the verge of melting. This makes for an unbelievably messy cone, and a good possibility of dark chocolate stains on your hands, face, and clothes (somehow, *this* chocolate ice cream leaves smears that are far more conspicuous than any other brand); but you *must* wait until the rich chocolate ice cream is soft. If you do, bliss is yours.

"Chocolate lace and cream" is another Dr. Mike's invention, made with a luxurious chocolate-covered hard candy produced by a local confectionery. The candy is broken into bite-size pieces and suspended in a pure white emulsion of sweetened cream: another dreamy experience, but in this case our warning is to get it in a cup. The crunch of the candy conflicts with the crunch of a cone.

We've named our two favorite flavors. Don't hesitate, though, if you find your personal favorite among the approximately six varieties available any particular day. Each one is made the old-fashioned way, using cream from dairy buckets, in five-gallon batches; and we have fond, fond memories of Dr. Mike's coffee, coconut, cinnamon, Heath Bar crunch, even prune, dazzling vanilla, and some real tongue-stunners made with fresh fruits in the summer.

After you have tasted the ice cream in its unadulterated state, please return to Dr. Mike's for a milk shake (none thicker this side of St. Louis) or a hot fudge sundae. Sundaes are huge, made so they literally fill up pint ice cream containers. The fudge is dark and dense, faintly granular, and a glorious complement to any of the light colors and fruit flavors. And the pure, sweet whipped cream is heaped on with a trowel.

Harry's Drive-In

| 104 Broadway St. | 860-537-2410 |
| Colchester, CT | LD (spring and summer only) | $ |

The person who tipped us off to Harry's Drive-In said that Harry's is to hamburgers what Abbott's (page 5) is to lobsters: the benchmark against which all others must be measured.

Standing at the pickup window (which is where you go after you have placed your order and paid at the other window), you have a great view of the grill on which the hamburgers are cooked. They are put on the hot, oily surface as a round patty a little smaller than a baseball, then they are flattened out with a spatula. Despite getting squished, the hamburgers remain thick enough to be overwhelmingly juicy. Hot dogs are cooked on the same grill, and they're plump and tasty ones, especially satisfying when bedded atop some of Harry's chili sauce.

Seating is al fresco on picnic tables along both sides of the capacious parking lot.

JK's

126 South St.   203-743-4004
Danbury, CT   BLD Mon-Sat | $

JK's looks like any modern fast-food restaurant, but photographs on the wall tell another story: decades of weenie history. The nostalgic black-and-white pictures show JK's with its hot dog sign hanging over Main Street many years ago; interior pictures show a spic-and-span diner that has served the Hat City's working-class clientele since the 1930s.

The place may have changed, but old-timers tell us that the Texas hot wieners on which JK's built its reputation remain precisely the same charming little frankfurters they've always been. They are plump sausages, split lengthwise and cooked until slightly crusty on the surface, loaded into a big spongy roll, then topped with mustard, onions, and hot sauce with a chile pepper kick. No single element of this arrangement has flavor to write home about, but the combination is powerfully attractive. You might order two, with a thick chocolate milk shake on the side, but midway through the second dog, you will likely be flagging down the waitress for a third, and possibly a fourth. The speedy gals who tend the short counter and the booths throughout the dining room are masters of balance, toting up to six or eight hot dog plates to different tables in a single trip from the semi-open kitchen in back.

There are all sorts of other things on JK's menu, from silver dollar pancakes at breakfast to New England's favorite Grape-Nuts pudding for dessert, but it's the devilish Texas dogs that put this restaurant on our map. Some connoisseurs order them with cheese, chili, and/or bacon in addition to the usual condiments; it's also possible to get a heap of excellent house-made slaw on top or to get the bun toasted: all interesting strategies, but we suggest first-timers stick with the original configuration . . . at least for the first round.

Lenny & Joe's Fish Tale Restaurant

1301 Boston Post Road (Route 1)   203-245-7289

Madison, CT   LD (check winter hours) | $$

Also at 86 Boston Post Road (Route 1), Westbrook, CT (860-669-0767),
and 138 Granite St., Westerly, RI (401-348-9941)

Lenny & Joe's opened as a roadside fried clam stand in 1979. It has since become three restaurants with vast seafood menus that range from all-you-can-eat Wednesday fish fries (winter months) to whole lobster dinners (summertime) and include virtually every kind of fried seafood known to the human race.

Despite expansion, all three L&Js remain casual eat-places; the "drive-in" operations in Madison and in Westerly, RI, feature do-it-yourself service—you wait for your number to be called and tote your own tray of food—and all three places have a breezy summer ambience that makes every meal feel like vacation. Although prices are on the high side compared to picnic table clam shacks along the shoreline, the quality of the food is impeccable, and the quantities are awesome.

The whole-bellied fried clams are big and succulent with golden crusts. We also love the fried shrimp and scallops, even simple fried fish. All fried items are available in an ample regular-size configuration as well as a "super" plate with double the amount of fish for about $5 more. This is one restaurant where the undecided customer who craves the crunch of fresh-fried seafood will be happy ordering a variety platter with some of everything. It is a gargantuan meal, including crinkle-cut French fries and a little cup of sweet cole slaw. The only other necessary item would be an order of fried onions; Lenny & Joe's onion rings are wicked good!

Lobster fanatics know Lenny & Joe's as one of the few reliable sources for a *hot* lobster roll, meaning nothing but chunks and shreds of lobster meat drenched in butter and heaped into a long roll. This is pure bliss, with none of the whole-lobster hassle of shell-cracking and meat extraction. In season, the kitchen also offers a softshell crab roll that is almost as luscious.

We admit to being fried-food addicts; but Lenny & Joe's is also a fine place for such unfried shoreline specialties as clam chowder (brothy, with a touch of milk), steamers by the quart with broth and butter, and—summer only—fine soft-serve ice cream by the cone, cup, sundae, or concrete-thick milk shake known as a "frenzy."

Lenny's

205 S. Montowese St.   203-488-1500
Branford, CT   LD | $$

"Where have you been all our lives?" we asked after our first meal at Lenny's, having lived within a fifty-mile radius of the place for almost as long as it's been open, some thirty years. A fixture of the Indian Neck section of Branford's coast well known to local cognoscenti, this excellent restaurant had somehow evaded our radar. Now that we know about it, we shall be regulars.

A well-worn seafood house with varnished wood booths, a taproom up front, and a scenic deck overlooking marshland behind the dining room, Lenny's is a neighborhood place with a menu that ranges from hamburgers and hot dogs to full shore dinners. The latter includes chowder (either creamy New England style or clear-broth shoreline style), a couple of cherrystone clams on the shell, a lobster, a heap of steamers, sweet corn, and a thick slice of watermelon for dessert.

Good as both kinds of chowder are, we intend never to begin a meal at Lenny's without "zuppa d'clams": six steamed-open cherrystones in a bowl of briny, lemon-laced broth, a half-loaf of bread on the side for dunking. Delicious! Swordfish is always on the menu, and always fresh, available in dinner-size steaks or in smaller sandwich cuts served on nice fluffy buns with lettuce, tomato, and mayonnaise.

So far, the meals we like best at Lenny's are the fried things: big, whole-belly clams, succulent oysters, scallops, fish and chips, and huge butterflied shrimp. Crunch-crusted and clean-flavored, these are exemplary fried seafood, and definitive proof that a crisp, clean crust can be the very best halo for seafood's natural sweetness.

Throughout the summer, strawberry shortcake is available for dessert. It is the true Yankee version, made from a sideways-split, unsweet biscuit layered with sliced berries in a thin sugar syrup, and a mountain of whipped cream. "I make it myself," our waitress boasted, then suggested that one might be enough for the both of us. "It's big!" she said. Yes, it is, but it is so good we don't recommend getting less than one per person.

Letizia's Pizzeria

666 Main Ave. (Town Line Shopping Center)   203-847-6022
Norwalk, CT   LD | $$

Dating back to "Uncle Joe's," which was Joe Letizia's grand old neighborhood restaurant that opened in Norwalk in the 1930s, this modern pizzeria is now run by a third generation of gifted cooks. The menu includes pastas with homemade marinara sauce, veal or chicken Parmesan dinners of Homeric size, baked ziti and ravioli, salads, and grinders . . . and all of these things are good. But the one item on the menu that puts Letizia's in the stratosphere is pizza—without doubt, some of the best pizza in Connecticut. Given the fact that Connecticut is home to the best pizza in this hemisphere, that's saying a lot.

The pie is Neapolitan style, meaning thin but not too thin, with an edge that rises in a crisp ring of dough with a bready crunch. Pizzas are brought from the kitchen on broad metal pans, along with small plates, if needed. What you will need, no doubt, is lots of napkins. Dainty pizza, this is not! In particular, we are fond of the pepperoni pie generously topped with chewy, thin-cut discs, plenty of mozzarella, and high-quality sauce, the clam casino pie made from clams, garlic, bacon, cheese, and onion, and the "garbage pie" heaped with a little bit of everything. There are "no cheese" pizzas, white pizzas (mozzarella, ricotta, and Romano), and Hawaiian pizzas topped with ham and pineapple.

As for the place, Letizia's location is extremely nondescript—in a small shopping center on a commercial strip—and the interior is just a simple room with a take-out counter and a few tables. The walls are plastered with New York sports team memorabilia and old photographs that tell the history of Letizia's and Uncle Joe's—a great culinary dynasty.

Louis Lunch

261 Crown St.   203-562-5507
New Haven, CT   L | $

Louis Lunch cooks hamburgers in fat-reducing metal broilers that predate George Foreman's Grilling Machine by almost a century. A handful of freshly ground steak is hand-flattened into a patty and placed inside a wire holder inside a vertical iron oven that holds the meat suspended between two heat sources. As the patty cooks, the grease drips off it and the meat sears. When it is done, the hamburger is removed from its wire holder and placed between two pieces of toasted white bread.

Hamburgers come on toast at Louis Lunch, because when Louis began serving them from his lunch wagon, there was no such thing as a hamburger bun. In fact, it is possible that there was no such thing as a hamburger. Some food historians believe that this is where the hamburger was invented. There are those who attribute it to the Tartars or to the Earl of Salisbury or to sailors from Hamburg, Germany; but Louis Lunch devotees contend that it was born of Louis Lassen's thrifty nature. The hamburger was his way of doing something useful with the leftover trimmings from the steak sandwiches he sold at his lunch wagon.

Whatever the hamburger's true origins, Louis Lunch is an essential stop on America's burger trail. The hamburgers are moist and crusty, available with a schmear of Cheez Whiz, if desired; and the place itself, now run by a fourth generation of the Lassen family, is a vivid taste of culinary history.

The Olive Market

19 Main St.   203-544-8134
Georgetown, CT   BLD | $$

Okay, we can't lie. We live around the corner from the Olive Market and we're good friends with the guys who run it. When we are home in the morning and need to grab a cup of really good strong coffee or a bacon, egg, and cheese sandwich, the Olive Market is where we go. So, although its main specialty—Uruguayan food—doesn't exactly fit the definition of Roadfood as an expression of indigenous U.S. culture, and although its inventory includes hoity-toity olive oils, imported cheeses, and boutique pasta, we do love it enough to recommend it to anyone passing through.

In fact, it is a swell place for a quick breakfast or lunch that's fairly easy on the wallet. The menu ranges from French toast and pancakes to exotic grilled sandwiches and ultra-thin-crust pizzas. Grilling things is the house forte. Pizzas and flatbread sandwiches inhale a smoky savor from being cooked on the grate. Especially notable is a sandwich known as a *chivito*. That's a protein-eater's delight of sliced filet mignon with thin layers of ham and provolone cheese plus a fried egg, all on a beautiful hunk of bread crowned with a single olive.

On weekends nights the Olive Market goes from casual to awesome.

That is when co-owner Fernando Pereyra shows off the cooking of his native Uruguay by offering, among other things, a stupendous "Gaucho dinner" for two or four people: an immense platter crowded with skewers of filet mignon, individual pork ribs, spicy chicken wings, teriyaki chicken skewers, and unbelievably luscious little lamb chops. In the center of this feast are ramekins of peanut dipping sauce, garlicky chimichurri sauce, and, of course, olives.

By the way, the coffee upon which Jane insists here is a specialty known as a *cortado*—strictly for those who like it ultrastrong. Normal coffee and espresso drinks are also available.

O'Rourke's

728 Main St.   860-346-6101
Middletown, CT   BL | $

Brian O'Rourke's diner just keeps getting better and better.

It's still the same unrestored beautiful dining car, circa 1946, it has always been, located at the far end of Middletown's Main Street, where the dawn air swirls with the wake-up scents of hot coffee, frying spuds, and the cologne of working people ready to start their day. You can claim a seat at counter or booth and eat the most basic kinds of blue-plate fare, including masterful omelets every morning and noontime meals that can be as simple as a pancake-flat grilled cheese sandwich for under $2 or as copious as a Reuben sandwich with French fries for about $5.

Among O'Rourke's good everyday dishes are the steamed cheeseburger (a central Connecticut passion), 3-way chili "Seeley style" (named for the diner's most devoted patron, J. Seeley), fish and chips, and a "tuna smelt" sandwich with red onion, bacon, and steamed cheese.

The homemade soups are spectacular; there are always two or three from which to choose, including such springtime wonders as potato-caraway and cream of portobello mushroom. As we plowed through lunch in our booth last March, we watched a small club of leather-clad bikers occupy one end of O'Rourke's counter and chat with one another about the extraordinary creaminess of the mushroom soup, sending their compliments back to the semi-open kitchen.

In recent years, Brian O'Rourke has been more and more inspired to create meals to suit special occasions, ranging from stunning Sunday brunches to holiday fare that is truly world class. Around Mardi Gras time, his daily lunch menu features moist blackened catfish, shrimp and crawfish jambalaya with hefty red Creole sauce, and an andouille sausage and chicken gumbo that he told us he learned to cook at the elbow of Paul Prudhomme.

As we swooned over the Creole cuisine in early March, Brian started to tell us his plans for the next week—St. Patrick's Day—which included oatmeal-turnip soup made with hard cider and Irish whiskey, as well as seven hundred pounds of corned beef that he was soaking and seasoning in brine for the holiday.

Pepe's Pizzeria Napoletana

157 Wooster St.   203-865-5762
New Haven, CT   D | $$

Adjacent to Pepe's is The Spot, owned by the same family and serving essentially the same pizza. The Spot is open Tuesday nights; Pepe's is not.

New Haven pizza is Neapolitan style, meaning it has a crust that is thin but has enough chew so that eating half a large pie can make your jaw ache the next morning. The circumference of the pizza, a circle of bread unladen with any of the stuff in the middle, rises in rugged puffs, occasionally charring to a crackable black blister at the outermost burst of stretched skin. Look underneath: the crust is speckled with grains of charred semolina flour. Semolina is used on the oven floor and baker's peel like tiny ball bearings, so the pizzas slide in and out easily. As they burn, the grains absorb the flavors of the smoke and sizzling pizzas, and many of them cling to the bottom, creating a friable web beneath the dough. It is this lagniappe of oven grit that gives the Wooster Street pizzas their extra measure of soul.

At Pepe's, the greatest (and most original) of Wooster Street's pizzerias, you walk into a room with an open kitchen in back where white-aproned *pizzaioli* reenact the ritual originated by Frank Pepe in the 1920s: bombs of dough are flattened on a marble table, clouds of spice are strewn in an instant, and six-foot wooden baker's peels inject pizzas deep into the wood-fired oven. It is a hypnotic scene, untouched by time or fashion.

Most regular pizza ingredients are available, but Pepe's premier pizza is an unusual one made without mozzarella or tomato sauce. It is called a white clam pie, available only when the kitchen can get the good, little clams from Rhode Island. It is elementary food—nothing but crust, freshly shucked littleneck clams, olive oil, garlic, oregano, and a dash of grated Parmesan. Without a mozzarella mantle, the dough's mottled surface is frosted gold with grated cheese.

Phillips Diner

Route 6   203-263-2516

Woodbury, CT   BLD | $

A modest town café tucked back from Route 6 (hunting grounds for antiques collectors), Phillips has changed shape since it opened in 1934. Mid-century it was a classic streamlined dining car and today it is a modest town lunch room with a convivial counter and a handful of booths and tables. One thing about it has remained consistent: chicken pie. Originally made by proprietor Bud Phillips's father, Phillips's chicken pies are not at all like a typical pot pie that is loaded with vegetables. Each individual-serving pie contains a big hunk of white meat and a coarse hash of smaller pieces under a flaky crust, served with a spill of gravy. If you want vegetables, you order them on the side.

Adjacent to the dining room is a vestibule with a take-out counter where people buy these superb chicken pies frozen to take home and bake, and also make their donut selection from a display in the bakery case. The fun thing about the counter, especially on weekends, is that there is almost always a large Lucite dish filled with bite-size pieces of broken donuts for munching while your order is prepared. It is entirely possible to consume two or three donuts' worth while waiting. These donuts are that good.

Not that there is anything swank about them. They are, in a sense, as plain as a donut can be. The baking powder batter is cooked until the outside is dark brown, and the exterior encases a perfect creamy cake. The four varieties include plain, cinnamon, powdered sugar, and chocolate. Heavily coated with cinnamon-sugar while still hot, the cinnamon donuts are the most popular. The chocolates bring us to our knees with a devastating union of tawny pastry and silken fudgy glaze.

Rawley's Drive-In

1886 Post Road
Fairfield, CT

203-259-9023

LD | $

Rawley's is pint-size: four booths plus a six-stool counter on what used to be a front porch, where an open picture window provides a scenic view into the lively short-order kitchen. Adjacent to the counter is a pay phone that rings often during the lunch hour as hopefuls try to place a phone order. We say "try" because when Rawley's is crowded, as it always is shortly after noon, the staff have their hands full taking care of dine-in and take-out business and simply don't have time to listen to orders over the phone. So it rings and rings. "Your chance of putting in a phone order during the week is ninety percent," advises proprietor Chico Bielik. "On Saturday, it's near zero. That's when we're busiest."

Chico, an indefatigable ringleader whose summer attire is chef's whites with white Bermuda shorts, is the one who cooks and assembles the hot dogs while the other three staff members dodge one another in the limited work space to take and pack orders, carry food to booths, and work the cash register. "What is the logic of this kitchen?" asks a curious customer between bites, just to throw out a question for discussion at the counter.

"It is pretzel logic," answers one employee tending a chocolate malt at the milk shake machine.

"This is like the bumblebee," a philosophical wiener-eater offers from the other end of the counter. "It isn't supposed to fly, but it does."

Rawley's defined a way of cooking hot dogs that has become gospel for many of the important frank emporia in southwestern Connecticut. It is deep-fried. When plump and darkened, it is pulled from the hot vegetable oil and rolled around on the griddle with a spatula—a finishing touch that strains off excess oil and gives the exterior a delectable crackle. The dog is then bedded in a high-quality roll that has been spread open, brushed with butter, and toasted on the griddle until its interior surfaces are crisp, in contrast to the outside, which remains soft and pliant.

The kitchen does the dressing, the most popular configuration being mustard and relish topped with sauerkraut and garnished with a fistful of chewy bacon shreds. To our taste, it is a perfect combination, although "heavy bacon"—twice as much—is a popular option. Chico says he cooks eighteen to twenty pounds of bacon per day, all for dogs.

As plebeian as a restaurant can be, Rawley's is known for attracting celebrities who live or summer in the area. Paul Newman, Meg Ryan, and David Letterman have all been spotted eating these fine hot dogs, and Martha Stewart used to be a regular. "Famous people, they wait in line, too," Chico notes. "At Rawley's everybody is equal, except maybe if you are a priest from Saint Anthony's—that's my church—and you need a phone order on Saturday."

Ridgefield Ice Cream Shop

680 Danbury Rd.   203-438-3094
Ridgefield, CT $

The Ridgefield Ice Cream Shop looks like one of countless Carvels around the country, and a Carvel store is what it used to be. But oh, what a difference! Using vintage silver machines that he maintains with parts salvaged from old Carvel stands that go out of business, proprietor Felix Lechner concocts what he calls "custard without the egg." That means his frozen dessert is made with minimal "overrun" (little air gets pumped into it), resulting in a velvety creation that is dense and full-flavored, robust enough to mound up impossibly high atop the store's superior wafer cones. Even a large serving, which rises a full six inches above the rim of the cone, will grasp a thick coating of chocolate sprinkles or a shell of quick-dry dip-top, either chocolate or cherry flavored.

Although it has a sunny, summertime feel, Ridgefield Ice Cream is open year-round, rain or shine. In good weather, customers lick their cones leaning on their cars in the parking lot or at one of the picnic tables out front.

Roseland Apizza

350 Hawthorne Ave.   203-735-0494
Derby, CT   D Tues-Sun | $$

Roseland Apizza (pronounce that second word the Neapolitan way, "ah-BEETS") started as a bakery in 1934. Today, it has a menu of hand-cut ravioli, four-star lasagna, and a board full of nightly specials featuring shellfish and pasta, but it is most famous for its brick-oven pies.

The crust is what connoisseurs know as New Haven style: thin but not quite brittle, with enough brawn to support all but the weightiest combinations of ingredients and to allay the pizza-eater's primal fears: slice collapse and topping slippage.

Baker Gary Lucarelli uses two ovens to cook pizzas, one that runs hot for those made with the sturdy meats and vegetables typical of pizzeria menus, the other slower for white pizzas topped with fragile seafood. Roseland makes some spectacularly lavish pies, such as a shrimp casino topped with bacon, mozzarella, fresh garlic, and too many jumbo shrimp to count; but for us, the one must-eat specialty is the relatively uncomplicated Connecticut classic, white clam pizza. Recommended configuration: no mozzarella, no tomato sauce, just a crowd of freshly shucked Rhode Island clams strewn across a crust frosted with olive oil and scattered with bits of basil, parsley, and oregano, thin-sliced garlic, a twist of cracked black pepper, and a scattering of grated Parmesan. The nectar of the whole clams insinuates itself into the surface of the crust, giving every crunch exhilarating marine zest.

Shady Glen

840 E. Middle Turnpike   860-649-4245

Manchester, CT   BLD | $

Connecticut is cheeseburger paradise. Nowhere else are beef and cheese combined on buns in such fantastic ways. In the center of the state, a ten-mile strip between Middletown and Meriden is home to several vintage hash houses equipped with steam cabinets in which portions of ground beef and blocks of Cheddar cheese are separately vapor-cooked in small metal tins to become the "steamed cheeseburger"—an oozing package of unspeakable succulence.

In Manchester, a sparkling mid-century dairy bar named Shady Glen makes some of the most dramatic cheeseburgers on earth. On a high-temperature electric grill, each circular patty of beef is cooked on one side, flipped, then blanketed with several square slices of cheese. The cheese is arranged so that only one-quarter to one-third of each slice rests atop the hamburger. The remainder extends beyond the circumference of the meat and melts down onto the surface of the grill. At the exact moment the grilling cheese begins to transform from molten to crisp, the cook uses a spatula to disengage it from the grill and curl it above the meat like some wondrous burgerflower. The petals of cheese, which may be topped with condiments and are crowned by a bun, are crunchy at their tip but chewy where they blend into the soft parts that adhere to the hamburger.

Shady Glen uses American cheese and 90 percent lean beef, which anyone can buy at the market. But creating spectacular cheeseburgers is no job for amateurs. It requires the right equipment and a finely honed sense of timing. "This is not about flipping hamburgers," said William J. Hoch, Sr., Shady Glen's executive manager. "It requires an education to make a cheeseburger as we do; you must train your eyes to know when the cheese is ready; and you need a sure and steady hand to curl it."

Mr. Hoch is second cousin to John Reig, whose wife, Bernice, invented the mind-blowing cheeseburger. The Reigs, now in their eighties and retired, opened Shady Glen in 1948 as an ice cream parlor adjacent to their dairy farm. They wanted something for the menu that would attract customers in the winter months. After three years of experimentation, Bernice perfected the creation that would become Shady Glen's signature, even better known than its excellent ice cream. The Reigs opened one other dairy bar in Manchester but never considered expanding further. "Bernice Reig has always been too much of a perfectionist to allow a franchised store out of her control," Mr. Hoch told us. "You cannot make perfect cheeseburgers from the golf course or from a backroom office. You can make them only at the grill."

Shiek's Sandwich Shop

235 E. Elm St.   860-489-5576
Torrington, CT   BL | $

Shiek's has been a Torrington town secret for decades. It's open for breakfast until early afternoon six days a week; and the counter and the shop's handful of tables are always mobbed at mealtime. In addition to building sandwiches and salads for the eat-in trade, proprietor/chef Gary Arnold also makes piles of lunches for walk-in customers to take out. Still, he manages to shoot the breeze with regulars at the counter, and even at the tables just beyond in the dining room.

Our tipster Charles Cramer said the sandwich to eat at Shiek's is the hot roast beef. Slices are cut to order from the roast and tossed on the grill to heat, then sandwiched in a grinder roll with provolone, romaine lettuce, roasted green peppers, grilled onions, and mayonnaise and/or mustard. A delicious sandwich.

The other spécialité de la maison is hot dogs. They are big plump ones available with all the usual condiments, plus a hot relish that is nearly as addictive as that served at Blackie's in Cheshire (page 6). There's a good meaty chili available as a topping, too.

The rest of the menu is a wide-ranging roster that includes such swanky-sounding fare as a Portobello Sandwich and an oinkers' delight known as a Pig-Out (pork loin and bacon with cheese on raisin toast). We've noted that a surprising number of customers actually come to eat salads, which appear several cuts above any ordinary diner salad. But next time we visit, it will be for roast beef again, and more of those good hot dogs.

Super Duper Weenie

306 Black Rock Turnpike   203-334-DOGS
Fairfield, CT   LD | $

In the autumn, when the temperature drops below 50 degrees, Super Duper Weenie chef Gary Zemola starts making fabulous soup, a single variety every day. It might be chili (vegetarian or meat), classic pasta fagiole, clam chowder, lentil and sausage, or any one of at least a dozen other kinds, each of which is a masterpiece that is far, far better than these humble surroundings might suggest. The soups are so liked by Weenie regulars that they usually sell out by the end of lunch hour. But that's okay, because Super Duper Weenie, as you might guess by its name, isn't primarily a soup place.

The thing to eat at this former dog-wagon, now a stationary restaurant with indoor seating, is a hot dog, with French fries on the side. The hot dog is a firm-fleshed, locally made sausage that is split and cooked on the grill until its outside gets a little crusty while the inside stays moist. It is sandwiched in a lovely fresh-baked roll and adorned with utterly amazing condiments. Homemade condiments, including relish made from pickles that Chef Gary has himself made from cucumbers! The sauerkraut, the hot relish, the meat chili, the onion sauce are *all* made from scratch.

You can get whatever you like on a hot dog, but Super Duper Weenie makes it easy (and fast) by offering certain basic configurations. These include "The New Englander," which Gary devised based on his own fond memories of the superior franks served at Jimmie's of Savin Rock in West Haven and at Rawley's in Fairfield. It's a dog topped with sauerkraut, bacon, mustard, sweet relish, and raw onion. "The New

Yorker," Gary says, was inspired by what is served from Gotham's street-corner carts (but we daresay it is 1000 percent better than any street weenie we've eaten in Manhattan): sauerkraut, onion sauce, mustard, and hot relish. There is a "Chicagoan" topped with lettuce, tomato, mustard, celery salt, relish, and a pickle spear; a dynamite "Dixie" dog that is topped with hot meaty chili *and* rests atop a bed of sweet homemade cole slaw (inspired by a North Carolina hot dog Gary likes); and there is a "Georgia Red Hot," which is a spicy sausage with the works.

Non-dog-lovers can get good hamburgers, a sausage and pepper sandwich on a Portuguese roll, a cheese steak, or a grilled chicken sandwich. Amazingly, S-D-W even accommodates non-meat-eaters with a tuna salad sandwich or a veggie burger.

Whatever you get, you must get French fries. These are beautiful, fresh-cut twigs of potato served fresh from the fry-basket and made extra delicious by a perfect sprinkle of salt and pepper. Dine indoors, where you cannot help feeling part of the counter-culture kibitzing that never ends; or choose a picnic table by the side of the eatery, under the sun . . . where hot dogs taste especially good.

Swanky Franks

182 Connecticut Ave.   203-838-8969
Norwalk, CT   LD | $

There's no place in America you can't find a hot dog, but if you are looking for a thriving hot dog culture, with multiple varieties of franks and scores of restaurants that inspire passion among their fans, travel between New York and Providence. Nowhere else are there so many different kinds of delicious hot dogs, from the big kosher-style franks of Manhattan delis to the teeny weenies of Rhode Island's personality-plus "Coney Island" shops.

Fairfield County, an otherwise upscale neighborhood, is home to more than its fair share of excellent déclassé dog houses. Among the oldest and most beloved is Swanky Franks of Norwalk. At the end of highway exit ramp 13, it is an unrepentant roadside shanty; even as the personnel behind the worn-out counter have changed, the hot dogs and ambience have, like fine wine, aged and improved. Sit at a wobbly table in the annex to the left or at the counter to the right and call out your order. There are hamburgers and clams and what is rumored to be good chicken salad on the menu, but at Swanky Franks, the hot dog is king.

Here sit truckers, working people, and junk food connoisseurs wolfing them down two at a time, their assemblage of paper plates also holding some of the finest French fries for miles around—cooked dark, lifted from the hot oil, and tossed directly into a wax-paper-lined basket.

The dogs themselves are well garlicked, porcine pink meat fried in hot oil until they develop a crackly darkened skin. If you pay extra you can get yourself a "lite" version—the frankfurter is bisected and cooked on a grill—but this has none of the wicked charm of the oily one. Relish, onions, mustard: pile 'em on. A Swanky Frank is strong; no amount of condiments can disguise its authoritative character.

Sycamore Drive-In

282 Greenwood Ave.   203-748-2716
Bethel, CT   BLD | $

Hamburgers at the Sycamore Drive-In are made in an unusual way that we only recently learned (by reading the menu) is known as "French style." What that means here in Bethel is that the grill man slaps a thick round circle of beef onto the grill, then uses his spatula to flatten it out so far that the edges of the resulting circle are nearly paper thin. As the burger cooks, the middle gets nice and juicy while the circumference turns into a crusty web of beef. You can get it plain, doubled, or topped with all sorts of ingredients, but the connoisseur's choice is the Dagwood burger. That's two five-ounce patties with cheese and nearly every garnish known to mankind piled into a bun.

Beyond hamburgers, the Sycamore also offers frankfurters topped with bacon and sauerkraut, a fine "pot o' beans," and good chili. It is famous for root beer, made on premises from a top-secret recipe and served in frosty glass mugs. The root beer varies from sweet to dry, depending on where in the barrel your serving comes from, but whatever its nature on any day, it always makes the perfect basis of a root beer float.

The Sycamore is a genuine drive-in with carhop service (blink your lights) and window trays for in-car dining. Indoors, there are booths and a long counter. And in the summer, on weekend evenings, "Cruise Nights" attract hordes of vintage car collectors in their finest restored and custom vehicles. It's a true blast from the past!

Ted's

1046 Broad St.   203-237-6660
Meriden, CT   L | $

Unique to central Connecticut, a steamed cheeseburger is very different from a regular cheeseburger. It is cooked not on a grill or grate, but in a steam cabinet, the meat held inside a square stainless steel tin as it cooks but does not sizzle. Adjacent to the beef patties in the steam cabinet are tins into which are placed small blocks of cheddar cheese. The effect of the steam on the cheese is to make it molten. The concept of steaming meat and cheese was devised in the 1920s, when steamed food was considered more healthy than fried, grilled, or baked. Local historians credit Jack's Diner as the source of the first steamed cheeseburgers. They say Jack's began as a horse-drawn eats-cart out of which Jack served steamed cheese sandwiches to local construction workers. When the men wanted something more substantial, he added beef to the steam box and the steamed cheeseburger was born.

Jack's is gone, but at Ted's—since 1959—you can eat a steamed cheeseburger made to perfection. Paul Duberek, proprietor of the little burger joint, assembles his masterpiece by putting a steamed rectangular patty onto the bottom of a hard roll, then using a spoon or spatula to slide a big gob of partially melted cheese out of the steel tin onto the top of the burger. Top with lettuce and tomato and, preferably, mustard, and you've got one heck of a messy cheeseburger!

Ted's is a tiny place with four booths, but the best place to sit is at the counter—a short slice of Roadfood heaven. Generally occupied by regulars who palaver with Paul as he attends the twin steam boxes, counter seats provide a view of the bin of chopped meat from which Paul grabs fistfuls of the burger boxes as well as a pile of hard rolls and big blocks of cheese ready to be melted.

Whistle Stop Muffins

20 Portland Ave.   203-544-8139
Georgetown, CT   BL | $

Located inside the Branchville train station, where many commuters hop Metro North on their way to the city, Whistle Stop caters to people with little time to sit and eat. We aren't commuters, but even when we buy a dozen swirly sticky buns to take home, which is a mere two miles away, it is not likely more than ten will arrive at the kitchen table. They're too much fun to eat while still warm; and frankly, licking the caramel goo off one's fingers is part of the pleasure. When Whistle Stop originally opened, muffins were the only thing on the menu; there are still about a dozen varieties baked every morning, as well as rich-textured scones.

Although most customers get their breakfast to go, it is a pleasure to take your muffin and a cup of coffee to the adjoining "waiting room," where there are a few tables for those in no hurry to eat, sip, and read the morning paper.

Beal's Lobster Pier

182 Clark Point Rd.   207-244-3202

Southwest Harbor, ME   D | $$

Beal's gives out a small map showing how to find Southwest Harbor, along with a drawing of a lobster and a slogan: "Dine on the Dock in a Lovely Maine Fishing Village." It doesn't get much lovelier than this. You sit at picnic tables on a pier over the water, with lobster traps for decoration and fishing boats for scenery. There is a shed where you pick your live lobster by size and choose raw or steamed clams, shrimp, or crab meat for an appetizer. They even make a lobster roll dressed with Miracle Whip. But we'll take a whole lobster every time. They are steamed for about twenty minutes and are served piping hot, their shells already cracked for easy extraction of the firm sweet, pink meat within.

Near the shed where you got the lobster is another, smaller shed that sells quahog chowder, which makes a great first course, and engagingly homemade blueberry cake or pie and ice cream for dessert. Carry all your own food to a table and, with the mountains of Acadia National Park for scenery and the sound of the lobstermen's boats rocking in their berths for background music, dig into one of this land's finest sleeves-up meals.

Becky's

390 Commercial St. 207-773-7070

Portland, ME BLD | $

Becky's opens before dawn every day of the year except Christmas and Thanksgiving (when it is closed); and its breakfast clientele includes a colorful gallery of men and women who work on or near the waterfront. The waitresses themselves are a lively bunch, always kibitzing with one another and the cooks behind the pass-through window (where orders are hung on a clothesline) and refilling your coffee cup until you are ready to float away.

Lunch is swell—the baked beans and franks are as classic a platter as you'll find anywhere in New England, and the Italian sausage sandwiches are true heroes. Friday's haddock chowder is exemplary. But breakfast is the great meal of the day. Fresh muffins can be had merely toasted or, for those of wanton taste, split and buttered and cooked on the same grill where millions of orders of bacon and eggs have grilled, thus absorbing the luscious flavors of breakfast past. Hash browns are soft and chunky; eggs are expertly cooked and arrive glistening with butter. On the side, Italian toast is the best available bread, served in hefty oval slices that are buttered and crisp-cooked.

Bob's Clam Hut

Route 1 207-439-4233

Kittery, ME LD (summer only) | $$

Bob's has been selling deep-fried seafood baskets since 1956, when even this outlet-store-crowded stretch of Route 1 was idyllic; and today, the sweet aroma of frying seafood in the parking lot is enough to make all the roadside sprawl evaporate in a dreamy haze of escalating appetite. For the roadside epicure, this clam shack is the ne plus ultra of eat-in-the-rough cuisine.

The method of ordering and getting food at Bob's is the immemorial Yankee clam hut ritual. You read the menu posted on the outside of the building, then place your order at a screened window and pay in advance. If you have been out in the bright sun for long, you will not see anything in the darkened interior, including the person taking your order, and it is all done so fast your eyes don't adjust. No matter. The order-taker hands you a number, then you dawdle outside around the pickup window (different from the order window) until your number is called over a loudspeaker. Dine either from the dashboard of your car or at one of Bob's picnic tables with blue-checked cloth.

The whole-belly clams are lovely—tan, gnarled, crunchy with briny insides; the fried scallops are pillow soft; the shrimp are brittle-crisp; the fish in fish and chips is snow-white inside its golden crust. On the side, Bob's onion rings are some of the crunchiest and tastiest anywhere in southern Maine.

Seafood rolls are showpieces at Bob's, most of them featuring one of the hot fried foods heaped into a top-sliced bun and served with pale twiggy French fries, secret-recipe tartar sauce, and a couple of pickle slices on a porous paperboard plate. Good as these fried sandwiches may be, the lobster roll is in a class by itself, cool and expensive (about $2 more than a clam roll). The bun is warm—buttered and grilled until toasty golden brown on both sides; the lobster meat inside is faintly chilled, but not so much that any of the taste has been iced. In fact, this lobster blossoms with bracing ocean flavor when you sink your teeth into the good-size pieces. There is plenty of meat, bound with enough mayo to help it hold together. The taste that lingers, though, is not the mayonnaise. It is lobster and its butter-sopped bun.

Chauncey Creek Lobster Pound

Chauncey Creek Rd. (off 103)   207-439-1030
Kittery Point, ME   LD Mother's Day-Columbus Day | $$

Situated along a quiet waterway far from the hubbub of Route 1, Chauncey Creek Lobster Pound is an oasis of calm and classic Maine cuisine. Operated by the Spinney family since the early 1950s, it offers no upscale amenities, but it has the best seating in the world: picnic tables on a lobster pier, under a tent, or inside a screened porch. Pick a live lobster and they boil it for you. It comes with butter for dipping and a nutcracker for cracking and some cole slaw and potato chips on the side. It is a simple meal, and a relatively cheap one (depending on the current price of lobsters), but ambience like this cannot be bought at any price.

In fact, there are a few nice things to eat other than lobster. A chowder of the day is always on the menu, as are peel-and-eat shrimp, shrimp cocktails, and lobster rolls. You can get oysters on the half shell or mussels steamed in wine with garlic. To drink, there is coffee, tea, or soda pop. For dessert: Dairy Queen Dilly Bars. BYOB.

The Clam Shack

At the bridge on Route 9   207-967-2560
Kennebunkport, ME   L | $

The Clam Shack is hardly bigger than a newsstand, with nowhere to sit, inside or out. Customers cluster in the sun devouring clam baskets, chowder, and lobster rolls standing up. Leaning against the whitewashed Kennebunkport Bridge rail is a favorite way to dine, too, although you must contend with greedy birds eyeing unattended onion rings (crunchy hoops with luscious warm insides). A posted sign warns: "Beware of Seagulls. They Like Our Food as Much as You Do." Some people simply eat in their cars; most take their food on picnics.

The fried clams are superb, sold by the pint or in a clam roll, but when you sink your teeth into a Clam Shack lobster roll, you ascend into Roadfood heaven. This is the best lobster roll anywhere. You can count the pieces of meat it contains. Six, eight, maybe ten pearlescent chunks of fresh-from-the-shell tail and claw are arranged in a round bun that proprietor Steve Kingston secures especially for the sandwiches. Some pieces of lobster meat are so succulent you can hear the juices ooze when you bite them, and each is so big that a single sandwich seems lavish. You have a choice of mayonnaise or butter on this roll; what that means is the meat is assembled on the bun and only then is the condiment spooned on. The result is an array of pure pink lobster merely frosted with a dollop of mayonnaise or veiled in a shimmering mantle of melted butter.

Cole Farms

Route 100   207-657-4714
Gray, ME   BLD | $

As devotees of comfort food, we salute a restaurant that makes four kinds of pudding daily: tapioca, bread, Grape-Nuts, and Indian. Plus about a dozen pies, including mince in the cold months. Plus good ice cream for banana splits, frappés (milk, ice cream, and flavoring), shakes, and sodas. Cole Farms is known for all these things, but dessert is only the finale to this story of inland Maine foursquare cuisine.

When Cole Farms opens at 5 o'clock in the morning, most customers come for muffins. A list of the day's repertoire is posted by the door. Muffin flavors include blueberry, apple, bran, even oatmeal; or you can get them absolutely plain—a purposeful breakfast breadstuff that Warren Cole told us is known simply as "old-fashioned egg muffins." These are truly wonderful, and the kind of ordinary food no tourist restaurant would ever dream of serving. They are warm and eggy, served hot from the oven, augmented with a pat of butter and a blob of honey.

Every day at lunch there is a choice of homemade soups and chowders, and clam cakes to accompany any meal. This is one of the few remaining dining rooms in New England where you can sit down to a simple and delicious plate of baked beans, with or without hot dogs, or that even rarer Downeast favorite, American chop suey (the Platonic ideal of Hamburger Helper). Meat loaf and chili are exemplary, and the weekend-only prime rib is a sight to behold.

The menu has something for everyone, but what we like best about it are the daily specials with a true Yankee accent, especially the New England boiled dinner every Thursday—that's corned beef, potatoes, cabbage, carrots, turnips, and beets. Tuesday is Yankee pot roast day. Wednesday means chicken pot pie. We should mention that prices are Yankee-frugal, too. The daily specials all run between $4 and $7, except for the prime rib, which is $9.95 or $11.95 depending on size, and the Monday special of macaroni and cheese—a hearty dinner, with rolls, for the grand sum of $2.95!

Cole Farms is a big café, four or five rooms strung together but partitioned by a kind of fencing, so that even though the space is sprawling, each booth seems cozy. Decor is a pedestrian mix of varnished pine and Formica. Place settings are marked by paper mats that ask *Did You Know?* and feature trivia questions.

Five Islands Lobster Company

1447 Five Islands Rd.	207-371-2990
Georgetown, ME	LD (summer only) | $$

Five Islands Lobster Company used to be called the Georgetown Fisherman's Co-Op. By contract, every five years the waterside site changes hands, and usually its name. But in our experience, you can count on it, whatever it's called, for one of the best and certainly most scenic lobster dinners along the coast.

From a picnic table on the dock, the sweeping view encompasses five small pine-covered islands just off the rocky coast. Nearby trawlers rock gently at their mooring, gulls squawk overhead, and the briny ocean air is tinged by the sweet smell of fresh-cooked lobster meat.

"Come on back, let's pick one out," is the greeting at the counter in the red clapboard shed on the pier when you walk in and say you'd like a lobster. When you find one the right size, it is boiled to order, along with corn on the cob or potatoes. Next door is a grill, where a broader menu offers crisp-fried crab cakes, lobster rolls, crunchy onion rings, fish and chips, etc., for whole-lobster-frowners (or for those of us who need things to eat while we wait the twenty minutes for our lobster to cook). And for dessert, the ice cream shop offers hot fudge sundaes or Maine blueberry cake.

Of course, the lobsters are beautiful and delicious, served on trays with drawn butter and accompanied by a nutcracker and a large smooth stone for cracking the shell. If you want to drink wine or beer, bring your own.

The Maine coast lobster-eating experience gets no better than this.

Flo's

Route 1
Cape Neddick (York), ME

No phone
L daily except Wednesday | $

The only choice you have to make when you walk into Flo's is how many hot dogs you want and how you want them dressed. Hot dogs are the only thing on Flo's menu, and that's just fine, for they are, in their own bite-size way, magnificent.

They are small, pale pink Schultz-brand franks, steamed taut and nestled in soft buns: a fine foundation for Flo's glorious hot sauce, a spicy-sweet onion relish that has inspired imitators up and down Maine's lower coast. In addition to relish, you want a dash of celery salt and, depending on which way you want to take your dog, either mayonnaise or mustard. Mayo makes it rich and luxurious. Mustard makes it snappy.

For those with a healthy appetite, half a dozen are a filling meal. But if you do drive away from Flo's filled, it won't be long before you wish you had gotten more. And when you are far from this roadside gem, you will dream of Flo's hot dogs, longingly. There is nothing like them anywhere else.

If the six little swivel stools at the short counter are filled (they almost always are), dine at one of the picnic tables outside or off the dashboard of your car.

Harraseeket Lobster

Town Landing 207-865-3635

Freeport, ME LD May–October | $$

Harraseeket Lobster is one of the nicest places west of Bath to plow into a shoreline meal. The specialty is boiled-to-order lobsters (also available live, to go), but don't ignore the seafood baskets. Whole-belly clams are giants, hefty gnarled spheres of golden crust enveloping mouthfuls of ocean nectar. On the side, you want onion rings: puffy circles of brittle sweet batter around a hoop of onion that still has crunch. Clam cakes are good, too, their dough dotted with dozens of little nuggets of marine goodness. The chowder is wonderful, but best of all is the lobster roll, served splayed open in a broad cardboard dish and packed with sweet chunks of meat. Have it with onion rings or an order of fried onion middles (slick nuggets that are to fried rings what holes are to donuts); and conclude with a fudgy, hand-fashioned whoopie pie.

Now that the management has put an awning up over the picnic tables, you can dine outdoors even when it rains. They tell us that it does rain in Freeport, but every visit we have made to town in search of our favorite clam baskets and o-rings, the sun was shining brightly and gulls were swooping overhead through the blue, blue sky. It is almost painfully picturesque, this eat-in-the-rough jewel of a clam shack overlooking the South Freeport Harbor. Even if it were ugly, we would recommend it for the seafood baskets and the lobsters.

Maine Diner

2265 Post Rd. 207-646-4441

Wells, ME BLD | $

It has been some twenty years since Bruce and Myles Henry of Drake's Island bought this old diner in Wells and turned it into one of the great culinary attractions of the lower Maine coast. Using family recipes and their own know-how, as well as occasional suggestions from friendly customers, they cooked up a menu that is equal parts Downeast and diner, with a dash of modern savoir faire. (Lobster Benedict, for heaven's sake!)

For us, no trip up Route 1 is complete without a visit to the Maine Diner, whether it's for a plate of homemade baked beans at dawn, chowder and meat loaf at noon, or lobster pie at supper time. Daily specials are truly special, including classic New England boiled dinner every Thursday and red flannel hash (made from leftover boiled dinner) on Saturday . . . while supplies last. We are especially fond of the fried clams, which are vigorously oceanic, just a wee bit oily, so fragile the crust seems to melt away as your teeth sink into them. If you are a serious clam lover, you can order the clam-o-rama lunch, which includes clam chowder, fried whole-belly clams, fried clam strips, and a clam cake!

Seafood rolls are outstanding—split buns piled with clams, haddock, scallops, or shrimp. And the lobster rolls are not to be missed. Yes, we said rolls, plural, for the Maine Diner is one of the few places that offers two kinds—a lobster salad roll of cool meat and mayo, or a hot lobster roll of warm meat with plenty of melted butter to drizzle on it. Either one is terrific; for us, the hot lobster roll is heaven on earth.

The menu is vast, including such all-American items as buffalo wings and barbecued pork sandwich, plus a superb chicken pot pie. When we visit, we stick to Maine cuisine, which the Henry brothers do so well, the best of which is lobster pie. Made from their grandmother's recipe, lobster pie is a casserole containing plump sections of lobster—soft claw and chewy tail meat—drenched in butter and topped with a mixture of cracker crumbs and tomalley. It is a strange, oddly colored dish, green and brown and pink, and shockingly rich.

Moody's Diner

Route 1	207-832-7785
Waldoboro, ME	BLD | $

Moody's is a roadside icon. The quintessential coast-of-Maine diner, it has been open round-the-clock since 1934. Although it has changed over the years, evolving from a lunch wagon to a full-kitchen restaurant with counter, stools, and booths, this welcoming establishment remains an honest roadside diner where you can count on a good, inexpensive meal, served fast, any time of night or day.

There is always a good selection of muffins and donuts in the morning—not spectacular pastries, and not even all that sugary. These are Downeast eats, honest and understated. We love the corned beef hash in the morning, especially alongside a couple of sunny-side-up eggs and home-fried potatoes. At lunch and dinner there are classic diner meals of meat loaf, corned beef, and pork chops, as well as some items that have a more distinct New England flavor. The seafood chowder and lobster stew are terrific, as are franks and beans and Yankee pot roast. You can even enjoy that little-known Downeast delight, fried tripe, and top it off with a dish of warm Indian pudding. There's an only-in-Maine meal for you!

We need to note (because to many travelers up the Maine coast, Moody's is best known as a pie stop) that Moody's makes pudding, a dish that has vanished from so many diner menus. Here, you can even get that strange local delight, Grape-Nuts pudding. Some five dozen pies are made daily and are available round-the-clock. Fruit pies and cream pies are lovely to look at and to eat; longtime favorites include nursery-nice custard pie dusted with nutmeg, four-berry pie, blueberry pie, and a wickedly sweet walnut cream pie that is known statewide.

To accompany your meal, there is coffee (fifty cents a cup!), of course, as well as a selection of soda fountain drinks with names that will make no sense to an out-of-stater. A *milk shake,* for instance, is milk and flavoring, whereas a *velvet* is what most of the rest of the world knows as a milk shake: milk, flavoring, and ice cream.

Nunan's Lobster Hut

Route 9	208-967-4362
Cape Porpoise, ME	D (summer only)	$$

At Nunan's Lobster Hut, you eat at a bare table with a raised rim to hold in the inevitable spillage caused by cracking into a lobster's shell. The lobsters are carried from the kitchen on pizza pans, accompanied by bags of potato chips and uninteresting rolls. Water comes in paper cups. Bring your own wine or beer, and the management will give you paper cups for that, too. Other than the lobster the only notable thing to eat at Nunan's is dessert, in the form of good homemade pie, preferably blueberry.

Nunan's offers no frills because it would be wrong to distract diners from the perfection of the lobster. Each one is steamed to order in a couple of inches of salty water just long enough to emerge with silky tender claw meat, its knuckles and tail succulent and chewy. It is served immediately, still too hot to handle.

Perhaps the term "no frills" is incorrect, for Nunan's is in fact designed to a fare-thee-well precisely for the enjoyment of lobsters. While it may resemble a World War II surplus Quonset hut, its interior is outfitted with capacious work-sinks for handwashing, and rolls of paper towels for hand drying. While these amenities might be a bit crude for some urban four-star dining room, they are precisely what the serious lobster eater needs, at least a few times during dinner.

As for decor, there isn't much other than the usual array of buoys and fish nets. However, there does happen to be a nice view out the small windows in the back dining room: the marshlands of Cape Porpoise aglow with twilight sun.

Red's Eats

Water St. and Main St.   207-882-6128
Wiscasset, ME   LD May-September | $$

Red's is a building about the size of a minivan that has been serving lobster rolls since 1938. It opened in Boothbay and moved to the north end of Wiscasset in 1954. It has no indoor seating, just a scattering of chairs in front and some picnic tables out back; and while service is brusque and eat-in-the-rough, this is a destination-diner for legions of summer visitors to the Maine coast.

The hamburgers, French fries, onion rings, and fried zucchini are all very good; and if you must eat chicken, there is a lovely-looking grilled chicken sandwich on the menu. There are decent hot dogs and ice cream, too. But really, there is only one reason to come to Red's, and that is Red's lobster roll. What a beauty . . . and what a whopper! It appears that nearly all the meat from a decent-size lobster has been extracted in big chunks, bathed in butter, and loaded into a buttered and grilled split bun. Note that this is a hot lobster roll, *not* a lobster salad roll with cold meat and mayonnaise to bind it. It is warm meat and meat only; and to eat such a lobster roll is no easy task, for pieces of lobster are likely to tumble out and the bread itself will start to disintegrate from the lobster's juices and the melted butter that is used as a condiment.

Lobster rolls are not cheap, and Red's rolls are relatively expensive. With a soda and an order of fries, you'll spend $15. Few meals we know are so deeply satisfying.

Shain's of Maine

Route 109   207-324-1449
Sanford, ME   BLD | $

Being citizens of Connecticut, we like to point out as often as possible that New England makes the best and eats the most ice cream; but within the region, we must tip our hat to the state of Maine for advancing the concept of strange, really strange flavors. (This is an ambition with roots in Massachusetts, where Howard Johnson's once boasted of "28 flavors," and it was taken to extremes recently in Vermont by Ben & Jerry's truly loony inventions, such as Phish Food and Chubby Hubby). At the venerable old Round Top of Damariscotta, you can order Morning Glory ice cream, which, like the familiar muffin, contains carrots and raisins. Smiling Hill farm offers Barnyard Scramble, which includes broken cone, nuts, jimmies, and chocolate chips. At Gifford's of Skowhegan, you can actually order Black Fly ice cream, which contains no actual insects, but does contain little bits of chocolate that resemble bugs. One of the truly great—but not too weird—flavors of Maine is Shain's Kahlúa Brownie: coffee ice cream chockablock with chunks of chewy brownie.

Shain's is a for-real ice cream factory (you can tour the plant) that sells its product in regional stores and markets; but it is also a fine restaurant to know about if you are looking for creamy clam chowder, a plate of fried seafood, or a hamburger. Whatever you have for lunch, consider it a prelude to ice cream (or frozen yogurt, available fat-free or sugar-free), in the form of cones, cups, sundaes, splits, and sodas, and in flavors that range from chocolate and vanilla to the old Yankee favorite, Grape-Nuts.

Thompson's Restaurant

272 Main St.   207-672-3245
Bingham, ME   BLD | $

We were led to this town dining room by Camille and Norman Dee, Roadfooders who described it as "simple, good . . . exactly what the romantic in us imagines Roadfood to be . . . even a waitress with big hair!"

We didn't meet the big-haired waitress, but we sure did have a wicked-good lunch. Tender, vividly beefy pot roast came with a veritable mountain of mashed potatoes. And our lobster roll was loaded with large hunks of moist, sweet meat. Custard pie had a fine, flaky crust and smooth elemental filling. The Dees also recommended Thompson's donuts, which looked great—they're made on-site every morning—but frankly, our lunches were so filling that we couldn't even think of taking some in the car for later.

Baxter's Boathouse

177 Pleasant St.   508-775-7040
Hyannis, MA   LD April-Columbus Day | $$

Eat in the rough: after studying the posted menu at Baxter's, place an order at the counter, then loiter nearby as the kitchen puts it together in approximately 120 seconds. You then carry your own tray to a varnished table indoors or a picnic table overlooking Hyannis Harbor. Or you can enjoy table service on the *Governor Brann,* a ferryboat converted into a floating dining room with seating for a few hundred customers. Or, if you choose, you can arrive by boat, tie up at Baxter's dock, and be waited on!

However you experience Baxter's, the thing to eat is summertime Yankee shore fare: crisp fried clams served with decent fries or indecently tasty clam fritters, which are deep-fried doughballs dotted with morsels of clam and served with honey for dipping. The lobster rolls are good, as is the Yankee-style (creamy) chowder. Or you can eat fine scallops, shrimps, or oysters. Steaks are available, too, for fish-frowners.

Baxter's is a restaurant and a club, and it is a popular pastime among the local drinking set to occupy the club long into the night, knocking back shots and beers. For us, the beverage of choice with our seafood dinners is the drink known here as "tonic," which is simply the eastern Bay State word for what the rest of us know as soda pop.

Boulevard Ocean View Restaurant

25 Western Ave.   978-281-2949
Gloucester, MA 01930   LD | $$

We wouldn't recommend Boulevard Ocean View Restaurant to just anybody. Certain aspects of the dining experience are—how shall we say?—less than refined. It's a perfectly pleasant place, in a great location facing the Gloucester sea (and with a deck for outdoor dining); and we admire the handsome formal portrait of Elvis Presley above the washroom doors. But it requires a sense of Roadfood humor to appreciate a waitress who stood near our table as we ate our fish stew and offered her running personal commentary on each piece of seafood as we pulled it from the serving bowl. (She loves clams, isn't so fond of lobster.) When we did as she suggested and used all our dinner rolls to mop the stew's juices from the plate, she volunteered to go back to the kitchen to bring us more rolls. It took a little while longer than we expected for the rolls to appear because while in the kitchen, Mademoiselle scooped herself a double-dip ice cream cone; and when she came out, our roll basket was in one of her hands, the cone in her other. As we continued with our supper, she leaned against a nearby counter, licking her ice cream.

The main reason we recommend eating at Boulevard Ocean View is not for its idiosyncratic service but for a repertoire of exquisite Portuguese seafood. That mainly means *mariscada,* which is a vast bowl full of littleneck clams, mussels, shrimp, scallops, and one large lobster in a rich wine/tomato broth with a handful of good olives. It also means salted cod. Our waitress explained to us that whole fields were once spread with cod that had been salted and set out in the sun to preserve it. But nowadays, she said, only the old-time Portuguese and Italians like it that way. "It's *so* 1600s," she said with disdain for the out-of-fashion technique. "I'm Portuguese myself, and I don't like it!" No question, salted cod, also known as *baccalà,* is an acquired taste; but this is a good restaurant in which to acquire it, for here the kitchen uses a thick hunk of really fresh (that is, freshly salted) cod that has been so well rinsed of its preservative that it tastes virtually salt-free. It is cooked over a charcoal fire so it develops a crunchy, flame-flavored exterior. The meat inside is intensely tasty, unlike any merely fresh fish.

When you see a plate of Boulevard Ocean View fried clams, you are reminded that you are on the North Shore of Massachusetts, where fried clams are simply better and more beautiful than anywhere else. Although we go for the *mariscada* every time, with maybe some clams as an hors d'oeuvre, it's also worth noting that the menu lists a whole roster of seafood that is not specifically Portuguese: swordfish, crab cakes, and plain or fancy lobsters.

Butler's Colonial Donut House

459 Sanford Rd.   508-672-4600

Westport, MA   B | $

In New England, donuts are an art, and Alex Kogler of Butler's Colonial Donut House is one of the top artists.

The donuts he makes are not like any ordinary sinker destined to be dunked in a cup of coffee. Each one is a giant, featherweight cream puff, holeless and sliced in half and filled with whipped, sweetened cream that is either plain or mocha flavored. Made from raised yeast dough, the donut is so fragile that you want to hold it very gently, lest you dent the surface with a heavy thumb. The cool filling is pure and white—or in the case of mocha, tan—and the counterpoise of silky whipped cream with ethereal cake, crowned by a spill of powdered sugar on the top, is angelic. Alex also creates a majestic long john, for which the same dough is fashioned into a rectangular shape, fried, then cut in half and filled with whipped cream and a thin ribbon of black raspberry jelly. The sweetness of the jelly tilts the flavor balance of this stout little hero toward delirious. As Alex likes to put it, his long john is "the ultimate."

He has been making donuts since 1976, when he bought the shop from Bill and Jeanette Butler, who opened the morning-only bakery in a shack in front of their house in 1955. Hours of operation are, as always, severely limited. The famous cream donuts are not even made in the summer months, when the delicate filling would wilt in the heat; and in winter, the bakery is open only Thursday through Sunday mornings. If all the donuts are sold before the midday closing time, the door is locked and Alex goes home so he can get some rest and, if it's a weekend, return to the bakery around midnight, when a new day's batch is begun.

Caffe Sicilia

40 Main St.   978-283-7345
Gloucester, MA   BL | $

Gloucester is a place for travelers in search of genuine local color. Yes, there are restaurants that serve the tourist trade and a fair number of shops catering to out-of-towners, but the town really is a working fishing port with stores, restaurants, and taverns that cater to the men and women who go down to the sea in ships.

Paul Ciaramitaro used to be one of those men, but now, with his wife, Anna, he runs Caffe Sicilia, a coffee bar and pastry shop on Main Street. Paul is a huge guy with huge enthusiasms, and his presence fills the tiny shop that is his domain down near the waterfront. He holds court behind the counter, where he makes espressos for friends who drop by for morning chats among the four small tables that barely fit in the store; and he delights in boasting to newcomers that *his* pastries are fresh, not like those sold by certain other shops across the street that get *theirs* from Boston. In particular, he is proud of his *cornetti,* which are featherweight confections that resemble croissants but have a ribbon of lemon filling inside and a dusting of powdered sugar. He also makes airy semolina bread, elaborate cakes, spectacularly colorful marzipan candies, and a "lobster tail" pastry like an Italian *sfoglia*—ultra-thin sheaves of dough shaped like a lobster tail, sugar-topped and filled with cream.

Mr. Ciaramitaro's gelati are delightful. He recommends the *nocciola,* which he tells us is hazelnut, and also the *zuppa inglese,* something like an English trifle, for which there is no proper English translation. "Marsala wine and fruit!" he rhapsodizes; and when we don't seem to understand quite how wonderful it is, he quickly dips spoons into the freezer case and offers us each a hearty taste. When we smack our lips and smile at its creamy sweet goodness, he beams with satisfaction, then, bursting with pride, he points us to a newspaper story displayed on the wall. "From the *Financial Times . . . of London!*" he says, stepping over to run his finger underneath a line that says his pastries put those of New York's Little Italy to shame. "No more need be said!"

Clam Box

246 High St. (Route 1A)   978-356-9707

Ipswich, MA   LD | $$

Every few years we eat our way along the North Shore of Massachusetts in a quest to decide where the best fried clams are. It's never an easy choice, because nearly all the fried clams you find are superb, in a class by themselves, beyond fried clams anywhere else. The clams are harvested here; and the tradition of frying them originated here (at Woodman's, page 57).

For the last several years, we have reached the same conclusion every time: The best of the best are served at the Clam Box of Ipswich. This conclusion especially pleases us because the Clam Box is such a likable place, even to look at. Shaped like a clam box, the trapezoidal container in which fried-clams-to-go are customarily served, it is a genuine roadside attraction that dates back some six decades. Under the stewardship of Marina "Chickie" Aggelakelis for the last several years, the restaurant has thrived; and the clams have maintained their preeminence.

The best way to have them is as a platter: a plate piled high with modest-size whole-bellied clams, French fries, and onion rings. You'll get a little tartar sauce for dipping and some wonderful sweet cole slaw, which is a necessary part of the clam-eating experience, for it helps cut the grease of so much fried food. But the truly wonderful thing about Clam Box fried clams is how *greaseless* they seem. They are luscious and crunchy, no doubt about that; but you'll have no oily fingers after plowing through a plate.

There is now some indoor seating, and across the parking lot from the building there are picnic tables for al fresco dining. Throughout most of the summer, expect a wait in line at mealtimes. The Clam Box is famous, deservedly so.

Durgin-Park

Faneuil Hall Marketplace   617-227-2038

Boston, MA   LD | $$

Like the Old North Church or the swan boats in the Public Garden, Durgin-Park is a landmark; no other restaurant is truer to the spirit of New England gastronomy yet so exceptional. Twice a day the open kitchen launches large portions of good food at reasonable prices into a dining room with all the charm of an army mess. Every customer begins with a square of grainy yellow corn bread. Then you can move on to such old favorites as whole lobster or Boston scrod (baby cod), or pot roast or pork loin. The house specialty is prime rib, a gargantuan cut that overhangs its plate. Side that with a mountain of mashed potatoes (into which the kitchen indelicately slides pats of butter, still in paper wrappers) and a scoop of fresh apple sauce, and you've got a mighty meal.

What could be more all-American than roast turkey with sage dressing . . . or New England boiled dinner of corned beef and cabbage? The beans Durgin-Park serves are real Boston baked beans, firm and silky, not too sweet, with a dash of molasses. This frumpy food traces its genealogy back to 1742, when the Faneuil Market was opened and a second-story eatery was established to serve the produce vendors. Although the market has been renovated into a modern urban grazing emporium with lattes and bagel shops galore, the old Durgin-Park dining room, with its red-checked linen, harsh lighting, and tables for twenty, is as rude and idiosyncratic as ever.

Nobody gets celebrity treatment; nobody is even treated nicely—and that's the fun of it. You better know what you want when the waitress comes around, because these gruff old birds give no quarter. And the food itself, slapped onto plates in the kitchen, comes in portions suitable for Elmer the Elephant. When you are finished, you pay the lady with cash or credit card and walk out the door with doggie bags fit for a whole wolf pack.

The Durgin-Park dessert list is tradition itself, featuring hot mince pie in the autumn, apple pandowdy, deep dish apple pie, strawberry shortcake on a biscuit, and the world's best Indian pudding, which is a steaming gruel of cornmeal and molasses that only a true Yankee could love.

Essex Seafood

143R Eastern Ave.   978-768-7233
Essex, MA   LD | $$

Cape Ann, Massachusetts, is to fried clams what Champagne, France, is to wine. The sweetest, tenderest, tastiest soft-shelled clams—perfect for frying—are harvested from the mud flats on Essex Bay; and although fried clams are served by pint and platter all along the eastern seaboard, none can compare to those dished out by the clam shacks of Essex and Ipswich.

Among the top places hereabouts to eat fried clams—as well as just about any other local seafood dinner, especially including big beautiful lobsters—is Essex Seafood. It is, in fact, primarily a lobster pound, where people come to buy them live to take home and boil, or already boiled and ready to eat. Adjacent to the market and the big holding pens is a quiet dining room with a window to the kitchen. This is the order window, where you select from a menu of various-size lobster dinners, as well as fried clams, scallops, and shrimp, plus excellent clam chowder and corn on the cob. The lobsters are impeccably fresh; and the fried seafood plates are beautiful to behold: a layer of French fried potatoes, topped with a layer of onion rings, topped with a heap of your seafood of choice. Clams are especially wonderful—big and crunchy, with a sweet ocean flavor.

Eat inside, at booths in the wood-paneled dining room that is decorated with charming nautical bric-a-brac, or choose a green-painted picnic table outdoors in back—a breezy retreat from Route 133 near the Essex-Gloucester town line.

J. T. Farnham's

88 Eastern Ave. (Route 133)   978-768-6643
Essex, MA   LD | $$

Farnham's has expanded its menu and its dining room since Joe and Terry Collucci bought it from the original owners in 1994. You can now get broiled scallops and three kinds of chowder (clam, fish, haddock), as well as wine and beer with your meal; and the seating capacity inside is more than forty.

Some things haven't changed. The fried seafood specialties, clams in particular, are still top-drawer, prepared according to the original recipes that made Farnham's a locals' favorite as well as a destination-diner for more than fifty years. Dipped in an egg wash, then pure corn-flour coating, shrimp, scallops, clams, calamari, oysters, and haddock all emerge from the deep fryer with a fine, fragile crust that has fully melded with the sweet fish it enrobes. When you take a bite, the crust will crunch, then virtually evaporate to become a lush complement to the primary flavor. Farnham's has long been known for serving clams with modest-size bellies, as opposed to the big, goopy ones that some clam fanatics prefer. (Belly-less strips, made from fresh, not frozen, clams, are also available.) We love the whole-belly clams this size because they have enough marine succulence to give full satisfaction without ever being grossly liquid the way a giant-belly clam can be.

Besides first-rate food, Farnham's offers accommodations that can't be beat. The indoor wood-paneled dining room is cozy and informal with all the vacation-time charm of an eat-in-the-rough seafood shack. Place your order and pay . . . and in this case, a waitress will actually bring the food to your table. However, a sign on the wall asks: "Please help us keep our dining room clean by clearing your own table." The best seats (when it's not horsefly season in late July) are outside—a row of picnic tables lined up over Essex Salt Marsh, a tranquil vista where modern life seems never to have intruded. Here, in the waters that thread through an endless sea of green, egrets perch and cormorants dive, and the salt air sweeps in to induce a ravenous appetite for more clams, with a cold Moxie or sarsaparilla on the side!

Flav's Red Skiff

15 Mt. Pleasant St.   978-546-7647

Rockport, MA   BL | $

Flav's Red Skiff, named for proprietors Mark and Victoria Flavin, is a tiny café with cute pastel-checked-cloth-covered tables and decor that consists of old magazine advertisements, a glowing review or two, and the paper napkin Tom Selleck signed for proprietor Mrs. Flavin the day he stopped in for breakfast while filming the movie *Love Letter* on the oh-so-picturesque streets of Rockport. It is a hangout for locals as well as visitors, and during the busy summer months, you can expect to wait for a precious table or seat at the counter any time after eight in the morning.

The restaurant is small enough that early in the morning, before the crowds arrive, conversations tend to be all-inclusive among diners at the counter and tables and the staff behind the pass-through window to the kitchen. By mid-morning, Flav's is so crowded that you might have a hard time hearing your tablemate talk.

The most interesting regional item on Flav's menu is anadama bread, which was supposedly invented in Rockport when a fisherman grew so angry at his lazy wife, Anna, that he baked his own loaf of bread from wheat flour, cornmeal, and molasses . . . all the while muttering, "Anna, damn her." Whatever its origins, Flav's makes a dark, sweet, and high-flavored anadama loaf that tastes just great when toasted and buttered. (Whole loaves are available to take home.) The unique bread is used to make interesting French toast, available plain or topped with strawberries, but in truth, we like simple toasted anadama bread better. The egg dip, frying, and strawberry topping tend to detract from the solid Yankee character of the bread itself. Other good breakfasts include elegant, plate-wide pancakes (buttermilk, blueberry, or chocolate chip) and a warm pecan roll that is served adrip with caramel frosting.

Four Seas

360 S. Main   508-775-1394
Centerville, MA   LD (summer only) | $

Four Seas is beloved by generations of Cape Cod residents and visitors for its ice cream, served in cones, cups, and sundaes. Long inventories inside and on the restaurant's outside wall enumerate which of several dozen flavors are available that day: vanilla, chocolate, strawberry, of course; maple walnut, black raspberry, and other fairly familiar names; plus such curious house specialties as penuche pecan and frozen pudding; and, on occasion, fresh cantaloupe. Likewise, the list of sundae sauces ranges from the familiar—hot milk chocolate (a.k.a. hot fudge) and hot butterscotch—to such soda-fountain Victoriana as claret, wild cherry, and soft walnuts in maple syrup. Frappé and milk shake flavors are also itemized—all are available plain, minted, or malted—and if you're not from around here, you need to know that a milk shake means nothing but a flavored syrup and milk; a frappé is what most of the rest of us know as a milk shake: flavoring, milk, and ice cream expertly blended together.

Sundaes are a delight; claret sauce on chocolate ice cream is our undoing. And there is one non–ice cream item we need to note, the perfectly proportioned lobster salad roll—available only between 10 A.M. and 2:30 P.M. But the pride of Four Seas is the cones: small (one generous globe), large (one extra-big triangle-shaped scoop), or double (two globes); the last is the maximum amount of ice cream any ordinary-size cone can bear. It is a pleasure to watch the boys and girls behind the counter construct the cones. They have perfected the correct circular scooping motion to retrieve just the right amount from the bucket, packed tight and even; and they know exactly how to use the scoop to force it onto the cone for maximum adherence and minimum drippage.

The cone, of course, is the perfect ice cream delivery system, allowing folks to eat on the stroll without cumbersome utensils, and also eluding any interference from sauce, nuts, cherries, or whipped cream. This is not to impugn fudge or marshmallow fluff; it's just that Four Seas' product is worth savoring with no adornment. It is honest and pure, luxurious but not ridiculously rich. This is ice cream you want to eat every night, all summer long.

Kelly's Roast Beef

Revere Beach Rd.   781-284-9129
Revere, MA   LD | $
Also in Danvers, Natick, and Saugus

Roast beef sandwiches are important north of Boston. In Lynn, Saugus, Salem, Beverly, and up toward Cape Ann, dozens of quick-service eateries make beef their star attraction. When we went looking for Kelly's Roast Beef in Revere (the original, and now one of four Kelly's around Beantown), we asked a gent outside an auto body shop if he knew where Kelly's was. "Whaddaya, hungry?" he asked with glee, pointing us to what he promised would be "one hunnerd fitty percent satisfaction."

Service is eat-in-the-rough: place your order at the broad window, gather your meal in your arms, and find a bench under the covered pavilion by Revere Beach. The roast beef is lovely indeed: soft, pink meat sliced thin and piled high on a butter-toasted, sesame-seed bun. Beyond its signature beef Kelly's serves dynamite shoreline seafood: crunchy hunks of fish (with chips), pints of toasty-flavored, plump-bodied fried clams served in such superabundance that they overflow their clam box, and sweet onion rings on the side.

By the way, the names for drinks at Kelly's are utterly local. Soda pop is called tonic, and what the rest of the world knows as a milk shake (ice cream, milk, flavoring) is a frappé.

Mrs. O's

Route 7   413-442-6830
Lanesboro, MA   BLD | $$

Route 7 south of the estimable Blue Benn Diner has always been a kind of Roadfood desert, so when we saw that Mrs. O's purported to offer seafood just like on Cape Cod, it was impossible to resist.

Service is eat-in-the-rough style: place your order at the counter; and if you stand around, you can watch your raw clams getting weighed out, dredged, and tossed into the deep fryer. If you've ordered a clam roll, a New England split-top bun is buttered and toasted on the grill. The whole shebang is presented in a Styrofoam container that includes a big ramekin of excellent tartar sauce and a couple of lemon wedges. Nice snack!

Mrs. O's menu offers more than just sandwiches. There are full-bore seafood platters of shrimp, scallops, clams (bellies and strips are available), and scrod with French fries, cole slaw, and a biscuit. Beyond shoreline seafood, the menu of this breezy café and raw fish market includes hamburgers and sandwiches, and breakfast from 6:30 to 11 A.M. every day.

Nick's Famous Roast Beef

139 Dodge St.   978-922-9075
North Beverly, MA   LD | $

Nick's motto—"We're the Only One"—is designed to set it apart from the many roast beef sandwich chains north of Boston. In our opinion, it's among the very best. Like all the local roast beef houses, it is a self-service joint. Place your order and wait for a number to be called, then carry your own tray to a table somewhere in the small strip-mall storefront eatery. The menu lists a large beef sandwich, a junior beef sandwich, and a super beef sandwich on an onion roll. Super beef is the way to go. It is a well-stacked pile of soft, pink beef inside a giant rectangular roll that is egg-yellow and studded with squiggles of onion. Many condiments and add-ins are available, including horseradish, cheese, mayo, and mustard, but the people's choice is barbecue sauce, which has a spicy sweetness that makes it beef's good companion. And speaking of companions, you definitely want onion rings! Nick's onion rings are beautiful—golden brown and wickedly crunchy—wanting only a hail of salt to attain perfection.

Decoration at Nick's consists of hundreds of snapshots taken of roast beef fans all over America and the world showing them standing in front of famous places holding up a Nick's Beef bumper sticker.

Santarpio's

111 Chelsea St.	617-567-9871
East Boston, MA	LD	$$

When someone writes *The History of Pizza in America,* Santarpio's will deserve significant mention as the Boston pizzeria that remained unaffected by fashion, in a city where pizza always has been plebeian food. A neighborhood tavern on the way to Logan Airport where locals come to chat over beer about sports (primarily boxing) and to eat thin-crusted pies, Santarpio's serves no boutique pizzas, nosiree! About the most exotic item on the pizza menu is the garlic pie, which is topped not only with huge amounts of garlic but with clouds of oregano, too. Other available toppings include onions, mushrooms, pepperoni, sausage, anchovies, and peppers in any combination you like; and Santarpio's will make a white pizza—without sauce. There is only one size available—about fourteen inches in diameter.

The toppings are good, but what makes these pizzas outstanding is crust. It is fairly thin, with a rim that puffs up a bit in the brick oven, resulting in a balance of crunch and chew all around the edge, where a few high spots have turned brittle. The thinness of the crust means that the center of the circle tends to soften under a lot of toppings—leading to the heartbreak of cheese slippage—but even the unwieldy parts of Santarpio's pizzas are easy on the tongue with a sort of creamy flavor to the cheese and mild red sauce that makes you want to keep eating more. In our experience, one pie is just about enough to satisfy a modest appetite.

Satisfying as the pizza is, it is wise in this place to consider the one other available kind of food: bar-b-q. At Santarpio's, "bar-b-q" means meat cooked on a grate over charcoal—lengths of homemade Italian sausage and skewered hunks of lamb. The sausage is in the form of a long, taut tube with the flavor of the charcoal fire permeating its highly spiced insides. Many people get sausage and/or lamb as a pre-pizza hors d'oeuvre on a plate with hot cherry peppers and crusty Italian bread.

Service at Santarpio's is, shall we say, colorful. Waitresses are fast, efficient, and actually helpful, although we imagine their brusque style might intimidate someone whose only experience in a pizzeria is at Wolfgang Puck's or one of the bland national chains. Metal trays carrying pizzas are clanged down onto bare tables without ceremony; drinks are delivered in a cluster for everyone to sort out; and when you order another round of pizza because the first one was not enough, the person bussing tables will dump the crumbs off your plate and return that same plate to you, along with the silverware you've already used.

There are two dining rooms. The front room, which is also a bar, is where the beef and lamb are cooked over charcoal. To the side is a wood-paneled annex where large parties of large people come to eat large amounts of pizza and drink all the beer necessary to wash it down.

Tom's Hot Dogs

37 State Rd.   413-665-2931
Whately, MA   LD | $

After all the eating we've done around America, you'd think we would know what's especially good in our own backyard. But we sure don't know everything, and that's what makes Roadfooding an eternal joy. Just recently we got a note from Greg P. of Springfield, Massachusetts, in which Greg noted (with great kindness) that we had neglected to cover any of the great hot dog places with which western Massachusetts is especially well endowed. In particular, Greg mentioned Tom's for its terrific hot dogs and roadside shack ambience that included Saturday morning polka music blaring from inside the order window. We headed north out of Connecticut on a hot-dog-eating binge.

Polka music faded into the background as we hefted a Tom's long dog from its cardboard tray and sank teeth into it. This big boy is so well packed that it audibly snaps when bitten! A foot long (extending far beyond the bun) and packed into natural casing, it is pale pink and quite literally bursting with flavor inside a steamed split bun. It is well-nigh perfect with nothing more than a line of mustard and spoonful of relish and raw onion spread across the top, but Tom's offers several nice variations, including a Mexican dog with spicy jalapeño cheese and a New England dog topped with baked beans.

On the side of the superlative dog, you definitely want French fries. These are gorgeous spuds cut from *locally grown* potatoes and fried until a rich honey color, served in a cardboard boat. At the order counter, as condiment for the potatoes, there is ketchup as well as squeeze bottles of cider vinegar and white vinegar. Vinegar is the pertinent French fry dressing in parts of the Northeast where fish and chips is part of the culinary heritage.

Tom's is a classic roadside eat-shack, where the expressed goal of the management is *ninety-second service* from the time you place your order. It is open year-round and, although good homemade soups are available only in cool weather, it is a special joy in summer . . . and not only because that is when tuna macaroni salad is available. Summer is when you can tote your well-worn tray to a picnic table out back and enjoy a quintessential roadside feast surrounded by the farmland of the Connecticut River Valley. Other than the picnic tables, Tom's has no sit-down dining facilities.

Turtle Alley

91A Washington St.   978-281-4000
Gloucester, MA   L | $

As a young girl growing up in Gloucester, Hallie Baker had a pet turtle. A few years ago, when she was about to realize her dream of opening a hometown candy store, it occurred to her that candy turtles should be her premier item. Triple-bite-size and made of chocolate, caramel, and nuts, turtles are among the most luxurious of confectionery sweets; and yet Hallie believes that mass-produced ones, totally enrobed in chocolate, have no personality.

Step into her candy store, named Turtle Alley, and behold a majestic school of terrapins: big, knobby candy rounds of dark, white, and milk chocolate, each as individual as a snowflake, and each bristling with nuts that poke out from the caramel like multiple turtle flippers from underneath the chocolate shell. Hallie makes them all by hand with pecans, almonds, peanuts, and macadamias, as well as cashews, which she believes are the ideal nut, at least cosmetically, because cashews most resemble turtle flippers. And while she may be right about cashews looking best and white chocolate tasting richest, the turtles we like best are the more traditional pecan-footed ones, dark or milk chocolate.

We need to say that turtles are just one of many things available in this joyous candy land. Hallie makes brittles and clusters and butter crunches, chocolate-coated candied fruits, snowflakes, nonpareils, and simple hunks of chocolate. The confectionery is a joy to visit, for Hallie's pleasure at running it is contagious—she is the proverbial kid in a candy store, but in this case grown up and doing exactly what she loves to do.

Turtles and chocolate samplers are available by mail order.

The Village Restaurant

55 Main St.   978-768-6400
Essex, MA   LD | $$

Although most of the eating we do on Cape Ann is "in the rough," meaning at picnic tables in restaurants where they call your number when the meal is ready, The Village is where we go for a more civilized meal. A town fixture for nearly half a century, it is the nice place in the area—not too fancy or overreaching, but not a summer picnic place, either. This truly is where the locals eat. One veteran staff member recalled to us that when it opened as a small-town café, the owner used to leave the door open so that before the kitchen personnel arrived in the morning, regulars could let themselves in and cook their own breakfasts on the grill!

Menus from those early days are posted in the vestibule, and they are a delight to read, not only for the prices (a dollar for a full dinner) but because they list so many of the very basic items that are still on the Village menu, and that still make this such a true regional eating experience. "We serve Essex clams," boasts a menu from 1956. They still serve Essex clams, fried to golden perfection. And for dessert, you can still have a dish of baked Indian pudding, Grape-Nuts custard, or strawberry shortcake on an old-fashioned biscuit.

Nowadays, the menu is *huge*, with something for everyone; and we must confess that there have been occasions, after long days of fried-clam eating, we have come to The Village because we needed a sirloin steak or even, on one occasion, vegetarian pasta! But still, it's local seafood that stars on these tables, simply fried or broiled, or in more deluxe configurations such as haddock Rockefeller. Lobsters are available boiled, fried, or in a luscious lobster pie, baked in a casserole dish with seasoned bread crumbs.

Among desserts, we recommend the Indian pudding. It is grainy with a powerful molasses kick, and it is served piping hot with a scoop of vanilla ice cream melting on top. A bit fancier, but every bit as much a reflection of local character, is blueberry bread pudding, made of cornmeal and molasses bread and set afloat in a pool of sweet rum sauce.

Wenham Tea House

4 Monument St. (Route 1A)   978-468-1398
Wenham, MA   L | $

The North Shore of Massachusetts is a place where traditions prevail. Among our favorites is the Wenham Tea House, the gentle-tempered eatery that is part of a philanthropic enterprise that sells books, antiques, china, and handiwork to benefit the community. Also on sale in the front room are bakery cases full of dainty cakes, pies, muffins, casseroles, and hors d'oeuvres one can buy to take home. Beyond the prepared foods is the tearoom, open only midday (and for afternoon tea), where lunch is served six days a week.

As connoisseurs of ladies' lunches, we find this place to be our idea of feminine heaven. Waitresses in crisp uniforms provide swift service; and a sign above the coffee and tea service on the sideboard in the dining room advises: "No cell phones, please." How civilized!

Of course, you can come to this place and have a lovely salad. Among the classics are a quite robust Caesar salad and a chicken Waldorf cut into bite-size pieces. There are demure little crab cakes, available as an appetizer or main course, with a nice sweet flavor and the soft texture of good white bread. It is possible to eat a club sandwich or a Cheddar crab melt on eight-grain bread, and even a modern vegetable wrap. Count on a quiche of the day as well as a soup; we love the creamy smooth lobster bisque. Meals are accompanied by warm, fresh-baked muffins.

Delicate foods are what you expect in such a setting (lace-curtained windows; decorative plates on the wall), but do not underestimate the satisfaction of such full meals as Yankee pot roast or turkey with trimmings that include moist sage dressing, mashed potatoes, whipped butternut squash, and cranberry-orange sauce, followed by hot milk sponge cake for dessert.

The White Hut

280 Memorial Ave.   413-736-9390
West Springfield, MA   BLD | $

Although this restaurant apparently does serve breakfast, we have no idea what's on the morning menu; and we don't care. There are exactly two reasons to dine at The White Hut: the cheeseburger and the hot dog.

The cheeseburger is a modest-size patty cooked through on a grill and sandwiched in a tender white bun. It is a likable lunch counter hamburger, flavorful and not too greasy; and the cheese atop it is standard American, melted soft by the heat of the grill below. What puts this hamburger into the stratosphere is a heap of grilled onions that regular customers know to order as a garnish. If you don't order onions, it is likely the waitress behind the counter will ask if you want them anyway, just as a reminder. In fact, if you order a hamburger, she's liable to say, "You mean cheeseburger?" The combo of meat, cheese, and onion is that good, and that popular. It is possible to get an onion-free, cheese-free burger, and it's a good one, but onions and cheese are what have made a White Hut hamburger something special since this high-energy eat-shack opened for business in 1939.

The hot dogs are mighty good, too. Cooked on the grill alongside the hamburgers, they are medium-size tube steaks that blossom under a mantle of mustard, relish, and raw onions; and they are served in a bun that is soft on the inside, but buttered and toasted crisp on the outside. There are no other things to eat on the White Hut lunch menu, and no side dishes other than bags of potato chips.

There are a few seats at a counter (above which a sign reads, "Please: No newspaper reading at counter between 12:00 and 2:00") and there are eating surfaces around the edge of the room, as well as a broad table where the lunch crowd can stand and scarf down weenies by twos and threes. When you are finished with this fine, $5 feast, walk over to the cash register at the far end of the counter, tell the man what you ate, and he charges you accordingly.

This is truly fast food: You can be in and out, and well fed, in less than five minutes.

There is a second White Hut at 1365 Main St. in Springfield. 413–736–7400.

Woodman's of Essex

121 Main St.	978-768-6451
Essex, MA	LD | $$

The Woodman family likes to believe that it was here that the fried clam was invented—on July 3, 1916, when Lawrence "Chubby" Woodman tried to drum up business by tossing clams into the deep fryer along with the Saratoga chips he was selling at his clam bar. Who knows if the story is true? Who cares? The fact is that today Woodman's is the Big Kahuna of North Shore clam shacks.

Overlooking a scenic marsh in the heart of the clam belt, where towns have bivalvular names like Ipswich and Little Neck, Woodman's defines a whole style of informal Yankee gastronomy. They call it "eat in the rough," which means you stand at a counter, yell your order through the commotion, then wait for your number to be called. The food is served on cardboard plates with plastic forks. Carry it yourself to a table . . . but pray you can find one that is not occupied. In the summer especially, Woodman's can be insanely crowded.

If your experience eating fried seafood means a vaguely ocean-flavored morsel of food inside a thick gob of breading, Woodman's clams (and all its fried shellfish) will be a total shock. The crust on a Wood-man's clam is lush and crunchy, but it exists only to play harmony to the sweet, soft lode of clam-meat goodness it contains. Although Woodman's clams are available by the pint, or on a bun (known as a clam roll), the way to enjoy them fully is as a platter, which means accompanied by both French fries and onion rings. It's a deep-fried pig-out beyond description!

Woodman's is a good place to eat clam chowder and clam cakes, and just about any kind of seafood that will fit in the deep fryer. On display out front is a table of cooked lobsters that, with chowder and corn on the cob, make for another kind of Yankee feast.

New Hampshire

Bishop's

183 Cottage St.   603-444-6039
Littleton, NH   April–Columbus Day | $

In 1976 for the bicentennial parade in Bethlehem, New Hampshire, Bill and Grace Bishop decided to hand-crank some ice cream. People loved it and ate all they made, so after the festivities were over the Bishops made more. Four years later, they bought a Victorian house across from the three-horse cemetery in Littleton and opened what has become one of the most beloved ice cream parlors in northern New England. From April to Columbus Day, Bishop's is a magnet for ice cream lovers of all ages.

Made every morning by Harry and Zellie Taylor, who bought the business in 1986, Bishop's ice cream flavors range from the baroque—Bishop's Bash is chocolate chips, nuts, and brownie chunks in dark chocolate—to basic. Vanilla is pure and creamy white; chocolate is more like iced chocolate milk than some ungodly rich chocolate mousse cake; the coffee is reminiscent of HoJo's—smooth and creamy more than ultra-caffeinated. Here, too, you can savor the old Yankee favorite, Grape-Nuts ice cream, in which the little specks of cereal are softened into grainy streaks of flavor in pudding-smooth ice cream.

There is something unusually civilized about coming to Bishop's for ice cream. You'd think that such a happy-time product would stimulate yelps of exuberance and that the interior of the shop would ring with rapture. On the contrary, there is a reverential hush about it, even when Bishop's is jammed and every little table is occupied with ice cream eaters and a hundred people are waiting to get inside. Perhaps it's the polite aura of the stately old house, or maybe it's the captivating charm of the young ice cream servers, who are extraordinarily solicitous as you choose between a S'more sundae and a maple sundae, and who want to know, if you order a sundae with buttercrunch and coffee ice cream, which flavor you want on top.

Four Aces Diner

23 Bridge St. 603-298-6827

West Lebanon, NH BLD Tues-Sat; BL only Sun-Mon | $

"Nothing Beats a Home Cooked Meal . . . Except Four Aces!" boasts the menu in this odd old diner that seems to have been partially ingested by a large Colonial house surrounding it on three sides.

Breakfast is served from pre-dawn until mid-afternoon, and includes lots of interesting pancakes (with blueberries, bananas, chocolate chips, or walnuts). For an extra $1.50, you'll get real maple syrup to pour on them. We are partial to the pork chop and egg plate with good home fries and a crusty grilled biscuit. Also on the menu are such traditional morning meals as hot oatmeal, corned beef hash, and creamed chipped beef on toast.

We automatically like any restaurant that makes a big deal out of franks and beans. Here, epicures in search of local tradition can come for a mighty handsome plate of genuine baked beans—al dente, not too goopy or sweet—with a brace of hot dogs and a biscuit. Other old-time favorites include chicken and dumplings, macaroni and cheese with hot dogs, and a fine whole-belly fried clam platter. The menu even lists that locally beloved supper specialty, fried tripe—in our opinion, a taste that needs to be acquired at an early age. Among traditional diner fare, you'll find superb liver and onions *and* bacon, meat loaf with a choice of either brown gravy or tomato gravy, and always those great pork chops, served with potatoes and apple sauce. Saturday night is all-you-can-eat fried chicken night.

Gilley's PM Lunch

175 Fleet St.   603-431-6343

Portsmouth, NH   LD | $

Gilley's is an old-fashioned night-owl lunch wagon, now semi-permanently anchored on Fleet Street, where it used to arrive each night around supper time. According to legend, the proprietor received a ticket every evening, but business was so good that he considered the fine simply a cost of doing business and kept coming back. Today, Gilley's has an address and even a telephone number; and while it is not, as far as we know, a scofflaw anymore, it has maintained a deliciously iniquitous ambience. If it is the wee hours of the morning, and all the normal restaurants are closed and even the bars are shut, you can count on Gilley's to be serving up hamburgers with chocolate milk on the side to a rogues' gallery of city folk who range from derelicts to debutantes.

Many dine standing on the sidewalk, but there is some limited indoor seating at a narrow counter opposite the order area and galley kitchen. Gathered here under some of the most unflattering lighting on earth are insomniacs, die-hard partyers, and late-shift workers with no other place to eat, feasting on such quick kitchen fare as hot dogs with sauerkraut, French fries gobbed with cheese, and fried egg sandwiches with coffee on the side. The best dish in the house, or at least the one that seems most appropriate in this reprobate restaurant, is the hamburger, actually the cheeseburger . . . no, make that a double cheeseburger, with bacon and onions, too.

L.A. Burdick

47 Main St.   603-756-2882

Walpole, NH   BLD | $$

We're not quite sure how to describe L.A. Burdick, but let us start with "ohhhh . . ." That would be a moan of pleasure, a chocolate-induced moan. Here is a magnificent chocolatier, specializing in the highest-quality bonbons. Among the stars are truffles with flavors that range from mint and honey-caramel to scotch whiskey (single-malt, of course), full-size tortes, chocolate fondue, marzipan, nougat, and pâté de fruits. The signature chocolate is a mouse—a small rodent-shaped delicacy (complete with ribbon tail) filled with dark ganache, milk chocolate and mocha or dark chocolate and cinnamon. Ourselves, we get weak-kneed over the chocolate-enrobed thin-sliced candied ginger. It has a sweet-spicy kick with a just a hint of saltiness that amplifies its confectionery intensity. Thin-sliced candied pears are another of our heartthrobs.

All these sweets are available in beautiful boxes to take home or to buy via mail order (check out www.burdickchocolate.com), but there is far more to this wonderful place than chocolate. It is also a café where you can come for coffee and amazing pastries (Viennese gugelhupf, anyone?) any time after 7 A.M., as well as for lunch and supper. The full-scale meals are swank indeed, featuring such upscale offerings as salad of arugula with truffled fennel and parmesan- and pepper-crusted yellowtail. The prices for these items are relatively high on the Roadfood scale, maybe $15 for lunch, twice that for supper. But for all its certified excellence, the eatery has the comfy, casual air of a town café, which is what it is.

Polly's Pancake Parlor

Route 117   603-823-5575
Sugar Hill, NH   BLD (closed in winter) | $$

New England boasts prolific maple sugar trees and a tradition of elemental grain cookery, and thus it is home to some mighty fine pancakes. Top of the line is Polly's Pancake Parlor in the White Mountains of New Hampshire. Polly's was opened in 1938 by "Sugar Bill" Dexter because he thought a tearoom would give him the opportunity to show passersby all the good things that could be done with the maple harvest on his farm. Named for his daughter and now run by his progeny, Polly's remains maple paradise.

Of course, pancakes are the specialty of the house; they are made from stone-ground flours or cornmeal, either plain or upgraded with shreds of coconut, walnuts, or blueberries. One order consists of half a dozen three-inchers; and it is possible to get a sampler of several different kinds. They come with the clearest and most elegant fancy-grade maple syrup, as well as maple sugar and mouthwatering maple spread. You can also get maple muffins, sandwiches made with maple white bread, a gelatinized dessert called maple Bavarian cream, ice cream with maple hurricane sauce (syrup and apples stewed together), and all sorts of maple candies to take home.

Polly's is a beautiful restaurant in a breathtaking location. It is surrounded by maple trees hung with taps and buckets in the spring, but the most wonderful time to visit is autumn as the sugarbush starts to turn colors. The dining room has a glass-walled porch that overlooks fields where horses graze; and its inside walls are decorated with antiques and tools that have been in the family since the late eighteenth century, when Sugar Bill's ancestors began farming this land.

Allie's Donuts

3661 Quaker La. (Route 2)   401-295-8036
North Kingstown, RI   B | $

Allie's is Rhode Island's premier donut stop, so popular that it has three doors, funneling into two lines of people to wait at two separate counters to place their orders. The waiting area is fairly small, but the open kitchen behind it is an immense workspace where powerful mixers whir and deep fryers bubble and Bud and Ann Drescher and their staff of waitresses never seem to pause for breath.

The variety of donuts made each morning is vast, including honey-dipped, glazed crullers, raised jelly sticks, plain cake donuts, coconut-glazed solid chocolates, and a rainbow of jimmies-topped extravaganzas. None are fancy-pants pastries; these are big, sweet, pretty things to eat. Regular customers love them so much that it is common to see people buy a dozen in a box (to take to the office), plus a bag of two or three to eat in the car—or in the parking lot on the way to the car—before the dozen is opened.

The joy of Allie's has as much to do with the people who run it as with the donuts they make and serve. It is a family operation, literally, including Aunt Velda, Allie's sister and overseer of the waitress staff, who explained to us that she and her girls think of the everyday customers as an extended family and know most of them by pet names. Lynn, not a relative but a nine-year veteran at Allie's, said that some of her favorite regulars included Spud, Sweet Pea, Smiles, Vanilla Man the cop, Speedo Man (named for his beachwear), Chicken Man (a local poultry farmer), Hello-My-Friend (his favorite greeting), and Liver Lips (whom she named in retaliation for his calling her Flipper Foot).

To demonstrate just how thoughtful the customers can be, Aunt Velda showed us a recent gift to the staff from a serious donut eater named Big Al. As thanks for their good service and cheery ways, Big Al brought the girls a pound-and-a-half bag of Belly Buster red licorice candy twists.

Evelyn's Drive-In

2335 Main Rd.	401-624-3100
Tiverton, RI	BLD (summer only) | $$

Evelyn's is a fair-weather drive-in with the nicest possible outdoor dining area: a row of covered picnic tables perched over Sakonnet Bay with a view of pleasure boats and the Newport shores. The outdoor dining is strictly self-service—carry your own food from the order window. We actually saw one couple spread a tablecloth and open their own wine to accompany lobster plates.

Regular customers tend to eat inside at tables or at a short counter, where the view is other diners and the tight quarters are filled with conversation and the hum of air-conditioning (rather than the lap of water and the screech of seagulls). We noted that many of the locals order non-seafood meals from the broad menu: meat loaf, burgers, chicken pie, and one oddity we couldn't resist ourselves: a chow mein sandwich. It is a plate of frizzled-crisp chow mein noodles, soy-sauce gravy, and vegetables (beef optional) with a hamburger bun floating in it. Weird!

Evelyn's is at its best being a seafood shack, where the blackboard menu lists market prices for fried clams, scallops, and lobster. Scallops and clams are available in small- and large-size plates, the large being immense. In our experience, the clams are extraordinarily uniform in shape—the classic diamond-ring formation, with a chewy hoop and a gooey belly. The lobster roll, available with a choice of butter or mayonnaise served on the side, is only pretty good—more shredded meat than chunked. Chowder and clam cakes makes a nice single-digit-priced meal—those market prices for seafood can take the better part of $20 for a single lunch. You want to have a little cash to splurge on Grape-Nuts pudding.

Gray's Ice Cream

16 East Rd.   401-624-3576

Tiverton, RI   I $

GIVEN: The best ice cream is made in New England.

QUESTION: Where in New England is the best of the best found?

Being fickle-tongued (and always eager to eat ice cream wherever we are), we have cast our votes for places ranging from Dr. Mike's of Bethel, Connecticut (page 11) to Bishop's of Littleton, New Hampshire (page 59). For years, we must confess, we never even considered Gray's of Tiverton, Rhode Island. Somehow, our sweet-tooth radar had totally missed this grand ice cream parlor, which is surely a contender for the blue ribbon.

Gray's is one of a kind—a general store/café and ice cream parlor that has been making its own since Miss Gray opened it in the kitchen of her home here in 1923. Owned and operated for the last twenty years by Marilyn Dennis, it remains a quirky kind of business, still offering a miscellany of groceries and household items and a very short counter for indoor dining. Most customers eat in their car in the broad parking lot or at one of a handful of picnic tables with a view of Mrs. Dennis's pet llamas and cows.

The ice cream is simple and dignified, as opposed to the giddy, silly sorts of high-priced pints that derive their personality from mix-ins of candy bars and cookies. Gray's myriad flavors include all the usuals, plus New England favorites such as Grape-Nuts and frozen pudding. Note especially the ginger ice cream, made from real gingerroot, flecks of which dot the creamy white custard. And the coffee ice cream has been honored with "best of" awards by *Rhode Island* magazine for more than a decade. It is an endearing kind of coffee flavor, very creamy and just sweet enough, robust but not at all bitter.

Indeed, Rhode Islanders love all manner of coffee-flavored creamery concoctions, ranging from "coffee milk" to Gray's high-quality "coffee cabinet." Coffee milk is like chocolate milk, but made with coffee syrup instead of chocolate. "Cabinet" is Rhode Islandese for a foamy blend of milk, syrup, and ice cream—known elsewhere as a milk shake; here at Gray's, order a coffee milk shake and you get coffee milk, i.e., nothing but milk and coffee syrup. Got that?

Haven Brothers

At the corner of Fulton and Dorrance 401-861-7777
Providence, RI   Daily 5 P.M.-3 A.M. | $

Over the last 112 years, the citizens of Providence have come to rely on Haven Brothers in the same way most of us rely on the sun coming up in the morning. Except in this case, the arrival of Haven Brothers signals the coming of night. Without fail, every day of the year just before 5 P.M., this diner-on-wheels drives to the city center from its berth less than a mile away on Spruce Street. Ivan Giusti unrolls a massive electrical wire and climbs twelve feet up his stepladder to plug into a streetlamp above the sidewalk for power. He opens a side door to the truck and attaches a wooden stairway, then flips on the lights. Haven Brothers is open for business!

This is no mere food truck with ready-made sandwiches to sell. It is a restaurant on wheels. You may dine in, seated at one of a half-dozen high chairs arranged around a narrow counter at one end of the truck's interior, where you are serenaded by the sounds of the grill and the deep fryer at the other end of the truck, and where you feel the entire restaurant rock and roll if a particularly heavy customer steps up the stairs onto the old Formica floor. Or you may place your order directly from the sidewalk at an outside order window that provides access to the kitchen. Many customers choose to eat on the street or seated on the steps of City Hall.

From the time the truck pulls up to closing, there is always a handful of regulars, inside and out, who keep up a continuous conversation with whichever members of the Giusti family are on duty that night, with customers, or—if no one will listen—with the voices inside their own heads. To say that the clientele of Haven Brothers is diverse is a ridiculous understatement. Among the diner's regulars are big-shot city politicians, police officers, drunks with no other place to go when the bars close after 2 A.M., and an assortment of street people who range from wildly entertaining early in the evening to wild and scary after midnight.

The Giustis, who are the latest family to carry on the legacy of street-eats begun by the Haven Brothers in 1888, include proprietor Saverio and his son Ivan, Ivan's sister Maria, and Saverio's niece Lora. On weekend nights, there are as many as four of them working in the kitchen, which is the size of a coat closet.

There is a full menu of sandwiches, including good lobster rolls and a great steak and cheese sandwich on toast, but the vast majority of orders are for hot dogs or hamburgers. The dogs are plump and pink, served in soft buns, available with chili and all the usual condiments. The hamburgers are modest-size patties, from plain to deluxe (lettuce, tomato, mayo, etc.), but devotees of great junk food want the Haven Brothers Murder Burger, which is topped with every condiment in the house plus bacon, cheese, and chili. Side a Murder Burger with cheese-glopped French fries and you have a seriously satisfying sidewalk feast.

The most popular beverage at Haven Brothers is coffee milk, or you can have a frappé (the Rhode Island word for a milk shake), made from ice cream, milk, and flavoring. Because power from the streetlamp is limited, Haven Brothers is equipped with a battery-operated milk shake mixer!

Iggy's Doughboys

889 Oakland Beach Ave.   401-737-9459
Warwick, RI   LD daily | $

In a glass-walled dining room overlooking Narragansett Bay, Iggy's serves many of the foods that are Rhode Island's alone. Actually, *serves* is not quite the right word, because—true to the spirit of the region's most enjoyable seafood restaurants—service is eat-in-the-rough style, i.e., self-service. To get your meal, you stand in line at a counter, place your order and pay for it, then wait for your number to be called . . . by which time you hope to have secured a table in the dining room to which you can tote your tray. Everything at Iggy's is presented in disposable containers—salads in plastic, chowder in a Styrofoam cup, stuffed clams in a cardboard boat, and doughboys in a brown paper bag—so that when you are finished eating, you can sweep everything from the table and dispose of it yourself.

Amenities may be sparse, but the food is plentiful and very, very good. Here's a place to taste that odd but beguiling dish unique to the Ocean State, a snail salad. The color of cooked artichoke leaves, these pieces of snail arrive as a heap of cool, thin slices that have been saturated in a garlic marinade. They have a nice chewy consistency and are presented on a bed of lettuce with sliced olives and tomatoes.

The term "doughboy," by which this restaurant likes to be known, is unique to New England's southern shores, but it is a food with cognates throughout the East and even, arguably, way out West. A doughboy is a small square of puffy fried dough, served hot and rolled in granulated sugar. Sold by the dozen, they make good sweet-bread companions for just about any meal. Elsewhere in New England, similar foodstuffs are known as flippers or cheats or (in Portuguese bakeries) *malassadas;* and they bear a remarkable resemblance to the scones of Utah and the sopaipillas of New Mexico. In any case, Iggy's doughboys are addictive to the point that we suggest getting only a half dozen, lest you eat nothing but dough and thereby don't give yourself the opportunity to eat the big, crusty clam cakes, red or white chowder, and good fried clams. We also suggest including in any meal a few stuffies—quahog clam shells piled with a luscious clam stuffing.

The beverage menu includes locally bottled white birch beer and sarsaparilla.

John's New York System

326 Cranston St.   401-861-7090
Providence, RI   BLD (closed in July) | $

Across from the old Cranston Armory in Elmwood, John's is one of the premier New York System weenie joints in Rhode Island. Dating back to well before World War II, the "New York System" restaurants of the Ocean State are, in fact, nothing like hot dog places in New York. The name comes from the fact that early in the century, hot dogs were considered New York food, and thus when hot dog men came to Rhode Island, they named their product accordingly, even though they made them in their own way, usually with a distinctive Greek accent. (Throughout the Midwest, hot dog restaurants are named Coney Islands for the same reason.)

At John's, you get a small pink frankfurter nestled in an untoasted bun, topped with yellow mustard, chopped raw onions, and dark sauce of finely ground beef. While it is possible to get this hot dog plain, there would be no point to that. It is the sauce that makes the Rhode Island hot dog unique. It is spicy but not hot, made without tomatoes yet vaguely sweet, reminiscent of the kaleidoscopic flavors that give Cincinnati five-way chili its soul.

An urban hash house with great personality, John's is run by Henry Degaitis (son of John) and his mother, Viola. We definitely recommend finding a counter seat, for Henry is a joy to behold at the grill. He dresses hot dogs with the speed of a three-card-monte dealer, slides plates of food along the counter to their intended recipient, and receives take-out orders on a headset telephone, all the while managing to carry on conversations with regulars at the counter.

A sign outside the restaurant notes that John's is "Where the Elite Meet to Eat."

Mike's Kitchen at Tabor-Franchi VFW Post 239

170 Randall St.	401-946-5320
Cranston, RI	LD | $$

If you happen to drive past Mike's Kitchen, you won't notice it's a restaurant. Located in a VFW hall with no sign outside other than the Post number, Mike's doesn't need to advertise. To those who seek out great Italian food at low prices, it is an appetite-stirring magnet. At mealtimes, its tables are always crowded. (Tuesday, Saturday, and Sunday nights, it is generally closed to the public; that's when the Vets meet and when private functions generally are held.)

The menu, posted on the wall, is extremely appetizing: a catalog of dishes that are mostly Italian, a little Portuguese, and very Rhode Island. You can begin a meal with a stuffie (a stuffed quahog clam) or the unique Ocean State appetizer known as snail salad, then move on to perfectly broiled swordfish or scallops. Or indulge in such delectable Old World favorites as sautéed broccoli rabe (or a rabe and provolone sandwich), gnocchi Sorrentino, sole Florentine, and chicken with cannellini beans. On the side of anything, you want polenta—a cream-soft block of steamy cooked cornmeal available with fennel-spiked sausage, meatballs, or a blanket of thick marinara sauce.

Many of the Italian dishes are familiar: veal cutlets in a variety of sauces, Parmesans galore, scampis, and even spaghetti and meatballs and linguine with nothing but oil and garlic. Seafood pastas are especially wonderful, offered with a choice of red or white sauce; the top of the line is seafood diablo—lobster, scallops, and shrimp in spicy sauce spread out across a bed of noodles.

To drink with your meal, wine and cocktails are available from a bar at one side of the dining room. You will pay for these separately, as the bar is run by the veterans who own the building.

Olga's Cup and Saucer

At Walker's Roadside Stand
261 W. Main Rd.   401-831-6666
Little Compton, RI   L | $

There are two Olga's, the original in Providence's historic jewelry district, and the other in Little Compton, which is the one we fell in love with, even before we walked inside. The setting on Route 77 along the water toward Sakonnet Point in easternmost Rhode Island is breathtakingly scenic; and Olga's is a small hut adjacent to a summertime farm stand. When we say small, we mean minuscule, with barely room for three customers inside at a time (but with two little stools and very short counters for dining-in). It has a few outdoor tables; and although many customers come to take food home, it is sheer pleasure to eat here on a nice day.

Olga's is best known as a bakery, with a large repertoire of such artisan breads as *pane francese,* golden raisin fennel, potato dill, roasted garlic boule, and country sourdough. In addition to lovely loaves, the ovens also produce one-serving meals, including tortes topped with fresh tomatoes and corn, and individual pizzas. Other available lunches include sandwich wraps and salads.

Our favorite things to eat at Olga's are desserts, especially the fruit crisps topped with streusel-type crunch and the small pies, which are sized for two. How deliciously we remember our first visit, late morning, when the peach-blueberry pies were just out of the oven, still so warm that the peaches sent puffs of steam into the air as soon as we plunged a fork through the flaky crust. The flavor was intense—powerfully fruity without being very sweet. It was nothing less than a pastry epiphany!

Sam's New York System Restaurant

2653 W. Shore Rd.   401-737-9566
Warwick, RI   LD daily; Fri-Sat until 2 A.M. | $

Rhode Island is passionate about "hot wieners," served in New York System restaurants, so named because long ago, when wieners arrived in

Rhode Island, they were associated with New York, where many of the dog men got their original training. Rhode Island's New York System restaurants serve not only a unique dog but also heaps of sass and color from the countermen.

Sam's is exemplary! A sign behind the counter advises, "Buy one wiener for the price of two and receive the second one absolutely free." Got that? Another sign notes that one wiener costs $1.05. After midnight (on Friday and Saturday nights), a single goes for $1.25. That's no joke: the wee-hour wiener surcharge, we were told, is management's way of making sure that people who wander into this happy little storefront in the Wildes Corner strip on West Shore Road are *serious* diners, not just hot dog dilettantes.

If you are a wiener connoisseur, Sam's delivers the goods. The dogs are definitive Rhode Island–style pups: fingerling-size, bright pink tubes with squared-off ends. They are plucked from their steam bath and inserted into sponge-soft buns. They're addictive plain—one is maybe three good mouthfuls—or you can have them served "all the way," which means mustard, onions, and a peppery dark chili sauce. Rhode Islanders sit at Sam's counter and ask for "wieners up the arm," a request for the grill man to line up six or eight along his forearm and dress them all at lightning speed. The whole ritual of New York System wieners in Rhode Island is mesmerizing, and while they are by no means gourmet frankfurters, they have a cheap-eats charm that is impossible to deny.

To complete the regional authenticity of your hot wiener meal, ask the man behind the counter for a cabinet, either coffee or vanilla flavored. "Cabinet" is Rhode Islandese for milk shake.

Vermont

Baba à Louis

Route 11   802-875-4666
Chester, VT   BL | $

While scarcely a restaurant—no hot meals are served in the morning, and only sandwiches at lunch—Baba à Louis in Chester is one of Vermont's most noteworthy breakfast stops. Since he opened his bakery more than twenty years ago, John McLure has won a reputation for masterful yeast breads. If you are serious about bread, you can stop in any day after 7 A.M., find a seat at one of the tables opposite the bakery shelves, and enjoy a cup of coffee while you tear off pieces from a warm baguette, anadama loaf, or sourdough rye. Morning-specific pastries are breathtaking, especially Mr. McLure's sticky buns. Ribboned with a wal-nutty brown-sugar glaze, these buttery cylinders are so fragile and fine that they verge on croissanthood.

Lunch is served cafeteria-style. There is pizza on the weekends, and Tuesday through Saturday, you can have a panini, open-face or regular sandwiches, quiche or soup or salad.

The place itself is beautiful: a sun-bathed baking cathedral with a full view of the open kitchen where doughs are kneaded and hot breads pulled from ovens.

Note: The bakery is closed during April and most of November, but open again at Thanksgiving.

Blue Benn Diner

314 North St. (Route 7) 802-442-5140
Bennington, VT BLD | $

We have seen the Blue Benn referred to as a "gourmet diner," but Roadfood devotees need not worry. This definitely is not an annoying reborn streamliner in which an ambitious chef recasts the image of a retro-chic eatery serving New American cuisine. An original Silk City diner manufactured in the 1940s and planted on its current site along Route 7 in 1949, the Blue Benn remains a true-blue hash house.

Yes, you can eat interesting (and very good) international dishes that are not at all typical of a classic diner, i.e., Syrian roll-ups or vegetarian enchiladas, but the traditional diner fare is not to be missed: pot roast, turkey dinner, meat loaf and mashed potatoes.

Breakfast is served all day, natch, and it is an especially good opportunity to squeeze into a booth or find a counter seat in the pint-size hut. The Blue Benn seems always overpopulated with customers, and its walls are plastered with a virtual confetti of hundreds of signs listing arcane and modern specials from creamed chipped beef on toast to soya sausage. The commotion is presided over by a team of waitresses whose dexterous repartee cheers on customers to greet the day. It's hypnotic to watch the coffee-pot-armed professionals maneuver the confines behind the counter and along the short line of wooden booths of the creaky old monitor-roofed diner.

And oh, what a joy it is to ease a fork into a steamy slice of corn bread French toast or a stack of crunchberry pancakes with turkey hash on the side. And don't tell anyone, but we love to greet the sun with Blue Benn Indian pudding, a primordial cornmeal and molasses samp that is, technically speaking, dessert . . . but makes a salubrious morning cereal when served warm and dolloped with cream instead of ice cream.

Curtis's Barbecue

Route 5 (exit 4 off I-91)   802-387-5474

Putney, VT   LD Tues-Sun, April-November | $$

An amazing culinary institution consisting of two old school buses semi-permanently parked just off I-91, Curtis's Barbecue calls itself the "Ninth Wonder of the World." For many years now, pitmaster Curtis Tuff has made this little oasis a genuine rarity—a worthwhile barbecue restaurant east of Cleveland and north of Washington, D.C.

The buses are open for business only in the summer, and dining facilities are limited to outdoor picnic tables. You step up to the window of one bus and place your order after perusing a menu that consists of listings written on white paper plates tacked to the side of the bus. Among the delicacies are smoky pork ribs that have been cooked over hardwood until bursting with piggy flavor. These ribs are a joy to eat, for although they are cooked to perfection, they provide just enough tooth resistance to give them the sort of substance that overly tenderized baby back ribs simply do not provide. To dress the meaty bones, Mr. Tuff makes a hot/sweet barbecue sauce. Also on the menu are chicken parts and chopped pork sandwiches, as well as side dishes of baked beans, ears of sweet corn, or baked potatoes.

The Dorset Inn

8 Church St.   802-867-5500

Dorset, VT 05251   BLD | $$$

The Dorset Inn sings of Green Mountain character. Its two-century history, its setting on the village green, its broad front porch just right for rocking, its inviting hearth and broad-plank floors all contribute to an enveloping sense of place that could be nowhere else. When you eat here—breakfast, lunch, or dinner—you are savoring Vermont at its very best.

Chef/owner Sissy Hicks calls the meals she makes comfort food, and they are. But like the town of Dorset itself, this is a very fine kind of country comfort with an unmistakable air of elegance. Yes, you can have meat and potatoes for supper, but the meat may be pot roast Provençale and the potatoes may be roasted reds stuffed with puréed yams. Not that there is anything ostentatious about the food service here. The dinner tables, especially in the tavern, are as cozy as a club room. While the

Dorset Inn is a destination for travelers in search of good food (and traditional accommodations for the night), it is also where locals come for lunch and supper to enjoy one another's company as well as the delicious meals.

It is not easy to define the Dorset Inn's cuisine. It is categorically local in terms of ingredients, from Green Mountain maple syrup for morning waffles to small-farm beefsteak tomatoes and wild-caught fiddlehead ferns at dinner. But Chef Hicks doesn't make a fetish of Vermont cuisine. "I pick up ideas here and there," she says. "I throw stuff together; I always find ways to put leftovers to good use. I cook the way it feels right. I never ventured off into nouvelle cuisine or anything like that. My mentors are James Beard and Julia Child. Like them, my joy comes from sharing good food. If there is a theme to what I do, it is 'natural simplicity.' " While she can dazzle guests with such culinary tours-de-force as breast of chicken stuffed with brie and coriander with pear and cider sauce, her repertoire is replete with masterful renditions of such down-to-earth dinners as braised lamb shanks, corned beef and cabbage, and turkey croquettes. Her own favorite dish—and, amazingly, the most popular meal at the inn—is liver and onions. There is none better, anywhere.

Dot's

| 3 West Main St. | 802-464-7284 |
| Wilmington, VT | BLD \| $ |

Year after year Dot's takes the People's Choice First Prize in the New England chili cook-off, and while Southwest chiliheads wouldn't even recognize it as their beloved bowl of red, this Yankee chili is terrific. It is listed on the menu as "Jailhouse Chili," but it's most respectable. Beefy, thick with beans, spicy but not ferocious, it comes in a cup or bowl under a mantle of melted cheese.

Dot's is a blue-plate lunch room (actually open for three meals every day), where the hot plates include turkey, roast beef, meat loaf, and pork roast. They are all served on bread with gravy and French fries or—when available—real mashed potatoes. At dinner (from 4 to 8 P.M.), the big platters include good fish and chips, fried chicken, broccoli cordon bleu(!), and baked stuffed scrod. All come with homemade soup, vegetables, potatoes, and homemade bread.

Breakfast is the great meal of the day, with a vast menu of choices from down-home sausage gravy and biscuits with home fries and eggs to a wide choice of muffins. There are omelets, French toast made from Dot's bread, waffles, and McDot breakfast sandwiches. But it's the pancakes we adore. You can get them plain, studded with blueberries, apples, or bananas, or—best of all—loaded with berries. The batter of "Berry-berry" pancakes contains an impossible number of blueberries, raspberries, blackberries, and strawberries. Each one retains its individual flavor, and the bunch of them together, packed into Dot's fluffy cakes, are a flapjack epiphany. For 75 cents extra, they are served with real maple syrup. A must!

Mrs. Murphy's Donuts

Route 30   802-375-9387
Manchester, VT   BL | $

Mrs. Murphy's is good evidence that New England donuts are the best. Forget about the national chains. Once you've had a real sinker at the counter of this storefront coffee shop, you can never go back to junk-food donuts.

All kinds are available and displayed on shelves behind the cash register: Boston creams, jelly-filled, iced, and jimmie-sprinkled. The kinds we recommend, especially for those in search of the Platonic donut, are plain or sour cream. They are the simplest pastries imaginable: sturdy circles with a good crunch to their skin and creamy-soft insides. If you're a dunker, they're ideal. In fact, no donut ever matched so well with multiple cups of coffee.

Mrs. Murphy's donuts are so respected in and around Manchester that several retail establishments sell them, but it's best to get them at the source, especially early in the morning. Walk into the eatery at dawn and you will see a do-si-donut line of dunkers sitting on the rows of stools at the counter bobbing theirs in and out of mugs.

P & H Truck Stop

Exit 17 off I-91   802-429-2141
Wells River, VT   BLD | $

P & H is a real truck stop, not for the fastidious epicure. You need to pass through the aroma of diesel fuel outside to get to the smells of fresh-baked bread and of pot roast blanketed with gravy in the dining room.

Enter past shelves of whole loaves of white and cinnamon-raisin bread for sale. This is a kitchen that means business, and is open 24/7.

Soups and chowders are especially inviting: tomato-macaroni soup is thick with vegetables, ground beef, and soft noodles; corn chowder is loaded with potatoes and corn kernels and flavored with bacon. We love the falling-apart pot roast and any kind of sandwich made using thick-sliced P&H bread, but the mashed potatoes *(purée de pommes de terre* on the bilingual menu, written for French-Canadian truckers) taste like they were made from powder, and the meat loaf is strictly for die-hard diner fans.

The homemade dessert selection is huge, including fruit pies, berry pies, custard pies, meringue pies, Reese's pie (a peanut-cream), a few types of pudding, and maple cream pie thick as toffee and topped with nuts.

Putney Diner

Main St.   802-387-5433
Putney, VT   BLD | $

Beautiful breakfast and fine pie are the main lures to this pleasant little town café only a few minutes away from I-91. In the morning, plates of sausage and eggs or three-egg omelets are accompanied by broad-topped muffins that are split and toasted on the grill. At lunch, after meals of meat loaf or roast turkey and stuffing, nearly everyone tops things off with a "baked by Karen" pie, the varieties of which include apple, candy-sweet maple walnut, chocolate cream, banana cream, and crumb-top four-berry. In the summer, look for superb strawberry rhubarb. The diner's pie is not big and flashy; it is served in farm-simple little slices—plain-looking, but delicious-tasting: pie made by a pro. One day after breakfast, we ordered four pieces between the two of us and our waitress arched her eyebrows but managed to contain her incredulity. "And four glasses of water, too," we added.

"Don't push it!" she said with the grin of a seasoned accomplice.

Simon Pearce Restaurant

Main St.   802-295-2711
Quechee, VT   LD Daily | $$

Warning: During leaf season or on sunny summer weekends, the restaurant at Simon Pearce can be maddeningly crowded. It is part of the Simon Pearce glassblowing factory (see it made!) and showroom (buy some to take home!), and it attracts hordes of tourists. Rightfully so: The glassware is gorgeous and it is hypnotic to watch it being blown; the setting of the dining room, perched above the rushing waterfall that powers the furnaces with a picture-window view of Quechee's covered bridge, is New England at its most scenic. And the food, reflecting Pearce's Irish heritage, is good and hearty.

Served on plates and in glassware made here, the menu includes such pubby dishes as shepherd's pie under a crust of Cheddar-laced mashed potatoes, lamb and rosemary pie with a traditional pie crust, suave Vermont cheese soup, and salmon and trout smoked on-premises. Alongside each meal comes a plate of dainty little soda bread scones and thin slices of Ballymaloe brown bread made from coarse-grain, whole-wheat flour imported by Simon Pearce from Ireland (and available here for sale). Available libations include a choice from an astonishing 900-label wine list, locally brewed beers and ales, and hot mulled cider. For dessert, we favor the old-fashioned Irish apple cake and pumpkin bread pudding, served warm with cranberries and caramel sauce and a dollop of rich vanilla ice cream.

Up for Breakfast

710 Main St.   802-362-4204
Manchester, VT   BL | $$

Green Mountain pancake paradise! Three kinds are available, with or without blueberries in the batter: buttermilk, buckwheat, and sourdough. The muffins are excellent, too: tender-textured quick breads with broad-risen tops and cream-colored insides, the best of them chockablock with blueberries and nuts. More elaborate meals include multi-ingredient frittatas, French toast made using big slabs of spice bread, and chicken-duck-cilantro sausage. Wild turkey hash—wildly assembled, not made from wild turkeys—is a cook's tour de force that combines big shreds of roasted turkey with peppers, onions, potatoes, and pine nuts, all griddle-cooked until crusty brown on the outside and topped with poached eggs and a film of fine Hollandaise. If you like omelets, let us suggest "The Metropolitan"—smoked salmon, chopped red onions, melting-warm cream cheese, capers, and a sprinkle of dill.

Coffee is good, as are morning champagne cocktails, including passion fruit mimosas.

Beware: Seats in this cozy little second-story café can be mighty scarce, especially on weekends or during leaf-peeping season, when an hour's wait is not uncommon.

Wayside Restaurant

1873 Route 302 (Barre-Montpelier Rd.)   802-223-6611
Berlin, VT   BLD | $

The Wayside Restaurant looks pleasant enough; inside, it is modern and comfortable—a wide, wood-paneled café with a couple of counters and rows of booths bustling with locals. There is nothing dazzling about the menu; the kitchen isn't trying to prove its regional character to anyone. In fact, it is entirely possible to come for a hamburger or a BLT or a plate of scrambled eggs. However, those are not the meals that have endeared the Wayside Restaurant to us.

Instead, we recommend dishes such as milk oyster stew or fish chowder, baked haddock (Friday) or fresh native perch, hot blueberry muffins or pancakes with real maple syrup. Or how about American chop suey? There aren't a lot of restaurants that offer this dowdy old dish, but somehow it seems so right here at the Wayside. It is a favorite Yankee way of getting the most out of one's larder by creating a one-dish meal of ground beef with macaroni and tomato sauce. The menu lists it as the "Vermont Special."

The most old-fashioned dish you can eat here is a plate of salt pork and milk gravy. Like American chop suey, it is a meal reminiscent of frugal farmhouse cookery. You see, way back when, most farm cellars held a pork barrel in which slabs of salt pork were kept in brine. The pork (or occasionally the brine itself) was used to season stews, vegetables, chowders, and main courses of beef or venison. But when there was no meat, no vegetables, nothing from which to construct a chowder, inventive Yankee cooks figured out ways to turn the salt pork itself into a satisfying meal. We've *never* seen salt pork and milk gravy served in any other restaurant. But in this part of Vermont, there are enough old-timers around to know just how delicious it can be; and so it is on the menu of the Wayside Restaurant once a week.

Most days, the kitchen offers hash. On occasion it is red flannel hash, made from a traditional New England boiled dinner of corned beef, potatoes, carrots, and beets. It is served mounded high in a boat-shaped dish—a damp heap of stick-to-the-ribs north country comfort food. On the side you get a basketful of freshly baked dinner rolls.

This is maple country, and so the dessert repertoire includes ice cream sundaes dripping with amber syrup and—our favorite way to end a Wayside meal—a slice of maple cream pie in which a toffee-thick layer of maple filling is topped with a lightweight ribbon of whipped cream.

Mid-Atlantic

Delaware ✳ District of Columbia ✳ Maryland ✳

New Jersey ✳ New York ✳ Pennsylvania

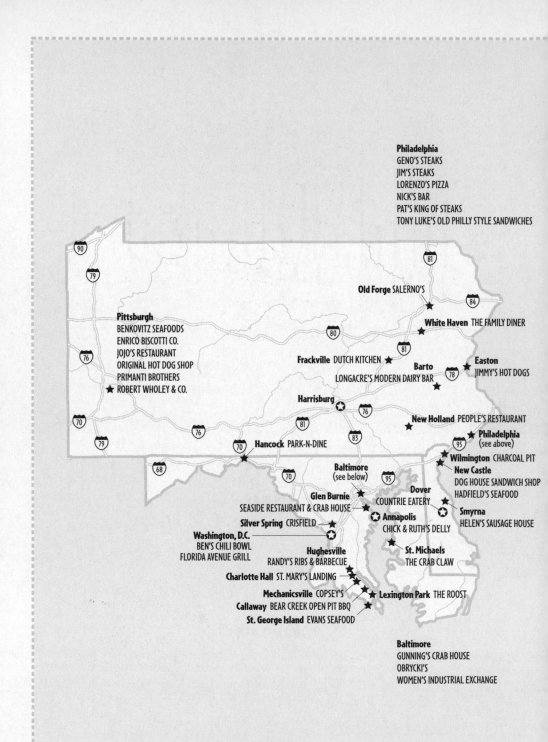

Philadelphia
GENO'S STEAKS
JIM'S STEAKS
LORENZO'S PIZZA
NICK'S BAR
PAT'S KING OF STEAKS
TONY LUKE'S OLD PHILLY STYLE SANDWICHES

Old Forge SALERNO'S

White Haven THE FAMILY DINER

Frackville DUTCH KITCHEN

Barto
LONGACRE'S MODERN DAIRY BAR

Easton
JIMMY'S HOT DOGS

Pittsburgh
BENKOVITZ SEAFOODS
ENRICO BISCOTTI CO.
JOJO'S RESTAURANT
ORIGINAL HOT DOG SHOP
PRIMANTI BROTHERS
ROBERT WHOLEY & CO.

Harrisburg

New Holland PEOPLE'S RESTAURANT

Philadelphia
(see above)

Wilmington CHARCOAL PIT

New Castle
DOG HOUSE SANDWICH SHOP
HADFIELD'S SEAFOOD

Hancock PARK-N-DINE

Baltimore
(see below)

Glen Burnie
SEASIDE RESTAURANT & CRAB HOUSE

Dover
COUNTRIE EATERY

Smyrna
HELEN'S SAUSAGE HOUSE

Silver Spring CRISFIELD

Annapolis
CHICK & RUTH'S DELLY

Washington, D.C.
BEN'S CHILI BOWL
FLORIDA AVENUE GRILL

St. Michaels
THE CRAB CLAW

Hughesville
RANDY'S RIBS & BARBECUE

Charlotte Hall ST. MARY'S LANDING

Mechanicsville COPSEY'S

Lexington Park THE ROOST

Callaway BEAR CREEK OPEN PIT BBQ

St. George Island EVANS SEAFOOD

Baltimore
GUNNING'S CRAB HOUSE
OBRYCKI'S
WOMEN'S INDUSTRIAL EXCHANGE

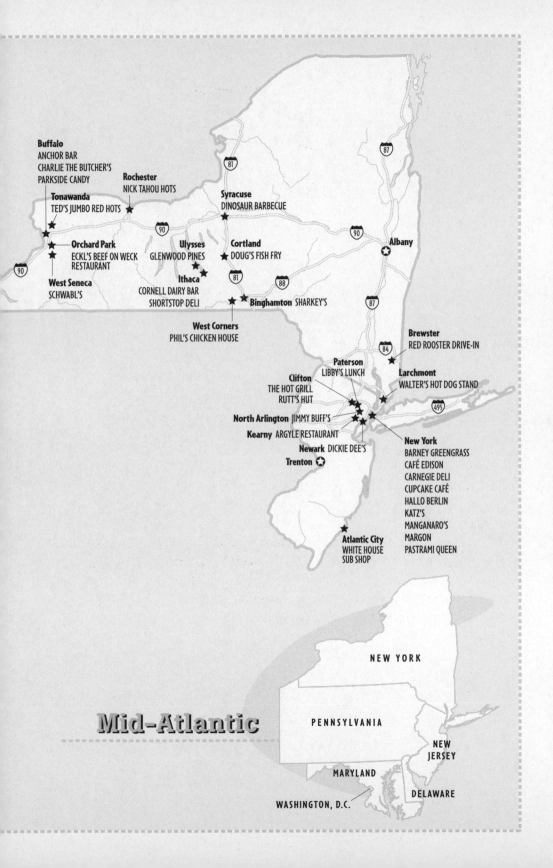

Buffalo
ANCHOR BAR
CHARLIE THE BUTCHER'S
PARKSIDE CANDY

Rochester
NICK TAHOU HOTS

Syracuse
DINOSAUR BARBECUE

Tonawanda
TED'S JUMBO RED HOTS

Orchard Park
ECKL'S BEEF ON WECK
RESTAURANT

Ulysses
GLENWOOD PINES

Cortland
DOUG'S FISH FRY

Albany

West Seneca
SCHWABL'S

Ithaca
CORNELL DAIRY BAR
SHORTSTOP DELI

Binghamton SHARKEY'S

West Corners
PHIL'S CHICKEN HOUSE

Brewster RED ROOSTER DRIVE-IN

Paterson
LIBBY'S LUNCH

Larchmont
WALTER'S HOT DOG STAND

Clifton
THE HOT GRILL
RUTT'S HUT

North Arlington JIMMY BUFF'S

Kearny ARGYLE RESTAURANT

Newark DICKIE DEE'S

Trenton

New York
BARNEY GREENGRASS
CAFÉ EDISON
CARNEGIE DELI
CUPCAKE CAFÉ
HALLO BERLIN
KATZ'S
MANGANARO'S
MARGON
PASTRAMI QUEEN

Atlantic City
WHITE HOUSE
SUB SHOP

Mid-Atlantic

NEW YORK

PENNSYLVANIA

NEW
JERSEY

MARYLAND

DELAWARE

WASHINGTON, D.C.

Charcoal Pit

2600 Concord Pike (Route 202)   302-478-2165
Wilmington, DE   LD | $

We were tipped off to the Charcoal Pit by a Roadfooder who said that he believed they hadn't changed their recipes since opening in 1952: "Everything has all the cholesterol and great taste from the old days." He recommended malts, sundaes, burgers, and fries.

Sure enough, the hamburger exudes mid-century Americana: a modest patty with a charcoal taste served on a big, spongy bun either plain or in the deluxe configuration, which adds lettuce, tomato, and pickle. For those who crave extra meat, there is also a double-size eight-ounce hamburger, but in our opinion, that's too late-twentieth-century, not really 1950s in spirit. The fries on the side are savory, normal-size twigs with a nice tough skin and soft potato flavor. And the milk shakes come in big silver beakers that hold at least two glasses full. (The shakes are so thick that a long-handled spoon is provided to help you get it from the beaker into your glass.) We even enjoyed the crab cakes, which were a couple of hardball-shaped spheres with crusty outsides and a fair measure of crab filling the interior.

It's an old-fashioned kind of place with comfy maroon booths and vintage menus decorating the wall. Waitresses go about their job with aplomb and attitude that make customers feel part of a cheap-eats ritual that has gone on forever.

There are other Charcoal Pits at 5200 Pike Creek, in the Fox Run Shopping Center, and in Prices Corner at Kirkwood Highway and Greenbank Road.

Countrie Eatery

950 N. State St.   302-674-8310
Dover, DE   BLD | $

Adjacent to the Blue Coat Inn and formerly known as the Blue Coat Pancake House, the Countrie Eatery is a three-meal-a-day coffee shop with Colonial-style primitive art and implements on its walls. Somewhat out of sync with Ye Olde Atmosphere are the paper place mats at every table that advertise bee pollen ("natural antibiotic and rejuvenator") and apple cals ("lose weight, protect bones"), both of which are available for sale at the cash register.

Breakfast is the meal we recommend: buttermilk pancakes or shillings (silver dollar 'cakes) filled with bananas or blueberries, or hefty biscuits topped with sausage gravy. The gravy, like the creamed chipped beef, is also available on regular toast or an English muffin. There are two noteworthy styles of French toast, one made with cinnamon bread, the other with seed-dotted sunflower bread. The latter is served as three long, thick pieces that are soft, moist, and nearly as eggy as pudding, dusted with powdered sugar. We got ours with a side order of scrapple—two thick slices from the loaf, fried until crunchy on the outside, but moist and porky within.

At lunch you can have a crab cake sandwich, a big sirloin burger, or a hot sandwich made with turkey, pork, or beef and *real* mashed potatoes. Every day the Countrie Eatery offers one all-you-can-eat special for $7.25. Monday = chicken 'n' dumplings; Tuesday = stuffed peppers; Wednesday = lasagna; Thursday = beef stew; Friday = fried chicken; Saturday = chicken livers.

Dog House Sandwich Shop

1200 DuPont Hwy.   302-328-5380

New Castle, DE   LD | $

Delaware's boisterous Dog House is a roadside attraction with a long counter that provides an excellent view of sandwich makers at work. Those who come for a to-go order jostle in an always crowded vestibule where placing and picking up orders is an adventure unto itself. This is not a place for anyone too timid to push through a crowd to get what they want, nor is it a restaurant to which you want to come for a calm, quiet meal or even for a normal-level conversation. This joint is loud and a little looney and lots of fun.

"Our dogs go out with the nicest people!" is the house motto, and much business is takeout. Make your way to the order counter and tell the lady what you want—a foot-long with chili and cheese, a cheese steak with light onions and extra cheese—then step back and wait . . . and remember exactly what you ordered. When your food is ready, someone from behind the counter will call it out, not by name or number, but by exactly what it is. Claim it, pay for it, and be out the door in a flash.

The hot dogs are excellent—bisected and grilled, served in soft buns and available with terrific hot peppers—and the cheese steaks are near-Philly quality, loaded with griddle-cooked, thin-sliced meat and soft sweet onions. About the only other item on the menu we care about is the turkey sandwich. This is the real thing, made from a bird roasted on premises using meat that is, as the sign above the counter boasts, "hand-picked for easy eating."

A separate area adjoining the Dog House sells only pizzas and sub sandwiches. It has its own number for call-ahead orders: 302–328–1838.

Hadfield's Seafood

192 N. DuPont Hwy. (Route 13) 302-322-0900

New Castle, DE   LD | $

There used to be makeshift tables at which to eat inside Hadfield's. Now there are none—only a few chairs for relaxing while you wait, if there is a line at the counter, or if you have to wait while they fry your softshell crabs or broil your lobster tails. Once you get your food, it is your responsibility to find a place to eat it.

A huge raw seafood market with everything from whole fish and bushels of oysters to oceanic fillets and steaks that are ready to take home and cook, Hadfield's makes a specialty of selling whole meals to go. Fried fish is the star of the show—scallops, flounder, oysters, whiting, and shrimp—but it is also possible to get broiled crab cakes, stuffed flounder, a pair of shells filled with creamy crab imperial, and hot chicken wings by the ten-count, up to 100 for $35.99, including blue cheese and celery. Dinners include cole slaw, French fries, a roll and butter, and tartar sauce; and it is also possible to get just about anything the kitchen makes by the pound or dozen.

In fact, what we like most about Hadfield's even more than the quickie meals to go, is simply browsing the glass cases and studying all the Mid-Atlantic seafood on display, especially the bounty of the Chesapeake Bay. Last time we visited, the counter contained a visual demonstration of different-size hard-shell crabs, from itty-bitty ones to the kind we all want to eat, here labeled "Texas monsters," and selling for $49 per dozen, live or cooked, and $189 a bushel (live) or $193 a bushel (cooked).

Speaking of crabs, you will have no trouble spotting Hadfield's as you travel north on Route 13. It is the shop with a crab statuette the size of a minivan hovering over the front door.

Helen's Sausage House

DuPont Hwy. (Route 13 at Black Diamond Rd.)   302-653-4200
Smyrna, DE   BL | $

Rush hour at Helen's Sausage House starts at four in the morning, when truckers heading up toward the Delaware River Bridge stop in for sausages, scrapple 'n' eggs, and pork chop sandwiches. Eating where the truckers eat isn't always a good plan, but in this case, following the 18-wheelers to Helen's tiny shack by the side of the highway will find you some truly magnificent meals.

The sausages are giants—thick and crusty, spurting juice at first bite—and you get two of them in a roll for about $3. Alone, they're delicious; with fried onions and green peppers, they are food of the blue-collar gods. We make a point of eating Italian sausage wherever we find it; and believe us when we tell you that Helen's is some of the tastiest anywhere.

The menu is large and, although there are platters that include home fries and toast, it is sandwiches that make Helen's a Route 13 beacon. There are breakfast sandwiches aplenty, made with eggs, bacon, and fried ham; as well as lunchtime sandwiches of steak, cheese steak, burgers, hot beef, and hot ham.

Other than the sausage, the one must-eat (and must-see!) meal is Helen's pork chop sandwich. When the menu says *jumbo* pork chop, you better believe it. This slab of meat is approximately three times larger than the puny pieces of white bread that are stuck on either side of it. It isn't all that thick a chop, but it is tender, moist, and mouthwateringly spiced. The only purpose of the bread, really, is as a mitt to hold the meat, so you can eat it with one hand as you steer your vehicle with the other.

While a majority of Helen's business is takeout for people who need to eat while they drive, there are dining facilities in the little sausage house. A few tables are located on the first level opposite the instant-order counter where sandwiches are wrapped, and up a few steps in back is the Elvis room: one small dining area with half a dozen booths where the walls are covered, edge to edge, with pictures of and odes to the King. We truly believe that Elvis—who started out as a truck driver—would have loved Helen's sausages and pork chops.

District of Columbia

Ben's Chili Bowl

1213 U St. NW   202-667-0909

Washington, DC   LD | $

Ben's is a national treasure in the nation's capital. When you walk in, look right. There you'll see a griddle lined up with ravishing hot dogs and half-smoke sausages, sizzling hot and ready to be bunned, dressed, and topped with chili. We ordered a chili dog and a chili smoke, as well as pieces of just-made sweet potato cake and chocolate cake. The man who took our order told us to find a seat, then shortly brought the food, the dogs each presented in a red plastic basket along with a pile of potato chips, the cake served in a see-through take-out box.

The half-smoke is sensational! A taut-skinned smoky link unique to the D.C. area, it is bigger than most hot dogs. Well browned on the griddle, it is firm-fleshed with an unbelievably luscious character, and as the name suggests, only a faint smokiness. You can get it plain or topped with chili that is thick, peppery, full-flavored, and positively addictive. The whole package—sausage, mustard and onions, and a heap of chili all piled into a tender bun—is extremely unwieldy, impossible to eat without making a mess. But that's okay. Dripping and licking is part of the dining experience.

The big hot dog has plenty of character, too. No bland tube steak here; it is hot and spicy and a fine balance for the chili. As for dessert, there are homey layer cakes. We especially liked the moist, spicy sweet potato cake with sugary frosting.

Florida Avenue Grill

1100 Florida Ave.   202-265-1586
Washington, DC   BL | $

You can eat your way around the world in the District of Columbia, but if breakfast Southern-style, is your definition of heaven on earth, there is only one place to start the day: on a stool at the counter of the Florida Avenue Grill. Aged country ham, griddle-fried until its fat halo glistens and the chewy lean parts turn a deep brick red, comes with a bowl of clove-scented stewed apples so tender they are nearly apple sauce. This supersweet / supersalty pair must be abetted by stout grits and a basketful of crusty biscuits. Or, have the split-open biscuits topped by cream gravy thick with clumps of sausage. Battered pork chops and corned beef hash are other morning favorites that have pleased Washington's plain folk and bigwig politicians since 1944. The small diner is Deep-South-friendly—expect to be *honey*'d, *dear*'d, and *darlin*'d by the waitstaff—and its air is scented by the irresistible perfume of hot hash browns and sizzling bacon. The walls are a gallery of 8 × 10 pictures signed by famous fans, including prizefighter Sugar Ray Leonard, who signed his, "To the Fla. Ave. Grill, from one champ to another," as well as attorneys general Janet Reno *and* John Ashcroft. Apparently, pork chops and pig feet make even stranger bedfellows than politics.

As for lunch, there are seriously soulful options such as neck bones and chitterlings, but you can also have excellent spare ribs glazed with a breathless hot sauce. For a tender meal, we suggest meat loaf with a side of mashed potatoes and a heap of pungent collard greens. The loaf is one of the kitchen's unexpected triumphs, its coarse-textured meat shot through with brilliant spices. True to Southern custom, there are lots of vegetables to accompany the entrees: candied sweet potatoes, rich macaroni and cheese, lavish potato salad, rice, beans, peas, and always sweet corn bread for mopping up a plate.

Maryland

Bear Creek Open Pit BBQ

Route 5   301-994-1030
Callaway, MD   LD | $

One of several good smokehouses in southernmost Maryland, Bear Creek is unique for its huge open pit. You'll see it on the left as you walk in the door. Here, pitmaster Curtis Shreve cooks pork and beef so tender that if you look at it hard, it falls apart. We are especially fond of the pork, either hand-pulled into shreds or sliced into pieces soft as velvet. It is so piggily good that we like it without any sauce whatsoever, all the better to savor the flavor of the meat.

Beyond superb barbecue, you can expect Bear Creek to have interesting game on the menu. Curtis Shreve is a hunter, and while he cannot serve what he kills (health department regulations forbid it), he does have a fondness for such non-supermarket meats as venison, alligator, and frogs legs. When we stopped in, the day's special was rabbit stew—a hearty meal that included big hunks of carrot and potato and easy-to-eat pieces of breaded and fried rabbit. On the side of the stew we had a block of delicious homemade corn bread.

Mr. Shreve originally hails from the Louisiana/Texas area, so his cooking reflects Southwest roots, too. The kids' menu contains corn dogs reminiscent of those at the Texas State Fair, and this is the only place in the region we know of that serves the unique Southwest specialty, Fritos pie. That's a bed of corn chips topped with chili, crowned with cheese and chopped onions. Mr. Shreve remembered, "When I was a kid years ago, they used to take a scoop of chili and put it right in the bag of Fritos and you ate it just like that. Now the bags are made of plastic that does not withstand the heat. So we serve our Fritos pie in a dish."

Chick & Ruth's Delly

165 Main St.   410-269-6737
Annapolis, MD   BLD | $

In the heart of historic Annapolis, Chick & Ruth's is one of a kind: cramped, colorful, and full of life. There is a short counter, booths that put you cheek by jowl with the stranger sitting next to you, and an upstairs dining room that throbs with conversation of informal and formal meetings of local folk from dawn through the breakfast hour.

The menu is huge, ranging from such traditional deli fare as corned beef and pastrami sandwiches to buffalo wings by the dozen to a stupendously good seasoned-crab three-egg omelet. The homemade soup repertoire is notable, including matzoh ball, chicken noodle, French onion, Maryland crab (spicy!), and cream of crab. Chick & Ruth's has a Jewish flair but is strictly kosher-style, meaning much of the food as well as the brusque service is typical of an East Coast urban deli, but that the menu offers *treyf* (non-kosher fare) galore.

Annapolis is near enough to the Beltway that many of the house specialities are named after politicians. A chopped liver and corned beef sandwich is known as the Governor Mandel; lox on a bagel is the Golda Meir; turkey breast on whole wheat is the Bill Clinton.

Upstairs above the deli is the Scotlaur Inn, which is, as far as we know, the world's only "Bed & Bagel," a hostelry with ten rooms.

Copsey's

Route 5   301-884-4235
Mechanicsville, MD   LD | $

There are two doors to Copsey's. The one on the right leads to a store that sells raw seafood and liquor; the one on the left is for the restaurant, where people come to eat spiced, steamed hard-shell crabs off tables covered with brown paper.

Whole Maryland crabs are not the only thing on Copsey's menu. In fact, we have had some pillowy-plump, sweet-meat crab cakes, pounds of peel-it-yourself steamed shrimp (infused with the same peppery orange spice mix that is used on the crabs), and raw oysters by the dozen. It is a distinctly local kind of place, and we have observed that many of the regular patrons come to eat fried chicken dinners; they are apparently that blasé about their great local seafood.

Generally, though, Copsey's dining room is filled with the sounds of energetic eaters pounding crabs, cracking the husks from cooked shrimp, and moaning with culinary ecstasy as they slide raw oysters down the hatch.

In the autumn, Copsey's is also a place to come for the unique St. Mary's County specialty, stuffed ham—a sweet (not salt-cured) ham stuffed with a mixture of kale and cabbage and boiled until the sweetness of the ham mellows the vegetables and the tonic zest of the vegetables insinuates itself into the ham, resulting in a plate of miscellaneous soft slices of pink meat jumbled with heaps of tender greens.

Note: There is a Copsey's take-out restaurant across the road in Mechanicsville. It is closed on Wednesday, the day we drove past; and when we asked Dagger Copsey, who was manning the liquor store/seafood market if that store was related to his, he answered, somewhat irked, "Not by money, but by blood."

The Crab Claw

Route 33 West   410-745-2900
St. Michaels, MD   LD (closed in winter) | $$

The great meal of Maryland's shore is a crab feast. Hard-shell blue crabs, steamed in spice, are served in a great heap on the table along with pick, mallet, piles of napkins, and plenty of beer. It is a royal mess; and crab-eating novices will expend nearly as many calories as they consume pulling and prying meat from the crustaceans' shells. But, oh, what delicious meat it is! Soft and sweet yet laced with spice, it is as addictive as food can be.

Perched high on a pier overlooking the Miles River, The Crab Claw of St. Michaels opened for business about a half century ago as a wholesale crab business. It is now one of the top places to indulge in such a feast; and it has customers who arrive by boat as well as by car. Some come to take away bushels full of crabs for waterside picnics; many come to sit at Crab Claw tables with rolled-up sleeves and dig in. The dining room clatters with the sounds of hammering, cracking, and slurping that are a crab feast's happy tune. Written instructions tell exactly how to extract meat from a cooked hard-shell crab, but if you find all that work a little daunting, the kitchen has a full roster of other crab-centric meals to offer, including crab cakes, softshell crabs, crab claws, crab soup, and crab cocktail. At one point many years ago, we actually ordered (but failed to fully excavate) a deep-fried hard-shell crab, which was the strangest-looking meal we ever have seen: a whole hard-shell crab, in its shell, blanketed with batter and fried until golden brown, then served with a knife and a mallet. The idea was to pick some of the batter off the exterior, then crack the shell and retrieve the meat inside. It was an adventure!

Oysters, clams, shrimp, and scallops are also available on the Crab Claw menu, as are filet mignon and chicken. But if you don't like crabs, this is the wrong part of the world to be in.

Crisfield

8012 Georgia Ave.   301-589-1306
Silver Spring, MD   LD | $$$

A second, more modern Crisfield is located at Lee Plaza, 8606 Colesville Rd. in Silver Spring. The number there is 301-588-1572.

Crisfield's is expensive, but no-frills. The room you enter is like a bar, with a long counter running along both sides and stools where people sit to eat and drink. The adjoining dining room has walls covered with white tile and cinder blocks, with all the charm of a locker room. Service is brusque and efficient and a full dinner can run over $20, even "light fare" meals are close to $15 and sandwiches are just under $10.

We'll happily pay these prices because some of the food served here is top-drawer. Crisfield is a fish house with regional specialities you simply don't find many places anymore. For example, seafood Norfolk-style (i.e., swimming in butter), and huge fillets of flounder, broiled or fried or heaped with mountains of fresh lump crabmeat, as well as oysters and soft-shell crabs in season.

On a recent visit, the "Crisfield special" (lump crabmeat mixed with a bit of mayo and baked until golden brown) wasn't as sweet as we remember it from years ago, but the crab-stuffed flounder was mighty fine: a gigantic, milky-white fillet covered with a full-flavored crown of crab. We also liked the "Combination Norfolk"—hunks of crab, whole shrimp, and pieces of lobster all crowded into a skillet and up to their waistlines in melted butter. It's a simple preparation, but unbeatable.

Evans Seafood

Route 249   301-994-2299
St. George Island, MD   LD (hours vary) | $$

Evans Seafood restaurant seems to be at the end of the earth, a long drive out a spit of land between the Potomac and St. George Creek. The land narrows and the water on both sides becomes ever wider, and finally, you are there, at a big seafood restaurant with an open deck overlooking the creek and an indoor dining room with big picture windows and a view of Indigo Point.

The setting alone is worth a million dollars, but the food at Evans happens to be extraordinary—some of the best seafood in a seafood-rich part of the world. Start with crab soup, the vegetable kind, please (there is creamy crab soup, too, and it is quite good). This is what crab soup should be: peppery, thickly laced with shreds of crab, and packed with unevenly cut vegetables to which hot spices cling. This soup has huge flavor and is a joy to eat; it leaves lips aglow with its beguiling heat.

There are two other glorious appetizers. Hushpuppies are simply about the best anywhere. Hot from the fryer, they are gnarled, dark brown, sandy textured, with a crunchy crust enclosing a soft, sweet corn interior. They are addictive! Another essential, noted on the menu as an old family recipe, is crab cake balls—half a dozen little rounds of crabmeat as lacy as macaroons, with an intensely oceanic sweet-crab flavor and so moist that they really seem to melt on the tongue.

Among the long list of entrees, beyond the obvious choice of hardshell crabs by the dozen, we recommend the local specialty, rockfish. Fresh as can be, a big slab of it pulls apart into big, juicy flakes with clean marine flavor. For a more exotic meal, how about the old-fashioned delight, crab imperial? It is nowhere better than in the small ramekin offered by Evans: toasty, full of meat, and creamy-rich.

Gunning's Crab House

3901 S. Hanover St.   410-354-0085
Baltimore, MD   LD | $$

Ed Gunning, who started this crab-eating institution many years ago, has since moved on to open Gunning's Seafood in a Hanover Street shopping center; but the original crab house is still one of the Charm City's best places to pound and pluck your way through a table full of steamed spiced crabs.

Featuring an outdoor crab garden where pitchers of beer seem especially right on a warm summer's night, Gunning's is a no-frills kind of place. Ordered by the dozen, the crabs are firm, meaty, and stuck with a vivid spice mix that sings perfect harmony with the pearly meat inside the shell. They are a royal mess to eat, but when you come to Gunning's, it's crabs you *must* eat. Although there is a menu with other seafood choices, and the crab cakes are pretty darn good, we are not so impressed with the fried seafood, and the French fried potatoes are lame. Maybe our taste buds have changed, but the fried green pepper rings that used to be so addictive now taste something like yesterday's Krispy Kreme donut: very sweet, very doughy, and not all that much fun to eat.

Still, the superb hard-shell crabs make Gunning's an essential stop on the Mid-Atlantic Roadfood tour.

Obrycki's

1727 E. Pratt St.   410-732-6399
Baltimore, MD   LD | $$

Obrycki's is no longer Olde Obrycki's, but the blue crabs on the table are as good as ever. Now located in a spacious new building across the street from the tavern that originally opened in Fells Point in 1865, this big eating hall provides the definitive urban crab feast: a table covered with brown paper and heaped with spiced, steamed, hard-shell crabs.

When you sit down, the waiter will ask if you are interested in crabs. If you nod "yes," he will spread the table with paper and tell you what size they are today and how much you'll be paying. Last time we visited—early June, 2001—they were large and cost $42 per dozen—plenty for a two-person feast. Crab eaters are given a large bucket lined with a paper bag to set by their table for debris, as well as the option of wearing a paper bib. The table is set with wooden mallets and knives; the cooked crabs are brought from the kitchen on a cafeteria tray, from which they are dumped on the table. Novices, of which the far-famed Obrycki's attracts plenty, are given lessons in crab meat extraction from the waiter or waitress, then it is time to start hammering, picking, and sucking. No music plays at Obrycki's, but it is filled with the most beguiling rhythms as people throughout the restaurant wield their mallets to pound shells holding meat.

The spice mix—a muddy gray-brown paste that clings to the shells—is addictively delicious, insinuating its peppery essence into every fiber of sweet, moist meat you pull from the carcass. Spices are what make Obrycki's steamed crabs so especially good; and although it is a huge amount of work getting all the meat you want from these stubborn creatures, you will keep picking, poking, and sucking until there is no more.

If the caloric output required to eat crabs seems like more than the nutrition the meat provides, Obrycki's has a full menu of easier-to-eat Chesapeake Bay seafoods, including softshell crabs, backfin crab cakes, sautéed crab meat (the lazy person's choice!), and highly spiced deviled crab cakes. The favored beverage is beer by the pitcher and mug, although if you don't mind crabby fingerprints on your glass, there is a high-tone wine list, too.

Park-N-Dine

189 E. Main St.   301-678-5242
Hancock, MD   BLD | $

If you are driving—or riding your bicycle—through the narrowest part of western Maryland in Hancock and find yourself hankering for meat and potatoes, pull up to Park-N-Dine. Located alongside I-70 and at the end of the bike trail from Indian Springs along the C&O Canal, this venerable establishment is a blast from the past where uniformed waitresses are pros and where the kitchen still practices the craft of from-scratch cooking.

High kudos to the old-fashioned roast turkey dinner with mashed potatoes, stuffing, and gravy, followed, of course, by wedges of apple pie or actual from-scratch pudding (banana, tapioca, chocolate). Yes, that's *pudding*, not mousse! Sandwiches and hamburgers are available, and breakfast is fine and dandy, but the charm of Park-N-Dine for us is its seven-day-a-week roster of Sunday dinner, i.e., pork chops, meat loaf, and plates of steaming pink corned beef and cabbage. Portions are vast and prices are low.

Randy's Ribs & Barbecue

Route 5 and Gallant Green Rd.   301-274-3525
Hughesville, MD   LD | $

"Whole pigs available!" boasts the menu at Randy's, which specializes in catered barbecues as well as a small roadside-stand menu that is a godsend for hungry travelers in need of pork along Route 5 in St. Mary's County. Generally, this is crab country: hard crabs, rockfish, and shrimp, amended by the local specialty of kale-stuffed ham, usually available only in autumn. But here at Randy's, the sweet perfume of slow-smoking pork fills the air throughout the year; and if you are one who considers barbecue foremost among the food groups, you will love what you find.

Sandwiches and platters are available: pulled or sliced pork, ribs and ham, whole chickens and slabs of ribs. "Slaw on that?" the order-taker will ask if you get a sandwich. "Yes!" we say, and then unwrap the foil around a big bun loaded with chunks of moist, full-flavored pork bathed in Randy's excellent spicy sauce, with which sweet slaw sings happy harmony. Ribs are large and chewy, their luscious meat infused with smoke; and on the side, you will relish collard greens, macaroni and cheese, and baked beans.

Randy also offers a mighty fine half-smoke, which is the locally preferred variant of a hot dog: an extra-fat sausage bisected lengthwise and smoke-cooked until its skin is taut and dark red, its insides dense and succulent. All the usual hot dog condiments are available, but we recommend topping it with only one thing: Randy's sauce. It is available by the pint and gallon: an excellent investment in one's future culinary happiness.

St. Mary's Landing

Route 5   301-884-3287
Charlotte Hall, MD   BLD | $$

St. Mary's County stuffed ham is a seasonal dish, generally served between Thanksgiving and Easter, but you can get it year-round at St.

Mary's Landing. It's wonderful stuff: a corned ham packed with heaps of kale, cabbage, onions, and spice, served for breakfast on a plate with delicious potato cakes or for supper as a main course.

Lucky for us, they were out of stuffed ham one December night when we came for supper. That meant we discovered the kitchen's marvelously crabby crab cakes, a plate of big, snapping-firm, spiced boiled shrimp, and barbecued ribs that had a delicate crunch to their outermost edges and meat that slid right off the bone.

This is a fascinating restaurant, a serious tavern as well as an eatery, with a wall-mounted TV monitor that displays Keno numbers and a countdown to the next game. One morning when we arrived at 7 A.M., we were the first customers to take seats in the restaurant, but bar stools in the adjoining taproom were already occupied by ladies and gentlemen having shots and beers to start their day. Contrary to general principles of detecting good Roadfood, St. Mary's County stuffed ham is almost always found in places where drinking and gambling are featured attractions.

Seaside Restaurant & Crab House

224 Crain Highway N   410-760-2200
Glen Burnie, MD   LD | $$

Beautiful crabs, especially big and too hot to handle, come to the table stuck with a peppery, salty spice mix. Grab your knife to pry away the outer shell and pick up the mallet to start pounding, and soon you will be rewarded with fat nuggets of the sweetest meat any crab ever delivered. Toss your shells into paper bags on the floor and hoist an ice-cold beer to quench the thirst that spicy crabs inevitably provoke: This is a true finger-licking feast and incomparable fun.

Beyond beautiful blue crabs, the Seaside Restaurant has a menu of other local specialties, well worth sampling, especially if crabmeat extraction is too daunting a task (it *is* hard work!). There are beautiful broiled shrimp, scallops, and flounder, and zesty crab cakes, plus as good a crab soup as we've had anywhere along the Chesapeake Bay.

A busy place, especially on weekends. Expect to wait at mealtime.

Woman's Industrial Exchange

333 N. Charles St.   410-685-4388

Baltimore, MD   BL | $

A spectacularly good restaurant in a spectacularly modest setting, the Woman's Industrial Exchange has been a Baltimore institution since 1880, offering needy women an opportunity to sell their handicrafts in the front room, and hungry patrons the chance to have breakfast and lunch in the back.

When we say it is spectacularly good, we don't mean that the Woman's Exchange serves any menu item that is extraordinary or exotic (although deviled eggs and tomato aspic aren't exactly as ubiquitous as Happy Meals these days); we mean that every item on the menu is honest, homemade, and old-fashioned good.

While lunch is the most notable meal of the day, and an opportunity to enjoy superb chicken salad or a crab cake sandwich, followed by Charlotte Russe, pie à la mode, or a cup of Jell-O, we love to come here at 9 A.M. for breakfast. The long dining room is quiet and peaceful, fans spinning overhead, only a few other patrons at the banquette along the side of the room or at the old steel-banded kitchenette tables. We eat decent breakfasts of bacon and eggs with a good biscuit on the side or pancakes served with bacon neatly arranged in an X-pattern across the top of the stack. During our most recent meal, there was pounding upstairs above the restaurant. "Renovation," the waitress said, explaining that profits from the restaurant and the crafts store up front were not enough to support the enterprise, so the upper floors were being turned into apartments, rent from which might help pay the bills and allow the Woman's Exchange to stay in business. "We've been here 121 years," she said. "So I don't think we'll be trying to go nowhere!"

Argyle Restaurant

212 Kearny Ave.   201-991-3900

Kearny, NJ   LD | $$

Fish and chips, hurrah! At the Argyle, each platter holds one very large triangular hunk of fish that has been dipped in batter and deep-fried until the exterior is brittle and the inside, nearly two inches in height, is a pillowy mound of snow-white, moist, sweet fish. Chefs Bill Gordon and John Nisbet bone and cut their cod or haddock in this kitchen, and it could not taste fresher. The soft flavor of the meat and the hard crunch of its golden jacket are a truly exceptional meal. The chips (French fries) are fried in the same oil as the fish—and these are supplemented by little cups of tartar sauce and larger cups of creamy cole slaw.

The Argyle is one of a couple of restaurants that feature fish and chips along Kearny Avenue, where you'll also find three different butcher shops specializing in such other British Isle faves as blood pudding, haggis, and pasties. Once known as "Little Paisley" for all the Scotsmen who came here to work in the fabric mills over a century ago, Kearny has gone more polyglot over the last few decades, but it still has a strong Scots accent. The Argyle, which hosts Robert Burns suppers every January, adjoins The Piper's Cove, an outfitting store for kilted marching bands and bagpipers.

The most delicious fish and chips in the Northeast is the star of this menu—the air all around the restaurant is perfumed by the aroma—but there are many other rare and enticing things to eat. A Scotch egg, for instance. That's a hard-boiled egg wrapped in sausage, breaded, and deep-fried. It is served cleaved in half, and to dress it properly, the Scots way, you want to pour on a little of the HP Sauce that is set out on every table (alongside the malt vinegar that experienced eaters use for their chips). Chicken pie and meat pie, accompanied by beans and chips, are true comfort food; and black pudding, albeit somewhat gruesome-looking (it's made with blood), has a truly appetizing smell rich with cinnamon.

For dessert, you want clootie dumpling, a.k.a. boiled baby, a not-too-sweet spice cake served in a pool of hot custard.

The Argyle is a true neighborhood lunchroom, occupied by locals as well as homesick Scots and Irish from towns and states far away. Its bare Formica tables are set with plain green paper place mats. Its walls display pictures of pipers and Scottish landscapes; and you will be well taken care of by Margaret Jones, who has been the head waitress here for well over thirty years.

Dickie Dee's

380 Bloomfield Ave.	973-483-9396
Newark, NJ	LD | $

Newark is a polyglot place with restaurants and stores that offer dozens of cuisines from around the world. For a meal that is distinctly American, go to Dickie Dee's and order a double dog. No ordinary weenie, Dickie Dee's dog is an Italian-style (a.k.a. Newark-style) hot dog, meaning it is deep-fried (like the Texas weiners so popular over in Paterson) and stuffed deep inside a half-loaf of Italian bread along with fried peppers and onions and fried potatoes. Although it is possible to get a single dog, stuffed into a quarter-loaf, the double is the connoisseur's choice because the ratio of tube steak to bread is better balanced; and besides, the half-loaf holds in all the messy ingredients better than a quarter.

Also on Dickie Dee's menu are sausage, burger, and cheese steak sandwiches constructed the same way—inside an Italian loaf with peppers, onions, and potatoes—as well as sandwiches filled only with potatoes and/or vegetables. There is nice thin-crust pizza, too; but it's the dog that has put this place on the map since the mid–twentieth century. All the ingredients are cooked in the same vat of oil next to the order counter; and they are plucked from the oil and inserted directly into the bread (no draining!), making for a wondrously oily double-handful of food. The fried potatoes are big and chunky; the fried peppers still have a bit of crunch to them; and the fried hot dogs themselves pack a flavor wallop.

Be prepared for serious attitude from behind the counter of this brash lunchroom. When it's crowded—it usually is—the line moves fast, and woe to whoever hesitates when placing an order. As the sandwich is made, the cook will demand to know what you want on it in the way of condiments; and this is another time you don't want to be slow responding. (We suggest that a spritz of ketchup is a nice complement for the potatoes that go atop all the other ingredients in the sandwich.)

Carry your tray to a table and ease into a permanently attached molded plastic chair. Lay out plenty of paper napkins for the inevitable spillage, and dig into a great hot dog meal that is a true North Ward original.

The Hot Grill

669 Lexington Ave.   973-772-6000
Clifton, NJ 07011   BLD | $

Texas weiners (spelled *e-i,* not *i-e*) are a big deal in this part of New Jersey, the word *Texas* being vintage hash-house code for chili. This particular branch of chili dog cookery dates back to a 1920s hot dog stand in the Manhattan Hotel in Paterson, and today, one of the best places to sample the Garden State specialty is the Hot Grill of Clifton.

Step up to the order counter, where empty trays await, and order a pair. *Nobody* gets just one Texas weiner! The counter man will holler out to the back kitchen, "Two, all the way!" And within ninety seconds, a pair of handsome little hot dogs will appear on the tray in front of you. Each is a deep-fried pup with rugged skin nestled in a too-short bun topped with mustard, onion, and spicy/sweet beef-chili sauce—exemplary eats! On the side you can get French fries topped with gravy, sauce, or cheese or any combination of the three, and the preferred beverage with a Texas weiner is always root beer.

It's fun to dine in The Hot Grill's vast modern dining room where, instead of music, you listen to the calls of the countermen back to the kitchen, and instead of sports, the overhead TV is tuned to "The Hot Grill Channel," which is a continuous program of hosannas to the hot dog.

Jimmy Buff's

390 Belleville Turnpike   201-998-7722 or 1-877-9HOTDOG
North Arlington, NJ   LD | $

Also at 60 Washington St., West Orange, NJ (973-325-9897) and 4 Elwood Ave.,
    Irvington, NJ (973-375-9883)

Newark hot dogs are an amazing local specialty little known anywhere else, but beloved to the dog hounds of the old neighborhood. Like a New Orleans muffaletta, a Newark dog is based on a round of fresh, tawny-crusted Italian bread. The bread is nothing at all like an ordinary, sponge-soft hot dog bun. It is sturdy, chewy, and delicious in its own right. It *needs* to be tough to hold all the ingredients that get piled into it. The bread is cut in half, forming two half circles. Each is squeezed open to become a pocket like a huge, spongy pita. Into the pocket go a pair of all-beef hot dogs that have been fried in hot fat until crunch-crusted, a heap of onions and peppers that have been sautéed until limp, and a handful of crisp-fried potato chunks. The ingredients are forked directly from the frying cauldron into the sandwich, which is why the bread needs oomph—to absorb drippin's from the garlicky dogs and sweet vegetables. Options include ketchup and/or mustard and/or marinara sauce, and fire-hot onion relish.

Some dozen sandwich shops in and around Newark specialize in Italian hot dogs. The dogs are slim, all-beef tubes that are always deep-fried; but each place that serves them has its own signature. Charlie's Famous in Kenilworth piles in peppers but serves fried potatoes on the side. Pacella's in Edison steams rather than fries its peppers and onions. Dickie Dee's deep-fries everything in the same oil. Jimmy Buff's in West Orange and North Arlington separately deep-fries the hot dog and the potatoes but sautés the peppers and onions.

James Racioppi, proprietor of Jimmy Buff's, believes it was his grandparents, James and Mary Racioppi, who started it at their home. Mr. Racioppi says, "He played cards there every week. My grandmother served sandwiches to him and his associates. After a while, people started coming just to eat; so in 1932 they opened a store at Fourteenth and Ninth to sell the sandwiches. That was the beginning." As for the name of the store, James explains: "My grandfather Jimmy was an excellent card player. He was known for his talent to bluff, but with their Italian accents, they used to call him Jimmy Buff."

The newer Jimmy Buff's in North Arlington doesn't quite have the old North Ward look of the original hot dog joint, but it is 100 percent New Jersey in character . . . and is sure to be filled with a handful of Jersey characters, most of whom appear to be relatives—or at least close friends—of Mr. Racioppi. As we ordered our doubles, one older gentleman called out to us from his table to recommend but simultaneously warn us about the hot sauce available. It is delicious, but it is *very* hot; and those with the cojones to survive it get their name inscribed in the honor roll posted on Jimmy Buff's wall.

Libby's Lunch

98 McBride Ave.   973-278-8718
Paterson, NJ   LD | $

Texas weiners (usually spelled *e-i* rather than *i-e*) were invented in New Jersey prior to 1920 by John Patrelis, who worked at his father's hot dog stand at the Manhattan Hotel in Paterson. According to hot dog historian Robert C. Gamer of Wyckoff, Mr. Patrelis devised a deep-fried frankfurter in a too-short bun, topped with mustard, onions, and spicy meat sauce, traditionally accompanied by French fries and a mug of root beer. In 1920 the hot dog stand was renamed the Original Hot Texas Weiner because Mr. Patrelis believed the sauce to be like Texas chili. In fact, it is more Greek than Texan; but the Lone Star moniker stuck, and today Paterson is rich with Texas weiner shops.

Libby's Lunch, since 1936, is the best of the best. Here in a dog house with no pretense but with impeccable pedigree, countermen dish out "dogs all the way" with the usual Texas weiner accompaniment of French fries topped with either beefy gravy or spicy chili sauce. Good as the spicy chili sauce is (you can buy it by the pint), it is the hot dog itself that makes this a memorable eating experience. Its insides are tender and succulent, while the exterior is blistered and chewy because of its hot oil bath. A pair of these tube steaks with a side of crisp French fries blanketed with gravy is a grand plate of food: true New Jersey, and uniquely American.

Rutt's Hut

417 River Rd.　　　　　　　　973-779-8615

Clifton, NJ　　　　　　　　　LD | $

Rutt's hot dogs are known as rippers because their skin tears and crinkles when they are deep-fried in oil. The deep fryer turns them rugged, dark, and slightly chewy on the outside, while the interior remains soft and juicy. (If you are a weenie wimp, you can order an "in and outer," which comes out of the fat more quickly and remains thoroughly pink and plump.) Most people order their rippers topped with Rutt's spicy relish, made from onions and finely chopped carrots and cabbage. These raunchy and irresistible pork and beef hot dogs are served in a wide-open dining room with high counters at the windows that provide a view of the parking lot while you dine. Stand and eat, and if you're bored with your company or by yourself, read the local *Pennysaver*. Or, the best thing to do: Listen to the exuberant calls of the countermen as they sing out, "Cheeseburger, dipped!" for a CB with gravy, or "Twins, all the way," meaning a pair of rippers with mustard and relish.

Rutt's serves real meals as well as real drinks in a taproom adjacent to the hot dog eating area. Here, amid wood-panel decor, one can quaff many beers with platters of such blue-plate fare as chicken croquettes, stuffed cabbage, Jersey pork chops, and bean-heavy chili by the cup or bowl. Prices are low, and the food we have tasted is mighty satisfying. But if you are coming to Rutt's only once, eat hot dogs at a counter. It is a definitive Roadfood experience.

White House Sub Shop

2301 Arctic Ave.　　　　　　609-345-1564

Atlantic City, NJ　　　　　　LD | $

It is easy to find submarine-style sandwiches almost everywhere in the USA. In some places they are well worth seeking. New Orleans has a passion for po-boys and oyster loaves. Miami and Tampa like Cuban sandwiches on fragile-crusted bread. Chicago's premier street food is the Italian beef sandwich. All these are truly great things to eat, but if you want to study the sub sandwich seriously, there is only one place to go: the Delaware Valley. This region, which includes southwestern New Jersey and easternmost Pennsylvania, is sub-sandwich-central, known for such glorious sub-genres as the cheese steak and the hoagie.

If you want the very best submarines, dished out with sass and attitude at no extra charge, pay a visit to the White House of Atlantic City. Built on loaves of superb bread that are secured fresh by the kitchen throughout the day, White House sandwiches are true heroes, ranging from the "White House Special," which is an immense stack of cold cuts tightly packed and lubricated with olive oil, to hot meatball subs that inevitably squish and ooze as soon as you hoist them toward your mouth. A full-size sub is about eighteen inches long. A half sandwich is, for us, a very satisfying meal. "Hot pepper, onion, lettuce, tomato?" the waitress will ask when you place your order. We like all of the above, especially the minced, marinated hot peppers when piled double-thick on the White House's superb cheese steak sandwich. Onions are available grilled or raw.

At mealtime, expect to wait in line for a table or for take-out orders; or, if you're lucky, get a seat at the counter where, to the right, you can watch the sub-makers assemble sandwiches with speed and precision. The counter is good also because it puts you in the midst of the cooks, waitresses, cashier, and other employees, where you are privy to their endless high-spirited palaver. We saw half a dozen sandwich men behind the counter and at least that many waitresses working the room, and not one of them was without gold chains and jewelry around his or her neck.

Since Tony Basile opened it in 1946, the White House has established and maintained the fundamental rule of good sub-shop decor, which is to cover the walls with pictures of celebrity clientele (Joe Frazier, Jerry Lewis, Wayne Newton, several Miss Americas, Mr. T, etc.). Some of the old celebrity pictures have faded with age, adding an especially sentimental aura to those who are now dead (Sinatra, Sammy Davis, Jr., etc.). For all the stardust of its famous clientele, the White House remains an extremely humble Naugahyde-and-neon eat-place with paper napkins, harsh lighting, and brusque service. It would be wrong to serve a great sub sandwich any other way.

Anchor Bar

1047 Main St.   716-886-8920

Buffalo, NY   LD | $$

The Anchor Bar was established in 1935, but it wasn't until July 29, 1977, officially proclaimed by the City of Buffalo to be Chicken Wing Day, that anyone other than its loyal local clientele gave a hoot about it. In the last quarter century, chicken wings have become an American obsession.

Teresa Bellisimo, who ran the bar with her husband, Frank, invented wings as we know them in 1964. Mrs. Bellisimo's genius was to cut the wings into two wieldy sections (drumettes and bows) and, after deep-frying them, stir them up in buttery hot sauce. Her presentation is now classic: They are presented under an upside-down bowl (for bones) with a few stalks of celery and a bowl of creamy blue cheese dressing. The wings are crisp, a lovely orange-yellow, not dripping sauce, but imprinted with it. They are available hot or mild. Hot is fiery and will burn your lips; mild is more buttery-flavored.

Mrs. Bellissimo's invention has proven to be a sublime combination of tastes and textures, as well a significant thirst-inducer, hence ideal bar food.

Barney Greengrass

541 Amsterdam Ave. (betw 86th and 87th Sts.)   212-724-4707
New York, NY   BL | $

What a great-smelling restaurant! Enter the small sales area where smoked fish, breads, and babkas are sold, and you inhale a delicious deli mix of bread, pickle, and spice. There are a few tables in this room, where you sit among the take-home crowd. While these seats provide no sense of privacy or peace, they offer a parade of Upper West Side life as it comes in to buy deli meats, plus a rare opportunity—if you are brave—to kibitz among waiters and countermen. We also like these seats because they provide a close-up view (and scent) of the fresh breads on the counter—seeded rye, pumpernickel, onion rolls—as well as of the gorgeous slabs of smoked fish behind the glass case. Sturgeon is the best (Barney Greengrass is the self-proclaimed Sturgeon King); it is lean, silky, and rich beyond description. The whitefish is snowy and a little drier. Sable is soft and garlicky. All are available on platters, with fresh bagels and bialys, cream cheese, onions, tomatoes, and olives.

Good as the smoke fish platters are, the single best dish in the house is the one known as eggs-and-Novie. If you come in the morning, especially on a weekend, you will smell plates of it being carried from the kitchen to customers as soon as you enter. It is eggs scrambled with plush morsels of smoked Nova Scotia salmon and onions nearly caramelized by frying. The combination tastes opulent; the textural range from the eggs' soft curds to the firm nuggets of fish they enfold to the slippery tangle of onions is a tongue's delight. Beyond smoked fish, Barney Greengrass is an excellent place to eat chopped liver, cool beet borscht, and just about any kind of cold-cut sandwich with garlic pickles.

As should be the case in a true New York deli, a visit here is always a personality-plus experience. Last time we came by, it was the middle of winter and the late Moe Greengrass still ruled the roost. We dashed from the car to pick up a pound of chopped liver, a loaf of seeded rye, and a babka. While at the counter, shivering from the cold outside, we asked Moe if he would let us take a copy of the menu.

"The menu, you can take," he answered. "And the chopped liver is nice. But it's a good overcoat you should be buying."

Café Edison

228 W. 47th St.   212-840-5000
New York, NY   BLD | $$

Known to regulars as "The Polish Tea Room," Café Edison offers a delicious taste of old New York that seems utterly unaffected by the corporate takeover of Times Square. Prices are moderate, the food is good, and the experience is unforgettable. In particular, we highly recommend ordering borscht, matzoh ball soup, braised brisket, kasha varnishkes, and homemade gefilte fish. Experts consider the cheese blintzes among the city's best, and we think the matzoh brei is superb.

Way back in the 1920s, this used to be a ritzy spot. Today, while it's no flophouse, the Edison Hotel is far from ultraluxurious. The café, which used to be the hotel's grand ballroom, still shows evidence of the glamour that once was, including salmon-colored bas-relief walls and elegant chandeliers. But now the walls are taped with signs advertising daily specials and the weary waitstaff will give any crabby deli help a run for their money in an angst-on-a-tray contest.

Carnegie Deli

854 7th Ave.   212-757-2245
New York, NY   BLD | $$

The motto of the Carnegie Deli is "There is only one!" Of course there are plenty of kosher-style delicatessens in Manhattan, and some of them make good pastrami sandwiches. But if you are looking for the biggest, in a place that literally reeks of New York deli, this is it. When we say "literally reeks," we are referring to the dizzying aroma of cured deli meats and sour pickles that smacks you in the nose the moment you walk in the door. Wow, what a rush! Almost instantly, a host will point you to the back, and as you walk toward the tables, you pass a counter full of meats and smoked-fish salads behind which sandwiches are made. Salamis hang like a curtain over the counter, adding their garlicky perfume to the air. At the back of the restaurant, or in the adjoining dining room, you will be directed to a place at a table where you will sit elbow-to-elbow with strangers.

Looking for privacy, peace, and quiet? Wrong restaurant! A Carnegie meal is a boisterous affair shared by blasé regulars, wide-eyed tourists, and showbiz celebrities (whose pictures line the walls). This is a New York landmark—the quintessential Midtown deli.

Featured in the Woody Allen movie *Broadway Danny Rose,* the Carnegie is best known for ridiculously outsized sandwiches made of corned beef, pastrami, brisket, turkey, and chopped liver, as well as triple-decker combinations of ingredients. Beyond sandwiches, the menu includes blintzes and potato pancakes, gefilte fish and pickled herring, borscht, and kreplach soup.

If it's your first time, you must have the pastrami sandwich. Although purists gripe that the meat is no longer hand-sliced, we have no complaints about the Carnegie's machine-sliced pastrami. It is mellow and not too zesty, utterly tender and infused with fatty savor. It is so tall that the top piece of rye bread appears to be merely an afterthought applied to the tower of meat. In fact, it is difficult to eat the ordinary way, by picking it up in your hands and taking a bite. Many customers go at it by piece by shred, directly from the plate. To accompany the monumental sandwiches, the Carnegie supplies perfect puckery accoutrements—half-sour and sour dill pickles arrayed in silver bowls along the tables.

Charlie the Butcher's

| 1065 Wehrle Dr. at Cayuga | 716-633-8330 |
| Buffalo, NY | LD \| $ |

Well situated for an impatient appetite arriving at the Buffalo Airport, Charlie the Butcher's is an essential stop for anyone who wants to sample the Nickel City's unique sandwich, "beef on weck." Slow-roasted beef, tender and pink, is sliced thin and piled on a hard roll that is crusted with pretzel salt and *kummel* (caraway seeds). The top half of the roll gets dipped briefly in beef juice, and the sandwich is served with only a pickle spear as garnish, although many customers slather it with eye-opening horseradish from the Broadway Market (where Charlie Roesch's grandfather started this beef dynasty in 1914).

Place your order at the front window with its fabulous view of the carving block, then pay and find a seat at the low-low counter or a table topped with oilcloth. All seats provide a nice view of the kitchen, where you'll see Charlie himself, with a large staff of accomplished helpmates, slicing cabbage, tending soups, and cutting beef to order. Sandwiches are served in cardboard boats, and it's customary to bus your own table.

By the way, Charlie's menu extends beyond beef on weck; and everything else we've sampled is first-rate: Buffalo-made hot dogs and sausages grilled over coals, chicken spiedie (a boneless breast that is marinated and grilled), and such daily special sandwiches as meat loaf (Tuesday) and double-smoked ham (Monday). The beverage list includes the local favorite, loganberry, as well as Charlie's personal favorite, birch beer.

Cornell Dairy Bar

At the Cornell Dairy Store, corner of Tower and Judd Falls Rd.
Stocking Hall   607-255-3272
Ithaca, NY   L | $

All the cow-sourced products served in this on-campus eatery are produced by the College of Agriculture and Life Sciences; even the maple syrup sold in the little grocery store upstairs comes from the Natural Resources Department, the apple cider from the Pomology Department.

The Dairy Bar is, as the name suggests, a casual joint with scattered tables inside and a few seats outdoors by the sidewalk. Although there are a limited number of other things to eat and drink, including soup from a Knorr Soup Bar and hot drinks from a cappuccino machine, it's ice cream that stars. Step up to the counter and browse among such flavors as Kahluá Fudge (coffee flavored with a fudge swirl), Mexican Sundae (with peanuts and fudge chunks), Espresso Chunky Chip, Sticky Bunz, even Green Tea. Order a cone, cup, or sundae and carry it to a seat. This is excellent ice cream: just rich enough to fully satisfy without cloying, and without the baroque flavor combos you find in boutique ice creams that sell for $3 a pint on supermarket shelves.

In addition to praising the good ice cream, we must also note that the whipped cream that goes atop sundaes is superb: thick, sweet, and dairy-fresh. And finally: chocolate milk. It's a beautiful thing, so smooth, so gently chocolaty, so perfectly juvenile.

Cupcake Café

522 9th Ave. at 39th St.   212-465-1530
New York, NY   BL | $

The Cupcake Café is a tiny old storefront with wooden floor, tin ceiling, and pink paint on the walls; and while much business is takeout, there are four scattered tables and some rickety chairs across from the order counter. Here you can spend a morning over cake and coffee while observing the ebb and flow of pastry eaters at the counter. Table seats also offer a leisurely view of the Cupcake Café's extensive inventory of colorful full-size cakes, individual cupcakes, and donuts.

The big cakes are great cylinders enrobed in multicolored frosting in the shape of sunflowers, peonies, and lilacs. Proprietor Ann Warren is known for her chocolate cake with mocha icing, decorated to fit whatever occasion you need to celebrate. Lovely as the big frosted beauties appear, they are not what most people come to eat at this corner bake shop west of Times Square, just down from the Port Authority terminal. The stars of the show are the simplest sort of coffee companions: donuts, muffins, and coffee cake.

The coffee cake is especially good: egg-rich and cream-textured, made with a sheet of apple topping or blueberries, or plain and cut into hefty squares. The donuts are plain as can be: perfect-circle cake donuts with a crunch to their skin and dense insides well suited for dunking. There are always buttermilk donuts; among the other available varieties are pumpkin, whole wheat orange, and glazed. On weekends only, the waffle irons are pulled off the high shelf behind the counter; and if you don't mind waiting a while for one of the few seats, they are one of the great, cheap Midtown breakfasts.

At lunch, the Cupcake Café offers a limited menu of soup, sandwiches, and small pizzas.

Dinosaur Barbecue

246 W. Willow St.
Syracuse, NY   LD | $$

Dinosaur Barbecue can be hard to find, and you will likely wait for a seat. But any inconvenience evaporates as soon as you sink your teeth into a pulled-pork sandwich or rack of smoky, dry-rub ribs enrobed in superior sauce (with fine corn bread and/or French fries on the side). The menu says that the ribs are "so good you'll slap yo' pappy."

Beyond the pork—which is *the* thing to eat—Dinosaur has a broad menu of such muscular items as "chili on the half shell" (that would be tortilla chips), barbecued wings with Wango Tango sauce, ribeye steak rubbed with coffee (!), and a Cajun-spiced Diablo Burger.

While it's the smoked meat that has earned this restaurant an honored place on the short-form honor roll of Northeast Barbecue, the ambience is delicious, too. Proud to note that it was founded by a trio of bikers who learned to cook over a 55-gallon drum, it is a true honkey-tonk rib joint, favored equally by students, bikers, travelers, and locals. Tables are covered with easy-wipe vinyl; blues blare, the dance floor throbs, and eaters literally moan with pleasure as they dine.

There are branches of the Dinosaur in Rochester and New York City.

Doug's Fish Fry

206 West Rd.   607-753-9184
Cortland, NY   LD | $$

Fried fish sandwiches are common throughout much of Upstate New York, appreciated by locals but little known by outsiders. A visit to Doug's is convincing evidence that this is regional food to take seriously. Your choice is either a sandwich, a fish dinner, or a fish-onion dinner. The titles are misleading because the sandwich is in fact two or three large hunks of fried fish piled in and around a modest bun that in no way is large enough to hold even half its alleged ingredients. Like a tenderloin from the southern Midwest, the presentation pushes the envelope of what, exactly, a sandwich is. A fish dinner adds beautiful chunky French fries to the pseudo-sandwich. A fish-onion dinner means it includes onion rings as well.

The fish is moist, sweet, and gently flavored, encased in a sandy crust with just the right amount of crunch. It comes with pickly tartar sauce that is surprisingly unsweet. Sweetness comes in the form of Doug's superb cole slaw, which is finely chopped and fetchingly spicy.

Service is eat-in-the-rough style. Place your order at the stand-up counter (from which you have an appetizing view of fish and fries coming out of the hot oil), pay for the meal, and wait for your name to be called. Fetch your own utensils and condiments from a table in the center of the dining room that holds plastic forks and knives and ketchup, mustard, and malt vinegar for spritzing on fries.

Bonus: Doug's is a source for excellent soft-serve custard, dense and alabaster-pure. Throughout the warm-weather months the custard is a foundation for warm fruit sundaes. The available compote, made right here from the fruit of the season, begins with strawberries and blueberries early in the summer, then moves to peaches and finally to apples in the fall. Glorious!

Eckl's Beef on Weck Restaurant

4936 Ellicot Rd.	716-662-2262
Orchard Park, NY	D	$$

Dale Eckl's menu offers many good things beyond the Buffalo-area favorite sandwich, roast beef on kummelweck (a salt-and-caraway-seed-spangled hard roll). The fish fry is legendary; the steaks are handsome; there is even a giant lobster tail dinner for about $30. But when we come to western New York, we cannot resist the famous sandwich, made of top round beef that is slow-slow roasted to pink perfection and shaved thin, then piled high on a delicious crusty roll (the top of which gets dipped in natural gravy). It is a dazzling combo, salty enough to have you ordering second and third and fourth beers. (Reputedly, inducing thirst for beer is the reason a German tavern owner invented beef on weck about a century ago.)

Eckl's is a polite kind of restaurant, a place for family celebrations and couples on dates. Its uniformed waitress staff is swift and efficient, and Dale Eckl is on hand to greet returning customers and make certain the beef-eating experience is flawless. Note to first-timers: Try to get a seat in the small dining room adjacent to the bar. Here you have an extremely appetizing view of the beef-carvers at work.

Glenwood Pines

1213 Taughannock Blvd. (Route 89)	607-273-3709
Ulysses, NY	LD	$

Glenwood Pines has been a destination diner for Cornellians since it opened in 1946. It has a broad menu, including eighteen-ounce steaks, farm-raised tilapia, spaghetti and meatballs, and multi-combo cold-cut sandwiches. But the main reason for coming to this friendly roadhouse overlooking Cayuga Lake is a Pinesburger. That's a six-ounce beef oval topped with a couple of slices of cheese wedged into a length of Ithaca Bakery French bread with lettuce, tomato slices, onion slices, and your choice of Thousand Island dressing or mayonnaise. Connoisseurs told us that we had to have it with the Thousand Island, and it would be hard to argue against that. The sweetness of the dressing is a grand complement for the smoky meat and all its dressings. On the side, good companions include ultra-crunchy fried onion rings and creamy cole slaw.

We said the Pinesburger was the primary reason to visit. The secondary one is the fish fry. A huge, thick length of haddock is breaded and fried crisp and served with either tartar sauce or cocktail sauce. It is sweet, moist, flavorful fish, and a giant meal.

Ambience at Glenwood Pines is old-time tavern. When you walk in, you see a few pinball machines and a bowling game on the right, a pool table ahead of you, and, beyond that, the bar where some folks sit and imbibe beers with (or without) their Pinesburgers as a TV delivers sports broadcasts from the upper-right corner. To the left are tables and a small separate dining room; also a small case of trophies—for baseball, bowling, and volleyball—earned by teams that Glenwood Pines has sponsored.

Hallo Berlin

| 54th St. and 5th Ave. | No phone |
| New York, NY | L Tues-Fri \| $ |

Hallo Berlin is usually parked at 54th and Fifth Tuesday through Friday, from about 11 A.M. to 3 P.M. Rolph and his wife, Bernadette, also operate the Hallo Berlin Food, Wine, and Beer Hall at 626 Tenth Avenue (212–977–1944) and the Hallo Berlin–North Tavern at Exit 1 off I-81 in Conklin, New York (607–775–4391).

Midtown side streets are crowded with hot dog carts that are pretty much the same, but Hallo Berlin off Fifth Avenue is something else. You will find no ordinary Sabrett's here. With signs boasting that it is "The 'wurst' pushcart in New York," and home of "The Soup Communist," this tiny piece of real estate at the northwest corner at 54th Street is the jocular domain of Rolf Babiel, whose specialty is old-world sausages: bratwurst, bockwurst, knockwurst, bauernwurst, and kielbasa. They are served whole in an excellent hard roll—preferably topped with red cabbage, kraut, onions, and mustard—or sliced into disks and spread atop a bed of fried potatoes in a cardboard boat.

One lunch hour, we finally get to the head of the Hallo Berlin line to order a pan-fried beef currywurst and the day's special, a "Freakin' Deal" platter of chopped Bavarian meatballs with alpenwurst sausage, German potato salad, and red and white cabbage. At the cart, Mr. Babiel assembles every order as a silent partner replenishes the spud trays and seasons the taut-skinned tube steaks as they sizzle on the cart. "Here or to go?" the wurstmeister asks.

When we say "here," he plants a couple of plastic forks in the meat-ball boat and directs us to an eighteen-inch-square ledge at the side of his cart that is topped with a red-and-white checked cloth. As we stand and eat at the microtable, Babiel makes us his audience while preparing lunch for the never-ending line of customers.

"The mayor of Chicago wrote because he wants me to open a sausage cart in the Loop," he announces. "And the mayor of New Rochelle is a fan, too. They approached me from the Empire State Building to open up there." With a straight face, he says, "I tell you, the world would be a better place with a Hallo Berlin on every corner." Then he shows us the dish he says we should have ordered, the German Double Soul Food Mix, a combo plate that includes bratwurst and a Berliner sausage, no substitutions allowed. "We call it the dictator special," he says. "Because you have no choice."

Katz's

205 E. Houston St.   212-254-2246
New York, NY   BLD | $

Oh, what a beautiful hot pastrami sandwich! Hand-sliced to order and piled as high as a water glass on fresh, seeded rye bread, Katz's pastrami is ribboned with flavorful fat, laced with spice, and tender as butter. Put a schmear of mustard on the bread and punctuate your mouthfuls of warm spiced meat with a taste of cool dill pickle and a swig of Dr. Brown's soda: here is a deli sandwich experience that sets the New York standard.

It isn't only the pastrami (or brisket or corned beef or knoblewurst salami) that makes eating a sandwich at Katz's such a joy. It is the place itself—a Lower East Side culinary landmark that is a cacophony of shouted orders and clattering carving knives and the wonderful smell of salami hanging all along the wall. Although it is possible to sit at a table and place an order, the way to fully enjoy a visit to Katz's is to walk up to the deli counter and go one-on-one with a counterman. Tell him what you want and he will cut and assemble it as you watch. It is impressive to see the old-timers fork a big corned beef from the steam box and glide their knife through it, piling a great heap of slices onto bread; and if your man likes you (and if you tip him), he'll cut it just the way you like (fat, lean, thin, thick) and maybe offer you a *schmeck* (taste) while he works.

Katz's has more to eat than sliced-meat sandwiches. The kosher hot dogs are among New York's finest; and the omelets are made deli-style, i.e., unfolded, allowing for heaps of salami, tongue, corned beef, pastrami, or baloney to nestle in big round plates of hot scrambled eggs.

Manganaro's

488 9th Ave. (betw 37th and 38th St.) 212-563-5331
New York, NY L | $

Manganaro's Groceria is one of those old New York places—since 1893—that seems never to change. It is a well-weathered Italian grocery store with salamis hanging from the ceiling, an old-world antipasto bar, and an inventory of odoriferous cheeses. While much of the business is takeout—cold cuts and cheeses by the chunk and pound, sandwiches to go, antipasti of all kinds—there is a scattering of tables toward the back where you can sit and have a fast, inexpensive, and full-flavored lunch.

Step up to the counter and order a pasta plate or a sandwich made on a hero loaf or a round focaccia bread. The sandwiches are big and handsome, filled with first-rate ingredients ranging from elegant prosciutto di Parma to a choice of Italian tuna or ordinary tuna. Available "extras" include roasted peppers, anchovies, sun-dried tomatoes, mozzarella, and pesto.

Party-length hero sandwiches are a major issue along this block on 9th Avenue. And we mean *an issue*. Signs all over Manganaro's caution that this establishment is *not related* to Manganaro's Hero Boy, the modern sandwich shop next door that boasts of being the original home of the six-foot hero sandwich. Six-footers are also a specialty here at Manganaro Grosseria (dial 1–888–SIX–FOOT); and when we asked Manganaro's proprietor, Linda Dell'Orto, if her store was the real originator of the big sandwich, she answered cryptically, "It started here." The details of what is a long-standing family feud are too complicated for us to understand; suffice it to say that the jumbo sandwiches we've watched carried out the door of this old shop (by two bearers, one at each end) are amazing-looking: ham, mortadella, two kinds of salami, capocollo, prosciutto, Swiss cheese, provolone, peppers, lettuce, and just enough vinaigrette to glisten around the edges of the great bread log. Now *that's* Italian . . . but only in America.

Margon

136 W. 46th St.   212-354-5013
New York, NY   BLD | $

Margon is a personality-plus hole in the wall around the corner from otherwise Disneyfied Times Square. Plush, it is not. A ramp leads downward to a long, narrow space with four stools jammed up against an impossibly uncomfortable counter near the front; tables are lined up on the right of an aisle that leads to the back.

On the left of the aisle is a buffet counter where arriving customers stand and place orders. A lot of business is takeout—people bringing lunch back to the office—but if you plan to dine here, this is how it works: Walk to the back with your eyes looking left. This allows full view of what's to eat, including pork chops smothered in gravy, glistening roast chicken, rice and beans, sweet plantains, and octopus salad. Place your order and have a seat. When it's ready, one of the counter help will call you to pick it up or, on occasion, they will bring it to your table.

The octopus salad can be a meal or a lip-smacking appetizer: tender leaves of meat glistening in a garlic marinade. While daily lunch specials include such exotica as tripe and pig feet (Monday and Thursday) and ox tail (Friday), everyday entrees include stews and chops and roast chicken that are beautiful to see and a delight to eat.

The Cuban sandwich is first-rate, a crisp-toasted length of bread enveloping roast pork, salami, ham, melted cheese, a surfeit of pickle slices, mustard, and mayo. Actually, any sandwich made on the good Cuban bread, then pressed and heated, is excellent. We love the plain roast pork, which is anything but plain-tasting.

On your way out, have a shot of espresso. It's dark, syrup-rich, and delicious, just about the best cup we've had anywhere in New York.

Nick Tahou Hots

320 Main St. West   716-436-0184
Rochester, NY   BLD | $

Also at 2260 Lyell Ave. (716-429-6388)

Nick Tahou is an unruly dog house, with chairs and tables scattered around and plenty of noise as customers call out for red hots and white hots with the works. The specialty of the house, and the late Nick Tahou's great legacy to American gastronomy, is a dish known as the garbage plate. Tahou's claim to garbage plate primacy is strong: Other restaurants in the Rochester area have tried to put garbage plates on their menu but have been legally enjoined to rename similar dishes they serve "Dumpster plates." At Nick Tahou, there is no one kind of garbage plate. It is up to each customer to choose the foundation: wieners, hamburgers (with or without cheese), Italian sausage, or steak. The meatstuff of your choice is plated with piles of baked beans and home fried potatoes, a scoop of cool macaroni salad, a dollop of spicy chili sauce, a squirt of two of mustard, and a sprinkle of chopped raw onions. It comes with plastic fork and knife, a bottle of ketchup, some hot sauce, and white bread with butter.

It is a wild, ridiculous, and delicious mess! Especially noteworthy is the sauce atop the hot dogs, a fine-grained, Greek-accented brew that is also available on such lesser variants of frankfurter cookery as Nick Tahou's peppery pork hots and the basic garlic-packed Texas hots, as well as on grilled hamburgers.

The hamburgers are fine, but upper New York State is hot dog country, and Nick Tahou's are dandy. They are called Texas hots, and they are split and fried, which gives them a chewy exterior and hash house raunch that boiled or even charcoal-grilled weenies do not offer.

Parkside Candy

3208 Main St.   716-833-7540
Buffalo, NY   LD | $

Candy by the pound is what keeps us coming back to this handsome 1920s sweetshop. In particular, we need chocolate-coated, spun-molasses sponge candy, the experience of which is like nothing else. It literally melts in your mouth, creating a delirious harmony of chocolate and molasses.

There are many other good candies available, too, all made in the small plant just behind the store: creams and chews, truffles and cordials, clusters, dixies, and barks. And there is a full repertoire of ice cream treats available at the old soda fountain to the left of the magnificent oval candy room. What a lovely place to gorge on such pleasures as frappés, parfaits and sundaes, pies, cakes, and cookies, or a lovers' delight, "Old

Granada Special," which is eight scoops of ice cream, four toppings, and two varieties of toasted nuts under a mountain of whipped cream and served with two spoons.

(There is a short sandwich menu, too, but we've never tried it. The aroma of chocolate when we walk in the Parkside door is a Siren's call.)

Pastrami Queen

1269 Lexington Ave.   212-828-0007
New York, NY   LD | $$

Any list of New York's best pastrami sandwiches needs to include the one made by Pastrami Queen. The meat is beautiful, laced with smoke, edged with a smudge of savory black spice around the rim of each brick-red slice, lusciously rich but not too fat, and about as tender as warm *schmaltz*. It is cut thin and piled high between pieces of fresh, sour-crusted seeded rye bread. Help yourself to mustard from the silver pitcher on the table, and occasionally give your tongue a break from the supreme luxury of the warm beef by biting into a sour or half-sour pickle served atop a bowl of cole slaw. With maybe a single crusty potato pan-cake on the side and a tall mug of icy Dr. Brown soda to drink, this is one of the great meals of New York City. It's not *unique* to New York, but nowhere is it nearly as good.

Beyond pastrami, there's a full menu of other deli sandwich ingredients including corned beef, tongue, brisket, hard salami, and chopped liver. And there are hot dinners galore, ranging from that Jewish mama delight, chicken in the pot, to Southern fried chicken. What's *not* on the menu is anything made from milk. Pastrami Queen is a true kosher restaurant under rabbinical supervision, and therefore can serve no cheese at all. If you order a bagel and want something to spread on it, you'll have to make do with margarine or tofu cream cheese.

Although Pastrami Queen is a relative newcomer to this storefront (having moved from Queens, where it was known as Pastrami King), the old, well-weathered location has a fine patina of age. In the afternoons, there is a comforting hush to the pint-sized dining area across from the counters where meats, knishes, and smoked fishes are displayed; at high noon, when the crowd spills upstairs to the second-story dining room, it is noisier. But even then, dignified serenity prevails. And in our experience, the staff couldn't be nicer. When we ordered a sandwich "to go" for a friend waiting in his double-parked car, the waitress offered to have someone go out into the street and deliver it to him so he could nosh on Lexington Avenue while we had our sandwiches inside.

Phil's Chicken House

Route 26   607-748-6855
West Corners, NY   LD | $$

If you think Memphians or Carolinians are the only cooks who fuss over smoldering wood, stroll down the condiment aisle at the Giant supermarket in West Corners on Route 26. In this otherwise ordinary grocery store, we counted more than six dozen different kinds of barbecue sauce and marinade—for beef, pork, and chicken, and for Binghamton's beloved spiedies.

Across the road from the Giant market is Phil's Chicken House, opened thirty-eight years ago by Phil Card, who learned his skills at Endicott's Chicken Inn. The folksy wood-paneled restaurant is decorated to the hilt with country-crafty knickknacks (souvenir plates, angel statuettes, lighthouse miniatures) and attracts customers that include local families and well-armed state police SWAT teams (who practice marksmanship nearby). There is a full menu, but Phil tells us that 95 percent of his customers come for one thing: barbecued chicken.

It is extraordinary chicken, glazed gold and haloed with the nose-tickling aroma of a sauce with which it has been basted for up to two hours on the rotisserie. The skin's glaze is a salty punch in a plush glove, its potency a dramatic contrast to velvety breast meat and basso harmony for thighs and drumsticks. The wings, with maximum marinade and moistest meat, reverberate with exclamatory gusto.

How Phil's chicken gets so good is no secret at all; in fact, Mr. Card relies on a recipe that is well known throughout the southern Finger Lakes region. "It's your basic Cornell chicken," he tells us, referring to a formula developed by Cornell professor Dr. Robert Baker back in the early 1950s. Dr. Baker's tomato-free vinaigrette, enriched with eggs and shot through with poultry spice, is now used as a marinade and/or basting sauce by cooks throughout the region.

"We baste our chickens on the rotisserie every seven to ten minutes for two hours," Phil explained. Although the technique has made his restaurant a thriving business for decades, Phil is not entirely happy with success. "We can never franchise this," he laments. "You can't do it on a timer. The chickens are different sizes, the rotisserie runs hotter some days; you need a cook who knows what he's looking at and when and how to baste. Years ago the Boston Chicken people came here and visited us to learn, but they walked out in frustration. 'You're too complicated for us,' they told me."

Red Rooster Drive-In

Route 22	845-279-8046
Brewster, NY	LD | $

Good-looking cheeseburgers, heaped with fried onions and sided by a genuine New York egg cream: drive-in life doesn't get much better than this blast-from-the-past eatery just north of I-684 in otherwise upscale Westchester County.

Although a roadside archeologist would definitely categorize this place as a drive-in, there is no car service and there are no carhops. Still, there is a vast parking lot and plenty of people eat in their cars (or in one of three improbably small two-person booths in the cramped interior), and the service, cuisine, and ambience are pure mid-century America.

The hamburgers are especially satisfying: not too big, not odd in any way, just fine handfuls fashioned by proprietor Jack Sypek or Andy the grill chef from freshly ground beef, then sizzled on a charcoal grill. They are served on tender buns—deluxe, please, with lettuce and tomato!—and accompanied by French fries, milk shakes, ice cream floats, or expertly made egg creams in a variety of flavors beyond chocolate. We are particularly fond of cheeseburgers gilded with a thirty-cent-extra order of onions that are grilled until limp and slippery. Also on the Red Rooster menu are hot dogs, cheese dogs, and chili cheese dogs.

In nice weather, customers can choose to eat at one of several picnic tables spread across the lawn in back. Adjacent to this open-air dining room is a modest miniature golf course where kids and carefree adults while away pleasant evenings in the Red Rooster's afterglow.

Schwabl's

789 Center Rd.	716-674-9821
West Seneca, NY	LD | $

Buffalo is the home of chicken wings, which are familiar to every American eater; but Buffalonians are even more passionate for beef on weck, which no one outside the city has ever heard of. Beef on weck is a sandwich of rare roast beef piled into a kaiser roll spangled with coarse salt and caraway seeds (kummelweck). It is one of the great beef sandwiches anywhere in this land, but among the reasons it hasn't gotten famous like Buffalo wings is the fact that it *must* be made on just the right kind of bun. These buns, or "wecks" as they are known in the Nickel City, are difficult to bake and virtually impossible to keep for any length of time. Furthermore, to cook and carve the beef properly requires a level of expertise that cannot be learned overnight.

The exquisite appeal of this unique sandwich is best understood at the family-owned tavern called Schwabl's, which itself dates back to 1946 and partakes of a Schwabl family tradition of running restaurants in the region since 1837. At Schwabl's, the hard rolls are heavily crusted with coarse grains of salt and infused with caraway seeds, fluffy inside, yet rugged enough to hold up well when sliced in half and dipped in natural beef gravy. Schwabl's beef is superb: thin, rare slices severed from a center-cut round roast just before the sandwich is assembled. It is piled high inside each sandwich, a tender and luxurious pillow of protein. The only thing this sandwich could possibly want is a dab of horseradish, which is supplied on each table and along the bar.

That is all you need to know about Schwabl's, except for the fact that the menu also lists a very nice hot ham sandwich on white bread in a pool of tomato-clove gravy, served with warm potato salad. The ham is an interesting alternative to beef, although it has none of the famous local sandwich's authority.

Schwabl's is a casual, well-aged beef house, attended by business people at noon and families at supper time. You can start your meal with a Manhattan or martini, and have a beer along with your sandwich, but the menu clearly states that this is not primarily a drinker's place. "We Cater to Nice Homey Family Trade" is the Schwabl motto; and a dry, nonalcoholic birch beer with the faint twang of spearmint is always available on draft. Waitresses are fast and professional, outfitted in nurselike uniforms, and refreshingly blunt. "You don't want the haddock," one advised us at the beginning of a meal one Friday night; and by golly, she was right. Beef is what you want at Schwabl's, beef on weck.

Sharkey's

56 Glenwood Ave.   607-729-9201
Binghamton, NY   LD | $$

Sharkey's is home of the spiedie. Other upstate New York restaurants sell them; and you can even buy spiedie meat in supermarkets in and around Binghamton, but if you want to eat the best, in a proper neighborhood setting, this family-run tavern is the only place to go.

Larry Sharak's father started making spiedies at a cookfire in the window by the bar more than fifty years ago. Skewered, marinated hunks of lamb were cooked on a charcoal grill and served with broad slices of bread. The custom was to grab the bread in one hand and use it as an edible mitt to slide a few hunks off the metal rod, thus creating an instant sandwich. Spiedies are still served and eaten this way at the bar and tables of Sharkey's. Lamb has grown too expensive, however, so today's spiedies are made from either pork or chicken. When you bite into a piece, it blossoms with the flavorful juice of a two-day marinade that tastes of garlic and vinegar, peppers and oregano, and, according to Larry Sharak, for whom the recipe is a family heirloom, "a lot of pinches of many spices."

Sharkey's city chicken is served on a skewer, too. City chicken is, in fact, not poultry, but pork; in this case, it is a juicy roll of meat packed into a tubular shape on a wooden stick, then steeped in something similar to the spiedie marination, after which it is quickly fried crisp, then baked until thoroughly done. The result is a crusty hunk of meat with insides as juicy and rich-flavored as the darkest dark meat. Like a spiedie, city chicken comes bedded on a slice of bread.

Beyond skewered things, Sharkey's serves Eastern European fare made by experts: holupkis (stuffed cabbage rolls) are the work of Larry's sister-in-law, Marie. Around Easter and Christmastime, the menu features homemade kielbasa sausages. And you can always count on buttery pierogi filled with seasoned mashed potatoes.

Sharkey's is a local institution to which families have come for generations. Old-timers know to enter through the back door rather than the front. Here, you walk into a dark dining room outfitted with ancient wooden booths and long family-style tables formed from pushed-together dinettes. Between courses, the young folks get up to play a few lines on the old Tic Tac Strike game, a pre-electronic diversion that seems at home in this historic tavern.

Shortstop Deli

204 W. Seneca St. 607-273-1030
Ithaca, NY always open | $

Until a few years ago, the only place to eat Hot Truck was at the Hot Truck itself, a mobile eatery that shows up on the Cornell campus during the school year every evening at 10:30 during the week, 11 on weekends, and which is so popular that a one-hour wait for a sandwich isn't unusual. When founder Bob Petrillose sold the Hot Truck to Albert Smith, Smith installed Hot Truck technology in his Shortstop Deli, and now the magnificent sandwiches are available year-round, round-the-clock.

More of a big convenience store than a sit-down diner, the Shortstop Deli features shelves of snack foods, countless varieties of coffee, and a counter where you write your own order for what is here formally known as a Hot Truck Pizza Sub. There are no tables and chairs, just some concrete benches outside the front window where it is possible to bring your wrapped sandwich and your cup of soda (ten cents with a meal!) and dine al fresco.

The pizza subs are fantastic. Made on loaves of Ithaca Bakery French bread (the same loaf that supports a Pinesburger; see Glenwood Pines (page 118), they range from the basic PMP (Poor Man's Pizza), which is nothing but bread, sauce, and cheese, to the extravaganza known as a Suicide (garlic, sauce, mushrooms, sausage, pepperoni, and mozzarella). Each one is piled with its ingredients, then baked open-face until the bread is shatteringly crisp, the cheese bubbles, and the meats sizzle.

The sandwiches have inspired a language all their own. Our Hot Truck tipster Marc Bruno explained that his usual order is a "Triple Sui, Hot and Heavy, G and G." That translates as a full Suicide (piled with a murderous quantity of ground sausage, pepperoni, and mushrooms on a bed of tomato sauce under a mound of melted mozzarella) with three extra homemade meatballs, a sprinkle of red pepper, extra garlic, mayonnaise, and lettuce. (G and G = grease and garden, i.e., mayo and lettuce.) An Indy includes link sausage, pepperoni, onion, sauce, and cheese, hot and heavy. A Flaming Turkey Bone (which contains no turkey and no bones and is not served on fire) includes chicken breast, tomato sauce, cheese, onions, extra hot and heavy, plus "spontaneous combustion" (double-X hot sauce).

Ted's Jumbo Red Hots

2312 Sheridan Dr.   716-834-6287
Tonawanda (Buffalo), NY   LD | $

Ted's began as a horse-drawn hot dog cart in Buffalo in the 1920s. It became a permanently anchored hot dog stand under the Peace Bridge in
1927, and opened as a bigger store on Sheridan Drive in 1948. There are
now eight Ted's in western New York, and one in Tempe, Arizona; but
the one to which we always want to return is Ted's of Tonawanda. It's
modernized since 1948 and is as clean and sanitary as any fast-food franchise; but the hot dogs are something special.

Sahlen's brand frankfurters, available regular, foot-long, or jumbo,
are cooked on a grate over charcoal that infuses each one with pungent
smoke flavor and makes the skin crackling-crisp. As they cook, the chef
pokes them with a fork, slaps them, squeezes them, and otherwise abuses
them, thus puncturing the skin and allowing the dog to suck in maximum smoky taste.

As the dogs cook, you must make some decisions. In consultation
with a person behind the counter known as "the dresser," you decide
how you want to garnish your tube steak. The stellar condiment is Ted's
hot sauce, a peppery-hot concoction laced with bits of relish. You also
want onion rings, sold as tangled webs of crisp fried batter and limp
onion. To accompany a foot-long and a basket of o-rings, the beverage
of choice in these parts is loganberry juice, which is like an exotic Kool-
Aid.

Ted's menu includes things other than hot dogs, such as excellent
hamburgers cooked over charcoal, as well as Italian sausage and Polish
sausage. But it's the hot dogs, topped with Ted's sauce, that has earned
this restaurant its place in the quick-eats hall of fame.

Tony's

Nassau and Wall Sts.   No phone
New York, NY   BL | $

It's nice to sit at a table and fork food off a plate, but sidewalk eating
stirs the soul. In the sun on office-building steps or on a brisk destination
hike, ad-hoc al-fresco meals are New York's most distinctive way to dine.
While other U.S. cities might sport a single stand-up specialty—fish tacos

in San Diego, custard in Milwaukee, coffee shots in Tampa—Manhattan's vendors put the world in your hands, ready to be devoured on a stroll.

On a recent eating/walking tour of Manhattan we started the day way Downtown—and way early—at Tony's, a food truck parked at Nassau and Wall. It wasn't yet dawn; Tony and his wife, Theodora Psaroudis, park here about 4 A.M., but there was already a short line of customers who work at or around the NYSE around the corner.

"Bread or platter?" Theodora asked when we got to the head of the line and said "Bacon and eggs."

"Platter," we say, assuming it the more comely choice.

"Wrong!" declares the man in line behind us, whose smock identifies him as a floor trader at the NYSE. "Bread's the best," he says. "Get a long roll."

The trader/tipster was absolutely right. Our $2.25 breakfast sandwich was a magnificent lode of buttery eggs and sizzled bacon folded inside a muscular hero roll with a silky seeded crust. The fresh bread is especially delicious when imprinted with the bacon's drippings. All sorts of morning sandwiches are available, as are plastic-fork platters. Tony's menu also includes burgers, gyros, and sausage heros.

Please note that Tony's fast food is not instantaneous. Eggs are cracked for every order, and there isn't room on the small griddle for more than a few. The five-minute wait for your order is an ideal opportunity to ask the folks at the juice cart next door to squeeze some fresh OJ or whip up a mango-banana-orange-pineapple shake; the cup for smoothies and shakes is presented in a brown paper bag, its lid heaped with chunks of fresh fruit.

Walter's Hot Dog Stand

937 Palmer Ave.   No phone
Larchmont, NY   L | $

Walter Warrington's great-granddaughter says that she could give you a raw Walter's hot dog (made of beef, veal, and pork from Walter's eighty-plus-year-old recipe) and you could cook it and still not make it taste like the ones they serve in Larchmont. That's because the grill on which the hot dogs are cooked is covered with what she calls a secret sauce. It looks like plain cooking oil to us, but when you take your first bite of a Walter's hot dog, split lengthwise and grilled so it glistens, there is an undeniable sparkle to the flavor of the crunchy flat surface that absorbs whatever it is they put on that ancient grill.

Many who grew up eating at Walter's (and that's generations, since 1919) believe that this roadside stand makes the best hot dogs on earth; and we dog lovers who have discovered it later in life cannot help hailing Walter's frankfurter as a paradigm of bunned excellence. It is a simple frank—not too big and only gently garlicked, so you easily can eat several and not regret it later in the afternoon. The split and grilled dog is inserted in a little bun that has been toasted on an adjacent grill (without the secret sauce) and is served either plain or with house mustard, made by Walter's son Gene according to the old recipe. Like the hot dog, Walter's mustard has a refined rather than explosive taste; it is slightly grainy and dotted with pickle bits. The combination of dog, bun, and mustard adds up to perfection. Some customers ask for their hot dog well done and therefore even more crisp than usual (not a bad idea) and others get a double dog (in our opinion, an imbalance of dog and bun).

Walter's itself is quite spectacular: an eye-catching exhibit of 1920s vernacular roadside architecture with a vaguely Asian flavor to its pagoda-shaped tin roof and bamboo-like letters on the sign. There is a small grove of picnic tables to the side, which is well suited to eating hot dogs and drinking excellent malts (or egg creams); but in inclement weather, you are on your own. Walter's has no inside seats. At lunchtime, both sides of Palmer Avenue are occupied by cars in which customers are eating hot dogs off their dashboards.

Pennsylvania

Benkovitz Seafoods

2300 Smallman St.   412-263-3016
Pittsburgh, PA   LD | $

At the back of Benkovitz Seafoods in Pittsburgh's Strip District, onlookers stand mesmerized as they watch skillful fish cutters turn whole fish into fillets and steaks ready to cook. While many loyal customers come for no reason other than to buy quarts of lobster bisque or pounds of fish for dinner that night, this exemplary fish market also has a good-size menu of cooked food to eat here, and they are willing to cook up just about any fish in the house to order, by weight.

Most people's favorite thing to eat is the fried cod sandwich—a pair of hot and crusty hunks fresh from the fry kettle stuffed into a torpedo roll. But you can also get "fish-in-a-dish" (a fish sandwich without the bread), and a fried fish hoagie that includes lettuce, tomato, onion, and cheese. You can also order shrimp—fried or simply boiled—soft-shell crabs, fish and chips, clams, oysters, smelts, squid rings, and crab cutlets. Recently a sushi bar was added, so you can pique your appetite for that good fried fish with raw fluke, yellowtail, or eel.

The only problem with Benkowitz as a restaurant is finding a place to eat. There are stand-up counters across from the order window and a couple of tables in the vestibule, plus a few available eat-stands outdoors in the parking lot, which are great on a sunny day. But you'll see plenty of people enjoying Benkovitz's treasures leaning on their car trunk, or off the dashboard of their vehicle.

Dutch Kitchen

433 S. Lehigh Ave.   570-874-3265

Frackville, PA   BLD | $

When Tom Levkulic and his wife, Jennifer, took over the reins of this thirty-year-old diner in Pennsylvania coal country, they made one seemingly minor but in fact monumental change from the way the previous generation ran it. They switched from instant mashed potatoes to real ones. "In this town, where people know good food and appreciate it, we thought it was just plain wrong not to do the work to serve real potatoes," Tom told us. Now, with the real mashed potatoes, a turkey dinner at the Dutch Kitchen is just about perfect.

Actually, better than perfect, for this is no standard turkey dinner. It also includes access to the salad bar, which goes way beyond ordinary salad ingredients with a spectacular array of vegetables that reflect Jennifer's Pennsylvania Dutch ancestry. Here are breathtaking pickled vegetables, seriously dark apple butter, chowchow, beets, beans, and fresh-baked bread to add to your plate of real daily-roasted turkey, hearty bread filling, *genuine* mashed potatoes (with an occasional reassuring lump in the smooth, swirly spuds), and gravy.

It is possible to stop at the Dutch Diner for a nice hamburger or sandwich, but we are always drawn to such hearty traditional dishes as smoked pork chops, turkey croquettes, and a stupendously good pot pie with homemade noodles, chicken and turkey, potatoes, and vegetables. During our last visit, a day's special was ham, cabbage, and potato stew loaded with big fall-apart-tender chunks of pink ham and sided by a block of brown-top corn bread nearly as sweet as cake. For dessert, of course, we chose shoofly pie, this of the wet-bottom variety with a ribbon of molasses at the bottom and a faintly eggy thickness to the crumbly coffee-cake top.

Aside from the excellent blue-plate fare, we love the Dutch Kitchen for its convenience. It always seems to be just where we need it to be when hunger strikes south of the I-81/I-80 junction. It is a big, friendly place, a former dining car (still intact inside) to which has been added a whole dining room that is decorated to the max with country crafts, speckleware, homily plaques for kitchen walls, and souvenirs of Pennsylvania.

Enrico Biscotti Company

2023 Penn Ave.   412-281-2602
Pittsburgh, PA   BL | $

As you stroll Pittsburgh's Penn Avenue along the Strip, where the air smells of aged prosciutto and fried fish sandwiches, fresh fruit and strong espresso, the smell of Enrico Biscotti will wallop you at 20th Street. Through the screen doors wafts the smell of a plum-filled crumb cake or a loaf of cornmeal biscotti as it is cut for its second bake. Inside the tiny store, you confront an array of jars that contain nearly two dozen different kinds of extra-large, hand-cut biscotti, including classic anise-almond and black pepper walnut as well as white chocolate with macadamia nuts. Macaroons are a regular part of the repertoire, sometimes dipped in chocolate; and macaroon-lovers everywhere agree that these are food of the gods. However, the inventory at Enrico cannot be predicted. Larry Lagattuta is one of those cooks who bakes what he likes to bake that day, all by touch and feel, the way he learned from his mother and his aunts when he was a boy growing up in Pittsburgh.

Behind the bakery, via a short sidewalk, there is a second part of Enrico Biscotti, a European-style café where Larry makes individual-size pizzas in his brick oven and little meals for snacks. Here, too, is the espresso machine, as well as a handful of tables both inside and outdoors in a sort of makeshift patio along the sidewalk. We know of no nicer place to start the day with strong coffee and biscotti, or to have a leisurely lunch of expertly made, true Italian food.

The Family Diner

302 Main St.   717-443-8797
White Haven, PA   BLD | $

Interstate 80 through Pennsylvania is a challenging route for people who like to eat. There are plenty of truck stops and restaurants at every exit, but many are mediocre. That is why we treasure The Family Diner, just a few minutes off the highway. There is something for everyone in this friendly place, from blue-plate liver and onions or meat loaf and mashed potatoes to one spectacular super-duper burger with the works to which the menu attributes a "college degree."

As in so many diners, breakfast is deeply satisfying, served here from dawn until the middle of the afternoon. The pancakes, while not what you'd call elegant, are colossal, so wide that they nearly eclipse the plate on which they're served. To add even more avoirdupois to this seriously high-caloric feast, you can get them blanketed with gooey, supersweet hot apple or blueberry topping. A real Pennsylvania favorite, creamed chipped beef, comes sided by hearty home fries or bite-size potato cakes. Eggs are available any way (including soft-boiled and poached) with a choice of bacon, ham, sausage, pork roll, and scrapple. Scrapple, as any true Pennsylvanian can tell you, is a local passion—thin slices from a loaf of ground pork and cornmeal that are sizzled in a pan until crisp.

Geno's Steaks

1219 S. 9th St.	215-389-0659
Philadelphia, PA	LD | $

We aren't going to get into the trap of saying which of Philadelphia's several cheese steak shops is the very best. (Frankly, that seems to vary from time to time.) But we will say that if you are on a cheese-steak-eating expedition through South Philly, Geno's needs to be on your short list. Virtually across the street from Pat's King of Steaks, Geno's is a definitive cheese steak joint. It's open late, brash and sassy, perfumed by sizzling meat and onions, and patronized by a motley crew of neighborhood wisenheimers, compulsive sandwich-eaters, and visiting Roadfood fanatics. Whichever cheese steak shop we happen to consider our favorite at any particular time, we have always appreciated a certain classicism about Geno's. It seems that here the meat is cut a little thicker than at other places (although it's still thin enough to be cooked through almost instantly when it hits the griddle), the rolls are sturdy, and the cheese choice includes provolone, American, or Whiz. Open into the wee hours of the morning, Geno's is a magnet for night owls who eat standing under carnival-colored neon, leaning forward at the waist so shreds of beef that fall from the sandwich hit the sidewalk rather than their shoes.

Be sure to order your steak properly: First give your choice of cheese, then say the word "with" or "without," indicating your decision on whether or not you want onions. In other words, "Whiz without" means a cheese steak made with Cheez Whiz but no onions. Red sauce is another option, but for most aficionados, sauce is not an essential cheese steak ingredient. On the other hand, you must have fries—or cheese fries—on the side.

Jimmy's Hot Dogs

21 Butler St.   610-258-7545
Easton, PA   LD | $

We're not cheapskates, but we must confess that there is something irresistibly alluring about a decent meal that costs considerably less than a fancy coffee at Starbucks. Maybe *decent* isn't exactly the right term to describe what's served at Jimmy's Hot Dogs on Route 248 in the 25th Street Shopping Center, for these dogs are sinful little franks—piggy and juicy and simply addictive.

Last we looked, the price of one was seventy-five cents including tax! So you can have two hot dogs, dressed, of course, the Jimmy's way, with mustard, onions, and pickle spears, along with a bag of potato chips and a Coke or chocolate milk for under $3. If you've got a big appetite, you might want three or four or five hot dogs; but even if you and a friend indulged in six apiece, you'd still walk out with change from a ten-dollar bill.

Want something other than a hot dog and chips? Too bad, because that is the extent of Jimmy's menu. There is no extra charge to chat with members of the Apostopolous family, who have run the joint, without changing a thing, for decades . . . and who have perfected the art of freezing and overnight-shipping their beloved weenies to ex-Eastonites desperate for a taste of home.

Jim's Steaks

400 South St.   215-928-1911
Philadelphia, PA   LD | $

Opened in 1939, Jim's is Philadelphia's second-oldest cheese steak shop (after Pat's; see page 142), and it definitely the sharpest-looking with its deco black-and-white-tile decor.

It's a very popular place, which is a good thing, because your wait in line will provide ample time for deciding how you like your steak garnished—"wit" or "witout" (onions), and whether you want the standard

Cheez Whiz or optional American or provolone. The wait in line also takes you past the back of the store where an automatic slicer produces heaps of rosy-colored beef ready to be fried.

The steaks are made by hacking up the meat on the grill (with onions, preferably!) so it becomes a kind of onion-flavored steak hash. If you get sliced cheese, it is layered in the roll before the meat and melts underneath it. Whiz is ladled atop the meat. Pizza sauce and peppers are optional condiments. The bread is excellent, the fried onions are appropriately slippery, and the optional hot peppers are breathtaking. Have a Dr. Brown's soda on the side, and you've got a cheap-eats meal to remember.

JoJo's Restaurant

110 24th St.   412-261-0280

Pittsburgh, PA   BL (from 11 P.M. to just after noon) | $

Pittsburgh's Strip District was once so full of foundries belching smoke that it was known as "Hell with the lid off." Hell is gone, and today the strip of streets along the Allegheny River is one of the most colorful— and appetizing—neighborhoods in America. Here are markets, restaurants, street food stands, and bakeries, as well as a vast all-night wholesale produce market to which truckers drive loads of fruits and vegetables from all over the South.

To serve the truckers and dockworkers at the market, the Strip has several restaurants that are open all night. One of the best-known and most colorful is JoJo's. When Joe Christina and John Cognetti created it as a trucker's haven in 1985, they featured a breakfast special at $2.49, its cost selected to honor Teamster's Local 249. Prices have since risen a bit, but produce haulers still are considered royalty in this former gas station perfumed by the smell of home fries on the grill. Professional drivers sometimes are the only customers between four and five in the morning, when JoJo's can be a meditative place. Before that, however, starting at midnight, the dining room rocks with face-painted post-game fans of the Penguins, Pirates, or Steelers, as well as with clusters of boisterous club denizens who don't want to go home at closing hour. During one all-night watch at JoJo's counter, we met a pair of home boys who invented a rap song for us about their delicious breakfast, a young married couple who live in their sleeper cab and had just trucked up a load of melons from Texas, and many chain-smoking insomniacs for whom

JoJo's is the only place to be at 4 A.M. As dawn breaks and the night shift drifts away, a new contingent of early risers occupies the booths and counter, ready to start their day.

JoJo's menu is headlined "Breakfast served all day, every day," and the flagship meal is a JoJo Special. Frank Mannetti, Joe Christina's son-in-law and current proprietor, explained to us that the Special was invented one day by accident. "We were making a frittata one day for ourselves, as a family," he said. "We all work here—my wife and my son—and after each of us tossed in a little of everything we liked, I thought that we should also fold in some potatoes. You need the potatoes as a dam, so all the other things don't squish out."

Mr. Mannetti is magnificent to watch as he assembles one of these impossibly large three-egg omelets. The eggs are swirled in a bowl and tossed into an individual skillet, where a few twists of the fork help them set just right. He gives the pan a quick shimmy, then tosses the omelet up and out, catching it on the flip side and immediately piling it with fistfuls of peppers, onions, mushrooms, provolone and American cheese, the customer's choice of breakfast meat (bacon, sausage, *and* ham if he is making the ultra "all meat JoJo"), plus the necessary spatula-load of hot fried potatoes. It is slid onto a plate and folded over to become a veritable mountain of food.

"Does anybody ever eat an entire Special?" we asked Mr. Mannetti.

"Many couples get one to split," he said. "But you watch the drivers come in after an all-night run up from Florida. They'll clean their plate of a JoJo Special and have a bowl of chili to top it off." With admiration and appreciation in his voice, he summarized: "Truckers have *good* appetites! JoJo's was created for them."

Longacre's Modern Dairy Bar

1445 Route 100   610-845-7551
Barto, PA   BLD Mon-Sat | $

Who doesn't love a true dairy bar with homemade ice cream, an armory of rainbow toppings, and all the fizz necessary to create any sort of float or soda? Such nostalgic sweetshops are particularly endearing when they are attached to a real cow farm, as is Longacre's, a working dairy since 1920.

The rolling land of eastern Pennsylvania, dotted as it is with black-and-white bossies roaming farm fields, is a perfect appetizer for one of

Longacre's excellent milk shakes or malts, or an old-fashioned ice cream soda in a tall tulip glass. If you need an ice cream dish that is more substantial, choose a sundae made from your choice of more than a dozen flavors of ice cream and nearly two dozen toppings, including the usual fudge and marshmallow and butterscotch as well as such old-time fountain oddities as wet maple walnut and crushed cherries. The supreme such concoction is known as the Longacre Special (a.k.a. Garbage Sundae) and features ten scoops of ice cream, ten toppings, whipped cream, and a cherry, all served in a thirty-two-ounce goblet.

It is also possible to come to Longacre's for a handy-size hamburger or hot dog, accompanied, of course, by a cherry Coke, vanilla Coke, or Hadacol (that's a Coke and root beer combo).

We like the fact that Longacre's little eating area—a short counter and a handful of booths—opens at 7:30 A.M., a time when most ordinary customers come for coffee and an egg sandwich. But the waitress assured us that it is not uncommon for the doors to open at dawn for customers who grab a booth or a stool at the counter and order up a cookie dough sundae or a CMP (chocolate marshmallow peanut sundae) for breakfast. Humankind's fundamental need for excellent ice cream is a craving that cannot be controlled by the hands of a clock.

Lorenzo's Pizza

900 Christian St.   215-922-3808
Philadelphia, PA   LD | $

Despite the name of this restaurant, we can tell you nothing about its pizza. We went there on a cheese-steak-eating expedition with the Roadfood.com team for the purpose of comparing it to the better-known shops around town. Located on a corner near the market, it is a real neighborhood kind of place with none of the tourist trade found elsewhere.

The steaks are made from frozen sheets of meat, which is not really a bad thing. After all, we are not talking about prime beef here. Anyway, the frozen sheets get thrown onto the grill along with a pile of raw onions. As the meat and onions sizzle together, the chef hacks away at them with a spatula, winding up with an oniony meat hash. The hash is shaped into an oval about the length of the Italian bread for which it's destined, and the oval is generously dolloped with molten Cheez Whiz. The cheese is insinuated into the hash, then the lengthwise-sliced bread is used to shovel up the whole mess and finally enclose it. We like this sandwich plenty; our Roadfood.com colleague Stephen Rushmore declared it the cheesiest steak in the city.

Nick's Bar

2149 S. 20th St. (at Jackson, South Philly)   215-463-4114
Philadelphia, PA   LD | $

It was an anonymous Roadfooder born and raised in Philadelphia, now retired in Arizona, who tipped us off to Nick's. Our informant told us that as far as he was concerned, Pat's made the best cheese steak in town, but for roast beef, Nick's at 20th and Jackson was the place to go (there are other Nick's roast beef restaurants in town); and he knows, because he has been going there since 1945!

Nick's is a corner bar, where some customers eat only as an afterthought to an afternoon and/or evening of Budweiser or Rolling Rock and a Flyers game on the TV above the bar; but for the serious beef hound, this particular Nick's is the North Star of Philadelphia. For each sandwich, roast beef is sliced to order, sopped with natural gravy, and piled into a bun that is itself moistened with beefy juices. The roast beef on a roll is wonderful; it is even better if you get a "combo," which is roast beef topped with a slice of provolone cheese, which semi-melts from the heat of the meat.

Also available are baked ham and roast pork, with or without cheese, and they look pretty good, but they are no competition for the beef, which is Nick's culinary raison d'être.

Original Hot Dog Shop

3901 Forbes Ave.   412-488-1295
Pittsburgh, PA   LD (late night) | $

The Original Hot Dog Shop (the Big O) has quite a large menu, including pizza, hoagies, fish sandwiches, and hamburgers; but if the name of the place doesn't clue you in to what's good, the view behind the counter will. There on a broad grill are row upon row of lovely hot dogs—pale pink ones barely warm and darker ones cooked through and ready to be bunned, as well as a formation of deep red all-beef kosher dogs. Regular or all-beef, these are fine franks with a seriously meaty flavor, available plain or gooped with cheese or in a "super" configuration with cheese and bacon, and with a full array of condiments that include ketchup, mustard, relish, onion, pickle, chili, mayo, and kraut.

On the side of whatever hot dog suits your taste, you must get French fries. Big O fries are legendary, crisp and dark gold with a clean flavor that makes them such a good companion for just about any sandwich. Even a small order, for about $2.50, is a substantial dish; but you can get them in sizes all the way up to extra large (currently $7.24) for a potato orgy. Although cheese for dipping is available, as are gravy, hot sauce, and ranch dressing, these exquisite potatoes want only a sprinkle of salt.

Aside from great fast food and post-midnight hours, one reason Pittsburghers are so fond of the Original Hot Dog Shop is that it can trace its heritage back to the Original Famous Sandwich Shop, where the foot-long hot dog was introduced in 1928. Syd Simon, who opened the Original Hot Dog Shop in 1960, worked fifteen years at the old Famous.

Pat's King of Steaks

1237 E. Passyunk   215-468-1546
Philadelphia, PA   always open | $

Street food historians believe that Pat Olivieri invented the cheese steak in Philadelphia in 1930. His family continues to operate the restaurant he began, and while aficionados of the cheese steak enjoy debating the merits of the city's many cheese steak restaurants (some operated by renegades from Pat's own family), this joint's shaved-beef-and-cheese sandwiches on serious Italian bread have stood for over half a century as the benchmark. Pat's sandwich is oily, salty, meaty, i.e., everything nutrition prigs dislike. Thin flaps of less-than-prime beef are sizzled on a grill alongside onions and hefted into a roll (with or without some of those onions), then a trowel of melted Cheez Whiz is dripped on top. Peppers, mushrooms, pizza sauce, and extra cheese are all extra-cost options; and if you wish to dude it up further, there are big glass jars with hot sauce and peppers near the take-out windows.

The combination of plebeian ingredients transcends its lowly status and becomes something . . . if not aristocratic, then certainly distinguished. Side your sandwich with a cup full of cheese fries (French fries blanketed with more of that melted Whiz), and eat standing up on the sidewalk under harsh lights. Observe the splattered hot sauce and dropped and crushed French fries underfoot. Listen to the rumble of trucks going past on their way to or from the Italian market. Smell the mingling of cheap aftershave lotion and fancy fragrances on customers in line—both aromas overwhelmed, as the line approaches the take-out window, by the powerhouse aroma of steak and onions sizzling on a hot grill. For our money, even at ten times the price, there is no meal in Philadelphia that can top this one.

People's Restaurant

140 W. Main St.   717-354-2276
New Holland, PA   BLD Sun-Fri | $$

Established in 1907, People's Restaurant has character that seems untouched by nearly a century of progress and development. It is a civilized lunchroom on the town's Main Street where locals and tourists come to eat honest Lancaster County food. Although accommodations are mostly tables with upholstered chairs, there is a short counter toward the middle of the restaurant where townsfolk gather and exchange sections of the newspaper as they discuss current events. This informal morning coffee klatch has a quiet, gentle pace about it; but even when People's dining room is packed—as it always is on Sunday—you can count on a dining experience that is serene.

This is the place to come for a well-balanced eastern Pennsylvania meal. There is a surfeit of big tourist-attraction restaurants in the area that boast of their groaning-board feeds; and although you are unlikely to leave People's hungry, neither will you walk out feeling like you've just eaten five pounds of dough. Suppers include such local delights as fresh-roasted pork with sauerkraut, smoked country ham steak, and lengths of light-bodied Lancaster sausage, as well as such all-American meals as tuna-noodle casserole and fried chicken. Meals are accompanied by a choice from a long list of freshly prepared vegetables: whipped potatoes, Cheddar-macaroni salad, three-bean salad, pepper cabbage, etc.; and for dessert, there are pies galore. Apricot crumb, coconut cream, French apple, strawberry Boston cream, shoofly (wet-bottom, of course), grasshopper, and peanut butter silk were the selection one day last March. In addition to pies, there are always cakes, custards, and pudding.

Our favorite time to eat at People's is early in the morning, when we feast on either old-fashioned oatmeal or "baked oatmeal," which is like a coarse-textured bread pudding made with cooked oats and brown sugar. Another excellent breakfast, and a true Mid-Atlantic specialty, is creamed chipped beef. This is the real stuff—spicy shreds of brined beef in a rich cream sauce, ladled over a plate of crusty fried potato discs. Of course, you can also get a dish of expertly crisped scrapple; and eggs are guaranteed to be only from local hens.

Primanti Brothers

46 W. 18th St.   412-263-2142
Pittsburgh, PA   always open | $

If you like big sandwiches, you need to eat around Pittsburgh. In this brawny city, where the Big Mac was invented in 1968 by a local McDonald's franchisee, "the more the merrier" is the basic rule of sandwich-making. The city's champion of huge sandwiches is Primanti Brothers, a raucous open-all-night beer-and-sandwich joint that throbs with the play-by-play broadcast of whatever local team is in action. Opened in 1933, the original Primanti's down in the Strip District is a city shrine where it is virtually criminal to drink anything other than Iron City suds, and where the walls are painted with caricatures of native sons who range from Andy Warhol to Mr. Rogers and Tom Mix to Roberto Clemente. (There are three other Primanti Brothers around town; none of these are open round-the-clock.)

The astonishing sandwiches were originally designed for truckers who hauled produce to the nearby wholesale market. While their trucks were being unloaded, they dashed over to Primanti Brothers with a big appetite but little time to eat a dagwood, slaw, and potatoes separately. The solution was to load hot French fries directly into the sandwich atop the customer's meat of choice, then top the fries with Pittsburgh-style (no mayo) cole slaw and a few slices of tomato. The sandwiches are assembled at the grill behind the bar at the speed of light, so when the sandwich is delivered, the fries and grilled meats are still steaming hot, the slaw and tomato cool.

Weird as this combination sounds, the regulars at Primanti's tables assert that such combinations as double-egg and pastrami (both sizzled on the grill) or steak and cheese simply do not taste right without a layer of crisp-fried potatoes and another of slaw. The barely hoistable meal is presented wrapped in butcher paper so that when appetite flags, the paper's edges can be gathered like a drop cloth to pick up the spillage.

Robert Wholey & Co.

1501 Penn Ave.　　　　　　　800-461-7292

Pittsburgh, PA　　　　　　　LD | $

Located in Pittsburgh's appetite-inducing Strip District, Robert Wholey & Co. seems more like a culinary amusement park than a mere store. It has a toy train running around and mechanical pigs singing to amuse children and an extensive kitchenware department to amuse recipe-obsessed adults.

Once strictly a wholesale fish market, Wholey now carries a vast inventory of foodstuffs that range from baked ham by the haunch (or sliced super thin, a.k.a. chip-chopped, the way Pittsburghers like it) to sides of tuna that are cut into steaks to order. For those of us who demand immediate gratification, there are a few makeshift tables for sit-down meals at the end of a cooked-food line, and more tables upstairs in the Pittsburgh Room. The meal most people come to eat is a fish sandwich, made of cod sizzled in the bubbling fry kettles toward the front. It is common to see grocery-browsers munching a sandwich on the stroll as they peruse this fabulous market.

Salerno's

139 Moosic Rd.　　　　　　　570-457-2117

Old Forge, PA　　　　　　　LD | $$

Salerno's is a tavern where many people come only to drink. We recommend a visit for Old Forge pizza, a style of pie unique to this area around Scranton. Most of the Old Forge pies are squared off rather than round, airy-crusted, and topped with sweet marinara sauce and a mild blend of Italian and American cheese. It's an easy-to-eat pizza, simple and friendly.

At lunch you can get only red pizza, which is a twelve-slice pie big enough for two healthy appetites. At dinner, Salerno's better-known creation is a white pizza—a double-cruster made with a blend of several cheeses between the crusts.

There is a broad menu beyond pizza in this neighborhood tavern: sausage and peppers, chicken Parmesan sub sandwiches, pasta i fagiole. Many customers take their food at the bar, where they can knock back draft beers and watch the wall-mounted TV.

Tony Luke's Old Philly Style Sandwiches

39 E. Oregon Ave.   215-551-5725

Philadelphia, PA   BLD | $

Located across the street from the Lucidonio family's other restaurant, Casa di Pasta, Tony Luke's is an old-time city haunt where it is easy to believe that the Delaware Valley in general and Philadelphia in particular is America's great sandwichland. Tony's is a small restaurant with uncomfortable counter seating for only a few dozen people and a small, semi al fresco patio with tables (there's a lot of take-out business). It is decorated in the traditional South Philly style, i.e., with autographed 8 × 10-inch pictures of celebrities. In this case, many of the glitterati are club boxers who apparently enjoy meals here between bouts.

The sandwich menu is huge, ranging from hot dogs (a.k.a. Texas Tommies) to traditional Philly cheese steaks topped with Cheez Whiz, and even cheese steaks made from ostrich meat. You can get roast beef, turkey, and cold cuts of all kinds. No sandwich we've ever pulled from its brown paper bag and unwrapped from its wax paper package (the traditional sandwich-shop presentation) has been less than excellent. The long Italian loaves on which they're made are fresh and chewy, with just enough crust to keep them sturdy.

The greatest of all Tony Luke sandwiches are the real Italian-style hot meats, including roast pork, which is garlicky slices of tender sweet meat piled inside the loaf with cooked-soft broccoli rabe. Chicken and veal cutlets are also particularly wonderful, with or without provolone and either a heap of broccoli rabe or spinach so well cooked it is more like a condiment than a vegetable.

Service is brash and fast. When you place your order and pay for it, they take your name; and when the sandwich is ready, they call you to the counter, front and center.

Mid-South

Kentucky * North Carolina * Tennessee *

Virginia * West Virginia

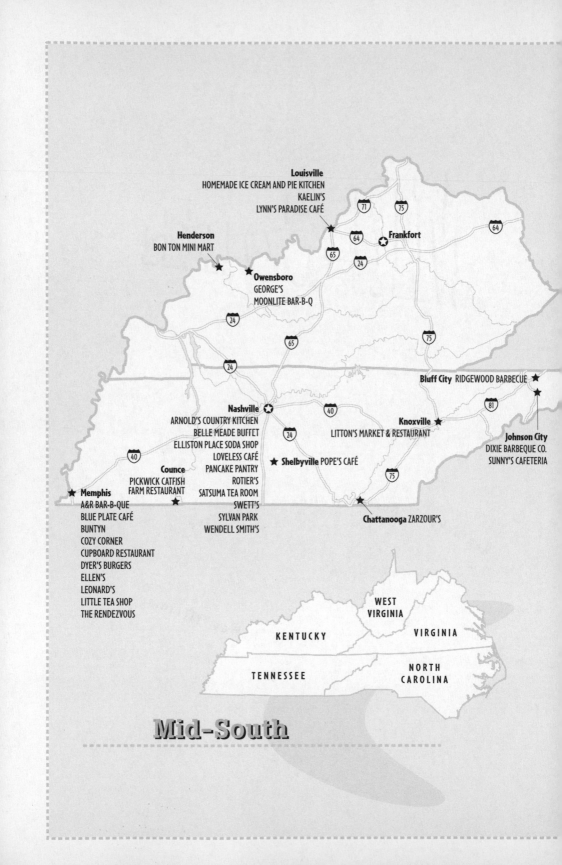

Louisville
HOMEMADE ICE CREAM AND PIE KITCHEN
KAELIN'S
LYNN'S PARADISE CAFÉ

Frankfort

Henderson
BON TON MINI MART

Owensboro
GEORGE'S
MOONLITE BAR-B-Q

Bluff City RIDGEWOOD BARBECUE

Nashville
ARNOLD'S COUNTRY KITCHEN
BELLE MEADE BUFFET
ELLISTON PLACE SODA SHOP
LOVELESS CAFÉ
PANCAKE PANTRY
ROTIER'S
SATSUMA TEA ROOM
SWETT'S
SYLVAN PARK
WENDELL SMITH'S

Knoxville
LITTON'S MARKET & RESTAURANT

Johnson City
DIXIE BARBEQUE CO.
SUNNY'S CAFETERIA

Counce
PICKWICK CATFISH
FARM RESTAURANT

Shelbyville POPE'S CAFÉ

Memphis
A&R BAR-B-QUE
BLUE PLATE CAFÉ
BUNTYN
COZY CORNER
CUPBOARD RESTAURANT
DYER'S BURGERS
ELLEN'S
LEONARD'S
LITTLE TEA SHOP
THE RENDEZVOUS

Chattanooga ZARZOUR'S

WEST
VIRGINIA

KENTUCKY

VIRGINIA

TENNESSEE

NORTH
CAROLINA

Mid-South

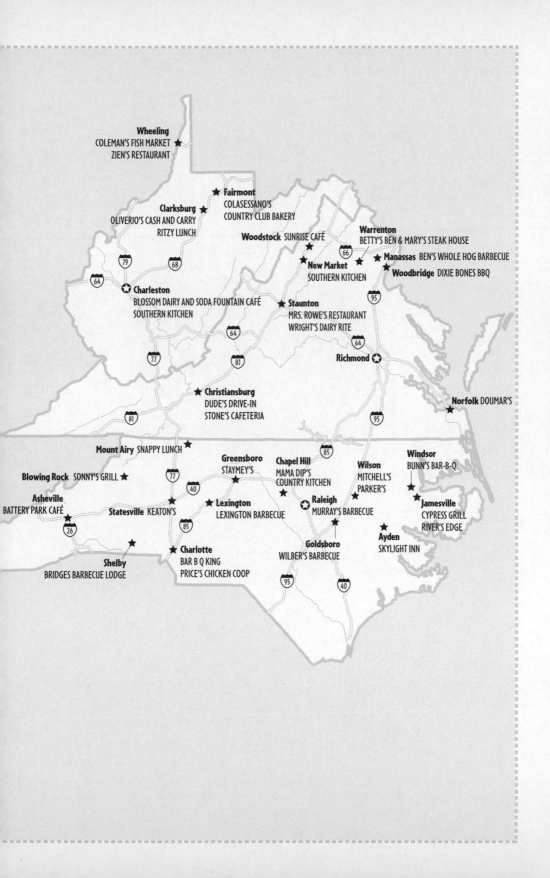

Wheeling
COLEMAN'S FISH MARKET ★
ZIEN'S RESTAURANT

★ **Fairmont**
COLASESSANO'S
Clarksburg ★ COUNTRY CLUB BAKERY
OLIVERIO'S CASH AND CARRY
RITZY LUNCH

Woodstock SUNRISE CAFÉ

Warrenton
BETTY'S BEN & MARY'S STEAK HOUSE

★ **New Market** **Manassas** BEN'S WHOLE HOG BARBECUE
SOUTHERN KITCHEN
Woodbridge DIXIE BONES BBQ

⭐ **Charleston**
BLOSSOM DAIRY AND SODA FOUNTAIN CAFÉ
SOUTHERN KITCHEN

★ **Staunton**
MRS. ROWE'S RESTAURANT
WRIGHT'S DAIRY RITE

Richmond ⭐

★ **Christiansburg**
DUDE'S DRIVE-IN
STONE'S CAFETERIA

Norfolk DOUMAR'S

Mount Airy SNAPPY LUNCH ★

Greensboro
STAYMEY'S

Chapel Hill
MAMA DIP'S
COUNTRY KITCHEN

Wilson
MITCHELL'S
PARKER'S

Windsor
BUNN'S BAR-B-Q

Blowing Rock SONNY'S GRILL ★

Asheville
BATTERY PARK CAFÉ

Statesville KEATON'S

★ **Lexington**
LEXINGTON BARBECUE

Raleigh ⭐
MURRAY'S BARBECUE

Jamesville
CYPRESS GRILL
RIVER'S EDGE

★ **Charlotte**
BAR B Q KING
PRICE'S CHICKEN COOP

Goldsboro
WILBER'S BARBECUE

Ayden
SKYLIGHT INN

Shelby
BRIDGES BARBECUE LODGE

Kentucky

Bon Ton Mini Mart

2036 Madison St. (junction of Hwys. 41 and 136) 270-826-1207

Henderson, KY   BLD | $

A first taste of Bon Ton fried chicken, like a first kiss, is a never-to-be forgotten event. It is as stunning as a bite of aged country ham: shockingly
spicy, salty, crunchy all at once. The meat is infused with a power-packed
spice marinade of cayenne and garlic that penetrates to the bone, and the
crust on the outside is dark and brittle like the best potato chip ever fried.
Dark or light meat, Bon Ton chicken delivers a taste thrill like no other.

The formula for this amazing dish dates back to the 1950s and a
restaurant in Henderson known as The Colonel's Lair. It was a favorite
haunt of local high school students and was run by a man named Bill
Koch, whom the kids called Bilko because that's the way he pronounced
it. All who remember The Colonel's Lair agree that Bilko made the best
fried chicken anywhere.

Bilko is gone, but Bon Ton proprietor George Markham and Koch's
former cook, Donna King, managed to get the recipe for the amazing
chicken; and now it is served every day at the unlikely tables of the Bon
Ton Mini Mart south of town. This pint-size restaurant, which is still a

secret to many residents of Henderson, began as a convenience mart and has slowly dropped the peripheral merchandise to concentrate on what's really important: fried chicken, as well as pork chops on Thursday and chicken pot pie on Friday.

"What we do in this kitchen is not opening a can," Donna King told us. "It is *cooking*!" By this, she means the from-scratch preparation of such dishes as fried apples, hash brown casserole, and scalloped potatoes, as well as big, sheet-cake desserts made from bananas and strawberries. "As a child growing up on a farm outside of Henderson, I learned how to put food on the table for my family of eight brothers and sisters," Donna recalled. "We had our own chickens; raised them and killed them and plucked them and cooked them in lard."

In Kentucky, where Harland Sanders began a commercial empire based on the secret spices used for the batter of the chicken he served in the dining room of his service station/café, the art of frying chicken is no small matter. A meal at the Bon Ton Mini Mart is casual as can be, but no chicken we know tastes more important.

George's

1346 E. 4th St.   270-926-9276
Owensboro, KY   LD | $

The inconspicuous, wood-paneled café named George's is one reason Owensboro lays claim to being the barbecue capital of the world. The meat of choice in this part of the world is mutton, slow-smoked over hardwood and served in chunks and shreds in hot red barbecue sauce. How does mutton taste? *Not* like chicken. It's sturdier, chewier, and a whole lot meatier-flavored than any other barbecued meat you will ever eat. In addition to mutton, George's serves fine platters of barbecued pork shoulder, beef, ham, chicken, and pork ribs.

Beyond mutton itself, Owensboro's star on the culinary map is also determined by the mutton-based stew known as burgoo. Supposedly invented during the Civil War by a Dixie chef whose speech impediment caused him to call *bird stew* "burgoo," it began as a catch-as-catch-can stew of birds and any other game animals the hunters could bag. Today it is a hearty bowl of soul concocted from various kinds of meat, almost always including mutton, along with a panoply of vegetables in a spicy tomato base. Around Derby Day, many Kentuckians enjoy burgoo cooked in huge cauldrons and served as a communal meal; in Owensboro, at George's, you can have it every day. It is a brilliantly spiced gallimaufry with plenty of the taste of meat from George's smoke pit, needing only a good draft of beer to become a fine one-dish, only-in-Kentucky meal.

Homemade Ice Cream and Pie Kitchen

2525 Bardstown Rd.   502-459-8184
Louisville, KY   LD | $

The ice cream in this sweetshop is homemade and hand-dipped, and includes such seasonal flavors as pumpkin, peach, and eggnog. The handsome repertoire of pies includes chess pie as well as lemon chess and chocolate chess, Key lime pie and Shaker sugar pie, seasonal fruit pies, mince pie in the autumn, and the number one customer favorite, Dutch apple caramel pie.

Even with all those good things to eat, it is cake that makes our heads spin. This Pie Kitchen is, for us, a cake kitchen, where we go for slices of grand layer cake swirled with buttercream frosting. A few favorite varieties include red velvet cake (a deep, dark chocolate) with cream cheese frosting, banana-pecan cake with buttercream, coconut cake, mandarin orange cake with pineapple-filled whipped cream, and jam-spice cake with caramel frosting. For plan-ahead parties, cakes are available with writing and candles and decoration in edible colors that range from black and gold for Halloween to pink and lavender for springtime.

Because we visit Louisville only for short periods of time, coming to this shop is inevitably frustrating. There is no way two people can even begin to sample all the lovely cakes available any one day. Nearly everything is sold by the slice as well as the whole cake, and there are a few dining tables scattered about for drop-ins who require instant gratification.

Kaelin's

1801 Newburg Rd.   502-451-1801
Louisville, KY   LD | $

Louisville's primary claim to culinary fame is the Hot Brown sandwich, a goopy melted cheese and bacon concoction invented at the venerable Brown Hotel downtown. Louisville is also known as a stronghold of burgoo (a hunter's stew traditionally served around Derby time) and the mint julep, which is the sweetest way to absorb bourbon ever devised.

As amateur culinary historians, when we think of Louisville, we think of cheeseburgers. Having spent many happy and satisfying hours tracing the hamburger's alleged origins in Connecticut, Wisconsin, St. Louis, and the suburbs of Chicago, we consider ourselves fairly well versed in the sub-specialty of culinary history, the burger. It is an interesting field, for claims of hamburger primacy are myriad, in and out of the United States.

But only one city we know purports to be the source of the cheeseburger, and that is Louisville. At Kaelin's restaurant, a plaque on the wall says that Carl Kaelin invented the cheeseburger right here, one day in 1934. According to the restaurant's menu, Mr. Kaelin was a restless soul "never satisfied with the ordinary." While cooking hamburgers on his grill the image of a piece of American cheese suddenly popped into his head. It occurred to him that "if he put a slice of cheese on top of a hamburger patty just before it was done, the cheese would melt down into the patty and add a new tang to the hamburger."

And thus the cheeseburger was begat. Cheeseburgers are still Kaelin's claim to fame, although it is worth noting that the kitchen's Hot Brown sandwich is a classic, and many Louisville citizens come to this family-style café not for sandwiches at all, but for a good ol' southern-style plate lunch of fried chicken with yams and greens on the side.

Cheeseburgers are available in several configurations: normal-size, double-size, and mini-burgers. The minis are available by the dozen as an appetizer. When you order a cheeseburger, the waitress will ask if you want it dressed, which refers to lettuce, tomato, and mayonnaise. It is a fine cheeseburger (although we wish the French fries were better)—a true taste of hamburger history.

Lynn's Paradise Café

984 Barret Ave.	502-583-3447
Louisville, KY	BLD | $

The phone number of Lynn's Paradise Café is spelled out 583–EGGS, which gives you a hint that breakfast is big. It is served from opening at 8 A.M. through the lunch hour, and it ranges from beautifully prepared (and locally laid) eggs with grits and biscuits on the side to fruit-sauced tropical French toast, bourbon-ball French toast, and banana split pancakes. You have a choice of classical omelets or Lynn's scrambles; we like the latter, especially the Manhattan scramble with corned beef, onions, Swiss cheese, and horseradish. There is also a plate of good ol' Kentucky country ham with eggs and warm Granny Smith apples. This is true country comfort food!

Not that we want to slight lunch and dinner. Lynn Winter's "Mom's Meatloaf" is a square-meal knockout made with marinara sauce, sided by real mashed potatoes and al dente lima beans. Hamburgers are particularly lovely, available with good French fries or one of the several side dishes always available. They include creamy polenta, braised rosemary cabbage, and grilled asparagus. Finally, Lynn's version of the Kentucky Hot Brown sandwich is magnificent: slices from a freshly roasted turkey on homemade bread topped with tomato, bacon, and melted cheese.

Of course, if you've been to Lynn's, you know we've saved the best for last. Visually, this restaurant is a blast. Decor in (and around) the former grocery store is an ever-changing exhibition of sculptures, collages, assemblages, paintings, and other forms of art that are sometimes so original they are difficult to categorize. Last time we looked, the bike rack was shaped like a carrot, the planters were shaped like coffee cups, the place was surrounded by blue concrete animals, and the outside wall was decorated like the South Dakota Corn Palace, with multicolored ears of corn, but here formed into a mural depicting Muhammad Ali and Secretariat.

Decide for yourself: Is this a great restaurant with amazing art . . . or an amazing art gallery with a great restaurant?

Moonlite Bar-B-Q

2840 W. Parrish Ave.   270-684-8143
Owensboro, KY   LD | $

"Y'all goin' buffet?" the waitress asks as she places sets of silverware (each wrapped in a paper napkin) and a pair of sauce pitchers on the table of our booth.

Unless one's legs are broken, buffet is the only way to go at Moonlite, which is the grandest of Owensboro's several fine barbecue establishments. It is a huge restaurant with spacious dining rooms, an annex selling sauce, meats to go, and souvenir hats, and a help-yourself buffet that is spectacular. Here you find chicken and ribs and pulled pork, even a pan of non-barbecued sliced country ham that is firm and salty and fits so well into Moonlite's buttery dinner rolls, with maybe a dab of sorghum. Beyond meats, there is a vast array of vegetables and side dishes, including broccoli casserole, macaroni and cheese, creamed corn niblets, ham and beans, and butter-drizzled mashed potatoes, plus the western Kentucky soup/stew known as burgoo.

The beef brisket is sensational. It is sliced half an inch thick and has a chewy crust blackened by hours in the pit. Its interior is butter-soft, so infused with long-cooked fat that it literally melts on the tongue into pure, non-corporeal meat-smoke flavor.

Mutton is unique to Owensboro and vicinity—on the menu of nearly every barbecue parlor in and around town. Cooked until pot roast tender, it is set out on the Moonlite buffet two ways: chopped or pulled. Neither has sauce on it; you apply your own at the table from the pitchers the waitress brings. One is a dark orange emulsion with gentle vinegar-tomato zest; the other is known as "mutton dip," an unctuous gravy that is used to baste the mutton as it cooks. For those who need heat, Moonlite also supplies bottles of "Very Hot Sauce," which is brilliantly peppered and will set your lips and tongue aglow. But we recommend sampling this meat sauceless. The chopped mutton is pulverized to nothing but flavor: tangy lamb and wood smoke in a bold duet. The pulled version is a textural amusement park—rugged and chunky with a lot of hard outside crust among soft, juicy chunks of interior meat that fall into shreds so supple they make us want to abandon all silverware and eat like happy cave dwellers.

North Carolina

Bar B Q King

2900 Wilkinson Blvd.   704-399-8344

Charlotte, NC   LD | $

Great Roadfood is often found by mistake. We have stumbled across what turned out to be some of our favorite restaurants when we were lost, on a back road, or in a strange town and wandered into a café to ask directions. At Bar B Q King, we discovered the perch sandwich because of our inability to speak English in the way it is understood in North Carolina soul-food restaurants.

Having just landed at the Charlotte airport from our home in the barbecue-deprived Northeast, we screeched to a halt when we saw Bar B Q King drive-in by the side of the road. We *needed* barbecue bad! So we pulled into one of the car slips, studied the Order-Matic menu, and asked the carhop for pork sandwiches. We were delivered a pair of buns stuffed with fried fish: perch sandwiches. Apparently, our alien pronunciation of "pork" sounded just like "perch" to Tarheel ears. Before the carhop turned away, we ordered again—*"Barbecue sandwiches, please!"*—having realized that in this part of the world, to order barbecued pork you need only say "barbecue." *Pork* is understood; it's the only barbecue meat that matters.

Anyway, the perch sandwiches, which hunger and curiosity demanded that we sample, turned out to be fantastic. The steamy moist fish was encased in golden crust and had a sweet succulence nearly as delicious as pork itself. In fact, it was so good that after we ate our sandwiches of barbecued pork (minced, veiled in a subtle sweet and tangy sauce), we went back to the menu and sampled the trout, shrimp, and oysters—all fried in that only-in-the-South soulful way that's guaranteed to convert even a die-hard fish-frowner.

Bar B Q King is a mid-century treasure. Although many customers eat in their car, phone-ahead service is popular, too: call in your order, then arrive to pick up meals packed in the sturdy cardboard boxes that have become the BBQK trademark.

Bridges Barbecue Lodge

US 74 Bypass	704-482-8567
Shelby, NC	LD Wed-Sun | $

Bridges has no written menu, just the slip of paper used by the waitress to take orders. Basically you get a sandwich, a tray, or a plate. A tray is barbecue and barbecue slaw; a plate also holds French fries, lettuce, tomato, and pickle. Both are accompanied by a basket of hush puppies, and whether you select sandwich, tray, or plate, you will have to decide if you want your meat (pork shoulder) minced, chopped, or sliced. It is a major decision, for they are almost like three different foods. Bridges is one of the few places that offers minced barbecue, an old-time configuration from traditional pig-pickin's. It is pulverized into moist hash with some little shreds of darkened, chewy crust among the distressed pork. The mound is held together by a good portion of uniquely North Carolinian sauce—tomato-based, but with a strong vinegar punch. Chopped is the more typical way modern North Carolinians like it— chunky and easily chewable, and with only a smidgen of sauce. Sliced barbecue comes as big, soft slices. All three kinds of Q are delightfully tender with a truly inspired smoky tang. With the pork comes a Styrofoam cup of warm sauce for dipping.

The hush puppies are curious: elongated crescents with a brittle, sandy-textured crust. The slaw is strange, too, if you are expecting anything like typical cole slaw. This is *barbecue* slaw, meaning finely chopped cabbage bound together with—what else?—barbecue sauce! It's got a brilliant flavor and a pearly-red color that handsomely complements your pork of choice. The small tray, by the way, is only about 3 × 5 inches and 1½ inches deep, but it is astounding how much meat and slaw get packed into it.

The Bridges dining room is plain and soothing, with the kind of meditative atmosphere unique to the finest pork parlors of the mid-South. Square wooden chandeliers cast soft light over green-upholstered booths and a short counter up front where single diners chat quietly among themselves as they sip buttermilk or ice tea and fork into barbecue. Five police officers with gleaming automatics in their patent leather holsters occupy a table toward the back. Even they speak in hushed tones, as if it would be sacrilegious to be raucous in this decent eat-place.

During our stay, more lawmen walk in to join their colleagues. As each one enters he gives us a not-so-subtle once-over. Unlike everybody else in the place, we are strangers. Apparently, we don't look like outlaws, because after scrutiny, we receive a friendly, informal salute as each trooper walks past. It can be unnerving to be inspected by regulars in a town café, whether or not they are cops. When you realize they aren't necessarily planning to kill you, that you are simply a curiosity because you are someone who does not eat here every single day, it can be quite a nice experience. To be the objects of notice in a small café can provide relief from the anonymity one sometimes feels on the road far from home.

Bunn's Bar-B-Q

127 N. King St.   252-794-2274
Windsor, NC   LD | $

Bunn's is yet more proof that great restaurants are found in former filling stations. That's what the building was before 1938, when it became a barbecue parlor. There's still an old Texaco pump outside, and the place is decorated inside and out with vintage signs, ads, and ephemera. The atmosphere is vaguely similar to what the Cracker Barrel chain aims to create, but in this case, it is real.

When you enter, you have a choice of sitting on a bench at a counter in a room to the left or at a table in a room to the right, in back. Wherever you sit, service is lightning-fast. That's because there is virtually no choice on this menu. What you eat is pork, with or without Brunswick stew, on a plate or sandwich, accompanied by tart, tangy cole slaw. The pork is chopped ultra fine, a mix of soft white meat from the inside of the roast laced with chewy brown shreds from its surface. It comes ever-so-lightly sauced with what the locals like: vinegar and spice; but if you want it moister or hotter, other sauces are provided on the counter and tables. Plates are topped with a lovely square of thin, extremely luscious corn bread that has a serious chew and is the ideal medium for pushing around Brunswick stew on the plate.

If you don't fill up on barbecue—you should, you should!—Bunn's has a huge selection of silly packaged cakes, cookies, and honey buns near the cash register.

Cypress Grill

1234 Brown Rd.   252-792-4175
Jamesville, NC   D January–April only | $$

The Cypress Grill may be the last of the herring shacks along the Roanoke River. It is quite literally a cypress wood shack overlooking the river, and it is open only for the herring run, January through April.

If, like us, you've known herring only as slippery little rectangular hors d'oeuvres that come in a jar with sour cream or some sort of pickling emulsion, the sight of a couple of cooked river herrings on a plate is a jolt. They look like fish! Heads are gone but not the tails; they are veiled in the thinnest possible sheath of cornmeal, and their flesh has been scored with notches so that when they were tossed in boiling oil, they cooked quickly, deep down to the bone.

The big issue among river-herring lovers is degree of doneness. Some ask for it sunnyside up, meaning minimal immersion in the fry kettle, resulting in a fish from which you can peel away the skin and lift moist pieces of meat off the bones. The opposite way to go is to ask for your herring cremated: fried until hard and crunchy and so well cooked that all the little bones have become indistinguishable from the flesh around them. The meat itself is transformed, its weight lightened so the natural oiliness is gone but the flavor has become even more intense. The crust and the interior are melded, and they break off in unbelievably savory bite-size pieces, finally leaving nothing but a herring backbone on the plate.

While some herring-crazed patrons fill up on four, five, six, or more of the plush fish, we must advise first-time visitors to the Cypress Grill to leave room for dessert. Every morning, proprietors Leslie and Sally Gardner make pies. When we stopped to visit one day around 10 A.M., Mr. Gardner led us right over to the pie case—a wooden cupboard built by a neighbor to be so sturdy, he says, "you could dance on it." He insisted we feel the bottom of a pie pan, still nearly too hot to touch. We sat down then and there and forked up a piece of chocolate pie that was modest-size but intensely fudgy.

Keaton's

Woodleaf Rd.   704-278-1619
Statesville, NC   LD Wed-Sat | $

An anonymous tipster led us to the chicken shack of our dreams with a note that said, "Keaton's is different than any chicken you've ever had . . . in business for years . . . Food so good it makes you almost cry." We get a lot of suggestions telling us where to eat; the passion of this one was convincing. It concluded: "Worth a long special trip."

Seven hundred miles from home, we came upon it: a cinder-block bunker in North Carolina cattle land between the High Country's natural beauty and High Point's unnaturally low-priced furniture outlets. Traveling the interstate or even secondary highways, you'd never accidentally pass by Keaton's. If you did happen to be profoundly lost on Woodleaf Road and saw the weather-beaten sign out front with the obscure boast "Best Taste by Taste Test," you'd likely drive on by. The dreary tan building looks more like a shot-and-beer honky-tonk than a place interesting food is served.

Wednesday through Saturday evenings, it becomes apparent that something special goes on here, for cars arrive in droves at supper time. Keaton's is little known beyond the Iredell County line, but since B. W. Keaton started making barbecued fried chicken in 1953, his unique recipe has been a fact of local life.

Step up to the counter and order an upper or a lower (the polite country terms for breast or thigh), a half or whole. Pick side dishes from a soulful repertoire of mac and cheese, baked beans, hot sauce slaw, or white mayo slaw; choose ice tea (sweet, of course) or beer; then go to your assigned table or booth, to which a waitress brings the food.

In Keaton's kitchen, the chicken is peppered and salted, floured and fried, at which point it is simply excellent country-style pan-cooked chicken. Then comes the distinctive extra step: just-fried pieces are immersed in a bubbling vat of secret-formula red sauce, a high-spiced, opaque potion similar to what graces High Country barbecued pork. This process takes only seconds, but the throbbing sauce permeates to the bone. You eat this chicken with your hands, pulling off crisp strips of sauce-glazed skin, worrying every joint to suck out all the flavor you can get.

Lexington Barbecue

10 Highway 29-70S   336-249-9814

Lexington, NC   LD | $

Welcome to Lexington, a small city with more than one barbecue restaurant per thousand citizens! Of the nearly two dozen eateries that specialize in hickory-cooked pork, Lexington Barbecue, which opened in 1962, is definitive. "Monk's Place," as locals know it (in deference to founder Wayne "Honey" Monk), looks like a barn with some smelters attached to the back. From those smelters issue the tantalizing aroma of burning hickory and oak wood and the sweet smell of slow-cooking pork, one of the most appetite-inducing aromas in the world. Honey Monk's is a straightforward place with booths and tables and little in the way of decor other than pictures of rural life on the wall. Much business is take-out.

There are no complicated techniques or deep secrets about Lexington barbecue. After about ten hours over smoldering smoke, pork shoulders are shredded into a hash of pieces that vary from melting soft (from the inside) to burnt crisp (from the "bark," or exterior). The hacked meat is sold in a sandwich (on a bun with finely chopped slaw and a mild, vinegar-thin red sauce) or as part of a platter, on which it occupies half a small yellow cardboard boat, with slaw in the other half. Like the meat, the slaw is flavored with a vinegar/sweet barbecue sauce. As part of the platter with the meat and slaw, you get terrific crunch-crusted hush puppies with creamy insides.

Historical note: In 1983 the North Carolina General Assembly designated Lexington as the "Hickory-Cooked Barbecue Capital of Piedmont North Carolina"; that same year the White House asked Mr. Monk to cook barbecue for President Reagan and other heads of state at the Williamsburg International Economic Summit.

Mama Dip's Country Kitchen

405 W. Rosemary St.　　　　　　919-942-5837

Chapel Hill, NC　　　　　　　　BLD | $

"Mama Dip" is Mildred Council, founder/owner/chef at Chapel Hill's beloved soul-food restaurant. Ms. Council, nicknamed "Dip" by her siblings because she was such a tall kid, wrote *Mama Dip's Kitchen* in 1999; it is a valuable cookbook that includes many of the recipes she has used in her restaurant.

Good as those written recipes are, they are no substitute for eating Mama Dip's food in its rightful place, which is her restaurant. It is our experience that soul food, perhaps more than any other cuisine, depends less on recipes than on the touch and feel of the cook who is making the food. At Mama Dip's, even if the proprietor is out of town demonstrating how to make corn bread dressing or sweet-potato biscuits on the Food Network, the food is prepared by experts.

Three meals a day are served; and although lunch and dinner offer great southern classics—fried chicken, chitlin's, Brunswick stew—we love to start the day at Dip's with eggs, pork chops, and gravy, sided by biscuits and grits. Other hearty wake-up meals include salmon cakes, brawny country ham, and blueberry pancakes.

Later in the day, what we love most about Dip's meals, aside from the crust of the fried chicken, are the vegetables. The vast daily vegetable list includes long-cooked greens, black-eyed peas, crunchy nuggets of fried okra, mashed potatoes and gravy, porky string beans, okra stew with tomatoes, corn-dotted cole slaw, always a sumptuous vegetable casserole, and cool sweet-potato salad. For mopping and dipping, there are buttermilk biscuits, corn bread, and yeast rolls.

There are many desserts, including a diabolical fudge pudding with ice cream and warm coconut cream pie, but the one that must not be ignored is sweet-potato pie. It is smooth, simple, and perfect.

Margie's Battery Park Café

1 Battle Square　　　　　　　828-255-2688

Asheville, NC　　　　　　　　B&L | $

Located on the first floor of an apartment building that once was the grandest hotel in Asheville, Margie's serves marvelous desserts. As we sat down, the waitress warned us that the mile-high coconut cream pie was almost gone; so we immediately reserved a piece, as well as some fresh strawberry cake and a piece of honeybun cake. To be absolutely certain they weren't spirited away by another sweet-toothed customer, our waitress brought the three desserts to the table and then took our order for lunch.

Perhaps because that trio of three sweet lovelies was occupying table space as well as our attention, we did not totally appreciate the lunch that was destined to precede them. Jane's choice of spaghetti was just okay, and while Michael's four-vegetable plate included excellent pinto beans and spectacularly good creamed corn made from kernels so fresh they still had a nice slightly sticky quality. Once we tasted the strawberry cake, we suddenly found ourselves engaged in a fork-duel as to who would get the most. Marvelous, marvelous cake, radiant with the flavor of fresh berries used in both the cake and its sweet, sweet icing. The honeybun cake also had terrific icing, a white sheath that surrounded cake that wasn't quite as sweet. And the tall coconut pie was exemplary.

No longer grand the way the old hotel restaurant used to be, Margie's is a quiet, serene place to dine with broad leatherette tables set with tidy white napkins. It is especially fun to look at the old hotel dining room menu posted on the wall near the cash register. Here are grand meals both Continental and Deep Southern, including such desserts as baked Alaska and cherries Jubilee. Much as we would like to go back in a time capsule to that dining room, we'd want to take a few slices of Margie's modern-day strawberry cake along with us!

Mitchell's

| 6228 South Ward Blvd. | 252-291-9189 |
| Wilson, NC 27893 | LD \| $$ |

There is no problem finding barbecue in Eastern North Carolina. It's as common as chile in New Mexico. And most we've eaten is very good. Mitchell's is a cut above, one of the very best.

A former roadside shack that is now a significant food-service enterprise, Roy Mitchell's restaurant serves meals cafeteria-style. You select what you want from an array of meats that includes chopped pork (the main attraction) as well as ribs, turkey, chicken, pig ears, feet, backbones, and chitterlings. The side-dish list is amazing: yams, collard greens, boiled potatoes, baked beans, mashed rutabagas, field peas, stewed cabbage, mac and cheese, corn, Brunswick stew, potato salad, and cole slaw. Plus hush puppies and corn sticks.

When you order a piece of chicken or ribs, the server will inquire, "In the sauce?" If you say yes, he drops the meat into a vat of tangy, vinegar-based hot sauce for a moment, long enough for its fibers to begin to absorb heat and flavor. Once you carry a tray full of food to a table, more sauce is available: traditional Eastern Carolina vinegar sauce in hot and mild versions, plus a sweet tomato-based sauce that Mr. Mitchell told us was his ode to Western North Carolina barbecue. Good as the sauces are, the pork itself is magnificent: juicy pale shreds and chunks along with crusty brown outside bits that have a sweet smoke aura that offers just a hint of pepper heat. With a pile of hush puppies and a bowl of bright, fine-chopped cole slaw, this is barbecue nirvana.

Murray's Barbecue

4700 Old Poole Rd.   919-231-6258
Raleigh, NC   LD Mon-Fri | $

Murray's is on the wrong side of town and looks like a rambling gas station. In other words, it has the appearance of a four-star house of barbecue. Further proof of its legitimacy can be found in the piles of hickory wood outside. This wood is made into coals for the pits, which send a sweet haze wafting through the air.

Hogs are cooked in Murray's pits for six hours, then chopped into chunks that are gentle-flavored, moist, and tender. This is the sort of refined Carolina barbecue for which any sort of heavy, sweet sauce would be anathema. Murray's sauce is merely a condiment; it is not overbearing, adding only an accent to the meat. The truly vital companions on a plate of pulled pork at Murray's are the crusty hush puppies and peppery cole slaw. For a special treat, get an order of yam sticks—like French fries, but made with sweet potatoes.

Parker's

Highway 301   252-237-0972
Wilson, NC   LD | $

The popularity of Parker's goes back to the 1940s when Wilson was the place many tobacco farmers sold their crop. A big barbecue meal was how tobacco men celebrated the harvest; buyers ate here and spread the word up and down Highway 301, which was the main north-south road prior to I-95. Still, the highway is only seven miles away, making Parker's an extremely convenient stop for those traveling along the interstate.

It's a vast eating hall with multiple dining rooms where customers crowd the lined-up tables for family-style combo platters of chopped pork, fried chicken, Brunswick stew, boiled potatoes, corn sticks, and cole slaw. Cooked over hardwood and chopped into hash, the pork is a mix of lean inside meat and crunchy shreds from the outside of the loins and hams from which it has been cut. There is scarcely any sauce on it at all, just a hint of vinegar and peppers to accentuate the wood-smoke savor. If you need to doll it up, tables are set with plain vinegar and a hot sauce that has a vinegar base. As for the fried chicken, we like it even better than the pork. It's seriously crunchy crust encloses juice-dripping meat, the dark pieces especially luscious.

From the moment it opens each day, Parker's always seems to bustle. As you enter, it's an adventure maneuvering your way to a table as waitstaff zoom past toting platters piled high with food.

Price's Chicken Coop

1614 Camden Rd.	704-333-9866
Charlotte, NC	LD (takeout only)	$

Ask anyone in Charlotte where to get the best fried chicken, and expect to be directed to Price's Chicken Coop. Far beyond the city limits, this longtime favorite, take-out-only chicken shack is known for fried chicken that smells so good it causes hungry people to salivate as soon as they exit their vehicle and head for the food. There will be a line of customers—there is almost always a line, often out the door—but it moves quickly; and once you get a cardboard box of hot, just-fried bird in your hand, our suggestion is to open the box and eat immediately—sitting in your car. If you like fried chicken, it will be love at first bite. The shattering crunch of the crust is itself a joy; the meat inside, white or dark, drips with flavor.

There are several other items on the menu that, someday, we might try. In fact, we have promised ourselves that the next time we get to the counter, we will get fried perch, gizzards, or shrimp. But each time, the thought of what that fried chicken feels like in the mouth wins out, and we break our promise, getting a box full of breasts, thighs, and legs . . .

accompanied by hush puppies, cole slaw, and a spongy white dinner roll. We fully agree with the Roadfood warrior who first tipped us off to this fantastic place, that it is "as close to fried chicken nirvana as you'll ever get . . . truly a five-star chicken emporium."

River's Edge

Water Street   252-792-2631
Jamesville, NC   LD | $$

We know two places that serve herring along the Roanoke River, the Cypress Grill (page 160), which is open only during herring season and has a strictly seafood menu, and River's Edge, just upstream, a year-round restaurant that supplements its fish menu with steaks, sandwiches, barbecue, fried-to-order chicken, even spaghetti and meat sauce.

Still, we were at River's Edge in March and therefore could not resist having herring. "Hard or soft?" asked the waitress. "Squeaky, the cook, can do it both ways." Soft means the meat inside the deep-fried crust is still lusciously oily; hard means long-fried so the inside firms up and you can eat virtually everything but the fish's backbone. If you adore fish, you'll like the former; otherwise, we suggest you get it hard, also known hereabouts as "cremated."

Other seafood choices include catfish, perch, flounder, trout, rock (a.k.a. striped bass), shrimp and oysters, all available with ultra-crispy, dark gold hush puppies, which are oval rather than round. "They're really, really hot!" said our waitress when she brought our basketful before the fish arrived.

River's Edge is a genuine restaurant (as opposed to a herring shack), meaning there are multiple dining rooms suitable for small parties and after-church groups on Sunday. The waitress assured us that the Sunday buffet was grand indeed, although that is the one day of the week no herring is available. "It's just regular home-cooked food," she said, reeling off a list of ribs, pork chops, and ham, corn and collards, cabbage and mac and cheese, plus banana pudding for dessert.

Skylight Inn

1501 Lee St.   252-746-4113
Ayden, NC   LD | $

Many cities, regions, and restaurants lay claim to being America's barbecue capital; this place quite literally *is* a capitol. The building is capped
with a capitol dome, as in Washington, D.C., with the U.S. flag flying
overhead. Not by looks alone can the Skylight Inn claim primacy. It is
one of the best—if not *the* best—barbecue in North Carolina. And in
North Carolina, that is saying a lot!

Known to one and all as Pete Jones's barbecue after its pitmaster, the
Skylight Inn is dedicated to pork. That's all there is to eat—pork served
on a bun, or in one of three sizes of cardboard tray with corn bread and
a mound of cole slaw, or by the pound. Hacked with a cleaver into meat
of nearly infinite variety, including wispy pale little fibers and brittle
shreds from the outside of the pit-cooked meat, all tossed together and
dressed with just enough hot sauce to make the natural sweetness blossom, it is aristocratic pork, however coarsely it is served. Compared to
heavily sauced and oversmoked barbecue many other parts of the country, this kind of barbecue, unique to Eastern North Carolina, is almost
ascetic in nature—a food to dote upon, to savor very slowly.

You know that pig meat is serious business the moment you walk in,
for just behind the counter is a window where big hunks of pork from
the pit are being chopped with a heavy cleaver on a cutting block. The
sound of pork being hacked to pieces is sweet music to accompany a Skylight meal.

Snappy Lunch

125 N. Main St.   336-786-4931
Mount Airy, NC   BL | $

As Yankees, we'd never heard of a pork chop sandwich until we traveled
south. Even in Dixie, it is not all that common, but you'll find it on
menus in various configurations ranging from a bone-in chop with superfluous bread that serves merely as a mitt so you can eat the meat without utensils, to the boneless beauty at Snappy Lunch. Surely, this is the
king of pork chop sandwiches. It is a broad slab of meat that is breaded
and fried similarly to the tenderloins of the Midwest, but with more

pork, and with more cushiony breading. It is soft and luscious, as tender as a mother's love.

Few customers of Snappy Lunch get a plain pork chop sandwich. The ritual here in Mount Airy (Andy Griffith's hometown, and the inspiration for TV's Mayberry) is to have it *all the way,* which means dressed with tomato, chopped onion, mustard, meaty-sweet chili, and fine-cut cabbage slaw speckled with green peppers and onions. The total package is unwieldy in the extreme. Served in booths or at the counter in a wax paper wrapper, this is a sandwich that requires two big hands to hoist and eat. There are no side dishes available other than a bag of potato chips; and the beverage of choice is tea—iced and pre-sweetened, of course.

There are, however, other items on the menu, including a weird Depression-era legacy known as the breaded hamburger, for which ground beef is extended by mixing it with an equal portion of moistened bread. The result is a strange, plump hamburger that resembles a crab cake. Definitely an acquired taste!

Pork chop sandwiches are the trademark specialty of the Snappy Lunch kitchen, but it is also a place to have breakfast. In the morning, big hot biscuits from the back oven perfume the vintage Main Street café with an aromatic steam that is irresistible if you just happen to be walking past. Brushed with butter while still hot, the biscuits are served with eggs or as sandwiches containing country ham, sausage, bacon, or sliced pork tenderloin. By a little after six every morning, seats and counter are occupied almost exclusively by locals, and the conversation is quintessential café banter. At a booth near ours one day, an elderly gentleman was informing two younger men that the finest pair of shoes he'd ever owned were made by hand for him in 1940. The shoemaker had measured him right there out on the sidewalk and charged him $6 for the pair. Now, he pays $79 for shoes and they don't fit nearly as well. Of course, those were the days you could drive clear from Burnsville to Asheville for a dime's worth of gas . . .

Sonny's Grill

1087 Main St.   828-295-7577

Blowing Rock, NC   BL | $

Blowing Rock has grown tremendously in the last half century, but Sonny's Grill, there since 1954, remains a simple town café. A small, square (literally) storefront restaurant on Main Street, it has eight stools at the counter and three tables that seat four people each. The floor is black-and-white linoleum; and on chill mornings, warmth is provided by the blue flames of a gas-powered wall heater. Instead of having napkins, each table is outfitted with an upright dowel that holds a roll of paper towels.

Sonny's ham biscuits are definitive: circular, golden-topped rolls with fluffy insides sandwiched around a few slices of deliriously flavorful grilled country ham. The power of the ham—its complexity, its salty punch, its rugged chewy texture—is perfectly complemented by the fluffy gentleness of the biscuit around it. A couple of these and a cup of coffee are a grand way to start the day.

We also love Sonny's sweet-potato pancakes, with a silky-soft texture and faint potato sweetness that almost makes syrup redundant. They, too, are a good companion for country ham. The dish we don't especially like on Sonny's menu is liver mush. One order of liver mush is three rectangular tiles of ground-up pig innards that are cut from a loaf and served warm. If you really like liver (for breakfast!), you might like them. For us, this mush is a taste we have no desire to acquire.

Breakfast at Sonny's is especially wonderful "off season," when the tables and counter are occupied by locals who carry on room-wide conversations, read the paper, and keep one another posted on news and gossip. At lunch, it is a more hurried scene (and during tourist season it can be a madhouse). But we do recommend lunch at Sonny's. It is the best place in town to have a hamburger. A real, short-order kind of burger, handmade and grilled to crusty succulence, served on a bun with lettuce, tomato, and mayonnaise. The hot dogs are excellent, too: all-beef beauties with a snapping-taut skin, available plain or in true Southern style, topped with chili and cole slaw.

Staymey's

2206 High Point Rd.   919-299-9888
Greensboro, NC   LD | $

Staymey's is a big modern restaurant on the outskirts of town, but its recipes go back to 1930, when Charles Staymey started smoking pigs under a tent in the town of Shelby. In 1953 he moved to Greensboro, and Staymey's is still run by his family.

Staymey's menu is minimal. There are no unnecessary adjectives, no mouthwatering descriptions, not even any cute pictures of dancing pigs. It lists the basics: pork, large or small, chopped or sliced, baked beans or hush puppies. Nor is there any folderol in the presentation. The food comes on heavy partitioned paper plates, which tend to soften but not disintegrate underneath the moist food.

The pork itself has two natures, depending on whether you get it chopped or sliced. Chopped, the pulverized meat seemed complex and zesty, especially if sprinkled with some of the peppery barbecue sauce on the table. Sliced, it's tender and mild: big, thick pieces of gently flavored pig meat, really quite an elegant food.

Hush puppies are tubular squiggles rather than spheres; beans are lush and hammy; cole slaw has some of Stamey's zesty sauce mixed into its dressing; and iced tea is wonderful: sweet but not overwhelmingly so, a perfect refreshing companion to a pig-out meal.

Wilber's Barbecue

4338 E. US 70 (Kinston Highway)   919-778-5218
Goldsboro, NC   BLD at the original,
                                        LD at newer locations | $

Two newer locations in Goldsboro at 502-A Eastgate Dr. (919-778-1990) and 1104 North William St. (919-735-7515)

Pilots who take off from Seymour Johnson Air Force Base have flown the fame of Wilber's far and wide; and legends abound regarding the pounds of barbecue carried aboard strategic flights. Even if it weren't at the end of the runway, Wilber's reputation for serving first-class Lexington-style North Carolina barbecue could never have remained merely local. This place is world-class! Since 1962, when Wilber Shirley stoked the oak and hickory coals in old-fashioned pits, he has been known for whole-hog barbecue, chopped and judiciously seasoned with a peppery vinegar sauce. After eight hours over coals, the meat is soft as a sigh, its natural sweetness haloed by the indescribably appetizing tang of hardwood smoke. It is served with potato salad, cole slaw, Brunswick stew (a pork hash with Veg-All type vegetables) and squiggle-shaped, crunch-crusted hush puppies.

Beyond terrific barbecue, the original Wilber's has the added attraction of serving breakfast, in the form of a buffet with smoky sausages, thick-cut bacon, chewy cracklin's, biscuits and gravy, grits, and sweet muffins. By late morning, chopped barbecue reigns, and it is served until about nine at night . . . or until the day's supply runs out. When that happens, the management locks the door and hangs up a sign that advises, "Out of Barbecue!"

A&R Bar-B-Que

1802 Elvis Presley Blvd.　　　　901-774-7444
Memphis, TN　　　　　　　　　LD | $

This smokehouse a few blocks north of Graceland radiates cooking-pork aroma clear across Elvis Presley Boulevard. When you enter and walk to the counter to place an order, you hear a blissful smokehouse lullaby coming from the kitchen: chop-chop-chop on the cutting board as hickory-cooked pork gets hacked into shreds and pieces for plates and sandwiches. The sandwich is the classic Memphis configuration: pork mixed with tangy red sauce piled in a bun and crowned with a spill of cole slaw. It occurred to us as we plowed through a jumbo that the slaw in a Memphis barbecue sandwich is as important for its texture as for its pickly sweet taste. The cabbage provides such nice little bits of crunch amid the velvety heap of pork.

Beyond pig sandwiches, you can have ribs (wet or dry), catfish dinner, hot tamales, meatballs on a stick (!), and that only-in-Memphis treat, barbecue spaghetti. That's a mound of soft noodles dressed not with ordinary tomato sauce, but with—of course—barbecue sauce, laced with shreds of pork. It's weird, but in this city, where restaurants also offer barbecue pizza and barbecue salad, it makes sense.

A&R is a big place with idyllic BBQ parlor ambience. Raw brick walls and fluorescent lights set a no-frills mood, and however hot it is outside, you can count on the air-conditioning system to be running so high that it's practically like going into hibernation. Or is the trance we experienced a result of hypnotically good food?

Arnold's Country Kitchen

| 603 8th Ave. S | 615-256-4455 |
| Nashville, TN | L \| $ |

"Just about the very best meat-and-three . . . wildly popular with lawyers, Music Row notables, and working stiffs," is how Arnold's was described to us by a cyberfoodie who had written to us primarily to praise the macaroni and cheese at Roscoe's House of Chicken and Waffles in Pasadena, California. We know Roscoe's mac and cheese, and we love it; so we took this tip seriously and found ourselves in a short cafeteria line one Monday in Nashville among a crowd of hungry locals pushing toward the food. On the wall were signed photographs of local and national celebrities singing the praises of Arnold's roast beef, meat loaf, fried oysters, and cream pies.

We piled our trays with hunks of fried chicken (the Monday special), whipped potatoes and gravy, turnip greens, corn muffins, and slices of lightweight but heavy-flavored chocolate pie, as well as classical Dixie banana pudding with vanilla wafers in the custard. Delicious, from first bite to last!

Arnold's is a funky little place that doesn't look like much from the outside—just a white cinder-block building with a decorative fence painted on its walls. But at high noon, expect to wait for a seat (and perhaps to share a table with strangers). To Nashville eaters who know good food, this little eat-place is a country star.

Belle Meade Buffet

| 4534 Harding Rd. | 615-298-5572 |
| Nashville, TN | LD \| $ |

Of America's many fine cafeterias, most of which are in the South, the crème de la crème is the Belle Meade. It isn't the biggest—there are no more than eight or ten entrees and a dozen-and-a-half vegetables, plus salads, desserts, rolls, relishes, and drinks. Still, it is a vista of beautiful things to eat that will make Roadfooders weep for joy and start to worry about all the good things that won't fit on a crowded tray. How can you possibly choose catfish, hush puppies, and chess pie, and by choosing them, *not* choose fried chicken, seasoned greens, and lemon meringue pie in a graham cracker crust?

Belle Meade food is beautiful merely to look at. Like the stars in a revue on Broadway, each item has its own spotlight in its pan on the steam table; or if already divvied into servings (pieces of pie, dishes of Jell-O, etc.), each plate is arranged for maximum eye appeal. Under the direction of co-owners Henry Kendall and Mickey Pope, the Belle Meade is shipshape; and unlike help-yourself buffets that can get very tired-looking as amateurs pick their way through the offerings, all the food here is maintained in perfect form by the serving staff. Drips, spills, and unsightly blemishes are anathema; and any time a serving pan starts looking empty, it is refilled or replaced to look bountiful and fresh. These servers know how to plate things, too, so you are guaranteed that the hill of mashed potatoes you get to accompany your meat loaf will be nicely swirled on the plate; and gravy, if desired, will spill down its sides in savory rivulets.

Belle Meade's best-known entrees include grilled chicken livers, chicken dumplings, roast chicken, roast pork, fresh ham, and chicken à la king on corn bread. Vegetables are especially noteworthy. They are cooked southern-style, which means they're super-seasoned and dolled-up. Cabbage gets stir-fried with bacon until it sops up the porky goodness. Whipped yams are flavored with vanilla, dotted with raisins, and streaked with marshmallow. There are sweet stewed tomatoes, green beans cooked with hog jowl, fried apples, and glorious macaroni and cheese. As for dessert, which is arrayed at both the beginning *and* the end of the cafeteria line, we defy you to choose only one item from among the chess pie, pecan pie, chocolate rum pie, coconut cream pie, egg custard pie, and smack-your-granny-down icebox pie. Did we mention that the muffins, yeast rolls, and corn bread sticks are fresh from the oven?

Once the bill is toted up at the end of the line (it is impossible to spend more than $10 for dinner no matter how you crowd a tray), a Belle Meade waiter carries the trays to a table in the dining room, sometimes showing off as he whisks it above the heads of diners he passes. (A tip for such service is customary.) The room is brightly lit; and just as the serving line moves fast, people eat fast, too. Since the whole meal is set out before you, there's no waiting between courses. And when you're done, you don't have to flag down the waiter for a check. Few people spend more than an hour at the Belle Meade, start to finish.

Blue Plate Café

5469 Poplar Ave.	901-761-9696
Memphis, TN	BLD | $

Listen up, waffle hounds! If, like us, you are perpetually on the lookout for slim, small-tread waffles (as opposed to the thick Belgium plumpies), put the Blue Plate Café of Memphis on your itinerary. They make plate-size round ones, crisp and golden brown, with plenty of little holes to hold gobs of butter and syrup. While it is possible to order one filled with pecans or topped with apple compote, blueberries, or other fruits, we like ours plain and hot from the griddle . . . with a huge slab of salty country ham on a separate plate.

In this cheery café that was once a private home, the menu goes way beyond waffles. Breakfast (served any time) includes pancakes, omelets with great hash browns or grits on the side, and flavorful knobby-top biscuits served with silky cream gravy dotted with bits of sausage.

Lunch is good ol' meat-and-threes, with a choice of such entrees as pot roast, baked pork chops, chicken and dumplings, and fried shrimp (that last one is every Friday). The vegetable roster from which you choose three is about twenty items long, including real mashed potatoes, turnip greens, creamed corn, mac and cheese, etc., etc. If you want something simpler than meat-and-three, there are salads, soups, and sandwiches, including a fried peanut butter and banana sandwich. Apparently, that one is health food: it is served on whole wheat bread.

Buntyn

4972 Park Ave.	901-458-8776
Memphis, TN	LD | $

About ten years ago, the venerable old Buntyn was passed along to a new generation of the Tull family, which started it, and it moved to a larger location on the far side of Audubon Park east of town. We were worried. However well-meaning, such changes often signal the end of greatness in a small restaurant that has honed its way of doing things for so long.

We are delighted to report that the new Buntyn is old-fashioned swell! Located in what appears to have once been a Polynesian-style steak house, it nevertheless maintains its vivid mid-South personality.

"I'm so sorry," says the waitress. "The rolls may be too hot to handle right now." Yes, they are! The big, gold-topped dinner roll vents clouds of steam as we gingerly tear off a big shred and savor its yeasty sweetness, and the crunchy top of the corn bread muffin literally sizzles a moment on our tongue as we take a first greedy bite. These breads are paradigms, and they signal the beginning of a dramatically excellent lunch.

The fried chicken is splendid, its red-gold skin hugging close to meat that is moist and flavorful. If you order meat loaf, you get a whole small loaf, crusted with a zesty Creole tomato sauce that gives it a soulful character. Side dishes are plentiful and good: festively spiced candied yams, luxuriant macaroni and cheese, bracing turnip greens, etc.

Save room for dessert, for Buntyn pies are among the best anywhere. We love the coconut cream, which is rich and thick and toasty, crowned with fluffy meringue, and the lemon icebox pie is beyond superb: very tart, very sweet, at once mellow and loud. It's a taste sensation, and proof positive that Buntyn's cooks are on the beam.

Cozy Corner

745 N. Parkway   901-527-9158
Memphis, TN   LD | $$

When we come to Memphis hungry for barbecue, the Cozy Corner is the first place we go. The spareribs are big and deep-flavored; baby back ribs are nearly too tender, their meat virtually evaporating on your tongue. Pork shoulder is our favorite meat, sliced into thick pieces with a devilishly blackened crust that is blanketed with spice, their centers velvet-soft, sweet, and moist. We're also fond of barbecued bologna, a thick oinky disc bathed in profound red sauce, available on a platter or on a bun with cole slaw dressing. The best-known specialty of the house, and a specialty found in few smoke pits anywhere, is barbecued Cornish hen—a small bird with burnished skin and meat of ineffably delicate texture.

The beeline we make for the Cozy Corner isn't only for its food; we love the place, which has the colorful character of a truly grand barbecue parlor. Its front room is clouded with haze from the smoker behind the self-service counter; it is a storefront that does a lot of take-out business but also has a small dining room to the side where Memphis blues provide a suitable beat for pork-eating. The place was established back in 1977 by Raymond Robinson with $2,500 he borrowed from his mother; and until his death early in 2001, Mr. Robinson presided over his small, sweet-smelling empire from behind the order counter, haloed by the glow of his smoke pit. When we first stopped in, about ten years ago, his mother was holding court on the couch near the order counter. Mrs. Robinson rhapsodized about the health benefits of eating barbecue as often as possible, pointing to a row of effulgent aloe vera plants growing in plastic spice buckets along the window. "They have been here for years," she said. "Look how healthy they are. They thrive on barbecue smoke!"

Cupboard Restaurant

1400 Union Ave.   901-276-8015
Memphis, TN   L | $

The Cupboard Restaurant cookbook is available for sale near the cash register, and it contains excellent recipes. But unless you live in the South, it's mostly a dream book. The kind of fine raw ingredients that make lunch here such a reliable treat make only rare and brief appearances in supermarkets in the Northeast. That's why we look forward to lunch at the Cupboard every time we visit Memphis.

Here are some of the best vegetable dishes in the city . . . and that is saying a lot in a city where vegetable cooking is a fine, fine art. Of special note are summer's plain sliced fresh tomatoes (and we do mean fresh!) as well as tangy fried green tomatoes. The sweet potato is one whole one, baked in its skin until marshmallow-soft. And we love the Cupboard's luxurious corn pudding. A printed menu, which is different for each day of the week, lists a choice of five entrees and eighteen to twenty side dishes, plus dessert. Among the entrees are such plate-lunch staples as baked chicken and dressing, beef tips with noodles, and a fried veal cutlet. One entree plus three vegetables—served on an unbreakable partitioned plate, so buttered squash doesn't mingle with rutabaga turnips—costs $7.78.

Not to slight the entrees, but an all-vegetable plate is a perfectly logical and satisfying lunch, accompanied by creamy-centered corn bread gem muffins, yeast rolls, and sweet tea, with blackberry cobbler and lemon icebox pie for dessert.

The Cupboard Restaurant lost something in the year 2000 when it moved to a former Shoney's on Union Avenue. Gone is the ramshackle charm of the older place, a favorite lunch spot since 1943. But the gains were worth the change: more seats (you'll wait less for a table at noon), plenty of parking, and a vast, comfortable dining room with broad enough aisles for waitstaff to tote big plates overflowing with good things to eat.

Dixie Barbeque Co.

3301 N. Roan St. (Kingsport Hwy.)   423-283-PIGS
Johnson City, TN   LD | $$

Johnson City is easternmost Tennessee, which means it is big on barbecue and the typical meat is sliced pork bathed in an opaque, dark red sauce radiant with spice. East Tennessee is not only a land of important barbecue; it is NASCAR country. Both these facts are easily gleaned from a look at the menu of Dixie Barbeque Co., which offers meat sliced or pulled (your choice) from pork shoulders that are slow-cooked over hardwood for a full twelve hours. If you want a full pound of meat (with Brunswick stew, two side dishes, corn bread, and apple sauce), ask for the meal of champions known as the Intimidator, which was the nickname of late, beloved NASCAR driver Dale Earnhardt.

In addition to pulled and sliced pork, Dixie makes mighty fine pork ribs. These are not the anemic-flavored, boiled-tender baby back ribs that national chains sell; no, these are big, hefty pork ribs with a real chew to their meat, and a deep, satisfying character that only hours over a smoldering pit can produce. When we asked proprietor Alan Howell what kind of wood he prefers for his barbecue, he answered "tree wood . . . whatever blows down . . . hickory, mostly."

To gild your pork (or beef or chicken), Dixie Barbeque offers a dizzying array of sauces: East Tennessee Red, classic Carolina Vinegar, Devil's Dew, South Carolina Gold, Alabama White, Texas/Oklahoma Style, and Sauce from Hell, all of which are made on the premises, plus Richard Petty brand sauce and Maurice's Gourmet Sauce from South Carolina. Any or all of them are brought to the table by your waitress, who patiently explains the fundamental qualities of each. We like most (except the bizarre white sauce that is mayonnaise-based: fie on it!); but for a true local experience, try the cinnabar-red East Tennessee sauce. Unless you say otherwise, this is what comes on sandwiches.

Although barbecue is serious business in this establishment, the ambience is plenty goofy, including sports-team pennants and amusing vanity license plates plastered all over the walls and a rack of fabulous rebel-themed bumper stickers for sale. (We could not resist plastering our bumper with one that says, "Don't Make Me Open This" next to a can of "Whoop-Ass.") Loud shag music blasts over the sound system, providing perpetual-party atmosphere; and dual television sets run continuous tapes of *The Andy Griffith Show.*

Dyer's Burgers

205 Beale St.   901-527-3937
Memphis, TN   LD | $

If you have a cholesterol problem, stop reading now. If you enjoy hamburgers with, shall we say, a generous measure of grease, please read on.

At Dyer's, a modest-size round of raw ground beef is held on the cutting board under a spatula and the spatula is whacked a few times with a heavy hammer, flattening the meat into a semi-compressed patty at least four inches wide. Now, the good part: The patty is submerged into a deep, black skillet full of bubbling-hot grease, grease that the management boasts has not been changed since Dyer's opened in 1912! It's the grease that gives a Dyer's burger a consummately juicy interior while it develops a wickedly crusty outside.

Our waitress explained that the grease is carefully strained every night after closing (usually about 4 A.M.; this is Beale Street, after all), and besides, the really old grease is always burning off, so the supply that supposedly never changes is, in fact, always changing. Whatever. The fact is that this is one heck of an interesting hamburger. We are especially smitten by the many ways in which it is served: as a double or triple, or as a double or triple "combo" (with layers of cheese), and with really good hand-cut French fries on the side. The menu boasts that each hamburger is served "Always on a Genuine Wonder Bread bun."

If hamburgers are not your passion, allow us to suggest another Dyer's specialty: the Big Rag Baloney sandwich. That's a half-inch-thick slab of baloney that is fried to a crisp in the same skillet and in the same vintage oil as the burgers.

Ellen's

601 S. Parkway E   901-942-4888

Memphis, TN   LD | $

"Call your pieces," says the waitress if you've come for fried chicken, meaning tell her which parts you like best. We are especially fond of thighs, an embarrassment of juices packed inside skin that crunches with brio. Favorite side dishes include stewed cabbage flecked with fire-hot pepper, fried corn dotted with bits of green pepper, and griddle-cooked corn cakes that tear easily into pieces well suited for mopping gravy. Desserts are such ingenious items as sock-it-to-me cake and 7-Up cake that is feather-soft and mellow-flavored. On the side, of course, you'll want plenty of sweet tea.

Now that Memphis's beloved Four Way Grill is gone, this is the soul-food café we'll happily visit whenever we crave a plate of neck bones, catfish, or fried pork chops sided by candied yams, purple hull peas, and a stack of corn bread. It is a South Memphis storefront with a tired, timeworn appearance but a staff that seems to be on a mission to make paleface newcomers—such as ourselves—feel at ease. "You are very welcome," the hostess told us as we walked in for the first time. She pointed us to a table where we sat in molded laminate seats and perused hand-written menus on 8½ × 11-inch paper, encased in plastic for protection from spills and drips. Apparently, more than one person does the writing. Jane's menu listed *pig's feet*. Michael's, in totally different handwriting, offered *pig feets*.

Elliston Place Soda Shop

2111 Elliston Place   615-327-1090

Nashville, TN   BL | $

Opened in 1939 and scarcely changed in the last six decades, the Elliston Place Soda Shop is now owned by former judge Charles Galbreath, whose team of waitresses upholds the little eatery's hallowed tradition of service with an attitude. Last time we visited, the attitude was extra nice, our waitress addressing Michael as "Precious," "Babe," and "Hon" as she brought our breakfast. We know one man whose father ate breakfast at Elliston Place five days a week for twenty years and had a fight with his waitress every single one of those days. He claimed never once to have had a good meal. And yet, of course, he came back every morning for more.

This is a restaurant with personality! Its tiny-tile floor is well weathered and its tables wobble. Each green-upholstered booth has its own jukebox with selections that are, suitably enough, country classics. Above the counter, vintage soda fountain signs advertise banana splits, fruit sundaes, sodas, and fresh fruit-ades.

The sodas, shakes, and floats are fine; but we like Elliston Place best for hot lunch and breakfast. Great biscuits are a fact of life here—crunchy brown on the outside with a luscious soft interior that begs to wrap itself around a slice of salty country ham. Many locals ignore the excellent ham and choose fried bologna as their breakfast meat. On the side comes a bowl of firm, steamy white grits—an excellent gentle-natured companion for full-flavored breakfast meat.

Elliston Place is one of Nashville's top meat-and-three spots. Choose sugar-cured ham, salt-cured country ham, southern-fried chicken (white or dark meat), a pork chop, or liver and onions, then select three vegetables from a daily roster of at least a dozen. On Mondays and Thursdays the house special is turkey and dressing, a casserole of shredded roasted white and dark meat with steamy corn bread dressing: delicious! Or if you want to skip the meat altogether (Elliston Place vegetables are so good, such a strategy makes sense), there is a four-vegetable plate, accompanied by hot bread, for about $3. Among the vegetable repertoire you will likely find whipped potatoes, turnip greens, baked squash, fried bite-size rounds of okra, black-eyed peas, baked squash, and congealed fruit salad (the local name for Jell-O).

For dessert, if you can resist a banana split, there is silk-smooth chess pie or a frosty wedge of the simple and nearly breathtaking Dixie classic, lemon icebox pie.

Leonard's

5465 Fox Plaza Dr.   901-360-1963
Memphis, TN   LD | $

You'll get barbecue sandwiches throughout the South, but the Memphis way to serve them is with cole slaw atop the pork inside the bun. This is a configuration invented by pitmaster Leonard Heuberger in 1922. Today, dozens of parlors throughout the city and beyond serve barbecue sandwiches that way, but Leonard's version remains the paragon—an ideal confluence of sugar and spice, meat and bread, and sauce.

Leonard's is worth visiting not only for its sandwich, but for its sign, which is one of the great images in porklore: a neon pig, all decked out in top hat and tails, wielding a cane and captioned: "Mr. Brown Goes to Town." For years, we were perplexed by what Mr. Brown was supposed to signify until one day about a decade ago, a Leonard's waitress named Loretta explained, "Mr. Brown was the term used for brownmeat barbecue. It is the outside of the shoulder that gets succulent and chewy from the sauce and the smoke in the pit. The inside part of the roast, which is moist but has very little barbecue flavor, is known as Miss White. People in Memphis used to ask for plates and sandwiches of 'Mr. Brown and Miss White.' " We were mesmerized by Loretta's explanation, but the smell of pit smoke and hot pork wafting off our sandwiches drew our attention to the meal at hand, and we forgot to ask why Mr. Brown, that delicious pig, is going to town. Might that mean that the sandwich is "dressed up" with slaw? We have returned to Leonard's many times since, but were always too occupied with ordering and eating pig sandwiches to uncover the full story of Mr. Brown's visit to town.

Little Tea Shop

69 Monroe Ave. 901-525-6000
Memphis, TN L | $

Around the corner from legendary Cotton Row on the banks of the Mississippi River, the Little Tea Shop opened in 1918 and continues today as a favorite eatery of commodities traders and financial types who work in the capital city of the mid-South. Despite the high-powered nature of its customers, the Little Tea Shop is indeed a little tea shop, serving only lunch on weekdays between 11 A.M. and 2:15 P.M. (with a take-out bakery open earlier for breakfast).

Many everyday people come for club sandwiches or BLTs or chicken salad, but if you are visiting just once, we recommend a traditional Dixie meal. Each day of the week has its own lunch special, from Creole chicken giblets and rice on Monday to catfish steak on Friday. These flowers of the Southern kitchen are accompanied by soulful vegetables such as black-eyed peas, candied yams, or scalloped tomatoes. Of course it is possible to make a meal of four vegetables without any entree at all, or you can base lunch around a mound of turnip greens.

Turnip greens are always on the Little Tea Shop menu, with salt pork, with baked ham, or with onions. They are *serious* greens, whole-leaf heaps of heavy vegetable goodness, soft and dark green, with a commanding tonic flavor enriched by the pork with which they have been cooked. They are served with their cooking liquid, known as pot likker, and it really is like some kind of invigorating liquor, only it's good for you. It is the essence of green leaves, the kind of liquid nutrition Popeye might drink to make his muscles bulge. Because it is so intense, so porky and focused, the Little Tea Shop serves it only by the cupful, with a couple of corn sticks, as a breathtaking appetizer before lunch.

Litton's Market & Restaurant

2803 Essary Dr.   865-688-0429

Knoxville, TN   LD | $

With a catalog of burgers that range from minimalist beef patties to a "Thunder Road" burger (named for the movie about moonshining in these parts) topped with pimiento cheese, onions, and hot peppers, Litton's is the most famous hamburger restaurant in the mid-South. For each burger, meat is hand-formed into a patty that is nearly half a pound and cooked to order, then sandwiched in a made-here bun, preferably with at least lettuce, tomato and onion, and, at most, bacon, pickles, or chili. Hamburgers—and other sandwiches—are available with French fries or—even better—a potato/cheese casserole known as Arizona Spuds.

At least as famous as the hamburgers are Litton's big desserts: coconut cream pie, old-fashioned red velvet cake, creamy banana pudding, and five kinds of freshly baked cookies every day. The one dessert that brings us to our knees is Italian cream cake, a creamy, buttery concoction with old-fashioned simplicity that goes perfectly with a cup of postprandial coffee.

Litton's has been around for years and its walls are covered with mementos of old Knoxville. It is a fun place to eat, but for those who prefer to dine rather than merely eat, there is a classier "back room" with its own upscale menu of continental fare. For a seat in either place, expect a wait at peak mealtimes.

Loveless Café

8400 Hwy 100   615-646-0067
Nashville, TN   BLD | $$

Eating at the Loveless Café isn't only a matter of fried chicken and biscuits. It is all about the South, Tennessee in particular, and Nashville, heart and soul. As comfortable as an old rocking chair and as welcoming as Grandma, this is a restaurant that resonates with country character. Recently renovated and now with an expanded menu featuring dinner, it is still rightfully best known for country ham with all the trimmings.

Foremost among those trimmings are biscuits: fluffy gold-topped discs that come in a basket that is replenished throughout the meal so you always have a pile of hot ones ready to push through cream gravy or red-eye gravy, or to adorn with made-here peach, blackberry, and strawberry preserves, local honey, or sorghum.

The other signature item is fried chicken—a traditional breakfast among locals, and, of course, a favorite lunch and supper, too. This is some of the best fried chicken in the South, with a good crunch to its skin and juice-dripping meat inside. With that cream gravy, nothing's better. Among the not-to-be-missed side dishes is the hash-brown casserole, a Loveless staple since it first opened for business in 1951.

New items on the menu include barbecued pulled pork and pork chops (smoked in a smokehouse just outside the dining room), catfish, a green-tomato BLT, and shrimp and grits. Now there is even a dessert menu featuring sensational coconut pie and an astonishing banana pudding that is made the classic way, with vanilla wafers, but in this case with homemade(!) vanilla wafers prepared from a recipe devised by new pastry chef Alisa Huntsman.

Truthfully, we were skeptical when we heard that the old Loveless had changed hands in 2004 and its new owner, Tom Morales, planned major renovations. But all is well, and we salute Tom for maintaining the good food and gracious country spirit of this roadside landmark while tastefully spiffing up the place and adding all sorts of delicious new items to the menu.

Pancake Pantry

1796 21st Ave. S   615-383-9333
Nashville, TN   BL | $

Rarely have we met a waitress more interested in our culinary happiness than the pro who guides us through our first meal at the Pancake Pantry. "Have you had our sweet-potato pancakes before?" she asks as she sets down a plate of five fluffy, five-inch discs. When we tell her we have not, she suggests that rather than pour on the cinnamon cream, we drizzle some of the golden syrup into a little ramekin she provides so we can dip a bite of the pancake and see how we like it. Her alert notwithstanding, we love the spicy syrup, and once the extraordinary tender cakes are slathered in butter, we use half a pitcher to flavor them.

She also suggests that rather than a whole order of cornmeal cakes, we get just one; that way, we can also have a half-order of Caribbean pancakes with bananas, pecans, coconut, and powdered sugar. And when we debate whether or not we want orange juice, she bends close over the table and in a gleeful whisper that is nearly conspiratorial, says, "It's fresh."

As for which kind of pancake a person should order in this restaurant, the hard truth is that there are too many good kinds to taste even half in a single visit. Among the outstanding varieties, after the sweet-potato cakes, which are the stars of the menu, there are wild blueberry, sugar and spice, creamy potato pancakes (with minced onion), and Swiss chocolate pancakes. In addition to the smooth cinnamon cream, every table is provided a cruet of warm maple-flavored syrup. All the usual breakfast meats are available on the side, including the Tennessee favorite, cured country ham, a big end-slab of which is sizzled to a crunch around its edges on the griddle.

Nearly always crowded (but with a fast turnover that usually precludes a long wait), the Pancake Pantry is a high-ceilinged restaurant with plenty of space among the tables and a tone of boisterous breakfast conversation throughout the dining room. This is a happy place. Of course it is: What's not to be happy about when you are eating excellent pancakes with plenty of butter and syrup and good coffee on the side?

Pickwick Catfish Farm Restaurant

4155 Hwy. 57   731-689-3805
Counce, TN   D weekends only | $

Catfish is popular throughout the mid-South, but there is none quite as good as that served at Pickwick Catfish Farm, 100 miles east of Memphis. Starting at five o'clock Thursday through Sunday, you can smell the hot corn aroma of hush puppies emerging from the oil. These 'pups are the perfect companion for thick steaks of Pickwick's own pond-raised catfish, which are moist and sweet, encased in a fine brittle crust. If you don't like a thick catfish steak (in our opinion, the best way to savor the luscious taste of the great Dixie fish), you can have thinner and crunchier fillets. And if you don't like fried fish at all, you can choose Pickwick's marvelous cured and smoked catfish. Marinated in brine, then hung over slow-smoking hickory sawdust, smoked catfish is a rich, peppery delicacy so treasured by Pickwick fans that the Knussmanns, who run the place, regularly ship it all over the country.

Catfish is our Siren song to this eat-place near the Alabama border; but the menu also offers ribs (smoked like the fish, over hickory), fried chicken, and u-peel-'em spiced boiled shrimp. As for side dishes, the hush puppies are crisp and faintly oniony, there are slaw and slices of sweet raw onion, and French fries, too.

Pickwick has been in the catfish business for more than a quarter-century. The restaurant is casual and friendly, and catfish dinners are served as an all-you-can-eat proposition. Please note the limited hours: Thursday through Sunday, starting at 5 P.M. In the winter, the dining area is warmed by a potbellied stove. In the summer, ice tea abets the air-conditioning to fight the heat.

Pope's Café

120 East Side Square   931-684-7933
Shelbyville, TN   BL | $

Even from the outside, Pope's Café looks just right: an ancient place (since 1945) on the square in Shelbyville, with a sign lettered on the storefront window boasting of Tennessee ham. The inside is well weathered, its yellow walls lined with red coat hooks front to back. There are six tables on the right, each topped with glass under which are hundreds of business cards from patrons, and a long counter with stools to the left.

Jukeboxes are arrayed every few seats along the counter and at each table, and the last time we stopped in, the waitress kept feeding quarters into the machine and playing the loveliest country tunes.

The one problem we have with Pope's is that we never can decide whether to plan our travels so we come for breakfast or lunch. Breakfast is classic: salty, chewy, resonantly flavorful ham with (or sandwiched inside) buttery tender biscuits. If such ham is too powerful, try Pope's good sausage, or even gentler (and more succulent), there are tenderloin patties that are made to slip inside one of these good biscuits.

If you come for late breakfast, look back into the kitchen and you'll see lunch being prepared. Ladies at big, steamy pots and skillets are seasoning and stirring such regionally flavored vegetables as fried apples, buttered corn niblets, spinach and eggs, spiced peaches, even—for heaven's sake—baked spaghetti. These, among a list of at least a dozen every day, accompany main courses of roast pork, roast beef, country-style steak (that's like chicken-fried), ham, or pork barbecue.

Then there's pie. Fabulous, homemade, only-in-the-Southland pie, including baby-food-gentle chess pie, fudge pie, meringues of all kinds, pecan pie, and a Pope's specialty named after a gaited Walking Horse named Charlie Pride. (Shelbyville is the Walking Horse Capital of the World.) Charlie Pride pie is a kind of mud pie—all dark and fudgy, but with cream cheese and Cool Whip heaped inside and a mountain of chocolate pudding on the top.

(In June 2004 Hazel the waitress told us that Pope's Café is for sale, but she guaranteed that if it did sell, it would stay the same. "Otherwise," she said, "It wouldn't be Pope's!")

The Rendezvous

52 S. Second St.	901-523-2746
Memphis, TN	D	$$

Overnight delivery: 1-888-HOGS FLY

Other than to visit Elvis World, barbecue is the best reason to spend time in Memphis; and Charlie Vergos's Rendezvous, across from the Peabody Hotel, should be high on any hit list. And yet, technically speaking, Vergos's ribs are not barbecue! They are charcoal-broiled and infused with the flavor of smoke, but instead of being bathed in sauce, which is the more traditional Memphis way, they are dry. Dry, but not drab. *Defi-*

nitely not drab. Indeed, these are some of the most flavorful ribs you will eat anywhere. Instead of sauce, the meaty bones arrive at the table encased in a crusty blanket of spice in which they have been cooked. The spice accentuates the sweetness of the pork and also seems to contain and concentrate its succulence. These ribs are ultra-lean yet drippingly moist, unbelievably tender, and flavorful beyond description.

Unique ribs put Vergos's on the good-eats map, but the kitchen's more traditional pork shoulder is well worth eating, too, as is the charcoal-cooked chicken. And to go with the beer you must drink before (as well as during) any meal, there are wonderful plates of sausage and cheese as hors d'oeuvres. Sound like a lot of food? Eating large is part of the Rendezvous experience; of all the restaurants in town, we nominate this one as the worst to visit on a diet.

As for ambience, the Rendezvous reminds us of a cross between an old southern speakeasy and a beer hall in *The Student Prince*. It is a rollicking, semi-subterranean place decorated with antique bric-à-brac and thousands of business cards left behind by decades of happy customers.

Ridgewood Barbecue

900 Elizabethton Hwy. (Old 19E)   423-538-7543
Bluff City, TN   LD | $$

Although the founder of the Ridgewood and its guiding light, Grace Proffitt, has passed away, the magnificent barbecue parlor she created in 1948 is in the good hands of her son Terry. After sitting down to pork platters as recently as mid-2004, we can say without hesitation that the Ridgewood remains, in our book, one of America's elite pits, a truly great restaurant.

If it is your first time, you will most likely get lost looking for it. Old 19E, now replaced by a four-lane, is a twisty little road that, coming from the south, takes you past such fascinating scenery as a church-pew padding store, weathered homes with La-Z-Boy recliners on their front porches, really ancient pre-plumbing log houses with apparently working outhouses, and, on our last trip, a man in overalls actually working his farm field with a hand-pushed tiller.

We arrived at the Ridgewood at 4 P.M. on a weekday, and it was already crowded. We dread to imagine what it's like on a weekend night at peak mealtimes, for despite its remote location, it is a magnet for barbecue fans from Bristol and beyond. We were lucky and got seated in one of the really choice booths adjacent to the open kitchen in the old dining room. From here, the view is magnificent. You see the cooks assembling sandwiches and platters. Once a meal is plated and ready to be sent to the table, it is set on a holding counter just inches from your booth, separated only by a short glass partition. If you arrive hungry and are waiting for your food to be delivered, this sight—and its accompanying aromas—is tantalizing beyond description.

Beef is available, but the meat to eat hereabouts is pork—hickory-cooked in the pit near the restaurant (what a sweet aroma it puts into the air!), then sliced into fairly thin pieces that are, when ordered, heated up on a grill and cosseted in the Ridgewood's very tangy, dark red sauce. A pork platter is a heap of this variegated meat—some soft pieces, some chewy—under a pile of delicious dark gold French fries, fresh from the kettle. Preceding the platter, you get a big bowl of crisp, cool, sweet cole slaw surrounded by crackers; and we also recommend a crock of beans. They are soft, laced with meat, and have a fetching smoke flavor. Sandwiches are huge, with pork spilling out all sides of the extra-large buns, which are also loaded with cole slaw. You can eat a sandwich with your hands, barely, but it is a multi-napkin task.

We recently received a note from an avid Roadfooder who proposed replacing the Mason-Dixon line with the unsweet-sweet tea line, since pre-sweetened tea is nearly ubiquitous in the Deep South, but virtually unheard-of in the North. If such a line exists, the Ridgewood in northeasternmost Tennessee might be precisely on the border. When you order tea, the waitress will ask if you want it sweet or unsweet.

Rotier's

2413 Elliston Place   615-327-9892
Nashville, TN   LD | $

Just as some people's lifelong quest is for the greatest fried chicken, best bowl of chili, or perfect piece of apple pie, many devoted red-meat-eaters are forever looking for the most delicious hamburger. High on the list of those in the running for the blue ribbon is a cheeseburger at Rotier's. Mama Rotier, who established this burger as one of the top contenders, is gone; but her progeny continue to make some spectacular beef patties that are quite unlike any others, anywhere.

A Rotier's hamburger, served on French bread, is monumental. Piled in with lettuce, tomato, pickle, and mustard (and preferably crowned with a slab of bright orange cheese, too), the rugged-textured meat patty is stuck inside its two tiles of bread with a long toothpick. It is a beautiful sight; and once the toothpick is removed, the diner faces a significant challenge keeping the sandwich intact as it is lifted from plate to mouth. To go with this hamburger are fresh, crisp French fries.

Although everyone in town knows Rotier's as the hamburger place, it also happens to be one of Nashville's premier hot lunch restaurants; and every day you can choose from a menu of such entrees as pork barbecue, country-fried steak, fried chicken, and meat loaf. On the side you pick two vegetables from a list of southern classics: black-eyed peas, turnip greens, fried okra, baked squash casserole, crowder peas, white beans, etc., etc. Or, it is possible to get a plate of nothing but vegetables—an excellent strategy if for some reason you are going meatless. (However, all-vegetable plates are *not* necessarily the ticket for confirmed vegetarians, as many of the green vegetables are cooked with pork for flavor.) With the vegetables come good rolls or warm corn bread; and if you don't want to choose a beer from a list of several dozen, the menu lists chocolate milk, sweet milk, and buttermilk.

Rotier's looks like a bar, and it is: beer-sign decor, dark wood-paneled walls, cozy back-room booths suitable for private rendezvous. Ambience notwithstanding, this is a restaurant that attracts families, well-dressed white-haired ladies, polite couples on dates, and just about every other sort of person in and around Nashville who appreciates a first-class hamburger.

Satsuma Tea Room

419 Union St.   615-256-0760
Nashville, TN   L | $

Satsuma (named for the orange) was a bastion of honest square meals for most of the twentieth century, since a pair of domestic science teachers founded it in 1918. It closed for about a week in 2001 but by popular demand—quite literally—it reopened and today remains one of the South's premier places to have an old-fashioned ladies' lunch. Don't misunderstand that term "ladies lunch." As many men dine here as women; but the menu and the rituals of service imbue the experience with a measure of grace you'd never find in a men's sandwich shop or tavern.

Captains of industry, politicians, shoppers, and even blue-collar types (who are willing to wash their hands and comb their hair) crowd into the vestibule around eleven every weekday morning, to eat meals that always include fluffy cupcake-shaped rolls and/or corn sticks, and entrees that range from southern fried chicken to American-style Italian spaghetti. We are particularly fond of Satsuma's delightful salads, including a banana salad with sweet poppy seed dressing, a frozen cranberry salad, and a great meal-size chef's salad. Satsuma's dessert repertoire is glorious, including such delights as lemon cake so moist it squishes when you push a fork down into it, sky-high chocolate pie with a hovering meringue cloud and crunchy nut crust, angel food cake with berries and cream, simple boiled custard, chess pie, pecan pie, and always home-made ice cream. Last time we visited, in the spring of 2001, the flavor was vanilla—perfect!—but we have fond memories also of coffee-sherry and eggnog-sherry flavors, both of them pale and creamy.

Dining at Satsuma is a unique experience. Once you are seated, you look over the menu (printed every day), and write your own order on a small pad set upon the table. The waitress, in white uniform and red apron, looks over the list and doesn't even blink if you order six good vegetables and four desserts for two people.

Note: To drink with lunch, we highly recommend Satsuma tea punch, an only-in-the-South, fruity-sweet beverage served in a tall glass that is refilled throughout the meal.

Sunny's Cafeteria

601 Spring St.	423-926-7441
Johnson City, TN	LD Mon-Sat, L only Sun | $

Sunny's is a cute red-trimmed, yellow corner building that serves four-star southern food, cafeteria-style. Its good-size dining room is partitioned into sections where fans spin overhead and music is provided by the local radio station. It is a one-of-a-kind restaurant, an independent; and so, unlike the big-name cafeteria chains (Piccadilly, Morrison's, etc.), the selection of dishes is somewhat limited—only about half a dozen entrees, a dozen vegetables, maybe ten kinds of pie, and five or six different-colored Jell-Os. But we have never chosen anything from this line that was less than exemplary.

Fried chicken breast? Moist and juicy with a brittle, savory crust. Chicken and dumplings? A totally mild food, with big squiggles of dough and significant shreds of meat lacing the creamy sauce, and yet for all its gentleness, it packs full-bore chicken flavor.

As is true of so many southern restaurants, cafeterias in particular, vegetables are stellar. Potatoes, billed as "creamed" rather than mashed, are dense and flavorful. Macaroni and cheese has a buttery richness that, somehow, our homemade mac and cheese never even approaches. The boiled cabbage is sigh-soft, with porky character. Squash casserole, veined with buttered bread crumbs, is as creamy-rich as dessert. There are sweet candied apples and vigorously green collard greens and crusty corn muffins for mopping up juices.

The Jell-O selection ranges from pure Crayola crayon colors to deluxe creations that include multihued layers of Jell-O and cream cheese dotted with nuts. Although the meringue pies are lovely, we can never resist the baby-food-for-adults dessert, banana pudding, made here to perfection.

"Y'all doin' all right?" asks the man at the end of the line as he tallies up our meal. Seldom do we feel as all right as when we sit down to a tray of Sunny's fine food.

Swett's

2725 Clifton Ave.   615-329-4418
Nashville, TN   LD | $

Note: Swett's has a second location inside the Farmer's Market at 900 Eighth Ave. North (615-329-418). Open for lunch.

Off the beaten path near Fisk University, Swett's is a brick edifice that looks fairly plain from the outside but serves meals that are anything but plain. Call it soul food or meat-and-three or southern comfort, lunch at Swett's is a regional paradigm of such deeply flavorful entrees as baked chicken, chicken fried steak, fried fish, and pork chops, sided by a mall constellation of two or three superb vegetables. These can include porky-flavored turnip greens, baked squash casserole loaded with buttery bread crumbs, black-eyed peas, and macaroni and cheese that is the quintessential chewy-creamy casserole. (Yes, in most of the South, mac and cheese is a vegetable.)

Desserts are deep Dixie: sweet-potato pie, warm blackberry or peach cobbler, lemon icebox pie that is the perfect exclamation point to a meal on a hot summer's day.

Swett's has been around many years and is the sort of place that locals tend to take for granted. If you are visiting Nashville and want a true taste of local food, we suggest you put it at the top of your eating agenda.

Sylvan Park

4502 Murphy Rd.   615-292-9275
Nashville, TN   LD | $

There is no way a modern restaurateur could create a place like Sylvan Park. This landmark of Nashville culinary life developed over time. Its character—weathered, worn, easygoing, and predictable—is the result of many years of high-standard food service in low-key surroundings.

How low-key? Just look up at the ceiling, its plaster cracked and uneven, or at the age-fogged plastic covers on the blue oilcloth tablecloths, or at the creaky oscillating fan near the cash register, its noise drowned by the rattling hum of the ever-present air-conditioning system. Sylvan Park is a single, small, square dining room with rickety tables a bit too close together, staffed by serene men and women who seem to take *everything* in stride, including the inevitable crowds at peak mealtimes. "You liked that chocolate pie?" asks the hefty waiter as he smiles at our emptied plate. When we nod "yes!" he laughs and boasts, "Well, then, I made it!" At the cash register, when we pay our bill, we admire waitress Betty's purple T-shirt, the front of which says, "I'll be back to get you soon. Love, Jesus."

Austere and humble it is, but Sylvan Park's kitchen is charismatic. There is no better place to luxuriate in the echt-Nashville meal known as meat-and-three. (You choose one meat and three suitable side dishes to go with it from a daily list.) The meat choices are fine, including muscular slices of fried Tennessee ham, barbecued chicken, and breaded pork chops; but it is the roster of sides, arrayed on a thick, unbreakable partitioned plate, that makes a meal here unforgettable.

Every day, there are at least a dozen side dishes from which to choose. Many customers forgo an entree in favor of a four-vegetable plate. Sliced tomatoes are flawless; a block of congealed fruit salad (a.k.a. Jell-O) has a jiggle that verges on seductive. Beyond simplicity, Sylvan Park is a fount of vegetable and fruit dishes that are cooked in ways unknown beyond the South. Turnip greens are boiled for hours until limp and heavy with hammy pot likker; mashed turnips pack a zesty pepper punch but are also shockingly sweet—an inspired companion for salty country ham. In a little bowl, a serving of glazed apples is dark brown, wallowing in syrupy essence, the fruits' skin still a little shiny but butter-soft; these apples have been reduced to caramel essence, one step before complete disintegration, and they radiate flavor like just-baked tarte Tatin. On the side of a breaded pork chop, nothing could be more right. Even familiar side dishes have a soulful southern accent: sensuously creamy whipped potatoes, soft-cooked green beans with a delirious pork smack, baked squash with flavor like a sunny summer afternoon, leaf spinach that is impossibly green, candied yams that are, in fact, vegetables turned into candy.

Good bread is as important to the vegetable service as gravy is to roast beef. For dipping and mopping the juices and for serving as uncomplicated punctuation among the assertive flavors, Sylvan Park offers tender little biscuits with great absorbent qualities, as well as tangy corn bread muffins with a rough texture that crumble nicely over a serving of creamy white beans.

Sylvan Park is known also for its pies: chocolate, butterscotch, egg custard, sweet potato. They aren't pretty. Cut to order in the kitchen, a slice often arrives half-fallen-apart on the plate. That's because these pies are very, very delicate, with fragile meringue on top of the creamy ones. A highly recommended alternative to pie, when available: banana pudding. Its flavor is colossal, and it is made the established southern way, with softened vanilla wafers and streaks of meringue throughout the custard.

Wendell Smith's

407 53rd Ave. N   615-383-7114
Nashville, TN   BLD | $

We're intrigued by restaurants that are more than places to eat: the catfish parlor that is also an upholstery shop, the roadhouse that is a used-book shop, the diner with a Laundromat in the back room. We knew we would like Wendell Smith's place in Nashville as soon as someone told us it was known to regular customers as "Booze and Biscuits," because the front of the place is a liquor store and the back is a café where hot biscuits are served with peppery gravy, grits, ham, and eggs.

Good as breakfast is at Wendell Smith's, it's the plate lunches that keep us coming back. Pork chops, hot beef, baked chicken, fried chicken, catfish and hush puppies, or barbecue is accompanied by a vast choice of soulful side dishes listed on the daily mimeographed menu. Turnip greens, mashed turnips, corn bread dressing, mac and cheese, fried corn, squash casserole, etc., etc.: three, four, or five of these profoundly flavored sides compose a wholly satisfying meal, with sweet tea to drink and a big slice of cream pie for dessert.

Featuring a staff of professional waitresses who are delightfully overfamiliar even with newcomers, Wendell Smith's is pure country. It is inexpensive, simple, and delicious, and attracts a diverse clientele of blue- and white-collar locals, as well as savvy travelers looking for a true taste of mid-Tennessee meat-and-three.

Zarzour's

1627 Rossville Rd.   423-266-0424
Chattanooga, TN   L | $

A gray-brick hut across from a junkyard, Zarzour's serves the best plate lunch in Chattanooga. Note that lunch is the *only* meal it serves, and only Monday through Friday. The fifteen-hour-a-week café is a minuscule place that is known for both meat-and-threes and huge, gnarled-crust, juice-dripping hamburgers hand-pattied to order.

When you walk in the door, Chef Shannon Fuller will call out, "Are you having a cheeseburger or dining off the menu today?" The menu is small: a 5 × 7-inch piece of paper with three entrees handwritten every day above a printed list of vegetables. Turnip greens, creamed potatoes, pinto beans, and cole slaw are always available; below them are inked such morning-market specials as butter beans, fresh corn, and black-eyed peas. The murky dark greens are especially delicious: pork-sweet, as tender as long-steamed cabbage, and heavy with tonic pot likker.

Certain meals are immemorial, including roast beef every Friday. We adore the antediluvian dish, baked spaghetti, which is timidly sauced, toothless pasta laced with crumbled beef, chewy shreds of cheese scraped from the edge of the casserole, and a web of hardened noodles on the top. No hot meal is more popular than the every-Wednesday salmon croquettes. "I make twenty-five or thirty plates of them," Shannon says, showing how she forms each one from a mix of salmon, egg, onion, flour, and milk, then pan-fries it so the luxurious pink mash inside is encircled by a good crunch.

It was Charlie Zarzour, great-grandfather of Shannon's husband, Joe, who established the café in 1918, making it Chattanooga's oldest family-run restaurant. At that time, Main Street was the thriving heart of the city and Zarzour's lunch room on Rossville Road was in the thick of it. Charlie had come from Lebanon via Syria, and shortly after opening day his wife died of influenza. He raised five children in the restaurant's back room, which has since become the smoking section. After Prohibition was lifted, Zarzour's was the place to go for hamburgers and beer.

Joe's mother, Shirley—Charlie's granddaughter—took over the café back in the 1950s from her Aunt Rose and Uncle George, and she continues to make the desserts. These include such exemplary Southern-kitchen sweets as lemon icebox pie and banana pudding, and the amazing millionaire pie. That's pineapple chunks, walnut pieces, green grapes, and mandarin orange slices suspended in a mix of frozen Cool Whip and sweetened condensed milk.

Ben's Whole Hog Barbecue

7422 Old Centreville Rd.   703-331-5980
Manassas, VA   LD | $

Less than an hour away from Washington, D.C., here is top-flight mid-South barbecue. That means velvet-soft shreds of pork exquisitely flavored by a long, slow bath in hickory smoke. Basically, this meat is delicious without sauce, but at Ben's you have two choices to dress it up: North Carolina–style sauce, which is a zesty vinegar-based emulsion (which must be requested at the counter), and a thicker, sweeter, mustard-flavored South Carolina–style sauce that is set out on the tables.

Side dishes include fried okra, collard greens, and the true smoke-pit specialty, hash. Hash is a whole-hog "pâté" made from parts of the pig best left unenumerated, served over white rice. Platters are immense, and also include a chunk of sweet corn bread.

Pulled pork is the barbecue meal of choice at Ben's, but the dry-rub, pit-smoked ribs should not be ignored. Also on the menu are chitlins and pig's feet.

Ben's looks the way a barbecue should: a wood cabin in a sort of noman's land, its interior decor consisting mostly of pig pictures and taxidermy. On weekend nights, you can find it not only by the smell of smoke from the pit but by the sound of blues from the bands that regularly play here.

Betty's Ben and Mary's Steak House

6800 James Madison Hwy.   540-347-4100
Warrenton, VA   D | $$

About the name: Betty was an employee of Ben and Mary when they opened their steak house along James Madison Highway about a half-century ago. Ben and Mary retired and sold the place to a third party who ultimately sold it to Betty. Betty was so devoted to the original restaurant concept that she simply added her name in front of the old one. It's a cozy old place, frequented by locals as well as travelers who have staked it out as a serious stop for traveling carnivores.

B's B&M's boasts that it is "Home of the Fabulous Filet Mignon," and while we are admittedly smitten with anyplace claiming to be the home of anything, this declaration carries real weight. The filets mignon served here are big, pillowy rounds of beef that run rivers of juice when severed. Our medium-rare filets were perfectly grilled with velvet-red insides and a nice crust. On the side came good French fries.

The menu is vast, including other kinds of steak, seafood, and chicken cooked on the broiler, but we can't imagine coming to the Home of the Fabulous Filet Mignon and ordering anything else.

Dixie Bones BBQ

13440 Occoquan Rd.   703-492-2205
Woodbridge, VA   LD | $

Roadfood adventurer Laura Key tipped us off to Dixie Bones for its macaroni salad, ice tea (available sweet or unsweet), and hickory-smoked pork. As far as we've tasted, the pork is the best barbecue in the greater D.C. area and an essential Roadfood stop along I-95.

Cooked at least a dozen hours over smoking hickory logs, the meat is velvet-soft and gentle-flavored, served in sandwiches heaped on a platter with such side dishes as Laura's favorite creamy-lush macaroni salad, French fries, baked beans, limp greens, and a terrific item known as muddy spuds. That last item is chopped-up baked potato dressed with barbecue sauce.

Dixie Bones offers three degrees of Carolina-style sauce (all of which are tomato-sweet/vinegar-tangy), the hottest of which is not incendiary. In addition to boneless pork, there are good ribs sold by the rack and half-rack, as well as in a "two-rib sandwich," whole barbecue chickens (falling-apart tender), fried catfish, and hamburgers.

Pies are made here, and we found the apple pie endearingly soulful, i.e., well sweetened and cooked long enough that the pieces of apple inside were as tender as the pork that preceded dessert.

Doumar's

20th St. and Monticello Ave.   757-627-4163
Norfolk, VA   BLD | $

Doumar's has been at the corner of 20th Street and Monticello Avenue in Norfolk since 1934, but it was thirty years before that and in the city of St. Louis that the Doumar name first gained fame. At the World's Fair of 1904, Mr. Doumar introduced a novel way of serving and eating ice cream: the cone. The cone made it possible for fairgoers to walk and eat ice cream at the same time, and without utensils—surely, one of the great ideas in culinary history.

Today's Doumar's of Norfolk is marked by a sign with two big ice cream cones on either side, but it's known also for pork barbecue, hot dogs, excellent burger-and-French-fry plates, and flattened grilled cheese sandwiches. As for ice cream, if you choose not to get a traditional waffle cone (still made in Doumar's kitchen), you can order what is here known as a Reggie (a chocolate milk shake with crushed cone chips), a June Bride (chocolate ice cream topped with strawberry sauce), a Scope (hot fudge atop vanilla ice cream and orange and lime sherbet), or a Kingston Flat (strawberry shortcake with bananas). Milk shakes are superb, served in shapely old-fashioned glasses.

Best of all, Doumar's delivers its classic drive-in fare in the classic drive-in manner—on trays that hang on the window of your car.

Dude's Drive-In

1505 Roanoke St. (Route 11)   540-382-7901
Christiansburg, VA   BLD | $

Dude's is one-half of a small world of car culture along Route 11 at the north end of Christiansburg. Just behind it is the Starlite Drive-In, a theater where you can view movies from the comfort of your front seat. At Dude's the sign says to toot your horn for service; but we have found that within nanoseconds of a car pulling up, a carhop is at the driver's-side window, eager to take an order—no honking required.

The menu is posted on the wall of the tiny restaurant (which has no seating indoors), and it is a pretty long one, including sandwiches of fish, barbecue, and chicken, dinners of fried shrimp and oysters, and a long list of hot dogs from plain to chili-slaw foot-longs. In our experience, the dish to eat is a Dude Burger. A plump patty formed by hand from quality meat that is just fatty enough to be really luscious, the Dude Burger is a deluxe configuration of meat, lettuce, tomato, and mayonnaise on a soft bun. Two Dudes and an order of French fries, with a Dr Pepper on the side, make a drive-in banquet. Those who have an especially demanding appetite for meat can get a double Dude; and of course, cheese Dudes are another option.

Carhop service is available for breakfast, too, but much of Dude's morning business is in the drive-through lane, which is unlike most fast-food windows in that you actually deal with a human being rather than a microphone; but if you are in a hurry, it is a great way to grab breakfast on the go without ever having to shut off your engine or leave the car. The breakfast menu is basically egg sandwiches and sausage sandwiches; the sleeper here is country ham—the real stuff, good and salty.

Mrs. Rowe's Restaurant

74 Rowe Rd. (Exit 222 off I-81)   540-886-1833
Staunton, VA   BLD | $

The restaurant founded by the late Mildred Rowe has expanded dramatically over the decades. At the end of a highway exit ramp, it is often mobbed by travelers, and to a first-time visitor unaware of the dining experience that awaits, it can seem like an assembly-line eatery where customers are processed rather than served. But once you are seated—and more important, once the food starts coming—you realize that while the ambience has changed, the culinary standards remain uncompromising.

For vegetables alone, Mrs. Rowe's restaurant deserves a place in the Roadfood firmament. The mashed potatoes are flawless. Squash casserole, gilded with buttery bread crumbs, is a southern paradigm. Yams have a spicy character that makes their sweetness all the more compelling. Greens are intense and salubrious; baked apples are baby-food soft.

Breadstuffs are the real thing, too. Buttermilk biscuits are plain; but there is hardly anything more delicious at seven in the morning than one of these lovely rounds, hot from the oven . . . unless you prefer the delirious nutty-topped, gooey-centered sweetness of a big sticky bun.

For dinner, unless you are in a hurry, we recommend the extra wait required for pan-fried chicken. It is golden brittle-crisp—a legend here in the Shenandoah Valley. The pork chop platter is succulence incarnate. The meat loaf, the barbecue, T-bone steaks: all, just fine.

And yet, beyond all those things, we must say that dessert is what we think of first when we think of Mrs. Rowe's. Cookies, cakes, sweet buns are all enticing; and the pies are ravishing. They range from cool meringues and fruit-filled double-crusters to hot mince pie with custard rum sauce in the fall. When it is on the menu, we simply cannot resist banana pudding. Semi-crumbled vanilla wafers, slices of banana, and yellow custard are all swirled together and piled into a dish under a cloud of whipped cream.

Southern Kitchen

9576 S. Congress St.   540-740-3514
New Market, VA   BLD | $

A conveniently located town café just minutes from I-81, the Southern Kitchen has remained true to its name for decades. If you want something real to eat, something *real southern,* drive past the fast-food franchised restaurants that cluster near the highway and find a seat in one of the old booths along the wall (beneath a deer head). Here you will find genuine country ham at breakfast and Virginia peanut soup at lunch (although a while back we convinced the waitress to warm up some of the latter for us at 7 A.M.).

The ham is from Turner's Ham House, not far away—whole ones are hanging on a rack near the cash register if you need one—and it is salty but not overwhelmingly so, delightfully chewy, and quite literally packed with flavor. We like it as part of the "Virginia Man's Breakfast," which includes a couple of eggs, home-fried potatoes, toast and jelly, orange juice and coffee. A less complex presentation is simply ham and biscuits—the soft blandness of the biscuits a perfect foil for the assertive cured pig meat. The other notable breakfast food is sausage gravy, a creamy, chock-full-of-sausage-meat potion to ladle on biscuits (or pancakes, as we saw one local gent doing!). Although thick and ridiculously rich, Southern Kitchen sausage gravy is not leaden the way so many others are. It is a pleasure to eat . . . but in very small increments.

Now, as for peanut soup, recent tastings have convinced us that the Southern Kitchen's version is the best—creamy but not too thick, nutty-flavored but not like liquid peanut butter, and laced with a fetching onion sweetness. A little of this goes a long way, too; it is an Old Dominion specialty that is a perfect appetizer before a country ham supper.

By the way, we are thrilled by this café's wine list, which includes the only vintage that we feel is right to accompany creamy peanut soup and/or salty country ham—right because it is sweet enough, even sweeter than sweet tea. That, of course, would be Mogen David blackberry or grape wine. In addition to these, the short list includes vintages from the Shenandoah Valley as well as Bartles & Jaymes wine coolers.

Stone's Cafeteria

1290 Roanoke Rd.   540-382-8970
Christiansburg, VA   BLD | $

Stone's has been in business since Dwight D. Eisenhower was president. It is a three-meal-a-day place featuring a breakfast buffet that includes ham and just-baked biscuits, plus other sorts of pig meat, eggs, pancakes, etc., but what we like best at Stone's is lunch. Here is the place to come for steak and gravy, sweet-tomato-gilded meat loaf and genuine mashed potatoes, or catfish with hush puppies. Some of the memorable side dishes along the short cafeteria line include big logs of soft, sweet yam topped with semi-melted marshmallows, buttery-soft macaroni and cheese, and moist hunks of corn bread.

For dessert, Stone's offers many options, including several colorful Jell-Os, but the only choice for the serious Roadfood explorer is pie. Here are magnificent homemade pies, including coconut cream pie in a fragile crust under a cloud of sugar-sweet meringue. As for the butterscotch pie we sampled on a recent visit, words cannot convey its perfection: light and fluffy, sweet but not sugary, with a faint toasty flavor to the few shreds of coconut that crowned its airy meringue.

Stone's is a small, independent cafeteria on the outskirts of Christiansburg. Now that the Interstate goes past, it is a terrific easy-off, easy-on dining experience for travelers in a hurry. Once you step inside, the speed of the interstate—and indeed much of modern life—feels very far away. A seat in one of Stone's tidy orange-upholstered booths is an opportunity to partake of culinary traditions in which quality is of much more value than speed and efficiency.

Sunrise Café

| 1032 S. Main St. (Route 11) | 540-459-5886 |
| Woodstock, VA | BLD \| $ |

Just around the corner and less than a mile away from the Sunrise Café are most of the fast-food franchises known to highway travelers. So if you want a bland and anonymous meal pretty much like the meal you'd get anywhere in the USA at the end of a highway exit ramp, you can take your pick from among the chicken buckets and assembly-line burgers. If, on the other hand, you want real local food prepared by women and men who know how to cook, served in a colorful little diner on the old high-way, and eaten alongside the local working people, you are in luck. The Sunrise Café is pure Roadfood.

Written on a white board above the pass-through to the kitchen, where you see the cooks at work sizzling ham on a grill and plating veg-etables, are such daily specials as fried catfish (the fillet, not the whole fish) and country-fried chicken with white gravy. Also on that board is the list of daily vegetables—cooked-soft, chopped green kale (served with a pitcher of vinegar on the side to use as a condiment), white beans (with or without chopped onions), buttered corn, and some terrific sweet-potato French fries served under a faint sprinkle of grated sharp cheese.

For our main course, we choose pig—either flavorful pork chops or a firm-bodied ham steak. If you order ham and if you look like a stranger, the waiter will likely suggest the sugar-cured variety. That is a nice pink color, sweet, and tender. The other kind, for serious ham lovers only, is country ham—a brick-red slab of hard-to-cut and tough-chewing pig meat that exudes piggy succulence and radiates salt flavor. For salt (and ham) lovers, it is heaven; but it is powerful stuff, make no mistake about it; and if you do eat this ham, you must be prepared with a quart or so of thirst-quencher in the hours that follow.

The Shenandoah Valley is apple country, and the signature dessert is an apple dumpling, served warm under a scoop of vanilla ice cream. Cooked-soft apple, sweet syrup, brittle crust, and melted ice cream all com-bine to make this one celestial dessert. Although it is modest-looking, the coconut cream pie is a minor masterpiece—sweet and cool, perched on a crust so flaky that it disintegrates on the tongue.

A very humble café with bare tables, crowded booths, and fluorescent lights overhead, the Sunrise is small enough that locals often engage in table-to-table conversations, and when Mike (cook and waiter) is too busy, you'll see regulars refill their own coffee cups and walk out the door after leaving the appropriate amount of money at the cash register for Mike to tally later.

A few words of warning. Despite its name, the Sunrise does not open for breakfast at dawn. Some days, you can't get in until fairly late—9 or 9:30 A.M.—and it closes before 9 P.M. If you do come for supper, especially any time after 6 P.M., we suggest asking your waiter to put aside an apple dumpling. It is not unheard of for all of them to be eaten before the last customer has a chance to order dessert.

Wright's Dairy Rite

346 Greenville Ave.   540-886-0435
Staunton, VA   BLD | $

In 1952, three years before Ray Kroc began franchising McDonald's and more than a decade before the creation of the Big Mac, Wright's Dairy Rite of Staunton started serving Superburgers. Two beef patties with cheese and lettuce, topped with special sauce and layered in a triple-decker bun, this monumental hamburger is still served as it was in 1952—by carhops at the window of your vehicle in a car slip at the side of the restaurant. Wright's added a dining room in 1989, so it is possible to eat inside, where decor includes a handsome Wurlitzer jukebox (with compact discs rather than 45s) and vintage Wright's menus from the 1950s and 1960s; but for us, the joy of this place is in-car dining.

If really, really hungry, forgo the Superburger for a Monsterburger. That is one-half pound of beef barely sandwiched in a bun, available in a basket, with French fries or, better yet, with Wright's homemade onion rings. To drink with this festive heap of food, one needs a shake. At Wright's, milk shakes are the real thing, available in chocolate, strawberry, or vanilla, as well as with real bananas or strawberries, and with or without malted milk for additional richness. While on the subject of dairy products, we should also note that this place knows how to make a fine banana split, a float (a big blob of ice cream set adrift in the soda pop of your choice), and a flurry (candy and/or cookies blended into soft-serve ice cream).

Wright's serves three meals a day, and the menu goes well beyond burgers. There are regular and foot-long hot dogs, pork barbecue on a bun, sandwich baskets with potato chips and a pickle, whole submarines, hearty chili with beans, and even some recently added low-fat wraps. In addition to milk shakes and soda pop, the beverage list includes pre-sweetened ice tea, served in cups that range up to one-quart size.

Blossom Dairy and Soda Fountain Café

904 Quarrier St.   304-345-2233
Charleston, WV   LD | $$

A fantastic art deco setting, a fancy menu, and a folksy waitress are what you'll find at the Blossom Dairy. A 1933 dairy bar that has been polished and restored to gleaming perfection, it is a vast, high-ceilinged room with tables and plush blue-upholstered booths, and a long counter facing vintage mixological tools.

During the day you can come for a late breakfast of coffee and pastries; at lunch there is a wide-ranging menu of sandwiches and salads, including some better-than-lunch-counter hamburgers; and at supper, the tables are covered with soft white linen and butcher paper and the menu is eclectic bistro fare. Beautiful filets mignon are a specialty, well charred and with butter-tender insides, served on a bed of caramelized onions and accompanied by a timbale of black-pepper-and-mushroom-infused potato hash. An appetizer of creamy polenta is described to us by our waitress, and we quote, as "better than S-E-X" . . . and we wouldn't disagree! Other interesting items are seared tuna steak, crawfish étouffée with jerk-seasoned shrimp, and a vegetarian grilled eggplant steak with portobello mushrooms. To accompany these deluxe dishes, you can choose a fine wine . . . or a chocolate milk shake from the soda fountain.

The most interesting aspect of the menu is the build-it-yourself pasta selection. You choose penne, spinach fettuccini, angel hair, linguine, or bowtie noodles, then pick the kind of sauce you want on them: marinara, Alfredo, creamy marinara, herb-infused oil, or Thai barbecue. After making that decision, you can then add any one or several accompaniments to the dish from a long list of such items as artichoke hearts, capers, roast Italian sausage, olives, pine nuts, shrimp, and scallops. We got angel hair pasta with marinara sauce, roasted peppers, and gorgonzola cheese: Mmm-mmm!

For dessert in this awesome sweetshop, we need ice cream (although exotic cheesecakes and pies are also available). The hot fudge sundae, made with creamy fresh ice cream, comes in a tulip glass with fudge spilling over the edge, whipped cream and a cherry on top. A beautiful sight!

Colasessano's

| 506 Pennsylvania Ave. | 304-363-9713 |
| Fairmont, WV | LD \| $ |

The West Virginia pepperoni roll is a simple concept: fold a few pencil-thin twigs of pepperoni inside a tube of yeast dough that is allowed to rise and is then baked. A typical pepperoni roll is a wieldy handful about six inches long, similar in heft to the border of a Neapolitan pizza, a fluffy tunnel of bread with its insides moistened by hot oil seepage from the resilient meat sticks it holds. In the opinion of many West Virginians, the best of all the state's pepperoni rolls are made at Colasessano's in Fairmont.

A former beer joint and dance hall, Colasessano's is now strictly in the business of making pizzas, hot sandwiches on broad homemade buns, and pepperoni rolls. A Colasessano's pepperoni roll is significantly bigger than the typical pocket-size torpedo. Hand-rolled in the back room by one of a team of women who carefully wrap each length of dough around a sheaf of chewy meat, one is a good-size meal. If you wish, you can have the baked bun opened up and the inside piled with tomato sauce, mozzarella cheese, and roasted peppers, thus transforming it into a kind of Italian-bread-based pizza. Located in the blue-collar Belleview neighborhood, the Colasessano family's business has been a popular meeting place for decades; and although there are no tables or chairs in the front room and all foods are sold to go, the old bar still has a footrest that makes for comfy waiting and easy conversation after you place your order with Joe or his mother, Josephine. On the wall is a portrait gallery of beloved family members and admired politicians, including John F. Kennedy, who swung through Fairmont on the presidential campaign trail in 1960. Joe Colasessano likes to remember that Ted Kennedy was about to sample a pepperoni roll that day, but was reminded that it was Friday, and therefore chose meatless pizza instead. So that he could eat lunch in peace, young Ted was ushered into the family's back-room kitchen, a quiet sanctum where, Joe's mother points out, wrestling greats Bruno Sammartino and Dominic DeNucci have both come to enjoy West Virginia pepperoni rolls.

Coleman's Fish Market

2226 Market St.   304-232-8510
Wheeling, WV   LD | $

There are thousands of loyal customers who believe that Coleman's Fish Market makes the best fish sandwich on earth. It is simplicity itself: two pieces of soft white bread holding a cluster of steaming-hot fried-fish fillets. If you want tartar sauce, you have to ask for it, and you pay a dime extra. The sandwich is delivered across a counter, wrapped in wax paper; it is your task to find a table somewhere on the broad floor of the renovated century-old Wheeling Centre Market House, unwrap it, and feast!

The golden crust on the North Atlantic pollock fillets is made of cracker meal, thin as parchment. When you break through it, your sense of smell is tickled by a clean ocean perfume, and as the pearl-white meat releases its warm, luscious sweetness, you taste a brand-new food, like no other fish sandwich ever created.

After you've eaten several dozen over time, you might want to branch out and try some of the many other excellent foods Coleman makes, all delivered over the counter in a bag for toting to a table: Canadian white fish sandwich (a bit blander and "whiter"-tasting than the regular fish), shrimp boats and baskets, fried clams, oysters, deviled crabs, and Cajun-spiced catfish. Coleman's really is a fish market, and if you wait in the "Special Line" (as opposed to the "Regular Sandwich Line"), you can ask the staff to cook up just about any raw fish in the case, and pay for it by weight. On the side of whatever fish you get, there are good French fries or JoJo potatoes (extra-thick French fries), and onion rings every day but Friday (when the deep fryers are totally devoted to making only fish sandwiches).

Coleman's was started by John Coleman in 1914 in the old city market (which itself dates back to 1890). Joe Coleman, grandson of John, keeps things up to date with the latest advances in nutritionally virtuous cooking oils. And the iron pavilion in which the market is located was handsomely renovated about fifteen years ago. In the heart of a muscular city better known for steel and coal than for cooking, Coleman's is a thriving legend of American gastronomy.

Country Club Bakery

1211 Country Club Rd.   304-363-5690
Fairmont, WV   BLD Thurs-Tues | $

Culinarily speaking, West Virginia has a curious character. At its best, it combines the rib-sticking foods of muscular immigrants who came to make steel and mine coal with the niceties of the Old Dominion plantation table, resulting in wondrous meals of stewed chicken and dumplings with spicy hot giardiniera relish on the side or country ham and red-eye gravy with sweet banana peppers.

As far as we can discern, there is but one single dish unique to the state, found mostly between Morgantown and Weston, but at its best in the old Italian-settled communities of Fairmont and Clarksburg. It is the pepperoni roll, a portable, self-contained meal similar to the Cornish pasty, but made of Italian-style dough wrapped and risen and baked around a fistful of pepperoni twigs scarcely bigger than matchsticks. Originally invented at the Country Club Bakery by Giuseppe Agrio in 1927, pepperoni rolls were a favorite food among miners, who could carry them underground without fear of spoilage and eat them with little mess.

Now pepperoni rolls are sold in every grocery store, convenience store, and gas station in the area, and not all of them are good to eat. But some of the best are still made by Country Club in a classic configuration. They are simple, small sandwiches, selling for less than a dollar apiece—a four-inch tube of warm, crusty dough with just enough pepperoni cushioned inside to add fetching zest to the bready wrap. It is not unusual for hungry locals to eat half a dozen rolls as a snack.

Oliverio's Cash and Carry

427 Clark St.   800-296-4959

Clarksburg, WV $

"This was once *the* spot in Clarksburg," says Angela Oliverio as she slides a long length of pig gut onto the spout of her hand-cranked sausage-making machine. "We had everything here in Glen Elk [the Clarksburg neighborhood where her grocery is located]: prostitution, gambling, big business, street-corner business, thriving industry. Now, there's not much left."

But Oliverio's is left! And what a gem it is: a vintage, family-run grocery store where Angela sits in back and with the help of her brother John cranks out lengths of coarse-textured Italian pork sausage seasoned with paprika, fennel seed, and plenty of hot pepper. She also prepares bowls full of peppered green olives that she will sell you by the pint. On the front shelves of the store are wide assortments of roasted peppers and vegetable relishes that Angela's other brother, Frank, makes in his workshop just down the street. Peppers are how Oliverio's has been best known, ever since mama Antoinette Oliverio began canning them in the back of this store in the early 1930s. Some of the choice varieties made by son Frank today include diced hot cherry peppers, a spicy giardiniera (garden mix), and hot peppers in sauce Oliverio.

We need to point out the rather obvious fact that Oliverio's is not a restaurant. It is a little grocery store; and unless Angela takes a liking to you and you happen to be lucky enough to arrive just when she's cooked up a batch of her zesty sausage for tasting purposes, you cannot eat here. But if you love good food, prepared with generations' worth of expertise, and are able to take some home, put this charming little cash-and-carry on your map of West Virginia's culinary treasures.

Ritzy Lunch

456 W. Pike St.   304-622-3600

Clarksburg, WV   LD | $

"A hot dog without chili is not a hot dog!" proclaims John Selario, known in Clarksburg as Hot Dog John. Mr. Selario's parents opened Ritzy Lunch in 1933, and he shows us pictures of his father in front of the same store some time in the 1940s when hot dogs were listed on the window for seven cents each, hamburgers a dime. "Ritzy Lunch has always been known for hot dogs," he tells us. "Clarksburg itself is an important hot dog town, not so much because of the weenies but because of the way we make our chili. There are so many immigrants and sons and daughters of immigrants—Greeks and Italians, mostly—that when we spice up our chili, we know how to do it right!"

Hot Dog John will get no argument from us. His dogs are lovely little pups, buried deep inside a steamed-soft bun and topped with a zesty ground-beef sauce that is gently peppered and earthy-flavored. If you want to add a sweet note, ask for a layer of cole slaw to go atop the chili.

Although hot dogs are the *spécialité de la maison,* you should also consider sampling an unusual kind of hamburger in one of Ritzy's old wooden booths. Listed on the menu as a Giovanni, it is a patty of meat topped with melted cheese and roasted peppers served between two slices of butter-and-garlic-infused toast. Excellent!

Ritzy Lunch is an immensely happy place, a sort of nonalcoholic tavern where old friends and town characters hang out on the ancient counter stools to kibitz back and forth among one another and the waitresses and where, on any pleasant day, two or three wiseacres are likely to be found out on the sidewalk joshing with one another and making friends with newcomers.

Clarksburg has many culinary wonders, including several top notch Italian restaurants and Oliverio's Cash and Carry grocery store (page 211), but no culinary tour is complete without a chili dog and a little conversation at Ritzy Lunch.

Southern Kitchen

53rd and McCorkle Aves.   304-925-3154
Charleston, WV   always open | $

Polly, Joyce, and Peggy are three fine-looking blond sisters who all used to work the dining room of the Southern Kitchen. But now you'll likely meet only Polly and/or Joyce, for Peggy went to truck-driving school and is now out on the road in a big rig. We love these gals, and if you are smitten by pure southern charm, you will love them, too. They worry if you don't eat every little scrap of your (delicious!) country ham with red-eye gravy and cream-textured biscuits; they are at your table to fill the coffee cups approximately every three minutes; and they simply glow with the joy they seem to derive from being part of a place as fine as the Southern Kitchen.

For us, this place truly is West Virginia's prime culinary landmark. When we first came across it some twenty-five years ago, it was already a quarter-century old; and in our experience, it has hardly changed at all. Still run by Delsie Mae Hershman, who opened it in 1947, it is a citadel of honest country cooking that is open round-the-clock every day of the year except Christmas.

No matter what time you come, you will want an apple dumpling. Served warm with or without ice cream, it is a whole cored and peeled apple enveloped in a pastry crust. Its sweet, starchy nature makes it an ideal companion for the savory impact of the excellent country ham.

Of the lunch specials, we recommend stewed chicken with dumplings, fried chicken, and homemade meat loaf with mashed potatoes. And although some consider the apple dumpling dessert, you must also get a piece of pie, for the pies here are legendary. In particular, you want peanut butter pie. It sets the world standard.

A word or two about decor: It is wild, crazy, over-the-top chicken mania, with Ms. Hershman's collection of chicken figurines occupying every available inch of shelf space, and larger busts and bas-reliefs of hens and roosters everywhere throughout the small, comfortable dining room. From the ceiling hang wire baskets filled with eggs, and at the front door, a tin chicken is posted to welcome newcomers.

Zien's Restaurant

105 Edgington La.   304-242-9320
Wheeling, WV   LD | $$

Zien's is a square American restaurant where good citizens of Wheeling have been coming for supper since the early 1980s. From the outside it looks like a banquet hall; the interior is a spacious place decorated with photographs of old-time Wheeling and outfitted with base laminate tables. The dining room is patrolled by a staff of uniformed waitresses who take good care of strangers as well as the vast number of regular friends and neighbors who make this cheerful place their culinary second home. There is a less formal dining area at the front of the building with booths and even speedier service, but throughout the restaurant, informality is the rule: napkins are paper and the tables are set with disposable place mats that feature display advertisements from a local attorney, a transmission specialist, a tattoo artist, and a T-shirt shop.

When you enter, you are faced with a large white chalkboard listing the day's specials as well as a roster of regularly available items. Choices range from a kingly grilled one-pound ribeye steak that arrives at the table still sizzling on its metal plate to a humble dish of beef and macaroni noodles with spaghetti sauce ("When I was growing up my mother called it goulash," our waitress advised). Baked whitefish leads the menu, and it is a beautiful hunk of fish—moist and mild-flavored, thick enough to fall into glistening forkfuls at the slightest prodding. If you're not from around here, you might wonder about "city chicken." The man at the cash register explained to us that city chicken used to be a mixture of veal and pork, but now that veal is so costly, the traditional mock chicken is always made only from pork . . . but only the finest cuts.

We could not resist ordering the item listed on the menu with these exact words: "Pierogies (made by Ukrainian ladies)." Whoever they are, the Ukrainian ladies do an extraordinarily good job, for these pierogi, available filled with seasoned mashed potatoes or with sauerkraut, have a motherly tenderness. You can get them plain (no butter sauce) or smothered with limp grilled onions. Another good dish with a Slovak accent is *golumbki,* a.k.a. cabbage rolls, presented in a gentle tomato sauce.

Of all the homemade desserts, which include a variety of pies and cakes each day, our personal favorite is one that somehow perfectly tops off a meal in this honest, old-fashioned restaurant: fruited Jell-O. It is bright red, firm enough to jiggle with real conviction, and crowned with pure white whipped topping.

Deep South

Alabama * Arkansas * Florida * Georgia *

Louisiana * Mississippi * South Carolina

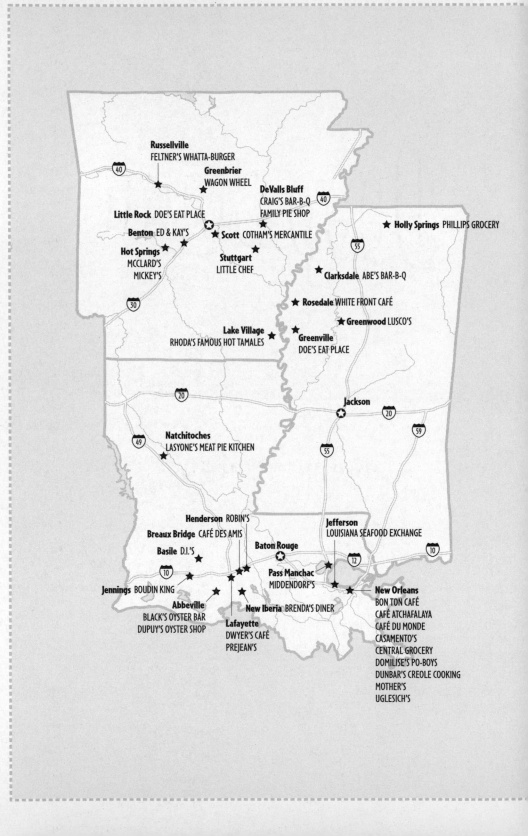

Russellville
FELTNER'S WHATTA-BURGER

Greenbrier
WAGON WHEEL

DeValls Bluff
CRAIG'S BAR-B-Q
FAMILY PIE SHOP

Little Rock DOE'S EAT PLACE

Benton ED & KAY'S

Scott COTHAM'S MERCANTILE

Hot Springs
MCCLARD'S
MICKEY'S

Stuttgart
LITTLE CHEF

★ **Holly Springs** PHILLIPS GROCERY

Clarksdale ABE'S BAR-B-Q

★ **Rosedale** WHITE FRONT CAFÉ

★ **Greenwood** LUSCO'S

Lake Village
RHODA'S FAMOUS HOT TAMALES

Greenville
DOE'S EAT PLACE

Jackson

Natchitoches
LASYONE'S MEAT PIE KITCHEN

Henderson ROBIN'S

Breaux Bridge CAFÉ DES AMIS

Baton Rouge

Jefferson
LOUISIANA SEAFOOD EXCHANGE

Basile D.I.'S

Pass Manchac
MIDDENDORF'S

Jennings BOUDIN KING

Abbeville
BLACK'S OYSTER BAR
DUPUY'S OYSTER SHOP

New Iberia BRENDA'S DINER

Lafayette
DWYER'S CAFÉ
PREJEAN'S

New Orleans
BON TON CAFÉ
CAFÉ ATCHAFALAYA
CAFÉ DU MONDE
CASAMENTO'S
CENTRAL GROCERY
DOMILISE'S PO-BOYS
DUNBAR'S CREOLE COOKING
MOTHER'S
UGLESICH'S

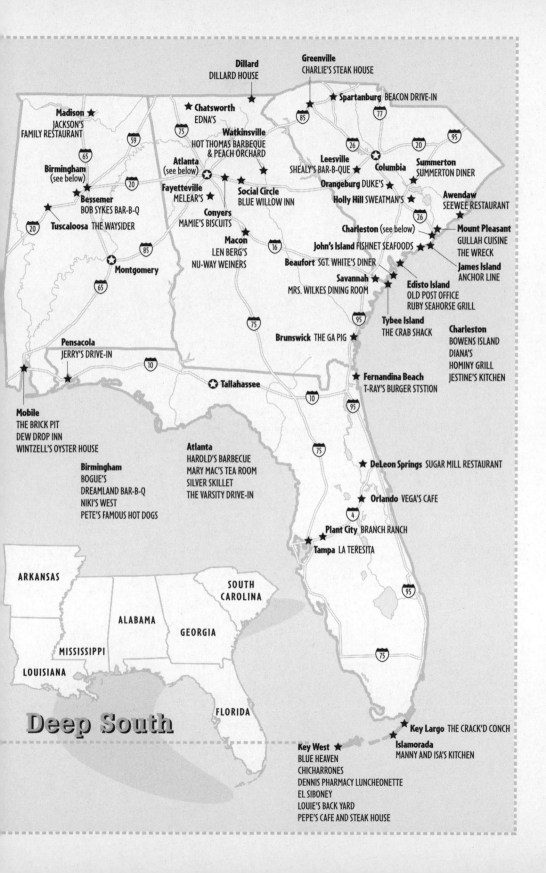

Dillard
DILLARD HOUSE

Greenville
CHARLIE'S STEAK HOUSE

★ Spartanburg BEACON DRIVE-IN

★ Chatsworth
EDNA'S

Madison ★
JACKSON'S
FAMILY RESTAURANT

Watkinsville
HOT THOMAS BARBEQUE
& PEACH ORCHARD

Leesville
SHEALY'S BAR-B-QUE

Columbia

Summerton
SUMMERTON DINER

Birmingham
(see below)

Atlanta
(see below)

Orangeburg DUKE'S

Bessemer
BOB SYKES BAR-B-Q

Fayetteville
MELEAR'S

Social Circle
BLUE WILLOW INN

Holly Hill SWEATMAN'S

Awendaw
SEEWEE RESTAURANT

Tuscaloosa THE WAYSIDER

Conyers
MAMIE'S BISCUITS

Charleston (see below)

Mount Pleasant
GULLAH CUISINE
THE WRECK

Macon
LEN BERG'S
NU-WAY WEINERS

John's Island FISHNET SEAFOODS

James Island
ANCHOR LINE

Montgomery

Beaufort SGT. WHITE'S DINER

Savannah
MRS. WILKES DINING ROOM

Edisto Island
OLD POST OFFICE
RUBY SEAHORSE GRILL

Tybee Island
THE CRAB SHACK

Charleston
BOWENS ISLAND
DIANA'S
HOMINY GRILL
JESTINE'S KITCHEN

Pensacola
JERRY'S DRIVE-IN

Brunswick THE GA PIG

★ Tallahassee

★ Fernandina Beach
T-RAY'S BURGER STSTION

Mobile
THE BRICK PIT
DEW DROP INN
WINTZELL'S OYSTER HOUSE

Atlanta
HAROLD'S BARBECUE
MARY MAC'S TEA ROOM
SILVER SKILLET
THE VARSITY DRIVE-IN

★ DeLeon Springs SUGAR MILL RESTAURANT

Birmingham
BOGUE'S
DREAMLAND BAR-B-Q
NIKI'S WEST
PETE'S FAMOUS HOT DOGS

★ Orlando VEGA'S CAFE

Plant City BRANCH RANCH

Tampa LA TERESITA

ARKANSAS

SOUTH
CAROLINA

ALABAMA

GEORGIA

MISSISSIPPI

LOUISIANA

FLORIDA

Deep South

Key Largo THE CRACK'D CONCH

Key West ★
BLUE HEAVEN
CHICHARRONES
DENNIS PHARMACY LUNCHEONETTE
EL SIBONEY
LOUIE'S BACK YARD
PEPE'S CAFE AND STEAK HOUSE

Islamorada
MANNY AND ISA'S KITCHEN

Bob Sykes Bar-B-Q

1724 9th Ave.   1-800-44SYKES
Bessemer, AL   LD | $

Cooked over slow-smoldering hickory wood, Bob Sykes's pork is finely chopped and succulent; ribs are hefty; chopped beef is particularly flavorful. "Big Bob" dinner plates include your barbecued meat of choice with baked beans, cole slaw, and French fries, plus rolls and a salad. For those with a lot of hungry mouths to feed, there are extra-large orders that range from the Working Mom Special (a pound of barbecue and all the fixin's) to the really big feed suitable for twenty-five people: six pounds of barbecue, a gallon of baked beans, buns, potato salad, and two gallons of tea. Carry-out orders are sold at a drive-through window that the menu advises is ideal for "church functions . . . hunting trips . . . tired mothers . . . unexpected guests."

Pies (whole or mini) are excellent, sold by the slice. You can get chocolate, pecan, and coconut, but the one that must be sampled is the meringue-topped lemon pie: sweet, creamy, and Southern to its soul.

Bogue's

3028 Clairmont Ave.   205-254-9780
Birmingham, AL   BL | $

Looking for an epicurean breakfast? For gracious service with a smile? For the trendiest restaurant in town? If you answer *yes* to any of the above questions, avoid Bogue's! In this city hash house, you can expect plebeian food served by wiseass waitresses to a clientele who have been coming to eat the same meal for decades.

Generally, that meal ought to include biscuits. Bogue's breakfast biscuits are richly endowed with enough cooking grease that your fingers will glisten after you split one in half, and the bottom gets as crusty-brown as a deep-fried potato. These biscuits make great companions to breakfasts in which eggs are only minor players on plates of pork chops or country ham or just a huge spill of pepper gravy and, of course, lots of grits.

If for some reason you don't want biscuits, we highly recommend the sweet rolls. "Are they made here?" we ask our waitress.

"Every morning," she reassures us, speaking loud enough to be heard over the blast of Bogue's high-powered air-conditioning and, without being asked, bringing us Tabasco sauce for a plate of eggs.

No, the pea green walls and upholstered booths are not exactly glamorous; but to connoisseurs of stick-to-the-ribs cuisine and of the no-nonsense waitresses who serve it, Bogue's is a gem in the rough.

The Brick Pit

5456 Old Shell Rd.   251-343-0001
Mobile, AL   LD | $

Legendary Texas pitmaster Sonny Bryan once explained the secrets of his delicious meats: "smoke and time." There is plenty of both involved in the barbecue of The Brick Pit, where Bill Armbrecht has built a room-size cooker into which he piles hickory and pecan logs and smokes meats at the lowest possible temperature for the longest possible time. Pork shoulder sizzles for some thirty hours; ribs for twelve; chicken for six. During the slow process, the meats' natural fat becomes their basting juices; and by the time they are done, each piece of pork and chicken is virtually fatless, yet moister than moist.

Brick Pit pork shoulder is what we like best, pulled from the cooked roast by hand. It is presented as a pile of motley chunks and shreds—some as soft as warm butter, others with crunchy crust from the outside of the roast. The meat is accented by a substantial film of house-made sauce that is thick and tomato-based, with laid-back character that does not distract from the fineness of the smoky meat. Ribs are blackened on the outside but extravagantly tender, with many areas so gentled by the smoke pit that the lightest finger pressure causes pieces of their meat to slide off the bone.

The low-slung dining room at The Brick Pit is painted white and completely covered in signatures, tributes, and other assorted happy graffiti. Orders are taken at a back window; once you've told them what you want, you find a seat and in no time, a waitress brings the meal in a partitioned plate that holds the meat of choice separate from the beans and cole slaw that come with it.

When most smokehouse devotees think of barbecue in Alabama, their thoughts turn to Birmingham and such legendary eateries as Dreamland. Birmingham is indeed a significant barbecue nexus, but we have a hard time disputing the sign above the breezeway that leads to the Brick Pit parking lot: "Welcome to the Best Damn Smoked Bar-B-Que in the Great State of Alabama."

Dew Drop Inn

1808 Old Shell Rd.   251-473-7872
Mobile, AL   LD | $

The Dew Drop Inn is one of several restaurants in the Deep South that takes credit for having been the inspiration for a Jimmy Buffett song. Buffett is a Mobile native, and when he was growing up, the Dew Drop Inn was *the* place in town to go for cheeseburgers, and is thus, perhaps, the original source of "Cheeseburgers in Paradise."

Now Mobile's oldest restaurant (since 1924), the Dew Drop Inn remains the city's premier source of cheeseburgers. But it is even better known for hot dogs. Dew Drop dogs are legendary, so beloved by natives that the waitresses here tell tales of former Mobilians now living in Memphis, Louisville, and even farther North who return like exiles to a beloved homeland so they can weep for joy over plates of Dew Drop dogs. The hot dogs themselves are merely bright red steamed franks of medium size, but the presentation is awesome—in toasted buns, topped with cool sauerkraut, a moist layer of sweet beefy chili, mustard, ketchup, and a pickle slice. A minority of hot dog connoisseurs order them "upside down" (the dog sits atop the condiments) and it is also possible to get them "shaved" (without kraut). The same unusual chili can be used as a topping for Dew Drop cheeseburgers.

Hot dogs and hamburgers are the main reasons to come to the Dew Drop Inn, but there is a whole large menu of po-boys, gumbo, Gulf shrimp, and hot dinners accompanied by such good vegetables as turnip greens and rice and gravy. Coca-Cola is served the true-South way, in its shapely classic bottle alongside a glass full of ice. Banana pudding is the choice dessert.

The setting is cool and comfy, a wood-paneled roadhouse of laminate tables with little flower arrangements in Coke bottles on partitions between booths. Service is speedy; checks are delivered with meals.

(Note to aficionados of old-time pharmacies: Across the road from the Dew Drop Inn, Nixon Drugs is one of the few remaining compounding pharmacies in the South. Mr. Nixon is a mortar-and-pestle man who regaled us with tales of adding such flavors as tutti-frutti and sarsaparilla to medications so that children—or, on occasion, sick pets—would gladly ingest them.)

Dreamland Bar-B-Q

1427 14th Ave. S	205-933-2133
Birmingham, AL	LD | $

The original Dreamland is at 5535 15th Ave. E in Tuscaloosa (205-758-8135); there is a third at 33104 Old Shell Rd. in Mobile (334-479-9898).

No slaw, no beans, no potato salad at this minimalist rib shack with wooden booths and sports-bar decor: just pork ribs with white bread to sop the mess, beer or soft drinks on the side. The ribs are available as a sandwich, a half-slab, or a whole slab, and that is all the choice you get. (The Mobile branch has added baked beans, slaw, and potato salad to the menu.)

Cooked over hickory coals, the ribs are meaty, moist, and crusted with sauce; and to Dreamland's many devotees, it is the sauce that's stellar: tangy, not too sweet, vigorously spiced and yet gentle on the tongue. Quarts of it, as well as slabs of ribs, are available via mail order at 1-800-752-0544.

Although the original Dreamland in Tuscaloosa has become a great shrine of southern barbecue since John Bishop founded it in 1958, we have had a special fondness for the Birmingham branch since it opened in 1993. In a residential area near the university, it can be a little hard to find unless you know to look for its perpetual smoke signal, a great, aromatic haze of smoldering wood and sizzling pork that perfumes the neighborhood for blocks around.

Jackson's Family Restaurant

234 Lime Quarry Rd.   256-772-0191

Madison, AL   BL | $

Halfway between Huntsville and Decatur, the small town of Madison is home to a great small-town restaurant. What a pleasure it is to ease into a Naugahyde booth and open up a menu to find a piece of paper clipped inside that lists all the various elements from which you can choose your fundamental southern plate lunch of meat-and-three. That means one meat and three vegetables from a choice that might include, among the former, country-fried steak or barbecue, and among the latter, fried okra, vinegar slaw, greens, beans, and hush puppies.

The star of the show is catfish, which is crusted with a fine, crumbly cornmeal coat and fried whole, meaning it is the customer's task to pull succulent hunks of flavorful meat from the bones (mighty easy with catfish). You get two catfish per order, the obligatory sides being hush puppies, cole slaw, and French fries. To drink: Coke or ice tea. And for dessert, you'll want a slice of pie that is baked locally for the café, preferably either pecan or apple.

Meat-and-three is a ritual of lunchtime; but Jackson's is also a terrific place for an early morning breakfast of country ham and biscuits. On weekends, it is open for dinner and the menu expands to include grilled (not country-fried) steak and slow-baked potatoes.

Martin's

1796 Carter Hill Rd.   334-265-1767

Montgomery, AL   LD | $

Oh, such biscuits begin supper at Martin's! Warm, flaky-crusted with gossamer insides, they would be insulted by the use of butter. There's fine corn bread, too, in the form of soft-textured muffins, also warm.

The dinner menu at Martin's is good-size, including such main-course choices as whole fried catfish, stuffed deviled crabs, and fried chicken livers. At lunch, choice is limited to daily specials: catfish fillets, smoked sausage, country-fried steak, chicken and dumplings. At either meal, you can count on a roster of side dishes that epitomize the southern way with vegetables: velvet-soft-cooked cabbage, pot-likker-sopped collard greens, pole beans, buttery mashed potatoes, plus, of course, Jell-O salad in rainbow hues.

Of all the things to eat at Martin's, the one essential, at lunch or supper, is fried chicken. Fried chicken has been the main reason Montgomery citizens have favored Martin's since 1931. Its crisp gold crust has a nice jolt of spice, it is easy to handle (i.e., grease-free), and it is dripping-moist inside. One serving includes a meaty white breast and a dark meat thigh. With biscuits, mashed potatoes, and greens, it makes a memorable meal . . . followed, of course, by a piece of Martin's coconut meringue pie.

A wood-paneled, colonial-theme restaurant that moved to its current location in a strip mall about ten years ago, Martin's is busier at lunch than at supper; at noon, you will likely wait, and watch, as early-arriving customers devour their plates of irresistible fried chicken with hedonistic gusto.

Niki's West

233 Finley Ave.   205-252-5751
Birmingham, AL   BLD | $

In the Deep South, vegetables are grown nearly year-round; and many of those vegetables are trucked to the produce center in Birmingham, where they are then shipped to destinations all over the country. Niki's West, surrounded by warehouses and loading docks, is where the produce haulers come to eat.

We counted more than three dozen vegetables in the long line—far too many to even contemplate sampling some of each; so prepare yourself to make some hard choices. Among the tasty-looking selection were yellow squash casserole, fried green tomatoes, black-eyed peas, and three different kinds of seasoned greens (turnip, collard, and spinach). The vegetables were guaranteed by one impassioned server behind the line to be "ninety-eight percent fresh, except for some dried peas we use." Some lovely items from the market are austere enough to please even the strictest dieter: unadorned sliced tomatoes, raw vegetable vinaigrette, and baby lima beans. But the truth is that the best of Niki's produce repertoire is prepared according to the more voluptuous southern café tradition. Broccoli is mixed with cheese and rice in a crazy-rich mélange; tomatoes are stewed with sugar and shreds of torn white bread until they become as sweet as cobbler; bright orange yams are infused with sugar; crunchy-fresh okra is sheathed in a deep-fried crust.

The decorative theme at Niki's is the Aegean Sea (fish nets, scenic art of fishing boats, etc.), and when it comes to choosing an entree, we recommend baked fish Creole, broiled mackerel, and grilled amberjack. For fish-frowners, there is always a selection of beef and pork as well as baked Greek chicken that is terrific.

Our only disappointment was dessert. In so many southern cafeterias, desserts are really big: cobblers, puddings, pies, cakes. Niki's has all of them, but only the pleasant banana pudding stirred our passion.

Although truckers favor Niki's, it is no truck stop. In fact, Niki's does not quite fit any genre of restaurant. It is a low-slung banquet hall with a sign in its vestibule warning customers: "No Tank Tops, No Bare Feet, No Rollers on Head." If you can live with such rules, you enter a cool, commodious space alongside whole families, blue-collar and white-collar workers, bargain-hunters, and big eaters from all over town who come to wind their way through the fast-moving line piling trays with plates and bowls of great southern food.

Pete's Famous Hot Dogs

1925 2nd Ave. N   205-252-2905
Birmingham, AL   LD | $

A true hole-in-the-wall downtown hot dog shop scarcely bigger than a modest-size SUV, Pete's Famous has been dishing out cheap eats since 1915. We first learned about it only a couple of years ago thanks to a Roadfooder who goes by the handle "The Don." The Don described Pete's hot dogs as "the absolute best in the land, perfectly grilled every time, always on a fresh steamed bun." He said that Pete's hot dogs (now made by a gent named Gus) are "so good I have to hit myself in the head with a brick to stop eating them."

We can relate. Pete's hot dogs are addictive. They are modest-size, loaded into soft steamed buns, and almost always served "all the way" with onions, sauerkraut, and chili sauce, as well as a shot of mustard. Cheese adds a whole other wonderful level of taste to the combo and is highly recommended.

Other than hot dogs and hamburgers, there is nothing else on Pete's menu, not even French fries. If you need something on the side, bags of chips are available; and the beverages of choice are Coca-Cola and a curiously tangy grape-flavored bubbly bug juice known as Grapico. Expect to dine standing up.

The Waysider

| 1512 Greensboro Ave. | 205-345-8239 |
| Tuscaloosa, AL | BL \| $ |

Alabama's great breakfast house for some forty years now, The Waysider is the place to go for four-star country ham with red-eye gravy and dainty-size, fluff-centered, crisp-topped biscuits and, of course, grits on the side. With the biscuits comes honey, a nice complement; the triple-whammy flavor combo of salty ham, creamy biscuit, and sweet honey makes a taste experience that is, for us, as close to heaven as earthly food ever gets.

Another fine way to eat pork is streak o' lean, served with brown gravy and biscuits. It is a dish Elvis loved: bacon-lover's bacon. You get four pieces of it on a plate, each about a quarter-inch thick, fried crisp. The word "luscious" does not do justice to the overwhelmingly rich quality of this pork, streaks of which are chewy but most of which just melts away on your tongue.

Waysider lunch is good café fare: fried chicken or steak with slews of such satisfying Southern vegetables as fried okra, field peas, collard greens, squash souffle, candied yams, and fried corn. Warm fruit cobbler and cream pies top things off with a super-sweet exclamation mark.

Wintzell's Oyster House

| 605 Dauphin St. | 251-432-4605 |
| Mobile, AL | LD \| $$ |

Wintzell's is goofy but great. A Mobile institution since Oliver Wintzell opened it as a six-stool oyster bar in 1938, it has survived hurricanes and floods, rebuilt, and expanded into a modern, comfortable seafood restaurant. It still has an oyster bar where you can sit and knock 'em back by the dozen; and it continues to keep score in the ongoing contest to see who can eat the most raw oysters in one hour. (Last we looked, the champ was Heather Andrews, who swallowed twenty-one-and-a-half dozen in 1997.) Its walls are plastered with thousands of little signs offering *bons mots* and politically incorrect rules of life put there by the late Mr. Wintzell, starting in the 1950s. For example: "When a wife looks high and low for her husband at a party, she usually finds him high." *Bits of Wit and Wisdom (The Signs at Wintzell's Oyster House)* and *Oysters and Politics,* Mr. Wintzell's self-published books, are available for sale at the cash register.

Aside from impeccable, opened-as-you-watch raw oysters and the vintage bar-room charm, Wintzell's is a worthy place for sampling many of the dishes that define Gulf Coast cookery: seafood gumbo and crisp-fried crab claws, oyster po-boys, and crusty-fried catfish, and a definitive version of the unique Mobile specialty, West Indies salad. No one knows how West Indies salad became such a favorite city dish, but it's one every visitor must try: nothing but hunks of crabmeat marinated in oil and vinegar with grated onions. It is simple, rich, and sweet—so addictive that many customers forgo it as an appetizer (its usual role) and get a couple of large orders for their main course, accompanied by nothing but saltine crackers.

Cotham's Mercantile

5301 Highway 161 S   501-961-9284

Scott, AR   L | $

Highway 161 southeast of Little Rock shoots through the Grand Prairie that is a mix of level rice fields and opulent roadside pecan groves, but with no apparent place to eat. In the dot-on-a-map town of Scott, past a low-slung barn built for drying cotton seeds, you'll find a riverside building on pilings over water in which cypress trees droop and ducks paddle. Built in 1917, Cotham's Mercantile has been a general store, a jail, and a military commissary. It is now a plate-lunch landmark.

Cotham's is fronted by a broad porch and a swinging door into a dining room packed with vintage household bric-a-brac. Bare wood tables are surrounded by people plowing into catfish, fried chicken, or chicken-fried steak with corn fritters, greens, and fried tomatoes. Big appetites order a Hubcap Hamburger, which is a circle of cooked ground beef that is the breadth of a '49 Fleetwood wheel cover and about a half-inch thick. It comes in a bun that nearly fits, dressed with a salad's worth of mustard, lettuce, tomato slices, pickles, and hoops of onion. Incredibly, it is possible to lift it with two hands from plate to mouth. This outlandish specialty has earned such renown that the store's pushpin map of the United States has no room left for any more pins to show where customers have come from; business cards from visitors around the globe are tacked up all around it.

Craig's Bar-B-Q

Route 70   870-998-2616
DeValls Bluff, AR   LD | $

Craig's is a one-room barbecue parlor with a handful of tables scattered inside and a lot of take-out business from barbecue connoisseurs who prefer to dine in the front seats of their pickup trucks. "Humble" isn't a humble-enough word to describe its physical presence, and yet it is an exalted culinary temple in a state where barbecue is virtually worshipped. In addition to the good ol' boys who dine wearing worn farm overalls, Craig's clientele includes a broad array of preachers, politicians, and Roadfood pilgrims.

The meat to eat is pork, torn into shreds and served on a soft bun with cole slaw, accompanied by silk-smooth beans. The pork has a gentle smoke flavor, but what puts this sandwich into the culinary stratosphere is Craig's taste-bud-boggling sauce, available mild, medium, or *very* hot. It is red-orange, slightly sweet, and so good that you really appreciate the wonderfully absorbent qualities of the bun that sponges up so much of the good stuff and morphs from drab white bread into soulful eats.

Doe's Eat Place

1023 W. Markham St.   501-376-1195
Little Rock, AR   LD | $$

First, we need to say that Doe's is not in the nicest neighborhood you'll ever visit. When we parked on the street for our first supper in this Little Rock version of the quirky Mississippi original (page 278), it was night and we had seen a few unpleasant characters on the prowl, so we hesitated before getting out of the car and sprinting the, oh, maybe five yards from vehicle to restaurant. Apparently the management saw us through the window and sent out an escort; when we were ready to leave, we were walked to the car by the same formidable gentleman. Our next visit was at lunch; the streets were populated by decent-looking citizens as well as several politicians, and the location didn't look nearly as scary.

Second, we must say that inside, Doe's is not pretty. The floor is worn, tables wobble, and the dishware is flea-market quality.

Why do we recommend visiting a restaurant that is a dump, outside and in? For the steak. Great, high-flavored, tender steak, char-grilled to perfection, has made Doe's a meat-eater's Mecca favored by all sorts of people who like to eat large, from the former president of the United States who discovered it while Arkansas's governor, to travelers in search of a taste thrill. Take your pick from among porterhouses, T-bones, and sirloins, sold by the pound in whatever size you crave, and get a pile of French fries on the side. Meat and potatoes get no better than this! On return visits, we have eaten tamales, tamales topped with chili, fried catfish, sweet tomato gumbo, and spaghetti, all of which are very good; but it's for the meat we'd send any serious Roadfood adventurer to this joint.

Ed & Kay's

15228 I-30	501-315-3663
Benton, AR	BLD | $

In a state where pie is a passion, Ed & Kay's is renowned for some of the best. The meringues are especially impressive, their tops a perfect volcano shape that is two or three times the height of the filling itself. Of course there are chocolate cream, coconut cream, and lemon meringue. Our personal favorite from this phylum is peanut butter cream. But neither should one ignore the non-meringue pies. Pecan is masterful, and the one known as PCP—pineapple, coconut, and pecan—is the ultimate.

Beyond dazzling dessert, Ed & Kay's belongs on the Roadfood honor roll for its plate lunch. There are only a couple of hot entrees any day, but the list of side dishes is awesome. Like many good books, it starts slowly, gets more exciting toward the middle, and has a satisfying conclusion. Here is how it read the day we stopped in:

Jell-O
Apple Sauce
Green Salad
Cottage Cheese
Cole Slaw
Skillet-Fried Potatoes

Buttered Spinach
Macaroni and Cheese
Pinto Beans
Green Beans
Purple Hull Peas
Creamed Corn

We didn't try them all, but we certainly can recommend the luxurious skillet-fried potatoes, buttered spinach, and creamed corn . . . as well as the excellent onion rings that you can order alongside a hamburger. Our entree of the day was a stuffed pepper, and it was fine, but next time we come, we'll likely forgo any entree and get a four-vegetable plate for $5.

Family Pie Shop

Highway 70 West   870-998-2279
DeValls Bluff, AR   Weds-Sat 9-5 (but call ahead to make sure) | $

Mary Thomas's culinary career began at Craig's Bar-B-Q (page 229), but in 1977 she moved across the road and opened her own place, the Family Pie Shop. Since finding it on one of our first Roadfood trips way back then, it has remained a country pie benchmark. Mary's hours have shortened and her menu isn't quite as broad every day, but the pies she does make, when she makes them, are superior.

One thing sure hasn't changed: the rudimentary facilities. The shop is nothing but a cinder-block garage hidden from easy view, and dining facilities, so to speak, are limited to four stools at a short counter in a disheveled storage room next to the kitchen. Most people get whole pies or small ones for two to eat in the car or at home. Mike Huckabee sends staff members to DeValls Bluff to bring his favorite, chocolate cream, and his wife's favorite, coconut, back to the governor's mansion. Mary tells us that when Bill Clinton lived there he stopped in all the time and ate pie at the counter with his friends and family. He didn't have a favorite. "He liked them all!" she confides.

We love Mary's simple sugar cream pie and her luxurious "Karo nut," a.k.a. pecan, and the sweet-potato pie is ideal. But filling almost doesn't matter; crust lifts these heavenward. Honey-brown, ready to flake with slight pressure from a plastic fork, it is as fine as a Viennese strudel. The crust's savor is amplified in Mary's version of the Arkansas favorite, fried pie—apple, peach, or apricot filling inside a crescent of pastry dough that is deep-fried until brittle. "Lard! That is the secret," we proclaim as we crunch into a hot fried pie at the counter.

Mary shakes her head. "I will not speak of crust." She does allow that there is no lard in it, but she is mum about details of the recipe, a legacy from her husband, who was a Mississippi riverboat cook.

(Note: Mary lists her hours as Wednesday to Saturday, 9 A.M. to 5 P.M. But sometimes she closes up to go shopping or do errands. Call ahead to make sure she's open.)

Feltner's Whatta-Burger

1410 N. Arkansas   479-968-1410
Russellville, AR   LD | $

Feltner's serves the best hamburger in Arkansas. There are Whatta-Burger shops throughout the Southwest, but none like this one, known for its "custom-made hamburgers," gorgeous French fries, and milk shakes too thick to suck up a straw and served in cardboard containers that are more like buckets than cups.

In addition to spectacularly big and good meals, Feltner's offers the kick of an only-in-America fast-food experience. The instant you enter the low-slung brick building, an eager order taker virtually accosts you at the door to find out what you want. You tell him the precise details of your order—from a simple Whatta-burger (that's a quarter-pound patty on a five-inch bun) to a Whatta-burger with double meat and double cheese). Then you snake through a short line where you have a view of the most bustling kitchen imaginable: a dozen green-uniformed enthusiasts flipping burgers, frying fries, drawing shakes, and bagging meals with the joy of kids putting on a musical at a summer theater.

At the end of the line, you pay and receive your meal on a tray in a white bag, beverage on the side. Find a booth in the big dining room, where the walls are lined with humorous and inspirational homilies: "We guarantee fast service no matter how long it takes"; "The hurrier I go, the behinder I get"; "Cherish yesterday, dream tomorrow, live today." When we visited, a sign warned customers, "We'll be closing Monday at 5 P.M. for our annual employee swimming party." Feltner's is *the* town burger joint, a favorite for families, teens on dates, and Arkansas Tech students. We shared the dining room with a happy stampede of approximately three dozen fresh-faced six-footers attending basketball camp at the college, each of whom carried a tray with a brace of double-doubles (double meat, double cheese) and a heap of French fries.

Little Chef

1103 E. Michigan   870-673-7372

Stuttgart, AR   BLD | $

The Little Chef is a Quonset hut in the Rice and Duck Capital of the World. It looks stark from the parking lot, but inside, it's cozy small-town café all the way. The dining room is decorated in antique memorabilia, and cakes of the day are appealingly set out on the counter. We arrived mid-morning to find a large table up front occupied by locals having their coffee break, some just sipping from their mugs, others plowing into eggs and biscuits topped with sausage gravy.

Jane had breakfast—pancakes and country ham—and Michael ordered lunch. The pancakes are elegant, thin and tender, served with regular corn syrup as well as butter pecan syrup. Alas, the plate-lunch special of fried chicken wasn't quite ready yet, so lunch was a four-vegetable plate: macaroni and cheese in a buttery sauce, rice topped with white cream gravy, ultra-porky brown beans, and a serving of oh-so-Southern five-cup salad made with equal parts mini marshmallows, pineapple chunks, Mandarin orange segments, coconut, and sour cream. On the side came a block of rich, buttermilky corn bread.

When we saw the banana pudding set out on the counter, we knew we needed some. It is balmy custard and banana slices interleaved with plenty of vanilla wafers, some still firm, others softened into streaks of vanilla grain in the pudding. And who could resist hummingbird cake, apparently named because hummingbirds like sweet things: spice cake chockablock with bananas and pineapple and spread with a thick layer of cream cheese frosting.

McClard's

505 Albert Pike   501-624-1247 or 623-9665

Hot Springs, AR   LD | $$

McClard's started serving barbecued goat in 1928, using a sauce recipe that a tenant at the McClards' trailer camp traded to the proprietors in lieu of rent. Now located in a 1942 stucco building that once offered carhop service, it is the best-known barbecue parlor in Arkansas.

Crowded, boisterous, and perfumed by the intoxicating aroma of smoked meats, McClard's is home to hordes of eaters who crowd the booths to work their way through plates of beef and pork (no more goat!) sided by cole slaw, French fries, and hot tamales. The pork ribs, crusted with eye-opening red sauce, are good enough to put McClard's in the upmost echelon of America's barbecue parlors.

Many regular customers get their ribs on a "rib and fry" plate, which is a rack of meaty bones completely covered over with a serving of French fried potatoes. Eating such a meal is an inevitably messy task, requiring nimble fingers and plenty of napkins, for utensils are useless; but the process of picking up a few fries every time you tear off a rib soon becomes an art unto itself; and the savor of the moist, sweet meat close to the bone is simply beyond description.

A whole section of McClard's menu is devoted to tamale plates, ranging from plain tamales with beans to a full spread. A spread is McClard's term for a pair of tamales topped with sauce-sopped chopped smoked meat, beans, crisp Fritos, raw onions, and shredded orange cheese. Spreads are addictive, reminding us of the locally favored Fritos pie, but with the added zest of genuine pit barbecue.

Mickey's

| 1622 Park Ave. | 501-624-1247 |
| Hot Springs, AR | LD | $ |

In and around Hot Springs, a handful of places serve grand smoked-meat meals where the pork is falling-apart tender and the sauce makes taste buds sing for joy. Mickey's is one of those fine places.

A casual, cafeteria-style eatery with a smoke aroma in the parking area outside, Mickey's has two dining rooms. There are a few seats in the front room that afford a view of the cafeteria line and the beautiful food being carved to order. Here, you get to observe Mickey, a big man who wields carving knife and fork with the skill of a martial artist, as he cuts the meat and assembles plates for salivating customers. For a somewhat more private dining experience, there is an adjoining "Hickory Nut Room," where half a dozen booths provide the comfort of rustic decor that includes napkin holders carved from tree limbs as well as wood paneling branded with scenes of animals that hunters like to see from behind the bead of a shotgun: deer, ducks, pheasants.

In addition to exemplary pork, beef, ham, and sausage, Mickey's deserves its place on the Roadfood honor roll for its side dishes. These include long-cooked bean pots filled with shreds and chunks and chewy debris off the ham roast combined with vivid red sauce and soft beans, as well as a handsome item known as a pit potato. The pit potato bakes nearly as long as the meat cooks, so it has a leathery skin enveloping insides that are soft as cream. It is available as is or, better yet, stuffed with well-sauced pork barbecue.

For dessert there is fried pie, a folded-over, flake-crusted pastry with warm peach or apple filling. "Y'all have enough?" Mickey is fond of asking customers as they tote loaded trays to a table. In this generous place, we can't imagine saying no.

Rhoda's Famous Hot Tamales

714 Saint Mary St.   870-265-3108
Lake Village, AR   BLD | $

Rhoda's is a tiny place that used to be a roadside convenience store. A handful of tables are scattered around the glass-front butcher cases behind which is an open kitchen where Rhoda Adams cooks. The cases are arrayed with pecan and sweet-potato pies and little cupcakes that are the stuff of bake-sale dreams. Rhoda is a cook who has a touch that makes anything taste great. One morning at eight, she prepared bacon and eggs so good that we laughed with joy as we ate them.

Then came her tamales, succulent beyond measure, infused with spice that made our lips tingle until noon. What's her secret? "Chicken," she explains. "I add it to the beef." This is not random parts of chicken, certainly not mild white meat. Rhoda uses only thighs, including skin— "all but the gristle," she jokes—thus imbuing her tamales with the flavor that gives so much soul food its soulfulness, chicken fat.

She learned the recipe from an Oklahoma woman many years ago, but if you ask Rhoda, it isn't the chicken that makes a difference. Blues guitarist Robert Johnson may have gotten his talents in a deal with the devil, but Rhoda Adams knows that her ability to make hot tamales comes from God. She points to the blue T-shirt she is wearing, which says, "When praises goes up, blessings come down."

Wagon Wheel

166 S. Broadview St.   501-679-5009

Greenbrier, AR   BLD | $

The best way to get to Bransom from Little Rock is up Highway 65, and if you pass through Greenbrier while hungry, you're in luck. Although it is a bland-looking roadside café from the outside, you smell that it's different the moment you enter. Pans filled with circular dough bombs are set out near the kitchen to rise, radiating yeasty perfume. We relished breakfast sandwiches of eggs and Petit Jean brand bacon enveloped in high-domed rolls and a bread basket piled with white toast that is rich as cake. And we gazed with awe on angelic meringue pies that are so perfect-looking they really ought to be emblazoned on the state flag. Morning biscuits are served with a choice of good cream gravy or—are you ready?—chocolate gravy. The latter is hard to describe, but in a strange way, it works.

This is the sort of place where it is nearly impossible to remain anonymous. While we were eating, we eavesdropped on a nearby table of regulars sipping coffee and exchanging news, as happens every morning. Apparently, they thought we were a little nutty taking pictures of everything before we ate it, so they designated veteran waitress Lynn Lockie to find out what was wrong with us. We told Lynn that where we're from, Connecticut, we don't see pies like this. Upon finding out our home, one of the guys at the table leaned over with a grin and said, "You do sound Northern!"

"And you sure sound Arkansan," Michael replied.

"No, no, up there, they're *Kansan*," a tablemate interjected with his finger pointed northwest. He does not like any variation of his state's name that isn't pronounced with *saw* at the end.

"Well, then, what do you call yourselves?" Michael asked.

"Razorbacks," he said with a good laugh. "You know about razorbacks in Canada, don't you?"

We didn't bother making the fine point that Canada and Connecticut are different places, which was of little consequence at this moment. Slices of coconut pie had arrived at our table and were demanding compete attention.

Florida

Blue Heaven

729 Thomas St.   305-296-8666
Key West, FL   BLD | $

"You don't have to die to get there" is the motto of Blue Heaven, which is the place that inspired Jimmy Buffett's song "Blue Heaven Rendezvous." For fans of the Key West lifestyle, this off-the-beaten-path eatery in old Bahama Village is truly divine. Its history is, to say the least, colorful: Before it was a restaurant, Blue Heaven was a boxing ring (Ernest Hemingway sparred here), a bordello (the tiny rooms upstairs are now part of an art gallery), a bookmaking parlor, and a cockfighting pit (heroic roosters are buried in a little graveyard behind the dining area).

There are some indoor seats, but the choice place to be is out in the patio under the shady banyan trees, where assorted hens and roosters peck around the tables for fallen crumbs. To call the ambience "laid back" does not begin to describe the air of supreme relaxation that pervades the air. We overheard one irascible patron, harassed by an impertinent chicken underneath his table and displeased by the offhand service, lecture to his wife: "These people get so accustomed to the easy life that they don't realize how low they've sunk, efficiency-wise."

Ah, but pleasure-wise, Blue Heaven has it all figured out! Three meals a day are served, but we like morning best. Pancakes are made from scratch, available with bananas, pecans, or strawberries. The granola is rugged and rich, available with soy milk or cow milk. And a big fruit plate comes with delicious banana bread. Coffee is served in miscellaneous souvenir mugs.

Supper ranges from mildly seasoned gumbo to spicy Jamaican jerk chicken and barbecued shrimp flavored with jerk seasonings. There is always a vegetarian special of the day and, of course, locally caught fish. Banana Heaven dessert is legendary: a Key West version of Brennan's Bananas Foster, made with spiced rum and vanilla bean ice cream on a slice of banana bread.

Expect to wait for a table at lunch and supper, especially on weekends. That is one other reason we like early breakfast best—because seats are usually available. True to its laissez-faire attitude toward life, Blue Heaven takes no reservations.

Branch Ranch

Branch Forbes Exit off I-4   813-752-1957
Plant City, FL   LD | $$

Mary Branch began serving meals to paying guests in the TV room of her family home in 1956. Her makeshift eatery became known to an ever-increasing circle of friends; and as new people crowded in for dinner, Mrs. Branch enlarged her dining room and kitchen. Today the Branch Ranch is still family-owned but has become a vast dining complex that can serve a thousand customers a day. In its reception room, where throngs wait for a precious table, the walls are plastered with calling cards of customers who have come from around the world to partake of the legendary Florida feasts.

The meal begins with a relish tray: pickled beets and bread-and-butter pickles that would do any farm cook proud. Buttermilk biscuits, warm from the oven, are accompanied by orange marmalade and jam made with whole, tender-textured strawberries. Everything is from scratch, the kind of idealized rural food you see wearing blue ribbons at state fairs.

Main courses are country ham, fried chicken, or steak; and they're all just fine. But the best part of a meal is the arrival of the tower of side dishes. The stack of pans is a yard high: candied sweet potatoes, scalloped eggplant, pole beans and white potatoes, baked yellow squash, and dumpling-topped chicken pot pie. These, we repeat, are merely the *side dishes*! And of course there are more biscuits, too.

Serve yourself, family-style; or designate one person at the table to dish out the food, just as dad does at home for Sunday dinner. For dessert, tradition demands peach cobbler or white cake topped with grated coconut. And if you like those pickles or homemade jams, we suggest you buy some to take home with you (or buy some via the Internet at http://www.branchranchdiningroom.com/mailorder.htm). Believe us when we tell you that after you eat relishes here in Plant City, no store-bought ones will ever taste the same again.

Surrounded by farmland, the Branch Ranch remains one of America's great country-style restaurants. Size and popularity have done nothing to diminish its glow.

Chicharrones

1223 White St.	305-292-0160
Key West, FL	LD	$$

For Cuban food in Key West, Chicharrones is a sure thing. It's dark and cool inside, where Latin songs provide background music with a lilting beat that isn't frantic, but gives the room a gentle sense of joy. Tables are arrayed around a semi-open kitchen; menus are heft volumes with spiral binding, each page devoted to a different type of meat.

Picadillo is our choice from the beef page; it is served with black beans and yellow rice and a goodly portion of caramel-sweet cooked plantains. We also savored a cooked-soft pot roast that fairly drips with flavor. Other beef selections include the Cuban favorite, oxtails, as well as *ropa vieja* (spiced shredded beef) and smothered steaks. The seafood page advertises cracked conch, Key West pink shrimp, and a tongue-teasing Jamaican jerk treatment for snapper fillets or shrimp.

We are particularly fond of Chicharrones's sandwich selection, which includes a magnificent Cuban mix of ham, salami, and cheese, in this case also including a layer of moist, high-flavored shredded beef and plenty of mustard, all packed into a broad length of fragile-textured, toasted-crisp Cuban bread. On the simple side of the menu, it is also possible to order cheese bread, which is nothing but American cheese on toasted Cuban bread. It's a comfort-food sandwich that goes great with a couple of cool beers.

The Crack'd Conch

Mile Marker 105, Ocean Side   305-451-0732
Key Largo, FL   LD | $$

Started as a fish camp in the 1930s, The Crack'd Conch remains a seafood shanty without airs, but with a big, brash personality. A white clapboard house trimmed in violet and green with picnic tables on its front porch, a breezy back patio, and a helter-skelter dining room in which wall decor consists of customers' business cards and foreign currency, it is the most casual of restaurants, the type of place that makes travel along the Florida Keys toward the Conch Republic such a dreamy experience.

Fried 'gator, steamed shrimp, and house-smoked chicken are all longtime favorites, and the fried shrimp are startlingly light and crisp-crusted. The house specialty is, of course, conch. Nuggets of sweet, tangy mollusk meat, tender but with mouthwatering tooth resistance, are encased in breading and served in a great, tangled heap. On the side, we like oily fried bananas—a soft, hedonistic tropical food to which there is nothing comparable in the Northeast where we live.

In addition to local seafood, The Crack'd Conch offers ambience that attracts a wide range of clientele from nice little white-haired ladies to clusters of leather-clad bikers, plus carloads of families on their way to or from vacation in America's Caribbean paradise.

Dennis Pharmacy Luncheonette

1229 Simonton St.   305-294-1577
Key West, FL   BL | $

Key West is rich with colorful restaurants as well as deluxe ones that cater to the tourist trade; but if you are in the Conch Republic and want to have lunch elbow-to-elbow with locals, come to Dennis Pharmacy Luncheonette. Here, as in all good pharmacy cafés, the scent of liniment from nearby aisles competes with that of the food; and in this case, the food smells terrific. Early in the morning, the air is perfumed by cups of thick espresso and *café con leche* served with lengths of hot buttered bread. At noon, the menu features the spicy ground beef/olive mix known as picadillo as well as Cuban sandwiches (Dagwood heroes of ham, pork, and cheese). This is one of many places where it is claimed

Jimmy Buffett learned to love cheeseburgers. At the Dennis Pharmacy, it is a lunch-counter classic: simple, tasty, and dignified.

The pharmacy's blond laminate double-horseshoe counter naturally encourages conversation among strangers. "I'm a Conch," boasts one leathery workman, spooning up rice and black beans from his steak platter.

"I'm new to Key West myself," responds the young woman across from him, having a glass of shockingly sweet sangria with her egg salad sandwich.

"You know, I've never seen mountains," the old-timer admits.

"I've never seen any place like this at all!" the woman answers.

The Dennis Pharmacy has special appeal for anyone who enjoys roadside hyperbole. It claims to be "the Southernmost Pharmacy, Luncheonette, and Photo Lab" in the continental United States. Around it in the neighborhood, signs proclaim the southernmost motel, deli, car clinic, hockey club, guest house, and private house; at the alleged southernmost point itself, marked by a 17,000-pound buoy (installed because souvenir hunters kept stealing the little sign), travelers from around the world line up to pose for pictures with the Straits of Florida in the background.

El Siboney

900 Catherine St.	305-296-4184
Key West, FL	LD | $$

When you consider El Siboney is just ninety miles from Cuba itself— closer to Havana than to Miami, you understand why its Cuban food tastes so right. This is the best place we know in Key West to taste grilled garlic chicken, a half-bird with a crisp skin and meat so tender that it slides off the bone when you try to cut it. Plantains on the side are slightly crusty and caramelized around their edges. And *yuca,* a cassava side dish served with roast pork, beans, and rice, is a revelation not quite like any other vegetable. Soft and glistening white hunks, reminiscent of a well-baked potato, but more luscious and substantial, are served in a bath of heavily garlicked oil and garlanded with onion slices.

The Cuban sandwich is a beaut, made on a length of fragile-textured toasted bread that is cut in half at a rakish angle and loaded with ham, roast pork, salami, and cheese with pickles, lettuce, and tomato. Conch chowder is thick with conch meat and provides a great opportunity for dunking shreds of the buttered Cuban bread that comes with every meal. The grandest dish in the house is paella Valenciana for two (call ahead; it takes an hour to prepare), a vast fisherman's stew served with rice, black beans, and plenty of Cuban bread for mopping juices. Dessert choices include Key lime pie, flan, and rice pudding, accompanied, of course, by espresso or *café con leche*.

El Siboney is a clean, pleasant place with red-striped tables topped with easy-wipe plastic and silverware presented in tidy little paper bags. If you don't speak Spanish, the waitresses do their best to help you understand the menu. Ours explained that El Siboney was a Cuban Indian, and that the Indian-themed art on the walls is a tribute to him.

Jerry's Drive-In

2815 E. Cervantes   850-433-9910
Pensacola, FL   BLD | $

Jerry's is not a drive-in. It is a joint, a Formica-counter café with a few tables and booths and help-yourself rolls of paper towels for customers to use as needed. The walls are decorated with college pennants and vintage graffiti going back decades. Jerry's originally opened for business in 1939; and frankly, it doesn't look like it's changed much in the last sixty-plus years.

Jerry's has character to spare . . . but it also has important hamburgers—hamburgers that local newspaper readers voted the best along the Gulf Coast. They are good-size, juicy patties of beef beautifully dressed with lettuce, tomato, chopped onions, mustard, and mayo, served with sweet cole slaw and crisp French fries. Not gourmet burgers, not unusual burgers: just good, satisfying hamburgers . . . in a classic lunch-counter setting.

Although many visitors to the "Redneck Rivieria" know Jerry's as the hamburger place, regulars come for three square meals a day. The breakfast menu features all the usual configurations of eggs and luncheon meat (with grits and/or hash browns), plus an extraordinarily luxurious chicken liver omelet. At lunch, you can have such regional delights as smoked mullet, deviled crab, and broiled grouper, as well as big, plump deep-fried oysters with hush puppies on the side.

La Teresita

3248 W. Columbus Dr.   813-879-4909

Tampa, FL   BL | $$

"Strong enough to make the rooster crow" is how one nearby La Teresita regular narrated the arrival of small cups of inky espresso to our place at La Teresita's counter. It *is* a powerful brew, with enough body to deliver a wallop even when you order it *con leche*. In the morning many customers sit at this counter with their newspaper (in Spanish or English) and drink cups of it *con leche* with lengths of toasted and buttered Cuban bread. It is elegant bread—crisp with fluffy insides—and needs nothing more than butter to attain a certain simple perfection. With coffee, it is a great breakfast.

At lunch, the long tubes of bread become the foundation for Cuban sandwiches, and shorter lengths are served alongside such Latin specialties as *ropa vieja* (spiced shredded beef), *bistec palomilla* (sirloin steak, thinly sliced, pan-fried and served with yellow rice), and the lush pot roast known as *carne asada*. Of course, black beans and white rice and that good bread come alongside the entrees. The food is brought to your place at one of the horseshoe counters (or at a table on the other side of the building) almost instantaneously after you order it. Five or $6 buys a meal that is actually large enough for two healthy appetites.

Louie's Back Yard

700 Waddell Ave.   305-294-1061

Key West, FL   LD | $$

When we visit Key West and think about dinner, we think of more than something to eat. We think of the ocean, of warm breezes, of tropical beverages in a magical place. Those thoughts logically lead us to a table at Louie's Back Yard, where the best seats are located on a multileveled terrace overlooking the Atlantic. Here you dine while pleasure boats sail past and pelicans graze the waves.

In truth, this gracious pink Classic Revival house could serve TV dinner and it would be irresistible on a moonlit night; but it happens to be one of the innovators of Key West cuisine, known for such tropical delights as Bahamian conch chowder with bird-pepper hot sauce, grilled local shrimp with salsa verde, and cracked conch with pepper jelly and ginger daikon slaw.

The Louie's supper forever etched in our book of great culinary memories was a pair of lovely grilled strip steaks glazed with hot chipotle chile sauce, sided by garlic mashed potatoes and red onion corn relish. To top things off, we had fancy coffee and feathery Key lime tarts. It was perfect! But who's to say that our judgment wasn't swayed by the romance of the setting? It was after dark. Soft island breezes made hurricane lamps flicker. Bulbs strung among branches in overhead trees formed a radiant canopy above the patio. The ocean glowed cobalt blue when distant, soundless lightning storms at sea ignited over the horizon.

Manny & Isa's Kitchen

81610 Overseas Hwy., Mile Marker 81.6   305-664-5019
Islamorada, FL   LD (closed Tues) | $

Key lime pie is one of America's most famous regional dishes, offered by dozens of restaurants in the Florida Keys and beyond, but the real thing is hard to find because Key limes are rare. Tahiti limes—the familiar bright green ones sold in every American supermarket—are far more common because they are easier to grow and harvest. Most people agree that Key limes have a more satisfying, profoundly limey flavor, but nearly every restaurant that sells "Key lime" pie is actually selling "Tahiti lime" pie. The counterfeit pies can taste quite all right, but they don't have the poise of the real thing, for which Key lime juice is combined with sweetened condensed milk to produce a pale yellow chiffon that precariously teeters on the line between sweet and tart.

If you want to taste real Key lime pie, head out Highway 1 a couple of hours south of Miami to Islamorada on Upper Matecumbe Key. Here is Manny & Isa's restaurant, which has built a powerful reputation on pies made from genuine Key lime juice. The crust isn't all that interesting—a basic pastry—but the filling is silk-smooth and tantalizing.

Before forking into authentic and original Key lime pie, have a whole meal at Manny & Isa's. The comfortable roadside café specializes in Cuban fare and takes full advantage of Gulf seafood. Feast on conch chowder spiced with herbs from a backyard garden, zesty Cuban picadillo, conch fritters, and stone crab. And be sure to accompany that piece of pie with a cup of strong Cuban coffee: Few elementary combinations of flavors are as satisfying.

Pepe's Café and Steak House

806 Caroline St.   305-294-7192

Key West, FL   BLD | $$

Pepe's is a personality-plus eatery that touts its status as Key West's "eldest" (since 1909). Although it calls itself a steak house, we like breakfast best, especially any omelet that comes sided by a creamy griddle-cooked mashed potato patty and a slab of the sweet bread of the day. Later in the day, Apalachicola Bay oysters by the dozen—raw on the half shell, baked, or roasted—make Pepe's a destination for rapacious appetites. Weekly traditions include a Sunday night barbecue and a full Thanksgiving dinner every Thursday. And who can resist a menu that offers both a blue-collar burger and a white-collar burger? (The former is six ounces, the latter four.)

As attractive as Pepe's food may be, it's the place that's irresistible. The old wood dining room is covered with knickknacks as miscellaneous as the contents of grandma's attic, including pictures of famous people and nobodies, a nude painting, nautical bibelots, and scenes of old Key West. Each varnished booth is outfitted with a shelf that holds about a dozen different hot sauces. Out back is a bar where locals congregate. And to the side on an open patio strewn with mismatched tables, illumination is provided by an array of fixtures that includes a crystal chandelier, green-shaded billiard lamps, and Christmas lights strung among the trees.

Sugar Mill Restaurant

Inside the DeLeon Springs State Recreation Area   386-985-5644

DeLeon Springs, FL   BL | $

At the suggestion of Roadfooder Sue Hawkins, we paid $4 to enter the DeLeon Springs State Recreation Area about an hour north of Orlando, and soon found ourselves cooking pancakes. Talk about serve yourself! At the Sugar Mill Restaurant, open now for forty years in an old mill building in the beautiful area where explorers once sought the Fountain of Youth, visitors sit around a table with a rectangular grill in the center. The staff brings two pitchers of pancake batter—a milled-here, stone-ground, buckwheat-style batter as well as more traditional buttermilk batter—plus whatever mix-ins you feel you need (bananas, blueberries, pecans, apple chunks, peanut butter, chocolate chips, apple sauce are all available for a slight extra cost), and you pour and flip your own! Sausage, bacon, and ham are also available . . . but cooked by professionals in the kitchen.

It's fun to punctuate the process of eating pancakes by cooking them at your own speed, and in your own favorite size; and as far as we could tell, you can keep pouring batter until you bust. At less than $5 per person (plus the park entrance fee), this is one of the bargain breakfasts of the South.

(Pancakes are served from morning until closing time, mid-afternoon. It is also possible to order a sandwich or salad.)

T-Ray's Burger Station

| 202 South 8th St. | 904-261-6310 |
| Fernandina Beach, FL | BL \| $ |

It's easy to drive right past T-Ray's. It looks like every other Exxon station . . . except for the fact that there are a whole lot of cars parked there every day around breakfast and lunch times. That's because inside this ultra-casual eatery are some of the best down-home meals around, at prices that are rock-bottom.

As its name suggests, burgers are the house specialty. They come in two sizes and dressed in many ways. We like the Big T Bacon Burger—extremely juice and full-flavored. For beef-frowners there is a portobello mushroom burger, and there are salads and fried chicken and delicious cheese grits, too. Locals know T-Ray's as the place to get superb chicken and dumplings every Thursday as well as classic banana pudding for dessert every day. And they flock here in the morning for masterful hot-from-the-oven biscuits.

Dine at counter or at one of the mismatched tables. Ray's the guy who does the cooking. His father, Terrell, runs the gas station.

Vega's Café

| 1835 E. Colonial Dr. | 407-898-5196 |
| Orlando, FL | L \| $ |

A quarter-century ago, the place that is now Vega's was a gas station. Today it is the best informal Cuban restaurant in central Florida. For the price of a soulless Happy Meal, you can walk in to this friendly little fast-food shop and not only satisfy your hunger but also uplift your spirit with the joy of real food, cooked by professional cooks.

There are soups and sandwiches of all kinds on the menu, as well as chicken and beef platters, but the one must-eat dish in our book is a Cuban sandwich. Thin slices of sweet ham, moist fresh pork, and Swiss cheese (nearly melting from the warmth of the other ingredients) are combined with dill pickles and mustard in a length of glorious Cuban bread (baked in Tampa and imported daily) that is toasted until fragile-crisp and buttered while still warm so the butter simply becomes part of the fleecy interior. This magic combination of ingredients is simply one of the great sandwiches anywhere. A whole one is a giant meal. A half, with a side of black beans and rice, is a perfect lunch . . . with caramelized flan and a cup of high-octane espresso for dessert.

(Special thanks to Jerry Weeks of Nashville for tipping us off to this fine restaurant that is all too easy to drive right past.)

Blue Willow Inn

294 N. Cherokee Rd.   770-464-2131

Social Circle, GA   LD | $$

The Blue Willow Inn serves Sunday supper twice a day, seven days a week. Located in a grand old mansion in the quiet town of Social Circle, it is the ultimate serve-yourself buffet. Pay one price and eat all of everything you want.

Once you find a seat and get your lemonade, you graze through the buffet room, where the day's food is set out, arrayed on several tables, including one dedicated only to dessert. The vista of things to eat fills us not only with insatiable hunger, but also with high anxiety. There is no way any one person can even taste everything, let along eat satisfying portions of all the food that looks so good. There is just too, too much. With at least four meats and a dozen vegetables on display, not to mention biscuits and corn bread and relishes, you either aim for a tiny bite of everything or you find yourself making hard choices: pass up the macaroni and cheese in favor of skillet squash; ignore corn bread dressing so there is room on the plate for sweet corn casserole. If you crave a feast of baked and smothered pork chops, then you likely won't sample the kitchen's magnificent streak o' lean—thick strips of bacony pork that vary in texture from wickedly crusty to meltaway-lush, blanketed with smooth white gravy. For those of us who travel far to eat at the Blue Willow Inn and can come only rarely, these decisions can be agonizing.

Certain foods are musts: the fried chicken is classic. Fried green tomatoes are exemplary. Collard greens, long-cooked to porky tenderness, are an only-in-the-South joy. Chicken and dumplings, which is served as a soup but is thick as stew, is supremely comforting—alabaster-white, soft, smooth, and aromatic. And, of course, biscuits. Using a recipe from Sema Wilkes's boardinghouse in Savannah (page 256), Louis Van Dyke's kitchen creates tan-crusted domes with fluffy insides and a compelling fresh-from-the-oven aroma. Their tops are faintly knobby because the dough is patted out rather than rolled.

As for dessert, there are pies, cakes, cookies, and pudding; but the one we recommend (assuming you have smidgen of appetite by the end of the meal) is warm fruit cobbler.

The Crab Shack

40 Estill Hammock Rd.   912-786-9857
Tybee Island, GA   LD | $$

It may not be the most romantic come-on in the restaurant world, but what Roadfooder could resist The Crab Shack's catchphrase "Where the Elite Eat In Their Bare Feet"?

Need we say that this is not a formal dining room? Park among heaps of oyster shells and eat off paper plates at picnic tables to the sound of Jimmy Buffett tunes. Toss your shells and refuse into big garbage bins provided. The dockside view of the broad tidal creek is lovely—a true waterside picnic—but even lovelier are the great heaps of sloppy, hands-on seafood that Savannahns come to gobble up with beer and/or frozen margaritas.

The fundamentals include boiled shrimp (served the Low Country way with corn, potatoes, and sausage), steamers by the bucket, raw oysters on the half shell, crawfish in season, and your choice from a list of four kinds of boiled crab: Alaskan, blue, golden, or, when available, stone crab (claws only, of course). In addition to these simple seafoods, The Crab Shack offers deviled crabs, crab stew, and shrimp and crab au gratin. Couples can always opt for a shellfish feast for two: mountains of whatever's in season accompanied by corn, potatoes, and sausage.

There are desserts—turtle cheesecake and Key lime pie—but we cannot tell you how they taste because we have never finished a crab feast at The Crab Shack with any dessert appetite remaining.

Dillard House

Off US 441	706-746-5348
Dillard, GA	BLD	$$

Dillard House is the Disney World of restaurants—it is huge, it is fun, and you'll likely wait in line. Located in the beautiful foothills of the Blue Ridge Mountains, it is a vacation complex that includes a motel, riding stables, and an amazing family-style eatery where large groups of people sit at large tables and help themselves to large bowls of food.

You never know exactly what you'll be served in the Dillard House dining room. The menu, which is written on a blackboard that you can read as you wait for a table, changes as all the pork cutlets are eaten up and country steak takes their place, or as fried okra is erased and replaced with butter beans. It is almost certain that among the three entrees always available there will be fried chicken and country ham. Vegetables, many of which come from the Dillard family garden, are served in abundance, and you will have your choice from among at least half a dozen, including squash soufflé, black-eyed peas, and stupendously rich steamed cabbage. Don't miss the calico salad, a refreshing mix of pickled tomatoes and cucumbers. Also, there are dinner rolls, biscuits, peach cobbler for dessert, and ice tea in Mason jars.

Lunch and dinner are deeply satisfying. Breakfast at Dillard House is awesome. Eggs are a merely minor note in a repertoire that includes sausage, ham with red-eye gravy, bacon, and pork tenderloin, fried potatoes, grits, stewed apples, biscuits with sausage gravy, cinnamon rolls, and blueberry muffins. Like the other meals, it is an all-you-can-eat affair; and it is an excellent opportunity to store up ballast if you plan to spend the day white-water rafting on the nearby Chattooga River.

Edna's

Highway 411 S	706-695-4951
Chatsworth, GA	LD	$

Mobbed at lunch with locals and visitors to Georgia's northern mountains, a little less crowded at supper time, Edna's is a meat-and-three feast. That means that every day there is a short list of entrees and a long list of vegetables, from which you choose one main course and three side dishes. In many meat-and-three restaurants, it is the vegetables that matter, and some customers forget the meat altogether and order a four-vegetable plate for lunch.

At Edna's the all-vegetable strategy would be a big mistake. We don't know about the meat loaf or the country-fried steak, but we love the ham shanks, and we can tell you that the fried chicken is delicious, a fact that becomes apparent if you look around the restaurant and note that probably half the clientele choose it. Edna's logo is a chicken wearing a chef's toque with the proclamation "Our chicken dinners are worth crowing about."

The side-dish list includes not only vegetables such as whipped potatoes, fried potatoes, yam patties, green beans, pole beans, etc., but also mac and cheese and Jell-O salads. And whatever you get, it comes with a corn bread muffin that crumbles very nicely over a heap of cooked greens. For dessert, the star of the show is Edna's peanut butter pie—a grand ode to the Georgia goober.

The GA Pig

Route 17 and I-95 (Exit 29)   912-427-2628
Brunswick, GA   LD | $

On the sign of The GA Pig you see a merry pig playing a fiddle and doing a jig. You, too, will dance for joy when you eat at this oh-so-convenient restaurant just yards from the exit ramp off Interstate 95. The perfume of hickory and sweet meat that laces the air tells you that you are in pork country; and GA Pig pork, slow-cooked over hickory wood, basted with a tongue-teasing red sauce, then hacked into juicy hunks and shreds to be served on a platter or stuffed into a sandwich, is among the best anywhere in the Deep South. There are ribs, too—a joy to gnaw—and on the side, sorghum-sweet barbecue beans.

A fun place to stop, The GA Pig is log-cabin rustic with picnic-table seating and a genuine pine grove set back from the road for al fresco dining. Eating here is a great break from the monotony of highway travel; or if you are really in a hurry, you can get anything to go and pig out as you drive along the highway. However you experience The GA Pig, we guarantee you will find a sweet place for it in your bank of culinary memories.

Harold's Barbecue

171 McDonough Blvd., SE   404-627-9268

Atlanta, GA   LD | $$

One of the South's grand old smoke pits, Harold's has built a half-century reputation on velvet-soft sliced pork, racks of meaty ribs, and bowls of old-fashioned Brunswick stew. Outside, a cheerful pig in sunglasses occupies the sign by the side of the road—a beacon of comfort in an otherwise scary neighborhood near Atlanta's federal prison. Although it is a stark building with bars on every window, Harold's interior has a comforting patina of age and hickory smoke. The wood-paneled walls are hung with earnest religious homilies, including this one above the door to the rear dining room: "God has time to listen if you have time to pray."

Tables are comfortable, but we much prefer seats at the worn counter to the right as you enter. From here you see the wood-fired pit, where just-sliced barbecue is heated over hot coals and white bread for sandwiches is toasted until light brown. It is a mesmerizing sight, unchanged for decades.

Sliced pork is unbelievably tender and fairly glowing with the perfume of wood smoke; pork ribs come as a magnificent rack—ultra-thick, heavily glazed with beguiling sauce, their crusty-lush meat pulling off the bone in messy strips. On the side of any platter comes squares of excellent, gritty-textured corn bread and a small bowl of Brunswick stew loaded with meat, corn, and tomato shreds. A couple of items we've yet to try off Harold's menu, but hope to some day: barbecue salad (green salad topped with pork and sauce) and a stew dog (a hot dog blanketed in Brunswick stew).

Hot Thomas Barbeque & Peach Orchard

3753 Highway 15   706-769-6550

Watkinsville, GA   LD Mon-Sat | $

Hot Thomas used to be only a peach orchard. It's still in the middle of fruit-growing country, and inside the restaurant you can buy jams, chutney, and syrup made from peaches and bearing the Hot Thomas brand.

The main reason for coming to this sun-bleached white building in Watkinsville, outside Athens, is to eat pork. Step up to the counter and order a plate, and while it is being assembled, nab yourself a Coke or Mr. PiBB from the cooler.

Find a seat and fork into delicious hickory-cooked pork, hacked to smithereens with a good measure of "Mr. Brown" (crusty dark meat from the outside) laced among the supple, sweet pieces from the center of the shoulder. Traditional Georgia side dishes to accompany this lovely entree (really, the only one on the menu) include Brunswick stew (a kind of tomato-onion-and-some-other-vegetable mélange with a mild pork flavor), sweet cole slaw, and soft, white bread suitable for dunking in the stew and mopping up hot sauce. The sauce is available mild, hot, and extra hot, that last one packing a breathtaking pepper punch. Like the peach products, sauce is available in bottles to take home.

Len Berg's

240 Old Post Office Alley   478-742-9255
Macon, GA   L | $

A tip of our hats to Roadfooder Anne Peck, who clued us in to Len Berg's, which has been Macon's favorite downtown lunchroom since 1908. If we were to make a list of restaurants that epitomize the glory of café lunch in Dixie, Len Berg's would be at the top—a great place to eat a civilized, inexpensive, and delicious southern meal.

The menu varies daily and as vegetables come in and out of season, but you can count on such meals as fried chicken with steamed cabbage and stewed apples on the side, meat loaf with mashed potatoes and a heap of likker-sopped turnip greens, shrimp Creole on rice with ham hock–flavored snap beans, creamed corn, and bright hunks of high-flavored garden tomato. Every meal comes with warm yeast rolls and corn sticks.

For dessert, the macaroon pie can't be beat, and there is bright, sweet strawberry shortcake; but if you come any time after June 1, there is only one proper way to end a meal—with Len Berg's fresh peach ice cream. Every summer, Macon citizens watch the newspaper for a small advertisement that says simply, "H.M.F.P.I.C. You know where." Translated, that means, "Home Made Fresh Peach Ice Cream . . ." and everyone for miles around who likes to eat does know exactly where.

Please note that the original Len Berg's is open only for lunch. A newer, take-out restaurant with the same good food (but without the vintage charm of the little dining rooms and white-coated waiters) is at 2395 Ingleside Avenue and is open from 11 A.M. to 8 P.M. Monday through Saturday.

Mamie's Biscuits

1294 Main St.   770-922-0131

Conyers, GA   BL | $

"We don't roll them with a rolling pin; we don't cut them with a can; we don't make them from a recipe. I will not allow anyone to cook from a recipe," proprietor Jack Howard says when we ask him to account for the goodness of the biscuits at Mamie's. He lifts a hot one off its paper plate and cups it in one hand, using a deft twist of his other hand to separate its top and raise it like he's a Tiffany jeweler showing what's inside a ring box. A buttermilk-scented cloud of steam wafts up. "This is what you call a 'scratch biscuit,' " he continues. "It is made from nothing but White Lily flour, buttermilk, and lard. *Pure, refined* lard," he emphasizes. "Enough of each goes into a big bowl where your biscuit maker kneads the dough, but not too much. She knows when to pull one off, pat it out, and put it in the pan." Fifteen hundred to two thousand biscuits are made this way six days a week at Mamie's Biscuits of Conyers, from before the doors open at 5:30 A.M. until closing time at 2 P.M.

Any time you order a biscuit at Mamie's, it comes hot from the oven. Its bumpy golden surface has a gentle crunch, and although the inside is fleecy, it is not fragile. This is a bun with enough substance to retain its pliant texture even as it absorbs savory red-eye gravy from the drippings of country ham, juices from a patty of country sausage, or melted butter from a heap of soft-scrambled eggs. It is substantial bedding for an open-face chicken biscuit: a broad piece of boneless, pan-fried chicken laid across a split biscuit and blanketed with gravy made from the juices in the frying skillet. It even holds up as a mitt for streak o' lean, the true pork-lover's breakfast meat, reminiscent of bacon, but chewier, fattier, and rimmed with hard rind.

Mamie's is a breakfast house, but it also serves lunch—a meat-and-three affair built around pork chops or chicken and dressing with a choice from among greens, squash, beans, peas, and potatoes. Even at noon, it's bread that stars: hot biscuits, of course, plus squares of corn bread and deliriously piggy cracklin' corn bread, loaded with melt-away nuggets of crunchy pork.

Mary Mac's Tea Room

224 Ponce de Leon Ave.   404-876-1800
Atlanta, GA   LD | $$

We lifted a fried chicken breast off the plate and bit into it. As the crust crunched, juices spurted everywhere. Full-flavored, inside and out, dark meat or white, this just might be the best fried chicken in the South.

Mary Mac's Tea Room inspires superlatives. Originally opened in 1945, it is an old-fashioned urban lunchroom in the heart of Atlanta that offers a broad menu of dishes that exemplify Dixie cooking at its best. You can start your meal with a bowl of pot likker—that's heaps of soft turnip greens wallowing in their flavorful cooking liquid—sided by a corn bread muffin. Entrees include such classics as baked chicken with cornbread dressing, pork barbecue with Brunswick stew, and country-fried steak with gravy.

The list of side dishes is a joy unto itself; many customers come to eat a four-vegetable plate with no meat at all. Standouts include a sweet-potato soufflé that is spiced Christmas-sweet, macaroni and cheese in which the noodles are suspended in an eggy cheese soufflé, fried green tomatoes, hoppin' John, and crisp-fried okra.

An airy place with soothing pastel yellow walls and tables covered with white oilcloth, Mary Mac's offers old-style tearoom service, which is great fun. When you sit down, you are given an order pad and menus. Once you've made your decisions, you write your own order and hand it to your waiter or waitress who, in the meanwhile, has brought you an immense tankard of what the menu lists as the table wine of the South—sweet tea.

Melear's

Route 85   770-461-7180
Fayetteville, GA   BLD | $

Melear's has been a big name in Georgia barbecue since 1927, when John Melear opened a smokehouse in LaGrange. The Melear's south of Atlanta goes back more than forty years, and is open seven days a week, even for breakfast Monday through Saturday.

Pork is the meat of choice, chopped, mixed with a bit peppery vinegar sauce, and served in a sandwich, on a tray, or as a dish with the irresistible name "bowl of pork." The sandwich is notable because it comes on grilled slices of bread (as opposed to barbecue's usual spongy-white companion slices), adding a nice crunch to the sandwich experience. The same pork, but more of it, is the anchor for a full-bore barbecue dinner that also includes potato chips, pickles, white bread, and smooth-textured, rib-sticking Brunswick stew. Extra-hot sauce is available, and it is good, but Melear's pork has a fine, subtle flavor that we believe is better complemented by the mild version.

To accompany Melear's classic "Q" the proper beverage is ice tea—dazzlingly pre-sweetened, as is the custom in this part of the country, presented in tumblers that are a full foot tall and about half again as wide at the mouth. When you get to the bottom of this tub, it is refilled on the house; and it will continue to be refilled for as long as you are parked in a high-backed chair at one of Melear's aged wood tables eating barbecue.

Mrs. Wilkes Dining Room

107 W. Jones St.   912-232-5997
Savannah, GA   L | $

Lunch at Mrs. Wilkes is one of the great culinary bargains in this land. From your seat at a bountiful table for eight, you reach out and help yourself to fried chicken, oven-hot biscuits, and a panoply of magnificently cooked vegetables that all add up to a good précis of Deep South boardinghouse cuisine. We imagine that when Mrs. Wilkes first started serving meals in this dining room in 1943, there were many similar places in cities throughout the region, where boarders as well as frugal local citizens gathered at the communal tables to enjoy the special pleasure of a meal shared with neighbors and strangers. Now, the take-some-and-pass-the-bowl style of the old boardinghouse is a rarity. Mrs. Sema Wilkes's establishment in the 1870-vintage red-brick building on West Jones Street is a prized opportunity to indulge in the delicious food—and the cordial foodways—of a culinary tradition that values sociability as much as a good macaroni salad.

As ever, there is no garish sign on the late Mrs. Wilkes's restaurant. "It would look so commercial," she once wrote, "not at all like home." Besides, everybody in Savannah knows exactly where it is.

Nu-Way Weiners

428 Cotton Ave.   478-743-1368
Macon, GA   BLD | $

There are ten Nu-Way Weiner shops in central Georgia. The Nu-Way on Cotton Avenue in Macon is the original, established in 1916 by James Mallis and now run by his descendants. It is a shoe box–shaped restaurant with tables and a counter, instantaneous service, and addictive hot dogs.

The dogs are bright red little private-label links. They are grilled and bedded in a steamed-soft bun; and although they are available plain, the glory of Nu-Way is a hot dog "all the way," which means topped with mustard and onions and a fine-grained chili that is sweetened with porky-rich barbecue sauce. One other good topping is cole slaw, which is creamy sweet. Or, you can order a "scrambled dog," which is a splayed-open bun topped with a hot dog and smothered with chili and beans.

Hot dogs have made Nu-Way a beloved culinary landmark in the South, but you'll find plenty of other quick-eats chow on the menu, none of which have ever disappointed us. In fact, we are big fans of the quarter-pound Mega-burger chili melt as well as the chili fries and chili cheese fries. Let's face it: Anything with Nu-Way chili sauce on it is pretty darn good.

Note the extra-chocolaty chocolate milk, and soft drinks served over Nu-Way's famous "flaky ice."

Silver Skillet

200 14th St.   404-874-1388
Atlanta, GA   BL | $

Be sure to go to the bathroom at the Silver Skillet. There's nothing great about the toilet itself, but the route to it leads through the kitchen, where you have an appetizing tour of fine food being created by masters in humble surroundings: onion rings pulled from hot oil, country ham drizzled with powerhouse red-eye gravy, great slabs of meat loaf plated alongside sweet yams and butter-tender cabbage and tangy fried green tomatoes.

The dining room itself, where glass windows rakishly slant outward at the angle of 1950s tailfins, is a blast from the past: green-and-orange

Naugahyde-upholstered booths at boomerang-pattern Formica tables. A sign on the wall advises, "Use a little sugar and stir like hell. We don't mind the noise." Each table is strewn with pencils. As you peruse the written menu and the long list of daily vegetables and specials posted above the counter, a waitress delivers you a couple of checks on which you write your own order.

Whatever else you get, and whether you're here for breakfast or lunch, you must get a slice of lemon icebox pie . . . if one is available. There is one pie per day, but believe us, it is well worth eating lunch at 10 A.M. if that's what it takes to get one. This is one of the five best pies in the nation: profoundly creamy, silk-smooth, and teetering on the precise balance point between sweet and tart.

We love Silver Skillet breakfast. Skillet-cooked ham is the real thing—strong and salty; biscuits are oven-hot; pancakes are plate-wide with a faint crispness at their edges; grits and gravy are pure country. And the people-watching is swell: high and low, rich and poor, the famous, the notorious, and the unknown all make themselves right at home in these old booths.

The Varsity Drive-In

| 61 North Ave. | 404-881-1706 |
| Atlanta, GA | BLD \| $ |

The Varsity is huge and fast, and while no one would mistake it for a four-star, blue-ribbon dining room, it is the epitome of its own style of dining: the Great American Drive-In. Since 1928, chili dogs with all the fixin's have earned this brash restaurant a place in the heart of Atlantans and visitors who appreciate cold Cokes, hot chili, crisp onion rings, and sweet fried pies.

"Gimme a yellow steak, a sideways dog, a ring and two strings," the counterman shouts back to the kitchen, using some of the most cultivated hashslinger slang you'll find anywhere in the USA. Within seconds, out come a hamburger with mustard, a hot dog with onions, an order of onion rings, and two orders of French fries. To say service is fast at The Varsity is an understatement. It is *instantaneous*. The line moves nearly as fast as you can walk, turning out forty-five customers per minute into vast dining rooms (each equipped with its own color TV, each tuned to a different channel).

A few facts from the restaurant press book: Two miles of hot dogs, three hundred gallons of chili, and five thousand fried pies are served every day to approximately ten thousand customers, twice that number when Georgia Tech plays at home. Senator Phil Gramm recalled that when he was at college in Atlanta, the *Journal-Constitution* had a party for its paperboys. The organizer stepped up and ordered *six thousand* steaks to go. Veteran counterman Erby Walker, without missing a beat, shot back, "Whatcha drinkin'?"

Varsity hot dogs are pink tube steaks served in steamy-soft buns, begging to be dolled up with condiments. The prime adornment is chili, a finely pulverized brew that perfectly complements either dog or burger. Chili dogs are best served with a line of mustard across their tops, and they are known among the staff as Yankee dogs, for their yellow streak. The best companion for a dog is a cardboard boat full of crusty onion rings and/or excellent French fries.

To drink with this good grub, there's a full menu of reliable southern favorites: ice-cold buttermilk, gigantic cups full of Coke, PCs, and FOs. PC is Varsity lingo for chocolate milk ("plain chocolate") as opposed to a chocolate milk *shake* (with ice cream). FO means frosted orange, which is the Varsity version of a California smoothie, reminiscent of a Creamsicle-in-a-cup. With or without chili dogs, frosted oranges are one heck of a way to keep cool.

Louisiana

Black's Oyster Bar

319 Père Megret   337-893-4266

Abbeville, LA   LD | $$

Abbeville calls itself the Oyster Capital of Acadian Louisiana. Black's is a good place to prove that claim. A Vermilion River town surrounded by cattle ranches and fields of sugar cane, Abbeville gets oysters every morning from nearby Grand Isle, and when you order a dozen at Black's (or at the venerable Dupuy's, across the street), you receive thirteen just-opened sweeties on the half shell for all of $4.75! The glistening steel-gray meat has a salty zest and ocean punch that makes eating them so elating that it seems a little wicked. Plain off the shell is grand, but of course tables at Black's are set with all kinds of hot sauces to spice them up.

There is a whole menu of hot foods, too: fried shrimp and catfish, stuffed crab, alligator, crawfish (in season), and some magnificent seafood loaves—whole long lengths of bread loaded with fried oysters, shrimp, catfish, or soft-shell crab.

Even if you sit at the bar, oysters are not opened before your eyes. That happens in a small, open area toward the back (where you can go and watch the shucker wield his knife). Up front in the barroom, Cajun music sets the tone, and decor includes neon beer signs and hundreds of pictures of family, friends, and oyster-lovers who have made Black's their destination for indulgence.

Bon Ton Café

401 Magazine St.   504-524-3386
New Orleans, LA   LD | $

Magazine Street was laid out in 1788; the Bon Ton Café is slightly newer, going back about a hundred years. Its menu is old-time Cajun, which means a rustic Louisiana cuisine that is *not* kicked up a notch, not over-spiced or overhyped or blackened or infused, but simply delicious. This is the place to know the joy of crawfish étouffée, an unspeakably luscious meal especially in May, the peak of the season when crawdads are plumpest. You can have étouffée as a main course or as one part of a wonderfully monomaniacal meal of bisque, étouffée, Newburg, jamba-laya, and an omelet, each of which is made with crawfish. Or you can start dinner with an appetizer of fried crawfish tails. They look like little fried shrimp, but taste like shrimp's much richer relatives.

Dinner begins with the delivery of a loaf of hot French bread, tightly wrapped in a white napkin. When the napkin is unfurled, the bread's aroma swirls around the table. Then comes soup—either peppery okra gumbo made with shrimp and crab or turtle soup into which the wait-ress pours a shot of sherry. Other than crawfish in any form, the great entree is redfish Bon Ton, which is a thick fillet sautéed until just faintly crisp, served under a heap of fresh crabmeat and three gigantic fried onion rings. Other exemplary Creole meals include pan-broiled oysters, crabmeat au gratin, and parchment-crusted soft-shell crabs. For dessert, you want bread pudding, which is a dense, warm square of sweetness studded with raisins and drenched with whiskey sauce.

A big, square, brick-walled room with red-checked tablecloths, Bon Ton is soothingly old-fashioned. There is no music, just the sounds of knife, fork, and spoon and happy conversation, interspersed by the oc-casional ringing of the pay phone at the back near the bar. Service, by a staff of uniformed professionals, is gracious and Dixie-sweet. As we pre-pared to take a picture of our redfish, a waitress rushed over and insisted on taking the picture herself so she could include the two of us along with the lovely meal.

Boudin King

906 West Division St.   337-824-6593

Jennings, LA   BLD | $

Yes, the boudin at Boudin King is wonderful—densely packed, spicy, and deeply satisfying. Buy it mild or hot by the link; it is a Cajun classic. But so is just about everything else on the menu of this unlikely source of greatness. We say "unlikely" because Boudin King appears to be a fast-food restaurant, and even includes a drive-through window. Meals are served on disposable plates. Prices are little more than McJunkfood.

And yet here is stupendously good gumbo, smoky-flavored and thick with sausage and big pieces of chicken. And speaking of chicken, we would rate the fried chicken served by Boudin King as some of the most delicious in southern Louisiana, a part of the world where frying chicken is a fine, fine art. Other specialties include crawfish in the spring and nice fried pies for dessert.

The late Ellis Cormier, who founded this place back in the 1970s, once told us, "Nowhere else in America, except perhaps where the Mexicans live, is food properly spiced." Monsieur Cormier was one of the leading lights in America's rediscovery of its regional food, of Cajun food in particular. It was primarily thanks to his good cooking that in 1979 the Louisiana State Legislature proclaimed Jennings "The Boudin Capital of the Universe."

Brenda's Diner

409 W. Pershing   337-367-0868

New Iberia, LA   BLD | $

Brenda's brought tears of joy to our eyes. "It doesn't get better than this," we agreed out loud halfway through lunch of fried chicken, fried pork chops, red beans with sausage, rice and gravy, candied yams, and smothered cabbage. Each dish Brenda Placide had cooked was the best version of itself that we have had since, maybe, forever. The pork chop was audibly juicy with a tender taste that had us gnawing to the bone. The chicken's fragile crust shored in juice-dripping meat. The red beans were New Iberia *hot*; the smothered cabbage, speckled with nuggets of garlicky sausage, brought high honor to the vegetable kingdom.

We ate this soul-stirring food in a tidy little dining room where a CD of Southern gospel music set a rapturous tone. There are seats for no more than twenty people. The neighborhood is run-down, but the diner is immaculate inside. The walls are a gallery of Brenda's gratitude: prints and posters celebrating African-American culture, as well as photos marking the achievements of Brenda's kin (graduations, weddings, reunions).

We had to ask her how she cooks such magnificent food, but we weren't surprised when she had no satisfactory answer. "It's from my mamma's kitchen," she said. "I cannot tell you how to do it because she never taught me to measure anything. You add seasoning and spice until it's right." It occurred to us that even if we studied Brenda as she cooked, taking scrupulous notes about every grain of every ingredient she used, we couldn't in a lifetime make food like this. It would be like watching Isaac Stern play the violin, then trying to copy his every move: something essential would be missing.

Café Atchafalaya

901 Louisiana Ave.   504-891-5271
New Orleans, LA   LD | $$

Café Atchafalaya, an easygoing corner eatery in the Garden District, is a reminder not only that New Orleans has its own distinct cuisine, but that it is also part of the Deep South. When you eat here, you are reminded that vegetables are grown nearly year-round in this part of the world; and they are so much a part of the cuisine that they can be the star of the menu in restaurants that are by no means "vegetarian."

Late one May, we found a table in one of the cozy dining areas toward the back of the restaurant (with a good view of the colorful blackboard on which daily specials are written) and ate a pair of amazing all-vegetable meals. Our table was crowded with small bowls and plates of fried corn fritters, crunchy fried green tomatoes, turnip greens, candied spiced yams, field peas, carrots, black-eyed peas, creamed spinach, mashed potatoes, baked Creole tomato, velvet-smooth butter beans, succotash, and a baked Vidalia onion so soft and sweet that it had nearly become syrup. To season the vegetables, half a dozen sorts of hot sauces and vinegar-soaked peppers adorn each of the café's tables; and all meals are accompanied by baskets of corn bread, both plain and jalapeño-cheese flavored.

Most people enjoy just two or three of these side dishes as companions to such serious entrees as pork chops with andouille and corn bread stuffing and a Jack Daniel's apricot glaze, fried chicken livers with pepper jelly, red beans with rice and sausage, chicken and dumplings, Creole crab cakes, and a full roster of fried seafood.

There is but one dessert to know about, and it is a New Orleans doozy: bread pudding, cooked to the consistency of soft custard, with crusty edges on the top and sides. It is served under a spill of intoxicating cognac sauce.

Café Atchafalaya's motto sums up the attitude—"Slightly sophisticated, rather southern"—but doesn't do justice to exactly how good a meal here can be.

Café des Amis

140 E. Bridge St.   337-332-5273
Breaux Bridge, LA   BLD | $$

A sign in the window of Café des Amis tells visitors they have found "The essence of French Louisiana." That means true Cajun food, a French-accented mix of South and Soul, with a dash of Caribbean spice and Italian brio. But it's ridiculous to try to define it by its roots; better to describe what it is.

At breakfast, it is beignets, little crisp-edged twists of fried dough under an avalanche of powdered sugar. It is "Oreille de Couchon," a long strip of fried dough named because it resembles a pig's ear, available plain or filled with boudin sausage, also spread with powdered sugar. It is biscuits topped with crawfish étouffée, omelets filled with tasso ham, and cheese grits with andouille sausage.

The menu for lunch and supper is a veritable encyclopedia of local favorites, including turtle soup, andouille gumbo, barbecue shrimp, corn bread filled with crawfish tails, soft-shell crab, and crawfish pie. Desserts include bread pudding with rum sauce, which is more of a New Orleans thing than a Cajun one, and *gâteau sirop*, which is extremely local. Made from sugar cane—grown and processed all around here—it is a block of moist spice cake with the distinctive smoky sweetness of cane sugar.

A friendly old brick-wall storefront that has been renovated to serve as an art gallery as well as a restaurant, Café des Amis is a gathering place for locals (who love swilling the excellent strong coffee) and an easy destination for passersby, just a short drive off I-10. If you are looking for a full, true, and joyous taste of Acadian Louisiana, you'll find none more satisfying than this.

Café du Monde

813 Decatur St.   504-581-2914
New Orleans, LA   always open | $

Café du Monde is a New Orleans institution, serving café au lait and beignets to locals and tourists for more than a century and a half. It is always open, and the characters you'll meet here—any time of day, but especially at odd hours in the middle of the night—are among the Crescent City's most colorful.

There are indoor tables, but the best seating is outdoors, where the chances are you will be serenaded by street musicians of the French Quarter as you sit under the awning and watch life go by.

There is not much to the Café du Monde menu: chicory coffee, either black or au lait (with a lot of milk), white or chocolate milk, orange juice, and beignets. Beignets are wonderful: square, holeless donuts, served hot from the fry kettle and heaped with powdered sugar.

After leisurely coffee-sipping and beignet-eating, you can buy all kinds of New Orleans souvenirs inside the restaurant, then stroll across Decatur Street to the place where fortune tellers, tarot card readers, and palmists set up shop every evening and discover your future.

Casamento's

4330 Magazine St.   504-895-9761
New Orleans, LA   LD (closed in summer) | $$

Casamento's is a tile-decorated neighborhood oyster bar that closes for a long vacation every year between June and September, but when it is open, there's hardly any room for customers. Its two small dining rooms have only a few dozen chairs, plus room for a couple of stand-up oyster eaters at the bar. Despite its modest appearance, this is one of New Orleans great restaurants, a place to feast on raw or fried oysters, fish or shrimp, or soft-shell crabs in the spring.

The signature dish is an oyster loaf. It is like a po-boy sandwich—the New Orleans version of a hero—but significantly bulkier. To make an oyster loaf, they fry the oysters so that each hefty one is crackle-crusted. Heaps of these briny-sweet nuggets are loaded into an entire loaf of sideways-sliced white bread, scooped out to become a fried-oyster trough. The bland yeasty quality of the bread is the perfect companion for crunchy, ocean-flavored oysters. One oyster loaf is a feast for two.

Central Grocery

923 Decatur St.   504-523-1620
New Orleans, LA   BLD | $

The Central Grocery is not exactly what it used to be, which was a convenient place to have a sandwich made in the French Quarter of New Orleans. The deli ladies won't make you a roast beef sandwich or a capocollo sandwich anymore, because the only sandwich they make is a muffaletta.

That's okay by us, because this muffaletta—the original muffaletta according to food historians—is a beautiful thing. A circular loaf of soft Italian bread is sliced horizontally and piled with salami, ham, and provolone, which are in turn topped with a wickedly spicy mélange of chopped green and black olives fragrant with anchovies and garlic. The hefty hunk of lunch is quartered and wrapped and sold ready to go . . . or to unwrap immediately and eat along the counters that have been installed at the back of the store. In our opinion, this mighty muffaletta (available as a half sandwich for puny appetites) is as delicious as it's ever been. Yes, other restaurants now make fatter ones on artisan breads with more exotic cold cuts and fancier ingredients in the olive salad, but this big fella has a classic dignity that simply cannot be bettered.

And the store, while a smidgen less quaint than it used to be, is still a fine place to shop. Yes, it is a magnet for tourists who mob the neighborhood, but it remains the same well-weathered, creaky-floored emporium it has been for decades, its grocery shelves a wonderland for all who like pickles, olives, peppers, and spice. What has not changed one bit is Central Grocery's distinct aroma: an irresistibly appetizing perfume of salamis, cheeses, garlic, and oil.

D.I's

Highway 97   337-432-5141
Basile, LA   LD | $$

Big, round, tin beer trays heaped with crawfish emerge from the kitchen trailing hot spiced steam through the dining room as accordion notes with a triangle beat bounce from the bandstand like runaway Superballs. Set back from the two-lane in the middle of nothing but rice fields and crawfish ponds, far from any town or major highway, D.I.'s is a brimful measure of Acadian pleasure. If it hadn't been for Sulphur policeman and good friend Many McNeil, we never, ever would have come across it. When we told Many we were on the lookout for a true Cajun eating experience, he said D.I.'s was it.

Daniel Isaac ("D.I.") Fruge has been known to neighbors for his well-seasoned crawdads since the 1970s. He was a rice and soybean farmer who began harvesting mudbugs, boiling and serving them on weekends to friends and neighbors: $5 for all you could eat. They were served in his barn the traditional way—strewn in heaps across bare tables—with beer to drink on the side.

D.I. and his wife, Sherry, now run a restaurant with a full menu that includes steaks, crabs, oysters, frog legs, flounder, and shrimp, but vividly spiced crawfish are the star attraction. The classic way to enjoy them is boiled and piled onto the beer tray—a messy meal that rewards vigorous tail-pulling and head-sucking. You can have them crisp-fried in to bite-size morsels with a salty crunch, and there is also crawfish pie, étouffée, and bisque.

No longer a makeshift annex to Monsieur Fruge's barn, D.I.'s is a spacious destination with multiple dining rooms and dance floor. The live Cajun music starts at 7 P.M., with an open-mike jam session Wednesday.

Domilise's Po-Boys

5240 Annunciation St.   504-899-9126
New Orleans, LA   L | $

From the outside, Domilise's looks like a small, no-frills neighborhood tavern; and in some ways, that is what it is. It would no doubt be possible to sit at the bar and knock back longnecks or boilermakers all day long. But we don't come to this out-of-the-way corner bar only to drink, and it sure doesn't look like many locals do, either. Midday, the bar may be packed, but it is a most unusual sight indeed, for nearly everyone sitting at it, drinking beer or Coca-Cola, is also eating big, beautiful sandwiches. Domilise's makes some of the best po-boys in New Orleans.

Of special interest are the loaves of bread loaded with fried shrimp or oysters. These shellfish are fried to order behind a stand-up counter near the door, where customers waiting for a place to sit can watch. It is a beautiful thing to see the golden-crusted crustaceans hoisted from the oil, strewn into a pan to drain, then piled into the fleecy bread in such copious numbers that nearly half seem to fall out.

Po-boys are also available made from all manner of cold cuts as well as several hot items, the best of which is hot smoked sausage. Get this one sopped with gravy and ask to have it dressed, meaning decorated with tomato, lettuce, and grainy Creole mustard. Domilise's large po-boys are constructed on loaves of bread so long that they are cut into thirds to fit on their plates. Plates, by the way, are paper.

Seating is precious. In addition to the bar, there are tables scattered about the room, which is supremely crowded during lunch hour. Strangers often share tables for four. In fact, we find the wait just inside the door a good experience, and not only because we can watch the ladies make their handsome sandwiches. It also gives us ample opportunity to study the menu, which is posted on the wall, and decide which of the great po-boys is the right one for us on this particular day.

Dunbar's Creole Cooking

4927 Freret   504-899-0734
New Orleans, LA   BLD | $

Dunbar's is the sort of place that you'd find only in New Orleans; but even in this food-rich city, it's a standout. Creole soul food, expertly prepared, served with grace but with a small price tag: What more does the hungry Roadfooder want? On Friday, the regular specialty is gumbo—a bowl of smoky soup/stew that is spiced to awaken taste buds and olfactory sensors. Every day, you can come to Dunbar's for crusty fried chicken or red beans and rice with or without sausage; and there is always intoxicating bread pudding for dessert.

Our favorite meal at Dunbar's is a shrimp boat, a magnificent rendition of the New Orleans sandwich for which a foot-and-a-half length of French bread is scooped out to resemble a canoe, then heaped with an amazing number of fried shrimp. These are medium-size and perfectly cooked shrimp—hot from the fry kettle, sheathed in brittle batter so thin you can see the firm, pink meat within. For anyone lucky enough to have eaten fried shrimp at the late, lamented Edisto Motel in Charleston, South Carolina, a Dunbar's shrimp boat (or any of the expertly fried seafood) will be a blissful trip down memory lane.

Fine as is the bread pudding, don't ignore Dunbar's cakes when it comes time to think about dessert. They are lunchroom classics—thick slices of coconut cake, heavily frosted, or strawberry cake that veritably glows pink.

Finally, a word of warning to those not familiar with pre-sweetened tea. Dunbar's sweet tea is really, really, really sweet! You can get unsweetened tea, too; or it is possible to order half-and-half, a mixture that, to our non-southern taste buds, tastes just about right.

Dupuy's Oyster Shop

108 South Main St.   337-893-2336
Abbeville, LA   LD (closed Tues) | $$

There's a broad menu at Dupuy's, including sirloin steak, fried catfish, pastas, and wonderful onion rings, plus a bountiful Sunday brunch, but as the full name of the place suggests, oysters are the star attraction. The very best way to have them is raw on the half shell by the dozen, served on a tray of ice with a full complement of condiments. Or, if you like things cooked, have them fried and stuffed into bread with mayonnaise and mustard. In addition, there is oyster stew and an intriguing grilled oyster salad.

The one other dish that is essential to eat at this friendly, always-crowded town café is Cajun seafood gumbo, a boldly spiced stew that you can practically eat with a fork.

When Dupuy's opened in 1869, the price of a dozen just-shucked oysters was a dime. Today, a dozen will cost you no more than $5.

Dwyer's Café

323 Jefferson St.   337-235-9364
Lafayette, LA 70501   BL | $

No one makes lunch sound as good as Mike Dwyer does. You will hear his pitch as you approach the cafeteria area of Dwyer's Café, where he enumerates the day's choices, one by one, with a pride and exuberance to make stomachs growl. It's a joy to hear him, but in fact, this food needs no hard sell. It is a superlative plate lunch.

Parenthetically, Dwyer's hamburgers are excellent. But it's the hot lunches we love. Dwyer's is a meat-and-three affair, and the daily meats including such expertly cooked stalwarts as smothered pork chops, lengths of pork sausage, roast beef with dark gravy, and chicken-fried steak with white gravy. One day in the winter, Mike was pitching craw-fish fettucine, a fabulous cross-cultural Franco-Italian-Cajun noodle casserole loaded with high-flavored crawdads. Among the notable side dishes are dirty rice, eggplant casserole, red beans, and sausage jambalaya. On cold days, you can get gumbo or chili.

Dwyer's is also a breakfast opportunity. We love the tender sweet-potato hot cakes with their faintly crisp edge (which Mike says he added to the menu for low-carb dieters!). When you order pancakes, the waitress will ask what kind of syrup you want: cane or maple. Sugar cane is a major crop around here, and the pancake syrup made from it is thick, dark, and resonantly sweet . . . but not at all white-sugar sweet.

Dwyer's is a Lafayette landmark that goes back to 1927. It was then that Mr. and Mrs. William Stinson first opened a café. Twenty years later, Stanley Dwyer became their head cook, and in 1965, Mr. Dwyer bought the place. Today it is in a new location and Stanley's son Mike runs it. Having been a downtown fixture for so long, it is the place citizens of Lafayette come to meet and greet, especially in the morning. While there is some counter seating, as well as tables for four along the wall, the center of the dining room is arrayed with tables for eight, where friends and strangers share breakfast and cups of locally roasted Community Coffee. In this place, it is customary to get up and help yourself to coffee refills when waitresses are otherwise busy.

Lasyone's Meat Pie Kitchen

622 Second St.   318-352-3353
Natchitoches, LA   BLD | $

Lasyone's meat pie, the renowned specialty of Lasyone's Meat Pie Kitchen, is a mash of pork and beef, onions and parsley, enclosed in a deep-fried half-moon pastry. Like a piquant Cornish pasty, it is practically a meal unto itself. Natchitoches used to have many places to buy meat pies—from street-corner vendors and from ladies who made them in their home kitchens and sold them from the back porch. But by the time James Lasyone opened his restaurant in 1967, meat pies were hard to find. Mr. Lasyone missed the food of his childhood, and so he rescued the idea and began making and selling his own meat pies, using a recipe that took him two years of experimentation to develop.

James Lasyone's meat pie is a vividly seasoned mélange enclosed in a luscious crust. It is deep-fried until the crust is golden crisp and the moist, seasoned meat inside is steaming hot. Most people get one for lunch, sided by "dirty rice" and a typical southern vegetable such as okra or greens, but it's not uncommon to see someone having a meat pie at

7 A.M. alongside a couple of fried eggs and a pile of warm grits, glistening with melted butter.

Lasyone's true Louisiana menu also lists fried seafood (shrimp, oysters), red beans and rice with powerhouse sausage, and such non-Creole Dixie classics as catfish platters and chicken and dumplings with corn bread and black-eyed peas. We have eaten first-rate banana pudding for dessert, but the sweet tour de force here is a dish invented by Mrs. Lasyone called Cane River cream pie—a variant of Boston cream pie, made with gingerbread instead of white cake.

Louisiana Seafood Exchange

428 Jefferson Hwy.   504-834-9395
Jefferson, LA   L | $$

Along Jefferson Highway between two sets of train tracks, the Louisiana Seafood Exchange is a wholesale and retail seafood market with a fairly nondescript café called Crabby Jack's in front. Inside this café you will find some extraordinary po-boy sandwiches.

As you might expect in this environment, those made with seafood are spectacular, available normal-size (eight inches long) or king-size (foot-long). A king-size oyster po-boy is enough to feed a family: several dozen fried oysters are so heaped into a loaf of French bread that the bread is invisible underneath the seafood when you unwrap the sandwich. And these are fabulous oysters—crunch-crusted with lush insides, nicely complemented by a virtual salad of mayo, tomatoes, and lettuce also stuffed inside the loaf. Likewise, the shrimp sandwich is overloaded with so many crisp-fried and impeccably seasoned shrimp that you want to ask for a whole other length of bread into which you can pile the overflow.

This place is known as a sandwich shop; indeed, non-seafood sandwiches such as muffalettas and roast beef po-boys are as good as you'll find anywhere. But beyond sandwiches, LSE serves New Orleans plate lunches to remember: grilled tuna or tilapia, definitive jambalaya, and seafood gumbo are all on the menu . . . as is bread pudding for dessert.

Middendorf's

US 51 N
Pass Manchac, LA

504-386-6666
LD Tues-Sun | $$

As you might expect at a Tangipahoa Parish seafood house situated among a string of bait shops and take-out stands, Middendorf's is extremely casual, noisy, and fun. Its crowded dining rooms have long been the great country catfish destination restaurant of New Orleans, good reason to drive forty-five minutes north of town, then stand in line waiting for a table.

We don't like waiting for a table, but Middendorf's catfish makes any inconvenience worthwhile. In our experience, there is nothing quite so good anywhere in the city of New Orleans; and there is nothing quite so good anywhere in the city of New Orleans; and there are times, when we crunch into a thin catfish fillet at a Middendorf's table after a long spell away from Louisiana, that we are willing to say there is none this good anywhere in America. It is sold thick or thin. Thick catfish is a meaty cross section of fish, similar to a steak wrapped in breading. It is sweet-smelling and has resounding vim that is unlike any seawater fish. Thin catfish is more elegant than thick. Sliced into a diaphanous strip that is sharply seasoned, lightly breaded, and quickly fried, a thin cat fillet crunches loudly when you sink your teeth into its brittle crust, which is sheer enough to let the rich flavor of the fish resonate. With the catfish, thick or thin, there are perfectly good and unsurprising companions: French fries, hush puppies, and cole slaw salad.

After catfish, just about any seafood on the menu is well worth eating. We have had some great gumbo here, made with shrimp and crabmeat, which was surprisingly delicate compared to the more overpowering versions sold in the city's best gumbo houses. There are sautéed soft-shell crabs, po-boy sandwiches, and Italian salads loaded with olives and spice.

Mother's

401 Poydras St.
New Orleans, LA

504-523-9656
BL Tues-Sat | $

Mother's might not be the best restaurant in New Orleans, but when we've been far away from the Crescent City for too long and start yearning for its marvelous food, it is Mother's where we imagine ourselves—

standing at the counter watching a big roast beef po-boy loaded with meat and "debris" (all the tiny bits and pieces that fall from the roast when it is carved) or sitting at a table plowing into glorious red beans and rice, then, of course, bread pudding with buttered brandy sauce for dessert.

A real Roadfood kind of place, Mother's is a proletarian cafeteria that's been in business since 1938, attracting a clientele of locals as well as tourists. It is a boisterous joint, noisy and unkempt-looking, with a staff of brash gals behind the counter who dish out sass along with meals.

Po-boys are the signature dish; beyond roast beef, between-the-bread choices include pork chops, fried oysters or shrimp, and soft-shell crabs, as well as a combination known as the Ferdi Special, which is ham, roast beef, gravy, pickles, mayo, and mustard.

Mother's also happens to be a great breakfast spot. The ham biscuit, made with debris of fried-black ham, is spectacular, as is a serving of grits with ham debris mixed in. There are omelets of red beans, shrimp Creole, and crawfish étouffée; and even the scrambled eggs have a flavor that simply does not exist beyond this city's limits.

Prejean's

3480 I-49 N   337-896-3247
Lafayette, LA   LD | $$

"I love to eat!" wrote Louisiana Roadfooder Laura B., who told us that the next time we were in Cajun country, we needed to try the gumbo and crawfish enchiladas at Prejean's.

Thank you, Laura, for a recommendation we gladly pass on to anyone who loves to eat to the beat of a Cajun band. Located in North Lafayette, where there are good Cajun eateries galore, Prejean's is big and noisy (the live music starts every night at 7 P.M., and be sure to wear your dancing shoes); and the food is classic Cajun. In some other part of the country, a restaurant this brash might seem too "commercial" to qualify for Roadfood—walls hung with Acadiana, a stuffed alligator in the center of the dining room, a gift shop with tacky souvenirs—but for all its razzle-dazzle, Prejean's is the real thing, a fact about which you can have no doubt when you dip a spoon into the chicken and sausage gumbo or the dark andouille gumbo laced with smoked duck.

The menu is big and exotic, featuring dozens of dishes you'll not find on menus outside Louisiana, from crisp-fried crawfish boudin balls and catfish Catahoula (stuffed with crawfish, shrimp, and crab) to eggplant "pirogues" (canoes) hollowed out, fried, and filled with crawfish and red snapper fillet, then drizzled with buttery lobster sauce. Laura's recommendation of crawfish enchiladas is a good one. The crawdads are rolled with chiles and cheese in flour tortillas, baked, and smothered in crawfish sauce with zesty "dirty rice" on the side. It is also possible to get a monomaniacal all-crawfish meal of crawfish bisque, fried crawfish, crawfish étouffée, crawfish pie, crawfish boulettes, and a salad dotted with crawfish. The one dessert you need to know about is bread pudding with Jack Daniel's sour mash sauce.

Robin's

| 1409 Henderson Hwy. | 337-228-7594 |
| Henderson, LA | LD \| $$$ |

It occurred to us as we traveled through southern Louisiana that a vast majority of restaurants have names with the possessive apostrophe. It makes sense, because these places tend to be defined by the personality of their owner/chef. Robin's is a perfect example. This is Lionel Robin's restaurant, with a menu that reflects his culinary taste and expertise. And chances are good that if you make any sort of inquiry about the menu or cooking techniques, you will meet Robin himself, who loves to come out of the kitchen to chat with strangers about his current culinary adventures, whether they be frozen and ready-to-heat crawfish étouffée or Tabasco ice cream.

Robin cooks some of the most distinctive restaurant meals in swamp country. Year-round, but especially in crawfish season from early in the year through spring, this is the place to have them either simply boiled or in all the many ways Cajun chefs like to celebrate crawfish. A Robin's crawfish dinner starts with bisque, which is smoky, complex, and rich. You then move on to a few boiled and fried ones, étouffée over rice, boulettes, stuffed pepper, and a superior pie in which the little crustaceans share space with vegetables and plenty of garlic in a translucent-thin crust.

The one crawfish dish we might not recommend here is gumbo—not because it isn't good (it is), but because the shrimp and okra gumbo is even better. And chicken and sausage gumbo, while containing none of the seafood for which Robin's is renowned, is wonderful—brilliantly spiced and thick with sausage you will remember for a long time.

When we last stopped in, Robin had been experimenting with ice creams, and among his proudest creations were fig ice cream (figs are a local crop), a Belgian chocolate ice cream for chocoholics only, and the amazing Tabasco ice cream with its fetching sweet heat.

Uglesich's

1238 Baronne   504-523-8571

New Orleans, LA   L Mon-Fri (closed July and August) | $$

Uglesich's has been around since 1924, and although it is not exactly a secret (Martha Stewart taped scenes for her TV show here), neither is it the least bit spoiled. It is pure, funky New Orleans, set in a neighborhood that is not at all quaint. Its ramshackle dining room features chairs that wobble, tables that are crowded too close together, and decor that is mostly crates of beer and soft drinks stacked up against the wall. Unless you are a fastidious epicure, all these qualities are part of its charm, for like an heirloom skillet, Uglesich's turns out meals that only the slow sea-soning of age and experience can yield.

Even when it's not totally mobbed by tourists and locals, it can be a confusing place to dine. Unlike in a normal restaurant, you place your order before you sit down. Just inside the door, Anthony Uglesich, or sometimes his wife, Gail, is standing at the counter and will help you if you need assistance perusing the long and appetizing menu. Once you've decided what you want, you tell Anthony. He writes it down and takes your name and gets the order to the back-room kitchen. Meanwhile, you move toward the back of the restaurant, where the oyster shucker is at work, opening them faster than you can eat them. You get a bottle of beer and slide a dozen freshly opened oysters down the hatch. At some point, a waitress will point you to a table that has opened up inside or, if you wish, to a table on the sidewalk outside. Shortly thereafter, the food you ordered starts arriving. "Do it justice!" our waitress invoked as she laid a few beautiful plates down on our table.

Oh, happy day! This is the food that we dream about eating when we've been away from New Orleans too long. At first bite of the peppery Shrimp Uggie or butter-grilled Trout Anthony, we are suddenly and dra-matically reminded that Creole food packs a flavor punch like no other cuisine, anywhere. It is spicy, it is powerful, it is complex, it makes your tongue and lips glow, and makes your whole body happy.

You can't go wrong on the Uglesich menu. Must-eats include soft-shell crab po-boys (when available), oyster po-boys (freshly shucked and fried for each order), oyster shooters (sautéed with oil, vinegar, and cane syrup), southern-fried grits topped with cream-sauced shrimp, fire-cracker shrimp in hot-hot horseradish cream sauce, fried green tomatoes with shrimp remoulade, and best of all, swoonfully tender barbecued oysters, swimming in a puddle of garlicky olive oil with great, flavorful clods of basil and parsley. Fortunately, such meals are served with baskets of toasted and buttered French bread, which is necessary for mopping all the delicious juices from the plate.

Abe's Bar-B-Q

616 State St.   662-624-9947

Clarksdale, MS   LD | $

Boston butt is hickory-cooked, cooled, then hacked into pieces and re-heated on the griddle until slightly crusty at the edge. It is moistened with a bit of tangy red sauce and served with a pair of sauces for extra flavor: hot and mild. Dark red, tangy, with the resonance of pepper and spice, the hot version of the sauce is a taste bud thrill ride; used judiciously, it is a sublime companion for the deep-flavored pork. Available on a plate or, better yet, on a toasted bun with a crown of rugged cole slaw, Abe's is first-rate barbecue.

The restaurant itself is fundamental, located not far from the junction of highways 61 and 49, where blues mythology tells us you sell your soul to the devil in exchange for the gift of music. Since Abe Davis started cooking in a small Clarksdale smokehouse in 1924, his place has become a legend among local musicians as well as among blues pilgrims who come looking for the real thing. Along with barbecue (good ribs, too), Abe's is well known for hot tamales, which are a specialty through-out the Delta. They are available plain or topped with chili; and while most people think of tamales as Mexican, these have a rugged cornmeal flavor that to the connoisseur of Roadfood is pure Mississippi.

Doe's Eat Place

502 Nelson   662-334-3315

Greenville, MS   D | $$

Like some of America's better-known steak houses, Doe's of Greenville has expanded in recent years and now has branches in Little Rock and in Fayetteville, Arkansas. We've never been to a Doe's we didn't love, but there is special magic about the original one in the Mississippi Delta. Built of whitewashed cinder blocks and located on the wrong side of town, it does not look like a restaurant, much less a great restaurant. Upon entering for the first time, you will think you are in the wrong place. It looks like a defunct grocery store . . . which is what it is. Beyond the old meat counter is a doorway that leads to the dining room, which also happens to be the big, open kitchen. Here, tables are spread helter-skelter among stoves and counters where the staff brews coffee and fries potatoes in big iron skillets. Plates, flatware, and tablecloths are all mismatched. It is noisy and inelegant, and service is rough and tumble.

Doe's fans, ourselves included, love it just the way it is. The devil-may-care ambience, which is at least a few degrees beyond "casual," is part of what makes it such a kick. Mississippians have eaten here for generations; for regular patrons the eccentricity makes the experience as comfortable as an old shoe. Newcomers may be shocked by the ramshackle surroundings, but even fastidious epicures will find Doe's impossible not to like once the food starts coming.

Start with tamales. They make them here, and sell them to go by the dozen. Peel away the corn husk and the peppery, steamy meal inside is positively luscious, messy enough to eat with a fork unless you are a tamale-eating expert and can eat it straight from the husk. Now you want steak. Doe's is famous for its well-marbled beef, and serves what many consider to be the best steaks in America. Describe the cut and size you like, and a few raw ones are brought from the meat locker for your selection and approval. The one you choose is carried out to the grill in the front room; and while it cooks, you eat some salad, which the waitresses fetch from a big bowlful they are constantly mixing and dressing (with lemon and olive oil) throughout the dinner hour.

Doe's is not cheap; but it shouldn't be. This unique combination of top-drawer steak and downscale atmosphere is priceless Americana.

Lusco's

722 Carrollton Ave.	662-453-5365
Greenwood, MS	LD | $$

Cotton planters around Greenwood came to know Charles "Papa" Lusco in the 1920s when he drove a horse-drawn grocery wagon to their plantations, bringing supplies from the market he and Marie "Mama" Lusco ran. Mama sold plates of her spaghetti at the store, and Papa built secret dining rooms in back where customers could enjoy his homemade wine with their meals. The clandestine cubicles remained, giving Lusco's a seductively covert character that has endeared it to generations.

Lusco's is still a restaurant fitted into a grocery store, but two big things have changed. First, the ceiling is clean. Until a little over a decade ago, it used to be a custom among partyers in the back rooms to use their flatware to flip butter pats upward so they stuck to the tin ceiling. "Well-bred southern ladies and gentlemen would get to yelling and screaming and pretty soon the butter would go flying," recalls Karen Pinkston, the third-generation Lusco who runs the restaurant with her husband, Andy. "It became a problem in the winter, when we turned on the heat. Heat rises, so the stuck butter melted. In 1989 the health department insisted something be done." Today, a sign in the waiting area warns that butter-throwing is classified under law as malicious mischief.

The other significant change at Lusco's is that there is a written menu. It used to be that a member of the serving staff entered your cubicle and recited what there was to eat in the most poetic and seductive terms. Despite the clean ceiling and the printed menu, Lusco's remains a restaurant like no other. Mama and Papa Lusco were Italian by way of Louisiana, so the flavors of the kitchen they established are as much Creole as they are southern or Italian. Gumbo, crab, and shrimp are always on the menu, and oysters are a specialty in season—on the half shell or baked with bacon. Because so many regular customers are big spenders from cotton families, the menu is best known for its high-end items. Lusco's T-bone steaks are some of the finest anywhere: sumptuous cuts that are broiled to plump succulence. Pompano has for many years been a house trademark (when available, usually the spring), broiled and served whole, bathed in a magical sauce made of butter, lemon, and secret spices.

Lusco's is also known for its New Orleans–style salad of iceberg lettuce dolled up with anchovies, capers, and olives and liberally soaked in a fragrant vinaigrette; but Karen Pinkston is a serious salad buff who has made it her business to concoct more modern alternatives. One evening's choices included Mediterranean salad, made with feta cheese; traditional Caesar salad; and a salad billed as Gourmet's Delight, made with arugula, radicchio, endive, red lettuce, and spinach. "Andy likes to tease me about that one," Karen said about the latter. "He tells me it's just weeds I've picked by the side of the highway. But the fact is that the Delta is different now than it used to be, and the new people have more educated palates. Even this place has to change with the times."

Phillips Grocery

541-A E. Van Dorn Ave. 662-252-4671

Holly Springs, MS L | $

Over the last several decades there has been much speculation about why Phillips's hamburgers are so delicious, but when asked for details, the cooks say only that the recipe has been handed down since 1948 when Mr. and Mrs. Phillips took over the old two-story building that started as a saloon in 1882 and became a grocery store in 1919. Some time ago a rumor went around Holly Springs that Phillips's trick was to mix the meat with peanut butter, which was categorically denied. Frankly, we wouldn't even hazard a guess as to these burgers' secret. To us, they taste simply like high-quality, freshly ground meat with enough seasoning to bring out their natural protein savor. Our honest suspicion is that the mystery is not any stealthy spice or condiment at all, but every Mississippian's most favorite flavor—tradition. Phillips's hamburgers are cooked on a grill that is over a half-century old. Five decades of sizzling meat have created a character that no mere ingredient could possibly beget.

The hamburgers are presented with or without cheese, wrapped in yellow wax paper inside a bag for easy toting. When you peel back the wrapping, particularly on a half-pound Super-Deluxe, it is a vision of beauty-in-a-bun. The patty is thick and juicy with a crunch to its nearly blackened skin. Burgers are the big deal here, but side dishes include deep-fried okra, corn nuggets (like hush puppies, but with kernels of corn), onion rings, and regular or spicy French fries. For dessert, you have a choice of moon pie (the favorite convenience-store snack of marshmallow, chocolate, and rounds of Graham cracker) or fried pies. The latter are another regional favorite: folded-over half-circles of dough fried until they are reddish brown and chewy, each enclosing a heavy dollop of sugary peach or apple filling.

Although much business is takeout, it's a pleasure to dine at Phillips. There is a short counter with stools that affords a good view of the open-kitchen action and a few tables (including a really odd one made from the cross section of a huge tree trunk). Outside on the front porch, a couple of picnic tables provide a view of the railroad depot.

(A branch of Phillips, outfitted to resemble an old country store, recently opened in Oxford, Mississippi, at 2406 S. Lamar, 662–236–5951.)

White Front Café

Rt. 1`	662-759-3842
Rosedale, MS	L | $

You can get anything you want to eat at the White Front Café, also known as Joe's Hot Tamale Place, just so long as what you want to eat is a tamale. Joe Pope's menu is one item, and one item only; and for it, his little wood-frame house by the side of Route 1 has become a Delta landmark to which people travel 100 miles from Memphis.

Many customers buy them by the dozen to take home for supper. We enjoy eating here at one of four kitchenette tables in the front room of the café. Order three or four and they are served tightly wrapped in their corn husk. You can eat them one of two ways: Pick up a tamale and squeeze out a mouthful of the succulent insides or peel away the husk and use a saltine cracker to scoop some up. (If you want saltines, you'll need to walk across Route 1 and buy a pack at the convenience store. Joe has only soda pop to drink, as well as a few jars of pickles and penny candies on the counter.)

Mr. Pope began serving tamales in Rosedale thirty years ago. He told us he uses a recipe he inherited from the daughter of John Hooks, who learned how to cook them from a Mexican from Texas who traveled through the Delta back in the 1930s. Today, tamales are a popular dish all along the Mississippi River from Memphis to Vicksburg. Most tamale cooks have their own way of doing things. Some use pork, some add chicken to mix; some tamales are ferociously spicy. We believe Joe Pope's are among the very best. They are all-beef (no pork), a well-nigh-perfect blend of meat, cornmeal, and just enough peppery spice to excite but not overwhelm your tongue.

South Carolina

Anchor Line Restaurant

2293 Folly Rd.   843-795-7518
James Island, SC   LD | $$

A sign on the road out to Folly Beach welcomes visitors to the edge of America. At the Anchor Line, that's a good thing. Seated at a picnic table on a sun-dappled porch overlooking Oak Island Creek, watching the occasional fisherman ply a line, life is restful . . . and very, very delicious. There are several eat-in-the-rough fish houses in the area, and while we haven't done a scientific compare-and-contrast of them all, we'd be very happy to return to the Anchor Line again and again.

Study a menu posted above the order counter and tell the nice people what kind of fish you want, how much you want, and how you'd like it cooked. They take your money, you find a seat (out on the screened porch for nice scenery; inside for chitchat with the staff and other customers), and pretty soon you are presented with a plate of wonderful cooked-to-order fish. And when we say pretty soon, we aren't kidding. As we were placing our order for a half-and-half plate of fried shrimp and oysters, the fry-man was eavesdropping, and before we had our wallet out to pay, our meal was bubbling in the fry kettles.

Three sizes of everything are available. "Are you really, really hungry?" the order-taker asked when we asked for large. It was indeed huge: multitudes of crunch-crusted shrimp—maybe a couple dozen, each of them one good mouthful—and a nearly equal number of oysters, all heaped on a disposable plate with good French fries and a pair of great rugged, red-gold hush puppies. Cole slaw came in a separate dish alongside.

While the fried food is superb, we found that a "large" order of broiled shrimp was equally excellent, and the blue crab gumbo with which we started the meal was another exemplary dish—exactly the kind of fresh, down-home seafood one hopes to find here at the edge of South Carolina's Low Country.

Beacon Drive-In

255 Reidville Rd.   864-585-9387
Spartanburg, SC   BLD | $

If you have time for only one meal at the Beacon Drive-In, we suggest you make it a Chili Cheese A-Plenty. That is a chili cheeseburger on a bun buried on a plate underneath piles of sweet onion rings and French fried potatoes. Second choice: Outside Pork A-Plenty, which is hacked-up shreds and chunks of hot, hickory-cooked pork on a bun with cool slaw, given the same delicious burial under o-rings and fries. The Beacon's menu is huge, ranging from succulent catfish (tail-on, bone-in) to banana-mayo sandwiches on white bread that Elvis might have loved; and nearly all the specialties are available as A-Plenty plates.

Malt A-Plenty, on the other hand, refers to a malted milk shake so thick that one literally can eat it with a fork! Delicious as the malt may be, however, it's nearly nuts to come to the Beacon and drink anything other than tea. Here is the great sweet tea of the South—supersugary, laced with a touch of lemon, served over a pack of shaved ice that somehow is colder and more refreshing than ice anywhere else. No surprise: The Beacon sells more tea than any other single restaurant in the USA.

The experience of dining at the Beacon is at least as enjoyable as the food itself. It is fast, loud, and big, the most intense restaurant you will ever visit. The moment you enter and approach the serving line, you are virtually accosted by an order-taker—J. C. Strobel, the senior man, if you're lucky—who will demand, *"Call it out!"* Say what you want to eat and say it quickly, or else J.C. will tell you to stand back and allow other, swifter customers to say their piece. On a good weekend day, the Beacon will serve five thousand people.

Once you manage to convey your order, J.C. or a comrade will shout it back to the huge open kitchen, then ask you in no uncertain terms to "Move on down the line!" Grab a tray and by the time you have moved twenty paces forward, there your order will be—miraculously, exactly as you ordered it, with or without extra barbecue sauce, double bacon on the burger. A bit farther down the line, you get your tea, lemonade, or milk shake and pay the cashier, then find a seat. Total time from entering to digging in—maybe two minutes.

The alternative to dining inside is eating in your car. "Curb boy" service has been a Beacon trademark since it opened in 1946; and there is a special joy in eating this sort of fast food off a tray hung on the car window. For over a half a century starting in 1950, the best thing about Beacon curb service has been Ezell Jackson, senior curb boy who, when he turned ninety two years ago, explained to us why he thought customers have made this restaurant a spiritual as well as gastronomic beacon of the Deep South: "If you've got something on your mind—worries at home or on the road—come to the Beacon," Mr. Jackson said. "Rich or poor, everybody belongs, everybody is respected."

Bowens Island

| 1870 Bowens Island Rd. | 843-795-2757 |
| Charleston, SC | D (oysters available September–April) | $$ |

Oysters, all you can eat! They are dug fresh, that morning, from Bowens Island oyster beds, and, when ordered, they are roasted under burlap on a big smoky pit. They are brought from the pit in a shovel and piled onto the table in great gnarled clumps, where it is the customers' job to separate them and shuck them (easy, once cooked), and to eat until appetite is only a distant memory. For a little under $20, it is a royal feast . . . and a royal mess, too!

When oysters are not in season, or for those who are oyster-frowners, Bowens Island restaurant has a short menu of other seafood, including colossal portions of fried fish or shrimp with grits and cole slaw on the side, and even Frogmore stew, the Carolina coast specialty that combines shrimp, sausage, and corn.

Fastidious epicures will not find happiness in this place. At the end of a bumpy dirt path off Folly Road on the way into Charleston, it is a cinder-block building surrounded by enough stuff that it resembles a yard sale. Inside, there is graffiti on the walls (customers are invited to add their own); tablecloths consist of pages from yesterday's newspaper; and you can expect your chair to wobble. Old-timers tell us that this beloved place has changed very little since May Bowen started cooking food for local fishermen in 1946.

Charlie's Steakhouse

18 Coffee St.   864-232-9541

Greenville, SC   D | $$

Most of America's great steak houses are found in the biggest cities, such as Chicago, Omaha, New York, Dallas, and Kansas City. But serious meat-eaters know that there is a good selection of world-class steak to be eaten far off the beaten path: in places such as Doe's Eat Place of Mississippi and Little Rock, Ranchman's Café of Ponder, Texas, and Charlie's Steakhouse of Greenville, South Carolina. Charlie's is a gem, the fine place to eat on Coffee Street since 1921.

Who could resist a menu that boasts "All beef shipped direct from Waterloo & Des Moines, Iowa; St. Joe & Kansas City, Mo"? Despite that honest boast, Charlie's is a low-key sort of place—polite, but not overly impressed by itself and not ridiculously overpriced like the national prime-steak chains.

Dinner is built upon time-honored rituals that citizens of Greenville (and their parents and grandparents) have come to know and appreciate over the decades: apply-your-own-dressing service for salad or slaw (the latter just a huge heap of cut cabbage), a bottle of Charlie's own steak sauce on every table, thick china plates rimmed with a pattern of magnolias, silver presented wrapped in thick linen napkins, and tables cushioned so well that highball glasses wobble as you slice into a steak.

If you are a gloppy blue cheese dressing fan like we are, you will love Charlie's; it is thick and creamy, with just a wee sweet touch to its mild cheesy flavor. In addition to considering what cut and size of steak to order, you also need to select a starch: fried onion rings or potatoes, or best of all, a half-and-half plate of both. The steak roster includes a T-bone, a filet mignon, and a porterhouse for one, but many regulars who come in groups opt for a jumbo sirloin cut into portions for two, three, or four people. The arrival of any steak at the table is a glorious event, for it comes on a hot metal plate (resting on a wood pallet), sizzling and sputtering so loud that all conversations stop in wonderment. It is nice meat, dense and juicy, although like so many modern steaks, it lacks the delirious beef taste of a good old prime cut.

We love Charlie's staff of waitresses. They are friendly as can be, but also real pros, constantly positioning and repositioning the dressings, sour cream bowl, bread plate, and butter-pat dish on the table so everything is arrayed for maximum convenience. As we photographed an extra large sirloin for our "What We Ate" picture album, our waitress suggested that when we got back to Wisconsin, we send her a copy so everyone at Charlie's could sign it. Earlier in the meal, we had told her we were from Connecticut, but we figure that to a lot of citizens of the Deep South, the difference between Connecticut and Wisconsin is a non-issue.

Diana's

155 Meeting St.   843-534-0043
Charleston, SC   BLD | $$

Diana's adjoins a downtown Day's Inn, but when we asked our waitress, Marie, if it was affiliated, she was adamant: "We are not connected to the hotel!" she said. "No way, whatsoever, not at all!"

It's apparent when you see the food that it is multiple levels above what one would expect in a chain-hotel snack shop. When you taste that food, you realize you are the beneficiary of master cooks. At breakfast, for example, if you order French toast you don't just get a couple of slabs of fried, egg-dipped bread. You get huge chunks of currant-berry bread stuffed with apples, cooked to a crisp outside, floating in an amber pool of apple-cider syrup. Sausage gravy is served over luscious homemade biscuits. And the Low Country favorite, shrimp and grits, is amended with crawfish, too, and topped with some of the most delicious fried green tomatoes we've eaten anywhere—thinly veiled in crust, cooked al dente with a vivid tang.

Tipster Susanne Hupfer told us not to miss the Southern fried chicken, served with chipotle whipped potatoes, and she was right. This is chicken with a rugged crust and succulent insides. Susanne also alerted us to Diana's pastries, which are on display as you enter the neat and tidy split-level café. A glass case holds such wonderments as red velvet cake, white coconut layer cake, and yellow butter cake with chocolate whipped frosting. Here also are handsome pies: coconut cream, lemon meringue, chocolate cream, and pecan. Everything we've sampled from this case has been outstanding.

Of special note are Diana's coffees. The back of the breakfast menu is devoted to beverages, with more various ways to have your caffeine than at a Starbucks. Fat-free variations of café mocha and café mocchiatto are available, and we were in heaven with a double-shot red-eye, here known as shot in the dark.

Duke's

789 Chestnut St.

Orangeburg, SC

803-534-9418

LD Thurs-Sat only | $

When connoisseurs of Southern food refer to Orangeburg-style barbecue, they mean Duke's. Here is the quintessential eastern South Carolina barbecue parlor, including—please note—the very limited hours of operation, Thursday through Saturday. The limited schedule harkens back to an old-fashioned pig pickin', which was a weekend celebration at which hogs were enjoyed from beard to tail, or "barbe à queue."

There's nothing at all charming about Duke's decor, at least not in a HGTV sort of way. It is a stark place with a single purpose: to celebrate hickory-smoked pork. Hacked into chunks at a cutting board in back, it is pork with a complex flavor that is just faintly smoky. Each piece is a tender mouthful that is a joy to savor in the peace of this room, where the only music is the cadence of more pork being hacked into hunks back in the kitchen.

You get the pork from a serve-yourself buffet line that also includes rice, hash (a stewlike mixture made from pig innards), a choice of red sauce that is four-alarm-hot or yellow mustard sauce that is sweet and tangy (unique to central South Carolina), and pickles. Dish out as much as you want in your partitioned plate, grab a plastic fork, and find a place at one of the long picnic tables in the cavernous eating hall.

The drink of choice is presweetened ice tea, and each table is outfitted with a few loaves of Sunbeam bread, which is just the right thing for mopping up a plate of good sauce.

Fishnet Seafoods

3832 Savannah Hwy.   843-571-2423
Johns Island, SC   LD | $

One of the most interesting places to find excellent seafood outside of Charleston is a dilapidated former gas station in Johns Island. Fishnet Seafoods is actually a market where customers come for raw flounder, trout, oysters, and shrimp sold by the piece or pound. There are no tables or chairs, but there is a waiting bench where you can sit while they cook to order whatever fish you want. It is then up to you to find a place to eat it; most customers take it home or dine in their car sitting in the spacious parking lot.

Fried food is the specialty, breaded and boiled in oil with the deft hand that only cooks in the Low Country seem to have. Shrimp are firm and brittle-crusted; local oysters are full-flavored; fillets of flounder are sweet, snowy white, available with two pieces of bread and labeled a sandwich . . . although the fish is about 200 percent larger than the bread. One of the best things on the menu is the dish that every other restaurant refers to as deviled crab. But that's not its name in this place. At Fishnet Seafoods, the highly spiced stuffed crabs are listed as Jesus crabs. When we inquired of a counter man how they got that name, he responded with no hesitation, "Because they are so good."

Gullah Cuisine

1717 Highway 17 N   843-881-9076
Mount Pleasant, SC   LD | $$

We love a restaurant on a mission, especially in the case of Gullah Cuisine, the mission of which is to celebrate the cuisine and culture of the Low Country. As you enter, you'll notice elegant woven sweetgrass baskets for sale near the cash register—they are a time-honored Mount Pleasant craft, and you will also see little jars of "Gullah seasoning." It's that spice that helps give so much of this food an indescribable zing.

For instance, take the "Gullah rice," which comes as a meal unto itself or as a side dish for such entrees as fried shrimp, smothered pork shops, or oxtail stew. It is stunning rice, chockablock with shrimp, shreds of chicken, discs of sausage, and nuggets of vegetables, the rice itself tinted a glistening mahogany color and fairly radiant with peppery flavor. It was a taste buds challenge for us to eat both Gullah rice and okra gumbo. Each is powerfully spiced, the gumbo dark and smoky and loaded with sausage, shrimp, and chicken. Midway through the meal, we felt we had gone into a kind of sensory overload from the overwhelming allure of so much flavor and aroma.

As balm for the tongue, the day's vegetable was broccoli casserole, and we must say, we were as impressed with it as we were the more complex Gullah specialties. It is a real Southern specialty—broccoli transformed from a plebeian vegetable into a dish that is rich and full-flavored by the addition of cheese, bread crumbs, and seasoning. Far, far from modern al dente broccoli, this casserole is soft, gentle, and profoundly comforting.

Desserts included a slice of superb pumpkin pie and a block of tawny bread pudding laced with raisins and soft peaches and topped with caramel sauce.

Hominy Grill

207 Rutledge St.   843-937-0930

Charleston, SC   BLD | $$

Our first meal at the Hominy Grill was breakfast, and it was spectacular. The sausage patties that came alongside our sunny-side up eggs were rugged and crusty and brilliantly spiced—a joy to eat when pushed through some yolk or sandwiched inside the tall biscuit that came alongside. Bacon was excellent, too—double-thick, crisp, and full-flavored, just begging to be cosseted in that hefty biscuit or eaten in alternating mouthfuls with a forkful of smooth-textured grits.

We were equally impressed when we returned for lunch and plowed into thick shrimp gumbo and a serving of Brunswick stew sided by good corn bread. And who could resist a distinctly Southern BLT made with crunchy discs of fried green tomato? Buttermilk pie was the perfect dessert.

The Hominy Grill building was at one time a barbershop, and the striped poles that signify the tonsorial profession still flank the front door (on the inside). It's a spacious room with an old stamped-tin ceiling, wood-slat walls, and slow-spinning fans overhead.

Jestine's Kitchen

251 Meeting St.   843-722-7224

Charleston, SC   LD | $

Jestine's is a modern restaurant that specializes in hand-me-down recipes. Some were contributed by the kitchen staff, but most were bequeathed to proprietor Dana Berlin by Jestine Matthews, the African-American woman who raised her (and who passed away in 1997 after celebrating her 112th birthday!). Jestine's is a hospitable Meeting Street storefront with a soundtrack of old-time jazz singers and decor that includes vintage cast-iron skillets, flour sifters, and juice squeezers. Quiet, inexpensive, and homey, it is a destination that makes customers feel as well favored as if Ms. Matthews herself were watching over them. "This is my all-time, number-one restaurant," boasts a young seaman from the nearby naval base to his date one afternoon as he guides her to a booth and chivalrously unwraps her silver from the clean green washcloth that serves as a napkin, then orders a pound of spiced, steamed shrimp and a basket of corn bread for them to share.

There isn't a nicer table anywhere to taste the time-honored coastal delights of shrimp and grits or crab and corn soup or the big loaf known as an oyster po-boy, loaded with crisp-fried oysters. On the side of such dishes as meat loaf or fried chicken come Low Country vegetables, including okra gumbo, red rice, and fried green tomatoes. Even common side dishes are uncommonly delicious: mashed potatoes pack eye-opening flavor, macaroni and cheese is threaded with chewy strips from the top of the casserole, cabbage is cooked with plenty of pork until its leaves are limp and sweet. The only proper beverage to accompany such powerfully flavored food is listed on the menu as "Jestine's table wine"— cool, sugary tea served in shapely tumblers. And for dessert, beyond celestial coconut cream pie, we recommend a dish we've never seen served in another restaurant, but which is a favorite among southern home cooks, Coca-Cola cake.

The Old Post Office

Highway 174 at Store Creek   843-869-2339

Edisto Island, SC   LD | $$$

We don't know of another restaurant where the table setting includes bags of raw grits. The Old Post Office is renowned for grits prepared Low Country style, meaning they are long- and slow-cooked, attaining a pleasant rugged texture but a deliriously creamy quality from all the butter and milk they absorb. They come alongside virtually every meal served here, and they are especially wonderful as part of that favorite Low Country duet, shrimp and grits.

Grits bags on the table are important not only because the grits at the Old Post Office taste so good, but because grits are fundamental to Low Country cooking, and here is a restaurant where the food traditions of the region are honored with enthusiasm. Ask any food-savvy person from Edisto, Charleston, or beyond where to eat meals that sing of South Carolina's coastal culture, and chances are good you will be directed to this unlikely place on Edisto Island.

Chef Philip Bardin changes his menu to reflect the spectacular vegetable crops of Edisto, as well as the seafood caught around here. That means that if it's oyster season (fall through early spring), you will likely have the opportunity to fork into Oyster Skillet, a dish the menu describes as "Low Country Escargots" but that puts smelly old snails to shame. A cast-iron skillet filled with small local creek oysters swimming in a pool of their own liquor with garlic and parsley comes with a toasted baguette that is great for shoveling heaps of oysters up from the skillet, as well as for sopping up those intoxicating juices.

The wide-ranging menu goes well beyond local seafood to include delicious roast duck, a "fussed-over pork chop" that's good reminder of just how important pork is in these parts, and "P.B.'s Ultimate Filet Mignon" (P.B. = Philip Bardin).

The Key lime mousse was a winning variation on Key lime pie, and we were brought to our knees by Coca-Cola cake, a truly Southern dish we've never found in any other restaurant.

Ruby Seahorse Grill

108 Jungle Road   843-869-0606
Edisto Beach, SC   LD | $

When Philip Bardin, chef at the Old Post Office restaurant (page 292) recommends a place to eat, we listen. Philip knows good food, and when we asked him where to go on Edisto Island, other than his own restaurant, "The Ruby Seahorse" was his instant answer. And what should we eat? Again, no hesitation: "A pimiento burger."

We found ourselves on Jungle Road near the ocean at a breezy eatery that looks pretty much like a million hamburger joints in other places. The short menu included a few salads and sandwiches, including an excellent French dip known as the Jacques Chirac and a classic grilled Reuben. Chicken wings are available by the dozen: medium, hot, teriyaki, and Calabash.

However, Philip's recommendation was quite specific so we directed our attention to the hamburger menu. Here we found bacon-cheese, chili-cheese, and mushroom-Swiss burgers, but it was the "Original Dairy Bar Pimiento Burger" for which we came. This house specialty is a handsome, good-size hamburger mounded with a huge spill of mostly melted pimiento cheese—a good-tasting mess. And if you want to make it even messier, you'll ask for it "all the way," which means mayonnaise, mustard, lettuce, tomato, onion, and pickle chips.

Suitable to a hamburger, the dining experience is extremely informal. You wait in line at an order window through which the kitchen is visible. Once you've ordered and paid, you wait for the meal to be assembled on throwaway dishware, then carry it to a rickety table on a back porch where the perfume of the ocean provides priceless ambience.

SeeWee Restaurant

4808 US 17 N   843-928-3609
Awendaw, SC   LD | $$

A former grocery north of Charleston along US 17, SeeWee is now a hugely popular restaurant that includes a lovely outdoor area for al fresco dining. It still looks a bit like a roadside store—shelves stocked with supplies, higgledy-piggledy decor of nautical bibelots. But Charlestonians now come here for local seafood, down-home vegetables, and magnificent cakes.

Daily specials are chalked up on a board. When we visited they included country-fried steak, whole catfish, Jamaican jerk chicken, Buffalo shrimp or oysters (fried in a spicy Buffalo-wing style), and fish stew by the cup or bowl. We zeroed in on the regular menu and its roster of fried seafood. In this part of the world, frying shrimp, scallops, and oysters is a fine art. You can get a platter or a sandwich with very good extra-large French fries and cole slaw on the side. Our shrimp were snapping firm and veiled in a fine, crisp crust.

One of the great only-in-the-South meals to get here is an all-vegetable plate. Choose four from a list of more than a dozen available, including such local faves as red rice, butter beans, fried squash, fried okra, and rice and gravy. We went for fried green tomatoes (deliciously al dente with a tangy smack), sweet-potato casserole (super spicy), macaroni and cheese (dense and thick with cheese), and collard greens (salty, oily, luxurious).

As you walk in the restaurant you will see a shelf of the day's layer cakes, and desserts are listed on a blackboard. When we saw chocolate cake with peanut butter icing, we knew we had to have a piece. So we ordered it as we ordered lunch. The cake came before the meal. "I cut this for you because I was worried there wouldn't be any left by the time you were ready," our waitress kindly explained as she set it down with our sweet teas. We are so grateful she was watching out for us, because this cake was superb . . . as was our caramel layer cake and goober pie.

No bill arrives after the meal. When you're done eating, the waitress will instruct you to go up to the cash register and tell the man your table number. He's got your check and will tally it up and get you squared away.

Breakfast is served on Saturdays only.

Sgt. White's Diner

1908 Boundary St.	843-522-2029
Beaufort, SC	LD | $

Immediately upon entering this little diner you are faced with the steam table from which the server puts together your plate. While it is possible to order off a menu—and the fried chicken and shrimp therefrom are exemplary—we cannot resist the array of barbecue and side dishes in the trays. You get either pulled pork, which is a medley of velvet-soft shreds from inside and crunchy strips from the outside of the roast bathed in the Sergeant's brilliant tangy-sweet sauce, or ribs, which are crusty and unspeakably luscious, also caked with the good sauce. Each side dish is a super-soulful rendition of a Southern classic: smothered cabbage richer than ham itself, broccoli gobbed with cheese, brilliantly seasoned red rice, a vivid mix of collard and turnip greens, *real* mashed potatoes, candied yams, etc., etc. A normal meal is one meat and two sides, served with a block of corn bread on top. Even that corn bread is extraordinary: rugged-textured and sweet as cake.

We are terribly sorry to confess that we were so delirious after eating meals here, we staggered out into the sunlight forgetting all about dessert! Looking at the smoky menu today, far from Beaufort, we see listings for sweet-potato pie and pecan pie. We'd bet money that they're mighty good.

Sergeant White, by the way, is a U.S. Marine, a former D.I., who offers business-size cards at the counter to remind guests of the Marine code of Honor, Courage, and Commitment.

Shealy's Bar-B-Que

340 E. Columbia Ave.   803-532-8135
Leesville, SC   LD | $

When George W. Bush ran for president, his South Carolina campaign included a stop at Shealy's Bar-B-Que. We don't know exactly what he piled on his plate, but we can guarantee he ate well. Only die-hard spoilsports could not enjoy themselves at this vast southern-style all-you-can-eat buffet.

We found out about it thanks to tipster Paul McCravy, who wrote that "the vegetables surpass any I've had at the three family reunions I attend each year in Pickins Country." Greens and beans, boiled, fried, and mashed, served plain and in elaborate casseroles, the array of vegetables is awesome. And they are merely the side dishes to some magnificent meals of fried chicken with cream gravy, including wishbones for those who are feeling lucky.

For us, the main attraction is pork barbecue, which is presented at the buffet with all the glory of a traditional South Carolina barbecue feast, meaning you will find just about every part of the pig but the oink. That includes meat, ribs, hash, skin, gravy, and a rather bizarre creamy/spicy mush apparently quite popular in these parts known as liver nips. Of special interest: On the tender shreds of smoked pork is Shealy's sauce (available by the bottle), an alluring mustard-tinged sweet-and-sour condiment unique to the South Carolina Midlands.

Summerton Diner

33 Church St.   803-485-6835

Summerton, SC   BLD (closed Thurs) | $

Straight off a plane from New York, we drove from the Charleston Airport to the Summerton Diner for meat-and-three. It was the height of lunch hour; the girls were shorthanded—two of them managed the counter and all the tables as well as take-out orders—and we were ravenous. The meal took no longer than an hour, start to finish, but as we waited for sweet tea and a bread basket, we found ourselves in the agitated state of hungry impatience that we so often bring with us from the Northeast when we head south. A few sips of tea, a sniff of the steamy insides of a warm biscuit, and we began to relax. When the partitioned plates piled with food arrived, serenity was ours!

The good old Summerton Diner is that kind of place: relaxing and reliable. Since Lois Hughes opened it for business in 1967, this little café on the outskirts of town has been a favorite of locals and a beacon for travelers along I-95. After Lois's daughter Lynelle Blackwell took over in 1987, she enlarged and remodeled it, but today the diner has the feel of an ageless eatery: well-worn Formica counter, blond wood-paneled walls, each table set with bottles of hot vinegar peppers for brightening up orders of collard greens.

There's a full menu, and such items as fried chicken or steak and quail are always available, but at lunchtime the thing to order is the special. For exactly $6, you get an entree, three vegetables, dessert, and tea. Plus corn bread and biscuits. The Monday we stopped in, meats included calves liver with onions and gravy, baked ham, beef stew, and baked chicken supreme. We love that chicken! It is crusty and fall-apart tender; the waitress asks if you want white or dark meat. Like all entrees, it comes on a partitioned plate along with two of the vegetables you choose. (The third vegetable, for which the plate has no room, comes in its own bowl.) As you might expect in a true-South café such as this, the side dishes are superb: earthy fresh rutabagas, spicy stewed apples, porky sweet greens that still have an al dente oomph to their leaves, mashed potatoes blanketed in gorgeous beef-shred gravy, hefty blocks of macaroni and cheese with crusty edges and creamy insides, rice infused with soulful gravy. Etc.!

The serving of pudding is small but classic: gentle custard in which sliced bananas and softened vanilla wafers are suspended, all under a Kewpie-doll spiral of whipped cream.

Note: The Summerton diner is closed Thursdays. It is open for three meals a day the rest of the week.

Sweatman's

Route 453   803-492-7583
North of Holly Hill, SC   LD Fri and Sat only | $

Please note Sweatman's hours of operation. Inconvenient, yes? But utterly true to the tradition of a country pig-pickin', the point of which is to pig out after a hard week's work. Decades ago, it used to be that the menfolk of the family did all the cooking and hosted these big feeds only for relatives and friends, but in the 1970s, the informal ritual became something like a restaurant. We say "something like a restaurant" because it is an unusual operation that is not a sit-down place with waiters, menu, and choice of food. At Sweatman's, you serve yourself, you eat in the former living quarters of the family home, and you come for one and only one thing: pit-cooked pig.

There are few dining rooms anywhere more truly homey than these: oilcloth-covered tables, calico-curtained windows, high ceilings, and wood-slat walls. The buffet line where everyone helps themselves is spectacular. Among the choice of things to eat are chunks of butt and shoulder meat, crusty ribs for gnawing, rib meat only (minus the bone), pigskin stripped and fried into mottled brindle strips with a wicked crunch, and pungent hash made from the jowls, liver, and other ignominious portions of the hog. The hash is used to ladle over rice. The chunks of barbecued pork are as succulent as food can be, presented plain and glistening with their own copious juices. This meat needs nothing in the way of condiments, but if you do want to gild it there are two sauces available, one made with hot peppers and the other a typical South Carolinian sauce built around mustard.

Sweatman's has few frills; but it is no rough-and-tumble smoke pit.

A barbecue meal in this smoky shrine is a serene and meditative experience, one that will linger in your memory as sweet as the aroma of pit-cooked pork.

The Wreck

106 Haddrell Point   843-884-0052

Mount Pleasant, SC   LD | $$

We are often asked to name the signs of a surefire-good restaurant along the road. In fact, the best sign of a great Roadfood eatery is *no sign at all*. You figure that all the locals simply know what it is and where it is, so the management doesn't need to bother with a sign. There used to be a terrific café specializing in tenderloins in central Illinois marked only by a small marker outside that said "Home of Wyatt Earp." In fact, it was not the home of Wyatt Earp; and the restaurant's legal name was something else altogether. But the regular customers who flocked there didn't mind; they knew where to eat the crispest, sweetest pork cutlet for miles around.

It goes without saying that such places can be a little difficult to find if you are a stranger in town and simply wandering around looking for a good place to eat. But if you happen to find yourself along the docks at Shem Creek in Mount Pleasant outside Charleston, South Carolina, ask just about any native to direct you to The Wreck. They'll point out Live Oak Road toward Haddrell Point, where, tucked between the Wando Seafood Company and Magwood & Sons Seafood, you will find a building that used to be a bait locker. It has no sign outside, but this is it: The Wreck, formally named The Wreck of the Richard and Charlene (after a boat hit by Hurricane Hugo). Its inside is as informal as its outside; decor consists of stacked-up cardboard beer cartons. Accommodations are plastic lawn chairs at tables clothed with fish-wrapping paper. Plain though it may be, the view from the porch of docked shrimp trawlers is priceless; and at night, the wobbly tables are lit by candles.

This out-of-the-way gem is mobbed at mealtimes with customers who come for crunchy fried shrimp and oysters, boiled stone crabs and shrimp by the pound, shrimp pilaf, and broiled grouper served with hush puppies and squares of luscious spiced grits. Depending on your appetite, you can get a meal either "Richard-size" (copious) or "Charlene-size" (normal portion). Everything is presented on cardboard plates with plastic utensils; beer comes in the bottle.

Although the restaurant is humble in the extreme, its culinary standards are impeccable. As we entered one afternoon through the open kitchen, we witnessed the man at the fry kettles lecturing a customer who wanted an order of fried oysters to go. The chef de cuisine absolutely refused to prepare oysters to go because, he explained, fried oysters *must* be served and eaten immediately; he would not allow anyone to eat a soggy oyster!

Midwest

Illinois * Indiana * Iowa * Michigan *

Minnesota * Missouri * Ohio * Wisconsin

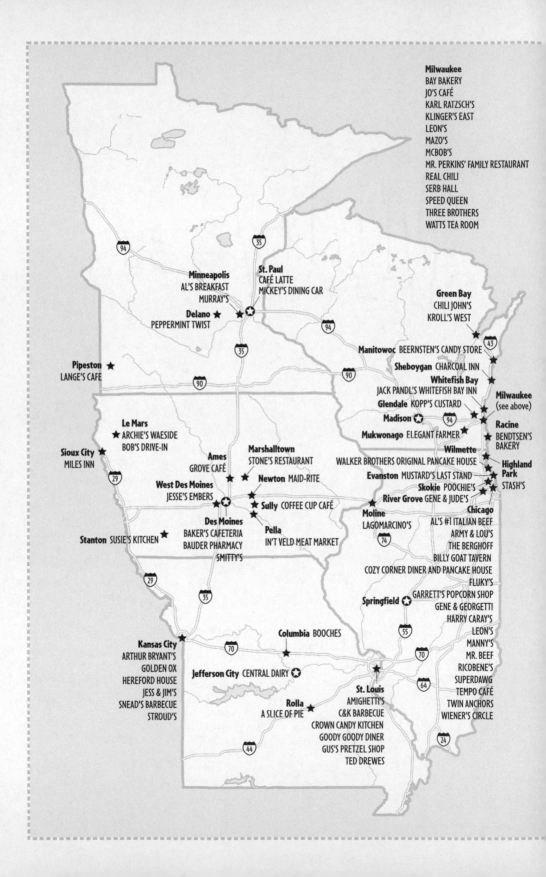

Milwaukee
BAY BAKERY
JO'S CAFÉ
KARL RATZSCH'S
KLINGER'S EAST
LEON'S
MAZO'S
MCBOB'S
MR. PERKINS' FAMILY RESTAURANT
REAL CHILI
SERB HALL
SPEED QUEEN
THREE BROTHERS
WATTS TEA ROOM

Minneapolis
AL'S BREAKFAST
MURRAY'S

St. Paul
CAFÉ LATTE
MICKEY'S DINING CAR

Delano ★
PEPPERMINT TWIST

Green Bay
CHILI JOHN'S
KROLL'S WEST

Manitowoc BEERNSTEN'S CANDY STORE

Sheboygan CHARCOAL INN

Whitefish Bay
JACK PANDL'S WHITEFISH BAY INN

Glendale KOPP'S CUSTARD

Madison ✪

Mukwonago ELEGANT FARMER

Milwaukee
(see above)

Racine
BENDTSEN'S
BAKERY

Pipeston ★
LANGE'S CAFÉ

Le Mars
★ ARCHIE'S WAESIDE
BOB'S DRIVE-IN

Sioux City
MILES INN

Ames
GROVE CAFÉ

Marshalltown
STONE'S RESTAURANT

Newton MAID-RITE

Wilmette
WALKER BROTHERS ORIGINAL PANCAKE HOUSE

Highland Park ★
STASH'S

Evanston MUSTARD'S LAST STAND

Skokie POOCHIE'S

River Grove GENE & JUDE'S

West Des Moines
JESSE'S EMBERS

Sully COFFEE CUP CAFÉ

Des Moines
BAKER'S CAFETERIA
BAUDER PHARMACY
SMITTY'S

Pella
IN'T VELD MEAT MARKET

Moline
LAGOMARCINO'S

Stanton SUSIE'S KITCHEN

Chicago
AL'S #1 ITALIAN BEEF
ARMY & LOU'S
THE BERGHOFF
BILLY GOAT TAVERN
COZY CORNER DINER AND PANCAKE HOUSE
FLUKY'S
GARRETT'S POPCORN SHOP
GENE & GEORGETTI
HARRY CARAY'S
LEON'S
MANNY'S
MR. BEEF
RICOBENE'S
SUPERDAWG
TEMPO CAFÉ
TWIN ANCHORS
WIENER'S CIRCLE

Springfield ✪

Columbia BOOCHES

Kansas City
ARTHUR BRYANT'S
GOLDEN OX
HEREFORD HOUSE
JESS & JIM'S
SNEAD'S BARBECUE
STROUD'S

Jefferson City CENTRAL DAIRY ✪

Rolla ★
A SLICE OF PIE

St. Louis
AMIGHETTI'S
C&K BARBECUE
CROWN CANDY KITCHEN
GOODY GOODY DINER
GUS'S PRETZEL SHOP
TED DREWES

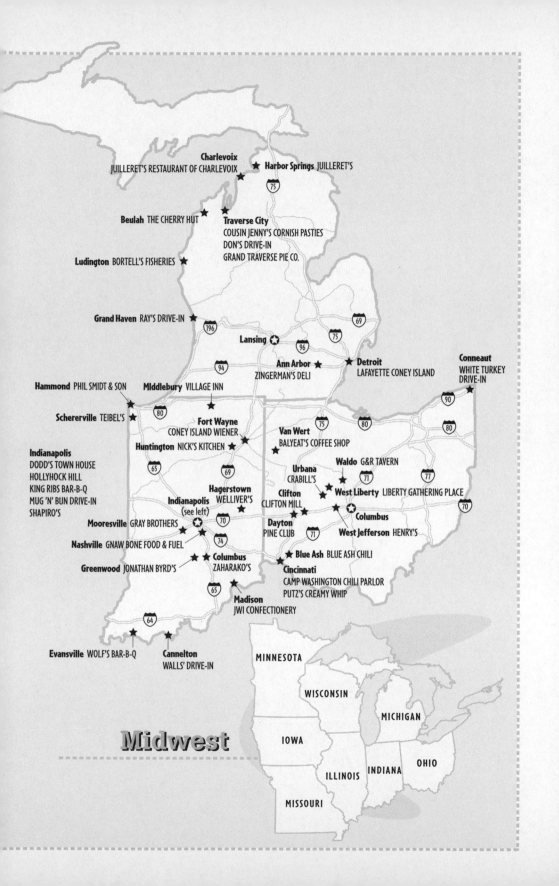

Charlevoix
JUILLERET'S RESTAURANT OF CHARLEVOIX   ★ **Harbor Springs** JUILLERET'S

Beulah THE CHERRY HUT

Traverse City
COUSIN JENNY'S CORNISH PASTIES
DON'S DRIVE-IN
GRAND TRAVERSE PIE CO.

Ludington BORTELL'S FISHERIES

Grand Haven RAY'S DRIVE-IN

Lansing

Ann Arbor ZINGERMAN'S DELI

Detroit
LAFAYETTE CONEY ISLAND

Conneaut
WHITE TURKEY
DRIVE-IN

Hammond PHIL SMIDT & SON

Middlebury VILLAGE INN

Schererville TEIBEL'S

Fort Wayne
CONEY ISLAND WIENER

Van Wert
BALYEAT'S COFFEE SHOP

Huntington NICK'S KITCHEN

Waldo G&R TAVERN

Indianapolis
DODD'S TOWN HOUSE
HOLLYHOCK HILL
KING RIBS BAR-B-Q
MUG 'N' BUN DRIVE-IN
SHAPIRO'S

Urbana
CRABILL'S

Hagerstown
WELLIVER'S

Clifton
CLIFTON MILL

West Liberty LIBERTY GATHERING PLACE

Indianapolis
(see left)

Columbus

Mooresville GRAY BROTHERS

Dayton
PINE CLUB

West Jefferson HENRY'S

Nashville GNAW BONE FOOD & FUEL

Greenwood JONATHAN BYRD'S

Columbus
ZAHARAKO'S

Blue Ash BLUE ASH CHILI

Cincinnati
CAMP WASHINGTON CHILI PARLOR
PUTZ'S CREAMY WHIP

Madison
JWI CONFECTIONERY

Evansville WOLF'S BAR-B-Q

Cannelton
WALLS' DRIVE-IN

MINNESOTA

WISCONSIN

MICHIGAN

IOWA

Midwest

ILLINOIS   INDIANA   OHIO

MISSOURI

Al's #1 Italian Beef

1079 W. Taylor St.   312-733-8896

Chicago, IL   LD | $

Italian beef is Chicago's premier street food. An Italian-American invention with only dim antecedents in the old country, this mighty sandwich is popular all over Chicago and, sad to say, is often very, very bad. If the sliced-thin beef is tough, if its gravy is bland or tepid, if the bun in which it nestles is wimpy, if the roasted pepper garnish is burnt or tired, or if the giardiniera condiment is undistinguished, you will wonder why Chicagoans even bother debating who makes the best. But if you sidle up to the counter at Al's in old Little Italy and order a big beef, double dipped (that's a large sandwich, momentarily immersed in a pan full of natural juices), you will understand. The beef is so tender you want to call it delicate, and yet its garlic soul packs a devastating punch. The juices are very essence of beef, so good that you will find yourself using shreds of roll to mop up puddles that spill onto the butcher-paper wrapper at your counter space. Al's is also notable for charcoal-cooked Italian sausages, and for its magnificent combo sandwich—beef *and* sausage loaded into a sturdy bun.

Al's accommodations are strictly stand-up: at counters inside the restaurant and at car trunks or off roofs in the parking lot outside. After a meal, stroll across the street to Mario's Italian Ice shop.

Army & Lou's

    422 E. 75th St.   773-483-3100
    Chicago, IL   BLD | $$

A friendly storefront open since 1945, Army & Lou's is the place to go for soul food—breakfast, lunch, or dinner, and, Friday evenings, jazz performed by South Side artists. We felt welcome despite being the only white people in the place the day we went for lunch; wall decor is exclusively pictures of African-Americans. It is said that the city's first black mayor, Harold Washington, ate here all the time.

While the menu features a wide array of soul food, including chitterlings (served with spaghetti!) and ham hock with mixed greens, there are plenty of items that appear to be just what you'd expect in any neighborhood café, black or white. We say "appear" because the smothered pork chops we ordered were soulful to the nth degree, and the fried chicken would never, ever be mistaken for KFC's flabby bird parts. Next visit, we intend to order the curiously labeled menu item "U.S. Prime Kosher Short Ribs of Beef" and, no doubt, more of that superb fried chicken.

All entrees come with a choice from a long list of appetizing side dishes, including candied sweet potatoes and corn bread dressing with giblet gravy. Dessert is a choice of fruit cobbler (ooey-gooey peach the day we were here), sweet-potato pie, or bread pudding with lemon sauce.

The Berghoff

    17 West Adams St.   312-427-3170
    Chicago, IL   LD | $$

The Berghoff (since 1898) has a German accent, but it is distinctly American. To dine at the bare wood tables in this dark-oak place is to recall a style of bountiful urban gastronomy that predates Prohibition. Vintage murals on the walls show images of old Chicago and the Columbian Exposition of 1893 and portraits of stern Berghoff ancestors. Longtime customers start their meal with a shot or two of The Berghoff's private stock, high-proof bourbon and/or flagons of brewed-here beer (light, dark, or red).

Appetizers range from creamed herring to Continental escargots; and while The Berghoff is best known for such Eastern European classics as sauerbraten with potato pancakes, rahm schnitzel with spaetzel, boiled pork shank, veal bratwurst, and pork knockwurst, it also happens to be a fine place to enjoy such Midwest meals as broiled Lake Superior whitefish and house-smoked baby back ribs with shoestring potatoes. We are particularly fond of The Berghoff's lunchroom basics, i.e., navy bean soup, meat loaf and mashed potatoes, hot turkey or roast beef sandwiches, fried calves liver with sautéed onions. A plate of corned beef, arrayed atop a heap of steamed-soft cabbage, is well accompanied by slices of the restaurant's two kinds of dark bread; and this kitchen's creamed spinach is some of the tastiest anywhere. Noteworthy desserts are warm, cinnamon-seasoned apple strudel and bread pudding with vanilla sauce.

Apron-clad waiters provide brisk and efficient service; when it comes time to settle up, the transaction is done the old-fashioned way. You give the man cash and he stands by the table making change from the money in his pockets.

Billy Goat Tavern

430 N. Michigan Ave.   312-222-1525
Chicago, IL   BLD | $

At the Billy Goat Tavern the cry of "Cheezborger, cheezborger" really does echo across the counter as satirized in the *Saturday Night Live* skit about the (semi-)fictitious Olympia Diner. A few other kinds of sandwiches are listed on the movable-type board above the Billy Goat counter, but if anyone orders ham or salami, the counterman will pause, scowl, and shoot back, "Cheezborger? Double cheese, that's the best." As soon as one is flipped and its cheese has begun to soften and melt, it is stacked inside a kaiser roll in a sheet of waxed paper on the counter, at which point the counterman calls out, "Double cheese!" As he does so, he finds you in the crowd of people standing in wait for lunch and makes eye contact. Then he calls even louder, "Sir! Double cheese." The calls from countermen to customers come every bit as fast as the countermen's calls to the burger flipper at the grill. It is a cacophony of "Double cheese!" "Two double cheese!" and "Triple cheese!" interspersed with "Cheezborger, cheezborger, cheezborger."

While by no means a gourmet meal, a Billy Goat double is immensely satisfying: an ideal greasy-spoon combo of meat, bun, cheese, and condiments. A word to the wise: Don't get creative when ordering. "May I have a slice of tomato?" an out-of-towner asks in a meek voice as she gets to the head of the Billy Goat order line.

"No tomato!" a counterman barks back.

"Well done?" queries her friend, also a neophyte.

"No well done!" the counterman replies. "All the same. Double cheese, double's the best."

The place itself, on Lower Michigan Avenue, is a trip. The tavern's door leads down a flight of stairs to a subterranean watering hole, a shadowy realm completely unlike the Magnificent Mile above. The interior is gauzy with smoke from the seven-days-a-week, twenty-hours-a-day grilling that fills the air with the scent of frying bacon in the morning and frying burgers in the afternoon.

One Tuesday at 9 A.M. two reporters who have pulled an all-nighter sit at a table in the bar with beers and bacon-egg-cheese sandwiches griping to each other about all the good autopsy details that an editor cut from a crime story. A hitchhiker with a knapsack on this back and a bottle of Schlitz in his hand keeps walking from his stool to the window and looking up, waiting for it to get light so he can hit the road. "No sun, no sun," a counterman keeps telling him, but the man has had too much beer to realize that down here, it is always dark.

Cozy Corner Diner and Pancake House

2294 N. Milwaukee Ave.   773-276-2215
Chicago, IL   BL | $

Cozy Corner calls itself a pancake house and offers nearly a dozen varieties of flapjack, including simple buttermilk 'cakes that are soft and fluffy. They're quite all right, but when we come to Cozy Corner for breakfast we skip the pancakes and order eggs and potatoes.

One good way to get them is as a "Skillet." A Cozy Corner Skillet is a pan filled with hash brown potatoes that are topped with eggs and enriched with onions and cheese (for The Hobo Skillet), ham, onions, mushrooms, and cheese (The Gypsy Skillet), grilled chicken breast, peppers, onions, mushrooms, and cheese (The Fajita Skillet), etc.

The hash browns are the main reason the skillets are so good. They are finely cut, cooked so the edges of the pile are webbed with crisp potato strips and the center is soft and oily. The potatoes come with all egg dishes, among the best being ham and eggs that include ham described by the waitress as "off the bone," meaning cut from a baked-here, sugar-cured ham. We also love the steak and eggs made with a charred skirt steak or New York sirloin.

Most of its fans consider Cozy Corner a house of breakfast ("served any time"), but in fact we have also enjoyed satisfying square-meal lunches, including roast beef, meat loaf, ocean perch, and broiled pork chops served with homemade soup (note: potato cabbage and beef barley soups on Wednesday!).

This is a bustling restaurant with fast turnover at the counter and in the booths, a team of efficient waitresses, and a lady at the cash register who flirts with every male between the age of eight and eighty-eight. The decorative theme is nostalgia; the walls are hung with pictures of pop culture icons including Jackie Gleason, Marilyn Monroe, Sammy Davis, Jr., Marlon Brando, the Beatles, and the Stones. In another context, such images might seem cloying; but this diner at the corner of Milwaukee and California has so much true urban character of its own (and so many *characters* off Chicago's streets) that the fun-time decor is pretty much irrelevant. The tone of the Cozy Corner is set by the elevated train rumbling past a block away, by the waitresses with their ever-ready pots of coffee, and by the plainclothes cop on the counter stool whose too-small shirt and too-large belly cause the .357 Magnum in his waist holster to dangle precariously as he forks through a Hungry Man breakfast of three eggs, three pancakes, and a double order of sugar-sweet, off-the-bone ham.

Fluky's

| 6821 N. Western Ave. | 773-274-3652 |
| Chicago, IL | BLD \| $ |

Frankfurter historians believe the Chicago red hot as we know it may have been invented at Fluky's, now a small chain of modern cafeteria-style hot doggeries where they know how to pile on the proper condiments, and where the poppy seed buns are impeccably fresh. We were not so impressed by Fluky's uninteresting French fries, but the Polish sausage—denser and crustier than a red hot—is superb. And we must mention that Fluky's is the only restaurant we know that also offers short, tubular lengths of hot-dog-shaped gum (cinnamon flavored) for chewing after the meal!

Garrett's Popcorn Shop

670 N. Michigan Ave.   312-944-4730

Chicago, IL $

Four other locations around Chicago

Chicago is known for many distinctive food passions, from prime steak to four-star hot dogs, and from pan pizza to Frango mints; but we have yet to see official recognition of the fact that no city is more caramel conscious. In the fall, candy stores all around Chicagoland produce spectacularly good caramel apples. Turtle sundaes, topped with fudge and caramel sauce, are ubiquitous on local ice cream parlor menus; and it was in Chicago that we ate one of the most wonderful slices of apple pie we've ever had—topped with warm caramel sauce and a globe of vanilla ice cream.

Of all Chicago's caramel-focused treats, the one that makes us dizzy with desire is known as CaramelCrisp. The place that makes it, Garrett Popcorn Shop, is so fussy about its product that one time, after we praised it on a radio show as "the best caramel corn on earth," we got an urgent message from the management informing us that what Garrett sells is *not* caramel corn. It is *CaramelCrisp,* a trademarked name for a product that, to us, looks a lot like caramel corn.

Legal niceties aside, we must agree with Garrett: This stuff is in a class by itself. Although it has the fundamental structure of caramel corn—popcorn sheathed in a dark-gold candy coat—its flavor and texture are dramatically superior to any other kind of candied corn. In fact, it doesn't really taste candied at all. The popcorn itself is a tender, earthy note within its caramel crust, which is deeply buttery and has a dark flavor that teeters at the edge of tasting burnt. Like the singed top of a well-made crème brûlée, the corn's crunch smacks of fire more than sugar.

Also on the menu in this little Michigan Avenue snack shop (one of five Garrett's about town) is rich cheese corn and unbelievably buttery, buttered corn. Some connoisseurs call for "a mix," which is CaramelCrisp and cheese corn for a sweet/savory one-two punch. But we are CaramelCrisp purists. We buy about a pound bag and eat it greedily until hunger is only a distant memory.

Don't be fooled by similar stores and similar caramel corns in other cities. Garrett's CaramelCrisp is available only in Chicago. They are all set up to mail-order it to you, which is great, but we must say that it is a real pleasure to stop in one of the Chicago stores where, as you wait in line to place your order, you watch the corn being popped, the butter being poured, and the CaramelCrisp stirred so it sticks together just a little bit but does not clump.

Gene & Georgetti

500 N. Franklin St.   312-527-3718

Chicago, IL   D | $$$

Gene & Georgetti is Chicago's great steak house. A manly supper club with out-of-fashion decor and waiters who are more efficient than obsequious, it serves meat that reminds you why steak is celebration food. Served unadorned and alone on an oval plate, G&G's sirloin strips and filets mignon are magnificent hunks of prime beef with glistening crust and succulent insides—the best meat money can buy. They are accompanied by thick cottage fried potato chips and, if you've got a big-time appetite, preceded by the cornucopic tossed antipasto known as "garbage salad": iceberg lettuce, celery, tomato, radish, slivers of cheese and salami, pepperoncini, and pink shrimp marinated in an Italian vinaigrette.

We only recently came to realize that Gene & Georgetti is a place to eat not only steak but also those two distinct Chicagoland specialties, chicken Vesuvio and shrimp de Jonghe. The former is a heap of chicken sautéed and then baked to utmost tenderness, piled on a plate with wedges of equally tender potato in a pool of super-garlicky white wine and spice. The skin on the chicken, plastered with herbs and permeated with the savor of chicken fat, peels off the pieces of meat like strips of crisp-fried bacon.

Shrimp de Jonghe is another garlicky meal, in this case involving bread crumbs, sherry, and nearly illegal amounts of butter. G&G's shrimp de Jonghe is not the baked casserole made by the handful of other Chicago restaurants that still serve the century-old specialty. It is a broad, deep plate that holds a golden pool of herbed garlic butter laced with crumbs so soft they have become tiny supple shreds of flavor. In this pool wades a spill of huge pink shrimp. You can cut the shrimp into bite-size pieces with a fork and knife, but you also need plenty of G&G's stout Italian bread for mopping all that garlic butter. Also on the menu, at twice the price of a two-pound porterhouse steak, is lobster de Jonghe, which is a seascape of white hunks of tail meat cosseted in the luminous pool of buttery juices. For this dish, so rich it is dizzying, we call upon a food-writer adjective we have never once used in two decades of describing things to eat: *sinful!*

Gene & Jude's

2720 N. River Rd.　　　　　　　708-452-7634

River Grove, IL　　　　　　　　LD | $

For most visitors to Chicago, Gene & Jude's is off the beaten path, but if you happen to arrive at O'Hare hungry, it's well worth a ten-minute trip in the other direction to stop at this venerable—since 1946—hot dog stand in River Grove. It is a classic Chicagoland street-food experience, and there are some hot dog connoisseurs who assert that Gene & Jude's way with Vienna franks is the original Chicago way, before arrivistes added pickle spears, tomato slices, and celery salt to the formula. Available condiments here include only mustard, piccalilli (great zesty-sweet piccalilli!), raw onions, and hot sport peppers . . . and also French fries, which we'll get to in a moment.

The menu is minimal. You get a hot dog or a double dog. The natural-casing, all-beef Vienna brand tube steaks are slim and snappy; they are inserted into soft buns and dressed as you request. It's a terrific hot dog, but it gets put over the top by French fries: whatever toppings are included, each dog gets heaped with a large fistful of them. And these are some of the best, freshest French fries in Chicago. As you wait for your hot dog to be prepared, you can watch the counter folks peel and cut whole potatoes, then fry them, drain them, and pile them onto waiting dogs. They spend a good long time in the bubbling oil, emerging a dark, dark brown with some pieces crunchy through and through, others thick and potato-creamy inside.

Fine dining? *Not!* Gene & Jude's is small and extremely modest. There are no tables or chairs at all; as is Chicago custom, the eatery offers a chest-high counter to which you may bring your meal, unwrap it, and eat standing up. When you're finished, use the waxed paper in which the food was served to gather up any scraps and heave them into one of the large garbage cans in the corners of the room. We find this arrangement comfortable and eminently practical for eating extremely messy food; however, many customers choose to dine in their cars in the parking lot.

Harry Caray's

33 W. Kinzie St. 312-828-0966
Chicago, IL LD | $$$

We tend not to frequent sports bars because the food is usually less important than what's on TV. Harry Caray's is one huge exception. It is the sports bar to end all sports bars—especially heavenly for Chicago team fans—and it is loaded with memorabilia not only from the Cubs, but from the life of legendary announcer Harry Caray.

Beyond his antics in the broadcast booth, which always included leading fans in a seventh-inning singalong of "Take Me Out to The Ballgame," Caray was known as a man who loved to eat. And the place he opened is testimony to that passion. This is one truly great Chicago restaurant. For example, there is not a better prime steak in Chicago. We like the sirloin best, grilled in a coat of cracked peppercorns. Other highlights of the menu include such familiar Italian specialties as lasagna, veal parmigiana, and a risotto of the day.

Among the "Italian" dishes is one that we've found only in Chicago, and it is magnificent: chicken Vesuvio. Chicken Vesuvio is several bone-in pieces of chicken, sautéed then baked to utmost succulence, encased in a dark, red-gold crust of lush skin that slides from the meat as the meat slides off its bone. Is it tender? Forget about it! The dark meat in particular sets new standards for chicken tenderness. Piled among the chicken are wedges of potato, long-sautéed in a bath of white wine, garlic, olive oil, and spice until they are soft as mashed inside with crunchy edges. Even if you don't get chicken Vesuvio, "Vesuvio" potatoes are available as a side dish to go with any steak or chop. The only problem about ordering them is that you likely won't also be ordering Harry Caray's garlic mashed potatoes, which are superb.

The setting is vintage: a 1895 Dutch Renaissance–style limestone building now on the National Register of Historic Places, its interior a luxuriously muscular space of mahogany woodwork and broad tables covered by thick white napery. Although a sumptuous place to which many customers come in pinstriped business suits, there is a democratic feel about this dining room that makes any decently dressed customer feel right at home. Harry Caray was a people's hero, and that's the way he liked it.

Lagomarcino's

1422 5th Ave.   309-764-1814

Moline, IL   LD | $

Started as a Moline, Illinois, candy store in 1908, Lagomarcino's is still renowned for hand-dipped chocolates, as well as fancy fruit baskets. You won't find better sponge candy anywhere. (Sponge candy is crunchy chunks of spun molasses enrobed in dark chocolate, also known as "fairy food," "seafoam," and "violet crumbles.") And the chocolate-dipped fruit repertoire includes orange, apricot, pineapple, pear, and kiwi.

What we like best is coming to Lagomarcino's and finding a seat in one of the fine aged wooden booths for a light lunch followed by a not-so-light hot fudge sundae. The fudge is made from a recipe acquired in 1918 from a traveling salesman for the princely sum of $25. It is a bittersweet, not-too-thick elixir that just may be the best hot fudge in this solar system or any other. When you order a sundae, the great, dark stuff is served in a manner befitting its distinction: in a small pitcher alongside the tulip glass full of ice cream and whipped cream, so you can pour or spoon it on to taste. This serving technique provides a fascinating demonstration of how one's soda fountain habits reflect one's personality. Do you pour on all the fudge at one time, willy-nilly, risking that some will spill over the sides of the serving glass? Do you pour it on spoonful by spoonful, carefully ensuring that every bite will have just the proper balance of ice cream and fudge? Or do you eat all the ice cream, with maybe just a dash of fudge poured on, so you can then conclude your snack by downing all the hot fudge that remains in one dizzy chocoholic binge?

Leon's

1640 E. 79th St.   773-731-1454

Chicago, IL   LD | $

Leon's other locations in Chicago are 8249 S. Cottage Grove, 1158 W. 59th, and 4550 S. Archer.

For the Roadfooder traveling through town, Leon's is a huge pain in the neck. That's because the food it serves is some of the messiest barbecue anywhere, and there is no place to eat it. Everything at Leon's is takeout.

On a pleasant afternoon, it would be great to dine standing up off the trunk of one's car, but local gulls are wise, and as soon as any food is out in the open, they start flocking and squawking and making threatening dives toward your meal. While we have never actually been attacked, these birds make outdoor dining feel downright dangerous. So you eat in your car, winding up with sauce on your fingers, the steering wheel, the seats, the gearshift, *everywhere*.

Rant over. The fact is, we love this place. The food is Chicago soul barbecue at its finest. Ribs, rib tips, and hot links are insanely luxurious—the rib meat pulling from its bones in long, savory strips, the hot link a real Chicago-style sausage, very soulful but with a distinct Italian accent. All these things are available with mild or hot sauce, the latter a serious lip-tingler. They are served in a cardboard boat, the meat topped with French fries, the fries sopped with sauce, the whole pile crowned with a few pieces of spongy white bread, the purpose of which is to absorb sauce and rib juice.

In our experience, Leon's looks scarier than it is. It's the only restaurant we know in which customers and staff are separated by bulletproof glass. As in a bank, you slide your money through a slot, and when your meal is packed, they send it out via a lazy Susan that ensures you can't shoot them or, we suppose, vice versa. We wouldn't likely visit Leon's at midnight, but every lunch we've had here has been a totally pleasant experience, the staff helpful and clientele friendly. It's only the birds in the parking lot that feel threatening.

Manny's

| 1141 S. Jefferson St. | 312-939-2855 |
| Chicago, IL | BL \| $ |

Manny's smells great: hot beef stew, roasted chicken, hot corned beef, and potato pancakes. It sounds good, too. Men behind the cafeteria counter call out above kitchen clatter to get customers' orders. At tables in the two big dining rooms, people chatter noisily the way happy eaters tend to do. There is a lot of table-hopping among them. Manny's clientele are old friends: police officers, cabbies, local businesspeople for whom this place has been home-away-from-home for years.

Manny's is a Jewish (but non-kosher) restaurant with traditional deli food (and more) dished out every day starting at five in the morning. The variety of choices along the lunch line is tremendous, including such

Old World favorites as knishes (potato dumplings), kasha (buckwheat groats) with bowtie noodles, and prune tsimmes (a sweet vegetable stew). The chicken soup is gold in color, thick with schmaltz (chicken fat), and holds a fall-apart-tender matzoh ball. Blintzes (order by the piece) are tender crêpes rolled around sweetened pot cheese, sizzled in butter, then garnished with sour cream.

Manny's is famous for its corned beef sandwich: three or four inches of hot, lean, rose-pink, thin-sliced corned beef stacked between slices of sour-crusted rye. These are so popular there are usually half a dozen of them already assembled atop the counter at the sandwich station in the cafeteria line. Along with sandwiches, instead of French fries or chips, Manny's serves magnificent potato pancakes: oval patties with gnarled skins encasing shredded potato with a trace of onion flavor. Potato pancakes are terrific on the side not only of sandwiches but of any stick-to-the-ribs main course, especially a pot roast. Or they are good all by themselves, accompanied by chunky apple sauce and/or sour cream.

There are all-American lunch counter favorites, too: turkey drumsticks every Wednesday, franks and beans on Saturday, macaroni and cheese on Friday. Or how about chicken pot pie; or a slab of meat loaf with mashed potatoes; you can even order that dowdy hodgepodge known as American chop suey. Manny's is a temple of honest food that tastes great but is not the least bit gussied-up.

Mr. Beef

666 N. Orleans   312-337-8500
Chicago, IL   BL | $

Italian beef is such a common feature of Chicago's gastronomic landscape that most native Chicagoans (M. Stern included) never think of it as something special until they move away, then realize with horror that one cannot get it anywhere else, certainly not in Italy. It is roast beef, slow-cooked and vigorously seasoned, sliced thin and sopped in natural gravy, loaded into bread torpedoes, garnished with either roasted peppers or hot pepper giardiniera.

Of all the Italian beef sandwiches in town, we put Mr. Beef right up there at the pinnacle of excellence. Its meat is lean, rare, maniacally garlicked, and it oozes vast quantities of natural gravy into the greedy jaws of bread that surround it. For a special treat, we suggest a Mr. Beef "combo sandwich"—beef plus a length of tough-skinned, juicy, sweet Italian sausage.

As for atmosphere, Mr. Beef's is superb: picnic tables provide a view of the parking lot and the Scala Packing Company across the street, where much of Chicago's finest beef originates.

Mustard's Last Stand

1613 Central St.   847-864-2700
Evanston, IL   LD | $

Chicago red hots are in a class by themselves, their claim to glory starting with the meat itself: all-beef, long and slim, dense-textured, and with a garlic kick. It is steamed until taut enough that a first bite erupts with savory juices on the tongue. Of penultimate importance is the bun. Expect a Windy City red hot to be nestled in a steamy-soft pocket of fleecy bread, preferably one from Rosen's bakery, spangled with poppy seeds across its tan outsides. The bun serves as a handy mitt and naturally plays a secondary note beneath the meat within, but it does provide a soft-flavor environment that is absolutely necessary for full appreciation of the spicy red hot and its condiments.

It is those condiments that elevate Chicago wiener culture to a higher plane. Bright yellow mustard and dark-green piccalilli are the basics; but every good dog house offers plenty more, including sport peppers, raw onions, full slices of tomato, long pickle spears, and a dusting of celery salt. When you ask for a dog with the works, only the tiny and ultra-hot sport peppers are considered "optional," and don't dare ask for ketchup—on a Chicago hot dog, it is taboo.

If you suddenly crave a true Chicago hot dog while in the northern suburb of Evanston, Mustard's Last Stand is an adorable little shop near Northwestern's stadium that has just the ticket: a Vienna-brand all-beef red hot in a poppy seed roll with all the Chi-town condiments available . . . even ketchup.

In fact, the house catchphrase is "Catch-up to Mustard's." As a test—and only as a test—we requested some on a frankfurter. "Really?" asked the counterman. "Are you sure?" When we told him we were only kidding, and wanted the ketchup for dipping French fries (a proper use for it in Chicago), he beamed with relief and took extra care arranging the condiments on our red hot like a horn of plenty.

Connoisseurs of cheap-eats interior decor will admire the counter stools at Mustard's, each of which is topped with a lovely portrait of a full-dressed hot dog.

Poochie's

3832 Dempster   847-673-0100
Skokie, IL   LD | $

To say that Poochie's is a no-frills kind of restaurant is totally correct in one respect: There are only two tables in the front room, plus three deuces in a dark corridor in the back. Most customers dine standing up or perched on stools. Service at the order counter, while fun and sassy, seems chaotic (but somehow always works), and is light-years away from the gracious rituals of fine dining. When the man behind the counter tells you your food is ready, you carry it yourself to the chest-high eating shelf at the perimeter of the room, unwrap it, and consume it. When done, toss your refuse in a can and be on your way. A ten-minute meal, if that.

Informal though it may be, the food Poochie's serves is exquisite. To us, a meal at Poochie's is more delicious and more deeply satisfying than the finest four-star dinner in New York. In its own way, it is abundant with frills . . . which include barely melted orange cheese available to top just about every dish in the house (dogs, sausages, burgers, char-cooked salami, French fries) as well as the full panoply of Chicagoland frankfurter condiments: mustard, ketchup, piccalilli, raw onions, sliced tomato, pickle spears, ground pepper, and celery salt, plus deliriously tasty sweet grilled onions.

Poochie's red hots are superb. Standard hot dogs are all-beef Vienna franks, boiled to perfect plumpness and served in tender, seeded Rosen's-brand buns. Char dogs, cooked over coals, are crusty, blackened versions thereof. Polish sausages are plumper, porkier variants that are slit in a spiral pattern to attain maximum crunchy surface area. And if one in a bun of any of these tube steaks is insufficient for your appetite, you can get either a jumbo dog or a double. Our personal favorite meal is a jumbo char dog with (superb) Cheddar fries on the side.

Poochie's is proud of its char-cooked hamburgers, and we like them very much, especially piled high with those sweet grilled onions. But if you are passing through Chicago and stop at Poochie's with time for only one street food indulgence, make it a red hot with the works and a side of fries. It is an only-in-Chicago meal, and a jewel in the crown of America's Roadfood.

Ricobene's

252 W. 26th St.

Chicago, IL

312-225-5555

LD | $

Italian beef gets all the glory when Chicago street food is discussed, and Ricobene's serves a fine beef sandwich with natural gravy; but the main claim to fame of this 1946-vintage Bridgeport eatery (now moved to spiffy new quarters) is its breaded steak sandwich. A great Italian-American neighborhood invention, the sandwich is a vast, pounded-thin sheet of meat that is lightly breaded and fried, then rolled into a bundle and stuffed inside a long loaf of Italian bread with a coat of red "gravy" (tomato sauce). Favored garnishes include fried hot peppers, spicy giardiniera vegetable medley, or shredded mozzarella. It is a meal—no, two meals—in a bun.

Beyond its bodacious breaded steak sandwich, Ricobene's serves virtually all the great Chicago street foods, including Italian beef, pizza, and hot dogs, as well as a delectable "Vesuvio Italian Classic" sandwich. This is a quick-eats version of the meal known in more upscale restaurants as chicken Vesuvio (garlic-flavored chicken with cooked-soft hunks of potato). In this case, you get a crisp breaded cutlet dressed with onions, lettuce, tomato, and mayo stuffed into a length of Italian bread.

Whatever else you order, be sure to get an order of French fries, either plain or gobbed with molten Cheddar cheese. These are some of the city's best—dark, skin-on, and crisp.

Stash's

610 Central

Highland Park, IL

847-432-6550

LD | $

If you are north of the city and in need of a great classic Chicago hot dog, find Stash's in Highland Park. It's not a charming edifice, located in Port Clinton Square along with a bunch of mall-style businesses, but the red hots and French fries are first-rate.

You can have your all-beef frank steamed, giving it a moist, luscious character, but we prefer ours charred, meaning its surface gets crusty all around the edges, while the inside still drips juice. It is pocketed in a fresh Rosen's-brand poppy seed bun and topped with your choice from a selection of nine different condiments, from mustard and relish to super-hot sport peppers and celery salt. If you get it "dragged through the garden," the hot dog itself will be completely eclipsed by long pickle spears, tomato slices, onions, etc. This is a beautiful wiener, and delicious. There are jumbo dogs and Polishes, too, as well as double dogs in a single bun, but it's our opinion that one of Stash's normal dogs, garnished with a plentiful supply of condiments, is one perfect food.

Beyond hot dogs, Stash's has a vast menu that includes a pasta bar from which the management will create whatever sort of dish you want from ten kinds of noodles, six different sauces, and all sorts of vegetable and cheese toppings. In addition, there are hamburgers, beef sandwiches, gyros, wraps, pockets, and quesadillas. We've never tried any of these things, but we do have one other important recommendation to make: French fries. With a Stash's dog, they are essential. These are four-star potatoes with a creamy center and crunchy edge. Cheddar cheese is available as a topping, but in this case, all we want is a sprinkle of salt.

Superdawg

6363 N. Milwaukee Ave. 773-763-0660
Chicago, IL LD | $

Superdawg has been in the upper echelon of Chicago's red-hot joints since 1948; and although it has recently remodeled, the old drive-in maintains tremendous kitsch appeal and still has genuine carhops and the "Suddenserver" automated order system. Its mascots, a pair of ten-foot-tall statues of a male and female hot dog (named Flaurie and Maurie), still stand atop the roof dressed in leopard-skin togas, flexing muscles and winking electrically like goofy airport beacons.

The hot dogs are Chicago classics: muscular, brick-red, all-beef franks with a good garlic kick, loaded into steamed-soft buns and topped with condiments of your choice. Of course, most Chicagoans want *all* available condiments (with the exception of grilled onions, which connoisseurs believe compete with the warm succulence of the dog itself). You get bright yellow mustard, sliced plum tomatoes, a dill pickle spear, hot sport peppers, beautiful spruce-green piccalilli relish, and a dash of celery salt. Sides include deep-fried Superonions (chips, rather than rings) or fine crinkle-cut Superfries that arrive perfectly salted. To drink, the choices include a Supermalt or Supershake that truly earns its name: no suction on a straw can draw it up; these are "beverages" that must be gulped or eaten with a spoon.

The grilled onions we eschew on our red hots do go great on Superdawg's excellent Superburgers and Whooperburgers (doubles), as well as Whoopercheesies and even Whoopskidogs (which is the house name for a Polish sausage).

Meals are presented packed in a cardboard box that announces, "Your Superdawg lounges inside contentedly cushioned in Superfries, comfortably attired in mustard, relish, onion, pickle, and hot pepper."

Tempo Café

6 East Chestnut St.   312-943-4373
Chicago, IL   Always open | $

On an unlikely corner of Chicago's Gold Coast, just blocks from the swankiest shops and hotels in town, Tempo Café is a 24/7/365 coffee shop that serves working-class food at affordable prices. Cops especially seem to make camp in the capacious booths, to which waitresses relentlessly bring coffee refills for bottomless cups.

Tempo is best known for eggs. Omelets are huge and handsome, served in silver skillets on wooden trivets. Special combinations include the Michigan, which is cheddar cheese and diced Delicious apples; the State Street (broccoli, ham, mushrooms, tomato), Jamaican (banana, walnut, honey), and Greek (feta, tomato, onion). The eggs and their filling are the top stratum in the skillet; below them is a thick layer of crunchy, crusty potato discs worthy of a good steak house. On the side comes a plate of Greek toast, which is thick and spangled with sesame seeds, and to dress the toast you get a globe of sweet butter and a ramekin of house-made, fine-cut marmalade. Before breakfast is served, everybody gets a single pitted prune and a wedge of orange. Nice rituals!

Breakfast is served round-the-clock, but if you come to Tempo for another kind of meal, there is a full menu of sandwiches, hot dinners, and stir-fries. In addition to good coffee, the beverage list includes latte, cappuccino, and vegetable juices.

Twin Anchors

1655 N. Sedgwick   312-266-1616

Chicago, IL   D | $$

Pop culture devotees know Twin Anchors for two big reasons: It was a favorite hangout of Frank Sinatra when he came to the toddlin' town, and it was transformed into O'Reilly's Italian Restaurant for the Bonnie Hunt melodrama, *Return to Me*.

Foodies know it for just one reason: ribs. Here are the best baby back ribs in a city obsessed with rib excellence. They are succulent beyond description, tender enough that teeth are optional to eat them, and basted with a wonderful "zesty sauce" that is just hot enough to tease even more sweet pork flavor from the meat. (Mild sauce is also available.) For the record, this type of rib is significantly different from the spareribs commonly offered in soul-food barbecues, the latter being larger, denser, and a good exercise for healthy dentition. We would not call Twin Anchor ribs soulful, but we would definitely say they're delicious.

There is a full menu beyond ribs, including steaks, fried chicken, and sandwiches. They look fine . . . on other people's plates. When we come to Twin Anchors, we know nothing but ribs.

The place itself is a charming corner tavern in Old Town dating back to the early twentieth century. It was a soda pop store (that is, speakeasy) during Prohibition, then christened "Twin Anchors" in 1932 by a proprietor who had twin sons whom he considered his anchors to reality. Today the walls are festooned with nautical knickknacks and abundant pictures of the Chairman of the Board.

Walker Brothers Original Pancake House

153 Green Bay Rd.   847-251-6000

Wilmette, IL   BLD | $$

There are nearly 100 Original Pancake Houses around the country, all vaguely related to the original Original, which opened in Portland, Oregon, in 1953. We've never eaten in a bad one—the formula of using top-notch ingredients and a repertoire of great recipes is sure success—but the Walker Brothers franchise in Wilmette, opened in 1960, raises the bar even higher. Decorated in art nouveau stained glass and wood, it is incredibly clean and comfortable. Everything served is eye-opening good, from the fresh orange juice and dark coffee (with a pitcher of heavy cream) to thick-sliced bacon and chicken-apple sausage. Order eggs and you may exclaim, as we have, "I forgot how good a fresh egg, cooked in pure butter, can taste!"

Granted, it is difficult to order eggs when the pancakes are so good. The plainer ones are simple excellence—rich buttermilk cakes, tangy sourdough flapjacks, old-time buckwheat; the snazzy "crêpe" menu includes banana crêpes, Cherry Kijafa crêpes, and luxuriant seafood Newburg with crusty potato pancakes.

Our favorite meals, and the kitchen's showstoppers, are the baked pancakes, either the German pancake or apple pancake, both of which are made with egg-rich batter that causes them to puff high above the skillet in which they are baked. Both arrive completely eclipsing the plate on which they sit. The German pancake is accompanied by lemon wedges and powdered sugar to create its own sweet-tart syrup. The apple pancake, a veritable mesa of breakfast, is a bubbling feast of fruit and cinnamon and tender batter—approximately ten thousand calories of deliciousness.

The only bad thing to say about Walker Brothers is that sometimes you can't get in. There is often a wait for a table, a long wait on weekends.

The Wiener's Circle

2622 N. Clark St.   773-477-7444
Chicago, IL   LD | $

The name of The Wiener's Circle is a typically Chicagoan bit of culinary wordplay, but there is no joke about the red hots served here. They are among the city's best, presented in steamy-soft Rosen's-brand poppy seed buns and topped with flawless condiments.

The mustard is classic yellow, the piccalilli is brilliant green and vividly pickly, the tomatoes are small and flavorful—four or five whole, fresh-cut discs per dog. And there are grilled onions or raw, sport peppers (hot!), and a sprinkle of celery salt. Have your frankfurter as you like it, from naked to loaded, and you will not be disappointed. The major decision to make, dog-wise, is whether you want it boiled or charred. At many of Chicago's red-hot joints, we recommend boiled or steamed because it yields the plumpest, tautest skin, but here at The Wiener's Circle, charred is the way to go. Cooked on the grate just behind the order counter, the char dogs get a good crunch from the flames. For us, that rugged tube steak nestled in its super-tender bun is the essence of Chicago.

Don't get a hot dog without French fries. These are beauties: hand-cut, freshly fried, served in ridiculously large amounts that totally overflow their cardboard boat and fall all over the waxed paper on which the boat is pushed toward you out the order window.

Inside, the perimeter of The Wiener's Circle is outfitted with counters and stools well suited for hot-dog eating and for gazing out the window at Clark Street. Orders are taken and food delivered by one of several gals at the open-kitchen window. "Char Dog!" one calls out to a customer, using what he ordered as his name, then continuing her conversation as the bill is paid by calling him *"sweetheart," "honey,"* and *"darling."* On other occasions, it is not unheard of for the staff to speak to customers the way baseball fans yell at umpires who have made a controversial call. Such personality is the extra condiment that helps make Wiener Circle hot dogs something special.

Coney Island Wiener

131 W. Main St.   219-424-2997

Fort Wayne, IN   LD | $

The Midwest has a number of notable Coney Island wiener stands, "Coney Island" being the old term for hot dog, which folks in the heartland used to associate with New York. Fort Wayne's Coney Island, a Main Street storefront formally known as The Famous Coney Island Wiener Stand, was established in 1914, and has built its reputation on what must be called the classic Greek-American frankfurter: a modest-size bright pink weenie nestled in a soft bun and topped with Coney sauce, which is a fine-grind chili with a rainbow of seasonings and a fetching sweetness. Although all condiments are technically optional, everyone orders their hot dogs with Coney sauce, as well as a line of mustard and a sprinkle of chopped raw onion. The only other things on the menu are baked beans, chili (more a soup than a stew), and hamburgers.

Seating is at counter stools, many of which offer a nice view not only of the doings behind the counter and between staff and customers, but also through the big window onto Main Street.

Tipster Brett Poirier, who encouraged us to eat Fort Wayne's famous Coney Island, pointed out that it makes a great way station for anyone traveling America's original coast-to-coast thoroughfare, the Lincoln Highway.

Dodd's Town House

5694 N. Meridian St. | 317-257-1872
Indianapolis, IN | LD | $

The Town House hand-cuts steaks from six-ounce tenderloins to one-pound strips and cooks them so the meat develops a savory crust and is loaded with natural juice. Slice into a ribeye or filet mignon and the natural juices spurt, then ooze onto the plate. That's fine, because it is a delight to push big hunks of chewy-skinned baked potato, or even one of Dodd's toasty French fries, along the plate to mop up all the juices. On the side of these all-American vittles comes a suitably all-American salad—a mound of iceberg lettuce with sweet-and-sour garlic dressing, or creamy cole slaw.

Nobody dresses fancy to dine at Dodd's, but somehow everyone who comes looks nice and acts polite. Service is fast but never brusque; and there is a feeling of well-worn familiarity about the whole experience. Most customers are regulars who have been dining with the Dodds for years, as well as a loyal clientele of out-of-towners (ourselves included) who wouldn't think of coming to the heart of Indiana without a visit to this wonderful old eatery.

No matter how much steak and potatoes or fried chicken you eat (and you will eat plenty), it is required that you have dessert. Pies like these you don't find too many places anymore: real blue-ribbon beauties, with light crusts and fillings rich with cream or with locally grown berries in the summer. You never know which pies will be available any particular day, but among the well-known specialties are chocolate cream, blueberry, and buttermilk, the latter a lesson in how to make something spectacular out of basic ingredients. Sugar, eggs, butter, buttermilk, and a sprinkling of lemon zest and vanilla flavor are combined in a crust and the result, so utterly simple, is sheer felicity—a fitting conclusion to a meal in a restaurant where dinner always tastes like coming home.

Gnaw Bone Food & Fuel

4947 State Road 46   812-988-4575
Nashville, IN   LD | $

Formerly known as Brown County Tack and Snack but now cleared of equestrian gear, Gnaw Bone Food & Fuel is a gas station/convenience store/live bait shop that serves some of the best tenderloins west of the Wabash. Chef and owner is Beni Clevenger, who credits the success of his outsized tenderloin to the fact that he cooks it in a Broaster. More commonly used to make chicken, a Broaster deep-fries food under pressure. "My tenderloin cooks from the inside out," Beni explains. "That keeps the pork plenty moist while the crust crisps up like the devil." He says he buys his meat just like anyone else around here—already cubed from the local IGA. "The less you mess with it, the better it will be," he says. "Nice and easy is the way to go. Don't fuss. Don't be pounding the life out of it; don't flap it around while it cooks. Start with good meat and treat it gentle. That's the Gnaw Bone way to cook."

The result of Mr. Clevenger's technique is a magnificently crisp, broader-than-its-bun, wavy disk of pork that defines tenderloin excellence. It is served as a "full meal" with a bag of potato chips and a pickle spear.

Accommodations at Gnaw Bone Food & Fuel are rustic indeed. Beyond shelves of sundries in the front room is a large storage room set up for indoor dining at picnic tables covered by checked-green oilcloth. The tables are surrounded by plastic bins of odd-lot bargain merchandise for sale including souvenir T-shirts from North Carolina and $3 audio CDs. Hot meals are served from 10:30 A.M. to 2 P.M., then again from 4 P.M. to 6 P.M. Service is tote-your-own from the order counter.

Gray Brothers Cafeteria

555 S. Indiana St.   317-831-5614
Mooresville, IN   LD | $

Gray Brothers is gigantic, and quite deluxe as far as cafeterias go: leaded-glass windows in the doors, plenty of tasteful decor. Almost any time you walk in, it will be crowded, but that's no problem because the cafeteria line moves really fast, and besides, your wait takes you along the "preview line," which allows you to study the dozens and dozens of food items from which you will soon be choosing. The trays are big ones, but if you're at all like us, you'll find yours fully occupied well before you get to the rolls and beverages at the end of the line.

It's hard to know what to recommend because we've never had anything at Gray's we didn't like. Among the most memorable dishes are the fried chicken, which has an ultra-flavorful crust that pulls off the bird like strips of pork cracklin'. The way things work in Gray's line is that you tell the servers what entree you want; they put it onto a nice flower-patterned partitioned plate then slide the plate down to the vegetable area, where it is piled with whatever sides you desire.

Who can resist the corn bread stuffing? Or mac and cheese? We also love the heartland salads, especially creamy pea and carrot-raisin-marshmallow. Desserts are dazzling, with whole pies arrayed on shelves below the individual slices (many pies get bought and taken home). The Indiana favorite, and a specialty of Gray's, is sugar-cream pie . . . as simple and pure and good as the name suggests.

Hollyhock Hill

8110 N. College Ave.   317-251-2294
Indianapolis, IN   LD | $$

In 1928, on a quiet street at the northernmost outskirts of Indianapolis, a restaurant named the Country Cottage started serving family-style chicken dinners. The city has grown around it and the name was changed to honor the hollyhock bushes on the lawn, but the specialty of the house is still fried chicken dinners.

The time to fully experience the bedrock character of this place is Sunday, after church. Pastels on the ladies echo the flowery murals in the fairy-tale dining room, which is partitioned with trellises and wrought iron the color of Easter eggs. Tables are draped with linen, and some of the really big ones have lazy Susans in the center so members of big families can spin the wheel and grab what they want.

The meal people come to eat is a ritualized banquet that begins with pleasant enough but unremarkable pickled beets and cottage cheese and salad with sweet-and-sour vinaigrette then upshifts to unforgettably good chicken. Fish, shrimp, and steak are options, but this chicken is skillet-fried and wonderful, served with pan gravy. To go with it there are bowls of mashed potatoes, green beans, and corn niblets, as well as hot breads with apple butter. All these trustworthy selections are replenished for as long as anyone at the table wants to keep eating them, but it's only the chicken that makes you want to eat 'til you bust.

Dessert is ingenuous and fun: Make your own sundae. Sauces of butterscotch, crème de menthe, and chocolate are provided to dollop as desired on your ice cream. The usual ice cream flavor is vanilla, but true Hoosiers opt for the state favorite, peppermint.

Jonathan Byrd's Cafeteria

I-65 and Main St. (Exit 99)   317-881-8888
Greenwood, IN   LD | $

Jonathan Byrd's boasts that it is America's biggest cafeteria, a claim with which we would not argue. The serving line is eighty-eight feet long with a minimum of twenty entrees at any one time (serving continuously from 10:45 A.M. to 8:45 P.M. daily) as well as countless vegetable side dishes, Jell-Os, salads, desserts, bread and rolls. In need of comfort food when we stopped by, we dined on turkey pot pie and a bowl of chicken and noodles, the latter an especially salubrious bowl of thick, soft pasta and shreds of chicken in just enough broth to keep it all moist.

Among the memorable side dishes were macaroni and cheese with a good portion of crusty, chewy top-cheese mixed in with the creamy noodles from below, a buttermilk drop biscuit that was a textural joy, and bread pudding laced with slices of cooked-soft apple and plenty of sweet caramel sauce.

Jonathan Byrd, the founder and proprietor, is a man on a mission from God. "I was impressed by how many significant biblical events involved people eating together," he wrote for a story in *Guideposts* (reprints of which are available in the vestibule). As a matter of principle, he serves no liquor in the cafeteria, not even in its banquet rooms, and the Jonathan Byrd function rooms regularly play host to gospel concerts.

JWI Confectionery

207 W. Main St.   812-265-6171
Madison, IN   L | $

A beautiful restoration, complete with nostalgic photos of long-gone high school days on the wall, makes a visit to this old soda parlor an irresistible taste of history as well as a worthwhile detour for Roadfood of the sweetest kind. The building that houses JWI Confectionery was built when Andrew Jackson was president . . . in 1835! Madison is an Ohio River town with a great historical feeling to it, and this Main Street storefront shop, which old-timers know as Betty Mundt's Candies, dates back to 1917. JWI still makes candies from heirloom recipes in vintage molds; and the ice cream is manufactured in a machine at the back of the store.

Lunch is served from about 11 A.M. until early evening, and the meals we've seen look dandy—meat loaf, roast beef, cold-cut sandwiches, soups, quiche, etc.—but to be honest, we've only seen them. When we come to JWI, we want pie, cake, candies, cookies, and ice cream. The ice cream is especially excellent, ranging from cones and single scoops in a dish to sundaes topped with real whipped cream. Of course we could not resist the top-of-the-line pig's dinner known as "The '37 Flood"—a ten-scoop, multi-topping extravaganza that JWI says will feed four to six people.

King Ribs Bar-B-Q

4130 N. Keystone   317-543-0841
Indianapolis, IN   LD | $

King Ribs is a former automobile garage with no dining facilities. All business is drive-through, walk-up, or home delivery. It is the sort of barbecue you smell before you see. The scent of more than a dozen drums lined up, smoldering wood inside them and pork sizzling atop the wood, perfumes the neighborhood for blocks.

The house motto is "Fit for a King," and of all the regal meals to eat here, ribs top the list. They are tender enough so that the meat pulls from the bone in heavy strips, barely glazed with sauce, but chewy enough that the pork flavor resonates forever. It is a pure, sweet flavor, just faintly tingling with the smoke that has infused the meat.

Side dishes include macaroni and cheese that is thick as pudding and intensely cheesy, with noodles so soft they are almost indistinguishable from the cheese. Also: baked beans, fine-cut slaw, and white bread for mopping. For dessert, there is a choice of sweeties: chess pies or sweet-potato pie.

Mug 'n' Bun Drive-In

5211 W. 10th St.   317-244-5669
Indianapolis, IN   LD | $

Writer Dale Lawrence described Mug 'n' Bun root beer as "legitimately creamy, yes, but also smoky, carrying hints of vanilla fudge and molasses, as rich and smooth as a dessert wine." In other words, not your average soda pop!

It truly is delicious root beer, served in thick frosty mugs and in sizes that include small, large, giant, quart, half-gallon, and gallon. As for the other half of the equation, the bun, what goes in that can be a hamburger, a hot dog, or a tenderloin (grilled or breaded and deep-fried). The tenderloin is a big one, if not the juiciest in town, but we were especially fond of the double cheeseburger that more than filled out its bun. Also, the onion rings are something special: battered thick, crisp and sweet.

There are no inside tables at Mug 'n' Bun. Dine either in your car or at outdoor picnic tables (where overhead radiant heaters make chilly weather meals feasible). In the car, blink your lights for service and the food will be presented on trays to hang on the window. Each picnic table is outfitted with a buzzer next to the menu. When you've decided what you want, buzz and a carhop will appear at the table to take your order almost instantly.

Nick's Kitchen

506 N. Jefferson St.   260-356-6618
Huntington, IN   BLD | $

In the heart of the heartland between Nebraska's Midlands and the Wabash River valley, a tenderloin is not just a cut of meat. It is a very important sandwich. When you ask for one in a café, drive-in, or diner, you can expect to get a slice of boneless pork loin that has been pounded flat, breaded, fried to a crisp, and planted in a bun (and, one hopes, dressed with mustard, pickle, lettuce, and tomato). The girth of the meat in a tenderloin ranges from generous, protruding maybe an inch past the circumference of the bun, to freakishly wide. In the latter category, you'll find tenderloins in which a plate-size pancake of pork extends so far beyond the bun that it is impossible for even the longest-fingered hands to grasp the bread to pick it up like a normal sandwich.

Historians believe the tenderloin was first served to the public just west of Fort Wayne in the town of Huntington. Nick Frienstein started frying breaded pork cutlets in 1904 to sell in sandwiches from a street cart in town; four years later he opened Nick's Kitchen. The method of preparation was changed one winter shortly after Nick moved to the café and his brother Jake suffered such severe frostbite that he lost the fingers off his hands. Jake, whose job it was to bread the slices of pork, found that his stumps made good tools for pounding the meat to make it tender. Since then, all tenderloins are either beaten tender (with a wooden hammer) or run through a mechanical tenderizer (or both).

Now run by Jean Anne Bailey, whose father owned it starting in 1969, Nick's Kitchen lists its tenderloin on the menu with a challenge that's ironic considering its culinary history: *Bet You Need Both Hands.* Two hands are barely adequate for hoisting the colossal sandwich, which is built around a wavy disc of audibly crunchy pork that extends a good two to three inches beyond the circumference of a five-inch bun, virtually eclipsing the plate. Soaked in buttermilk that gives a tangy twist to the meat's sweetness and tightly cased in a coat of rugged cracker crumbs (not the more typical fine-grind cracker meal), the lode of pork inside the crust fairly drips with moisture. Jean Anne tells us she buys the meat already cut and cubed. She pounds it, marinates it, breads it, and fries it.

For dessert, you want pie. Jean Anne told us, "My father served frozen ones. I knew I wanted something better." Made using a hand-me-down dough recipe that incorporates a bit of corn syrup, her fruit pies have a flake crust that evaporates on the tongue, melding with brilliant-flavored rhubarb or black raspberries; the butterscotch pie—which she learned to cook from her grandmother—is more buttery than sweet, nothing at all like cloying pies made from pudding filling. And we won't even get into the hot apple dumpling . . .

Phil Smidt & Son

1205 Calumet Ave.	800-FROGLEG
Hammond, IN	LD	$$

Phil Smidt started as a fisherman's shanty on the shore of the lake and today it is a majestic 450-seat banquet hall with weekend entertainment in a renovated area of the Indiana shoreline. Not exactly a Roadfood jewel in the rough, it is nonetheless an essential stop on the regional food trail.

The primary reason to come to Smidt is pan-fried perch, the formal name for which is "a mess of perch." It is available whole, boned, buttered, or boned and buttered. Old-timers do their own boning and make it look easy. The rest of us get fillets, swimming in butter. They are small sides of fish, pan-crisped, firm, freshwater-luscious. Plates of perch are preceded by five relish trays, lined up in formation on the table: potato salad, kidney bean marinade, pickled beets, slaw, and cottage cheese.

If perch is not your dish, the other house specialty is frog legs, either crisp-fried or sautéed. They are messy and delicious and make chicken wings seem like second-class appendages. Smidt offers half-and-half plates of perch and legs, as well as a full menu of more traditional lake seafood, steaks, and chicken. For dessert, the one thing to know about is gooseberry pie, served warm and available à la mode.

Shapiro's

| 808 S. Meridian | 317-631-4041 |
| Indianapolis, IN | BLD \| $ |

Funny, Shapiro's doesn't *look* Jewish—at least not like the familiar Jewish delicatessens in New York or Miami or Los Angeles. It looks like a modern midwestern cafeteria-style restaurant, with ample parking outside and a spacious interior dining room with plastic chairs and Formica tables. Instead of crabby old men who traditionally staff deli counters in the East, the servers here are a heterogeneous group of men and women—some rather pleasant.

Despite the anomalies, this genuine delicatessen is the best in Indianapolis, and one of the best in the Midwest. We would stack Shapiro's corned beef sandwich against any corned beef sandwich from anywhere. The meat itself is lean but not too much so; each slice is rimmed with a thin halo of smudgy spice and glistens underneath the fluorescent lights of the dining room. The slices are piled high and heavy inside slabs of rye bread with a shiny, hard, sour crust. Slather on the mustard, crunch into a dill pickle to set your taste buds tingling, and this sandwich will take you straight to deli heaven.

Get some *latkes* (potato pancakes), too. They are double-thick, moist, and starchy: great companions to a hot lunch of short ribs or stuffed peppers; Shapiro's supplements ordinary latkes with cinnamon-scented ones—wonderful when heaped with sour cream. And soup: bean, lentil, split pea, and chowder are daily specials; you can always order chicken soup with rice or with matzoh balls.

Shapiro's serves breakfast every morning, including classic platters of bagels and lox with cream cheese, onions, tomatoes and olives; also salami omelettes, fried matzoh, cold corn flakes, and hot oatmeal. Even after breakfast, desserts here are mighty fine. We like a gigantic slice of cheesecake with a cup of coffee; but if you want an end for your meal that is more midwestern than Jewish, Shapiro's peanut butter pie is grand.

Teibel's

1775 Route 41	219-865-2000
Schererville, IN	LD | $$

Teibel's is one of a handful of restaurants that continue to serve the favorite big-eats Sunday-supper sort of meal so beloved in northern Indiana, buttered lake perch. When it opened in 1930, it was a mom-and-pop café, and today it is a giant-size dining establishment (run by the same family), but the culinary values that made it famous still prevail.

The ritual feast starts with a relish tray—scallions, olives, celery, and carrots—followed by a salad (superfluous), then a plate piled high with tender fillets of perch glistening with butter. It is a big portion, and this fish is full-flavored; by the time our plate was empty, we were more than satisfied. Our extreme satisfaction was due also to the fact that we had to have an order of Teibel's fried chicken, too. Perhaps even more famous than the perch, this chicken is supposedly made from a recipe that Grandma Teibel brought from Austria many years ago. It is chicken with a good hard crust and juicy insides, in a whole other league from the stuff that comes in a bucket from fast-food franchises. Some other interesting items from Teibel's menu: frog legs (another local passion) and walleye pike. For fish- and frog-frowners, there is a turkey dinner.

After a family-style feed like this, what could be nicer than a hot apple dumpling? Teibel's flake-crusted, cinnamon-scented dumpling is served à la mode with caramel sauce on top.

Village Inn

107 S. Main St.   574-825-2043

Middlebury, IN   BL | $

The traffic patterns in Middlebury are frequently determined by the comings and goings of the somber black buggies driven by all the Amish people who live around here and visit town for trading and livestock auctions. If you are looking for a meal fitted to the mighty caloric needs of such hardworking people, we recommend a booth at the Village Inn.

Of course, you can get eggs and potatoes and toast, just as in any regular town café, but here you can also plow into a vast plate of cornmeal mush accompanied by head cheese. Lunches are huge, too: chicken and noodles or meat loaf or beef stew and mashed potatoes, smothered steaks and stuffed peppers, all served with plenty of richly dressed slaws and salads and well-cooked vegetables enriched with bread crumbs, butter, and cheese.

You cannot say you have truly partaken of this monumental heartland cuisine unless you follow breakfast, lunch, or dinner with a piece or two of pie. The Village Inn offers a dozen different kinds daily, including blueberry (from locally picked berries), lattice-topped raisin, and the pie known among Indiana farm folks as O.F., meaning "old fashioned": little more than sugar, eggs, and cream, whipped into a jiggly custard perched atop a flaky pastry crust. Whole pies can be ordered in advance, to go.

Walls' Drive-In

Highway 66   812-547-8501

Cannelton, IN   LD | $

Among the most trustworthy rules of finding Roadfood is to stop any place that boasts it is The Home of Anything. We figure that any restaurant that has so proprietary a feeling about a dish probably makes it well, or at least tries to. Such boasts can range from quite significant, such as the claim by Kaelin's of Louisville that it is Home of the Cheeseburger, to mysterious, such as the café we came across in the Midwest that advertised itself as Home of the C.L.O.T.H. sandwich. Needless to say, we were intrigued by the latter and sat down for lunch, only to discover that C.L.O.T.H. was the acronym for cheese, lettuce, onion, tomato and ham on ordinary bread, i.e., a fairly unremarkable sandwich.

The sign above Walls' Drive-In along the Ohio River in southern-most Indiana announces that it is "Home of the Big Square Burger," a promise that drew our car into the parking lot like a magnet. Even without the sign, we would have wanted to eat at Walls'. It is a pretty little place by the side of the road, painted red, white, and blue outside, with picnic tables out back and order windows in the front.

The Big Square Burger turned out to be a patty of meat that is squared off at the edges, similar to Wendy's; but it isn't really all that big. It is a quarter-pound patty, available in the "Big Square Box" configuration, which means fully dressed with French fries and baked beans on the side. If you arrive with an appetite for a really big one, we suggest you order a double or, better yet, a "Wall Banger Special," which is a Big Square topped with melted cheese and a round of Canadian bacon.

Beyond hamburgers, Walls' has an exemplary fast-food menu featuring crisp-fried tenderloins (those are pounded-thin rounds of pork on a bun that are a passion in these parts), hot dogs, and plump Polish sausages. Good ice cream, too, either hard-packed or soft-serve.

Welliver's

40 E. Main St.	765-489-4131
Hagerstown, IN	D Thurs-Sun | $$

Special thanks to Roadfooder James Bogan, who not only tipped us off to what he called his favorite restaurant in Indiana but actually provided a map link so we could find the place when traveling along I-70. The map link was hardly necessary. We could have followed the dozens of other vehicles that were heading to this landmark restaurant the Friday night we happened to visit.

Opened in 1947 as a counter café serving home-cooked meals, Guy Welliver's establishment has grown to an awesome eating complex with half a dozen dining rooms serving hundreds of customers on weekend nights. Service is buffet-style, and the selection is overwhelming, with some six dozen different items from which to build a salad and more than 150 buffet choices ranging from great onion soup to an array of breads that includes homemade yeast rolls, cheese balls, and sweet cinnamon bread with a mantle of white icing, to chilled steamed shrimp, pan-fried chicken, and chicken livers for which chicken liver lovers travel for miles every weekend.

The dessert selection is overwhelming: handsome Hoosier pies of every height, color, and substance, plus a very fine hand-dipped ice cream bar.

Welliver's is not cheap. It is possible to spend $25 for dinner. But it is impossible to leave hungry.

Wolf's Bar-B-Q

6600 1st Ave.	812-424-8891
Evansville, IN	LD | $$

Nowhere in America is barbecue terminology more esoteric and precise than around Evansville, Indiana, which is one of about a half a dozen cities that claims to be the barbecue capital of the country. When you come to Wolf's you need to know if you want beef pit or beef and sauce, pork pit or pork and sauce. At least you don't have to know about soaks, because they don't sell soaks at Wolf's (but they do at other local BBQ parlors).

Soaks are similar to what Kansas Cityans know as brownies: shreds, scraps, ends, chunks, and odd-lot pieces of meat that are heaped together and simmered in sauce. Similar to soaks, but less sloppy, are the items Wolf's calls beef sauce and pork sauce. For these, the meat of choice is pre-cut and long-simmered in sauce until the meat and sauce are nearly indistinguishable. It's like barbecue syrup, meat and sauce reduced to a saturated essence. Beef pit or pork pit refers to meat that is sliced when you order it, and only then brushed with sauce. Whereas the already-sauced stuff verges on flavor overdose, beef pit and pork pit are by comparison almost elegant, and have a certain discreet poise that allows you to actually savor the taste of the fire that has infused the meat.

Wolf's serves barbecue according to exacting procedures shared by many pits of the southern Midwest and western Kentucky. When you order a "plate," beef or pork, sauce or pit, you get your meat of choice along with the peculiar slices of bread, which are vaguely tan and precisely square, known as rye but actually every bit as bland—and suitable for barbecue-mopping—as supermarket white. You also get pickle, onion, and a bag of chips.

Zaharako's

329 Washington St. 812-379-9329
Columbus, IN LD | $

Columbus is a spectacular city in several respects. Per capita, it has more great architecture than Chicago, including an impressive collection of Victorian edifices, as well as fifty buildings designed by renowned modernists such as I. M. Pei, Venturi and Rauch, and Harry Weese. Columbus is also home to the Wee Scots, a nationwide group of people who love Scottie dogs and Scottie memorabilia. It was while researching Wee Scots for a magazine story several years ago that we discovered our favorite Columbus attraction, Zaharako's.

Zaharako's is a century-old sweetshop. It boasts a magnificent mahogany back bar, twin onyx fountains, and an eye-and-ear-boggling self-playing organ on the back wall that blares out John Philip Sousa marches from 185 pipes as well as on its drums, triangles, and cymbals. The woodwork around the booths in the back room and around the candy shelves and soda fountain up front is itself a beautiful thing; but of course the main reason we return is for the great ice cream treats and a unique sandwich known as a cheese-br-gr.

This is the place to sit across from your sweetheart and enjoy sarsaparilla, a fireball, a cinnamon Coke, fresh lemonade or orangeade, or a dazzling tutti-frutti sundae. As for the cheese-br-gr, it is like a cheeseburger in that it combines beef and cheese, but it does so in its own very special way. In this case, the beef is a spicy chili sauce reminiscent of a sloppy joe; the cheese is a thick slab of school-bus-orange Velveeta. These two elements are sandwiched between slices of white bread that are toasted on a grill. Suggested beverage to accompany a cheese-br-gr: a sixteen-ounce chocolate soda served in a green-tinted, bell-shaped glass.

Iowa

Archie's Waeside

224 4th Ave. NE   712-546-7011

Le Mars, IA   D | $$$

Archie's Waeside serves splendid steak, some of the best in the Midwest, some of the best anywhere in America. The meat is choice and prime; it is hung and dry-aged in a back room of the restaurant. Steaks are grilled so they get a little crusty on the outside. They are overwhelmingly juicy and exude the full, resonating character of corn-fed beef. Even the filet mignon, usually a tender cut that is low on flavor, virtually sings with the succulent authority of blue-ribbon protein. Bone-in ribeye is deliriously succulent. And at the suggestion of a tipster in the know, we ordered an off-the-menu item, the Benny Weiker, named for a good customer of years ago who used to be a cattle buyer in the Sioux City stockyards. This is an eighteen-ounce, center-cut, twenty-one-day-dry-aged filet mignon that was simply the most handsome piece of meat we have ever seen presented on a plate.

Side dishes are special, too. Along with salad you get a relish tray and—oddly enough—a plate of cured-here corned beef: super-lean, high-flavored, beautiful to look at. The waitress suggested we do like regular customers do and shred the spicy beef on our salads. Available companions for meat include a well-browned patty of hash brown potatoes and a trio of substantial corn fritters.

A steak-eaters' destination since Archie Jackson started it in 1949, Archie's is now run by grandson Bob Rand, who is a fanatic for excellence. Bob is an oenophile who regularly travels to the Napa valley to build the restaurant's wine list, and he likes nothing more than rhapsodizing about the dry-aging process that makes his meat so good. His restaurant is a big, happy place with capacious booths and hordes of customers who come from miles around to enjoy this Siouxland prize.

Baker's Cafeteria

7400 Hickman Rd.   515-276-8432
Des Moines, IA   LD | $

Baker's celebrated its half-century anniversary in 2000, and for those of us who treasure old-fashioned American square meals, dished out by polite people in pleasant surroundings, it was a golden anniversary indeed. They don't make restaurants as nice as this one anymore. Once you've carried your tray to a table (if you ask, it will be carried for you), you are taken care of by a staff whose job it is to refill your ice tea glass and instantly replace that fork you dropped in your eager grab for some of your dining partner's Harvard beets.

The cafeteria line starts with a salad carousel, spinning the choices on ice. There are always Jell-Os: clear, opaque, molded, and cubed, in colors of a large-size Crayola crayon box. If Jell-O is too sweet for your first course, select from a nice array of Heartland salads: kidney beans with cheese chunks in mayonnaise, slaws, pea salad, and single hard-boiled eggs. Main course choices include such stalwart entrees as scalloped ham and potatoes, tuna noodle casserole, turkey and dressing, and roast beef, all of them available with mashed potatoes and made-from-scratch gravy. On the side, have a hunk of corn bread, a sticky bun, or an oven-warm whole-wheat roll.

The best of the pies for dessert is the Heartland favorite, raisin pie—heaps of bloated cooked raisins in sweet goo spilling out their triangle of fragile crust. We also like crumb-topped apple pie; and the chocolate cream is a simple classic.

Bauder Pharmacy

3802 Ingersoll Ave.   515-255-1124

Des Moines, IA $

Mark Graziano, proprietor of Bauder's Pharmacy, is a man who knows how to make one heck of a fine cherry Coke, a green river, and a lime phosphate. He also constructs a grand turtle sundae (that's caramel, nuts, and hot fudge topping), as well as shakes, malts, sodas, and floats of every stripe. All the ice cream treats are made from Bauder's own ice cream (well known to all who visit the Iowa State Fair in August), the flavor rotation of which always includes fresh strawberry and peach in the summer months.

The nostalgic reverberations of this old drugstore take you back to an America that long predates modern franchised restaurants. The business was founded in 1922 by Carolyn Bauder, a pharmacist whose motto was "Cleanliness, order, service." After World War II, Mark Graziano's father became a partner and started making ice cream in the front window. Today, the fixtures are comfortably familiar, but not prehistoric: colorful octagon-tile floor, blue-upholstered counter stools, a couple of booths back near the prescription counter, a small glass case of warm salted nuts for sale, and a waist-high cooler with pints of delicious ice cream packed and ready to take home.

Bob's Drive-Inn

Highway 75 S   712-546-5445

Le Mars, IA   LD | $

Although it is the signature dish of Bob's Drive-Inn, you will not find loosemeats listed on the menu that hangs above the order window. That is because it is listed by one of its several Northwest Iowa aliases, a tavern. At many restaurants that serve it, loosemeats is called something else: tavern, Big T, Charlie Boy, or Tastee. When Roseanne Arnold opened her Big Food Diner over in Eldon out Ottumwa way, journalists unfamiliar with Iowa cuisine made a fuss over the fact that her menu did list loosemeats, a name that to outsiders sounds vaguely taboo.

At Bob's Drive-Inn, they don't even offer a hamburger. If you want beef, you get loosemeats. Bob's loosemeats are definitive: moist, full-flavored, and deeply satisfying.

"Tomatoes? No way!" says Myles Kass, son of founder Bob Kass, when we try to pry loose the loosemeats recipe. "You know how when you eat a sloppy joe you get that orange ring around your mouth?" He grins, using a spoon to stir a batch of ready-to-serve loosemeats. He lifts the spoon to show that it is clean and tomato-free—no orange color whatever. "We brown the ground beef; we strain it; we pressure-cook it in the sauce; then we strain it again. That's why it has so little fat and so much flavor." As it is scooped out of its metal pan for a sandwich, the meat looks just like cooked ground beef with no visual evidence of any spice or of the sauce in which it has been cooked. But the flavor is kaleidoscopic.

Whereas most loosemeats are served on factory-made burger buns, Bob puts his inside morning-fresh rolls he buys from Le Mars's Vander Meer bakery. He takes a similar approach to everything in his unprepossessing restaurant. As soon as we start asking questions, he becomes positively evangelistic about his entire menu, and he is in and out of the kitchen a dozen times to bring tastes and samples and to clue us in to other wonders of his quick-eats cuisine. "Our hot dogs, they're natural casing from West Point, Nebraska, made by Wimmers with a snap to their skin. The malts are mixed with real fruit—strawberries, black raspberries, blueberries, wild cherries. We hand-ice our onion rings; they're the best! The root beer is made from an old recipe my father used." It adds up to a dining experience superior to any other $5 drive-in meal we know.

Coffee Cup Café

616 4th Ave., On the Square   641-594-3765
Sully, IA   BLD | $

An ad hoc convention of local farmers was in process as we entered the Coffee Cup about 9 A.M. one spring morning. Two tables for eight were lined up in the center of the small main dining room, and sixteen men in seed company caps and overalls sat over coffee trading weather observations and other news. Occasionally, one got up, walked out, and drove away in his pickup truck (not a single sedan was parked anywhere near the Coffee Cup on the town square) and, as if on cue, another pulled into his space, entered the restaurant, and sat down for coffee and conversation. So it went for well over an hour until mid-morning, when the tables started to empty and the Coffee Cup began setting up for lunch. If you are driving southeast of Des Moines and looking for the sort of place where locals eat three meals a day, this little cinder-block café with its laminate tables and short counter is definitely it.

Breakfast is lovely—plate-wide golden pancakes and big rounds of sausage; there are eggs and potatoes, of course, and modest-size but big-taste cinnamon buns with a translucent sugar glaze, served warm with butter on the side. The meal we like best is lunch. The menu lists hot beef sandwiches and tenderloin steaks, and there is one square-meal special every day—last visit, it was baked ham with mashed potatoes and apple salad. Any time of day you can order Dutch lettuce, a locally preferred salad of crisp, cold iceberg leaves bathed in a warm sweet-and-sour creamy mustard dressing with pieces of bacon and slices of hard-cooked egg.

No matter what meal you eat, or what time of day you eat it, you must have pie at the Coffee Cup Café. Iowa is major pie country, and it is in just such inconspicuous small-town cafés that some of the very best are eaten. Looking for a good cream pie? Have a wedge of Coffee Cup banana cream. It quivers precariously as the waitress sets it down on the table, the custard jiggling like not-quite-set Jell-O, the foamy white meringue on top trembling like just-spun cotton candy. Below these ribbons of white and yellow is a thin, tawny crust that doesn't *break* when it is poked with a fork; it *flakes*. The whole experience of cutting a mouthful, raising it to one's mouth, and savoring it is what we imagine it would be like to eat pastries on the moon or some planet where gravity is only a fraction of Earth's, for the word "light" barely does justice to the refinement of this piece of pie.

Even more wonderful than Coffee Cup cream pies are the fruit double-crusters. No words are dainty enough to describe the fragile-brittle crust, dusted with glistening sugar crystals, that encases the cherryberry pie, which is balanced perfectly on the line between sweet and tart. This pie is so good that we never even consider having it à la mode; and frankly, we often skip whatever meal is supposed to precede dessert, just so we can have a piece or two of fruit pie, plus whatever meringue cream pie is on the menu that day.

We have long believed that Iowa is the best place in America to eat pie, and the modest Coffee Cup Café, of which the locally known address is "On the Square in Sully," is one convincing reason why.

Grove Café

124 Main St.   515-232-9784

Ames, IA   BL | $

When you order a pancake at the Grove Café, the word will take on a new meaning. In this place, a pancake is truly a pan cake—a good-size layer of cake that has been cooked in a pan, or in this case, on the grill. Nearly an inch thick in its center, it is wide as its plate—a round of steamy cooked batter that has an appealing orange hue. It comes with a couple of pats of butter and a pitcher of syrup (all of which this cake can absorb with ease). With some peppery Iowa sausage patties, one of these cakes is a full-size meal. Two of them, listed on the menu as a "short stack," are a breakfast for only the tallest of appetites.

Grove Café also offers omelets with hash browns and happy little slices of French toast for breakfast, as well as hamburgers, hot beef, and meat loaf at lunch. But to many of its longtime fans, including hordes of Iowa State alumni who have consumed tens of thousands of calories in these bare-tabled booths and at the low stools of the counter, pancakes are all that matter. To its most devoted fans, Grove Café is a pancake parlor.

Located in the old business district, it has a weathered character with faded cream-colored walls decorated with photos and mementos from the riding exploits of the proprietor. Among them is a blue ribbon he won at the state fair showing Appaloosa horses. A large sign painted on the wall above the grill jokes, "Just Like Home: You Don't Always Get What You Want."

In't Veld Meat Market

820 Main   641-628-3440

Pella, IA   BL | $

Most customers come to In't Veld to shop for meat rather than to eat; and even those of us who are just passing through will find such good travel companions as summer sausage, dried beef, and wax-wrapped cheeses. For those in search of regional specialties, the meat to eat is ring bologna, also known as Pella bologna, because this town is the only place it is made. It is a tube of sausage about as thick as a pepperoni stick, curled into a horseshoe shape, smoked and cured and ready to eat. It is delicious sliced cold with a hunk of cheese and a piece of bread; it's even better when you can warm it up and cut it into thick discs like kielbasa. Smoky, vigorously spiced, and firm-textured, this bologna is an only-in-Iowa treat.

For Roadfooders, what is especially good about In't Veld Meat Market is that you can sit down right here and have a hot bologna sandwich: five thick slices on a fresh bakery bun . . . pass the mustard, please! In fact, a whole menu of meat-market sandwiches is available for eating here (or taking out) until mid-afternoon each day. In addition to the famous bologna, you can have house-dried beef on a bun, homemade bratwurst with sauerkraut on a Hoagie roll, ham and Swiss, or a ground-here beefburger. Side orders are limited to potato salad, macaroni salad, beans, slaw, and Jell-O; and for dessert, we suggest a walk across the square to Jaarsma Bakery, a Dutch-accented shop with some of the most beguiling pastries, sweet cakes, and cookies in the Midwest.

Jesse's Embers

265 50th St.   515-225-9711

West Des Moines, IA   D | $$

Also at 3301 Ingersoll, Des Moines, IA (515-255-6011)

Jesse's Embers has been Des Moines's steak house since the 1960s, known for an open-pit grill where you can watch the chef cook steaks and where the room tone is set by the sizzle of the beef. Both the older branch downtown and the newer one to the west are set up with similar ambience: cool, dark, comfortable, a retreat from the world for those who want the best in life, which includes expertly made cocktails and beautiful hunks of steak. Jesse's is not like one of the super-expensive steak house chains; it is a restaurant for people who pay for meals rather than put them on expense accounts. And the meat here, while not of the butter-knife-tender $30+ per cut variety, has character that in some ways is more satisfying than an overpampered hunk of prime.

Take, for example, the Jesse's Embers special—a pound-plus circle of sirloin that is at least an inch thick with a thin ribbon of fat along one edge. You want a steak knife to slice through it; and when you do, juices flow. Seared over the fire, it bursts with flavor. Cottage fries or baked potatoes are ideal for pushing through the juices on the plate. The menu also lists seafood, chicken, etc., but we have never had much interest in trying anything other than red meat.

Begin the meal with a cool iceberg-lettuce salad topped with creamy blue cheese dressing and some wonderful warm croutons; have a few cocktails with the nice little dinner rolls that begin each meal; and the only natural anchor, in our book, is a big sirloin, bacon-wrapped filet, or maybe a slab of slow-cooked prime rib. Jesse's is a restaurant where red meat reigns.

Maid-Rite

215 1st Ave. W   641-792-4166

Newton, IA   BLD | $

We don't generally recommend chain restaurants because they lack the character and distinctive local specialties that make one-of-a-kind cafés so enjoyable. For the Maid-Rite chain of Iowa, we set aside that rule. Although it is a chain, and although every Maid-Rite we've ever visited serves the same specialty, we are charmed not only by its unusual food, but by the old-fashioned sandwich-shop ambience. In business since 1926, the Maid-Rite shops specialize in a very unglamorous but addictive version of what the people around Sioux City known as a "tavern" or "loosemeats" sandwich: seasoned ground beef that is stirred and worried as it cooks so it never clumps. The result is best described as sloppy joe without so much slop: a heap of pebbly beef that gets piled into a bun . . . and spills out as you try to eat it.

One exemplary Maid-Rite shop to which we've returned a few times over the years is in Newton, Iowa, east of Des Moines. Last time we stopped in, it was nine o'clock in the morning. The breakfast crowd had cleared out, and the girls behind the counter told us that the meat was just ready for serving. It was only a few hours before lunch, so we plowed into a Maid-Rite and a Cheese-Rite, both with the works, while a veteran customer across from us called out an order of "meat and coffee." Alongside his cup of coffee was presented a good-size bowl filled with nothing but hot, seasoned Maid-Rite meat—no bun, no condiments, not even a pickle to distract his taste buds as he spooned his way to the bottom.

Miles Inn

2622 Leech Ave.   712-276-9825
Sioux City, IA   LD | $

At the Miles Inn, Siouxland's passion, the loosemeats sandwich, is known as a Charlie Boy after Charlie Miles, son of founder John Miles. The senior Miles was a bricklayer who built the Inn in 1925. Charlie Boys are the only food you can buy other than Beer Nuts and potato chips. Sitting at the bar, you have a view of the steam box in which the meat is kept and of Charlie Boys assembled as you drink beer from a frosted goblet. The waxed paper in which they are presented unfolds to become a drop cloth for catching meat that falls out as they are eaten.

Miles Inn's Charlie Boys are small and addictive, their fine-grind meat so soft and gently seasoned that it hits the tongue smooth as cream. They have a concentrated beef flavor that even a sirloin steak cannot match. (It is our opinion that the one meal that most fully satisfies the deepest hunger for red meat is ground beef, even more than a great steak.) Two or three Charlie Boys make a wonderful lunch, and of course the proper libation is plenty of draft beer.

Smitty's

1401 SW Army Post Rd.   515-287-4742
Des Moines, IA   LD | $

Iowa is one of the midwestern states mad about tenderloins, which are cutlets of pork that are breaded and deep-fried, customarily served on buns with pickles, onions, and mustard. A good tenderloin starts with a pounded-thin sheet of meat, and it requires the hand of a skilled fry cook to pull it from the oil exactly when perfectly golden crisp.

One of the best places to eat a perfect tenderloin is Smitty's, out by the Des Moines airport, a friendly little eat-shack where you'll find a ten-inch-diameter "King Tenderloin" with brittle breading that hugs a thin ribbon of savory moist pork. The wide cutlet of meat is served on an ordinary burger bun, which is irrelevant except as a means of holding ketchup, mustard, onions, and pickles close to the center section of the impossibly broad cutlet.

"Home of the REAL whopper," says a cartoon on the wall that shows Smitty and his truly kingly sandwich.

Stone's Restaurant

507 S. 3rd Ave.   641-753-3626

Marshalltown, IA   LD | $$

Stone's is in the most unlikely location, below a viaduct by the railroad tracks, near where the old vinegar works used to be. You'd think by that description that it was some sort of disreputable, wrong-side-of-town eat-shack. Nothing could be further from the truth. Of all the upright midwestern restaurants we know, Stone's is among the politest. Not fancy—all are welcome—and not expensive, either, this is a place where you are greeted by a kindly hostess, treated well by an efficient waitress, and served handsomely by a kitchen that upholds old-fashioned culinary values. For more than a century, Stone's has been Marshalltown's nice place to eat.

In the front room there is a counter, mostly for single diners. Here, last visit, we watched an octogenarian gent in jacket and tie enjoy his lunch of Jell-O salad, then chicken and noodles, and finally grasshopper pie. Throughout the meal, he held a round-robin conversation with virtually every waitress and hostess in the place as they passed, as well as several of the regular customers who were apparently old friends.

The menu is a broad one ranging from familiar sandwiches and salads to the very old-fashioned oddity "tender young beef heart," served with bread dressing. All hot meals come with a choice of moist corn bread squares or big, puffy whole-wheat dinner rolls. Among the odd hot sandwiches is the artistically arranged Robert E. Lee, which is chicken, bacon, and olives on rye with white sauce on the side, all arranged to vaguely resemble the Confederate flag. Different specials are featured each day of the week: chicken and noodles, meat loaf and rivel soup (with tiny dumplings), ham and scalloped potatoes, chicken casserole, fried cod on Friday. Saturday night, Iowans come to eat pan-fried walleye pike. At night, the salad bar is resplendent: marinated vegetables, pasta salads, bean salads, relishes, slaws, pickles, ambrosia, etc., etc.

Everyone who comes to Stone's finishes their meal with a piece of pie. There are fruit pies and cream pies and a graham cracker custard pie that is superb, but the one amazing pie is lemon chiffon, which is significantly taller than it is wide.

Susie's Kitchen

404 Broad Ave.   712-829-2947
Stanton, IA   BL | $

Known as the "Little White City" since the 1920s, when passersby re-
marked how clean and tidy it appeared with all its houses painted white,
Stanton calls itself the Swedish Capital of Iowa. Aficionados of roadside
extravagance mark Stanton on the map for its forty-thousand-cup
coffee-pot—the largest in the world—which sits ninety feet above town
to honor native daughter Virginia Christine. Ms. Christine played Mrs.
Olson, the kindly Swedish lady who was the spokesperson for Folger's
coffee back in the 1960s and 1970s. Stanton has recently added the
world's largest cup and saucer to its wonders.

Coffee is a big deal in Stanton because it signifies hospitality, and one
excellent place to drink it, and to experience country-style hospitality, is
Susie's Kitchen, also known as Susie's Kök. At Susie's, a basket full of
money on the counter says "Coffee—50 cents" so that those who help
themselves to a cup when the waitress is otherwise occupied can pay and
make their own change. The coffee is good, served in sturdy mugs, the
right companion to a slice of Susie Johnson's superb pie. She makes all
kinds, cream pies and double-crusters, the most spectacular being "Fruit
of the Forest," a multi-fruit extravaganza of apple, rhubarb, strawberry,
blueberry, and raspberry heaped into a luscious golden crust that is light,
flaky, and deliriously unctuous. When we asked Susie to tell us why the
crust is so good, she shrugged and said, "It's just regular crust . . . made
with lard." In Iowa, "regular crust" is what those of us in the other 49
states would call blue-ribbon-wonderful crust!

Susie's decor has a Swedish theme—painted woodwork, *Valkom-
men!* stenciled on the wall. Her lace-thin Swedish pancakes with ling-
onberries are a memorable breakfast, but for many visitors, it is simply
a good, all-American café. At lunch we love the big hot beef sandwich . . . followed, of course, by a piece of Susie's pie.

Bortell's Fisheries

| 5510 S. Lakeshore Dr. | 231-843-3337 |
| Ludington, MI | L May–Labor Day \| $ |

Ludington is the heart of Michigan's year-round fishing country. Winter anglers catch panfish on frozen lakes. Steelhead spawn in the spring. Walleye, muskie, and northern pike crowd the rivers in May; and by mid-summer, along come the Pacific salmon, then the cold-weather steelhead.

Everybody who comes to fish these prolific waters knows about Bortell's, a century-old fish market that has all the decorative charm of a gas station. There is no formal menu, no waitstaff, no indoor seating, and few restaurant-style amenities of any kind. Most locals come to buy fish for cooking at home; but visiting fishermen and passers-through with an appetite know this well-weathered place by its enticing aroma—the smell of wood smoke.

In addition to smoking local walleye, catfish, trout, and whitefish to finger-licking goodness, Bortell's imports ocean perch and Alaskan salmon; so if you walk in with a raging appetite, you will have a wide variety of flavorful smoked fish from which to choose. Buy it by the piece or pound, BYOB, and find yourself a picnic table to eat outside in the shade under Bortell's grove of ancient beech trees.

The Cherry Hut

246 Michigan Ave.   231-882-4074
Beulah, MI   LD Memorial Day-Mid-October | $

The Cherry Hut is a roadside snack shack that opened in 1922 and has dedicated itself to the glories of Michigan's sweetest crop, the cherry. There is a full menu of sandwiches, turkey dinner, and wonderful cherry chicken salad, plus excellent cinnamon rolls, but the one most important thing to eat is a slice of cherry pie. Loaded with bright red cherries, it is sweet and a little tart, with a crust that adds a savory note. This superb pie is made from the same recipe that has defined cherry pie excellence now for more than three-quarters of a century.

Dining includes outdoor picnic tables as well as indoor facilities, and part of the Cherry Hut experience is buying things to take home. The restaurant shop sells not only whole fresh pies (500 per day) but also jellies, jams, and a wide array of Cheery Jerry, the Happy Pie-Faced Boy, souvenirs.

Driving around this part of Michigan in the summer is a cherry-lover's delight. Throughout the region, farm stands along the side roads sell bags of washed cherries ready to eat. They are dark maroon, nearly black; their skin is taut, and their flesh is firm and full of nectar. When you buy them by the side of the road they are usually warm from the sun, and there is something about summer-temperature cherry juice flooding the tongue at first bite that makes these fruits one of the greatest car snacks anywhere.

Cousin Jenny's Cornish Pasties

129 S. Union St.   231-941-7821
Traverse City, MI   BLD | $

Pasties are as much a passion on Michigan's Upper Peninsula as green chile cheeseburgers are along New Mexico's Rio Grande. They arrived in the northland over a century ago with Cornish miners who came to dig ore. The men who went down into the mines were tough as mules, and therefore known colloquially as Cousin Jacks; their wives were Cousin Jennies. These hardworking immigrants made their native land's pasty a

Michigan tradition; and although the mines are closed, the pasty persists. Essentially a kind of beef stew inside a flaky pastry crust, they were originally favored by miners because they were easy to carry and easy to eat—a hearty pocket meal.

Cousin Jenny's restaurant introduced pasties to Traverse City in the 1980s. It is a modern cafeteria-style restaurant where pasties are available in two sizes, neither of which you would want to carry around in your pocket. Cousin Jenny's pasties are knife-and-fork meals! They are listed on the menu as "Gourmet Pasties," but the steak pasty is the traditional configuration, filled with beef, potatoes, onion, and rutabaga. In addition, you can get a meatless seven-vegetable pasty with cream and cheese; and there are always novelty pasties available, such as Italian (with pizza sauce and pepperoni) or German (Swiss cheese, ham, and sauerkraut in a rye-flavored crust). There are some hand-holdable pasties, but for breakfast only. They are filled with eggs, hash browns, and bacon or sausage.

Pasties can be bought partially cooked, ready to bake at home, or fully frozen and ready to ship to any friends you have from upper Michigan who miss their native specialty.

Don's Drive-In

2030 N. US Highway 31 N   231-938-1860
Traverse City, MI   LD | $

Don's is a real drive-in that opened the year Elvis joined the army (1958). Selections on its jukebox evoke days of American mid-century car culture at its prime, and the ambience is pure rock and roll: hubcaps and album covers decorate the walls and you can dine inside or in your car, where meals are served on window trays. The menu, basically burgers and fries, features the old-fashioned "basket" presentation, meaning a sandwich heaped with French fries and cole slaw.

The tough decision to make at Don's is whether to get a hamburger or a brace of Coney Island hot dogs. The burger is thick and juicy; a Coney, topped with chili sauce, is a Midwest paradigm. Whatever you get to eat, there should be no question about the beverage. Make it a milk shake. Don's blends its shakes to order, either large or small, both of which are big enough to fill at least a couple of glasses, and both of which are thick enough to require powerful suction with a straw. Chocolate and vanilla shakes are good all the time; in the summer, strawberry shakes are made with fresh fruit.

Grand Traverse Pie Co.

525 W. Front St.   231-922-PIES

Traverse City, MI $

One of the great sensory thrills of the upper Midwest is walking into Grand Traverse Pie Co. For those of us who enjoy eating, the smell in here is more devastating than any rare perfume. It is the unspeakably delicious aroma of baking crust and bubbling-hot fruit filling.

As the name suggests, it is a limited-service restaurant where pies are virtually all that matter. Indeed, other than coffee and a few kinds of cookies, pies are the only thing on the menu, and much cross-counter business is whole pies to go.

Although you can't come here for a square meal, there are a handful of tables inside and (when weather permits) outdoors, to which you can carry a warm, just-cut slice and appreciate the absolute goodness of a pie that is individually crafted out of raw fruit and sugar in a crust rolled from dough made daily from scratch.

Because northern Michigan is the fruit capital of the Midwest, where apples, cherries, and blueberries are harvested in abundance, the double-crust fruit pies are what we like to eat here. Among the varieties available, most of them named after sights and places around Traverse Bay, are Suttons Bay blueberry, Front Street apple, lakeshore berry, Union Street peach strawberry, and Long Lake berry cherry. Some thirty varieties are in the kitchen's repertoire (though not all are available every day), and in addition to fruit-filled ones, there are Key lime, coconut cream, and (in season) autumn harvest pecan, and Northport pumpkin.

(In addition to the original store in Traverse City, Grand Traverse Pie Co. has shops in Brighton and Okemos, Michigan. Mail-order pies are available, shipped second-day-air Monday through Wednesday.)

Juilleret's

130 State St.   231-526-2821
Harbor Springs, MI   LD | $$

Juilleret's planked whitefish is an old-time presentation for which milky-white fillets are spread out on a seasoned hardwood plank and broiled in rivers of butter until their edges turn crisp and brown. They are strewn with slices of lemon and tomato and surrounded by a wall of piped-on mashed potatoes that shores in all the juices. What a feast!

Planked whitefish is available only for dinner, after five in the afternoon, for any number of people from two to ten. The size of the plank and the number of fillets are adjusted accordingly. An odd dish worth knowing about on the side—with anything you order in this place—is pea and peanut salad. It's a Michigan farm-country concoction we've encountered a few times at church suppers: plump green peas and crunchy peanuts with little bits of gentle-flavored onion, all bound with plenty of sweet Miracle Whip.

Juilleret's is beloved for its soda fountain. Soda jerks are proficient at using house ice cream to make sodas, sundaes, banana splits, tin roofs, cream puffs, coolers, rainbows, and a couple of exclusive items, the velvet and the thundercloud. The thundercloud is vanilla ice cream, bittersweet chocolate sauce, and chopped nuts all layered in a slender tulip glass and topped with a blob of marshmallow fluff. A velvet is the same ingredients, minus the nuts, blended smooth.

Many customers come to Juilleret's only for sandwiches or hamburgers, and some come just to hang out. It is a big, tin-roofed town lunchroom, favored by generations of vacationing Michiganders for the last century, and its ambience is noisy, extremely casual, and fun. It is a place to table-hop, carry on across-the-room conversations, and flirt with the new kids in town.

A historical note: The once-famous fox-trot "Sleepy Time Gal" was written by Joseph Alden and Ange Lorenzo in Juilleret's dining room in 1923.

Juilleret's Restaurant of Charlevoix

1418 S. Bridge St.   231-547-9212
Charlevoix, MI   BL (closed in winter) | $

By the time Juilleret's opens at five-thirty in the morning, its air is perfumed by the smell of cinnamon bread hot from the oven. Many local people come to buy whole loaves of the restaurant's sweet bread to take home and toast. For those of us just passing through, and for legions of loyal locals, the scent of cinnamon augurs extraordinary French toast, either at a seat inside, where you can pore over the morning paper, or—on any pleasant morning in June, July, or August—at a picnic table outdoors under a pink umbrella.

Besides cinnamon-bread French toast, Juilleret's renowned breakfast menu includes crisp American-fried potatoes to accompany eggs and plate-wide buttermilk pancakes. Orange juice is fresh-squeezed and coffee cups are refilled as often as necessary.

Lunch is simple and local: broiled whitefish, on a plate or in a sandwich, hot sandwiches of beef or turkey, homemade soup, and a couple of kinds of pie.

Warning: Northern Michigan is a popular vacation destination, and at the height of summer any time after about seven in the morning, you can count on a wait for a seat. Especially on Sunday morning!

Lafayette Coney Island

118 W. Lafayette   313-964-8198
Detroit, MI   Always open | $

"The American [Coney Island restaurant] is okay," wrote a Roadfooder named Charles in an elaborate note explaining exactly where we needed to eat in Detroit. "On a slow evening, the guys at the American might try to steer you into their establishment. But hold out for the Lafayette!"

The Lafayette and the American are an adjoining pair of storefront Coney Island hot dog joints in Detroit (two of many Coney Islands in the area); and while to the casual observer, their cuisine might seem similar, if not identical, true Coney Island aficionados definitely have their preferences. Following Charles's impassioned plea ("Forget that Nathan's crap from the east!" he wrote), we found ourselves under the fluorescent lights at Lafayette with a brace of weenies for each of us, one set served plain in their steamy little buns, the other topped with chili, raw onions, and mustard. We also got a couple of bowls of chili, one with and one without beans, both topped with shredded cheese (which is also available on the hot dogs).

The chili is finely ground meat that is fairly peppery unless supplemented by the starch of beans and the pleasant fatty mantle of bright orange cheese. The dogs are far from fancy, but in their déclassé way, they are mighty good: porky-sweet inside, with a skin that has a nice little snap, they have a succulence that is perfectly complemented by the spongy bun that cradles them. In our opinion, the condiments are essential. A plain Coney is as erroneous as a pancake without syrup.

Tasty as the hot dogs are to the true frank-o-phile, it is the ambience of Lafayette Coney Island that endears it to die-hard Roadfooders. Open round-the-clock, and especially interesting in the wee hours of the morning when there is no place else to eat and the bars are closing, it is staffed by cranky old gents who have seen it all and who remember exactly what everyone eats and don't have to bother with written checks: everything is in their heads.

A word to the wise: The beverage of choice here is Vernor's, a locally made ginger ale with zest that puts all other brands in the shade.

Ray's Drive-Inn

20 N. Beacon Blvd.   616-842-3400
Grand Haven, MI   LD | $

A tipster who identified him/herself as Flame On Catering of Muskegon advised us exactly what to eat when we went to Ray's: a triple beefburger with only cheese. Flame On explained, "I would never order a burger with nothing else but cheese from anywhere else." Nor would we, as we are big fans of all sorts of burger condiments. However, in this case, the suggestion was a good one. Ray's uses gobs of cheese, and while the beef itself is just fine, it's all that cheese that puts this one over the top. When you unwrap your triple, you will definitely see bun and cheese, but the meat itself is completely smothered. It is a delightful, goopy mess.

French fries are especially excellent, and while all the usual milk shakes are available, we took good advice and ordered pineapple. A great drive-in meal!

Zingerman's Deli

422 Detroit St.   734-663-3354

Ann Arbor, MI   BLD | $

Here is a world-class deli that serves every kind of sandwich the human race has devised—from Italian salami subs to brisket-and-schmaltz on rye and a pile of hot pastrami parenthesized 'twixt two potato pancakes. We get dizzy thinking of Zingerman's smoked whitefish salad, redolent of dill and red onion, piled on slices of freshly made onion-rye bread. The immense menu is an hour's read, and ranges beyond sandwiches to such traditional specialties as noodle kugel (a sweet pudding), cheese blintzes (cheese-filled crêpes), and knishes (heavyweight potato-filled pastries). Or you can choose Thai noodle salad, Arkansas peppered ham, or ratatouille with polenta. Brash, crowded, and invariably delicious, this one-of-a-kind place is an essential stop for all traveling eaters.

Zingerman's stocks a tremendous inventory of smoked fish, meats, breads, coffees, etc., for retail sale. It also features a full-service mail-order department, selling such specialties as rugelach (the best!), babkas, poppy seed cake, brownies and blondies, cheeses, oils, vinegars, and multiple-item gift baskets. To see what's available, check out www.zingermans.com.

Al's Breakfast

413 14th Ave. SE
Minneapolis, MN

612-331-9991
BL | $

Al's is a closet-size diner wedged perpendicular to 14th Avenue among the shops of Dinkytown, near the University of Minnesota. Customers waiting for a stool stand hovering just above and behind those who are seated and eating. On a shelf underneath the aged yellow counter are accumulations of newspapers to read. Behind the counter, where the hash slingers race with seasoned aplomb, decor consists of pictures of Elvis and Wayne Newton, foreign currency, and a sign that advises, "Tipping is not a city in China." Also behind the counter is a pile of $20 meal ticket books, each inscribed with someone's name. Many of Al's customers buy these books and keep them here so they know they can come eat, using coupons instead of dollars, even when their wallet is empty.

The specialty of the house is blueberry pancakes, which are made with either a whole-wheat or buttermilk batter and are also available studded with walnuts or corn kernels. We choose blueberries and buttermilk—a balance of sweet fruit in a faintly sour medium, infused with butter. They are just barely sticky, delicate-textured, and profoundly satisfying, especially when lightly drizzled with maple syrup. Al's flap-jacks are sold as a short stack (2), regular (3), or long (4); and you can also have your waitress garnish them with sour cream and/or straw-berries.

The short-order chef up front spends a lot of his time making eggs, omelettes, and truly excellent corned beef hash, as well as luscious hash browns, which he drenches with seasoned oil from a small pitcher as they turn crisp and brown on the grill. It is an old-fashioned pleasure to watch this guy work, handling about a dozen orders at a time, always snatching whatever he is frying, poaching, or grilling away from the heat at the peak of its perfection.

Café Latte

850 Grand Ave.   651-224-5687
St. Paul, MN   BLD | $

We cannot visit the Twin Cities without at least one meal at Café Latte. The last time we visited, we virtually staggered in the door after spend-ing a very long and very delicious day up in the town of Braham, Min-nesota's pie capital. We had just judged the small town's pie-baking contest, and after sampling eighteen of the finest apple, rhubarb, and berry pies imaginable, all we could imagine for supper was a green salad!

Café Latte filled the bill perfectly. It is a breezy cafeteria that offers all sorts of fresh, healthy salads to order, e.g., Indonesian rice salad, grilled chicken Caesar salad, asparagus-lemon salad. It is entirely possi-ble to eat a meal of which any nutrition warden would approve. There are lovely sandwiches available, different interesting soups every day, and small-size pizzas ranging from au gratin roasted vegetable to a "Mediterranean" with olives, cheeses, artichokes, and basil-flavored sauce.

What we "forgot" when we headed for Café Latte to find relief from our pie-eating pig-out was that this place also happens to make the best layer cakes on earth: chocolate banana, chocolate-chocolate, German chocolate, and the king of all pastries, turtle cake. Inspired by the candy of the same name, turtle cake is three chocolate layers gobbed with an obscene amount of caramel frosting and loaded with walnuts. It is a dessert no sweet tooth can refuse, even after eighteen pies.

As the restaurant's name suggests, all sorts of espresso-based drinks are available (as are wine by the glass and afternoon tea, the latter served with scones, cookies, and little sandwiches). The fancy coffee beverage of our choice is a Mandarin cocoa latte with candied orange slivers and chocolate sprinkles.

Lange's Café

110 8th Ave. SE (Route 23)   507-825-4488
Pipestone, MN   BLD | $

The moment we walked into this inconspicuous café and saw the caramel rolls we knew we had hit pay dirt. Sure enough, as we ate our way through as much of the menu as possible, we swooned with pleasure over and over again. Beef is the entree not to miss. It is the upper Midwest fave, "hot beef," served on a plate with mashed potatoes, green beans, and gravy . . . or in a sandwich with mashed potatoes on top and gravy all over.

The caramel rolls that so many people eat for breakfast must be sampled any time they are available. They are immense blocks—a three-inch-square cube—of sweet, yeasty dough, and they are bathed in buttery warm caramel syrup that has a burnt-sugar smack to its sweetness.

Now, we have saved the best for last: sour cream raisin pie. It's a specialty of bakers in Minnesota, Wisconsin, and Iowa, and over the years we have made it our business to sample every one we come across. Lange's is built upon a custard that is dense, packed with raisins, creamy and sweet with the sour-cream edge that makes its sweetness all the more potent. Its meringue is air-light; the crust flakes when poked by a fork. It was our supremely lucky day, for we walked into Lange's about 10 A.M. and the SCR pie was just out of the oven. Our pieces were faintly warm, and as we ate, we declared this the best sour cream raisin pie ever made . . . 10 on a 1 to 10 scale . . . the crème de la crème . . . the mother lode—you get the idea.

Mickey's Dining Car

36 W. 7th St.   651-222-5633
St. Paul, MN   BLD | $

The best thing about Mickey's Dining Car is Mickey's Dining Car itself—a stunning yellow- and red-enamel streamliner built by the Jerry O'Mahony company in 1937. Although it has been well used over decades of twenty-four-hour service, it is still in magnificent shape. Complementing the deco dazzle of the diner (which is listed on the National Register of Historic Places) is a jukebox featuring Elvis and Del Shannon, and a waitstaff who have honed the art of service with a snarl. It's not mean service, and it's not bad service; in fact, it is efficient and polite . . . unless you are one of the frequent gawkers (we plead guilty) who come in to look around at the handsome joint and its colorful regular denizens. Those who are too preoccupied to place their order swiftly and with no hesitation can find themselves at the mercy of the hash slingers, one of whom once told us, in no uncertain terms, "A museum, it's not. You gonna eat or kick tires?"

We're not going to tell you that the cuisine at Mickey's Dining Car rates four stars. There are some things they serve we wouldn't recommend at all. The pies, for example, are more easily identifiable by their color (red, yellow, blue) than by their designated ingredient (could it be fruit?).

On the other hand, breakfast is foursquare. Eggs are whipped up in a flash, blueberry-buttermilk pancakes are pretty fine, and the hash brown potatoes are available O'Brien-style, meaning mixed with diced ham, onion, and green peppers. We like the French toast made from the diner's extra-thick white bread, and the morning special of pork chops or steak and eggs. While these chops bear little resemblance to the thick, tender ones you'll get for supper in a high-priced restaurant, they have a flavorful hash-house charm all their own. The milk shakes are real, blended to order. And how many other joints do you know that still offer mulligan stew?

Murray's

26 S. 6th St.   612-339-0909
Minneapolis, MN   LD | $$$

Rippling pink drapes hang heavy on the walls of Murray's, a plush supper club where a piano/violin duo serenades the room with "Polonaise," "Bali Hai" from *South Pacific,* or "Happy Birthday" as weekend customers' moods require. Murray's lavish menu includes such regional exotica as walleye cheek appetizer and hickory-smoked shrimp; but aged beef has been the beacon for generations of Twin Citians who crowd the white-clothed tables to eat hearty and toast life's good moments. Murray's is renowned for immense "butter-knife" steaks: the silver butter-knife sirloin or golden butter-knife porterhouse, available for two or three people. These roast-size blackened hunks of beef arrive whole from the kitchen and are sliced tableside into thick cuts that are indeed tender, but substantial enough that you'll want to use the steak knife that is part of each place setting's battery. Because the steak is so immense, sliced pieces offer an appealing textural range from juicy center to seasoned crust.

Alongside the steaks come au gratin potatoes or French fries, an assortment of dinner rolls, a salad, and a basket of garlic toast. The toast, which is put on the table when you first sit down, is pre-buttered, so lush that it seems to melt when you crunch into it. Nothing goes better with cocktails. For years, the word around town was that once all your toast was eaten, the basket was replenished only if your waitress liked you. She must have loved us, as our table of six went through three baskets one evening while laying waste to approximately eight pounds of golden butter-knife porterhouse.

Peppermint Twist

115 Babcock Blvd.   763-972-2572

Delano, MN   LD Tues-Sun | $

An hour west of Minneapolis is a bright pink building that is a trip back in time to the glory days of car culture: a genuine, order-from-your-front-seat drive-in with carhop service and trays built to hook on the window.

The hamburgers are big and juicy, the French fries are fresh-fried, and the malts and shakes are thick and full-flavored. The house specialty is a Delano Burger (heaped with Swiss cheese, mushrooms, and onions), and there is a peppermint milk shake dotted with little bits of pink candy. For those who choose not to dine off the dashboard, Peppermint Twist offers picnic tables spread out on an adjacent lawn.

Amighetti's

5141 Wilson   314-776-2855
St. Louis, MO   LD | $

Amighetti's is a serve-yourself sandwich shop that has become a beloved culinary institution on "The Hill," St. Louis's old Italian neighborhood. Eating here is casual and fun, especially on a pleasant summer day. Place your order at the window and wait for your name to be called. Find yourself a seat on the sunny patio, and feast on an Italian sandwich.

Amighetti's bakes its own bread—a thick-crusted loaf with sturdy insides awaiting slices of ham, roast beef, Genoa salami, and cheese, garnished with shreds of lettuce and a special house dressing that is tangy-sweet. All kinds of sandwiches are available, including a garlicky Italian hero, roast beef, and a three-cheese veggie sandwich—all recommended primarily because of the bread on which they're served.

Each sandwich is wrapped in butcher paper secured by a tape inscribed with Amighetti's motto: "Often imitated, never duplicated." That's not entirely true. There are now several other Amighetti's around town.

Arthur Bryant's

1727 Brooklyn Ave. 816-231-1123
Kansas City, MO LD | $

Arthur Bryant used to shock reporters by calling his esteemed barbecue restaurant a "Grease House." Although the master of Kansas City barbecue passed away almost twenty years ago, his business heirs, bless them, never tried too hard to shed that moniker. The "House of Good Eats" (another of Mr. Bryant's appellations) remains a cafeteria-style lunchroom with all the decorative charm of a bus station. The menu is written on the wall; you can order food by the sandwich, plate, or pound.

Because Arthur Bryant and his brother Charlie (who started the smokehouse) hailed from Texas, it makes sense that the smoked brisket—a Texas passion—is the best meat in the house. It drips flavor. It is sliced into fall-apart lengths that get heaped into white bread sandwiches; or if you come as a large party, you can order a couple of pounds of beef and a loaf of bread and make your own at the table.

The pork ribs are wonderful, too, glazed with blackened burnt edges and lodes of meat below their spicy crust. The skin-on French fries are bronze beauties, and the goopy barbecue beans are some of Kansas City's best.

What makes Arthur Bryant's unique is the sauce, a gritty, red-orange blend of spice and sorcery that is not at all sweet, like most barbecue sauces. It packs a hot paprika wallop and tastes like a strange soul-food curry, a nice complement to any meat. Once you've tasted it, you'll understand why this old Grease House is a foodie legend.

Booches

110 S. 9th 573-874-8772 or 573-874-9519
Columbia, MO LD | $

A billiard parlor / tavern where the beverages of choice are beer (in a bottle) and ice tea (in a pitcher), or maybe Coke in a paper cup, Booches is a magic name to hamburger aficionados. The hamburgers—known among old-timers as "belly bombers"—are thick, juicy, and maddeningly aromatic, served unceremoniously on a piece of wax paper. It is difficult to say what exactly makes these hamburgers so especially delicious. They are normal-size, available with or without cheese, and the condiments are standard-issue onions, pickles, mustard, or ketchup; yet their smoky/meaty flavor is extraordinary from first bite to last. In 1999, Booches won kudos from the *Digital Missourian* as an especially earth-friendly eatery, not only because each hamburger is cooked to order (thus, no meat is wasted), but because "no one can leave a Booches burger half-eaten."

Some of the food's charm is no doubt due to the offhand way in which it is served in colorful surroundings. Booches is the oldest pool hall in Columbia, and it is likely your burger—or good chili dog—will be eaten to the wooden clack of pool shooters, as well as the noise of whatever sports event is blaring on the television. Decor is a combination of sports memorabilia, kudos from famous artists who have enjoyed the beer and burgers, and some delightful politically incorrect humor, including one sign that advises, "Parents . . . Keep your ankle-biting little crumb-gobblers on a leash or I will put them in the cellar to play with the rats."

C&K Barbecue

4390 Jennings Station Rd.	314-385-8100
St. Louis, MO	D | $

St. Louis has always been a great barbecue town; C&K represents the best of this tradition. It is a small, out-of-the-way place with no seating (all takeout) and late-night hours well suited to those of us who get a craving for ribs after midnight.

Ribs, rib tips, chopped meat, even chicken, all bathed in proprietor Darryle Brantley's exclamatory red sauce, are served in Styro boxes with sweet-potato salad and soft white bread that makes a good sponge for drippy extra sauce. These are extremely messy meals, so even though each order is packed with napkins, we recommend getting extras.

In addition to all the expected smokehouse specialties, C&K offers a few rarer items, such as snoots (pig snouts baked until crisp and bathed in sauce) and ears (yes, pig ears, cooked until butter-soft and served between two slices of white bread, with or without sauce). These items are for the advanced barbecue connoisseur. We recommend the first-time visitor start with a slab of ribs!

Central Dairy

601 Madison St.   573-635-6148

Jefferson City, MO $

Missouri is a dairy state, and Central Dairy is one of its top bottlers, turning out 7 million gallons of milk per month. It is known to local sweet tooths for its repertoire of outstanding ice cream. Central Dairy ice cream tastes great, but what's truly amazing about it is the way it is portioned out at the old-fashioned soda fountain store in the capital city's downtown. Ask for a cup of ice cream, and you get a pint container nearly full! Never make the mistake of having a banana split in a flimsy low-rimmed boat, from which vast amounts of ice cream and syrup will spill over the edge onto the table of your Formica booth as you spoon into it; be sure to ask for your split or sundae in a quart container. It, too, will brim over the top, but once the first dozen or so spoonfuls are consumed, the quart is a good holding vehicle for the remaining pounds of ice cream and syrup.

Sundaes and splits are the pièces de résistance at Central Dairy, but for those who don't have time to plow in at a table, it is possible to get a tall triple-dip ice cream cone, then face the challenge of trying to lick enough off the pile of cool, creamy globes before they start to melt down one's wrist. Ice cream sodas are grand-size, too; and we want to thank Roadfooder Tony Gawienowski, our Central Dairy tipster, for pointing out that the ice water tap serves cold soda water—just what ice-cream-sated taste buds require!

Crown Candy Kitchen

1401 St. Louis Ave.   314-621-9650

St. Louis, MO   LD | $

Opened in 1913 by Harry Karandzieff and Pete Jugaloff, the Crown Candy Kitchen is the oldest soda fountain in St. Louis. The walls are packed with turn-of-the-century memorabilia, including an impressive collection of Coca-Cola advertising trays. For a nickel, a rickety machine will tell your weight and read your horoscope. Overhead, hanging from the tin ceiling, fans spin slowly.

Punch up a tune on the jukebox in your booth, and order a mile-high "Lover's Delight" or a strawberry-pineapple-marshmallow-sauced French sundae studded with toasted cashews and chocolate sprinkles or a fruit salad sundae topped with fresh and frozen fruit. The Crown Candy Kitchen's turtle sundae is exemplary. Silken vanilla ice cream is shrouded with hot fudge, the fudge covered with caramel sauce, and the caramel sauce mounded with buttered and toasted pecans. Everything is served in its proper soda fountain glass, accompanied by long-handled spoons.

They make malted milk shakes here the old-fashioned way, using malt powder, ice-cold milk, their own ice cream (not too rich, not too sweet), and the full repertoire of soda fountain syrups, including cherry, pineapple, marshmallow, strawberry, and, of course, vanilla and chocolate. They serve them the old-fashioned way, too—in 24-ounce silver beakers, filled nearly to the top. Drink five such malteds in thirty minutes (that's approximately one gallon) and you get them free!

The most unusual of the malted flavors is banana, for which a fresh banana is pulverized along with the ice cream and milk. If you really want to gild this lily (you do!), have chocolate syrup added to the brew. Top it with a blob of whipped cream and a sprinkle of chopped nuts and it is known as the "Johnny Rabbit Special."

Golden Ox

1600 Genessee   816-842-2866
Kansas City, MO   LD | $$$

In the lobby of Kansas City's Golden Ox is a panoramic photo taken high over Genessee Street ninety years ago. It shows the stockyards stretching to the horizon along the Kansas River, an area once known as the West Bottoms. The infinite meat market is gone, but the Golden Ox remains: a stockman's haven with chairs cleverly designed for gents to rest their cowboy hats just beneath the seat and a brandy-colored rug inscribed with a yippi-yi-yea cattle brand design. Ranchers, truck drivers who haul "swinging beef," rodeo stars, and Future Farmers of America all consider "The Ox" *their* restaurant in Kansas City.

"Ta-da!" croons our waitress when she presents the steaks crosshatched with char-marks from the white-hot hardwood grill. "Now there is a sight to remember," she adds with the heartfelt sentiment of a person who truly loves the beef business as she sets the meat on the table. The big filet mignon is lovely; T-bone tends to be the cattleman's choice; and guys on dates go for extra-heavy prime rib; but if you can eat only one thing at the Ox, make it the KC "royal cut." It is a boneless pound of center-cut sirloin with a thin amber ribbon of fat along one edge and a pliant center that glistens with juice sealed inside by the fire. Side dishes are predictable, but the cocktail menu is extraordinary, including a long list of single-malt Scotches and small-batch bourbons, as well as giant-size versions of those aperitifs tradition-minded beef-eaters like: martinis, Manhattans, and Rob Roys.

Goody Goody Diner

5900 Natural Bridge
St. Louis, MO

314-383-3333
BL Mon-Sat | $

Hamburgers have been Goody Goody's pride since 1948. Hunks of ground meat are mashed down hard on the grill so they become thin, rugged patties with a crisp circumference; and they are served on soft yellow buns. You can have a single, a double, a cheeseburger, or a barbecue/slaw burger, each made to order with the garnishes of your choice. Side dishes include French fries, onion rings, slaw, potato salad, chili, and chili with cheese.

The chili, which can be ordered as a side dish, is stout and salty, made with chunks of beef; it is the fundamental element in a once popular but now rare midwestern diner dish, chili mac, which Goody Goody prepares with hash-house finesse: a plate of noodles topped with chili and crowned by a mass of shredded Cheddar cheese. You can even come here and eat chili for breakfast—as part of an amazing platter of food known as "The Wilbur." Don't ask us how it got its name, but a Wilbur is a variation of what other St. Louis diners call a Slinger; in this case, it is a three-egg omelet filled with chili, hash brown potatoes, peppers, onions, and tomatoes.

Breakfast is our favorite meal in this busy, comfortable diner, where it seems like half the business is carryout. Curiously, breakfast is served all day on Wednesday and Saturday, other days only until 11 A.M. (but Goody Goody is closed Sunday). In addition to that hefty Wilbur, the morning menu includes a bone-in ham steak with grits on the side, a country-fried steak with sausage gravy, and—are you ready?—a catfish fillet with eggs and hash browns!

Gus's Pretzel Shop

1820 Arsenal   314-664-4010
St. Louis, MO $

St. Louis is a serious pretzel town, and Gus's has been known for excellent soft pretzels since 1920. They are available as twists or sticks, numbers and letters, and—best of all—as the casing for sausage, e.g., pigs in blankets. The varieties of sausage available inside the pretzel include a diversity typical of St. Louis's savory ethnic heritage: Italian salsiccia, German bratwurst, and all-American hot dogs.

To complement its first-class pretzel repertoire, Gus's offers cups of Poupon mustard and melted Cheddar cheese, plus servings of Ted Drewes ice cream. The proper method of dining is to dip one's pretzel, bite by bite, in the little cups, swilling a mug of beer on the side. The only problem is finding a place to do this. Gus's has no tables or counter; business is all takeout, for eating at home, in the car, or on the sidewalk. Frozen cooked pretzels are available, as are bags of "Bake UR Owns."

Hereford House

2 E. 20th St.   816-842-1080
Kansas City, MO   LD | $$$

Going out for steak in Kansas City is not necessarily a dress-up occasion; nor need it be dauntingly expensive. In the American West's original cow town, a good T-bone now and then is a fundamental right of all citizens. On Saturday night, a big percentage of those citizens gather at the Hereford House. Opened in 1957 but modernized in recent years, this vast, multiroom restaurant attracts meat eaters by twos and by twenties.

Those who face a long wait are given a beeper that vibrates when a table is ready, allowing them to go outside for a smoke. There is also a lounge, where we found standing room near the doorway and watched two women try to edge toward the bar for a drink. As they brushed past one rotund reveler in a farm cap, the old boy exclaimed with glee, "Ladies! You ain't a-vibratin', are you?"

Sirloins, strips, filets, T-bones, and ribeyes are available from six ounces to pound-plus "cowboy cuts," accompanied by such beefy delights as steak soup and meat-laced "cowboy beans" with a sweet chili flavor. For those who lust after the meatiest red meat, Hereford House has a "baseball cut" top sirloin, which is a heavily marbled hunk known also as the coulotte, fairly dripping with juices. Note also the lunch-only hamburger, made from steak cuttings: With the possible exception of the renowned Tubby Burgers dished out from a truck behind Kemper Arena in November during the American Royal rodeo, there isn't a tastier round of chopped beef anywhere in town.

Jess & Jim's

517 E. 135th	816-941-9499
Kansas City (Martin City), MO	D | $$$

"What do vegetarians eat when they come here?" we asked Marilyn, a seasoned waitress at Jess & Jim's, where a statue of a bull stands atop the roof as an ode to animal protein.

She considered the unlikely occurrence, shaking her head in pity and sorrow, then whispered so no other diner could hear the awful words: "Salad, cottage cheese."

A hungry meat-frowner *could* eat nothing but marvelous potatoes: cottage fries, French fries, or one of the astounding bakers on display along with cuts of raw steak in a glass refrigerator case near the front door. But of course none of these alleged vegetables are prepared to please the culinary prig. Even if you demur on sour cream, bacon, and shredded cheese condiments, the pound-plus baked potato will be served split open and twice-baked, with a scoop of butter that looks to be nearly one-eighth of a pound melting into it.

Yes, broiled fish is on the menu; chicken, too (fine fried chicken!); but who cares when there's great Kansas City beef to be eaten? All around Jess & Jim's every evening, the air is perfumed by the smell of cooking beef; several parking lots are full and streets are crowded with customers eager to savor hand-cut T-bones, filets, porterhouses, and strips. (The management offers a "call ahead" system in lieu of reservations: Phone an hour before you expect to arrive, and chances are good you won't have to wait too long.)

Steaks arrive from the kitchen exuberantly sputtering, crusty from an iron griddle. The top-of-the-line twenty-five-ounce "KC Playboy Strip" is a full two inches thick, and unlike the super-tender bacon-wrapped filets, it demands some serious chewing. Not that it is tough; but neither is it a cut of meat for milquetoasts. Dense and intense, this is a steak-lover's steak!

A Slice of Pie

601 Kingshighway St.   573-364-6203
Rolla, MO   LD | $

The pies are glorious at A Slice of Pie: the velvet-cream meringues, the Boston cream, and the Tahitian cream are especially noteworthy, that last one being a layered pie of sliced bananas, pudding, and pineapple with a mantle of toasted coconut on top. Phillip Quintana, the tipster who directed us to this little eatery halfway between St. Louis and Springfield, said that his favorites were apple and peach with cinnamon cream, as well as any of the pies filled with fruit. We did our best to sample some of everything, but there are far too many pies (not to mention cakes and cheesecakes!) for even two big appetites to try some of everything in just a few visits.

The problem of eating one's way through the dessert menu is compounded by the fact that lunch and supper at A Slice of Pie are hearty. After bowls of wonderful homemade creamy tomato soup and potato soup with bacon, we forked into a pair of flake-crusted chicken-mushroom pot pies. After polishing off those savory pot pies, it took some mustering of appetite to ask for several sweet pies . . . especially considering each slice served was enormous!

Snead's Barbecue

171st and Holmes   816-331-7979
Kansas City, MO   LD | $$

Snead's is a wood-paneled house of barbecue with a magnificent giant oak tree in the parking lot and laminated tables inside. The dining room has windows that look out onto what is still countryside (though the city is steadily encroaching). It remains a long drive from downtown Kansas City, but is required eating for anyone who wants to savor pit-cooked excellence.

Snead's lists so many good things on its menu that it is impossible to sample all of them in one visit. To wit: beef and/or ham brownies, which are the crusty, smoky chunks stripped from the ends and tips of the meat. Order a sandwich or a plateful. They aren't as soft as the ordinary barbecue, but they fairly explode with the flavor of meat and smoke. French fries are freshly made; barbecued beans pack a smoky punch; and the finely chopped cole slaw is a brilliant palate-refresher.

Regular pork barbecue, cooked over hickory wood, is sweet and tender, and with satisfying heft. The beef brisket is shockingly fatless, and yet somehow supple and luscious. Then there are log sandwiches, named for their shape: a mix of finely ground barbecued beef, pork, and ham, all minced together and wedged into a tubular bun. The result is a salty, powerful mélange reminiscent of northwest Iowa's loosemeats—not as potent as the burnt ends, but in some long-term satisfying way, even more complex.

Stroud's

1015 E. 85th St.   816-333-2132

Kansas City, MO   D | $$

Stroud's is one good reason Kansas City is known as a fried chicken city. The home of pan-fried chicken with all the trimmings for over half a century, this dilapidated roadhouse on a bleak street south of the city defined a meal now served by the most popular restaurants in town, including even some of the best barbecue parlors and steak houses. As memorable as other chicken dinners may be in other regions and cities around the nation, there are none as sublime as Stroud's.

Each piece Stroud's serves is tightly enveloped in a red-gold crust imbued with the succulence of chicken fat exactly the way a crisp strip of bacon is charged with the nectarous goodness of pig fat. When you heft it in your hands (no one here uses knife and fork) and penetrate the tender wrapping, the flavor of sizzled skin is so profound that you might suddenly think you have never really tasted fried chicken before. Great fried chicken, for which this is a paradigm, is as different from mediocre stuff as is a *grand cru* burgundy from a screw-top wine cooler. Inside its crust, each breast is steamy-moist and white. Dark meat fairly oozes juice as soon as the exterior is broken, and it pulls from the bone as easily as if it had been stewed.

On the side come long-cooked green beans and superb mashed potatoes: fluffy-textured, with an intense flavor of . . . *potato!* As you fork up big mouthfuls of these spuds you learn new respect for real mashed potatoes and new intolerance for bogus ones. The only way these lovelies can be improved is if you ladle some of Stroud's gravy on them. It is zesty, pan-dripping gravy, redolent of chicken and powerfully peppered.

At the risk of sounding hysterical, we must tell you that the cinnamon rolls that accompany this meal are fantastic, too. Tasting more of yeast and cinnamon than of sugar, they are glistening buns with only the faintest hint of caramelized cinnamon butter around the base.

(Note: There is a second Stroud's, in a lovely old house furnished with antiques. The menu is almost identical to the original's, except fry-frowners can get a skinless broiled chicken breast. It is at 5410 Northeast Oak Ridge Drive in Kansas City. Phone: 816-454-9600.)

Ted Drewes

6726 Chippewa   314-481-2652 or 481-2124
St. Louis, MO

Also at 4224 S. Grand (314-352-7376)

For anyone in search of America's most delicious ice cream (and who is not?), here's a name to put on the short list of candidates for greatness: Ted Drewes. Drewes's frozen custard is fresh, pure, and tons of fun, manufactured only as vanilla, but mixable with your choice from a list of dozens of different flavoring agents from chocolate and strawberry to fudge, cherries, cookies, nuts, and candy bars.

The best-known dish in the house is called a concrete, which is a milk shake so thick that the server hands it out the order window upside down, demonstrating that not a drop will drip out! Beyond concretes, there are sundaes, cones, floats, and sodas.

Both Ted Drewes locations are mobbed all summer long with happy customers spooning into huge cups full of the creamy-smooth delight. As winter approaches, the custard operation closes and Ted goes into the Christmas tree business.

If you are far away and seriously crave this superb super–ice cream (as is the case for many St. Louis expatriates), Ted Drewes is equipped with dry ice to mail-order its custard anywhere you need it.

Balyeat's Coffee Shop

133 E. Main St.   419-238-1580
Van Wert, OH   BLD Tues-Sun | $

Van Wert, "Peony Center of the World," is a vintage town along the old Lincoln Highway. It has an imposing 1876 courthouse, a drive-in movie theater on the outskirts, and Balyeat's Coffee Shop on Main Street (next to the courthouse). With its boast of being "Nationally Famous Since 1924," Balyeat's appears to be where the locals come to eat every day at breakfast and lunch, but it no doubt attracted more tourists back when the Lincoln Highway was the primary thoroughfare through Ohio. Now superseded by the efficient monotony of Interstate 30, the Lincoln Highway remains a beautiful two-lane route; and Balyeat's is just the sort of restaurant you'd hope to find along the way.

Outside, a lovely neon sign advertises "Young Fried Chicken Day and Night." Good as the chicken is, it is just the lead item on a menu that is an honor roll of mid-American square meals. Balyeat's is the place to sit down for a plate of roast pork or roast beef, cooked that morning, served hot and large, with piles of mashed potatoes and gravy. Sauerkraut and sausage is on the menu every day but Friday; and you can usually count on a choice from among barbecued ribs, meat loaf, and liver and onions. If mashed potatoes don't ring your chime, how about the fine alternative, scalloped potatoes?

Ahh, dessert! Pie's the thing in this part of the world, and Balyeat's pies are pastries to behold. There are cream pies, fruit pies, custard pies, and pecan pie; but our personal favorite is the one known as "old-fashioned pie" (O.F. pie). It is like custard, but tawnier, and has a sort of layered effect that happens as its cream rises to the top. It is pure, simple, and utterly satisfying: culinary synecdoche for a visit to Balyeat's Coffee Shop.

Blue Ash Chili

9565 Kenwood Rd.   513-984-6107
Blue Ash, OH   LD | $

The way to order chili in Cincinnati is to build a plate, layer by layer. It is, for instance, possible to order only a dish of spaghetti (traditionally, the bottom layer) or a bowl of chili (the meat sauce that usually goes atop the spaghetti). You can get a dish of chili *and* spaghetti, or you can get a three-way (chili, spaghetti, and cheese), four-way (chili, spaghetti, cheese, and raw onions), or five-way (add beans). You can even get a five-way, hold the onions, extra cheese. The possibilities are nearly endless, all the way up to what the menu lists as a gallon of chili (to go, we assume!) for $20.

A layered plate of three- to five-way is a beautiful thing. The chili meat is dark and resonant, not too spicy but with complex character, and the spaghetti noodles are always fork-friendly: not overly long, and squiggly enough that they stay on the tines of a fork with virtually no slippage.

Good as the chili is at Blue Ash, we think of this Naugahyde-and-linoleum eat-place more as a sandwich shop, for the sandwiches are nothing short of spectacular. "We think we have the best sandwiches in town," the menu advises, and in Cincinnati, sandwiches are a very big deal, almost as big as chili. As in every Cincinnati chili parlor, double-deckers reign. A double-decker means two ingredients of your choice are sandwiched amid three slices of bread, making a sandwich that is so tall it is a challenge to lift it from its plate. Ingredient choices for double-deckers range from bacon and egg to hot ham and cheese to turkey, beef, and bacon. Any combo is possible, including "turkey and turkey," "beef and beef," etc., meaning your double decker is simply a double dose of a favorite ingredient. We are especially fond of hot ham, which is sliced thin and packed into the bread in moist clumps, especially when paired with American cheese, lettuce, tomato, and mayo. Bacon is quite wonderful in any double-decker; it is thick and curly—great with turkey, eggs, or cheese.

On the side, for variety's sake, many customers get one or two Coneys—small hot dogs in tender buns, customarily dressed with chili, onions, and mustard and completely covered with a great fistful of grated orange cheese.

Camp Washington Chili Parlor

3005 Colerain Ave.	513-541-0061
Cincinnati, OH	Open 24 hours Mon-Sat | $

When we met John Johnson in 1977, he was beaming with pride, having just bought Camp Washington Chili Parlor from its founders, his uncle Steve Andon and Anastasios "Fred" Zarmbus. John had worked at Camp Washington since his arrival in America in 1951, so he knew the secrets of five-way chili as well as any cook in the chili-crazed city of Cincinnati; and he explained to us with conspiratorial glee that when he took over, he actually tinkered with the hallowed recipe and improved it! The result was an American success story—a restaurant beloved by Queen City eaters for decades, now recognized far and wide as a Roadfood original. Even a move in 2000 to spanking new quarters a stone's throw from the old building hasn't dimmed the luster of this superb chili parlor, although we must admit to missing the fluorescent hash-house ambience of the original.

Camp Washington sets the standard for Cincinnati's unique style of chili, which is a sweet, spicy, fine-ground beef mixture served atop noodles and generally garnished with beans, shredded American cheese, and raw onions, plus oyster crackers. Beyond chili, John Johnson's menu remains a simple one—eggs for breakfast, Coney Island hot dogs and double-decker club sandwiches all the time. Coneys and double-deckers, which are favorite menu items in several of the city's important chili parlors, make good companions to a plate of piled-high five-way chili. (Five-way is the term for chili *all the way*, with everything.)

Clifton Mill

75 Water St.   937-767-5501
Clifton, OH   B&L | $$

A genuine water-powered grist mill—the largest in the United States—Clifton Mill is the place to come for such country comforts as cornmeal mush, buckwheat cakes with rugged-textured sausage, and biscuits the size of softballs accompanied by a vast bowl full of creamy sausage gravy.

The mush is swell: three tiles of cornmeal fried into crunchy squares with a sticky interior—great with a little syrup poured on top. Biscuits and gravy is a daunting meal . . . although we did watch a ten-year-old boy at a nearby table polish off the whole thing with precise strategy, mopping the last of the gravy with his last piece of biscuit. The assortment of pancakes, made from grain ground on premises, is vast, including whole-wheat, buttermilk, buckwheat, cornmeal, apple-cinnamon, banana-walnut, and oat bran–honey. Blueberries, raisins, or chocolate chips can be added to any kind you like. Lunch specials include hamburgers, buffalo burgers, and ostrich burgers. Sandwiches are made on baked-here bread.

You can buy the mill's grains as well as country-style knickknacks in an attached gift shop. Christmas aficionados should note that Clifton Mill puts on a display that is *way* over the top: 2.5 million lights on the building, in the gorge, and in the waterfall that powers the mill, plus a collection of 3,000 different Santa Clauses, and a live Santa who goes up the chimney every half hour. Starting the day after Thanksgiving and continuing through New Year's, the lights display goes on every night at 6 and runs until 9:30, weather permitting.

Crabill's

727 Miami St.   513-653-5133
Urbana, OH   L | $

Size matters, but when it comes to hamburgers, bigger isn't necessarily better. In fact, some burger hounds prefer minuscule two-bite "sliders." The best place we know in Ohio to gobble such mini-burgers is at the counter of Crabill's, where fifty-cent hamburgers are served on itty-bitty buns, with small squares of cheese if desired, and with mustard and/or relish for a few cents extra. Eating one of these gems is a unique experience: cooked in deep oil on the grill, it has an outside surface with delicious crunch, and it is so skinny that there is virtually no interior! Six or eight make a decent meal, but if you have a competitive spirit, you might want to try to beat the single-sitting record-holder, Dave Woods, who ate thirty-one on February 22, 2001.

G&R Tavern

103 N. Marion St. (off US 23)   740-726-9685
Waldo, OH   BLD | $

Waldo, north of Columbus, is known as the town with the fried baloney sandwich. Merely driving through Waldo, you will home in on this culinary attraction if you keep your eyes open for the handsome mural that depicts a bologna sandwich on the outside of the G&R Tavern.

Since 1962, the G&R has built its reputation on bologna sandwiches that put pale, pink, thin-sliced supermarket bologna sandwiches to shame. In this family-friendly sports bar, the bologna is dark and smoky, firm as a knoblewurst salami, and sliced as thick as a good-size hamburger patty. It is fried until its exterior turns a bit crisp, and loaded into a sandwich with sweet pickles and onion (a great condiment combo), or your choice of mustard, mayonnaise, or tomato. Fitting side dishes include a variety of deep-fried vegetables and curly fries.

If for some reason, you are a fried-food-frowner, G&R also offers a bologna salad sandwich; and because this bologna is so much better than the spongy packaged stuff, the salad reminds us of something made with good ham, but smoother.

While you stand along the bar waiting for a seat (at mealtimes, you will likely wait), your appetite will be whetted by the sight of the kitchen staff carrying great big logs of this very special bologna into the kitchen.

Henry's

6275 Route 40   614-879-9321
West Jefferson, OH   LD | $

Highway 40 was once the National Road, a way to cross the country east to west before the interstate highway system. It is now a side road parallel to I-70, so that millions of vehicles zoom past, utterly oblivious to the existence of Henry's. Even if you are on the two-lane and you do see Henry's on the south side of 40, chances are good you will drive on by. It looks defunct. It needs paint. The gas pumps that used to be outside are long gone and what remains of the refueling islands is rusty. But a sign in the window says Open. And for those who take a chance, walking through that door is a pass into Roadfood heaven.

The meals are just fine, very good country-style fare: baked ham, hot roast pork sandwiches with mashed potatoes and gravy, creamed chipped beef on corn bread. But it's not the hot meals that put this unlikely knotty-pine-paneled roadside café on the map. It is pie. Here are some of the best pies in Ohio, in the Midwest, anywhere. Every day, baker Shelley Kelley has a list of six or eight she has made: peach, banana, chocolate, peanut butter, cherry, coconut, etc. We tried three kinds on our last visit. The butterscotch pie was thick and dense, full-flavored the way only real (not from a mix) butterscotch can be, and it was topped with a creamy meringue. Custard pie was modestly thin, a sunny yellow wedge dusted with nutmeg. It was balmy, lightweight, melt-in-the-mouth tender. The flavor of the rhubarb pie was as brilliant as a bright summer sun, intensely fruity, sweet but not cloying, and balanced by a crust that flaked into luscious shards.

Liberty Gathering Place

111 North Detroit St.   937-465-3081
West Liberty, OH   BLD | $

While waiting for The Pine Club (page 380) to open for supper one day, we drove north of Dayton into the farmland around Urbana and West Liberty. We marveled at the Crystal Sea and the Devil's Tea Table (formed from stalactites and helactites) in the Ohio Caverns; we toured Mac-A-Cheek and Mac-O-Chee, two late-nineteenth-century Gothic-style castles filled with sublime woodwork and surrounded by waves of cornfields; and we came upon a stupendously good lunch at the Liberty Gathering Place.

"We have girls who come in at four in the morning to make the cole slaw and macaroni salad," the Gathering Place waitress boasted when we asked if the side dishes were good. "Good" turned out to be not a good enough word to describe them; for the little bowl of macaroni salad set before us was inspired: blue-ribbon, church-supper, Independence

Day–picnic fabulous! It was creamy with a pickle zip, dotted with hunks of hard-cooked egg and a few crunchy shreds of carrot; the noodles themselves cooked just beyond al dente but not too soft.

Noodle rapture proved to be a paradigm for the dining experience at what appears to be a typical Main Street café, but is in fact an extraordinary one. During a week in Dayton, the Gathering Place became our destination lunch stop for moist ham loaf and deep-flavored smoked pork chops sided by mashed potatoes and bread-crumb-enriched scalloped corn. We were astounded by the fried tenderloin sandwich—totally unlike the brittle-crisp, foot-wide 'loins typical of Midwest cafés. Here, the tenderloin is a thick pork steak with only a hint of crust—a slab of meat that is folded over inside the bun so you get a double layer of pork as juicy as a pair of chops. For dessert, we had cool coconut pie and peach crunch pie, the latter served hot and veined with melted butter.

The Pine Club

1926 Brown St.   937-228-7463
Dayton, OH   D | $$$

It was still daylight when we arrived at The Pine Club late one afternoon, and upon entering, we were suddenly blind. This is the darkest restaurant you can imagine, darker than walking into a movie theater for a sunny-day matinee. It was so impossible to see that the hostess literally led us to a booth by holding Michael's hand, while Michael held Jane's, as if we were sightless people without dog or cane. Even an hour later, after our eyes had adjusted to the camera obscura, we were shadow-people across the table from each other, and the primary gathering points of light in the room were the radiant Manhattans, martinis, and Cosmos in their stemmed glasses, being carried on trays from the bar to booths, trailing the alluring perfumes of gin, vermouth, and blended whiskey.

The bar is at the center of The Pine Club, spanning two small dining rooms, with stools all around to accommodate people waiting for a table. Because there is always a wait, the bar dwellers are an unlikely mix of serious drinkers with shooters and beer, church ladies sipping rock 'n' rye, and youngsters burbling through their straws on Shirley Temples and Roy Rogerses. A big, good bar is one of the essential elements of a supper club.

What else defines a supper club in these parts? According to Pine Club VP and general manager, Dan Nooe, a supper club is a restaurant that has honed the evening meal to its fundamentals. "We have no party rooms, no specials, no lunch, no soup, and no dessert," Mr. Nooe says. Credit cards are not accepted, nor are reservations. Open weekdays until midnight (1 A.M. on Friday and Saturday), The Pine Club is simple and predictable, known for superior sirloins, filets mignon, and porterhouses. Good as the deluxe cuts are, what wows us more is a medium-rare chopped steak, the crust of which encloses meat that is pink at the edge and velvet red at its soft center: the flavor is as intoxicating as steak tartare, but with the added pleasure of warm, dripping juices.

All steaks come with a tangle of skinny onion rings and choice of potatoes that includes a crusty pancake of shredded spuds woven with veins of sautéed onion. As for salad, although a mesclun mix was added to the menu a while ago, the traditional and proper Pine Club salad is iceberg lettuce—cold, crisp chunks of it topped with either the house vinaigrette or served "red and bleu," which means jolly sweet French dressing loaded with enormous clods of dry blue cheese.

In lieu of dessert, The Pine Club offers such drinkable confections as Golden Cadillacs, Grasshoppers, and Pine Cone Cocktails (crème de cacao and Crème de Noyaux).

Putz's Creamy Whip

Putz Place and West Fork Rd. (Exit 17 off I-74)   513-681-8668
Cincinnati, OH   LD (closed in winter) | $

Putz's is a drive-up stand with a menu of hot dogs, foot-longs, burgers, and barbecue, but it's ice cream that stars. Smooth and rich, it is soft-serve custard that is great swirled into a sugar cone or waffle cone or heaped into a cup and enjoyed for its simple, pure, creamy goodness. Or you can have it whipped up for an extra-thick milk shake or malt or mixed into a soda.

The best way to enjoy Putz's Creamy Whip, in our opinion, is to come for a sundae or banana split. Banana splits are long plastic boats that hold three mounds of ice cream plus all the toppings. Sundaes are medium-size plastic cups filled with custard and topped with whatever you like. The best of all sundaes is the turtle, for which the bottom of the cup is filled with caramel, the caramel is topped with custard, then the custard is topped with chocolate syrup. And the chocolate syrup is mounded with whipped cream, chopped nuts, and a cherry.

Putz's is just off the highway in a little grove all its own (on a street that was rechristened to honor the longtime favorite destination dessert place). There are pleasant picnic tables alongside that are an ideal place to spoon into creamy-whip perfection. For us, a sundae here defines summer in Cincinnati.

White Turkey Drive-In

388 E. Main Rd.   440-593-2209
Conneaut, OH   LD Mother's Day through Labor Day | $

"If you find yourself along Lake Erie in the northeast corner of Ohio, pull into the White Turkey, a seriously vintage drive-in." So wrote a Roadfood tipster in a note with no return address and no ID. So we don't really know who to thank for this suggestion, but we sure would like to! This Richardson's Root Beer stand is a quintessential Roadfood stop along old US 20, offering seats at high stools where you can feel a lake breeze and watch the cars cruise past while you dine on true mid-American, mid-century drive-in fare.

The namesake turkey sandwich is the real thing. No turkey loaf here! You can get a plain one or a "Large Marge," which also includes cheese and bacon. And beyond turkey, there are Big Ed ⅓-pound burgers, hot dogs, and chili cheese dogs.

While only one flavor of ice cream is available—vanilla—the variety of soda fountain drinks and desserts is mesmerizing. Of course there are cones, shakes, and malts; there are sundaes topped with your choice of pineapple, cherry, chocolate, hot fudge, butterscotch caramel fudge, strawberry, and grasshopper. You can get a black cow (here, a blend of root beer and ice cream). And the root beer floats are divine, available in sizes from kiddie (eighty cents) to Super Shuper, created with a quart of root beer and a quantity of ice cream to match.

Bay Bakery and Delicatessen

423 E. Silver Spring Dr.   414-332-5340
Milwaukee, WI   Tues-Sun | $

"Butter!" said the girl behind the counter at Bay Bakery as we stood in the store devouring a piece of yellow cake by hand—no plate or utensils to get in the way—and speculating out loud about why it tasted so extremely wonderful. "Some bakeries, they use lard," she scoffed. "We do not."

Here in the state with license plates that proclaim it "America's Dairyland," good pastries made with butter are not uncommon. But those made at Bay Bakery are some of the best we have eaten anywhere. Known to many customers as a place that makes elaborate celebration cakes (see www.theunionstation.com/baybakery/), it is, for us, an opportunity to get bags and boxes full of sour cream donuts, cupcakes, fruit flips, caramel buns, single-serving bundt cakes, and fritters.

Fresh-baked bread is also outstanding. There are warm loaves on the shelf every morning, but the day we like stopping in is Friday, when you can count on caraway rye. We would describe this rye as "heaven on toast," but in fact we've never had the opportunity to toast it. We buy a loaf and tear at it as we drive around Milwaukee looking for other good things to eat.

Mostly a take-out store, Bay Bakery does have a couple of tables for customers desperately in need of eating pastries now.

Beernsten's Candy Store

108 N. 8th St.   920-684-9616

Manitowoc, WI   L | $

Beernsten's has been the town sweetshop since 1932, and little has changed in the years since the store passed from Joe Beernsten to his son, Richard, to Richard's son, Tom. Tom loves this old confectionery, pointing to the original black walnut woodwork and boasting, "There isn't a knot in the place."

In back, past the confectionery shelves and through an elaborately carved archway, handsome wooden booths are occupied by customers who come for such ice cream fancies as a Sweetheart (caramel, vanilla ice cream, marshmallow, crushed nuts) or a Sunset (strawberry and vanilla ice cream, pineapple, marshmallow, crushed nuts). Up front are more than a hundred different kinds of hand-dipped candy, including a chocolate cosmetology set (brush, mirror, hair dryer), smoochies (like Hershey's kisses, but bigger), raspberry and vanilla seafoam dainties, and—pièce de résistance—a bonbon known as fairy food, which is a two-inch square of brittle spun sugar molasses shrouded in deep, dark chocolate. We are very happy we live nowhere near Manitowoc, and that fairy food is too delicate to be shipped; otherwise, we'd be addicts.

Bendtsen's Bakery

3200 Washington Ave.   262-633-7449

Racine, WI $

Bendtsen's calls its kringle "the world's finest Danish pastry," a claim with which we would not disagree. If you don't know what kringle is, think of an ordinary Danish, like you have with morning coffee. Now, imagine its crust buttery and feather-light, almost like a croissant's, and fill it with a ribbon of pecan paste and chopped nuts, or a layer of almond macaroon paste, or a tunnel of cherry and cheese. Picture it as big as a Christmas wreath, a ring that is about a foot and a half across and iced with sugar glaze or flavored frosting. There you have one of the great breakfast (or teatime) treats in America, a dish that is virtually unknown outside the city of Racine.

Bendtsen's has pictures on the wall that show the time they made the world's largest kringle, but size isn't what makes their pastry so wonderful. Each kringle made here, whether simply filled with apricot jam or fancy-filled with a mash of cranberries and walnuts, is a beautiful sight— a broad oval rather than a perfect circle, quite flat, and ready to slice into small pieces (of which you'll want three or four).

There is no place to eat at Bendtsen's, although samples of kringle are often available for tasting on the counter. And we must warn you that this is not really car food. It's rather a mess to eat (it crumbles and the filling oozes), and it really should be served warm, buttered, and with hot coffee. Nevertheless, we have been known to devour the better of two whole rings between Racine and Chicago, leaving a hail of crumbs on the seat and floor of our car.

Charcoal Inn

1313 S. 8th St.   920-458-6988
Sheboygan, WI   L | S

Also at 1637 Geele Ave. (920-458-1147)

"My dears, everything we make is charcoaled except the BLTs and the egg salad," a waitress informs us when we ask about the specialties at The Charcoal Inn, a luncheonette on the south side of Sheboygan. She points to a grill behind the counter where flames are licking up above the grate, and where sputtering Sheboygan brats are sending their pork sausage sweetness into the air. *(Brat,* short for bratwurst, rhymes with *hot.)*

She suggests a double brat with the works. "People in Sheboygan like everything they eat with pickle, mustard, and onions, and butter oozing out on every side," she informed us. Some brat enthusiasts add ketchup to the mix or delete the pickles or choose fried onions over raw ones, but every Sheboygan hot meat sandwich—brat, burger, or butterflied pork chop—drips butter.

A Charcoal Inn double brat is brought to the table without a plate. It is wrapped in wax paper, which you unfold and use as a dropcloth to catch dripping condiments. Each of the two brats inside the Sheboygan-style roll has been slit and flattened before being grilled, which makes for an easily stacked sandwich. These are brats from Henry Poth, the esteemed butcher shop just down Eighth Street, and they are deeply perfumed with spices that burst into blossom when they sizzle over a smoky charcoal fire. Thick and resilient but thoroughly tooth-tender, they are as luscious as sausage can be, oozing a delectable blend of meat juice and pure melted butter.

For dessert after a brat, one eats a torte. Tortes are another passion in the dairy state: the best way to get the maximum amount of cream flavor into a single piece of food. At the back of its little square dining room, The Charcoal Inn has a glass refrigerator case in which the day's selection is kept. The lemonade torte is about four inches square and two inches high. It is white and smooth, sitting on a pallet of graham cracker crumbs, and there are other sweet crumbs on top, too; but in this dessert, the crumbs aren't even a distraction. The thick band of faintly lemon-flavored torte has tremendous gravity, as if a pint of cream had been reduced, thickened, and sweetened. It is similar in texture to a cheesecake, but it is so pure and rich you want to call it cream cake.

Chili John's

519 S. Military Ave.   920-494-4624

Green Bay, WI   LD | $

No food-conscious explorer is allowed to head up the shore of Lake Michigan without a stop at the historic Chili John's. Here, in 1916, "Chili John" Isaac invented Green Bay–style chili, now popular throughout the state: a concoction of ground round with a kaleidoscope of secret spices combined with spaghetti noodles, beans, and cheese. It is served with minuscule oyster crackers, which were invented at Chili John's request. Some time in the 1920s, he came to believe that the old-fashioned store cracker, at least an inch in diameter, was too unwieldy to garnish his chili, so he convinced cracker manufacturers to downsize.

The style of chili that John invented is now popular throughout Wisconsin, but the best place to have it is at the original location. Here in Green Bay, many people know it as "Texas-style" chili, apparently referring to the fact that it's peppery; but in fact, it's unique. Made from ground round and secret spices, the meat sauce would be unbearably hot by itself. But with noodles and beans, cheese and oyster crackers, and maybe a dab or two of sour cream to cushion the blow, it is irresistibly delicious.

The Elegant Farmer

1545 Main St.   262-363-6770
Mukwonago, WI   L | $$

America's best apple pie is baked in Mukwonago, Wisconsin, at a Waukesha County produce market called The Elegant Farmer. Its crust is as crunchy as a butter cookie, so brittle that when pressed with the edge of a fork, it makes a cracking sound; grains of cinnamon sugar bounce off the surface as it shatters. The bottom crust is softer than the top, but browned and breakable. Where the top and bottom meet at the circumference, there's a knotty cord of dough that can be pinched away in bite-size nuggets, its crunch impregnated with enough seepage of fruit filling that it has become chewy. Inside the pie is a dense apple pack of al dente Ida Red crescents bound in syrupy juice. There is no wrong time or place to eat this pie. We have loved it for breakfast and cold from the refrigerator shelf at 3 A.M.; warm from the oven at The Elegant Farmer (where it is available by the piece or by the whole pie with a diameter of four, eight, or nine inches) or heated at home, its tart fruit filling makes us moan.

While there is nothing eccentric or innovative about the product—it is basic apple pie—how it's baked is unusual: inside a brown paper bag. A woman behind the counter at The Elegant Farmer explained to us that inside-the-bag cooking allows the juices of the fruit to simmer, mellowing its tang. When the pie is mostly baked, a large hole is cut in the top of the paper bag, which makes the crust harden. She pointed to the fact that the bag in which each pie is baked (and sold) gets blotched with dampness drawn from within.

Housed in a cathedral-size 1930s dairy barn, The Elegant Farmer isn't just a pie place. Its shelves contain hundreds of Wisconsin cheeses, nine kinds of locally grown popcorn, cider-baked ham and peppered bacon, jumbo muffins guaranteed to be one-third fruit, bricks of butter sculpted into the shape of sheep, and an enchanting frozen cider lick: apple or berry juice made into a popsicle on a stick. And there are hot meals and sandwiches available for lunch every day.

(Note: Baked and ready-to-heat apple pies are available by overnight delivery.)

Jack Pandl's Whitefish Bay Inn

1319 Henry Clay   414-964-3800

Whitefish Bay, WI   LD | $$

Jack Pandl's (since 1915) serves German-flavored Dairyland cuisine in a friendly, wood-paneled dining room with a wall of windows that looks out over elegant Lake Drive. Waitresses wear dirndl skirts and there is lots of Old World memorabilia for decor (including one of the planet's biggest collections of beer steins), but the menu is at least as Midwestern as it is Middle European. At lunch, when the steel-banded tables are set with functional paper place mats, you can eat a julienne salad or a Reuben sandwich made with Wisconsin cheese, or pork chops, or a Denver omelet. In addition to superlative broiled whitefish ("always purchased fresh," the menu guarantees), there is that lean but luscious local specialty, walleyed pike, filleted and broiled to perfection. This being Milwaukee, Friday is fish-fry night, of course. Pandl's perch is lovely—whole fish filleted so their two halves hold together, encased in a golden crust and accompanied by first-class potato pancakes.

We love schaum torte for dessert. That's a crisp meringue dolloped with freshly made custard. On the other hand, we never can resist the German pancake. It's not really a dessert item, and many people have it as their main course, but somehow it makes a grand conclusion to a meal. This gorgeous edible event, a Jack Pandl's specialty, is a big puffy cloud of batter similar in texture to Yorkshire pudding, but slightly sweeter. It arrives at the table piping hot and shaped like a big bowl, its circumference crisp and brown, risen high in the oven, its center moist and eggy. Dust it with a bit of powdered sugar and give it a spritz of lemon, creating a sophisticated syrup, then dig in immediately. It is a big plate of food, a joy to share with friends.

Jo's Café

3519 W. Silver Spring   414-461-0210

Milwaukee, WI   BLD Mon-Fri | $

"Jo" is Josepha Platzer, the omnipresent woman who runs this tiny weekday-only café, makes the jelly on the counter, and collects the souvenir trivets (from nearly every state) that decorate the walls. She is a character who always has something to say—when she is busy preparing food behind the counter, at one of the four tables, or with the small group of people waiting near the door for seats to open up. She laughed out loud when she saw us taking pictures of the morning hoffel poffel, but then understood when we told her we were from Connecticut, where hoffel poffel is unknown.

Hoffel poffel isn't widely known anywhere else in the U.S. that we are aware of, although we have seen versions of it (called hoppel poppel) in Iowa. It is one gigantic breakfast plate of a few eggs scrambled with chunks of potato, some onions, and, at Jo's, lots of nuggets of spicy salami and, optionally, some cheese on top. The only reason we would recommend not getting it for breakfast at Jo's is that the *other* kind of potatoes—the thin-cut hash browns—are delicious. Cooked in a flat patty until brittle-crisp, they too are available under a mantle of melted cheese. Actually, either potato dish will leave precious little room for Jo's terrific pecan rolls and cinnamon rolls; nor should a first-time visitor miss out on one of the large omelets cooked on Jo's griddle.

That griddle, just behind the counter at the far end of the restaurant, is hypnotic to watch. The short-order cook, Donna, wields her spatula like a culinary maestro, creating gorgeous piles of potatoes and perfectly cooked eggs, sizzling sausages and bacon, and orchestrating every table's meal so all plates arrive at the same time. You'll not likely have a choice of seats when you come to Jo's, because they are always in short supply; but if you can sit opposite the grill, the good view of food being made adds a whole other dimension to the meal—and you get to see the work-ings of the Bunn-O-Matic coffeemaker, above which a sign toasts, *Guten Appetit.*

We generally think of this place for breakfast, but lunch is not to be ignored. Blue-plate cuisine is the order of the day, including such daily specials as meat loaf, beef stew, pork chops, and country-fried steak with real (of course!) mashed potatoes, homemade gravy, and a yeasty fresh-baked dinner roll. Every day you can order good barbecued pork ribs or chicken.

Jo's is simple, personal, inexpensive, and delicious. Pure Roadfood!

Karl Ratzsch's

320 E. Mason   414-276-2720
Milwaukee, WI   D | $$$

Milwaukee has an abundant supply of good cheap eats that fill the Road-food bill, and while Ratzsch's is by no means cheap, nor typical Roadfood, it deserves a slot on any serious eater's itinerary. It is a grand urban restaurant founded in 1904 and now justifiably famous for its expertly prepared German food. The staff are Teutonically costumed professionals and the dining room is intensely atmospheric: dark woodwork, antique steins, romantic murals, sentimental paintings.

The Old World menu includes such stalwart classics as liver-dumpling soup, roast goose shank, beef rouladen, and sauerbraten with ginger-snap gravy. There isn't a more beautiful roast duck in the state of Wisconsin; the wiener schnitzel is magnificent; and the crackling pork shank we had on a recent visit is one of the most awesome-looking (and tasting) meals imaginable—a veritable mountain of succulent meat ready to fall from the bone when tugged with fingers or prodded with a fork. The beer-on-tap list includes some from Germany as well as local Milwaukee brews (and the waitress will gladly describe each one, if you have any doubts), and there is a whole array of Kümmel, Kirschwasser, and Rumpleminze liqueurs for after dinner.

Most people come to Ratzsch's for the German food, and rightfully so. But here's a secret: The normal American food is grand, too. Steaks and prime rib are utterly regal (get Ratzsch's thick, crusty potato pancakes on the side), and the $79 porterhouse-for-two is one of the Midwest's most magnificent meat monuments. Whitefish is a Great Lakes treasure—tender, sweet, and juicy—served on a wood plank in a ring of mashed potatoes, and every Friday night, you can count on fried lake perch. Recently, a "lighter fare" menu has been added, too, for those who prefer angel hair pasta or a veggie plate to stuffed pork chops and spaetzle or potato dumplings.

Klinger's East

920 E. Locust   414-263-2424
Milwaukee, WI   D | $$

When we went to Milwaukee on a mission to eat its best fish fries, our buddies Jessica Zierten and Brad Warsh, both lifelong Milwaukeeans, insisted that any significant expedition needed to include a visit to their favorite tavern in the Riverwest neighborhood, Klinger's East. We're glad they recommended it, because this shadowy bar is not one that we would necessarily feel obligated to enter. It doesn't look like a great place to eat.

The swinging door opens onto concrete stairs that lead up and inside. "These five steps take you to northern Wisconsin," Brad declared as we came in off the sidewalk late one Friday night. He said he was reminded of summer places far from the lights of Milwaukee every time he stepped up into the beery air. It is so dim that we saw nothing other than a few neon window signs when we walked in; ambient light at our table under a corner television seemed to go from noon-bright to twilight and back again as the TV's image flickered light and dark.

Despite the fact that half of Klinger's East is a pool hall and the bleak decor shadowed by the dining room's dropped acoustic-tile ceiling includes a sickly green rug and tables covered with matching green oilcloth, it's a cozy place to eat, even for out-of-towners like us. Customers include wholesome-looking families you'd never see dining in such an establishment in other parts of the country. But in Milwaukee, taverns aren't just for drinkers; they are community centers.

The fish fry is brilliant. Of course cod is on the menu, sheathed in a crunchy coat of beer batter. You can also get smelt, which Brad informed us is properly pronounced "shmelt" hereabouts. It is a fish-lover's fish with vivid oily character—a heap of crunch-coated two-inch sprats well accompanied by a short stack of silver-dollar-size potato pancakes. The night we visited, the potato-slicing machine was broken so fresh-cut French fries were unavailable. Bartender Tammy Galioto apologized for their absence, but wanted to know if we agreed that the fish was fantastic. "People say it should be patented!" she exclaimed. When we asked how to ID her for this entry, she pondered a moment and said, "How about 'An East Side Sicilian Icon'?" But she didn't kid around when we asked her to describe Klinger's East. "You are in a neighborhood tavern," she declared. "This is what makes the city of Milwaukee what it is."

Kopp's Custard

5373 N. Port Washington Rd.   404-961-3288
Glendale, WI   LD | $

Also at 18880 W. Bluemound Rd., Brookfield, WI (404-789-9490), and 7631 W.
Layton Ave., Greenfield, WI (404-282-4312)

Kopp's is a great place to stand up and have a cooked-to-order hamburger (there are no table seats), but it is best known for custard. Custard, not ice cream. Here in the Dairy State, such custard is a nearly sacred food, made by Kopp's in great silver machines behind the order counter. It is ivory white, pure, rich, and densely flavorful.

The plain vanilla is superb . . . and *very* unplain in character—the true choice of a serious custardhead. No matter what else we get, we always need to dip a spoon into one dish of that. Beyond vanilla, Kopp's makes a new and different flavor every single day of the year. Among our fondest memories are caramel-apple with mixed nuts back in August 1995, Key lime pie custard in September 2000, and Snickers chunky cheesecake in October 2000. Throughout July 2000, the favorite "magic flavor" (a changing every-Monday specialty made of various flavors) was cherry bomb, made by swirling together burgundy cherry, Key lime pie, and passion fruit. And the sundae of the month for August 2000 was French silk pie, made of Swiss chocolate swirled with cream cheese custard and thick shards of chocolate, all dished out in a pie crust.

Some of Kopp's sundaes are so elaborate that the management has been known to offer architectural diagrams pointing out various ingredients and their place in the structure of each concoction. The blueprint for the staggering Kopp's Special shows pineapple and raspberry sauces, sliced bananas, hot fudge, toasted pecans, and a cherry on top.

Kroll's West

1990 S. Ridge Rd.	920-497-1111
Green Bay, WI	LD | $

You don't have to be a Green Bay Packers supporter to enjoy Kroll's, but it helps. When the home team plays at Lambeau Field just across the way, Kroll's West beer garden is open from early in the morning for game prep and celebrating. Any other day of the year, Kroll's is known among non–football fans as a premier source of Wisconsin's wonderful butter burger.

There are many other items on the menu, from peanut butter and jelly sandwiches to broasted (pressure-fried) chicken and battered perch; but it is Kroll's way with hamburgers (or cheeseburgers, or Big K extra-large burgers) that puts this rollicking diner/bar on the Roadfood map. The meat patties themselves are not extraordinary. Normal-size lunch counter rounds of beef, they are cooked through and juicy enough; their magic is in the way they are packaged. As is Wisconsin custom, each hot burger is topped with a pat of butter that melts into the meat, making merely decent beef absolutely delectable. In addition to butter, a Kroll's burger ordered with *everything on* includes ketchup, onions, and pickles; it is sandwiched in a hard roll and presented wrapped in wax paper. Bacon, lettuce, and tomato are available at extra cost; and it is possible to ask the kitchen to substitute margarine for butter (practically a mortal sin here in the Dairy State).

Some of Kroll's other sandwiches are delicious, too, all of them prepared with butter and the same condiments as on the hamburgers. Shaved prime rib is especially succulent, as is its less sumptuous but irresistible cousin, shredded beef. And as you might expect, the bratwurst is excellent (instead of ketchup, the brat gets mustard). There are milk shakes and malts to drink (and, of course, beer) and pie and hot fudge sundaes for dessert.

Leon's

3131 S. 27th St.   414-383-1784
Milwaukee, WI $

Milwaukeeans love Leon's, especially on warm summer nights. If you appreciate custard, you will love it, too. Here, across the street from Mazo's (page 394), is an old-fashioned drive-in that is a neon-edged fun ride for anybody with a sweet tooth and an appreciation for the profound goodness of frozen dessert that is a cut above.

Custard looks like soft-serve ice cream and the broadest definition of frozen desserts might lump the two together. But as Leon's makes it, there is virtually no similarity to the aerated soft-serve available in national chains outside of America's Dairyland. And to compare it to the sort of ice cream that comes in supermarket pints—even the super-premium brands—is like comparing vintage Burgundy to screw-top wine. This custard is densely flavored, smooth as alabaster, sweet but not cloying, and uncomplicated. No mix-ins, no silly names for flavors, no cookie dough or brownie chunks. Choose vanilla, chocolate, strawberry, or butter pecan. Have it in a cone or cup. Or have a sundae topped with sauce of your choice and some of the most delicious toasted nuts on the planet: pecan halves that have a wicked crunch, a salty punch, and an earthy flavor that only helps accentuate the heavenly clarity of this superior custard.

Mazo's

3146 S. 27th St.
Milwaukee, WI

414-671-2118
BLD Tues-Sat | $

One of Milwaukee's lesser-known culinary attractions is its excellent hamburgers. Many connoisseurs believe Mazo's serves the best. It is a tiny place, now run by Nick Mazo, whose grandparents started it in 1934, and if you come at lunchtime, prepare to wait awhile once you find a precious seat in the dining room. These burgers are *not* fast food, but they are worth the wait.

They are not spectacular; they are very normal patties of good ground beef grilled in butter—the Milwaukee way!—and served in lovely toasted buns. Available toppings include fried onions, sautéed mushrooms, and of course a layer of cheese. Other choices for dressing up the burger are bacon, lettuce, and tomato as well as Thousand Island dressing. On the side, have cole slaw, French fries, or baked beans.

Bonus: Mazo's is directly across the street from the excellent Leon's custard stand (page 393).

McBob's

4919 W. North Ave.
Milwaukee, WI

414-871-5050
LD | $

McBob's Pub & Grill is a Central City bar that attracts an especially boisterous thank-God-it's-Friday crowd. Six other days a week the big draw, other than drinks, is corned beef sandwiches: smoky red brisket cut into hunks and served on rye with horseradish mustard or in a Reuben with sauerkraut and Swiss cheese. One of these days we need to do some serious research into Milwaukee's extraordinary corned beef sandwiches, but for now we're happy we know about this great one.

Friday night is, of course, fish-fry night. (Wednesday is, too.) You will not find common cod with its soft white meat as part of McBob's fish fry; the options are perch, walleye, and grouper, or a combination of two or three. Hot from the fry-kettle, with a fine, brightly seasoned crust, they are served atop a velvety trivet of onion-laced potato pancakes. They are elegant fillets—especially the milk-white walleye.

Beyond corned beef and fish fry, McBob's makes all kinds of sandwiches, including fresh liver sausage on rye with raw onions and a mighty fine half-pound hamburger. Tuesday, Thursday, and Saturday are taco days, and breakfast is served Saturday and Sunday. As Bob's is a serious drinking place, all patrons must be at least twenty-one years old.

Mr. Perkins' Family Restaurant

2001 W. Atkinson Ave.   414-447-6660
Milwaukee, WI   BLD | $

Mr. Perkins' is a city lunchroom with a mostly African-American clientele, but all visitors are made to feel welcome at this counter and in these booths. With a large menu (and a reliable rotation of daily specials, i.e., pork neckbones every Wednesday), this neighborhood Milwaukee café is one of the great soul-food restaurants anywhere.

While certain dishes may be an acquired taste—chitterlings, for example—many of Mr. Perkins' specialties are comfort food for anyone. Baked chicken with dressing is tender and vividly spiced; meat loaf is firm and satisfying; those pork neckbones on Wednesday are some trouble to eat (they're little), but the meat virtually falls from the bone as you savor it. We must also mention the fried perch, which is a plate of about three large boneless fillets encased in a sandy cornmeal crust. The meat of the fish is amazingly juicy with flavor as lusty as beefsteak.

One of the most delightful aspects of lunch and supper at Mr. Perkins' (which also serves breakfast) is choosing side dishes. The list is cornucopic, and nothing we've sampled is less than dazzling. Macaroni and cheese has a perfect balance of tender noodle and crusty edges; fried okra is vegetable-sweet; fried green tomatoes are tangy and brittle-crisp; there are pot-likker-sopped turnip greens *or* turnip bottoms, made into an intriguing squash-like mash with butter and sugar. One week in late September, the kitchen was offering homemade pear preserves, the pieces of fruit sweet as candy and flavored with cloves.

When you order lunch, you'll be asked if you want corn bread. Say yes! This is Tennessee-style corn bread, i.e., a pair of griddle-cooked corn cakes. They are buttery, tender, and golden-colored, and they are ideal tools for mopping gravy and vegetable drippings from a plate. Desserts include pineapple coconut cake, individual-size fried peach pies, sweet-potato pie, or a plate of sweet yams. To drink, the beverages of choice are lemonade and ice tea, both served Southern-style, i.e., supersweet!

A joyous place that almost always seems a little too crowded, especially up front where so many customers come to pick up orders to go, Mr. Perkins' is a kind of community center for people from all walks of life. It is now run by Willie Perkins's son, Willie Jr., who told us that his father still comes in nearly every day to check up on the operation and make sure it is running smoothly, as it has now for more than thirty years.

Real Chili

419 E. Wells St.   414-271-4042

Milwaukee, WI   BLD | $

Real Chili serves bowls of chili mild, medium, or hot, with spaghetti or beans, or spaghetti *and* beans, the latter arrangement known as the Marquette Special (to honor the original Real Chili established near Marquette University in 1931). The degree of heat is adjusted by how much meat sauce the server puts atop the beans. More meat equals more heat; and the hottest version costs about eighty cents more because it has so much of the dense, fine-grained chili meat piled on it. (If one bowl is not enough, seconds are available at half the price of the first bowl.) Atop each mighty serving of chili, you have your choice of sour cream, cheese, or onions; and on the side, you'll get some oyster crackers to crumble on top or to eat as a sort of palate-cleanser between bites of chili. Available condiments include a cruet of cider vinegar to sprinkle on if you need to cut the heat and a cruet of pepper vinegar to up it.

Real Chili is a working-person's eatery of the sort you once found in most big cities throughout the region: cheap chili the speciality of the house, served with plenty of attitude under fluorescent lights to a clientele that ranges from men and women in fine pinstripes to, shall we say, more rugged individuals who look like they might only recently have been wearing prison stripes. With the exception of Cincinnati, which still has an abundance of chili parlors, most Midwest cities have lost these democratic lunch counters; and although Heartland chili gets little respect from gastronomes who prefer the southwestern kinds, Real Chili is a true taste buds adventure and a reflection of America's urban culinary history.

The menu is posted on the back wall. You sit at a counter where you can watch the bowls assembled or at one of a couple of communal tables with backless stools in the center of the room. The preferred beverages are beer and cherry Coke. Alas, the bumper sticker we got here several years ago is no longer available. It said, "Real Chili: it's not just for breakfast anymore." Current bumper stickers boast that Real Chili is a Milwaukee legend. As well it should be.

Serb Hall

5101 W. Oklahoma Ave.   414-545-6030
Milwaukee, WI   D Friday only | $$

Of all the major fish-fry cities between New York's southern tier and the Great Plains, Milwaukee is the biggest. Here the ritual is so much a part of life that it is rare to find a restaurant that does not dedicate Friday night to it. The opportunity to feast on fried fish is found in places that range from Taqueria Azteca to Benji's Jewish Deli, including even the Bya Wi Se Nek Buffet in the Potawatomie Bingo Casino.

The most awesome place to have your Milwaukee fish fry is Serb Hall, where Friday night is the *only* time meals are served to the public. The scale of the place is stunning. It is a chandelier-crowned eating stadium with a capacity to seat one thousand diners at hundreds of four-tops and dozens of big-party tables. A disembodied loudspeaker voice reverberates above the dinner din with announcements of birthdays and anniversaries as clusters of diners cheer from a hundred yards away. By 6 P.M., the South Side banquet hall is filled, but the line of people waiting outside stretches for city blocks. When we inquired about Serb Hall serving hours, our very busy waitress took time to carefully explain that the door closes precisely at 8 P.M., but that customers already seated are allowed to finish eating and drinking.

The standard fish to fry here is Icelandic cod—thin-crusted blocks of soft white meat served in a plastic basket with French fries, tart cole slaw, and rye bread on the side. Beer-battered cod is frequently available, its hopsy coat shoring in an abundance of cream-rich fish juices.

Speed Queen

1130 W. Walnut St.   414-265-2900
Milwaukee, WI   LD Mon-Sat | $

We are sure the woman at the order window of Speed Queen has a system, but whatever that system is, its logic defies our brainpower. She simultaneously takes orders, takes money for orders, calls orders back to the kitchen, assembles platters that come out of the kitchen ready for bread and cole slaw, calls people's numbers when their orders are ready, and delivers the right meal to the right customer. It appears to be total chaos, but it works . . . and it works fast.

It's a good thing it works fast, because the aroma inside Speed Queen is so appetizing that it makes us weak with hunger. You smell it even in the parking lot—a come-hither perfume of smoldering hickory, apple-wood, maple, and oak combined with slow-sizzling beef and pork—and the moment you enter, the aroma wallops your brain directly in the place where desire and hunger reside. Simply walking into this simple barbe-cue restaurant is a joy.

Speed Queen is Milwaukee's best barbecue, serving pork, beef, and turkey cooked until ridiculously tender and served in a glaze of spicy sauce. The mild sauce is robust and slightly sweet. Hot sauce is explo-sive, a dark orange emulsion that reminds us of Arthur Bryant's dizzying potion in Kansas City. For many customers, the mild is a little too mild, the hot is too lip-burning; so it is not uncommon to hear orders for "half and half." (Sauce is sold in bottles to take home: *highly recommended!*)

There are two kinds of pork available: shoulder or outside meat. Shoulder is thick slices that are almost chunks, tender as velvet. Outside meat is a motley pile of nearly blackened shreds and nuggets, some of which are tender, some of which are crusty, and some of which quite lit-erally melt on the tongue. It is smokier-tasting than inside meat, like essence of barbecue.

A favorite way to eat at Speed Queen is to order a half-and-half plate (ribs and outside, rib tips and shoulder, etc.) that consists of meat, sauce, a couple of slices of spongy white bread (necessary for sopping sauce), plus a cup of cole slaw. Beans and potato salad cost extra. You can also get a sandwich; but beware: These "sandwiches" are, in fact, lots of meat and sauce piled onto white bread in such a way that it is inconceivable to hold it in your hands like a sandwich. If you want to pick something up, you can get pork or beef on a bun, a somewhat more manageable configuration.

Everything is delivered at the order window in a Styrofoam con-tainer; and while most business is takeout, Speed Queen offers a row of functional booths for dining-in. Decor is minimal, consisting of two identical photo murals of the Wisconsin Dells on opposite walls. Al-though there is a jukebox, it seems seldom to be plugged in or playing. Room tone is a hush punctuated by lip-smacks, sighs of pleasure, and the quietest kind of reverential conversation—the pensive calm induced by truly wonderful barbecue.

Carry your own meal from the window and please bus your own table when you are through.

Three Brothers

2414 S. St. Clair St.   414-481-7530
Milwaukee, WI   D | $$

Three Brothers is a neighborhood tavern that has been serving Serbian food for the last half century. It is best known for its *burek*, a plate-wide circular plateau of phyllo leaves layered with beef, cheese, or spinach/cheese and slow-baked until the phyllo is brittle gold around the top and sides and permeated with flavors of the filling within.

We like to start a Three Brothers meal with lemon-and-wine marinated rice-stuffed grape leaves, which are served with black olives and firm sticks of nut-sweet *kashkaval* (a goat's-milk cheese) and a glorious "Serbian salad" of tomatoes, green peppers, and onions. The salad is veiled with finely grated *Bryndza*, a very soft goat's-milk cheese that is like mild feta.

All of Three Brothers' recipes come from the family of proprietor Branko Radiecevich, whose parents arrived in Milwaukee mid-century. Now Branko and his wife, Patricia, run the place (and live upstairs), doing all the cooking, food shopping, and hosting. As we watch Branko greet people at the front door or adjust the spices of chicken paprikash in the tiny back-room kitchen, we marvel at the delight he shows in the very existence of his restaurant and the food of his heritage that people come to eat.

One autumn when we came for supper, Branko told us it was leek season. "This is when we make leek pie!" he exulted, bringing out a savory pastry pie layered with caramelized peppered leeks. He was even more enthusiastic about roast lamb, a Three Brothers signature dish that is basted four hours in its own juices with tomato, pepper, onion, and garlic, and served *just barely* on the bone. Poke it with fork tines, and bite-size hunks of meat separate from the haunch and fall into the juice on the plate. Surrounding the meat are a pile of soft pickled cabbage and thick discs of carrot cooked until supple and sweet, bathed in butter. The menu describes this meal as "A must for the lamb lover"; but we suspect that even non–lamb lovers might find its refined taste irresistible.

The rare charm of Three Brothers' old-country meals is immeasurably enriched by the setting, a very Midwest-urban corner tavern built in 1897. For decades early in the century it was operated by the Schlitz Brewing Company, whose insignia—a globe—still crowns the peak of the roof. There are no longer seats at the old bar, which runs the length of the front room and is now a service area, but the wood-floored saloon retains the warmth of a community gathering place. While a visit to Three Brothers is a special night out for many Milwaukeeans, we also noted several small tables occupied by single diners who frequently stop by for a leisurely meal of roast pork loin in mustard sauce, and who read a book or newspaper or chat with Branko when he is not in the kitchen resolving culinary crises.

Watts Tea Room

761 N. Jefferson St.   414-291-5120

Milwaukee, WI   BL and T, Mon–Sat | $

When we wrote the cookbook *Square Meals* in 1984, we described the ritual of ladies' lunch as culinary history. We were wrong. At the Watts Tea Room, on the second floor of George Watts & Son fine china shop, ladies' lunch is alive and well . . . along with afternoon tea and lovely breakfasts of ginger toast and hot chocolate.

Such a pleasant place! At the front door downstairs, you are greeted by a member of the staff and directed to the elevator. Past display cases of Limoges and Wedgwood, you find yourself on the second floor in a broad lunchroom with a window view of Jefferson Street below. The tables are well-worn bare wood, the floral carpet is a muted blue. Coffee is served in Royal Worcester Hanbury–pattern cups, and napkins are white linen. Of course, waitresses wear tidy uniforms.

Most people think of Watts Tea Room for lunch or a teatime snack, which are its specialties. Midday, sandwiches are served on tender-crumb homemade whole-wheat bread; and while we adore the mixed green and black olive salad sandwich, and the BLT is exemplary, and a quiche of the day is always available, what dazzles us about the menu is its many ways with chicken. You can have chicken salad, minced chicken, all-white chicken, sliced chicken, or chicken salad Polynesian, that last one mixed with coconut shreds, pecans, and a citrus vinaigrette.

To drink, there are tea and lemonade, and the wonderful house specials known as a Waterford spritzer (lemonade, lime, and sparkling water) and a cold Russian (coffee, chocolate, and whipped cream). Dessert is splendid: filled sunshine cake, made from a decades-old recipe for triple-layer sponge cake with custard filling and seven-minute frosting.

Only recently, we discovered breakfast at Watts. It is a short menu of eggs and pastries and perfectly likable French toast, made from Watts bread, and one wonderful item we've never seen anywhere before: ginger toast. Ginger toast is like cinnamon toast, but made with ground ginger instead of cinnamon. A mixture of ginger, sugar, and butter is melted atop the whole-wheat toast to form a frosting with a dainty spice flavor. Ginger toast is also available at afternoon tea (as is filled sunshine cake).

Great Plains

Idaho ✳ Montana ✳ Nebraska ✳

South Dakota ✳ Wyoming

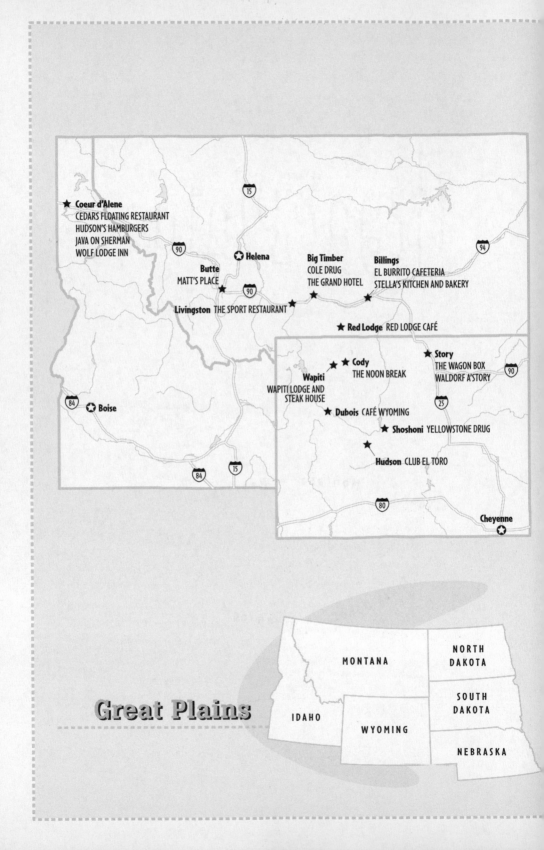

★ **Coeur d'Alene**
CEDARS FLOATING RESTAURANT
HUDSON'S HAMBURGERS
JAVA ON SHERMAN
WOLF LODGE INN

✪ **Helena**

Butte
MATT'S PLACE

Livingston THE SPORT RESTAURANT

Big Timber
COLE DRUG
THE GRAND HOTEL

Billings
EL BURRITO CAFETERIA
STELLA'S KITCHEN AND BAKERY

★ **Red Lodge** RED LODGE CAFÉ

★ **Cody**
THE NOON BREAK

★ **Story**
THE WAGON BOX
WALDORF A'STORY

Wapiti
WAPITI LODGE AND
STEAK HOUSE

✪ **Boise**

★ **Dubois** CAFÉ WYOMING

★ **Shoshoni** YELLOWSTONE DRUG

★ **Hudson** CLUB EL TORO

✪ **Cheyenne**

MONTANA

NORTH DAKOTA

IDAHO

SOUTH DAKOTA

WYOMING

NEBRASKA

Great Plains

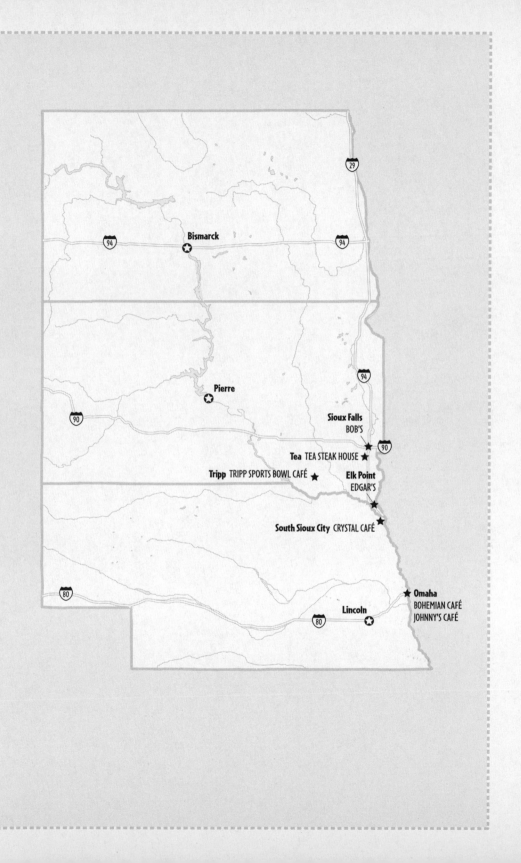

Bismarck

94 · 94

Pierre

90

94

Sioux Falls
BOB'S ★

Tea TEA STEAK HOUSE ★

Tripp TRIPP SPORTS BOWL CAFÉ ★

Elk Point
EDGAR'S
★

South Sioux City CRYSTAL CAFÉ ★

80

★ Omaha
BOHEMIAN CAFÉ
JOHNNY'S CAFÉ

Lincoln
80

Idaho

Cedars Floating Restaurant

1 Marine Dr. (Blackwell Island)   208-664-2922
Coeur d'Alene, ID   D | $$

Rugged as it is, the landscape of northern Idaho can be irresistibly romantic. This fact is especially evident at dinner hour in Cedars Floating Restaurant, which is one of the few eateries that take full advantage of the city's auspicious setting at the north end of Coeur d'Alene Lake. In fact, Cedars is located *in* the lake, moored about a hundred yards out at the head of the Spokane River and reachable by a walk down a long, narrow gangplank from the parking lot. Permanently berthed on three hundred tons of concrete, the dining room does not bob with the waves (as the original structure did in the 1960s!); but the window tables are virtually on the waterline. We happened to visit one drizzly September evening when the lake was steel gray, reflecting stormy skies and low clouds creeping down over a forested horizon.

A crackling fire and the lively sounds of an open kitchen provide cozy ambience to the circular dining room, where every seat affords a view of waterfowl skimming over waves and the distant rocky shoreline. Cedars's multipage menu has something for everyone, including steaks and prime rib, but the blackboard in the entryway tells what's special: fresh fish from Pacific waters. Salmon, ahi, sea bass, halibut, shark, and mahi mahi are some of the frequently available choices; they are cut into thick fillets and charcoal-broiled, served with a choice of clear lemon-butter-caper sauce, tropical fruit salsa, or cucumber dill sauce. Our fillet of Hawaiian wahoo was a handsome piece of meat, well over an inch thick: firm and sweet-fleshed with a savory crust from the grill, accompanied by a baked potato with tawny skin and flavorful insides. "An Idaho potato?" we asked the waitress. Blushing, she confessed the spud was grown in Washington State.

Preceded by a pair of creamy crab cakes dotted with red and yellow pepper bits and followed by fresh raspberry crème brulée for dessert, the wahoo and potato were an exemplary Far West meal. But if we don't dwell too much on Cedars's food, please understand that we were overcome by the setting and the view. Rolling waves slapping in from the lake, a brewing tempest in the sky, and the heavy mists settling down over the far mountains at dusk were a vision of primal beauty that made us linger in this magic place long after coffee was poured and plates were cleared away.

Hudson's Hamburgers

207 Sherman Ave.	208-664-5444
Coeur d'Alene, ID	L	$

"Pickle and onion?" the counterman will ask when you order a hamburger, a double hamburger, or a double cheeseburger at Hudson's, a counter-only diner that has been a Coeur d'Alene institution since 1907, when Harley Hudson opened a quick-eats lunch tent on the town's main drag.

Your garnish selection is called out to grill man Todd Hudson, Harley's great-grandson, who cuts the raw onion to order, using his knife blade to hoist the thin, crisp disc from the cutting board to the bun bottom; then, deft as a Benihana chef, he slices eight small circles from a pickle and arrays them in two neat rows atop the onion. When not wielding his knife, Todd hand-forms each burger, as it is ordered, from a heap of lean ground beef piled in a silver pan adjacent to his griddle—all at warp speed. Customers enjoy the mesmerizing show from the sixteen seats at Hudson's long counter, as well as from the small standing area at the front of the restaurant where new arrivals await stool vacancies from mid-morning through the afternoon.

Each patty is cooked until it develops a light crust from the griddle but retains a high amount of juiciness inside. One in a bun makes a balanced sandwich. Two verge on overwhelming beefyness. Chef Hudson sprinkles on a dash of salt, and when the hamburger is presented, you have one more choice to make: Which condiment? Three squeeze bottles are deployed adjacent to each napkin dispenser along the counter. One is hot mustard, the other is normal ketchup, the third is Hudson's very spicy ketchup, a thin orange potion for which the recipe is a guarded secret. "All I can tell you is that there is no horseradish in it," the counterman reveals to an inquisitive customer.

Hudson's is a *hamburger restaurant*. In other words, there is nothing else on the menu to eat, except for some pies in a pie case. There are no side dishes at all: not even any potatoes here in Idaho, not a leaf of lettuce or a slice of tomato in the house. This is not to say the staff isn't attuned to the fine points of hamburgerology. When a man sits next to us and orders a glass of buttermilk to accompany his double cheeseburger, the counterman asks if he wants the beverage now, or three minutes from now, when his sandwich is assembled—thus ensuring the buttermilk will be served properly, ice cold.

Java on Sherman

324 Sherman Ave. 208-667-0010
Coeur d'Alene, ID BLD | $

Coeur d'Alene is Northwest enough to have a high coffee-consciousness, so it is no surprise that the Idaho panhandle's hub has one terrific coffee bar (actually, there are four Javas around the state). During a week's stay a couple of years ago, we sampled breakfast all around town; but nothing we ate in the morning was as alluring as this stylish storefront, which by day seven had become our morning home. We were not alone. We came to know a small handful of locals as well as visitors who had staked out Java on Sherman as their source for terrific coffee and masterful muffins.

All the usual drip-brewed and espresso-based beverages are made to order; house specialties include such caffeine infusions as the "Keith Richards," made from four shots of espresso and Mexican chocolate, and one wonderful beverage named "bowl of soul"—a mix of coffee and espresso with a sprinkle of chocolate and cinnamon served in a big ceramic bowl.

Java offers a repertoire of hot breakfasts, including bulgur wheat with apples and raisins, non-instant oatmeal, and eggs scrambled then steamed at the nozzle of the espresso machine, but it's the baked goods that have won Idahoans' hearts: handsome scones, sweet breads, and sour cream muffins, plus a trademarked thing known as a "lumpy muffin"—big chunks of tart apple with walnuts and raisins all suspended in sweet cinnamon cake. Considerably more top than base, this muffin breaks easily into sections that are not quite dunkable (they'd fall apart), but are coffee's consummate companion.

Wolf Lodge Inn

12025 E. Frontage Rd. (Exit 22 off I-90)   208-664-6665
Coeur d'Alene, ID   D | $$

Naturalists know the Wolf Lodge District, just east of Coeur d'Alene, for a population of bald eagles that congregate at the Mineral Ridge trail and on Beauty Bay in the late autumn to feast on the spawning kokanee salmon. Year around, human carnivores are drawn to the Wolf Lodge Inn for meat and potatoes of legendary scale. A vast red barn-board roadhouse just yards from the highway, this exuberant Wild West domain features oilcloth-clad tables and walls festooned with trophy animal heads, bleached bovine skulls, antique tools, old beer posters, vintage snowshoes, silly backwoods homilies, and yellowing newspaper clippings of local-interest stories. It is a sprawling place with miscellaneous booths and dining nooks in several rooms; at the back of the rearmost dining area is a stone barbecue pit where tamarack and cherrywood burn a few feet below the grate. On this grate sizzle slabs of beef ranging from sixteen-ounce sirloins and filets mignon to porterhouses well over two pounds. (Seafood is also available, cooked over the wood.)

Cowboy-cuisine aficionados like to start supper with a plate of "swinging steak"—sliced and crisp-fried bull testicles, served with cocktail sauce and lemon wedges. We relished a bowl of truly homey vegetable beef soup that was thick as stew with hunks of carrot, potato, beef, green pepper, and onion. All dinners come with saucy "buckaroo" beans, a twist of krebel (fried bread), and baked or fried potatoes, the latter excellent steak fries, each of which is one-eighth of a long Idaho baker that has been sliced end-to-end and fried so that it develops a light, crisp skin and creamy insides. We split the forty-two-ounce "Rancher," which turned out to be a hefty porterhouse supplemented by an average-size sirloin ("to make up weight," the waitress explained). It was exquisite beef, loaded with juice, redolent of the burning wood over which it was cooked.

As we exited into the brisk autumn air, we noticed that whenever the Inn's front door swings open, a cowbell clangs.

Cole Drug

136 McLeod St.   406-932-5316

Big Timber, MT   L | $

The staff of Cole Drug are blasé about making milk shakes, malts, green rivers, and root beer floats; but when we walked in and asked for a Big Timber sundae, they were thrilled. A Big Timber is the biggest ice cream dish on the menu, the top of the line: nine scoops of ice cream (your choice of flavors), six sauces (butterscotch, chocolate, strawberry, caramel, pineapple, and marshmallow), whipped cream, and nuts.

"You don't *both* want one, do you?" asked Laurie, the mixologist behind the counter. When we told her we intended to split one, she breathed a sigh of relief, confessing that Cole Drug has only one bowl big enough to hold a Big Timber sundae. "I've never made one in my life!" she further confessed.

Two comrades who were having lunch in one of the four booths toward the back of the pharmacy overheard our conversation and came forward to join Laurie in the creation of a Big Timber. The three of them discussed, debated, and consulted with each other regarding nuances of soda fountain technique (Must the pineapple sauce go atop the chocolate ice cream? . . . Should caramel sauce cover strawberry? . . .) and eventually designed and constructed a monumental ice cream dessert. When it was finished, they set it before us on the counter with a spoon on either side of the bowl and stood there watching with pride as we plowed into it.

If a pig's trough of ice cream is not on your diet when you come to the charming town of Big Timber, Cole Drug's "lesser" specialties are excellent, too. Among them are a Crazy Mountain sundae, a Big Sky Sundae, huckleberry sundaes and milk shakes, and a Bitter Root float. That last one is root beer and chocolate syrup with vanilla ice cream: an inspired combination.

El Burrito Cafeteria

310 N. 29th   406-256-5234
Billings, MT   BLD | $

A one-room storefront with too many customers and not enough seats, El Burrito is a downtown dining adventure in Billings, and the best Mexican food for miles around. For newcomers, it is a rather bewildering place to dine. First, place your order at the back counter, then grab a tray and pile it with tortilla chips, salsa, and hot peppers. Now, scan the dining room and hope to find a seat. While dipping chips and gasping for air (the salsa is hot!) at the table, you need to keep an ear pricked toward the back counter because when your order is ready, one of the women in the kitchen will call out above the din of the dining room to tell you to come and get it. The confusing thing is that she calls it out not by your name or number, but by exactly what it is you ordered. So you need to remember whether you ordered a red-chile-smothered pork burrito or a bowl of green chili with beef.

The menu bills itself as California-Mexican, featuring burritos of all kinds: filled with pork or beef, or meatless with beans, potatoes, rice, and/or cheese, topped with red or green chili. The tacos are excellent: soft-shell or hard, filled with vigorously seasoned shredded beef or chicken. We also like El Burrito's simple bowl of spicy chili beans, and the tamale plate with rice and fresh red salsa. Although we don't necessarily *love* it, menudo is on the menu, too—that is tripe stew—available in one size only, which is *large*. If you like menudo, you really like it!

For breakfast, El Burrito serves eggs with shredded beef or chorizo sausage, huevos rancheros, and sweet fried pastry dough known as buñuelos that are great to munch with coffee.

A humble restaurant with low-low prices, El Burrito attracts Billings citizens from all walks of life, including well-dressed executives in suits and ties who could afford a much fancier meal. But you don't have to be a blue-collar person to appreciate this downtown gem that bills itself as "The Working Person's Eating Place."

The Grand Hotel

McLeod and 2nd Sts.   406-932-4459
Big Timber, MT   LD | $$

Our Crazy Mountain Suite in Big Timber's Grand Hotel was the nicest room in the hotel (with its own bath and telephone), but we still found it impossible to connect a notebook computer to the Internet, thus going cold turkey off e-mail. By Stern standards, this was roughing it! However, one thing we did not give up during our stay was good eating. Of all the joys of staying at this historic inn in its grand western landscape, delicious meals are at the top of the list.

Foremost, the lamb is extraordinary. It is indigenous, contracted from local ranchers; and the rack of spring lamb, herb-roasted and cut into rosy chops tableside, is glorious. Ordinarily, it is served with baby red potatoes; but if you are a true potato fan, you need to inquire about the provenance of the mashed potatoes the night of your dinner. If they're Montana spuds, get some.

"Whenever possible, I use potatoes from Manhattan, Montana," says Chef Amy Smith. "I believe they are much better than Idahos. They are firmer, they bake longer; and when you mash them, they have a fluffiness like no other." Local fans of Amy's cooking tell the story that when *The Horse Whisperer* was in production, the catering company hired to feed the cast and crew became ever more frustrated because each day when shooting was over, Robert Redford didn't stick around to eat dinner on the set; instead he came to town so he could have supper at the Grand Hotel, where he especially liked those mashed potatoes, served on the side of cedar-plank-grilled salmon, with peach pie for dessert.

During the growing season, other vegetables are bought from a produce lady north of town in Melville. She supplies tomatoes and string beans as well as pansies to be used as a kitchen garnish. Decorative pansies on a dinner plate are a culinary stretch in this meat-and-potatoes land, where newcomers to the Grand dining room have been known to mistake rosemary for a pine twig that has accidentally fallen on their food. "I tell them to smell it," Amy says, "and I suggest to the wife what a nice potpourri it will make in a dresser drawer or the kitchen counter."

Matt's Place

2339 Placer Rd.   406-782-8049
Butte, MT   LD | $

Opened in 1930, Matt's Place is Montana's oldest drive-in restaurant, featuring beautiful old murals of the mountains on the wall, a short curved counter, and an ancient, bright red, waist-high Coke machine—the kind in which the green glass bottles tinkle when you pry open the top to fetch one. The soda fountain behind the counter is fully equipped: six wands for blending milk shakes, dispensers for syrup, and three tall seltzer spouts; the menu features a root beer float, ice cream sodas, malted milks, and nut sundaes, plus "hot Silex coffee." To eat, there is the Montana classic, a pork chop sandwich, and all sorts of hamburgers, including a Wimpy special (two patties on one bun), a hamburger with an egg on top, and a nutburger with ground peanuts mixed into the meat.

No jukebox plays, there is no music at all; in fact the mood around supper time is as polite as a tearoom. In the back kitchen, hamburgers sizzle slowly on a grill, and at the counter a few stools away from us, a quartet of elderly Butte ladies, fresh from an afternoon at the beauty parlor with immaculately coiffed white hair in tidy waves and tightly sprung curls atop their noggins, converse in gentle tones as they each pack away a pork chop sandwich, loaded, with heaps of French fried potatoes on the side.

"Poor Grace, she just can't seem to get ahead," one reflects, gripping her heft sandwich by its wax-paper wrapper in one hand while drawing a French fry through a puddle of ketchup with the other.

The lady on the next stool blots her lips with a napkin and agrees. "Her washing machine can't be ten years old, and it's broken already."

A third customer, the oldest of the quartet, simply shakes her head and tsk-tsks in agreement, but is too focused on her meal to say anything just now. She carefully pours a second helping of her milk shake into a glass from its icy silver beaker. She uses two unsteady hands to do the job, then two to lift the full glass to her lips. It is a strawberry milk shake; she takes a hearty draft, unfazed by her age-weakened grip, sets the glass down, smiling with a little milk shake mustache. She and her three comrades and their loaded pork chop sandwiches and pink milk shakes in Butte, Montana, are a sweet counter scene we won't soon forget.

Red Lodge Café

| 16-18 S. Broadway | 406-446-1619 |
| Red Lodge, MT | BLD \| $ |

From its height at Beartooth Pass, the spectacularly beautiful Beartooth Highway coasts down to the old frontier settlement of Red Lodge. In the world of rodeo, Red Lodge is known as the home of the Greenough family—three generations of roughstock champions; it also is where legendary mountain man Jeremiah Johnson became the first village constable. For us Roadfooders, Red Lodge is also recognized as home of the Red Lodge Café, a three-meal-a-day eatery with a western theme (lighting fixtures made of wagon wheels) and fun for everyone. There are keno games, weekend karaoke, and the strangest-shaped pool table we've ever seen. The ceiling is stamped tin, and the walls are bedecked with painted wooden totem poles and murals of local scenery.

For breakfast, you'll want to eat jumbo omelets or blueberry buckwheat pancakes, for lunch country-fried steak and potatoes or buffalo burgers. On one merry occasion, the daily special was tuna noodle casserole, expertly made. For dessert, everybody has pie: apple or berry pie or, best of all, banana cream pie, which is a tender pillow of pale yellow custard that eats better with a spoon than a fork.

The Sport Restaurant

| 114 S. Main | 406-222-3533 |
| Livingston, MT | LD \| $$ |

Cruising through the breathtaking scenery of Big Sky country along a highway where 100 mph seems reasonable, it can still be a long way between meals. That is why we especially like the town of Livingston, where The Sport Restaurant offers a menu of hamburgers to suit every appetite.

The burgers are not particularly huge—about one-third pound—but they are broiled just right; and best of all, they are available in virtually any configuration you desire: topped with chili and/or cheese, with lettuce and mayonnaise, marinated in teriyaki sauce and topped with melted Swiss cheese and a broiled pineapple slice, with bacon, guacamole, mushrooms, jalapeño peppers, salsa, etc., etc. Each burger comes on a white or whole-wheat bun with a small pile of tortilla chips.

Beyond burgers, sandwiches range from broiled skinned chicken breast (available with all the same toppings as hamburgers) to pork chop, to French dip and a "sea burger" (fried cod).

The Sport also serves significant dinners, including steaks and ribs (beef or baby back), barbecued chicken, Mexican plates, and broiled seafood. (On weekends, dinner reservations are a good idea.) In our experience, dessert is spectacular—a giant hunk of peach or apple pie that looks like rugged shortcake.

The Sport goes back some ninety years, and its decor pretty much reflects most of the last century: a High Plains hodgepodge of mounted game trophies, antique shotguns hung in nooses from the ceiling, giant pairs of Levi's, and rusty farm implements, plus stacks of vintage magazines for customers to browse.

Stella's Kitchen and Bakery

110 N. 29th St.   406-248-3060
Billings, MT   BL | $

If you like cinnamon rolls, you need to know about Stella's, where one roll pretty much fills a normal-size plate and makes breakfast for two or more hungry people.

Everything is large at Stella's, especially pancakes. "You've got to see 'em to believe 'em," the menu boasts of the "monster cakes," created many years ago when Stella had a cook who simply could not pour a normal-size pancake. So rather than change cooks, she changed pancake descriptions and monster pancakes were born. Each one is a good twelve inches, edge to edge. You have your choice of buttermilk, apple-cinnamon, blueberry-wheat, or a combo. If you can polish off four of these cakes in a single sitting, you get just what you need after a five-thousand-calorie breakfast . . . a free cinnamon roll!

There are normal-size breakfasts at Stella's: omelets, hot cereals (oatmeal, seven-grain, and "Cream of the West," i.e., of wheat), and egg sandwiches; and the lunch menu includes such regular-size items as club and sub sandwiches, chili by the bowl, and a French dip, as well as hamburgers that range up to the half-pound Ziggyburger, served on an outsize bun to match.

For dessert? How about one of Stella's giant peanut butter chocolate chip cookies?

Bohemian Café

1406 S. 13th St.   402-342-9838
Omaha, NE   LD | $$

"Czech Us Out" says the marquee in front of the Bohemian Café, where Omahans have been coming to eat roast duck and drink pilsner beer since 1924. It is a corny place, no doubt about it; if you are eating your way through Omaha, this multiroom eating hall is an essential culinary experience. Its walls are decorated with colorful Old-Country wood-work and pictures of men and women in traditional peasant attire; tables are patrolled by veteran waitresses in bright red dirndl skirts; and perpetual polka music plays on the sound system (CDs are for sale at the bar). We are particularly fond of the upholstered booths in the front dining room—plush aqua accommodations reminiscent of bench seats in a 1956 Bel-Air.

Start with liver dumpling soup and a slice or two of sour rye from the bread basket. The big menu includes steaks and seafood, a quartet of specials every day of the week (the Bohemian Café is open every day, all day, from 11 A.M.), and a long list of Czech specialties. Foremost among the kitchen's accomplishments is roast duck—half a bird with crisp skin and flavorful meat that pulls off the bone with ease. We are particularly fond of the sauerbraten, which is a stack of pot-roast-tender hunks of beef in gravy with none of the cloying sweetness that characterizes icky sauerbraten. We also like Czech goulash, a vivid red, smoky pork stew. There is a large choice of side dishes, but the two for which the Bohemian Café is best known are dumplings and kraut. The former is a daunting pair of saucer-size slices of doughy matter covered with whatever gravy your main course demands; the latter is a fetching sweet-and-sour mix, thick as pudding, dotted with caraway seeds. These two sides will flank your entree and present a challenge to any appetite.

Paper place mats remind diners that this restaurant is home of the Bohemian Girl Jim Beam commemorative bourbon bottle (there is a huge collection of Jim Beam commemoratives in the entryway); and the mats also list the lyrics of the house song, which has been used in radio advertisements:

> *Dumplings and kraut today*
> *At Bohemian Café*
> *Draft beer that's sparkling, plenty of parking*
> *See you at lunch, okay?*

Crystal Café

4601 Dakota Ave.	402-494-5471
South Sioux City, NE	always open | $

Here is a round-the-clock truck stop serving haute highway cuisine: big food in abundance. Plate-wide buttermilk pancakes, chicken-fried steak with a patty of oily hash browns, sausage gravy on big, crumbly biscuits are some of the morning specials. The Texaco Deluxe is an omelet with ham, bacon, or sausage plus cheese, tomato, onions, and green peppers. The morning item we especially like is the caramel sweet roll, which is thick and goopy.

The lunch menu features breaded pork tenderloin, bowls of chili, and hamburgers that include ⅓-pounders and a ten-ounce king-of-the-road Texaco Burger. We never did get to try the sour cream raisin pie (not ready yet!), but the chocolate pie was grand. It was exciting to watch the waitress cut a piece, using a moistened warm knife to slide down through a full eight inches of whipped topping, then balance a taller-than-wide slice on a plate.

At the counter and in booths, each place is set with a clean over-turned coffee cup and a water glass. The waitress flips your cup right-side up and pours coffee and refills throughout breakfast; pour your own water from a pitcher on each table.

This is a great place to rub elbows with professional drivers. We picked up a rather unusual souvenir on our last visit: a booklet from the adjoining truckers' store entitled *Beef Spotter: A Guide to Midwest Feed Lots*. And we were tickled by the truck-stop humor evident at the penny bowl by the cash register. Above the stash of coins, a handwritten sign says: *Need a Penny . . . Take a Penny. Need 2 Pennies . . . GET A JOB!*

Johnny's Café

4702 S. 27th St.
Omaha, NE

402-731-4774
LD | $$

If you want steak in Omaha—and who does not?—the place to go is Johnny's, a family business at the edge of the old stockyards for more than three-quarters of a century. Once a café for cowboys and cow shippers, it is now a supersize dining room with upholstered chairs, broad-loom carpets, and modernistic chandeliers. We love the baronial ambience, especially because it is balanced by service that is as folksy as in any small-town café, courtesy of waitresses unafraid to scold you if you don't finish your T-bone but then want dessert.

Beef is king, but not just steaks and chops. True to their meat-market heritage, the Kawa family also offers ribs, liver, tongue, and oxtail. Ourselves, we stick to the basics, which are just fine, from the $20 filets and chateaubriands at supper time to a jim-dandy hamburger at lunch.

Dessert is corny and ingratiating, including crème de menthe sundaes and clear blocks of Chuckles-colored Jell-O. Turtle pie is a weighty af-fair—a solid block of vanilla ice cream, chocolate, nuts, and caramel. Johnny's serves the pie well frozen, so you will have all sorts of fun try-ing to fork off a piece. Once defrosted, it is as gooey and sweet as candy, but even richer.

Bob's

1312 W. 12th St.	605-336-7260
Sioux Falls, SD	BLD | $

Behold the Megabob Challenge: If you ingest a three-quarter-pound hamburger, three-quarters of a pound of French fries, and a cookie, plus drink a large bottle of soda pop faster than Jason Carpenter did on March 7, 2002 (it took him 5 minutes, 9.82 seconds), you get your supper free. If you don't beat the time, the megameal will cost you $7.25.

Eating contest notwithstanding, Bob's is a Roadfood joy. A tiny diner with a curvy counter and about a dozen seats, all with a view of the grill, it specializes in plentiful hash-house breakfasts, burger baskets, broasted chicken, and sides of ribs. What fun it is to sit at the counter in the morning and watch Bob work the grill—as he has done since 1951—all the while kibitzing with customers, buttering toast that pops from the toaster, and stacking pancakes hot off the griddle. Incongruously for a joint so steeped in blue-plate tradition, Bob's partner in the operation tallies up bills on a computer opposite the grill.

Fans of diner food will think they've entered heaven the moment they walk into this place, take a sniff, and see what's on other people's plates. Bob is a true grillmaster. Eggs are made exactly as you like them; bacon (extra thick) is cooked under a press so it gets crisp and flat; hash browns sizzle alongside, absorbing the flavors of the very well-seasoned grill.

Edgar's

107 E. Main St.   605-356-3336
Elk Point, SD   L | $

With its pink-and-white tin ceiling, quartet of creaky wood booths, and steel-rod chairs for a scattering of tables, Edgar's is an absolutely charming little place inside the Pioneer Drug store on the main street of Elk Point. Its nucleus is a soda fountain that was first installed in Schmiedt Drug in Centerville in 1906. In the 1960s, the old marble fountain was removed and put into storage. It was only recently discovered by Edgar Schmiedt's granddaughter, Barb Wurtz. Barb brought it to Elk Point where it is once again part of a pharmacy (run by Barb's pharmacist husband, Kevin) and general store.

It is mesmerizing to watch the experts at Edgar's make a soda. First, syrup and a little ice cream are smooshed together at the bottom of the deep vase-shaped glass to form a sweetshop roux; next, soda is squirted in and mixed vigorously; penultimately, a globe of ice cream is gingerly floated on top; finally, a crown of whipped cream is applied and, to that, a single cherry. It's a monument of soda fountain art.

The same high standards apply to tulip sundaes, malts, and shakes, and a long roster of more elaborate, daring delights that range from the relatively familiar turtle sundae (vanilla ice cream with hot caramel, chocolate syrup, and pecans) to the rocket, a vertical banana split that the menu promises "will send you for a blast!"

Tea Steak House

215 S. Main St.   605-368-9667
Tea, SD   LD | $$

Off the interstate in the tiny town of Tea, steak-lovers congregate at tables covered with seafoam-green oilcloth to slice into T-bones, sirloins, porterhouses, and filets mignon. The Tea Steak House, a low-slung, wood-paneled restaurant that shares a building with O'Toole's Bar, is one of the top beef dens of the Great Plains. Dress-up clothes are not required, but it is a weekend-splurge kind of place; on Friday night (when fried perch joins the meaty menu), the dining room is packed until midnight with couples, families, and star-crossed meat-eaters on big dates.

Service, by ladies in nylon uniform blouses, is instantaneous. Iceberg lettuce salad arrives in a little beige wood-grain plastic bowl along with a silver caddy with three dressings you ladle on at will. The steaks are available charbroiled over coals or grilled in a pan. Of the three types of potatoes, French fried and baked are nothing notable; but the hash browns, soft inside with a hard-crusted surface, are delicious. Every table is outfitted with ketchup and Heinz 57 Steak Sauce.

It is a Midlands meal of the highest order. And who can resist a restaurant with this motto, printed on its menu: "We're Glad You Brought Your Sugar to Tea."

Tripp Sports Bowl Café

210 S. Main St.   605-935-6281
Tripp, SD   BL | $

Ultimate comfort food: creamed chicken on toast. That was the special of the day when we found the Tripp Sports Bowl Café. This extremely gentle plate of food was preceded by vegetable beef soup (homemade, of course) and followed by a modest dessert of canned pear sections in syrup. From the everyday menu, we highly recommend the Dakota burger. It is not a hamburger at all, but a pile of chunky roast beef slices that are moist and flavorful, topped with a slice of cheese and served on a burger bun. Our waitress explained that hot beef is a frequent daily special at the café, served with mashed potatoes and gravy.

The menu has a few other items—fried chicken, hamburgers, sandwiches—and you can have ice cream for dessert. But variety is not why we'll return. We'd bet on the daily special every time. And the truth is that the joy of eating in this place goes beyond its honest, inexpensive food. It's a true small-town café and bowling alley. On the wall in a place of honor are posted the records held by Doug Janssen (a 300 game!) and Dorothy Schnabel (267).

Club El Toro

132 S. Main St.   307-332-4627
Hudson, WY   D | $$

Sixteen different cuts of beef are listed on El Toro's menu, including a ribeye as big as its plate. There are French fries or a foil-wrapped baked potato, but the one and only proper companion to such a steak (or any of El Toro's beef) is "cowboy fries," which are what some know as jo-jo potatoes: spiced potato logs accompanied by ranch dressing as a dip.

The house specialty is prime rib, which is available in four sizes. The top-of-the-line "Royal" cut is a mesa of meat rising high off the plate and weighing well over two pounds. Heavy with juice and so tender that a butter knife glides through with ease, it is a plush cut with enough flavor to win over even those of us who generally prefer the more assertive character of steak. It is accompanied by a cup of dark juice for dipping.

Every dinner starts with a relish tray and a salad, then hot appetizers—individual plates with two spicy ravioli in tomato sauce and a small portion of *sarma* on each. Sarma is an unusual treat, a staple of the Serbian kitchen—and of Hudson's two great steak houses (Svilar's being the other one). It is a thick, boiled-tender leaf of pickled cabbage rolled around a tightly packed filling of ground pork and beef with onions.

Club El Toro is a spacious restaurant brimful of character. One large room is set up with a U-shaped banquet table and flags for meetings of the Marine Corps League. Have a few drinks at the bar and co-owner Mike Vinich will tell you how he was wounded in the foot with the first wave of leathernecks to hit Iwo Jima; have a few more and he'll explain his special connection with John F. Kennedy, whose pictures and memorabilia decorate the walls. Adjacent to the bar is a room that is mostly dance floor, where Carl F. Baxter performs on keyboard weekend nights, occasionally joined by volunteer locals on sax or drums. Mr. Baxter's repertoire of 554 selections is mimeographed and bound in clear plastic so patrons can choose their favorites, ranging from "Misery and Gin" and "Heartaches by the Number" to "Coca-Cola Cowboy."

Café Wyoming

106 East Ramshorn	307-455-3828
Dubois, WY	LD | $$

"Very Wyoming" is how our California tipster described this log cabin adjoining a True Value hardware store parking lot overlooking Horse Creek. The note said that the chef made deluxe dinners every night for which reservations were advised. It sang of homemade soups and salad dressings, and a whole repertoire of house-smoked meats.

While the menu is broad, it's ribs that made a deep impression on us. They are beautiful racks heavy with smoke-infused meat and spiced and sauced with brio. A smoked pork chop was equally delicious, and the steaks that others around us were eating looked great. Sandwiches are served on homemade bread, and there are a BLT and a catfish sandwich in particular that are numbers one and two on our list to eat next time we visit.

The Noon Break

927 12th St.	307-587-9720
Cody, WY	BL | $

It's laid back and it's far enough off the beaten path for few tourists to find it; but the main reason to come to The Noon Break is green chili. There are two kinds available, regular and "Code 10," the latter a hot jalapeño soup made with little chunks of pork sausage, available in cup or bowl or as the topping of a tasty burrito in a bowl.

There are a few more excellent reasons to find this small café. One is the breakfast hour, when regulars sip endless amounts of coffee with platters of huevos rancheros, buckwheat pancakes, or biscuits and gravy. Another is the fact that many of the zesty Mexican dishes on the short menu are in fact heart-healthy: the red and green chiles, posole topped with yogurt rather than sour cream, burritos stuffed with beans or potatoes.

One last reason we like this kooky place, which is strewn with newspapers and magazines to read and decorated with old Wyoming license plates, is a lunchtime item listed as "Louie's Ethnic Plate." It's a Spam sandwich, grilled to order, with potato chips on the side.

The Wagon Box

Story, WY   307-683-2444
                                   D | $$

The Wagon Box attracts beef-eaters from miles around. Most of the menu is devoted to big cuts of cow, including filets mignon that come plain or peppered or with mango relish and a handsome "XIT Striploin," a boneless sirloin named for the XIT ranch of Texas, which sent its cattle up this way about a hundred years ago. The house specialty is juice-heavy prime rib that delivers maximum beefy savor. It is served with epicurean mashed potatoes (with a few lumps and flecks of skin) and a nice salad garnished with bright red, crisp tortilla strips. Accommodations include a civilized dining room with a big stone fireplace and a cool outdoor patio surrounded by fragrant Ponderosa pines.

Waldorf A'Story

19 N. Piney Rd.   307-683-2400
Story, WY   BLD | $

The Piney Creek General Store, on the Bozeman Trail between Sheridan and Buffalo, has the feel of a base camp for wilderness expeditions in the winter and is a party store in the summer. (The population of Story goes from 450 to 1,500 when the weather turns warm.) Built of pine logs and featuring some gorgeous outdoor accommodations in the form of benches and tables made of rough-hewn wood, this something-for-everyone outpost is just ten minutes from I-90. We are astounded by the stocks of gourmet groceries that crowd its limited-space shelves—hot sauces, interesting pasta, exotic chips, etc., not to mention cookware, automotive supplies, videotapes for rent, souvenirs, and stores of wine and beer that would do a serious urban liquor store proud. Take-out meals are available for picnics or cabin-cuisine; "bring yer own wheelbarrows," advises a store brochure.

As you enter the retail commotion, look to the left and you see Waldorf A'Story, a very small dining room with mismatched tables where locals come to greet the day with biscuits and gravy, fresh-baked coffee cake, or a superb breakfast sandwich of bacon, eggs, cheese, tomatoes, and onions on French bread crisped on the grill.

The lunch menu ranges from single- and double-deck sandwiches, soup, and chili to hot wings with blue cheese dressing and celery sticks. Daily specials include theme meals of Mexican huevos rancheros for Sunday morning, Chinese egg rolls with fried rice, and Native-American "Indian tacos" made on crisp fry bread. Soup and chili are always available; and every Friday is bisque day. Saturday the little eatery becomes a "Happy Moose Rib Shack" with a mix-'n'-match menu of baby backs, smoked brisket, sausage, and chicken accompanied by potato salad, slow-baked barbecued beans, and French pan toast.

Wapiti Lodge and Steak House

3189 Northfork Hwy.   307-587-6659
Wapiti, WY   D | $$

Eighteen miles west of Cody, Wyoming, is "downtown" Wapiti . . . which consists of the Wapiti Lodge and Steak House. The motto of this handsome rustic eatery suggests "You have been UPTOWN, By getting OUT OF TOWN, In DOWNTOWN Wapiti, Wyoming." We cannot tell you what that means, but we can tell you that this is a good place to dine, western-style. It is casual (wear jeans), but the food is quite deluxe. If you are in the vicinity of Cody hankering for a nice steak or, for that matter, a pound of steamed crab legs with melted butter, this is the place you want to know about.

The choice of beef is big, including various-size ribeyes, sirloins, and filets mignons as well as prime rib from twelve to twenty ounces, regular or blackened. Blackened food is a house specialty: blackened chicken breast and red snapper are also listed on the menu; and although we've tried neither, we can tell you that the blackened prime rib is delicious. Many people come to eat racks of baby back ribs, tender little lovelies presented under a glaze of good barbecue sauce.

Dinner includes a relish tray, soup, salad, bread, and potato, but there are some extra-cost appetizers worth knowing about. Rocky Mountain oysters (testicles) are quite tasty, served with cocktail sauce for dipping; and as munchables with cocktails, we like the kitchen's hot wings and jalapeño poppers. About the only thing conspicuously missing from the menu is the Wyoming favorite (but restaurant menu rarity), elk, the Native-American name for which is wapiti.

Yellowstone Drug

127 Main St.   307-876-2539
Shoshoni, WY   L | $

There aren't a lot of good reasons to detour into Shoshoni, Wyoming, but to the adventurer in search of Americana, Yellowstone Drug on the town's main street is a meaningful destination. Since it was built in 1909, it has boasted "the best malts and shakes in the state." Made with a triple-wand shake maker behind the long counter, they are amazing—served with a spoon because their thickness defies a straw. Although only three flavors of ice cream are available (vanilla, chocolate, strawberry), fifty-nine different flavors of malt or shake are available, from almond to wild cherry. The menu suggests that you can mix any of these two flavors, thus allowing a serious soda fountain hound to taste a different shake every Sunday from now until the middle of the century. Yellowstone makes more than fifty thousand shakes every year; and last time we checked, the single-day record (July Fourth, of course) was 624.

Great shakes are Yellowstone's pride, but there is also a nice short-order menu of burgers, hot dogs, and BLTs. The double bacon cheeseburger with French fries (and a huckleberry malt) is, in our opinion, a great lunch counter meal.

Beyond food, the place is spectacular. It is located in a former bank building, and the old vault now serves as a display room for World War II memorabilia. In addition, there is a huge collection of old patent medicines, as well as shelves of interesting merchandise and souvenirs. This is the place to shop if you need a gun rack made from horseshoes, a horsehair bridle made by an inmate at the state prison in Rawlins, or a bumper sticker that says "Christian Cowboys Have More Fun." We were delighted to buy several old black-and-white postcards that show the town decades ago, the cards captioned with a note boasting that Shoshoni was the home of the grandfather of former U.S. president Gerald Ford. So, not only is this a great milk shake stop; it's educational!

Southwest

Arizona * Colorado * Kansas * Nevada *

New Mexico * Oklahoma * Texas * Utah

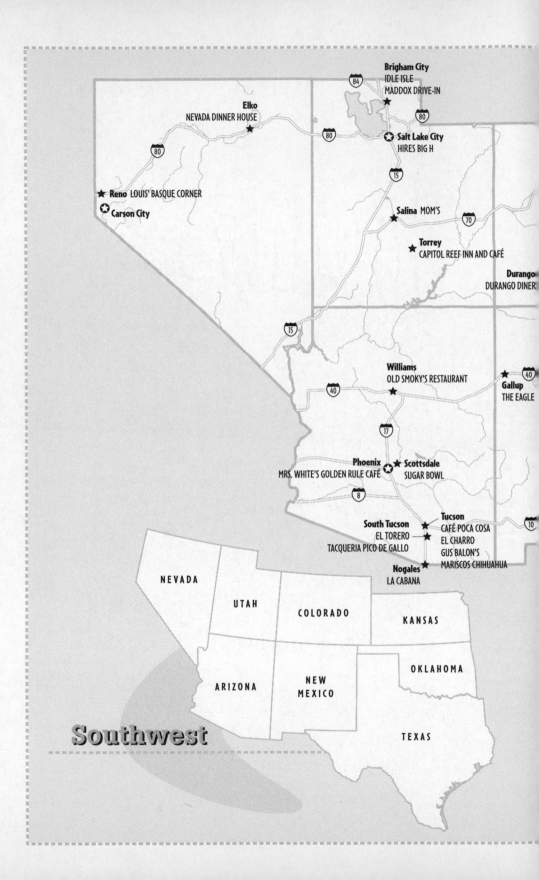

Brigham City
IDLE ISLE
MADDOX DRIVE-IN

Elko
NEVADA DINNER HOUSE

Salt Lake City
HIRES BIG H

Reno LOUIS' BASQUE CORNER

Carson City

Salina MOM'S

Torrey
CAPITOL REEF INN AND CAFÉ

Durango
DURANGO DINER

Williams
OLD SMOKY'S RESTAURANT

Gallup
THE EAGLE

Phoenix
MRS. WHITE'S GOLDEN RULE CAFÉ

Scottsdale
SUGAR BOWL

South Tucson
EL TORERO
TACQUERIA PICO DE GALLO

Tucson
CAFÉ POCA COSA
EL CHARRO
GUS BALON'S
MARISCOS CHIHUAHUA

Nogales
LA CABANA

NEVADA

UTAH

COLORADO

KANSAS

ARIZONA

NEW
MEXICO

OKLAHOMA

TEXAS

Southwest

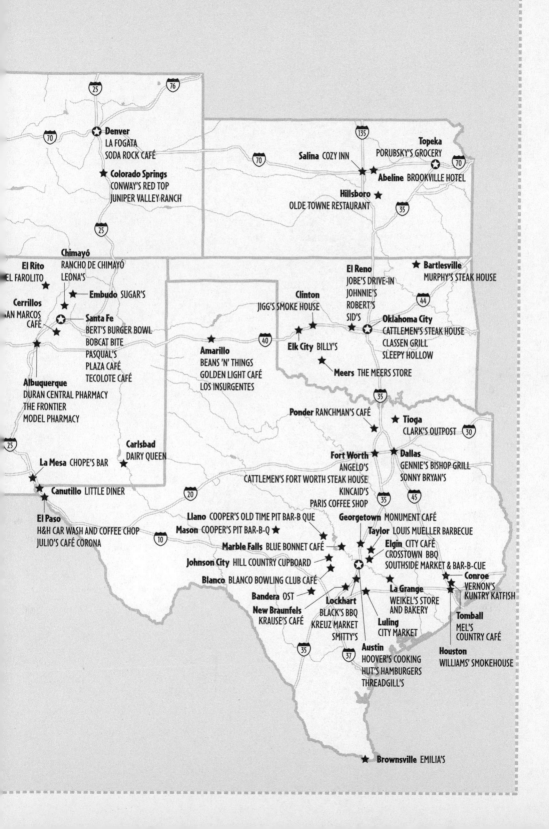

Denver
LA FOGATA
SODA ROCK CAFÉ

Colorado Springs
CONWAY'S RED TOP
JUNIPER VALLEY RANCH

Topeka PORUBSKY'S GROCERY

Salina COZY INN

Abeline BROOKVILLE HOTEL

Hillsboro
OLDE TOWNE RESTAURANT

Chimayó
RANCHO DE CHIMAYÓ
LEONA'S

El Rito
EL FAROLITO

Embudo SUGAR'S

Cerrillos
SAN MARCOS CAFÉ

Santa Fe
BERT'S BURGER BOWL
BOBCAT BITE
PASQUAL'S
PLAZA CAFÉ
TECOLOTE CAFÉ

Albuquerque
DURAN CENTRAL PHARMACY
THE FRONTIER
MODEL PHARMACY

El Reno
JOBE'S DRIVE-IN
JOHNNIE'S
ROBERT'S
SID'S

Bartlesville
MURPHY'S STEAK HOUSE

Clinton
JIGG'S SMOKE HOUSE

Oklahoma City
CATTLEMEN'S STEAK HOUSE
CLASSEN GRILL
SLEEPY HOLLOW

Amarillo
BEANS 'N' THINGS
GOLDEN LIGHT CAFÉ
LOS INSURGENTES

Elk City BILLY'S

Meers THE MEERS STORE

Carlsbad
DAIRY QUEEN

La Mesa CHOPE'S BAR

Canutillo LITTLE DINER

Ponder RANCHMAN'S CAFÉ

Tioga
CLARK'S OUTPOST

Fort Worth
ANGELO'S
CATTLEMEN'S FORT WORTH STEAK HOUSE
KINCAID'S
PARIS COFFEE SHOP

Dallas
GENNIE'S BISHOP GRILL
SONNY BRYAN'S

El Paso
H&H CAR WASH AND COFFEE CHOP
JULIO'S CAFÉ CORONA

Llano COOPER'S OLD TIME PIT BAR-B QUE

Mason COOPER'S PIT BAR-B-Q

Georgetown MONUMENT CAFÉ

Taylor LOUIS MUELLER BARBECUE

Marble Falls BLUE BONNET CAFÉ

Elgin CITY CAFÉ
CROSSTOWN BBQ
SOUTHSIDE MARKET & BAR-B-CUE

Johnson City HILL COUNTRY CUPBOARD

Conroe
VERNON'S
KUNTRY KATFISH

Blanco BLANCO BOWLING CLUB CAFÉ

La Grange
WEIKEL'S STORE
AND BAKERY

Bandera OST

Lockhart
BLACK'S BBQ
KREUZ MARKET
SMITTY'S

New Braunfels
KRAUSE'S CAFÉ

Luling
CITY MARKET

Tomball
MEL'S
COUNTRY CAFÉ

Austin
HOOVER'S COOKING
HUT'S HAMBURGERS
THREADGILL'S

Houston
WILLIAMS' SMOKEHOUSE

Brownsville EMILIA'S

Café Poca Cosa

88 E. Broadway

Tucson, AZ

520-622-6400

LD | $$

Chef/owner Susanna Davila has made Café Poca Cosa one of the great destination dining experiences in the Southwest. Since opening in the old café of the Clarion Hotel in downtown Tucson, she has developed a loyal following of locals as well as travelers who know her restaurant as a source of Mexican food like nowhere else. We cannot tell you exactly what to order when you eat here because the menu changes throughout the day to reflect what chiles, spices, vegetables, and ingredients are fresh in the kitchen, and what Susanna's whim dictates. When you are seated, you are shown a portable blackboard with about a dozen choices on it, virtually all of which need to be explained. Nothing on this menu is familiar; do not expect tacos, enchiladas, or burritos!

You might find a glorious chicken molé, or the variant of molé known as pollo pipian, for which boneless chicken is cosseted in sauce made from bitter chocolate, crushed red chiles, Spanish peanuts, pumpkin seeds, and cloves. You will definitely find a tamale pie—always on the menu as a vegetarian alternative. Even if you are a devoted meat-eater, you must have this tamale pie, for it is creamy comfort food supreme, tender as a soufflé, always dressed up a little differently, topped with vivid green chile puree or a sweet mango sauce.

Usually, there is shredded beef (*deshebrada*) infused with smoky chile flavor; there are seafood dishes and pork, too. Each entree is heaped upon a plate along with a bright, fresh salad, so that whatever your main course is, it mixes with the greens and makes a happy mess of things. On the side come small, warm corn tortillas, and for dessert, do not neglect the Mexican-flavored chocolate mousse (is that cinnamon we taste in it?) and the sultry square of flan, for which the soft custard is floated on a dish of deliriously sweet burnt-sugar syrup.

El Charro

311 North Court   520-622-5465

Tucson, AZ   LD | $$

El Charro opened in 1922 and created many of the dishes that are now taken for granted as classic Mexican-American fare. The tostada grande, first made here by founder Monica Flinn, is a broad cheese crisp known on local menus as a Mexican pizza. Most people get it with a veneer of creamy melted cheese on top; other options include green chiles, guacamole, air-dried beef, and refried beans. El Charro's round-the-world version is a majestic appetizer, served on a pedestal, garnished with fresh basil leaves.

El Charro's carne seca (dried beef) is cured high above the patio in back of the restaurant, where strips of thin-sliced tenderloin hang in an open metal cage. Suspended on ropes and pulleys, the cage sways in the breeze over the heads of customers, wafting a perfume of lemon and garlic marinade into the Arizona air. Sautéed after it is air-dried, carne seca is customarily served in concert with sweet onions, hot chiles, and tomatoes, making an explosion of flavor like no other food. El Charro has a full menu of tacos, enchiladas, and chiles rellenos, plus such rarer regional specialties as enchilada Sonorese (a patty of fried cornmeal garnished with chile) and chalupas (small cornmeal canoes filled with chile, meat, or chicken and whole beans). Beyond the indisputable goodness of these meals, the kitchen offers a full repertoire of nutritionally enlightened fare—lo-cal, lo-fat, good for you, and good-tasting!

El Charro is noisy and sociable, almost always packed with tourists, Tucsonans, health nuts, and burrito hounds who spoon up fiery salsa picante with corn chips and drink Tecate beer served in the can with a wedge of lime on top. Mariachi music sets the mood as the sturdy wood floors veritably rumble with the crowds and the air fills with the inviting aromas of hot tostadas grandes. Wall decor is a kaleidoscope of vintage south-of-the-border advertisements, straw sombreros and rawhide bull-whips, and years' worth of El Charro calendars, many of which feature melodramatic scenes of Mexican horsemen (known as charros), proud steeds, and pretty maidens all making flirty eyes at one another amid stormy landscapes. The calendars are a house trademark, and a good memento of the high spirits of an El Charro meal.

El Torero

231 E. 26th St.   520-622-9534
South Tucson, AZ   LD (closed Tuesday) | $$

South Tucson is surrounded by the City of Tucson, but legally and culturally they are separate. In this part of town, buildings are festooned with brilliant painted tiles, streets hum with low riders cruising in their chopped-roof custom *caruchas,* and at least a dozen different restaurants serve Mexican food that most of us gringos have never experienced.

One of the best is El Torero, a place that is all too easy to drive right past. Despite a sign on 4th Avenue, a set-back location off 26th Street makes it seem nearly hidden. If you do realize that it exists, chances are good that you will assume it isn't open for business. The front door of the pink-painted building, far at the back of the parking lot, is inconspicuous to say the least. From the outside, it looks like a tiny place, perhaps abandoned a while back.

Once you push that door open, you instantly realize you have entered a very inviting region of Mexican-food heaven. The jukebox will likely be belting out party tunes; the bar you walk past to get inside may be occupied by happy people knocking back longneck beers; and at the tables in the brightly lit dining room, where the walls are decorated with bullfighter paintings and one large stuffed swordfish, people are plowing into gorgeous plates of expertly prepared true-Mex food.

Start with a wafer-thin tortilla crisp of cheese and green chile strips, presented on a silver pedestal so all at the table can pull away slices. This crisp is among the thinnest and tastiest in a neighborhood full of excellent crisps. The main menu is a broad one, featuring all the familiar tacos, burritos, enchiladas, and chimichangas, plus a few items that are truly special. These include off-the-bone turkey topped with a spectacular spicy-rich dark molé sauce or, on occasion, the similar sauce known as *pipian*, which includes pumpkin seeds. Our Tucson friends, the Sparks, who directed us to this out-of-the-way gem, are hooked on the shrimp or flounder Vera Cruz, and they also insisted on ordering a topopo salad—an amazing sight. *Topopo* means volcano, and El Torero's topopos are so shaped: great conical mounds of lettuce and other vegetables packed with your choice of chicken, shrimp, chile, guacamole, or carne seca, and surrounded by columns of hard cheese.

Gus Balon's

6027 E. 22nd St.   520-748-9731
Tucson, AZ   BL (closed mid-July to mid-August) | $

Yes, Gus Balon's does serve lunch; Saturday's baked chicken and dressing is quite all right; the baked ham sandwich is okay, too; and there are a score of different homemade pies for dessert every day. But the primary reason Tucsonans come to this café once known as Gus's Catalina is breakfast. Since 1966, Gus Balon's has been the city's number one breakfast house.

If you like to see your eggs sunny-side up or over easy, this is the place. They arrive glistening with butter, accompanied by bacon, ham, sausage, ground steak, strip steak, or pork chops. The French toast, made from Gus's own bread, is light and eggy. We love the omelets, from the basic cheese-filled variety to the big Spanish omelet loaded with peppers, onions, tomatoes, and cheese. Best of all—and the one must-eat dish on the menu—is Gus's cinnamon roll. Huge, sweet, and gooey, it arrives warm and aromatic, sugar-glazed and begging for a little extra butter to melt into a torn-off piece.

Service is fast and familiar; coffee cups and water glasses are kept filled throughout the meal; and you can expect the waitress to address you as "Dear," "Hon," or, if she really likes you, "Sweetheart."

La Cabana

840 N. Grand Ave. #12   520-287-8208
Nogales, AZ   BLD | $

Our South Arizona friend Margaret Bond took us to La Cabana when we asked her and her husband, Paul (the estimable boot maker), where to go in Nogales to get a real local meal. Margaret walked into the inviting little cantina with us in tow and she was greeted warmly by the staff, who know her as a regular.

Hostess Lupita had a worried look on her face when we sat down around 10:30 in the morning, between breakfast and lunch. Lupita knows what Margaret likes to eat when she comes here, and she warned us, "The chiles rellenos are not ready yet. Can you wait ten minutes?" For rellenos like these, we are happy to wait longer than that. They are packed with deep green-chile flavor, oozing melted cheese, and enrobed in a luscious fried crust.

The meal started with made-to-order guacamole, a bowl of chunky mashed avocado mixed with little bits of cheese and tomato. Margaret advised that we might want to spruce it up with a dab of the hot salsa provided to every table, as well as a spritz of tiny Mexican limes. We also sampled steamy corn tamales, spicy enchiladas, a crisp-crusted taco, and a beef burrito filled with meat that was moist and pot-roast tender. Among the most memorable flavors on the table were the simple flour tortillas, served in a bread basket. They are suitable for mopping one's plate of sauce and refritos, but just by themselves, these are superb: warm, delicate, with an earthy wheat flavor so rich they taste pre-buttered.

La Cabana is an inconspicuous little adobe restaurant/bar in a cluster of shops on the main drag. It is outfitted with tables and a couple of comfortable booths. For serious eating, we recommend the booths, where you can lounge like royalty.

Mariscos Chihuahua

| 2902 E. 22nd St. | 520-326-1529 |
| Tucson, AZ | LD \| $$ |

There are two other Mariscos Chihuahuas in Tucson. The others are located at 1009 N. Grande Ave. and 3901 S. 6th Ave.

Mariscos Chihuahua is a big, bright place with sunlight streaming in picture windows all around, illuminating a tempestuous seascape mural that covers one wall. The staff are friendly, and the sound system belts out Mexican tunes that make every meal feel like a celebration. Seafood stars on this menu: oysters raw or cooked, fish grilled or fried, stews and soups. And oh, such shrimp! The menu lists a dozen different styles including cool cocktails and "drowned raw"—meaning ceviche-style, i.e., cooked by immersion in a lime marinade—to breaded and fried.

We stuck to the basics and got an order of cooked shrimp in garlic sauce and an order of shrimp *endiablados,* which means extremely hot. The shrimp are presented in a most appetizing way, strewn across a field of crisp French fries on a broad fish-shaped plate that also holds a mound of rice, a green salad, and a warm tortilla wrapped in foil. They are served with the hard tail still on, providing a nice handle for picking them up and nabbing one good mouthful. What's great about the presentation is that whatever the shrimp are sauced with—be it garlic butter, soy sauce, oyster sauce, or that devilish *endiablados*—seeps down and flavors the French fries that are their bedding. That means that as you approach the end of your shrimp, you then get to savor these good, crisp fries infused with whatever flavor it was that made the shrimp so delicious.

Beverages include excellent pre-sweetened (and lemon-flavored) ice tea as well as *horchata,* the locally favored sweetened rice milk. A large cooler in the center of the dining area holds bottles and cans of Dos Equis, Tecate, Corona, and Bud and Bud Light.

Mrs. White's Golden Rule Café

| 808 E. Jefferson St. | 620-262-9256 |
| Phoenix, AZ | L until 5 P.M. \| $ |

Looking for inexpensive home cooking in downtown Phoenix? This is the place. A destination lunch for citizens from all social strata, Mrs. White's usually gets mobbed shortly after opening at 11 A.M., but don't worry if you have to wait. Meals are served quickly and customers don't generally linger. The cuisine is southern-style soul food, including smothered pork chops and crunch-crusted fried chicken, always accompanied by hunks of corn bread. On the side come such vegetables as creamed corn, scalloped cabbage, stewed tomatoes, and salubrious, pork-flavored greens. For dessert, spoon into a bowl of warm fruit cobbler. We love the do-it-yourself decor of this ramshackle little eatery, where strangers instantly feel right at home.

Old Smoky's Restaurant

624 W. Bill Williams Ave. (old Route 66)   928-635-2091

Williams, AZ   BL | $

Before Interstate 40 replaced Route 66, Williams was known to travelers along great Mother Road as the "Gateway to the Grand Canyon." For vacationing families as well as highballing adventurers, it was an oasis on the road west, an opportunity to buy souvenirs, spend the night, establish a base camp, and eat a good meal. There are two restaurants in town that maintain the flavor of the old road. At Rod's Steak House, you eat a big meat-and-potatoes supper; and at Old Smoky's, you fuel up for the day on three-stacks of hotcakes starting at six o'clock every morning.

Old Smoky's, opened in 1946, appears to have changed little in the last half century. It is a cozy, wood-paneled diner where tourists and truckers rub elbows at the counter and exchange news over the backs of well-worn upholstered booths. Open only through the lunch hour, it has a midday menu of chile cheeseburgers and bowls of homemade chile topped with biscuits, but it's breakfast—served anytime—that pulls our car into the lot like a magnet.

Bread is featured on the front of the menu: white, wheat, rye, Cheddar-wheat, and Swiss rye, all of which are available by the half order, whole order, or two-and-a-half-pound loaf. In addition to these yeasty delectations, there is a long roster of sweet breads available: cinnamon raisin, banana nut, banana chocolate chip, pumpkin raisin, apple walnut, etc. Select your toast to accompany a scramble of chorizo sausage and eggs, a green-chile cheese omelet, or huevos rancheros on a corn tortilla. Of course there are pancakes—buttermilk or buckwheat—as well as a Billy Hatcher omelet made from the kitchen's exemplary red chile, cheese, and beans (named for the Chicago Cub who came from Williams).

Old Smoky's has an old-time highway atmosphere that makes us think of what it must have been like to drive through the Southwest before superhighways. We were strangers when we first stepped in the door several years ago, but were soon drawn into conversations among the staff and pancake-eaters about everything from the current price of cranberries to major detours on the road ahead. Before we knew it, we had put away about a dozen cups of coffee and the morning was mostly gone. It was just the sort of genial café experience that makes Route 66 through Arizona a necessary course for any Roadfood scholar.

Sugar Bowl

4005 N. Scottsdale Rd.   480-946-0051

Scottsdale, AZ   LD | $

No expanding urban metroplex has a restaurant scene more fluid than Phoenix, with great new places opening all the time, and some great new places closing almost as quickly. But since 1958, there has been at least one culinary institution that locals have learned to rely on: the Sugar Bowl in Scottsdale's Old Town. With its pink-upholstered booths and counter stools and a swift young staff who look so cheerful carrying raspberry glaciers (Sprite and sherbet), golden nuggets (Sprite, sherbet, and ice cream), and Turkish coffee sodas, it is the quintessential ice cream parlor. In particular, we recommend the Camelback sodas, made with either vanilla or coffee ice cream, and the "extra-luscious malts," which are infused with marshmallow and fudge or caramel sauce.

There are sandwiches, soups, and salads, too, which look quite fine; but in truth, when we walk into this happy place, we instantly become too obsessed with eating ice cream to consider anything else.

Taqueria Pico de Gallo

2618 S. 6th Ave.   520-623-8775

South Tucson, AZ   LD | $

Tucson is an especially food-savvy city. Many citizens maintain a high food-consciousness characterized by an abiding loyalty to one or another of the several excellent Mexican restaurants in town. Much as we like to eat around, we enjoy a fairly monogamous relationship with Taqueria Pico de Gallo. We would feel unfaithful (not to mention unfulfilled) if we came to South Tucson and did not put ourselves at a table crowded with Pico's ceviche tostada, plenty of tacos *de barbacoa,* a cool "cocktail" of marinated *pulpo* (octopus), a bowl of *albondingas de camaron* (shrimp meatball soup), and tall red plastic party cups filled with the city's best *horchata* (sweetened, cinnamon-flavored rice milk).

A tiny, tidy taqueria that has grown into several small rooms by enclosing its al fresco porches, it remains self-service, low-priced, and low-key. Study the day's menu posted on the wall, discuss things you don't understand with Adam Delgado, son of proprietors Ignacio and Antonia (he explained to us that the purple beverage in the vat next to the *horchata* is wild-berry lemonade, and that the day's special taco, *cahua-*

manta, was manta ray), place your order, and pay. When the food is ready, one of the staff will summon you to the counter to fetch your plates and carry them to a bare-topped table. Everything except for big bowls of soup comes on disposable dishware with plastic utensils.

Marshaled in a refrigerated case at the counter are plastic red party cups filled with the restaurant's namesake, pico de gallo. In this case, the nip of the rooster is a salty chili powder mix that is sprinkled on top of a gorgeous bouquet of giant chunks of watermelon, coconut, pineapple, mango, and even some jicama . . . the whole shebang stuck with four or five long wooden picks for fetching the pieces you want. The red-hot spice elicits the fruit's sweetness and packs its own lip-tingling punch. It is a heady culinary collusion like nothing else we've ever eaten.

Colorado

Conway's Red Top

1520 S. Nevada Ave.   719-633-2444
Colorado Springs, CO   LD | $

Also at 390 N. Circle (630-1566), 3589 N. Carefree Circle (596-6444), and 1228 E.
Filmore (329-1445)

Conway's motto, referring to its hamburger, is "One's a Meal." The colossi they dish up in these restaurants are genuine whoppers—half a foot across, served on broad-domed buns, accompanied by shoestring French fries and titanic pitchers of soda. Panavision-wide but not gourmet-thick, they are lunch counter patties with enough oily smack to imprint the bun with their savor. They are sold whole or half, topped with regular cheese (or, as the ingenuous menu advises, "a generous serving of Velveeta cheese") or zestier jalapeño cheese, or served as a "Hickory Dickery Top," infused with smoke flavor and smothered with chopped onions and barbecue sauce.

One definitely is a meal, especially if accompanied by good French fries and a large soda. But it would be a shame to visit the Red Top without a taste of the soups and stews that are still made from Grandma Esther's (Phyllis Conway's mom's) original recipes. The navy bean soup, for example, has a long-simmered flavor redolent of hickory-smoked ham and spice. With its accompanying sourdough roll, it is enough to be a filling lunch. Beef stew is another homespun delight—hours in the making, so all the juices of the beef and vegetables have a chance to mellow and blend and soften. It is so thick you only need a fork to eat a bowlful. We concur with the menu's description of it, which promises a stew that is "delicious, nutritious, and healthy."

The Red Tops have been a family operation since 1962, when Norb Conway bought the hamburger shop he worked in and he and his wife and ten children went to work. The Conways instilled an unshakeable pride in the business that is as much a part of this restaurant's charm as are the giant hamburgers. An honest menu, homemade food, and genuine hospitality make a Red Top meal delightfully oldfangled.

Durango Diner

957 Main Ave. 970-247-9889

Durango, CO BLD | $

It was pancakes that made us fall in love with the Durango Diner—plate-wide pancakes, preferably with blueberries, glistening with butter and running rivers of syrup. We branched out to other breakfasts, and liked them plenty, especially the "half and half" plate of biscuits with gravy and green chile, and the big warm cinnamon roll. Breakfast is a particularly good meal to eat in this Main Avenue hash house; you will share it with some locals who claim to have been having coffee an' at these seats for more than thirty-five years.

Then we discovered hamburgers. If you are a connoisseur of hamburger excellence, put Durango on your treasure map, for here they make one really wonderful variation known as the Bonus Cheeseburger Deluxe: one-half pound of meat under a mantle of melted Swiss cheese and a heap of diced green chiles, French fries on the side. We love the Durango Diner's bacon double cheeseburgers almost as much as we love the chiliburgers (available red or green), and although some customers combine all these toppings on one mound of meat, we must confess that bacon and chili together atop a cheeseburger are just too much for our delicate palates.

Juniper Valley Ranch

Highway 115 S
Colorado Springs, CO

719-576-0741
D Wed–Sun, April–December
| $$ (reservations advised)

A one-story adobe house on the old road to Canyon City, open only part of the year, only for dinner, and only if you have a reservation in advance (generally three to four days in advance), Juniper Valley Ranch serves some of the nicest food in the West. It is a family-style retreat with antiques around the fireplace and a menu that lists the same two entrees every day—an opportunity to sit down with a serene square meal and a glass of ice tea.

Start with curried consommé or spiced apple cider. Then skillet-fried chicken or baked ham in an oval casserole. These satisfying entrees are accompanied by hot biscuits and good apple butter, cole slaw, okra and tomato stew, and delightfully fluffy riced potatoes. Help yourself to seconds, thirds, as much as you like, then top things off with the homemade dessert of the day: bread pudding, fruit cobbler, or cake. It is a simple meal, the same year after year, served on faded calico tablecloths and seasoned with the rare and irresistible ingredient of tradition's charm.

La Fogata

5670 E. Evans Ave.
Denver, CO

303-753-9458
BLD | $

There is another La Fogata at 2797 S. Parker Rd.

Although La Fogata means "the bonfire," the green chile stew served in this bilingual hole-in-the-wall isn't really all that hot. But, oh, it is delicious: zesty, glowing with sunny chile flavor, and packed with the punch of cumin. If you are looking for excellent Mexican food in Denver, served with speed and sass by a staff who all seem to be related to one another, Evans Avenue is the place to be.

Many items on La Fogata's menu are Tex-Mex staples—enchiladas, chiles rellenos, tamales—expertly made and served in abundance; but this is also an opportunity to be adventurous. If you are blasé about beef in your taco, you can order tacos filled with crisp-roasted pork (wonderful!), or with beef tongue (spicy!); or you can spoon into a bowl of menudo, the Mexican tripe-and-hominy stew that is alleged to have magical powers to cure a hangover. For those who are not hungover, La Fogata's breakfast menu features burritos and huevos rancheros, as well as a repertoire of omelets.

A fun place to dine, where the crowd is equal measures of downtown business executives, blue-collar beer drinkers, and foodies who appreciate this rare taste of high-quality but utterly unpretentious Mexican food served in a pink-walled café with giant sombreros and serapes as decor.

Soda Rock Café

2217 E. Mississippi Ave.   303-777-0414
Denver, CO   BLD | $

Located on a quiet street where people live, Soda Rock Café is an old-fashioned neighborhood soda fountain that has been buffed, cleaned, and polished to gleam like it was 1950 again. In fact, the soda fountain itself dates back much further than that, to the early years of the twentieth century; and it still has all the proper equipment to squirt out bubbly fruit ades the likes of which are simply not available bottled.

The menu includes good hot dogs and hamburgers and sandwiches of all kinds, but the main reason to visit is ice cream. More than a dozen flavors, made here, are available at any one time—alone in a bowl or as the basis of a soda, sundae, or float.

It isn't necessary to polish off a cheeseburger or a hot fudge sundae to enjoy this lovely piece of vintage Americana. Soda Rock Café also has a nice menu of coffee drinks for leisurely sipping; and last we heard, Friday acoustic guitar sessions were planned for the late-night crowd.

Brookville Hotel

Lafayette St.   785-263-2244

Abilene, KS   D Tues-Sun; L Sat-Sun only | $$

Originally known as The Cowtown Café, the Brookville Hotel started earning its reputation more than a century ago, when cowboys were driving cattle up from Texas to the railheads in Kansas. At the time, Brookville was expected to become a major metropolis as a roundhouse town. As it happened, the train lines bypassed Brookville, and its fortunes waned, but the hotel never closed; and over the years, its tables became the town's primary attraction. A tradition of chicken dinners began in 1915, and as soldiers from the nearby Smoky Hill Air Base came to eat, its fame began to spread across the country. By mid-century, the Brookville Hotel was a destination eatery, especially on weekends, for Kansans from as far away as Kansas City.

Alas, the old Brookville Hotel closed at the end of 1999; but the good news is that a new version opened in Abilene. It's not a rickety old way station anymore, although its design is reminiscent of the old one, and the lonesome charms of the old town of Brookville are lacking, but the Brookville Hotel menu is still a bonanza for seriously big eaters in search of Sunday supper six days a week. The ritual meal includes sweet-and-sour cole slaw made from an old Pennsylvania Dutch recipe, plenty of relishes, corn, creamy cottage cheese, mashed potatoes and chicken gravy, baking powder biscuits, and half a chicken that has been skillet-fried until its surface has a crunch. Dessert is ice cream, and a wine list is available.

Reservations are suggested, especially on weekends.

Cozy Inn

108 N. 7th St.   785-825-9407

Salina, KS   LD | $

Back when the McDonald Brothers opened their first hamburger stand in California after World War II, the Cozy Inn had already been around a quarter century. This is one of America's original hamburger stands; and although its management has changed over the years, and it was threatened with extinction (saved by a consortium of local hamburger patriots!), it serves burgers that are pretty much the same as they were in 1922.

The first great thing about Cozy burgers is their aroma. When you walk into the Cozy Inn, the smell of grilling onions and beef with a hint of dill pickle tickles your senses like some exotic hash-house perfume. Sit at the Cozy counter on one of the six stools for a twenty-minute lunch of maybe half a dozen little sliders and a bag of potato chips, and that smell will saturate your clothes and stay with you the rest of the day. Freeze a bag of Cozies, then heat them in the microwave oven six months later, and their perfume will billow out when you open the oven door.

The other exceptional thing about them is their taste. These are no Salisbury steaks or even quarter-pounders. They are thin-as-a-nickel patties in little buns that somehow form a perfect combination with pickle, mustard, and ketchup. It is a combination so consecrated that according to Cozy Inn folklore, some years ago when a Cozy cook tried to put a piece of cheese on his own, personal burger, he was fired on the spot.

The best way to eat a Cozy burger is straight from the grill (which holds fifty-five at one time), at the counter in Salina, any time between nine-thirty in the morning and eleven at night, Monday through Saturday, and eleven to eleven on Sundays. (It has been reported that the management will ship Cozy burgers packed in dry ice to desperate people elsewhere in the country, but it is not a house policy.) As always, the price is right: Cozy burgers, which started selling for a nickel apiece when the Inn opened in 1922, now go for sixty-nine cents, or six (a nice-size meal for one) for $4.16.

Olde Towne Restaurant

126 N. Main St. 620-947-5446

Hillsboro, KS LD | $$

In a big old limestone building on Main Street in downtown Hillsboro, Olde Towne Restaurant really is Olde! Located in what was built in 1887 as the town's bank (with a vault in the basement), it served for many years as an egg factory where women candled, sorted, and crated eggs. Lower-story decor includes vintage egg crates made of wood as well as antique farm implements and a mural of old Hillsboro showing the great yellow bank building.

Olde Town is the one nice restaurant in Hillsboro, and so it has a menu with something for everyone, from sandwiches, soups, and hamburgers every day at lunch to an all-you-can-eat Mexican smorgasbord on Friday nights. But the main reason to drive out of your way, other than for a taste of prairie history, is to eat German food. Hillsboro is the heart of America's Mennonite community, and home to many of today's three thousand citizens descended from Germans who came to the USA (some via Russia). One of those who upholds the culinary heritage is Linden Thiessen, proprietor of Olde Town Restaurant, a man who makes a point of serving such melting-pot dishes as *verenika* (cottage cheese dumplings), zwiebach bread, beet borscht, and New Year's cookies, as well as locally made German whole-hog sausage and slow-smoked beef brisket reminiscent of Texas Hill Country cuisine (where the original settlers brought some of the same likings).

Dessert measures up to grandmotherly standards and includes an array of cream pies, bumbleberry pie, hot fruit cobbler, and elegant cream puffs. If you are the type who worries that there is never enough to eat, come to Olde Towne on Saturday night between five and eight-thirty P.M. That's German buffet night, featuring help-yourself servings of just about all the kitchen's Old World specialties.

Porubsky's Grocery

508 N.E. Sardou   785-234-5788

Topeka, KS   L Mon-Thurs | $

For half a century, customers have been coming to the dining room at the side of Porubsky's Grocery store to eat cold-cut sandwiches and chili (the latter during chili season only—October to March). Curiously, no coffee is served for the simple reason that this is an eat-it-and-beat-it type of establishment where few midday customers have long lunch hours to while away sipping coffee. Regulars include a large blue-collar crowd as well as Kansas politicians and other public figures whose autographed pictures, inscribed with praises of the place and the family that has run it since 1950, line the walls.

The sandwiches are well apportioned and low-priced, but it's the extras that make lunch well worth a detour off Highway 70. The most famous of the extras are Porubsky's pickles. These big, firm discs, which start as dills but are then infused with horseradish, mustard, and hot peppers, are guaranteed to snap your taste buds to attention. They are a favorite complement, along with crumbled saltine crackers, atop a bowl of Porubsky's chili.

Note: Chili is served only Monday through Thursday. The Porubsky family likes to keep the store aisles clear on Friday and Saturday for neighborhood residents who still come to shop for their groceries.

Louis' Basque Corner

301 E. 4th St.   775-323-7203

Reno, NV   LD | $$

We ate at Louis' Basque Corner on our first trip across the USA in the early 1970s. At the time, Louis' was only about five years old—Mr. and Mrs. Louis Erreguible, who had only recently come to Reno from southern France, were ebullient hosts in their New World dining room. After supper, we walked out utterly inspired, thinking that *someone* really ought to be writing about marvelous local restaurants in unlikely places across the country. We've been writing about such restaurants ever since, and Louis' Basque Corner continues to serve what Mrs. Erreguible described long ago as "simple food cooked to perfection."

By average American-meal standards, the food at Louis' is far from simple. What you eat at the long, family-style tables are copious feasts that start with soup, salad, bread, and beans, then move on to a plate of beef tongue, paella, oxtails, lamb stew, or Basque chicken. That's the *first course*! After that comes the serious eating: an entree of sirloin steak, pork loin or pork chops, lamb chops, or a fish of the day. Dessert is inconsequential, but do consider a glass of Picon punch, the bittersweet Basque *digestif*.

Louis' is a colorful place with waitresses outfitted in native attire and walls decorated with travel posters of the Pyrenees as well as pottery from Ciboure. Its clientele is a mix of travelers passing through for whom a meal here is a special treat, as well as plenty of locals who make Louis' a regular part of their regime.

Nevada Dinner House

351 Silver St.   775-738-8485
Elko, NV   D | $$

The emblem of the Nevada Dinner House is a shepherd drinking wine from a *bota* bag. It is not necessary to drink wine to enjoy a meal in this family-style eatery on Silver Street in Elko's old downtown, but it is the sort of meal that makes you want to shout, celebrate, and dance.

A casual tavern/dining room decorated with paintings of life in the Pyrenees, the Dinner House is also a spacious bar, where it is a joy to linger before or after dinner over Picon punch, the high-octane Basque very adult beverage made of brandy, Picon liqueur, and a twist of lemon. At capacious tables in the dining area a speedy waitstaff serves meals that are fundamentally western, but with Basque seasonings. Simply put, that means nearly everything but the liquor and after-dinner ice cream is shot through with garlic. The ritual big feed starts with powerhouse salads—no exotic greens or any such wussy ingredients; just good ol' iceberg lettuce—glistening with lemony vinaigrette. After that come such "first course" casseroles as paella or oxtail stew, then pork chops, lamb, sirloin steaks, shrimp, halibut, or falling-off-the-bone garlic chicken accompanied by mouthwatering mashed potatoes (are they garlicked, too?).

After supper, Elko is a great place to stroll; its attractions include a casino reminiscent of Las Vegas in the pre-Disneyfication era, where farmers, cowboys, and visitors come to whoop it up at the gaming tables.

Bert's Burger Bowl

235 N. Guadalupe St.   505-982-0215

Santa Fe, NM   LD | $

Bert's says it invented the green-chile cheeseburger, and while we cannot confirm or deny the claim, we can tell you that the one made here is a doozy. Flat patties of beef are sizzled on a grate over charcoal, from which flames lick up and flavor not only the meat, but also the bright orange cheese laid upon it. Dollops of fiery minced green chile are mounded atop the cheese from a bucket near the fire, and unless you say otherwise, your burger will come dressed with mustard, pickle, lettuce, onion, and tomato. Experienced customers, who dine under umbrellas on a sun-drenched patio overlooking Guadalupe Street, gradually peel back the wax paper in which the sandwich is wrapped as they eat, thus avoiding too much spillage.

Other popular burger configurations include barbecue and mayo/relish, and if the normal one quarter-pounder seems insufficient, a half-pound hamburger is available. Anyone who eats four half-pound burgers in thirty minutes gets them free. The menu also lists taco carnitas, *flautas de pollo,* chili dogs, and Fritos pie.

Bert's is a quick-order joint, but the food doesn't come right away. You tell them what you want, they take your money and give you a number. Then you hang around listening to hamburgers sizzle. Every one is cooked to order. A sign on the cash register advises: "All our food at Bert's is specially made for you and the approximate wait is 12 minutes once order is placed."

Bobcat Bite

420 Old Las Vegas Hwy.   505-983-5319
Santa Fe, NM   LD | $$

Bobcat Bite at first appears to be dilapidated, an impression reinforced when you pull into the rock-and-pothole parking lot around the low-slung 1950s-vintage adobe café. And yet, when you enter the little shoe box dining room and admire the polished wood on the five tables and the tidy nine-seat counter built on log-cabin lumber, you see that it is as natty as a highway hash house from a postwar Hollywood film noir.

The menu is simplicity itself—steaks, chops, sandwiches, chili in the winter, and a superb green-chile cheeseburger year-round. Like everything else about this singular place, the presentation of the chile cheeseburger is impeccable and precise, and a little eccentric. In a plastic basket lined with yellow wax paper, the burger arrives displayed on a bun bottom that rests on a bed of potato chips. On top of the meat, instead of the usual chile-on-cheese configuration, cheese is melted over the chile, the two elements melding into one. Hidden beneath the bun top, which also rests atop the potato chips, are tomato slices and lettuce. It is barely possible to put everything together and eat it with two big fists. The meat is extraordinarily tasty—high-quality beef, a full inch thick—complemented but not overwhelmed by chile that is tangy more than hot.

Chope's Bar

16145 S. State 28   505-233-3420
La Mesa, NM   LD | $

Chope's is two places to eat: a bar and a house, about fifty yards apart. Both have their charms, but we like the house better, because if you sit at the right table, the one nearest the Coke machine, you look into the back-room kitchen while you eat. You can watch the staff carry skillets full of lard to the stove for deep-frying sopaipillas, see them count out the warm flour tortillas that are allotted to every table, and gasp at the beauty of the huge tray of big roasted green chiles carried in from another room, ready to be battered.

The chiles are the basis for Chope's chiles rellenos. They are quick-fried and served three to an order, or singly alongside any of the combination plates. They are some of the finest you will find here in the heart of chile country: bright-flavored but not overwhelmingly hot, glowing with the sunny taste of the native pods, encased in a crisp coat with a few flecks of melted cheese on top. Also terrific, and milder than the rellenos, are red enchiladas. Green enchiladas are available, too, and they are hotter; but the man who took us to Chope's insisted we get red. Since this man was Dr. Paul Bosland, America's foremost chile breeder, we took his advice. We were not sorry. They sang with chile flavor, and had only enough heat to set our taste buds glowing pleasantly. We recommend a stack, with a fried egg on the top.

Meaty, gritty tamales are available by threes or as part of combination number one, which also includes an enchilada, a soft (and tasty) taco, rice, and beans. The menu is typical for this part of the country, featuring bowls of chile with or without beans or con queso (with cheese), as well as airweight sopaipillas for dessert. Nothing we have sampled is less than exemplary.

A word of warning: Although Chope's is in the middle of nowhere in a one-horse town, it gets crowded at lunch with chowhounds from Las Cruces, local chile planters carrying their cellular telephones, and hot food pilgrims from throughout the state. By 11:45 in the morning, customers are lined up outside waiting for the dining room to open. The turnover is fast, but it is likely you will have to put your name on the waiting list if you arrive much after noon.

Dairy Queen
902 South Canal   505-885-8739
Carlsbad, NM   LD | $

In our business, we often judge restaurants by their looks. And if they look like some sort of national franchise, we tend to drive on. Dairy Queen of Carlsbad is a big exception to that rule. Yes, you can get all the predictable ice cream things served at every other Dairy Queen. But the hot-food menu at Danny Gaulden's place is extraordinary. For nearly a quarter century, this inconspicuous DQ has dished out conspicuously excellent barbecue.

Ribs, beef, sausage, and ham are slow-cooked in a big pit that gives the restaurant an appetizing scent unlike that of any other Dairy Queen we've encountered. The beef brisket is especially flavorful, available as a pile of tender, spice-rimmed slices or as a chopped mélange that makes a super sandwich. On platters, alongside the fine smoked meats you have a choice from among sweet/tangy beans, brilliant garlic-flavored cole slaw, and chunky potato salad. Barbecue and side dishes come as dinners or by the pound and pint for take-out big feeds.

For those resistant to the allure of great barbecue, the menu also lists tacos, nachos, burritos, and hamburgers that are a cut above fast-food fare. The one must-eat item other than barbecue is the unique New Mexico treat, a green-chile cheeseburger.

Duran Central Pharmacy

1815 Central NW   505-247-4141
Albuquerque, NM   L | $

One of our favorite views in the scenery-rich Southwest is from a stool at the lunch counter in Duran Central Pharmacy. To the right is the kitchen, where you can view one of the staff using a dowel to roll out rounds of dough into broad flour tortillas that are perfect tan circles. Straight ahead is the grill where they are cooked. To see them puff up from the heat and blister golden-brown, then to smell the warm bready aroma, is to know for certain that good food is on its way.

These superlative tortillas, available plain or glistening with butter, come on the side of most lunches, including the wondrous Thursday-only carne adovada. They are used to wrap hamburgers and as the base of quesadillas. We like them best as a dunk for Duran's exemplary red or green chile, which is available either plain (nothing but chiles and spice) or loaded with your choice of ground beef, beans, potatoes, or chicken. The green is hugely flavorful, hot and satisfying with an earthy character; the red is pure, essence of plant life, liquefied with a full measure of sunshine.

Duran, by the way, is a full-service pharmacy.

The Eagle

220 W. 66   505-722-3220
Gallup, NM   BL | $

Outside The Eagle café in Gallup, car and truck traffic rumbles past. When the train rolls through town, its horn toots and the signal gates clang. Sitting on a chrome-banded, red-upholstered stool at the counter in this deep storefront diner, we find the outside noise is good background to an old-fashioned, way-out-west meal.

With its pea-green walls, high ceiling, and decor consisting of cut-out images of a taco, a chicken basket, a hot dog, a hamburger, and French fries, The Eagle is a humble place favored by locals and visitors who come to buy or sell at the venerable Richardson's Trading Post next door. The menu is Southwest-café cuisine, including hamburgers, Navajo tacos, and enchiladas. And lamb. Lamb is part of the culinary heritage of this region, primarily thanks to Navajo shepherds who have raised it for centuries; but it isn't all that common on café menus. That is why we felt compelled to order a bowl of Eagle café lamb stew one afternoon for a snack.

"It'll be kinda huge," the waitress warns. Huge it is, and unforgettable. A stark dish with hominy and spuds on the side, it is little more than a bowl full of seasoned meat, much of it still on the bone, soft and tender and rich as cream. The bones necessarily make it finger food, so there is no way to eat this meal fast. To work through it at the ancient porcelain counter with the big neon "Welcome" sign on the back wall and the beveled mirrors that look like something from an Edward Hopper painting, is to have a dining experience that could happen only on Route 66.

El Farolito

1212 Main St.   505-581-9509
El Rito, NM   LD | $

We were tipped off to El Farolito by Michelle Sullivan, who called it "an adobe-covered house trailer *way* out in the middle of *nowhere* with fabulous green chile." Her description led us northwest of Espanola across the River Chama and into the Carson National Forest, where grazing cows and stately rock monuments vastly outnumber humans and houses.

In fact, El Farolito is not a house trailer, but it is the shape of a double-wide: seven picnic tables up front, kitchen in back. It was opened twenty years ago by Carmen and Dennis Trujillo, and its name comes from the little lantern that hangs like a beacon on the front porch—the only light in town after dark.

In the fall, the modest diner smells of roasting chiles; year around, it serves eye-opening red and green chile that are odes to the luminous flavor of the state vegetable. Green is an opulent stew of tender pork, tomato bits, and ribbons of hot, *hot* chile. Red is opaque and meatless—pureed pods and spice. It is more of a sauce for dipping tortillas or cloaking a burrito, but you can get a bowl of red with ground beef and/or beans added to it.

"You've had the Fritos pie at Woolworth's on the Plaza?" asks Dominic Trujillo, son of Carmen and Dennis. "Ours blows it away!" As popular in northern New Mexico as enchiladas, the Fritos pie is said to have been invented at Woolworth's some fifty years ago, and the traditional way of serving it is in the bag of Fritos so you can stroll around town and fork it up while you walk. El Farolito serves its version in a bowl, and it is ravishing: a massive layer of beefy red chile garnished with shredded cheese, lettuce, and tomato completely blankets a foundation of salty corn chips. Beyond the persuasive combination of flavors, the magic here is the textures of the dish. The Fritos soften but retain a fragile ghostly crunch.

As we left El Farolito, Dominic asked us to sign the guest book. We browsed through comments left by previous guests—"great meal" . . . "*Wowee—hot* chile!!!!" . . . "Where am I?" . . . and added our consensus to a page where one happy customer had written, "This is the way it should be. *Life is good!*"

The Frontier

2400 Central SE   505-266-0550
Albuquerque, NM   Always open | $

The Frontier is gigantic. It occupies a full block, and its several dining rooms are decorated with a vast collection of western-theme art that includes one mural-size portrait of John Wayne, antique rifles, steer horns, and romantic paintings of soaring eagles, bold stallions, and Pueblo pottery. Signs on the front door warn "No Study Groups or Meetings, Sat

& Sun 9–1." Across from the University of New Mexico, this mess hall is a favorite of students, as well as travelers and just about everyone else who values cheap food, served fast, round-the-clock.

Lunch and supper are great examples of quick-eats, New Mexico–style. There is green-chile stew by the bowlful, there are big broad enchiladas that can be had with beef or vegetarian-style with meatless green chile, cheese, and onions; there are chalupas and tacos and blue-plate hamburgers. We are particularly fond of the Frontier burger special, a big goopy sandwich made with hickory-flavored sauce, cheese, and Thousand Island dressing, served with French fries on the side.

For breakfast, we love the morning burrito, which is a soft flour tortilla tightly hugging scrambled eggs, melted cheese, hot green chiles, and some of the tastiest hash brown potatoes for miles around. Even if you don't like sweet rolls, you have to order one at The Frontier just to say you have seen one. Frontier sweet rolls are an Albuquerque legend, served fast and eaten hot. They are not exactly refined or delicate, but they are satisfying the way only several thousand calories of hot dough and sweet sugar glaze can be.

One thing that makes dining at The Frontier fun is its breakneck pace. Because meals are ordered fast, cooked fast, and served instantaneously, you are guaranteed that things that are supposed to be hot are piping hot; we've gotten hamburgers still sizzling from the grill. Although many students come to linger over coffee and homework, it is possible to be in and out, with a good meal under your belt, in five minutes. The system is serve-yourself. While you wait in line, study the overhead menu and make your decision. When the green light flashes, indicating someone is ready to take your order, step up to the counter and say what you want. Approximately two minutes later, you are carrying your meal to an open table.

Leona's

Behind the Santuario   505-351-4569
Chimayó, NM   LD (closed Tues and Weds) | $

The village of Chimayó is off a winding road in the foothills of the Sangre de Christos, but it isn't obscure. Generations of weavers have made its cloth a western legend; and its early-nineteenth-century Santuario is a destination for religious pilgrims who believe that dirt from the earthen floor has miraculous healing powers. For four decades, hungry travelers have come to Chimayo to eat Leona's tortillas.

Leona Medina-Tiede knows wheat. When she was growing up, her mother grew it and harvested it with a sickle. "We rubbed it on a screen to get off the thistles," she remembers. "We'd hurt our hands bad doing that. Then we'd pick it up and the wind blew the thistles away." She and her mother took the wheat to the Chimayo mill where, Leona recalls, "They wouldn't grind it too well, so you'd get little crispy nuggets of unground wheat in your flour. It was *so* good!" Leona's mother rolled out fresh tortillas three times a day for Leona and ten siblings.

The first time we drove through New Mexico in the mid-1970s, Leona had a roadside stand on Highway 76 where she sold tortillas and chiles. At harvest time in the fall, you could pull over and get a sandwich of just-roasted chiles wrapped in a fresh tortilla—one of the great roadside snacks of all time. She now makes and sells flavored tortillas (apple cinnamon for breakfast; onion, garlic, piñon or pesto) and she runs a little restaurant, shaded by an ancient catalpa tree just below the Santuario. Here she serves tamales that radiate corn flavor, red- and green-chile stew, posole, and the traditional hangover cure of posole and tripe known as menudo.

Leona's serves exceptional burritos stuffed with fiery *carne adovada* (chile-marinated pork), rice and beans, or *chicharrones* (rendered pork fat like nuggets of bacon only piggier). The one that knocks our socks off is the chile relleno burrito. Rellenos, which are cheese-stuffed, breaded-and-fried chiles, are popular throughout New Mexico, but too often the chile and its crust turn to mush. Leona's has crust with crunch; the chile pod it sheaths is al dente and full-flavored, with enough mellow melted cheese inside to balance the heat. Wrap it in one of her tortillas and you have what Leona calls a "handheld burrito," easy to pick up and eat with no utensils. This is a valued quality to pilgrims for whom Leona's sanctuary is a blessed part of the walk through Chimayo.

Model Pharmacy

Lomas at Carlisle   505-255-8686
Albuquerque, NM   L | $

You enter this neighborhood drugstore near the pharmacist's counter, navigate along perfumes, soaps, and sundries, then find the little lunch area: a few tables scattered about and a short marble counter with a Pueblo-deco knee guard of colorful enamel tiles. If you are like us, your attention will be drawn to the right of the counter, where the cobblers are displayed under a spotlight. Three or four are made every day—geological strata of flaky crust atop syrupy tender hunks of apricot, peach, blackberry, or a mix thereof—and they are available simply warm or warm with a globe of ice cream melting on top.

The soda fountain is impressive: a fully stocked armory of milk shake mixers, syrup dispensers, and soda nozzles, plus a modern espresso machine (so you can get an espresso milk shake—mmm). As for lunchtime entrees, locals love the walnut chicken salad, and some come to eat hamburgers and cold-cut sandwiches; but we'll choose green-chile stew every time. It is more a soup, actually, chock-full of carrots, tomatoes, and bits of green chile with good flavor and alarming heat.

Pasqual's

121 Don Gaspar Ave.	505-983-9340
Santa Fe, NM	BLD | $

Pasqual's is a modest corner café with terrific food. At any mealtime in this crowded, split-level dining room, you are lucky to find a seat at a small table or at the large shared one, where a local yokel or a stranger from just about any part of the world might break bread with you.

For breakfast, we love the pancakes, the blue-and-yellow cornmeal mush, big sweet rolls, and giant bowls of five-grain cereal with double-thick cinnamon toast on the side, accompanied by immense bowls—not cups—of latte. For lunch, we can never resist the expertly made soups. Little things mean so much: fresh bread for sandwiches, flavorful roasted chiles on quesadillas; even the coffee is a tasty surprise.

After a few meals at Pasqual's, it is easy to feel affection for its unpretentious, sometimes clamorous ambience; this is a restaurant with character that perfectly complements the good stuff from the kitchen.

Plaza Café

54 Lincoln Ave.	505-982-1664
Santa Fe, NM	BLD | $

Opened in 1918, the Plaza is the oldest restaurant in Santa Fe. Its interior is a blast from the past, especially attractive to those of us who appreciate traditional diner ambience . . . but the tidiest version thereof. At the back of the room is a neon-edged map of New Mexico; the floor is lovely tiny-tile checks; and tables are chrome-banded, luncheonette-style.

The Plaza seems not to be impressed by itself as a piece of history or an example of classic counter culture. It is an easygoing kind of café, one of the last vestiges of the Santa Fe Plaza as a town gathering place. The menu is an appetizing combination of Americana (burgers, chicken-fried steak, hot turkey sandwich), Greek diner standards (lamb meat loaf, souvlaki, Greek salad), and real New-Mex specialties including chiles rellenos, posole with pork, menudo, and pure red chile or green chile stew. Every day starting at 11 A.M., the Plaza kitchen turns out what may be the city's most delicious sopaipillas. Fresh and hot and cloud-soft, these golden pillows of quick-fried bread are served with a squeeze bottle of honey to sweeten them, and they are simply wonderful to eat plain or on the side of red or green chile. The Plaza's green chile is a viscous stew with chunky vegetables; red is thicker and hotter.

More than any other downtown restaurant, the Plaza feels like a real part of day-to-day Santa Feans' lives. Locals eat here, but so do travelers in search of a good square meal. Below the clock on the wall is a movable-letter board on which are spelled out "Important Phone Numbers." These include the mayor, the governor, the representatives in Congress, the president of the United States, and the police chief.

Rancho de Chimayó

Route 520
Chimayó, NM

505-351-4444
LD | $$

North of Santa Fe, through the foothills of the Sangre de Cristo Mountains, the road leads towards the ancient village of Chimayó. It is a beautiful journey, past apple stands and adobe homes draped with bright red chile *ristras* (ropes of pods) hung out to dry. Built a century ago by the Jaramillo family, whose ancestors arrived in the 1600s, Rancho de Chimayó is a spacious home of wide wood planks and low-beamed ceilings, hammered-tin chandeliers, and a capacious fireplace. It became a restaurant in 1965, and since then it has gained fame not only for its charm and ambience, but for a kitchen that exalts the cuisine of New Mexico.

Native New Mexicans seldom sit down for a "bowl of chile." In fact, chile as a meal isn't listed on the Rancho de Chimayó menu. But there are few dishes this kitchen makes in which the chile doesn't play a vital role. New Mexican cooks use their native pod in stews and omelets, on top of steaks, stuffed into sopaipillas, and as a marinade for the fire-breathing native specialty known as *carne adovada*—pork infused with a pepper bite. If you are coming to Rancho de Chimayó only once, and if you like hot food, carne adovada is the dish to order. The pork glistens red, and has turned tender from its long marinade in a sauce made from hot red chile pods. On the side of this fiery pork the kitchen provides a mound of posole (hominy corn)—mild little lumps of tenderness to soothe the tongue.

For those who want something a little less incendiary, Rancho de Chimayó's menu also offers sopaipillas rellenas, in which the triangular fried breads are stuffed with beef, beans, tomatoes, and Spanish rice, and topped with red or green chile sauce. There are flautas, too—rolled corn tortillas filled with chicken or pork and fried crisp, topped with cool sour cream.

To drink, you want frozen margaritas or Chimayó cocktails, the latter made from tequila and Chimayó apple juice.

On a warm evening, the place to enjoy this great American feast is outdoors at a candlelit table. Strolling guitarists strum southwestern tunes, and the air smells of sagebrush and native cooking.

San Marcos Café

Highway 14	505-471-9298
Cerrillos, NM	BL | $$

When we came across the San Marcos Café along the Turquoise Trail to Cerrillos, a heretofore unrecognized rule of finding good Roadfood dawned on us: Look for restaurants with live poultry strutting around. Blue Heaven in Key West (page 237) was the first such place on the good-eats honor roll. Now we can add the San Marcos Café, where peacocks and peahens, wild turkeys, and roosters all cavort around the front and back of the restaurant. They are not allowed in the dining area, but about fifteen years ago there was one very famous leghorn rooster named Buddy, who served long tenure as unofficial maître d' of the restaurant. Dressed in black tie, Buddy cheerfully greeted guests at the door and crowed through the breakfast hour.

Wandering chickens notwithstanding, San Marcos Café is a real find. A cozy, charming ranch house decorated in country-kitchen style (old enameled stoves, wooden cupboards, knickknacks galore), it serves one of the best cinnamon rolls we've ever devoured. It's an unusual roll in that it's taller than it is wide, and, rather than being dense and doughy like so many others, it is crisp and lightweight, almost croissantlike in character. A beautiful thing!

Other breakfasts are dandy, too. We sampled eggs San Marcos, which is a large serving of fluffy scrambled eggs wrapped inside a tortilla and sided by beans, chile, and guacamole under a mantle of melted cheese. We also had a half-order of biscuits and gravy, the gravy hugely sausage-flavored and yet not the least bit unctuous. Some of the other breakfast choices include a pork chop with eggs, *machaca* (beef and eggs with pico de gallo), and smoked chicken sausage.

(San Marcos Café is a destination breakfast spot, especially on weekends. If you plan on coming Saturday or Sunday morning, we suggest calling ahead to make sure there's room.)

Sugar's

1799 Highway 68, Mile Marker 18   505-852-0604
Embudo, NM   L | $

Sugar is a beauty. She is the proprietors' bulldog, whom you can usually see in the yard to the left of the tin trailer where you place your order at a window then wait while they cook it inside. Her picture also adorns the wall-mounted menu, which is a roadside roster of burgers and green-chile cheeseburgers, corn dogs, burritos, and of course, Fritos pie.

We never tried any of those things because we were too busy eating Sugar's excellent barbecue. It's brisket, slow-cooked until pot-roast tender, ridiculously juicy, and infused with the flavor of smoke. Basically there are two ways to have it: in a sandwich, veiled in a tangy red sauce, or wrapped in a tortilla with green chiles and cheese. We prefer the latter because, in our opinion, that sweet-tangy sauce on the sandwich distracts from the lovely, subtle taste of the brisket. On the other hand, the barbecue burrito is pure virtuosity: thick shreds of beef accented by the snap of peppers and even further enriched by melted cheese. We could eat these burritos all day long. But alas, where we live, they are nothing but a memory. Such a fine cheap-eats meal is an only-in-New-Mexico experience.

During the summer, Sugar's also offers barbecued ribs and sausage. The winter smokehouse menu is strictly brisket.

Tecolote Café

1203 Cerrillos Rd.   505-988-1362

Santa Fe, NM   BL | $$

When Bill and Alice Jennison opened Tecolote in 1980, they did so with a sense of mission. Their goal, stated on the back of the menu, was "to serve a wholesome, tasty meal, at a reasonable price, in a comfortable and cheerful environment." On occasion they have opened up for evening meals, but the Jennisons' specialty, and the distinction of Tecolote, is breakfast. Lines of morning customers waiting to get in are testimony to their fulfillment of the mission.

Personally, we like Tecolote's atole (corn flour) piñon hotcakes best of all. Made with blue cornmeal and studded with roasted piñon nuts, they actually resemble wide, low-rise cakes more than ordinary flattened-out flapjacks. Pale blue inside with a faintly crusty exterior from the grill, each cake is ethereally fluffy, and gosh, what joy it is to bite into a little lode of those roasty-rich nuts! There are blueberry hotcakes, too, made with a similar, from-scratch batter, and plain ones—each available singly, as a short stack (two), or a full stack (three).

Of course there are omelets galore and eggs of every kind, including shirred on a bed of chicken livers; as the crown of corned beef hash; "rancheros" style—fried and served on a corn tortilla smothered in red or green chile and topped (at your request) with cheese. One nontraditional meal we hold dear at Tecolote is a gallimaufry called "sheepherder's breakfast"—new potatoes boiled with jalapeño peppers and onion, cooked on a grill until crusty brown, then topped with two kinds of chile and melted Cheddar cheese.

Tecolote, by the way, is an Aztec word that means owl, chosen by the Jennisons because Bill had been fascinated by a nearly deserted village by that name in northern New Mexico. "We like to think of him as our 'wise friend,'" says the Tecolote menu, "and hope that you will think of those of us at Tecolote Café that way."

Oklahoma

Billy's

210 N. Madison   580-225-3355

Elk City, OK   LD | $

Billy's is a burger joint. In Oklahoma, that means a lot, for this state has some of the highest hamburger-consciousness in the nation. Nowhere else is there such an abundance of excellent and unusual fried meat patties, ranging from simple rounds of charbroiled beef to the sloppy Caesarburgers of Oklahoma City. In El Reno and points west, you'll find an especially good variation, the onion-fried burger. For this aromatic Wimpy, a fistful of thin-sliced onion is mashed into the raw beef as soon as it is slapped on the grill so that the two elements—meat and onion—become virtually one. At Billy's they make a King-Deluxe version, served on a five-inch bun decorated with pickles, cheese, lettuce, and tomato.

Proprietor Billy Wilson learned his culinary skills at the venerable Sid's in El Reno, so he's a pro, knowing just how to squish the elements of the onion-fried burger together so they meld while the patty of meat retains its juicy character. The other dish Mr. Wilson learned to prepare in El Reno is the local-style "Coney," a modest-size hot dog topped with fine-textured beanless chili and a spill of zingy greenish-yellow slaw that crowns the whole package with a sweet note.

On the side of these quick eats, you can have rugged-cut French fries and chocolate milk shakes, and all the counter-palaver you desire. Mr. Wilson is always on duty, and he cannot resist joshing. When we wanted to write down his hours of operation, he informed us that he opens every morning at 11:02 and closes every evening at 7:35. His boast, posted on the wall sign outside, is that Billy's is "The largest in the world of its size."

Cattlemen's Steak House

1309 S. Agnew   405-236-0416
Oklahoma City, OK   BLD | $$

A steak at Cattlemen's is magnificent just to see, alone on its white crockery plate, higher in the center than around the rim, surrounded by a puddle of its own translucent juices seeping from within.

"If y'all would cut into your steaks," the waitress says when she sets the plates on the unclothed dinner table, "we'll see if they're done just the way you like them." To carve the steaks, Cattlemen's provides each customer a wood-handled knife with a serrated blade. The blade eases through the meat crust and down into its warm red center—medium-rare, as requested. You don't really need the sharp edge—a butter knife would do the job—but it sure is mouthwatering to feel the keen steel glide through beef that, although tender, has real substance. In contrast, a filet mignon, however sumptuous, seems wan. This is beef with corn-fed character.

On the side come French fries and big-topped yeast rolls, both of which are great to push through the meat's juices. Who cares that baked potatoes are accompanied by bright yellow globes of mediocre margarine instead of butter? So what if the dinner salad is little more than iceberg lettuce with thick white dressing? When one is in the company of this steak's greatness, secondary culinary issues dwindle to nothingness.

In addition to cuts of seared beef, Cattlemen's is a good place to eat such local favorites as Rocky Mountain oysters (fried testicles, served with cocktail sauce for dipping) and chicken-fried steak. Arriving in a spill of white cream gravy, the chicken-fry is an inherently lowly cut of beef, pounded tender but still fibrous. Its charm, for those who relish it, is the way its plebeian personality endures, and yet somehow the eating experience is transcendent. The only problem with Cattlemen's version is that no mashed potatoes are available . . . a grievous omission.

Finally, be aware of breakfast at Cattlemen's—a special time to come to this place in the old stockyards. Starting at six in the morning, the counter is home to genuine cowboys and the truck drivers who are cowboys' spiritual heirs, and it is an opportunity to start the day right, western-style, from a menu that features breakfast steaks and platters of brains and eggs.

Classen Grill

5124 Classen Blvd.	405-842-0428
Oklahoma City, OK	BLD | $

For a quarter century now, Classen Grill has been our favorite place to eat breakfast in Oklahoma City. We love early morning plates of taquitas (tortilla-wrapped packets of eggs, cheese, and vegetables) or chinook eggs (salmon patties topped with poached eggs) accompanied by a block of cheese grits. When we arrive with insatiable appetites, we go for "biscuits debris"—two big ones split open and mounded with gravy chockablock with ham and sausage chunks, cloaked with melted Cheddar cheese. On the side of breakfast, you have some serious potatoes—either home fries or the specialty known as Classen potatoes, which are mashed, seasoned with garlic and rolled into little balls, then deep-fried until brittle gold on the outside. The result is a kind of prairie knish.

Lunch is great, too, ranging from spicy barbecue pork sandwiches to grilled fish and sophisticated pasta. Our personal favorite midday meal at Classen is the tuna steak sandwich, garnished with a bit of avocado and jalapeño-peach relish.

Jiggs Smoke House

Route 2 Box 42 (exit 62 off I-40)	580-323-5641
Clinton, OK	L | $

Jiggs's beef jerky is tough as shoe leather. Ordinarily, that would not be an encomium we'd use for food we love, and if you are dentally challenged, Jiggs's jerky must be cut into matchstick-size pieces that won't hurt weak teeth. But if your jaw is strong and your tongue salivates for that mystic combination of beef and smoke, there are few eating experiences more emphatically satisfying than tearing off a plug from a foot-square sheet of Jiggs's dried meat and worrying it like a happy dog with a hunk of rawhide.

Although proprietor George Klaassen can send jerky by mail, he doesn't really like doing that, so we recommend a trip through Oklahoma along old Route 66 and a visit to Jiggs in person. The place looks the way an Okie smokehouse should: a weather-beaten wood shack with creaky wood steps and a front porch where you can sit in the shade and chew your meat. Inside, two construction spools are used as tables opposite the butcher counter; and there are a few kitchenette tables in an adjoining cubicle where the paneled walls boast odes to meat-eaters' heroes John Wayne, Bob Wills, and Marty Robbins.

Unlike the formidable jerky Mr. Klaassen makes, his short menu is a list of sandwiches that are easy on the jaw muscles. We are particularly fond of super-tender "pigsickles"—patties of smoked boneless pork rib bathed in spicy sweet sauce—as well as barbecue sandwiches that are nuggets of fall-apart smoked beef brisket on a five-inch bun. Mr. Klaassen smokes hams, bacon, and summer sausage for local customers, but cannot produce enough to ship them. "I semi-retired a while ago," he told us. "But there's too many people who won't let me quit. Once they get a taste for smokehouse jerky, they need it all the time."

Jobe's Drive-In

1220 Sunset Dr.   405-262-0194
El Reno, OK   LD | $

A weathered drive-in where each car slip has an Ordermatic menu and an intercom to communicate with the Touchmatic terminal at the kitchen window, Jobe's is a thriving remnant of yesterday's car culture. An American flag flaps out front along the highway that used to be America's favorite trail west, Route 66.

Although you can come to Jobe's for a fine Fritos pie (always a good idea, wherever it appears on a menu) or a chicken-fried steak sandwich (not necessarily a good idea!), the main things you need to know about are hot dogs and hamburgers. The menu in this bustling roadside enterprise is a veritable encyclopedia of hot dog and hamburger culture.

In the category of Hot Dogs (subtitled "Large All Meat"), listings include, and we quote, "Mustard Only ... Catsup Only ... Chili ... Chili & Onions ... Chili & Slaw ... Corn Dog." We recommend the chili and slaw variation; Jobe's slaw is sweet, pickly, and perfect harmony for chili. As for hamburgers, you can choose from among "Charburger . . . Big Burger . . . Triple Decker w/cheese . . . Double Meated Big Cheeseburger . . . Chiliburger w/Cheese," etc., etc. Please note that "onion burger" is *not* listed on Jobe's menu. Charburgers are automatically cooked the El Reno way, with smooshed-in onions, unless you specifically tell the kitchen to hold the onions. Available extras include bacon, cheese, and the deluxe treatment (lettuce and tomato).

It is possible to have a Coke or Dr Pepper brought out on the tray that attaches to the car window, but in a place like this and with hamburgers as good as these, who can resist a chocolate malt, a float, or a freeze?

As much fun as it is to dine in one's car, it is well worth stepping into Jobe's for a meal. Decor is fun Southwest memorabilia, including souvenir Indian arrows, road signs, and advertisements from the days when Ordermatic service was the latest thing in fast-food technology.

Johnnie's

301 S. Rock Island	405-262-4721
El Reno, OK	BLD | $

Johnnie's is one of a handful of restaurants in El Reno that are renowned for hamburgers. A 560-square-foot diner opened by W. J. "Johnnie" Siler in 1946, it looks like a bland town café from the street. The inside has wallpaper with a Route 66 theme, but the real clue to its greatness lies in the air: the smell of onions on the grill.

Onion-fried burgers are Johnnie's pride. Grill man Otis Bruce makes one by slapping a sphere of beef onto a hot griddle. He grabs a fistful of thinly sliced yellow onions—about the same cubage as the beef—and gingerly places them on top of the round of meat. He uses a spatula to flatten the onions and the meat together, creating a broad circular patty with an uneven edge; he presses down three or four times, slightly changing the angle of attack with each press, and pressing only one-half to two-thirds of the patty each time. The ribbons of onion are mashed deep into the top of the soft raw meat, which assumes a craggy surface because of the uneven, overlapping use of the spatula. Once the underside is cooked, the burger is flipped. The air around the grill clouds with the steam of sizzling onions. After another few minutes, the hamburger is scooped off the grill with all the darkened caramelized onions that have become part of it and it is put on a bun, onion side up. Lettuce, tomato, mustard, and pickles are all optional if you like them, but no condiment is necessary to enhance this simple, savory creation.

Beyond four-star onion-fried burgers, Johnnie's is a good place to eat El Reno's own version of a Coney Island hot dog, topped with meaty chili and a strange, soupy slaw that local epicures hold dear. (Some customers get this slaw on their burger, too.)

We also like breakfast at Johnnie's, when the little place is packed with locals eating Arkansas sandwiches (that's a pair of pancakes layered with a pair of eggs) and three-dollar all-you-can-eat platters of biscuits and gravy. It was at breakfast one day that we decided we had to stick around El Reno for a mid-morning pie-break, for as we were finishing our coffee, in walked Everett Adams, Johnnie's baker, wedging his way through the thirty-seat restaurant toting a battered tray above his head on which were set the coconut meringue pies and Boston cream pies he had made that morning for the lunch crowd.

The Meers Store

Highway 115	580-429-8051
Meers, OK	BLD | $

Tulsa World magazine once declared the hamburger at The Meers Store the best burger in Oklahoma, which is a bold pronouncement indeed. Border to border, Oklahoma is crazy for all kinds of interesting and unusual burgers, including the unique giants—seven full inches across!—known as Meersburgers.

A Meersburger is special not only for its size but because it is made exclusively from longhorn cattle that are locally raised. Longhorns are less fatty than usual beef stock and supposedly have less cholesterol than chicken, and yet the meat has a high-flavored succulence for which no excuses need be made. In addition to Meersburgers The Meers Store has a menu of steak, chicken-fried steak, prime rib, and barbecue, plus a salad bar; and, being the only place in town, it also serves breakfast: biscuits or pancakes with sausage, cured ham, or thick-sliced smoked bacon.

Meers itself is a sight. In the southwest corner of the state, it is a ghost town that sprung up in the wake of a gold strike in the 1890s but is now populated by exactly six citizens—the Maranto family, who run The Meers Store. The Store is the only open business, located in what was once a mining-camp emporium. Its walls are blanketed with antiques, memorabilia, pictures of famous and not-so-famous customers, and business cards left behind by happy Meersburger and Meerscheeseburger eaters.

Murphy's Steak House

1625 W. Frank Phillips Blvd.   918-336-4789
Bartlesville, OK   LD | $$

There are many ways a savvy passerby can identify an unknown eatery that's worth a try: a cluster of pickup trucks gathered in the parking lot before dawn, the aroma of hickory smoke wafting from the smokestack of a barbecue pit, or a huge animal on the roof. We've been eating at big-animal-on-the-roof places for so long that we can't quite remember exactly when this strategy for finding good meals crystallized; but at some point early in our career, we came to believe that a looming bull above a steak house, a 3-D rooster on a fried chicken joint, or a jolly plaster pig atop a barbecue was a near guarantee that there were good meals inside.

Murphy's Steak House does not have a lifelike cow on top of it, but its sign is shaped like one—a not-so-subtle hint that beef is king in this restaurant where the locals come to eat. The steaks are fine, but in fact, it isn't meat alone that puts Murphy's on our good-eats map. It is the kitchen's way with beef *and* potatoes. In particular, we refer to the meal known as a "hot hamburger." This is a mountain of food that adds up to a plate of perfection, Oklahoma-style. Pieces of toasted white bread are topped with French fries, a patty of beef that's been hacked into bite-size pieces, dark gravy, and—if you're smart enough to request them—sautéed onions. We love the way the crisp logs of fried potato soften in places where the gravy blankets them, imbibing a beef flavor for which the squiggles of onion are an ideal accent.

In fact, it is possible to ignore the hamburger part of the equation. Longtime customers who come to Murphy's for T-bones rather than chopped-up burger know to order a side dish of fried potatoes and gravy garnished with limp, sweet onions.

Robert's

300 S. Bickford Ave. 405-262-1262
El Reno, OK BLD | $

Starting at six o'clock every morning, the fourteen-stool counter at Robert's is occupied by early birds who come for coffee and eggs and home fries, many of them truckers who make this 1926-vintage hash house a regular morning stop on their way west of Oklahoma City.

The breakfasts are fine diner meals, but the main reason for Robert's place on the Roadfood honor roll is its superb onion-fried hamburgers. This striking white-fronted café is the oldest hamburger restaurant in the hamburger-crazed town of El Reno, and proprietor Edward Graham, who started in the business by slicing onions as a kid, is a master of his craft. It is a joy to sit at the counter and watch him slap a round of beef on the grill, top the beef with onions, then use his spatula to mash the patty into a juicy round as it cooks. He knows how to apply just the right amount of pressure with his spatula, and at the right angle of attack, so that the onions gradually turn into glistening limp squiggles of sweetness that only partially adhere to the meat and tend to fall from inside the bun as soon as the sandwich leaves its plate. The hamburger patty itself, saturated with the taste of onions, is juicy and rugged-textured.

Robert's is a good place to sample El Reno's second passion (after onion-fried burgers)—slaw-topped hot dogs, which are known here as Coney Islands. Mr. Graham makes a coarse, pickly slaw that seems to be an ideal complement for the chili sauce that tops the dog.

Sid's

300 S. Choctaw 405-262-7757
El Reno, OK LD | $

You can study the history of the Osage Frontier on the walls and tables of Sid's, where proprietor Marty Hall has sealed hundreds of pictures of local life under epoxy on the counter and tabletops. Some images are vintage sepia tones that go back to the days of the land lotteries and the Cherokee Strip; some are less ancient photographs of drive-ins, local school teams, and roadside businesses in the halcyon days of Route 66.

The Mother Road, as Route 66 was once known, passed right through El Reno; and there was a time in those pre-interstate days when this small metropolis just west of Oklahoma City was known for its smell. A delicious smell. The smell of hamburgers and onions combined on a grill and cooked so the onion and meat form a perfect union. Now, most travelers drive past El Reno on Interstate 40, but if you have an appetite, it's a fine place to stop, because it remains what it has been since at least the 1920s: the home of the onion-fried burger.

Sid's is one of the elite burger places in town. Before opening it in 1990, Mr. Hall learned to cook burgers a few blocks away at Johnnie's, one of the older burger joints in town. His burgers are beauties with a style all their own, cooked on the grill in such a way that the onions mashed into the patty of beef become slightly charred and caramelized from their time on the grill, giving the sandwich a sweet and smoky zest.

If you are not a burger eater, be advised that Sid's also specializes in El Reno's *other* great culinary passion, the Coney Island. As you might imagine, this is a hot dog topped with chili. Local custom demands that it be a bright red weenie, and that the chili be a fine-ground, meaty blend. El Reno's twist on the formula is to add a thick ribbon of superfine cole slaw with a unique sweet-mustard punch to the top of the package. On the side, have a milk shake, served with a spoon as well as a straw.

Sleepy Hollow

1101 N.E. 50th St.   405-424-1614
Oklahoma City, OK   LD | $$

There are a lot of reasons to have good thoughts about Sleepy Hollow, starting with daily-made biscuits. They are modest-size, fragile-crusted, and fluffy inside, and they come with every meal. So it has been since this OK City institution opened for business in 1948, and while it has had some ups and downs over the years, we are delighted to report that dinner today is as good as it's ever been.

The menu is limited. Steak and pan-fried chicken are the entrees to know about. (There's shrimp, too, but we've never tried it, nor do we know anyone who has.) The chicken is golden-crusted, heavy with juice, absolutely delicious. Steaks come in a couple of sizes. The one-pound sirloin is a beaut, its exterior blackened by flame, its rosy insides radiant with flavor. Before the entree, you get a nice little salad, and with entrees come with family-style mashed potatoes, gravy, peas, and those slap-yo'-mamma biscuits. Dessert is a little cup of pineapple sherbet.

Angelo's

2533 White Settlement   817-332-0357
Fort Worth, TX   LD | $

Angelo's is a dining hall with a remarkable exhibition of game animal trophies, including big fish and at least two brown bears, one of which wears a souvenir T-shirt. Notwithstanding the sprawl of its two rooms and its daunting popularity, and despite the fact that beer flows into frosted goblets at an amazing pace, there is something distinctly meditative about the Angelo's experience. Perhaps its odd sense of tranquility is induced by the haze of hickory-and-brisket vapors that waft from the smoke pit . . . which we sniffed two blocks away, through rolled-up car windows, long before we ever saw the old rugged eatery. Although illuminated by functional fluorescents, it seems softly lit inside, like some living diorama in a natural history museum entitled "Texas Barbecue Parlor, Late 20th Century."

"You are in the Land of Brisket!" proclaims the counterman when an out-of-towner gets to the head of the line and innocently asks what type of beef is served on the beef plate. To prove his point, the counterman steps aside, providing a full view of the cutting block behind him, where a kitchen carver plunges his fork into a slab of smoked beef, holds it aloft like a trophy, then plunks it back down on the wood board and begins slicing pieces nearly half an inch thick. As the knife severs the dark crust and glides into the meat's center, each slice wants to disintegrate. But miraculously, it holds together enough to make it intact onto a Styrofoam plate, where a row of slices is accompanied by beans, potato salad, cole slaw, a length of pickle, a thick slice of raw onion, a ramekin of sauce, and two pieces of the freshest, softest white bread in America. Tote your own meal to a table, and if you pay an extra twenty-five cents, you can stop at the bar along the way and fill a small cup with scorching hot peppers to garnish the meat.

Angelo's hickory pit also yields pork ribs, hot link sausages, ham, and salami. In the relatively cooler months of October through March, Angelo's posts a sign below its regular menu advertising bowls of chili. Strangely, a simple bowl of red is hard to find in modern Texas; Angelo's is an unctuous soup/stew of ground beef and pepper, here served in a plastic bowl with plastic spoon and little bags of oyster crackers on the side. Most people get an order to accompany a rib or beef plate or a few sandwiches, for this type of real-Texas chili is too focused a food to be a meal unto itself: just meat and oil and spice.

Beans 'n' Things

1700 Amarillo Blvd. E   806-373-7383
Amarillo, TX   BLD | $

We came across Beans 'n' Things a few decades ago when it was run by Wiley Alexander, a Marine whose no-nonsense personality dominated the barbecue parlor. Mr. Alexander is gone, but this Amarillo lunchroom is still a fine stop for plates of hickory-smoked brisket with sides of pinto beans and vivid cole slaw. Two sauces are available—hot and mild—and beer is the preferred beverage.

It's good barbecue, but a recent visit reminded us that Amarillo is also a significant Fritos pie place. Beans 'n' Things version is a Southwest classic, heaped with cheese that melts into the meat that softens the chips directly underneath.

Beans 'n' Things opens at 7 A.M., so if you're blasting along old Route 66 and need a quick breakfast, it's a good place to stop for egg-centered burritos.

Black's BBQ

215 N. Main St.   512-398-2712

Lockhart, TX   LD | $

Black's is one very good reason the town of Lockhart lays claim to being the barbecue capital of Texas . . . which, to most Texans, means it is the barbecue capital of the world. It has been smoking brisket and making sausage since 1932, when Edgar Black, Sr., added barbecue pits to his meat market as a way of making something good to eat from parts of the cow that were hard to sell over the butcher's counter.

Although ribs, ham, and chicken are on the menu, and the pork loin is delicious indeed, the one great meat to eat is brisket—slow-smoked in double-wall brick pits over smoldering post oak to a point of maximum tenderness, literally dripping with its own juices. You can get it served the old-fashioned way, by the pound on a piece of butcher paper, or you can go through a cafeteria line and have it served on an actual tray, with such side dishes as pinto beans, potato salad, macaroni salad, and Jell-O. The sides are immaterial, but there is one other item that must be eaten at Black's—a sausage ring. Taut twin crescents made of beef and pork, a ring is spicy, smoky, and a rather exciting diversion for taste buds as you eat your way through a pound of the gentle-flavored brisket.

Black's is no smoke shack. It is a commodious barbecue parlor with decoration that includes mounted jackalope heads, pictures of Lockhart a hundred years ago, and a spectacular collection of longhorn cattle horns.

Blanco Bowling Club Café

310 4th St.   830-833-4416

Blanco, TX   BLD | $

The book of *Bowling Alley Fine Cuisine* has yet to be written, and perhaps it never will be; but we know of at least one bowling alley that is well worth a meal stop: the Blanco Bowling Club Café, just off the town square in a small Texas town famous for its beautiful 1886-vintage courthouse. The nine-pin bowling teams roll only at night, and in the morning, dominoes are played at tables near the alleys; most of the day, the alleys are curtained off, although customers in the back dining room do enjoy such decor as bowling trophies, racks of balls, and ball bags piled atop league members' lockers.

Dining accommodations are basic: wood-grain Formica tables set with flatware wrapped in paper napkins. Service is fast and efficient, and checks arrive with the meal. There is a short counter in the front room with a view of the pass-through to the kitchen and one big table where locals come and go for coffee and terrific cinnamon buns and glazed donuts all morning.

The lunchtime menu includes hamburgers and hot beef sandwiches and an array of tacos, chalupas, and enchiladas. Desserts—pies in particular—are breathtaking. Meringues are spectacularly tall: frothy white crowns that rise three times as high as the filling they top. Crusts are masterful, with a real savory goodness to complement the sweet stuff they contain. And the fillings themselves are delicious. Coconut pie has an indescribably creamy flavor, accented by little bits of toasty coconut scattered across the top of the meringue. Fudge pie is dense, rich, and super-chocolaty. In the category of meringue pies, we place these in nomination for the best in Texas.

Blue Bonnet Café

211 Highway 281   830-693-2344
Marble Falls, TX   BLD | $

At 11 A.M., when we want to stake out our pieces of pie as we order lunch, our waitress at the Blue Bonnet Café advises us to hold off a short while. "I'll come back and ask you what you want," she says. "All the pies aren't up yet. Some are still in the oven and I don't know what they are." You will have no doubt that pie is big in this café the moment you walk in the door from the parking lot in back. A short hallway leads into the dining room past a case that displays pies ready to be cut: cool meringue-topped beauties and hot-from-the-oven double-crusters.

Pre-pie, Blue Bonnet food is mighty fine. Meals start with a bread basket of four-by-four-inch yeast rolls with a bakery sweetness that perfumes the whole table as soon as you tear one apart. With the rolls are rugged-textured corn bread muffins. The menu is a big one, including chicken-fried steak, "mama's famous pot roast" that is falling-apart tender, and such daily specials as chicken and dumplings (Tuesday) and meat loaf with red sauce (Wednesday). With any entree, you get a choice of three vegetables. We love the fragile-crusted fried okra, pork-rich pinto beans, and butter-sopped leaf spinach.

Now, about those pies. Eight or ten are available every day, plain or à la mode; and while we enjoy the apple pie and pecan pie, the one we'll come back for is peanut butter cream. Smooth and devilishly rich, topped with a thick ribbon of white cream, it is accompanied by a small paper cup full of chocolate sauce to either pour on or use as a dip for each forkful: an inspired condiment!

Cattlemen's Fort Worth Steak House

2458 N. Main St.
Fort Worth, TX

817-624-3945
LD | $$

Full-body black-and-white portraits of monumental Herefords, Anguses, and Brahmans decorate the walls at Cattlemen's Fort Worth Steak House, located in the historic stockyards district. Captions identify each corn-fed bovine, telling not only its name but its glory as a top-producing bull or cow. At the back of the main dining area, known as The Branding Room, raw steaks are displayed on a bed of ice in front of a charcoal fire where beef sputters on a grate. Before placing a dinner order, many customers stroll back toward the open broiler to discuss their appetite with the chef, and to admire the specimens on ice and compare and contrast ribeye and T-bone, demure filet mignon and ample porterhouse, K.C. sirloin strip and pound-plus Texas strip.

That Texas sirloin is the steak-lover's choice, a bulging block of aged, heavy beef with a charred crust and robust opulence that is a pleasure simply to slice, and sheer ecstasy to savor. Sweet dinner rolls make a handy utensil for sopping up all the luscious juices that puddle onto the plate. Start with a Gulf shrimp cocktail or a plate of lamb fries—nuggets of quivery organ meat sheathed in fragile crust; get the zesty house dressing on your salad; plop a heap of sour cream into your baked potato; and accompany the big feed with frozen margaritas, longneck beers, or even a bottle of Texas's own Llano Escatado cabernet sauvignon. Such a meal is a cow-town institution that has been favored by true Texas cattle ranchers as well as hordes of beef-seeking tourists for more than fifty years.

City Café

19 N. Main St.   512-281-3663

Elgin, TX   BLD | $

The City Café is an ancient building on a raised-sidewalk street with a big awning out front for shade. It has been remodeled in recent years, but its brick walls resonate with a century of history. First a drugstore, then a bakery and barbershop before it became a café in 1910, it used to be the place in town to which cowboys rode in from cattle-punching for a cool beer late in the day.

History aside, we savor this place for its chicken-fried steak, one of the best in Texas. Gnarled and crusty, golden brown with a brittle crust and a lush ribbon of tender meat inside, it is a portrait of Texas soul food. It comes sided by chunky peppered mashed potatoes and glazed carrots, as well as a basket of moist corn bread muffins.

The City Café menu goes beyond such country classics as chicken-fried steak and chicken and dumplings to include modern salads, fajitas, hamburgers, and all-vegetable plates with a choice of four from a repertoire of at least a dozen. In addition to those sweet carrots and fine mashed potatoes, our favorite vegetables are black-eyed peas and fried okra.

You'll see the pies in a glass-fronted case as you walk in. We thought the lattice-top cherry pie didn't taste as good as it looked, but the coconut cream pie, made from scratch, is a four-star classic.

City Market

633 E. Davis St.   830-875-9019

Luling, TX   LD | $

The dining area at the City Market in Luling is cool and comfortable with faux-granite tables and clean tile floors. To fetch the food, however, you must walk into hell. A swinging door leads into a back-room pit, a shadowy, cave-like chamber illuminated by the glow of burning logs in pits on the floor underneath the iron ovens. It is excruciatingly hot, but apparently at ease in their sweltering workplace, pit men assemble meats on pink butcher paper with gracious dispatch. They take your money, then gather the edges of the paper together so it becomes a boat-like container you easily can carry back into the cool, pine-paneled dining room.

City Market's specialties are sausage rings with chewy skin and coarse-chopped all-beef filling as well as overwhelmingly succulent pork ribs.

Uncharacteristically (for Texas), the City Market also makes a significant barbecue sauce—a spice-speckled, dark orange emulsion that is so coveted by customers that signs on the wall above every booth implore *"Please Leave Sauce Bottles on Tables."* One-serving Styrofoam sauce containers are available to go for forty cents apiece; if you need more, the management finds a clean, empty jar, fills it, and charges you accordingly.

Clark's Outpost

101 Highway 377 (at Gene Autry Dr.)   940-437-2414
Tioga, TX   LD | $$

An hour north of Dallas, Clark's Outpost is a destination restaurant favored by local horse breeders, city folk hungry for a country meal, flamboyant high rollers who arrive by helicopter in the field across the road, and food pilgrims from all over the U.S. in search of Texas on a plate.

Clark's fame is built on beef. Briskets are put into smokers over smoldering green hickory or pecan wood, where they bask in the pungent smoke at 175 degrees for a few hours, then are turned down to a superslow 150 degrees to cook for three days more. Nothing is put onto the beef as it cooks—no seasonings, no sauces, no marinade. The result is beef and smoke laced together in harmony that words cannot convey. Rimmed with a smoke-black crust, each slice is so supple that the gentlest fork pressure separates a mouthful. The warm barbecue sauce, supplied on the side in Grolsch beer bottles, is dark, spicy, and provocatively sweet.

Pork ribs are another Clark's treasure. Neither tenderized nor marinated, they are rubbed with a seasoning mix and cooked until they are soft enough that the chef can easily poke his finger into the meat between the bones. Rib dinners arrive at the table severed into individual bones glistening with juice but also begging for some of that sauce.

Clark's offers country-style side dishes that include crisp-fried okra, jalapeño-spiked black-eyed peas, and a marvelous oddity, French-fried corn on the cob. Lengths of corn, unbattered and unadorned, are dipped in hot oil a minute or so, just long enough to begin to caramelize. The result is corn with a mere veil of a crust around kernels that are astoundingly sweet. Each piece is served with blacksmith's nails stuck in its ends to serve as holders.

Despite success and renown, Clark's is rustic. Located in a town that is little more than a farmland crossroads, it is a small agglomeration of joined-together wood buildings surrounded by a gravel parking lot and stacks of wood for the smoker, with the flags of Texas and the U.S. flying above.

Cooper's Old Time Pit Bar-B-Que

604 W. Young (Highway 29)   915-247-5713
Llano, TX   LD | $$

Old-time and big-time, Cooper's may lack the quaintness of a backroom smoke pit, but its food lacks no flavor. Here is delicious barbecue, Texas-style. That primarily means long-cooked brisket—brisket so tender that its meat and smoke essence veritably melts across your tongue. On the side, you can have creamy cole slaw, beans and/or potato salad, and corn on the cob, as well as a thin, slightly spicy dipping sauce that adds a certain unctuous extra charm to the meat. Also on the table are white bread (for mopping) and pickles (for a jolt to jaded taste buds). To drink, you want a Big Red soda, which is sweet as sugar.

Beyond brisket, Cooper's also smokes pork chops that are as big as softballs and butter-knife-tender, nicely gnawable pork ribs, taut lengths of sausage, and goat shoulder. Tuesdays and Fridays there are beef ribs.

Service is the old-time Texas way: You stand at the pit closest to the door (one of five steel pits in which meats are smoked) and tell the pit man what you want. He retrieves it from the grate and cuts it to order.

Cooper's Pit Bar-B-Q

US 87   915-347-6897
Mason, TX   LD | $$

At the northern edge of the Hill Country in Mason County is a grand barbecue shrine, Cooper's, where the ritual is that you eyeball the meat on its grate, tell the pit man what you want, and he hoists it off. Once it is sliced and priced, you find a seat at one of a handful of tables inside the cinder-block dining room (or at a picnic table outside) and feast. The repertoire of meats is huge, including brisket, all-beef sausage, pork chops, pork tenderloin, and lamb ribs. The brisket is among the best in the state: dripping-moist, radiant with beefy flavor, and so tender that it literally falls to pieces when you lift it toward your mouth. There's a tangy sauce that is delicious, but we recommend a few good samples of this meat au naturel. Sided by cole slaw and jalapeño-spiked pinto beans, it is the foundation of an only-in-Texas feast.

Although they were originally related and do business pretty much the same way, this Cooper's is now an entirely different operation than the one in Llano (page 483). The Llano one tends to be much more mobbed at mealtime, and while some local connoisseurs consider this Mason store to be far superior, we've had great meals at both.

Crosstown BBQ

211 Central Ave.   512-285-9308
Elgin, TX   LD | $$

Crosstown BBQ is a relative newcomer in the world of Texas smoked meats, located in Elgin across the street from where the venerable Southside Market was before it moved to the outskirts of town. It is a stark tin building with little decorative charm, outside or in, but the allure of pit smoke is a seductive perfume impossible to resist.

Service is cafeteria-style. Tell the man what sort of meat you want, and how much you want. He slices it out, puts it on a plate, and sides it with white bread and, if desired, beans. The available choices are ribs, brisket, mutton, and sausage. They're all exemplary, and we would recommend the ribs, brisket, and sausage to anyone. Mutton has a sharp flavor and isn't as fall-apart tender as the beef, but if you are a serious barbecue person, you will find it immensely satisfying.

We took our place at the long communal table in the center of the room and dug in to vast platters of meat, using the bread to mop juices and slaking our thirst with tall cups of ice tea. In the corner of the big dining room, a television was tuned to a show of celebrity gossip from Hollywood . . . but everyone was way too interested in their lunch to pay attention to such nonsense.

Emilia's

605 W. Elizabeth   956-504-9899
Brownsville, TX   BLD | $

South of Corpus Christi and Laredo, culinary pickin's get slim as you approach the Rio Grande. For many years, our last dependable outpost was Abe's barbecue north of Laredo off I-35. But now we have a culinary goal at the southernmost tip of the Gulf Coast, just across the border from Tamaulipas in the city of Brownsville: Emilia's.

Here, you feast on homespun, true-Mex food at rock-bottom prices. From sunny-side up, salsa-garlanded *huevos* with wheaty tortillas to dip into yolks at six in the morning to plate-wide *entomatadas* at supper time, locals and travelers have learned to count on Emilia's for three squares a day. Many items on the menu are Tex-Mex dishes that were once unique to homes and restaurants along the border, but are now familiar to anyone who eats at Taco Bell—chalupas, fajitas, enchiladas, etc. But to savor these meals at Emilia's is to discover the spice and spirit of Mexican food all over again. The meal we recommend highest is picadillo, a South Plains version of the Cuban ground-beef dish in which sautéed beef, well spiced and laced with sweet bits of onion and nuggets of fried potato, is folded into one of Emilia's giant-size flour tortillas. It is a joyful, falling-apart mess.

Don't worry if you speak no Spanish, as eating is universal; but in Emilia's, English is most definitely a second language.

Gennie's Bishop Grill

321 N. Bishop Ave.   214-946-1752
Dallas, TX   L | $

Stroll through an abbreviated but nonetheless magnificent cafeteria line that is everything good about southern-style Texas cookery. Vegetables are bought daily at the farmer's market, seasoned with brio, and served with homemade yeast rolls and corn bread muffins to accompany blue-plate vittles such as chicken-fried steak, meat loaf, beef stew, chili, catfish fillets, and stuffed peppers. The best meal in the house (when available) is garlic chicken. Oozing juice, slipping off its bones as you lift it, fragrant with spice, it is a deeply sensuous eating experience. As for potatoes, Gennie's sweets are cooked until all tooth resistance is gone;

mashed potatoes are whipped smooth, crowned with a spill of peppered cream gravy.

Other side dishes include turnip greens sprinkled with peppery vinegar, baked squash, and corn bread stuffing that is soft and sweet. For dessert, you want peanut butter pie.

"If Our Prices Were Higher, We'd Be Famous," says the movable-letter menu above the buffet line. But the management is disingenuous. Since it opened in 1970, Gennie's has become quite famous among American café connoisseurs, to whom this modest lunchroom is a taste of paradise.

Golden Light Café

2908 W. 6th
Amarillo, TX

806-374-9237
LD Mon-Sat | $

Opened in 1946 as a hamburger stand on old Route 66, the Golden Light Café is struck by brilliant western rays in afternoons when the sun is low in the south. The old brick front fairly glows and the otherwise dusty interior—where decor is neon beer signs, vintage license plates, and a bumper sticker that says "God Bless John Wayne"—is touched with highlights wherever light beams through glass in the door and windows. The high counter chairs toward the front are occupied by locals, the miscellaneous tables and booths crowded with longneck beers and burger platters. Ambience alone is an inspiring remnant of life along "America's Main Street" before it became Interstate 40.

The hamburger is cooked cowboy-style *(well* done!), served with mustard, lettuce, tomato slices, onions, and pickle chips, complemented by layers of cheese and chili on top. Available extras include roasted green chiles, jalapeño peppers, and fried onions. We also like the Fritos pie (here known as "Flagstaff Pie")—an oval plate of Fritos chips topped with the stout house red chili, cheese, and onions. What's great about Fritos pie is how different every chip is, depending on how close it gets to the chili. Those corn ribbons that are totally smothered turn to soft, salty cornmeal; some remain untouched and crisp; most are half-and-half crisp and tender, or on their way to disintegration.

The most memorable dish in this old café is French fries: thin-cut and superbly crisp, they have a starchy savor that calls only for a sprinkle of salt to attain perfection. If you want to walk on the wild side, get a bottle of the delicious, pepper-hot Southwest Sensations smoked jalapeño, garlic, and corn hot sauce that the Golden Light has made especially for its tables. As a ketchup-alternative condiment, it is dynamite.

A notable house motto, on the place mat menus: "We serve good food, *not fast food,* so please be patient." At the peak of lunch hour, it may take a while for the two harried waitresses to get your burgers out, but they always manage to keep the frosty mugs of Shiner Bock coming.

H&H Car Wash and Coffee Shop

701 E. Yandel   915-533-1144
El Paso, TX   BL | $

Three tables, topped with blue boomerang-pattern Formica, provide a view of vehicles being soaped, scrubbed, and toweled, but despite the undeniable interest of the attached car wash, we recommend counter seats at H&H. Here you have a view of the pint-size food-prep area, where the cooks are busy peeling chiles and tomatoes, brewing sauce, stirring refried beans, and chattering among themselves and with customers in a language that is approximately two-thirds Spanish, one-third English.

They give us a once-over, confer about the heat level of the huevos rancheros, then inquire if we want ours *"Muy caliente."*

"Si," say we, and as the eggs fry, one brings out a plastic cup filled with salsa along with a couple of warm-from-the-griddle flour tortillas, each folded into quarters. The salsa is olive green, chopped fine. It is made of jalapeño peppers—*muy caliente,* indeed!—and has a smoky zest that plays reveille on the tongue.

The huevos rancheros are fierce themselves—smothered in cheese gravy flecked with incendiary bits of green chile pepper. Amused by the tears of hot-pepper joy in our eyes, a waitress turns to a cabinet and fetches a plastic bottle filled with house-brewed pink salsa, and she carries it toward the counter as cautiously as a pyrotechnician toting pure nitroglycerine. She sets it before us and whispers with conspiratorial glee, *"!Mas caliente!"*

We squeeze some onto a tortilla and taste. *"¡CALIENTISSIMO!"* we exclaim, emboldened by our pepper-induced rapture to speak our own brand of pigeon-Spanish. It *is* blazing hot, but totally different from the jalapeño salsa or the peppers on the eggs: more sheer inferno and less intrigue.

Not everything posted on the H&H wall menu is four-alarm. You can eat ordinary eggs for breakfast or a hamburger for lunch (the café

closes at 3 P.M.). Burritos are available seven ways: stuffed with chiles rellenos, egg and chorizo sausage, picadillo, red chile, green chile, carne pi-
cada, or beans. Specials include chicken molé, red and green enchiladas,
and—always on Saturday—menudo, the tripe and hominy stew
renowned for its power to cure a hangover.

Hospitality at the well-worn cook shop is enchanting. If you speak
Spanish, so much the better: you will understand the nuances of the chatter. But if, like us, you are limited to English, you will still be part of the
action. We were wearing ten-gallon hats, so we soon became known to
one and all as the cowboys. *"Vaqueros,"* called the waitress as we
headed out the door, *"Vaya con dios."* With our car newly cleaned and
the radio tuned to the rollicking Mexican polka rhythms of *Tejano*
music, we highballed north along the Rio Grande.

Hill Country Cupboard

Highway 281   830-868-4625
Johnson City, TX   BLD | $

Hill Country Cupboard claims to serve "The World's Best Chicken-Fried
Steak," backing up that claim with the humorous parenthesis "(NEARLY
3 DOZEN SOLD)."

We reckon this big barn of a café along the highway through Johnson City has sold plenty more than three dozen chicken-fried steaks; and
while we are reluctant to proclaim any single C.F.S. the best in the world
(perfection is always just out of reach), we would definitely put this one
in the pantheon. It has a golden-brown crust that is rich and well spiced,
virtually melting in the mouth to harmonize with the thin ribbon of tender beef it encloses. Alongside the slab of fat-crusted protein comes a
great glob of skin-on mashed potatoes; and of course, there is thick white
gravy to blanket the whole shebang. It is possible to get a "Mexican
chicken-fried steak," which is covered with spicy sauce and melting
Cheddar cheese: not a terrible idea, but neither is it an improvement on
the excellent simplicity of the basic formula.

Beyond chicken-fried steak, Hill Country Cupboard has a full menu
of Southwest eats. (The menu itself is something to behold: glued onto
two sides of a brown paper bag!) There is all manner of barbecue, including smoked brisket that has a good taste but is dry enough that it is
dramatically enhanced by generous applications of spicy barbecue sauce;

there are sausage, spareribs, and smoked turkey, too. You can even have a salad . . . enriched by pieces of chicken-fried steak or chicken-fried chicken!

The Cupboard is a place where locals eat. Truckers, cowboys, field hands, and farm families saunter in at mealtimes and occupy tables topped with easy-wipe blue-checked cloths, quenching thirsts with huge tankards of ice tea. There are two airy dining rooms crowned with circulating fans, illumination provided by fluorescent tubes shaded by what appears to be burlap feed-sack material. Service is no-nonsense; checks are put down on the table along with the meal.

Hoover's Cooking

2002 Manor Rd.　　　　　　　512-479-5006
Austin, TX　　　　　　　　　LD | $$

Hoover's is a big restaurant that serves big portions of food. "We proudly present honest-to-goodness good cooking," the menu boasts; and it is true. Without too many frills, but with expertise born of proprietor Hoover Alexander's childhood memories of his mother's own home cooking, this restaurant serves Texas comfort food in grand style.

Although it always seems crowded and extremely noisy (background music, loud conversation, the commotion of people having a great time eating well and drinking plenty), Hoover's commodious dining room, with plenty of room between the tables, is made for comfort. This is a restaurant for people who are serious about eating.

We knew we were in for a bigger-than-life treat as soon as our glass of lemonade arrived. In fact, it arrived not as a glass, but as a pitcher with a straw. We had to ask if a glass would be forthcoming; our waitress told us that the pitcher *is* the glass: maybe a quart of lemonade to be drunk straight from the tankard. And it is good lemonade—sweet, fresh-squeezed, refreshing.

The choice of meals is wide. Hoover's has its own smokehouse, perfuming the parking lot outside, from which come pork ribs, Elgin sausage, highly spiced Jamaican jerk chicken, and lesser-spiced (but nonetheless delicious) regular-spiced barbecue chicken. On the side of these delicacies you choose from a large selection of vegetables that include chunky mashed potatoes, macaroni and cheese, black-eyed peas, sweet and hammy mustard greens, crisp-fried okra, and jalapeño-accented creamed spinach. The vegetables are so good, and served in such abundance, that Hoover's offers a three or four vegetable plate, *sans* meat.

Other than smoked fare, the menu lists chicken-fried steak with cream gravy, meat loaf dotted with onion bits and peppers, ham steak, pork chops, catfish, and a full array of sandwiches. For dessert, hot fruit cobbler is de rigueur, especially good if topped with a scoop of Blue Bell ice cream.

Hut's Hamburgers

807 W. 6th St.	512-472-0693
Austin, TX	LD | $

Hut's is a hoot. It's a burger joint, no doubt about that, with nineteen different varieties of hamburger listed on its menu (not to mention the options of buffalo meat, chicken breast, or veggie burgers), each one topped with a different constellation of condiments that range from hickory sauce (delicious!) to cheeses of all kinds to guacamole to chipotle mayonnaise. Beyond burgers, there are other sandwiches, a different blue-plate special every day (chicken-fried steak, meat loaf, catfish, etc.), and a beverage list that includes cherry Coke, pink lemonade, and a root beer float.

Decorated to the rafters with neon beer signs, team pennants, and clippings celebrating its long-standing fame—since 1939—it is a small place that is always overstuffed with people, with noise, and with a spirit of fun. You will likely wait for a seat in the small vestibule or on the sidewalk outside, but once you're seated, the food comes fast.

We don't know about the salads or plate dinners, but we can tell you that the hamburgers are excellent. American classics. We are particularly fond of the Buddy Holly burger with the works, the double-meat Dag burger, and the Hut's favorite with bacon, cheese, lettuce, and mayonnaise. The French fries are very good, and the onion rings have a peppery zest that make them a joy to overeat.

Julio's Café Corona

8050 Gateway E.   915-592-1294
El Paso, TX   LD | $$

Roadfooder Mike Riley of El Paso tipped us off to Julio's, saying that he and his wife have eaten there for the last ten years and never have been disappointed. In fact, Julio's is a spin-off of a restaurant in Juarez and goes back to the 1950s. Today El Paso's Julio's is a comfortable place with polished service and a mariachi band on Sundays.

Meals start with a hot chile green salsa and chips, and after that you can move on to any of the Tex-Mex standards, from old-fashioned tacos and burritos to newfangled fajitas. The dish that stands out in our memory is the flautas—a rack of 'em, lined up and topped with guacamole. So named because they resemble flutes, these flautas are made of shattering-crisp fried tubes of corn tortilla filled with moist and spicy beef. They're irresistible!

Kincaid's

4901 Camp Bowie Blvd.   817-732-2881
Fort Worth, TX   L | $

Kincaid's serves a half-pound hamburger, lean yet drippingly juicy, sandwiched between halves of a big warm bun that oozes a surfeit of onions, tomato slices, and shreds of lettuce. What an unholy mess it is, compounded by the fact that Kincaid's accommodations are—how shall we say it?—less than deluxe.

In fact, it is the ambience of Kincaid's that gives these hamburgers their extra pizzazz. Kincaid's is not quite a normal restaurant. It started as a grocery store and is still configured that way. The old grocery shelves are cut down to approximately chest-high and surfaced so customers can find a convenient place to stand and scarf down lunch. Many years ago when we first discovered the place, we saw one old couple arrive with their own folding chairs, wait in line at the counter, get their burgers, find an unoccupied length of shelf space, tuck napkins into their collars, and dig in with gusto. They told us they eat lunch at Kincaid's at least three days every week. A while back, tables and chairs were added up front so people can dine more normally, but somehow this place makes us want to be in the aisles where the action is.

The makeshift tables are strewn with magazines for reading while you chew. And dangling from above is what must be called interior decoration: a menagerie of plastic yellow happy faces, inflatable anthropomorphic hot dogs, and similar amusing gewgaws.

Krause's Café

148 S. Castell Ave.   830-625-7581
New Braunfels, TX   BLD | $

Historians have not yet convincingly documented the history of chicken-fried steak, which native Texans consider their fundamental comfort food, but it has long been our contention that this pounded-tender beef cutlet, breaded and fried crisp and served with mashed potatoes under a blanket of cream gravy, most likely traces its heritage back to the many well-trained European cooks who found themselves in Texas but without the fixin's for a fine, tender wiener schnitzel. Instead, they took a hunk of cow and beat the chaw out of it, then fried it up like Southern-style chicken.

Our genealogical speculation is supported by the fact that the Hill Country, with its preponderance of German great-grandmas, is home of the best chicken-fried steaks anywhere, among them the one served at the venerable Krause's Café. This place has been a New Braunfels town favorite since 1938, and its Old/New World menu lists both wiener schnitzel *and* chicken-fried steak (as well as homemade sausage, Old World potato pancakes, and red-white-and-blue blackened Cajun catfish).

Kreuz Market

619 N. Colorado St.   512-398-2361
Lockhart, TX   LD | $$

Kreuz Market isn't what it used to be, and it isn't *where* it used to be (see Smitty's, page 499), but its barbecue is as good as ever . . . probably as good as it was 100 years ago when it opened as an eat-place annex to a meat market. For decades, the dining area consisted of an area near the pit outfitted with communal tables, each of which had a single knife chained to a post for customers to use to cut their meat. Service was do-it-yourself: Tell the man at the pit how much meat you want, and that's what you got, sliced off the brisket to order, served on a piece of butcher paper with a stack of saltines on the side.

Today Kreuz (say "Krites") has moved to big, modern, relatively smokeless quarters; but the menu remains simple—beef brisket, smoked prime rib, beef sausage, or pork chops. On the side, you might want a firm hot sausage link; and your meal will be rounded out by crackers or white bread and condiments consisting of pickles, onions, and jalapeños. Barbecue sauce? Forget about it! In a real Texas barbecue, sauce is anathema; the meat speaks for itself. To drink: beer and more beer. Service is still tote-your-own, and it is a special pleasure to stand at the counter and watch the flaps of glistening brisket severed from the whole with a sharp knife and piled onto the butcher paper. Once seated, you will want to eat with your fingers; each piece is so soft and juicy, the tactile experience is nearly as good as the taste. That's why every long table is outfitted with rolls of paper towels for hand-wiping throughout the meal.

Little Diner

7209 7th St.   915-877-2176
Canutillo, TX   LD Thurs–Tues | $

The Little Diner is an out-of-the-way eatery that serves some of the finest flautas and gorditas in West Texas. Flautas, which means flutes, are tightly rolled, crisp-fried tortillas packed with either seasoned chicken or beef. The chicken is moist and savory, the beef is brisket, cooked until falling-apart tender. About the size of a hefty asparagus stalk, a Little Diner flauta is perfect finger fare: pick it up and crunch away; juices from inside will dribble down your chin. Gorditas are sandwich pockets made of cornmeal, stuffed and then griddle-cooked. They have an earthy corn taste and moist insides with just a hint of flaky crispness all around their skin. Many cafés in this region serve them, but Little Diner's are notable for their refined texture and gay orange hue. Inside is ground beef, along with melted cheese, lettuce, and tomato. To spice it up, the restaurant offers dark red, chunky sauce with a Tex-Mex wallop.

Curious about the punch of the table salsa, we visited the kitchen, where two ladies sat at a dinette table hand-shredding cooked brisket for the flautas. Here we found Lourdes Pearson, who bought the Little Diner from her mother, Irene Gallegos, in the early 1990s. Lourdes grew up in the business, and with casual expertise she explained that Sandia peppers were the secret of the sauce. "They have the most heat, so we wouldn't stuff them for chiles rellenos," she said. "For rellenos, mild Big Jim peppers are best. We try not to serve anything too terribly hot at the Little

Diner. Late in the summer, though, the salsa can get pretty powerful. That is when we get our chiles straight from the Mesilla Valley."

Los Insurgentes

3531 W. 15th Ave.　　　　　　　806-353-5361
Amarillo, TX　　　　　　　　　LD | $$

Early November in the Texas Panhandle: "Order Your Christmas Tamales Now!" suggests a sign on the front door of Los Insurgentes, an Amarillo neighborhood restaurant named for the revolutionaries (Zapata, Villa, etc.) whose pictures decorate its walls. The stern attitude of these fighters all around is balanced by a small selection of festive sombreros and a soft light from lanterns that illuminate the back dining room; and the staff is as friendly as can be. When we came for dinner one Friday night, the waitress warned us at the end of the meal that the flan was still a little warm. "Do you mind waiting?" she asked. We did mind waiting, so we got the balmy custard still slightly tepid, the temperature of baby formula—and just as comforting.

Before the flan, which is an every-Friday specialty, we enjoyed the best Tex-Mex food we've had in the Panhandle, starting with baskets of warm tortilla chips (replenished as needed), bowls of hot sauce, and creamy guacamole. We ate enchiladas, chalupas, chiles rellenos, and tacos, and were especially impressed by the savor of the chunky beef in the tacos. Most of all, we liked the refritos (refried beans), which have a lardy avoirdupois that made us scoop the last of them from the plate with tortilla chips. Alas, the kitchen's much-loved *cabrito* (goat) was not in season for our visit mid-November, and neither were we able to determine precisely *when* goat season is hereabouts. But no matter; we'll definitely return to Los Insurgentes any time we're in Amarillo, whether or not *cabrito* is on the menu, and whether or not we are in the market for Christmas tamales.

Louis Mueller Barbecue

206 W. 2nd St.　　　　　　　512-352-6206
Taylor, TX　　　　　　　　　LD Mon-Fri, and Sat until the barbecue is
　　　　　　　　　　　　　　gone (early afternoon) | $

Now run by a third generation of Muellers and with new seats amending the old communal benches, Louis Mueller's is *the* Texas barbecue parlor—a cavernous old building where beef brisket and hot link sausages are served the true Lone Star way—with no frills, but with oceans of flavor.

The meat is smoked over hardwood, then wrapped in butcher paper to steep until it becomes more tender than pot roast. Tell the pitmaster how much you want and he forks a big chunk from the pit and lops off enough to fill your order. Each individual slice is gorgeous, halved by the ribbon of fat that runs through a brisket, separating the leaner, denser meat below from the more luscious stuff on top. All around the edge there is a smoky-tasting crust; and if you want to add a bit of punch to this gentle-flavored meat, you are provided with a little cup of brothy sauce speckled with red pepper flakes. Other than hot sausages, side dishes are inconsequential: white bread, potato salad, cole slaw. They exist only to provide a breather from the intense pleasure of the meat.

When you walk into Louis Mueller's, even when it's crowded, you will be shocked by the quiet. Reminiscent less of a restaurant than of the Cathedral of Notre Dame, there is a reverential hush in the air; for people come here not merely to eat smoked meat, but to meditate upon its greatness. Louis Mueller's is the heart and soul of Texas barbecue.

Mel's Country Café

24814 Stanolind Rd.   281-255-6357
Tomball, TX   LD | $

McDonald's advertises the Quarter Pounder like it's something extra large. We've seen a few restaurants that specialize in half-pound hamburgers, which really do seem oversize, especially when fitted inside any kind of ordinary bun. But a mere four or eight ounces of beef is scarcely worth discussing if you want to talk about a really big hamburger. How about a One-and-a-Half-Pounder? Yes, a twenty-four-ounce meat patty—known as a Mega-Burger—actually served on a bun, is the signature dish of Mel's Country Café. And if the thought of eating a pound and a half of meat seems a wee bit monomaniacal, rest assured a Mel's Mega-Burger is not served plain. It comes topped with a pound of bacon and a half pound of cheese, some lettuce, tomato, and onions, plus whatever condiments you prefer. So, not including all the dressings and bun, this sandwich weighs just about three pounds!

Is it good? Who the hell knows? At this dimension of girth, ordinary standards of hamburger excellence seem rather inadequate. Let us simply say that it tastes like good hamburger meat (not like meat loaf, as we expected), there is enough juice to drip down your chin, and frankly, we found ourselves utterly unable to eat all of one. Too bad, because for those who do manage to eat a Mega-Burger in under two hours, there is a wonderful prize: a second Mega-Burger, for free.

You don't have to order a section of cow when you come to Mel's. Monday through Friday at lunchtime, there is a fine steam table for help-yourself meals that include an inviting selection of at least a half-dozen southern-style vegetables. While most people amend their choice of two or three vegetables with an entree (country steak, fried chicken, etc.), we've actually seen customers who eat vegetarian, choosing a quarter of non-meat items from among beans, corn, okra, potatoes, etc. On the other hand, meat-eaters of normal appetite can come to Mel's and enjoy regulation-size hamburgers (about a quarter pound) on normal buns with all the trimmings.

Monument Café

1953 S. Austin Ave.   512-930-9586
Georgetown, TX   BLD | $

Inside and out, the Monument Café looks extraordinarily simple. It is a rectangular building with a plain neon sign and glass brick corners; inside, there is a long counter with stools opposite the door and steel-banded tables surrounded by well-worn wooden chairs. Fans spin overhead, and even when it's crowded and the waitresses are bustling, the dining room has an air of serenity that makes every visit a slow-food joy.

Three meals a day are served, and we have had excellent catfish as well as charred chicken with poblano sauce at lunch, and this is one of the few cafés in central Texas that still makes a serious no-bean chili; but it is breakfast we like best. The kitchen's *migas* just might be the best anywhere: eggs scrambled with cheese, diced tomatoes, and small ribbons of tortilla that variously soften and turn crisp depending on where they are in the pan, giving the dish an earthy corn flavor. On the side comes a nice red salsa to heat it up if desired, along with grits or hash browns and a soft flour tortilla that is good for mopping and pushing food around on the plate. Pancakes and waffles are lovely, as are the big squarish biscuits; the pastry that makes us swoon is sour cream coffee cake, its top blanketed with sugar and frosting, its inside layered with local pecans.

"Our pies, cakes, and cookies are made here fresh every day," the menu notes. "We use only the best ingredients, including real butter, yard eggs, and real whipping cream." Of this boast, you will have no doubt if you order a piece of cream pie. This is some of the best pie in Texas, some of the best *anywhere*! Chocolate pecan pie looks big and gooey like any show-offy café pie, but when you fork up a piece and taste it, you are suddenly in another world of fine chocolate and master baking. This pie is rich as truffles, devilishly fudgy, and loaded with nuts. Coconut cream pie is equally amazing, but at the opposite end of the pleasure spectrum: light, silky, fresh, and layered on a flaky light-gold crust.

Oh, one more thing: lemonade, limeade, and orange juice are *fresh*. You can watch the fruits squeezed if you sit at the counter, which is also a great place to view beautiful plates of food as they are sent out the pass-through window from the kitchen.

OST

305 Main St.	830-796-3836
Bandera, TX	BLD | $$

Even die-hard Texans have to agree that the majority of chicken-fried steaks served in restaurants are tough, spongy, and tasteless, and have given the dish a bad reputation. But anyone who is a chicken-fried-steak skeptic needs only to come to Texas Hill Country to realize there is another way. Dine at OST (Old Spanish Trail) and you will know just how wonderful a well-made chicken-fried steak can be. It is the Platonic ideal of the dish, a tantalizing balance of crunch and tenderness, with gravy that is cream-soft but pepper-sharp.

OST has been Bandera's town café since 1921, and its roomy cypress booths and bar stools made of Western saddles make it an especially appealing destination for hungry travelers in search of cowboy culture. One whole wall is devoted to images of John Wayne; its spur collection includes rowels dating back to frontier days; and the buffet is set out under a downsized covered wagon. The buckaroo trappings make a lot of sense in Bandera, which is surrounded by dude ranches and has proclaimed itself "The Cowboy Capital of the World."

Paris Coffee Shop

700 W. Magnolia   817-335-2041

Fort Worth, TX   BL | $

By 7 A.M., the Paris Coffee Shop on the south side of Fort Worth is bustling. An airy room with a counter, booths, and tables, Paris (named not for the capital of France, but for the original owners) smells delicious in the morning, its air fragrant with the smell of sausages, bacon, pork chops, corned beef hash, as well as tangy biscuits smothered with gravy. Beyond biscuits, breadstuffs include soft, glazed cinnamon rolls and a choice of eight-grain, sourdough, or sun-dried tomato toast.

The Paris Coffee Shop is also a legendary lunchroom, known for meat loaf, fried chicken, and chicken-fried steak with mashed potatoes and gravy as well as one of the best bowls of chili in the Metroplex. The café's signature dish is an "Arkansas Traveler": hot roast beef on corn bread smothered with gravy. Such Lone Star comfort fare is accompanied by your choice from a wide variety of southern-style vegetables such as turnips and/or turnip greens, pole beans, and butter beans. And every meal *must* be followed by a piece of Paris pie. One morning, when we spotted a single piece of custard pie we wanted behind the counter and ordered it for breakfast, the waitress warned, "It's not today's." (Today's pies were still in the oven.) But then she thought a while and agreed with our choice, declaring, "Hey, yesterday's egg custard pie is better than no pie at all!"

For locals who have made the Paris their neighborhood café since the 1920s (when it opened across the street), a meal here is like coming home. For the rest of us, it is a treasured Fort Worth souvenir.

Ranchman's Café (a.k.a. Ponder Steak House)

110 W. Bailey St.   940-479-2221

Ponder, TX   D | $$ (reservations advised)

In a sleepy encampment by the train tracks at the northern fringe of the Dallas/Fort Worth Metroplex, the Ponder Steakhouse (actually named Ranchman's Café) has been a destination meat house since 1948. Since that date, indoor bathrooms have been added; but the steaks are still hand-cut, and the ambience is Lone Star to the core.

"Welcome to Texas!" chimed one well-fed good ol' boy at us as he pushed his way out the creaky swinging door, looking like he just sold his prize bull for a million dollars. Handing his denuded T-bone to the hound that had faithfully gazed in at him through the storefront window as he dined, he strolled along the dusty Ponder main street enjoying a smoke. The dog settled in on the raised sidewalk to savor his bone.

Ponder serves cowboy-style steaks—platter-size, sizzled on a hot griddle until they develop a wickedly tasty crust. Although tender, they are not the silver butter-knife cuts of expense-account dining rooms; they are steaks of substantial density that require a sharp knife and reward a good chew with tides of flavor. French fries come on the side, but if you call an hour and a half ahead, they'll put a baked potato in the oven and have it ready when you arrive. "Y'all did good!" exclaimed our waitress after we polished off a few pounds of beef, potatoes, and a couple of slices of buttermilk pie that Granny had made just that morning.

Smitty's

208 S. Commerce	512-398-9344
Lockhart, TX	BLD | $

If you are a barbecue devotee, the address of Smitty's will be familiar even if the name is not. The location at 208 S. Commerce is the old store where Kreuz Market (page 492) used to be before it moved to its modern digs. Smitty's was opened by the daughter and grandkids of Edgar "Smitty" Schmidt, who ran Kreuz forever.

Genealogy aside, what's important is the beef; and Smitty's beef is beautiful. Here is one very good reason to take seriously Lockhart's claim to be the Barbecue Capital of Texas. The beef is brisket, velvet-soft and sliced to order, served on butcher paper along with your choice from the roster of traditional side dishes of sliced onion, wedges of avocado, sliced tomato, pickle spears, and cheese. To accompany the brisket, many customers choose a length of hot sausage (delicious!), and there is an option of pork chops, which are mighty good . . . but *not* as celestially good as the beef. (Added to the menu, and utterly heretical in a Texas barbecue parlor, is an option of beans on the side of any meal.) All servings of food come with saltine crackers or soft white bread. Utensils? You get a little plastic picnic knife. But no one uses utensils to eat this food. It is finger food—incredibly messy finger food, truly finger-licking good.

Sonny Bryan's

2202 Inwood Rd.   214-744-1610

Dallas, TX   LD | $

Other locations around Dallas

Sonny Bryan's serves sandwiches of piled-high brisket so delicious that it needs no condiment. However, Sonny Bryan's sauce also happens to be superb, a tangy companion to gentle-flavored beef. Turkey, ham, pork, pork ribs, and sausage are also on the menu, and it is possible to have sandwiches that include two kinds of meat, and even cheese. But if you are coming to Sonny Bryan's for the first time, please have a simple brisket sandwich—chopped or sliced, it doesn't matter—and you will understand why Texans are passionate about barbecue.

On the side with whatever meat you choose, Sonny Bryan's offers a slew of side dishes, including French fries, barbecue-sauced beans, potato salad, black-eyed peas, cole slaw, potato chips by the bag, and corn on the cob.

The Bryan barbecue dynasty goes back to 1910, when Elijah Bryan, Sonny's grandfather, opened a smoke shack in Oak Cliff. The Sonny Bryan's on Inwood Road opened in 1958, and it still features awkward school-desk seating. Sonny Bryan himself has since passed on, but the family tradition of great barbecue continues at about a dozen Sonny Bryan restaurants all around the Metroplex.

Southside Market & Bar-B-Cue

1212 US 290 W   512-281-4650

Elgin, TX   LD | $

Elgin (pronounced with a hard "G," as in *gut* rather than *gin*) has been the sausage capital of Texas since the Moon family opened the Southside Market in 1882. Like so many of the great Texas barbecues, the smoked meat business was an annex to a butcher shop, with a dining area added so that customers could sit and eat smoked brisket and sausages by the pound.

Several kinds of barbecued meat are available at Southside, including mutton ribs, pork ribs, and slices of brisket. Diners who love the chewy, crunchy, semi-burnt ends of the brisket (as opposed to the soft inner sections) can order a mess of "brisket trimmings" from the cutting board—just about the most condensed barbecue-eating experience imaginable.

Of all its smoky delights, Elgin is best known for muscular tubes of ground beef sausage known among connoisseurs as Elgin hot guts, their succulent insides flecked with pepper, their exteriors ready to pop at first bite. We noted that as a measure of just how appreciated this product is among connoisseurs, it is the only sausage the King family serves at the annual Sheridan, Wyoming, "King Days Rodeo." Friends truck up pounds of it every year because there is nothing like Elgin sausage anywhere else in the West.

It used to be that the only place to eat this good food at the Southside Market was at a long bench facing a tiled wall in the un-air-conditioned room adjoining the barbecue pit, and the only way to order it was by the pound, with nothing but saltine crackers on the side. Ten years ago, the operation moved from downtown to a big old bank building by the highway, and while it looks antiseptic, the food is still 100 percent Texan. Today, you will dine at a nice table in a clean, barn-size dining room and actually order from a menu. The meats are available by the sandwich and plate, but old-timers can still buy what they want by the pound and have it served not on plates, but on pieces of butcher paper.

Threadgill's

| 6416 N. Lamar | 512-451-5440 |
| Austin, TX | LD | $ |

Threadgill's is a bonanza for appetites in search of southern and/or Texas food. The vast menu starts with fried green tomatoes as an hors d'oeuvre and features chicken-fried everything (steak, pork chops, even chicken) as well as a long list of vegetables, from virtuous (okra with tomatoes) to wicked (garlic cheese grits). Many hungry customers come to Threadgill's to eat *only* vegetables, accompanied by big squares of warm corn bread. If you choose right, a meal of five vegetable selections is, in fact, every bit as satisfying as a few pounds of beef. Among the excellent choices from the regular list are the San Antonio squash casserole, turnip greens, and crisp-fried okra.

If, for some reason, we arrive in Austin not wanting something fried, we go for Threadgill's T-bone steak with side of scalloped or mashed potatoes and a dish of black-eyed peas. Those of lighter appetite can choose either an all-vegetable meal or a very handsome (albeit gigantic) Caesar salad piled with grilled chicken.

Aside from great food, Threadgill's is worth visiting for its history (the Austin music scene started here; Janis Joplin used to waitress here) and its Texas-to-the-max ambience. Although the original beer joint/gas station that Kenneth Threadgill opened in 1933 burned down twice and virtually none of it remains, the restaurant today has the feel of an antique: creaky wood floorboards, wood-slat ceilings, and a devil-may-care floor plan that gives the impression that the sprawling space just kept growing through the years. The main decorative motif is beer signs. Even before it became a legal beer joint in 1933 (with the first post-Prohibition beer license in Travis County), Threadgill's was known for the dime-a-bottle home brew suds it served; and long into the thirties, it was still famous for its moonshine. Today's beer list is prodigious, including Live Oak Pilz on draft, and bottles of Salado Creek Honey Bock and Fat Tire Amber Ale.

Vernon's Kuntry Katfish

5901 W. Davis	936-760-3386
Conroe, TX	LD | $

Hugely popular—you will wait for a table any weekday at lunch—Vernon's Kuntry Katfish serves not only Mississippi-raised catfish, but also a passel of country-style vegetables every day. Mustard greens or turnip greens, northern beans, field peas, fried okra, mashed potatoes, and cheese-enriched broccoli are some of the selections; and crunchy, dark-cooked hush puppies, studded with bits of onion and jalapeño pepper, are accompanied by bowls of pickled green tomatoes.

If catfish is not your dish, try the chicken-fried steak. It's a Texas benchmark, gilded with pepper gravy and served with biscuits or corn bread squares on the side.

Dessert is significant: fruit cobbler, banana pudding, or an item known as "good pie," which is a uniquely American pastry edifice of pineapple chunks, bananas, cream cheese, nuts, and chocolate syrup.

Weikel's Store and Bakery

2247 W. State Highway 71   979-968-9413

La Grange, TX   BL | $

In the Hill Country east of Austin, *kolaches* appear with some regularity on bakery shelves. A Danish-like pastry with Czech lineage, the kolache has become a tasty symbol of the Eastern European roots that have helped make this part of Texas such a culinary adventureland. Although it does physically resemble a Danish, a good kolache is in a league by itself, made with dough that is fluffy and elegant, and filled with top-quality apricot or prune preserves, cream cheese, or a sweetened paste of poppy seeds.

One of the least likely places to find superior kolaches is Weikel's Store and Bakery, a convenience store attached to a gas station by the side of the highway. At first glance when you walk in, it looks like any other quick-shop highway mart: refrigerator cases full of beer and soda, shelves stocked with junk food chips and candy, an assortment of pre-fab sandwiches, a serve-yourself coffee bar, and sundries for traveling truckers.

But look to the left and take a few steps back. Here you find the bakery cases, usually topped with at least half a dozen good things to sample. We picked small pieces of cream cheese pound cake, pecan sandies (the house special cookie), brownies, chocolate chip cookies, and cinnamon rolls. Below the freebies were shelves of strudel, cake, and the day's repertoire of kolaches.

There are a dozen sorts of kolache listed on Weikel's menu; but not all are available all the time; alas, prune had sold out by the time we walked in; but the cream cheese kolache, the apricot kolache, and the poppy seed kolache we sampled were superb, as good as any kolache we've ever had, even from fine-looking non–highway bakeries. You know this place is serious about its kolaches when you consider the house motto: "We Got'cha Kolache." Those who plan to pass through La Grange can order their kolaches in advance at the Weikel website, www.weikels.com.

There are more good-looking cakes and pastries on the shelf than we had appetite to sample, but we did manage to sample one more house specialty, which we highly recommend: Weikel's pig-in-a-blanket. It is a taut-skinned, rugged-textured kielbasa sausage fully encased in a tube of tender-crumb bread that is finer than any hot dog bun we've ever eaten.

Williams' Smokehouse

5903 Wheatley   713-680-8409

Houston, TX   LD Tues-Sat | $

If you need ribs in Houston, Cedric Williams is your man. Son of Willie and Hattie Williams, who started the smokehouse in the late 1980s, young Mr. Williams is a true pitmaster, turning out gorgeous ribs, smoky hot links, butter-tender brisket, and glistening half-chickens for lunch and supper. The meats are all exemplary, with or without a dab of the Williams family's semi-incendiary sauce; or if you want a real bargain, order the "beef potato"—a huge baker piled with chopped smoked beef. Finally, you want some of Mrs. Williams's peach cobbler, an old family recipe she has used for decades to make dessert for church picnics.

Capitol Reef Inn and Café

360 W. Main St.	435-425-3271
Torrey, UT	BLD | $$

At the west end of the town of Torrey in the wilds of south-central Utah, the Capitol Reef Inn and Café is a rare oasis of good food and elevated cultural consciousness. It is not only a restaurant; it is a lovely (and inexpensive) motel with hand-hewn furniture in the rooms; it is a bookstore featuring practical and meditative volumes about the West; and it is a trading post with some intriguing Native-American jewelry and rugs.

The restaurant serves three meals a day and appears to be as informal as any western motel dining room, except for the fact that you are likely to hear the gurgle of an espresso machine in the background and Bach played to set the mood. The house motto is "Local, Natural, Healthy"; and while it is entirely possible to sit down to a breakfast of bacon and eggs, you can also choose to have those eggs accompanied by smoked local trout, or you can have an omelet made with local cheeses . . . with fresh-squeezed juice to drink.

At lunch and dinner as well as breakfast, the Capitol Reef dining room is a blessing for traveling vegetarians. A few notable meatless menu items include spaghetti with marinara sauce (also available with meat), fettuccine primavera, and plates of steamed, stir-fried, or shish-kebabed vegetables. Beef, chicken, and seafood are always available for vegetable-frowners (that trout, broiled with rosemary, is what we recommend); and desserts include a hot fudge sundae and/or apple pie.

Hires Big H

425 S. 700 E   801-364-4582

Salt Lake City, UT   LD | $

Also at three other locations in SLC

Hires Big H is an eager-to-please fast-food restaurant the likes of which have virtually disappeared everywhere else in America. "If for any reason you are not satisfied with the food, drink, or service, please contact your server or the manager," the menu says. We have not ever considered such a move, because the food, drinks, and service at the Big H have never failed to satisfy. For what it attempts to be and to do, this restaurant is perfect.

The menu is a drive-in bill of fare: a long list of hamburgers including a "New York H" (garnished with grilled onions), a Danish H (with a slice of ham), a Roquefort H, a Pastrami H, and a Big H, which is garnished with lettuce, tomato, special sauce, and cheese. There is even a Harvest H, a patty made entirely of vegetables for meat-frowners. The bun on which Big H burgers are served is gentle-tempered sourdough with a floury top (as opposed to what the combative menu describes as "some preservative-enhanced, wilted crust studded with obnoxious seeds"). Extra-cost options include bacon, grilled onions, a side of pickles, a side of mayonnaise, or the deluxe treatment (lettuce and tomato, if your sandwich of choice doesn't already have them).

Beyond burgers, the Big H menu has a variety of choices that are expertly made. The grilled cheese sandwich is a jim-dandy (and we are real fussbudgets about grilled cheese sandwiches!); the BLT is an unassuming masterpiece; and the "country club" with cranberries is worthy of a tea-room kitchen: white turkey meat with crisp bacon, lettuce, tomato, and cranberry sauce on good toast. Also noteworthy is the grilled lemon chicken sandwich, another dish that is a cut above the drive-in setting in which it is served.

On the side of whatever H hamburger or sandwich suits your fancy, you want French fries or onion rings. Both are available with dipping sauce reminiscent of French dressing; the potatoes can be ordered with a mantle of homemade chili and melted cheese.

To drink, we recommend root beer, which comes in five sizes, from "baby" to "large." Of course, there are root beer floats, milk shakes, and freezes; or you can sip a limeade or a marshmallow-chocolate malt.

Idle Isle

24 S. Main St.   435-734-2468
Brigham City, UT   BLD | $

Every time we visit Idle Isle, we find ourselves astonished and delighted that it still exists. A piece of culinary history that opened for business in 1921, it is the sort of cordial town café once found on Main Streets everywhere. In the twenty-first century, its charm is a rarity. For us, merely walking in the door is enough to lower our blood pressure. Carpeting keeps sound at a pleasant hush and fans spin slowly from the high ceiling; only the occasional whir of the milk shake machine or the hum of an electric lemon squeezer (for lemonade) rises above the chatter of the good citizens who eat here.

You can have a lovely burger and a malt at the marble-and-onyx soda fountain; and there is a slightly more boisterous back room with oilcloth-covered tables where regulars congregate at noon; but the choice seats, at least for us travelers, are in polished wood booths up front, each outfitted with a little ramekin of Idle Isle apricot marmalade for spooning onto the fleecy rolls that come alongside dinner. Before taking your order, a waitress sets down a little card that says, "Your Server Is . . ." with her name written on it, then she guides you through a menu of blue-plate fundamentals, including divinely tender pot roast with lumpy mashed potatoes shaped like a volcano crater to hold gravy, as well as such daily specials as Wednesday braised beef joints, Friday trout, and Saturday prime rib.

Serving sizes are temperate, so you will have room for Idleberry pie—a resonating purple blend of blue, black, and boysenberries—or baked custard pudding, which is simply the tenderest food imaginable. "I'm sorry," says our waitress, Cariann, when she places a jiggly bowl of it before us. "The pudding might still be a little warm. They just took it from the oven." An apology is hardly necessary: balmy, smooth, golden-sweet, this is food fit for the god of comfort.

(Adjacent to the restaurant is a confectionery where Idle Isle chocolates, hand-dipped in the basement, are sold by pound and box.)

Maddox Drive-In

1900 S. Highway 89   801-723-5683
Brigham City, UT   LD | $

Attached to the Maddox Steak House (famous for beef, corn sticks, and water drawn from its own well), the Maddox Drive-In is a survivor of mid-century car culture. The long, covered tramway where you park is festooned with enthusiastic signs apparently meant to stimulate appetites: "We serve only grain-fed beef . . . . We invite you to visit our entire operation." And there is a huge spinning sign high above the restaurant where futuristic letters boast of "Maddox Fine Food."

The hamburgers are indeed fine, but so is the lesser-known drive-in specialty, a chicken basket: fried chicken and French fries piled into a woven plastic trough. To drink with diner meals, the beverage that goes best is Maddox's own unique concoction known as "fresh lime," which tastes something like Sprite doctored with lime juice and extra sugar.

Mom's

10 E. Main St.   435-529-3921
Salina, UT   BLD | $

At the crossroads in the old cowboy town of Salina, Mom's café isn't really all that motherly, but it's been a notable Roadfood stop since long before we hit the road many years ago. In fact, this square brick edifice has been a gathering place for travelers and ranchers for more than seventy years now, and it bears the well-weathered look and seeming permanence of the rock mesas that surround the town.

Mom's offers a full menu, including laudable liver and onions at supper, but we like breakfast best, for that is when the scones are fresh and hot. The scone is a Utah specialty, always on the menu. It is similar to New Mexican sopaipillas and to the Indian fry breads served at roadside stands throughout the Southwest, but generally big enough and weighty enough to be a nice little meal all by itself.

As the sun rises, Mom's fills up with breakfasters for whom the close quarters are an invitation to socialize with one another. Our dining companions one morning include ranch hands with rodeo-trophy belt buckles, Paiute Indians wearing spectacular porcupine-quill hatbands, and a pair of German-speaking tourists with backpacks on their way to hike around Bryce Canyon. The waitress uses hand gestures to explain to the foreigners the difference between "over easy" and "sunny-side up"; the cowboys show the newcomers how to dip their biscuits in the thick, white gravy; and a Native-American coffeehound demonstrates that a squeeze bottle of honey-butter on the table was put there so they could frost their scone.

The German couple takes all the good advice looking a little confused. But finally they beam with joy when their chicken-fried steak arrives. *This* is food they recognize!—the ranch kitchen cook's version of a wiener schnitzel—made perfectly at Mom's, the pounded-tender slab of meat encased in a luscious meltaway crust. At eight in the morning, the two well-fed travelers finally top things off with wide slices of blueberry sour cream pie, then head out the door for a day of hiking.

West Coast

California * Oregon * Washington

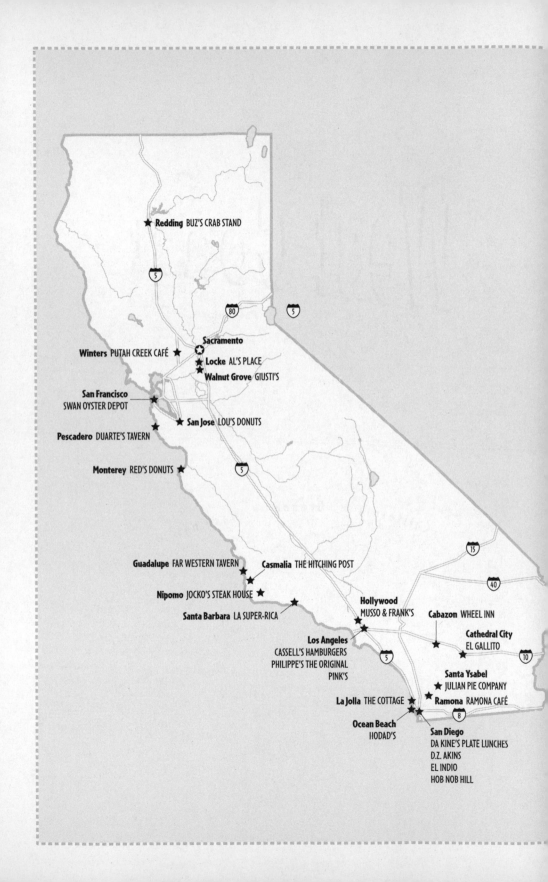

Redding BUZ'S CRAB STAND

Winters PUTAH CREEK CAFÉ

Sacramento

Locke AL'S PLACE

Walnut Grove GIUSTI'S

San Francisco
SWAN OYSTER DEPOT

San Jose LOU'S DONUTS

Pescadero DUARTE'S TAVERN

Monterey RED'S DONUTS

Guadalupe FAR WESTERN TAVERN

Casmalia THE HITCHING POST

Nipomo JOCKO'S STEAK HOUSE

Santa Barbara LA SUPER-RICA

Hollywood
MUSSO & FRANK'S

Cabazon WHEEL INN

Cathedral City
EL GALLITO

Los Angeles
CASSELL'S HAMBURGERS
PHILIPPE'S THE ORIGINAL
PINK'S

Santa Ysabel
JULIAN PIE COMPANY

La Jolla THE COTTAGE

Ramona RAMONA CAFÉ

Ocean Beach
HODAD'S

San Diego
DA KINE'S PLATE LUNCHES
D.Z. AKINS
EL INDIO
HOB NOB HILL

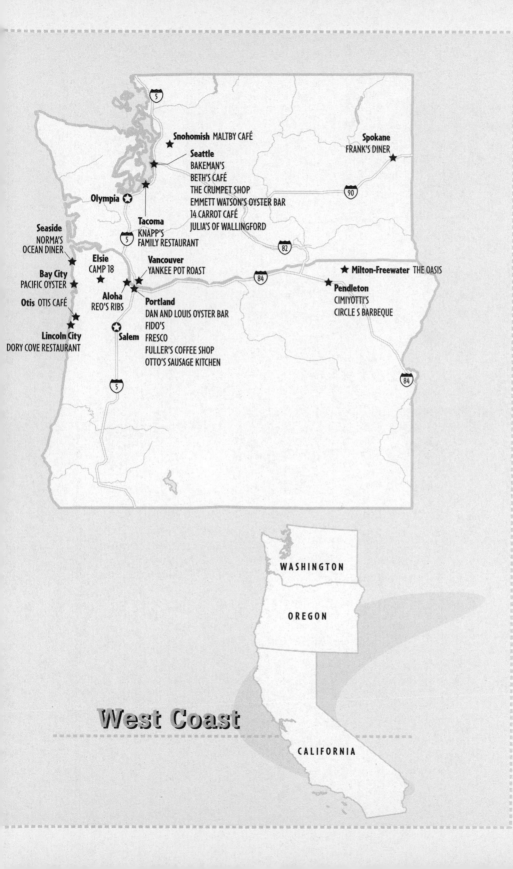

Snohomish MALTBY CAFÉ

Spokane
FRANK'S DINER

Seattle
BAKEMAN'S
BETH'S CAFÉ
THE CRUMPET SHOP
EMMETT WATSON'S OYSTER BAR
14 CARROT CAFÉ
JULIA'S OF WALLINGFORD

Olympia

Tacoma
KNAPP'S
FAMILY RESTAURANT

Seaside
NORMA'S
OCEAN DINER

Elsie
CAMP 18

Vancouver
YANKEE POT ROAST

★ **Milton-Freewater** THE OASIS

Bay City
PACIFIC OYSTER

Aloha
REO'S RIBS

Pendleton
CIMIYOTTI'S
CIRCLE S BARBEQUE

Otis OTIS CAFÉ

Portland
DAN AND LOUIS OYSTER BAR
FIDO'S
FRESCO
FULLER'S COFFEE SHOP
OTTO'S SAUSAGE KITCHEN

Salem

Lincoln City
DORY COVE RESTAURANT

WASHINGTON

OREGON

West Coast

CALIFORNIA

Al's Place

13936 Main St.   916-776-1800
Locke, CA   LD | $$

Al's Place, known to legions of fans by its proper, albeit politically incorrect, name, Al the Wop, is a fantastic destination for travelers in search of culinary color. It is located on the main street of Locke, a forgotten town in the Sacramento Delta, originally built by and for Chinese Californians. Once famous as an anything-goes enclave of vice, Locke is ghostly today, with few Chinese left; but its weathered wood-frame main street remains a magical sight; and in the middle of it is Al's Place, thriving since 1934, when Al Adami, fresh out of prison as a convicted bootlegger, opened up the only non-Chinese restaurant in town. Al had no menu—he asked you how you liked your steak, which was the only thing to eat amid the slot machines and card tables in the Tong Dining Room behind the front-room bar. Legend says that at some point in time, a crop duster came in with jars of peanut butter and marmalade and asked Al for some toast to spread it on. Al liked the idea, and started putting peanut butter and marmalade on every table.

The menu remains simple, now including hamburgers, cheeseburgers, and steak sandwiches in addition to steak. The burgers are juicy ones, served between slices of grilled-crisp Italian bread with lettuce, tomato, onions, pickle, and olives on the side. The steak sandwich is, in fact, not a sandwich, but a sandwich-size steak on a platter accompanied by a second plate of toasted pieces of Italian bread. Horseradish or a little dish of minced garlic is available to spread on the meat.

Proprietor Stephen Gianetti suggested we use the peanut butter and jelly on the bread, although he says some customers actually spread it on their steak!

Buz's Crab Stand

2159 East St.   530-243-2120
Redding, CA   LD | $

Thanks to Roadfooders Karen Meyer and Paul Duggan for clueing us in to Buz's as one of the essential Roadfood experiences of Northern California. They especially recommended cracked Dungeness crab (fresh from November through May), fish and chips, and charbroiled salmon; and they noted that Buz's kitchen is supplied by its own fishing boats out of Eureka on the coast. Calling itself "Redding's own Fisherman's Wharf," Buz's truly is a seafood bonanza, not only a restaurant but a fish market, deli, crab feed caterer, and mail-order source of cooked crab, smoked salmon, and sourdough bread.

In the restaurant, you'll find something on the menu for every kind of seafood fancier (and even charbroiled chicken and chicken nuggets for fishphobes), ranging from the glorious fisherman's stew known as cioppino to fish tacos and salmon burgers (the latter advertised as low-fat and low-cal). When Dungeness crab is coming in fresh from the cold Pacific, that's all we care to know about, but any other time of year, we will gladly plow into one of Buz's umpteen different kinds of fried seafood basket, featuring prawns, oysters, catfish, and calamari (or all possible combinations thereof). In addition, there are seafood wraps, salads, sandwiches, and burritos, and a long list of fish available charbroiled with barbecue sauce, teriyaki sauce, garlic sauce, or lemon butter.

It is especially fun to come to Buz's during Dungeness crab season because the crab is cooked in big outdoor kettles; its sweet aroma, combined with that of the sourdough bread baked throughout the day, makes an irresistible appetizer.

Cassell's Hamburgers

3266 W. 6th St. (near Bernardo St.)   213-480-8668
Los Angeles, CA   L | $

Several places stake a claim for inventing the hamburger, but it is fair to say that its proliferation definitely can be traced to Southern California, where the McDonald Brothers invented the quick-cook/quick-serve system that Ray Kroc bought and then franchised. One can infer from historical accounts that those original, pre-franchise McDonald's hamburgers were nothing special to eat; it was the unique way of cooking and serving them that led to nationwide success. Similarly, Cassell's of Los Angeles has its own way with hamburgers, but they *are* something special. And unlike McDonald's, Cassell's has remained unique. And unlike all assembly-line hamburgers, the one-third and two-third pounders Cassell's serves are utterly delicious.

Proprietor Helen Kim says that Cassell's special goodness is due to their being cooked using a double broiler, meaning the heat hits them from top and bottom, sealing the juices inside a crunchy charred crust. It also helps that the meat is ground fresh daily and the burgers are made to order and customers dress them as desired with the finest condiments, including homemade Thousand Island dressing and mayonnaise, lettuce, tomato, pickles, and onions.

Service is cafeteria-style, and the menu is short and simple. The basic choice is which size you want: big or bigger. We definitely recommend the bigger boy. It can be cooked all the way to medium and still stay succulent in its rosy center. Whichever size you get, it is juicy enough on the inside to make your chin glisten at the first jaw-stretching bite. Hamburgers are served on a large sesame seed–spangled bun unless you choose to pay twenty cents less and get yours bunless. You can add Swiss or American cheese to make a cheeseburger, and available side dishes include steak fries, potato salad (wonderful!), fried zucchini, and onion rings.

The Cottage

7702 Fay Ave.   858-454-8409

La Jolla, CA   BL | $

California abounds in great breakfasts; The Cottage of La Jolla serves some of the best. As you walk in the door, look right. There's the bakery case holding the nut-topped cinnamon rolls, muffins, and buttermilk coffee cake with cinnamon and walnut crumb topping.

The pastries are superb . . . but so are the hot meals. In particular, we recommend Cottage Irish oatmeal, served with a full complement of brown sugar, sliced bananas, raisins, milk, and a dish of sensational sticky-crunchy caramelized walnuts. Also pretty wonderful are meat loaf hash crisped with cottage-fried potatoes and topped with eggs, French toast stuffed with strawberry compote and mascarpone, and "crab Benedict," which is like eggs Benedict, but heaped with pure rock crab instead of Canadian bacon. Even the granola is extra special—dark and toasty, a delightful chew.

Lunch at The Cottage is an opportunity to taste a high-tone version of San Diego's favorite fast food, the fish taco; these are built around grilled mahimahi, dressed with cilantro-avocado sauce, and accompanied by bowls of creamy black beans and chunky papaya relish. The pork and beef chili has a true Southwest pepper zest, and the hamburger is a So-Cal classic, served with an abundance of Cheddar cheese, tomato, lettuce, onion, and mayo.

The Cottage is a casual place: sunlight streaming in the windows, a palm-shaded patio outside, the occasional bird hopping in the open front door to peck at a crumb near the counter. It is located in a small house that was built early in the twentieth century and served as a private home in the days La Jolla was a little-known community of sun-and-surf worshippers. It still exudes end-of-the-earth charm that makes this seaside community so appealing.

Da Kine's Plate Lunches

4120 Mission Blvd. #208   858-274-8494
San Diego, CA   LD | $

Also at 1635 Sweetwater Rd., Suite H, National City, CA (619-477-8494)

Belen Ishii, who owns this unusual lunchroom with her husband, Nelson, told us that Da Kine means "the stuff" in Hawaii's pidgin English. Beyond that, she couldn't really explain the name, except to say that Da Kine is a true and pure Hawaiian phrase. How appropriate, for this oddly situated restaurant (above a Tony Roma's in a pod of stores along Mission Boulevard) strikes us as a true and pure taste of Hawaii.

In other words, it is *not* a romantic or upscale version of Polynesian cuisine; it is what many ordinary people really like to eat. That means very, very large portions of such exotica as kalua pig, which is a supersoft kind of steamed/barbecued pulled pork mixed with faintly pickly cabbage; it means chicken katsu and soy/sesame marinated ribs; it means broth of noodles and green onions; and it means Spam. Hawaiians eat lots of Spam, and you will find it on Da Kine's menu cooked with eggs, sliced into twigs in the saimin soup, and as a big rectangular flap of pinkness atop a tube of sticky rice that is wrapped in seaweed like a jumbo hunk of sushi.

In our experience, many of the meals served at Da Kine's are—how shall we say it?—very luscious, i.e., on the fatty side. The Thursday special of sweet/sour spareribs in a pineapple sauce is a joy, but not for the fatphobe. Similarly, grilled teriyaki chicken is way this side of lean . . . but it sure is delicious. On the other hand, to be fair, Da Kine's fire-grilled mahimahi is a dieter's delight, served with lemon and chopped scallions and twin mounds of rice.

Mrs. Ishii told us that the restaurant's mango cake is "so good it breaks the mouth." It truly is wonderful, although light-years away from the sort of expensive boutique cakes served in swank restaurants. This giant-size pink rectangle, totally enrobed in frosting, is supersweet and uncomplicated. Likewise, the chocolate macadamia cake reminded us of the best cafeteria desserts (but about three sizes larger).

Service is totally without ceremony. You read the menu at the cash register and place your order, then carry it yourself to a table when your number is called. Although the accommodations have all the luxury of a McDonald's and the mall setting is less than romantic, the ambience of the second-story patio is priceless: lots of San Diego sun overhead, and the ocean to the west, beyond some nearby hotels.

Duarte's Tavern

202 Stage Rd.   650-879-0464
Pescadero, CA   BLD | $

Down-home dining, California-style, doesn't get much better than this. There are pork chops served with homemade apple sauce and chunky mashed potatoes; pot roast; beef stew; roast turkey with sage dressing. Seafood is something special, including big servings of Dungeness crab cioppino, calamari, sea scallops, and oysters baked in puddles of garlic butter. Even the house salad—a perfunctory gesture in so many restaurants—is topped with beets, pickled beans, and tomatoes that come directly from Ron Duarte's gardens.

The farmland around Pescadero is thick with the thistle-topped stalks of artichoke plants, and artichokes are a Duarte's specialty. You can get them simply steamed or elaborately stuffed (with fennel sausage), in utterly wonderful omelets at breakfast, or as the foundation of renowned cream of artichoke soup.

To conclude any meal at Duarte's, you want pie made from local olallie berries, rhubarb, apricots, or apples heaped into feather-light crusts that are all the more delicious for being homely rather than symmetrical.

Dining at Duarte's is a joy. It is a vintage small-town tavern that started as a stage stop more than 100 years ago. Today, locals and strangers share mismatched tables in the knotty pine–paneled dining room, which is cozy, crowded, and full of life. Town geezers occupy chairs for hours holding court; babies squall; townsfolk trade gossip; and travelers are made to feel right at home.

D.Z. Akins

6930 Alvarado Rd.   619-265-0281
San Diego, CA   BLD | $$

As often as we've visited San Diego in the last few decades, D.Z. Akins eluded us until recently. But one day while wandering around in search of the KPBS studio at San Diego State University, we walked inside this mammoth deli and found ourselves grinning ear to ear. The air was perfumed with spiced beef and the bakery shelves up front held a spectacular array of ryes, pumpernickels, bagels, hard rolls, and challahs, plus countless macaroons and cookies, all baked right here.

The sandwiches we got were fantastic: hot, fat-striated corned beef radiant with flavor, cut thick and piled between two slices of the best rye we've had in years: soft inside with a nice sour smack and a hard savory crust. Full-flavored roast beef was presented in a poppy seed–spangled hard roll that was also impeccably fresh. And the kosher salami (Vienna brand, of course) packed a garlic wallop.

We liked our sandwiches so much that we returned to D.Z. Akins the next day for breakfast and plowed into a platter of matzoh brei that was nearly as good as the brei Michael makes (and he makes the best), homemade blintzes, and a plate of bagels and lox. Nothing was short of excellent.

This full-service restaurant also features a soda fountain, the menu of which includes sundaes and sodas of all kinds, from a traditional banana split to one called "Prenatal Silliness": Chocolate ice cream and pickles, with your topping of choice!

El Gallito

68820 Grove St.   760-328-7794
Cathedral City, CA   LD | $

Popular, crowded, and straightforward, El Gallito has been serving Mexican food in the Coachella Valley since 1978. It has a broad menu of mostly familiar dishes such as tacos, chiles rellenos, enchiladas, and burritos. They're all quite good, in our experience, but we are especially fond of El Gallito's daily specials that include carnitas (shredded pork) every Thursday, chicken molé (Friday), and menudo (Saturday). The molé is smoky with a pepper zest, cosseting on-the-bone chicken that is ridiculously tender.

We also like El Gallito's chilies. They are California-style, meaning not fire-hot, and they are mighty tasty: either chili colorado, which is bite-size pieces of beef in a peppery red sauce, or chili verde, which is beef cooked with green peppers, onions, and shreds of tomato. The "El Gallito Especial" is a half-and-half plate of both kinds of chili. It is also worth noting that breakfast is available starting at 10 A.M., when the restaurant opens: huevos rancheros, shredded beef and scrambled eggs, and egg burritos with rice and beans.

El Gallito is an extraordinarily clean and tidy place, outfitted in classic Mexican restaurant decor (serapes, sombreros, velvet paintings). It operates according to a lot of rules that are posted throughout the dining room and written in the menu. A sign above the cash register warns, "Cash only." A placard hanging over the dining room notes: "If you have reservations, you are at the wrong place." To discourage unsavory clientele, a sign in the entryway advises: "WE ARE NOT A BAR. Beer/wine is only served to those who dine with us." And on the menu, the management notes that daily specials are in limited supply, so customers who want them should come early; it is further noted that "it is impossible to debone the chicken entirely, so it is possible that you may find a bone in your chicken entree." Finally, be advised that there is a limit of three drinks per customer, and "persons who seem to have been drinking will not be served."

El Indio

3695 India St.   619-299-0333
San Diego, CA   LD | $

El Indio is a quick-service, cafeteria-style taqueria adjacent to Interstate 5. Meals are served on Styrofoam plates with throwaway utensils. There are a few shared seats at a counter and some tables to the side of the order line, but many people choose to eat on the sunny, fenced-in patio across the street. Here, one is serenaded by vehicles passing on the raised highway.

The menu is classic Cal-Mex. An on-premises tortilla press turns out big, warm wheaty ones for burros and chimichangas; there are crunchy, freshly fried, hot corn tortillas; and there are all sorts of combo plates topped with gobs of sour cream. One of the best things to eat is the San Diego specialty, a fish taco. El Indio's version is a hefty meal served in a foil wrapper along with a wedge of lime. When the foil is pulled back, you find a double layer of warm corn tortillas loosely wrapped around a log of crisp-fried cod with a golden crust. The fish is nestled on a bed of ruggedly shredded cabbage, a few tomato shreds, and a faintly peppery pink sauce. Give it a spritz or two from the wedge of lime provided—an ideal complement for the sweet meat of the white fish and its savory crust.

Above the windows where you order your food at El Indio are portraits of fierce Mayan gods, including the god of war, the gods of rain and wind, and the god of Mexican food who, according to this portrait, goes by the name of El Indio. We are not up to date on our Mayan theology; but there is no doubt in our minds that El Indio is indeed the reigning deity of San Diego Mexican food.

Far Western Tavern

899 Guadalupe St.   805-343-2211
Guadalupe, CA   LD | $$

The Far Western Tavern is a place to eat barbecue, California-cowboy style. The dining room features a spectacular suite of hairy brown-and-white cowhide curtains, and meals are served on cowboy-fantasy dishware festooned with little images of brands, spurs, and cows' heads. The wall across from the bar is one sweeping painted mural of ranch life; other displays include a portrait of Will Rogers, a poster that shows how to break a wild pony, an autographed 8 × 10 of Ralph Edwards (from *This Is Your Life*) praising the steaks, and a photograph of the all-women bowling team sponsored by the Tavern along with a display of their trophies.

Specialty of the house is a "bull's-eye" steak (a ribeye) cooked over flaming live-oak wood, served Santa Maria–style, meaning it is sided by firm pinquito beans, French bread, and salsa. The bull's-eye is available at breakfast in a smaller version, served alongside eggs, hash browns, beans, and biscuits.

Even if you can't come to Guadalupe to taste the great steak meals for which this region is known, there are ways to approximate it at home. You can almost exactly duplicate Far Western beans, thanks to Mr. Minetti's daughter, Susan Righetti, who has begun a mail-order business featuring dried local pinquitos along with packets of bean seasoning and salsa (http://www.susieqbrand.com/). All that's needed to complete the picture is some live-oak wood and a pit, a selection of good steaks, French bread, and a passel of friends to enjoy it with. Cowhide drapes in the dining room and plates with pictures of spurs and lassos on them are optional.

Giusti's

14743 Walnut Grove-Thornton Rd.   916-776-1808
Walnut Grove, CA   LD | $$

A weathered roadhouse surrounded by farm fields, Giusti's is a ram-shackle building with a wood-plank porch that squeaks when you walk to the front door. Enter the bar room, spectacularly decorated with well over a thousand farmers' caps hanging overhead like some sort of multi-colored tapestry, their crowns advertising every brand of fertilizer, trac-tor, seed, and tool that makes a country gent feel loyal.

The dining area is at the rear of the drinking area—a linoleum-floor, wood-pancled space with bare tables, where local citizens congregate to eat "the usual." For supper, that means family-style meals of minestrone soup, salad, and a salami plate followed by steak, prime rib, fried chicken, or veal cutlet, accompanied by *vin ordinaire*. Thursday is Italian night, featuring sausage lasagna and linguine with clam sauce. At lunch, you pay $7 for a herb-spangled Italian baked chicken or a dish of fettuccine Alfredo served with a sweet-dressed salad and a glass of wine.

Giusti's offers a taste of robust farm-country California all too often eclipsed by the upwardly and downwardly mobile urban parts of the state.

The Hitching Post

3325 Point Sal Rd.   805-937-6151
Casmalia, CA   D | $$

The Hitching Post's top sirloin is pungent with age, oozing juice, an easy chew; but the filet mignon is even better. Its delicate fibers seem to glow with the flavor of burning wood, and with the smack of a wine vinegar and oil marinade that is applied as the meat cooks. "We've had people throwing one-hundred-dollar bills at us to try to get the recipe for that marinade," proprietor Bill Ostini says of the magic potion developed by his father. "Sometimes I make bottles of it up for local friends. Other than that, all we use is salt, pepper, and garlic. But the real trick is in how the steaks are handled. You've got to know how to cook which steak which way—some are made to be cooked rare, some well done; it de-pends on the marbling, and how much age they have. It takes two to three years to train a cook to do it the right way. Cutting and cooking steaks is practically a lost art."

Steak at The Hitching Post is part of a full dinner, which includes a relish tray with sweet peppers and chile peppers, celery ribs, carrot sticks, and olives, plus shrimp cocktail made with teensy-weensy shrimp, a green head of lettuce, garlic toast, and potatoes, either baked or French-fried.

Ambience is cattle country supreme: a big, dimly lit roadhouse with linoleum floors and red tablecloths, each table supplied with a basket full of cellophane-wrapped saltines. Above the bar, a TV is always playing; the mirror is plastered with decals from NASA, *Voyager,* and the Army Corps of Engineers; a bison head on one wall wears a Buffalo Bills cap. In the dining room, which affords a view of the kitchen, there are mounted deer heads and old black-and-white family photos of young Bill and his brother on hunting and fishing trips with their dad when they were young. The hallway that leads to the restrooms is lined with cattle hides.

Hob Nob Hill

2271 1st Ave.   619-239-8176
San Diego, CA   BLD | $

Every city ought to have a Hob Nob Hill—a comfortable three-meal-a-day coffee shop where the food is homey, the service fast, and the prices low.

At mealtimes, especially breakfast, chances are you will have to wait in line. But the line moves quickly, and once you are seated you are set upon by a team of waitresses who could not move faster if they flew through the aisles—taking orders, filling coffee cups, making sure everyone is happy.

When it's time to order, you are faced with hard choices, for Hob Nob Hill's repertoire is broad, and there isn't a clinker on the menu. There are pecan waffles, pigs in blankets (buttermilk pancakes rolled with ham, sausage, and sour cream), blueberry hotcakes, grilled smoked pork chops, etc.—plus a bakery's worth of coffee cakes, muffins (try carrot), and a not-to-be-missed pecan roll. Even little amenities are special: syrup is served warm; jelly comes in hollowed-out orange halves; coffee is strong and rich.

At dinner, it's meat-and-potatoes time: leg of lamb with sage dressing and mint jelly, chicken and dumplings, roast tom turkey with giblet gravy, corned beef and cabbage, pot roast and buttered noodles every

Sunday. There are turkey croquettes with cranberry sauce, a nursery-nice breast-of-chicken curry, and baked ham with fruit sauce and yams on Thursday. Accompaniments are such comfort-food side dishes as warm apple sauce (homemade, of course), marinated bean salad, and puffy yeast rolls.

Hodad's

5010 Newport Ave.	619-224-4623
Ocean Beach, CA	LD | $

Hodad's motto, on a sign above the cash register: "No Shirt, No Shoes, No Problem!"

Here is the definitive Southern California beachside burger joint, its clientele including true surfers still wet from the ocean, surfer wannabes, counterculture denizens of Newport Avenue, and a large number of foodies who come not because of the colorful ambience but because the hamburgers are terrific. Available in three sizes (mini, single, and double), as cheeseburgers or bacon cheeseburgers, plain or as part of a basket with a pile of French fries, these are amazing pieces of food. Even the "mini" is impressively opulent; a "double"—two patties—is huge beyond belief. The amount of meat is not what's so impressive, although it's quite enough; it's the beautiful, only-in-California way it is dressed. The menu warns that all burgers come with lettuce, tomato, onion, pickle, mayonnaise, mustard, and ketchup "unless you say otherwise"; and this heap of condiments, piled with the beef inside a broad sesame bun, makes for a sandwich that is virtually impossible to fit between upper and lower jaws.

The hamburger is presented partially wrapped in yellow wax paper, which provides a necessary way to raise it from the table and to keep it relatively together as you try to eat it: a joyous package of good food! The French fries in the basket (or available as a side dish with Hodad's short menu of other normal sandwiches) are thick wedges of potato with pleasantly tough skins and creamy insides. To drink there is lemonade, beer and wine, and milk shakes or malts (vanilla, chocolate, strawberry) served in a glass and silver beaker with a straw as well as a spoon. The straw is of little use; these shakes can be ingested only by gulping from the glass or using the spoon.

In terms of local color, Hodad's is a rainbow. Seating includes the front half of a VW minibus; the walls are festooned with vanity license plates from around the nation (as well as local awards given to Hodad's for serving the best hamburger in town); and surfboards are strung overhead in the boisterous dining room. Seating includes hard wooden booths and a counter along the wall with stools. Each booth is outfitted with a cardboard container that once held a six-pack of beer bottles. The half-dozen compartments are now used to store sugar and sweeteners for coffee.

Jocko's Steak House

125 N. Thompson Ave.   805-929-3686
Nipomo, CA   D | $$

We found Jocko's many years ago when we were students at Gary Leffew's bull-riding school north of Santa Barbara. (That's another story . . .) When the week of riding rank bulls was over, cowboys who hadn't broken too many bones and had some jingle in their jeans headed for Nipomo to eat beef at Jocko's on Saturday night.

Nipomo isn't much of a town, but cars from afar crowd around Jocko's on weekends; and even if you've made a reservation (highly recommended), you may have to wait a while for a table. That's fine. Waiting allows time to belly up to the bar and imbibe a colorful roadhouse atmosphere of taxidermized game animal heads on the wall and the good-time shenanigans of California country folk (a whole 'nother breed from those who live in the big cities). Although the steaks are first-class, the experience of dining at Jocko's is absolutely nothing like a meal in one of the high-priced, dress-up steak house chains. Wear your jeans and boots and Stetson or farm cap and you'll be right at home.

Meat is the only thing to eat. (One Roadfooder wrote to us suggesting that this must be the place where bad vegetarians go when they die, for it truly is a kind of beef-frowners' hell, where smells of roasting meat permeate the air.) Shockingly thick steaks and hefty lamb chops and pork chops are cooked on an open pit over oak wood and served Santa Maria–style, meaning accompanied by tiny pinquito beans and salsa. It's a great, filling meal; and even if you get a relatively modest-size filet mignon, chances are you'll be taking meat home in a doggie bag for lunch the next day.

Julian Pie Company

21976 Highway 79   760-765-2400
Santa Ysabel, CA $

Apple pie is the specialty of the Julian Pie Company, a sweet oasis at the western edge of the desert. Merely walking into the big modern building is an olfactory joy—the air is thick with the aroma of cooked apples, cinnamon, and hot crust. You can watch the pies being made behind the counter; you can buy whole pies to take home; or you can get a single slice and a cup of coffee and find a seat at the counter and indulge.

Varieties of apple pie in the Julian repertoire include Dutch apple with a crumb top, boysenberry apple crumb, natural strawberry apple, and apple rhubarb. Also on the regular menu are peach, peach melba, blackberry, and pecan. Basic apple pie with a pastry top is the classic, and we can't think of a better pie anywhere. Its crust is flaky, and the insides powerfully fruity/sweet. When you choose to dine here, you have the option of getting it à la mode, which is nice . . . but unnecessary.

While not a full-service restaurant by any means, this bakery does have a few other excellent food items worth knowing about. One unusual snack is pie crust—two bite-size, heart-shaped pieces of crust that are baked in a veil of cinnamon sugar to become irresistibly delicious cookies that fall into flakes as you bite. The other handsome things in the glass display cases are donuts. They are plump cider donuts enrobed in either cinnamon sugar, chocolate, or supersweet (and super-good!) maple frosting.

La Super-Rica

622 N. Milpas St.   805-963-4940
Santa Barbara, CA   LD | $

La Super-Rica is barely a restaurant. It is a taco stand where service is do-it-yourself and customers are expected to clean their own tables when they're finished eating. All plates and utensils are disposable, and seating is at wobbly tables on a semi–al fresco patio. Since Isidoro Gonzalez opened for business in 1980, this extremely modest eatery has built a reputation as source for some of the very best Mexican food anywhere in the USA.

Tacos cost between $2 and $5 each, and the roster includes basic beef, beef with green chile and cheese, and a "chorizo especial" of spicy sausage, melted cheese, and tomato. We are especially fond of the taco adobado (grilled pork) and the frijol Super-Rica (chorizo and pinto beans with bacon and chile). In addition to tacos, La Super-Rica makes some sensational tamales, and beverages of choice include *horchata* (sweet rice milk), hibiscus, and Mexican beer. Each of the three kinds of salsa is excellent: chunky tomato, spicy red chile, and even spicier green chile.

Expect to wait in line at mealtime. The line is actually a good thing. La Super-Rica has no signs outside, so the crowd of people you see on North Milpas Street will let you know you have arrived.

Lou's Donuts

387 Delmas   408-295-5887

San Jose, CA $

For the discovery of Lou's, we thank a Roadfood correspondent who identified herself only as Nancy. Nancy said that she and her husband go to Stan's in Santa Clara for raised donuts and to Lou's in San Jose for cake donuts. The original Lou's goes back to 1955, and the current location, also known as Lou's Living Donut Museum, was established by the Chaviras family (who worked for Lou many years) in 1995.

Lou's donuts are simple, well sized, and weighty enough to be great dunkers, but good to eat even without coffee. You can watch them being made, by hand, through the window on Auzerais Avenue; and when you walk into the shop in the morning, the sweet-cake aroma is profoundly appetizing. To have a Lou's donut while it is still warm is an education in bliss.

Raised donuts are available and they are good, but it is the cake donuts that Lou's does best. They come glazed with vanilla, chocolate, or maple; and depending on the whim of the bakers, there are chocolate ones with vanilla glaze, blueberry cakes, and in the autumn, apple and pumpkin donuts. If you have your heart set on a particular kind of donut, we suggest arriving early. Lou's opens at six and closes early in the afternoon; by late morning, favorite flavors may be gone.

Musso & Frank's

6667 Hollywood Blvd.   213-467-7788
Hollywood, CA   LD | $

When Musso and Frank opened for business in 1919, Hollywood was young and fresh and Hollywood Boulevard was a magic address. The boulevard went to honkytonk hell in a handbasket and is now trying to rebirth itself with entertainment complexes and shopping malls competing for attention with cheap souvenirs and hookers' wig shops, but the moment you step inside Hollywood's oldest restaurant, the battle of the lifestyles is left behind.

In fact, now that meat and potatoes have enjoyed a well-deserved renaissance, this vintage eatery almost seems trendy. The menu is printed every day, but Musso's is known for dowdy kinds of meals: flannel cakes (for lunch, named because they are flannel-thin and soft), Welsh rarebit, chicken pot pie on Thursday, classic corned beef and cabbage every Tuesday, lamb shanks, baked ham, chiffonade salads.

There are so many things we love to eat from this kitchen's extensive repertoire, but pay special attention, please, to the potatoes. Ten different kinds are listed, from mashed and boiled to lyonnaise and candied sweet. Steaks and chops, cooked on an open broiler where those sitting at the counter can watch—are grand. From the dessert list, note bread and butter pudding, and its deluxe variant, diplomat pudding—topped with strawberries.

Many adventurous gourmets of our acquaintance do not understand the appeal of Musso and Frank's. They compliment its antique Tudor decor and comfortable red leather booths but complain that the food is ordinary. Yes, indeed! It is some of the tastiest ordinary food anywhere.

Philippe's the Original

1001 N. Alameda St.   213-628-3781
Los Angeles, CA   BLD | $

Philippe's (say Phil-EE-peez) claims to have invented the French dip sandwich. The story is that a carver accidentally dropped a sliced roll in beef gravy and the customer was in too much of a hurry to wait for another roll to be cut and more beef to be sliced, so he took the sandwich "wet." Today Philippe's makes French dips from beef, pork, lamb, ham, and turkey. Beef is the standard, available single-dipped or, for serious juice-lovers, double-dipped.

Philippe's moved from its original location in 1951 when the freeway was built, but the "new" location is as comfortable as an old shoe, and still features cafeteria-style service. The floors are strewn with sawdust, the chest-high tables are communal, and coffee has now gone all the way up to nine cents a cup. The French dip sandwiches are delicious as delivered at the counter, but connoisseurs know to slather them with plenty of Philippe's roaring-hot mustard (available for sale in jars by the cash register). The menu also lists such lunchroom fare as chili and stew and a soup every day; and you can still come to this old joint to eat pickled spiced eggs, which are hard-boiled and displayed at the carving counter in glass jars of pink beet juice.

We love Philippe's for its superb people-watching opportunities. Like a through-the-looking-glass Spago, this downtown institution is where you can see only-in-Los-Angeles characters, but not necessarily of the *People* magazine ilk. Philippe's regulars include municipal employees from the nearby post office and court house, as well as Santa Anita touts who frequent the bank of old wooden phone booths, racing forms in hand. "We got the Rodney King jurors on a few occasions," recalled proprietor John Binder several years ago. "They came during lunch hour and we sequestered them in an upstairs dining room. Let me tell you, though, you wouldn't want to be judged by them. They had real attitudes. They always demanded extra cups of gravy. I said, 'You can't talk to me. You want more gravy, tell your bailiff.' "

Pink's

709 N. LaBrea Blvd.   323-931-4223
Los Angeles, CA   LD | $

The thing to eat at Pink's is a hot dog—an all-beef dog in taut natural casing that is nabbed in a spongy bun, then topped with mustard, raw onions, and a spill of Day-Glo orange no-bean chili that was originally invented by founders Paul and Betty Pink. Service is lightning-fast (under a minute, once your order is placed), and the place to dine is standing on the adjoining sidewalk or strolling along Melrose Avenue.

Tube steaks with chili have made Pink's a preferred dive for decades, but the menu lists lesser-known breeds of pup worth eating, too: the Polish pastrami Swiss cheese dog, the Guadalajara dog piled with taco top-pings, a burrito dog (that's two, wrapped in a tortilla), and giant foot-long jalapeño dogs. There are even hamburgers, and some Pink's fans could not dine here without an order of onion rings.

For dessert, there is cake; but Pink's connoisseurs avail themselves of the on-premises candy machine and top things off with a couple of Atomic Fireballs.

Putah Creek Café

1 Main St.   530-795-2682
Winters, CA   BL daily; D Thurs-Sat | $

Offspring of the fancier Buckhorn Steak and Roadhouse across the street, the Putah Creek Café is the town gathering place for locals and a destination diner for bicyclists from Davis and breakfast fans all the way to wine country.

Oatmeal is the old-fashioned kind, long-cooked and coarse-cut, served with a dish of brown sugar and (optionally) raisins and locally grown walnuts. You can get a nice chicken-fried steak with a hunky bis-cuit or warm bread pudding with espresso sauce, but the breakfast we like best is known as the Putah Creek Scramble. It is a version of what Tex-Mex cooks know as *migas*—eggs scrambled with a corn tortilla, cheese, chiles, and crumbled chorizo sausage. The shreds of tortilla are mostly softened as they cook and become little earthy flavor cushions for the chiles and chorizo; and the parts of tortilla that get sizzled crisp on the griddle serve as a high-contrast corn crunch among the creamy eggs.

The lunch menu is broad. In particular we recommend the sirloin beef sandwich: delicious slices from a dry-rub-seasoned and slow-smoked tri-tip piled into a bun with sweet grilled onions.

And don't walk away without at least one apricot bar. They are made by manager Janet Valadez from locally grown fruit.

Ramona Café

628 Main St.   760-789-8656
Ramona, CA   BLD | $

Looking for a big breakfast? We suggest a meal called "The Kitchen Sink" at the Ramona Café. It is a ceramic skillet filled with about a pound of fried potatoes plus bacon, ham, mushrooms, tomatoes, onions, peppers, garlic, sausage-dotted gravy, and two kinds of cheese, topped with a pair of eggs cooked as you like them and accompanied by a square biscuit. The biscuit is unusual in that it is cut from a broad biscuit sheet rather than baked individually. If you want a meal that is a little less complicated, but equally calorific, consider "The Belly Buster": corned beef hash and fried potatoes topped with three eggs and sided by a biscuit. Even simpler is the cinnamon roll—a half-pound circle of hot, sweet pastry swirled with thick veins of cinnamon sugar and accompanied by two paper cups full of butter. Not all things served at this town café are huge, but we guarantee that no one walks away hungry.

In addition to omelets of all kinds, breakfast options include an array of "Home Fry Specials," which are broad hills of good fried potatoes topped with any four ingredients from a long list that includes ham and bacon, taco meat and sausage, chiles, peppers, four different kinds of cheese, sausage gravy, and garlic. If you really like garlic, check out the "Gilroy Omelet" (named for the California town that has proclaimed itself the garlic capital of the world): ham, bacon, mushrooms, Cheddar and jack cheese, plus lots of garlic.

Ramona Café also happens to be a fine lunch place. There are cheeseburgers, hot meat loaf sandwiches, turkey pot pie, and fried chicken that is crusted with breading made from the café's breakfast biscuits. The list of pies is a long one, including apple and rhubarb and chocolate peanut butter pie that we once had as dessert for breakfast before a long drive inland, where good eats grow scarce.

The café has been here since the mid-1920s (originally as El Patio, open 24 hours); and it has a comfy Roadfood feel about it: two broad rooms decorated with personal airplane memorabilia from the owner, who is an flying fanatic. Waitresses are swift and friendly, and there is a nice outdoor seating area on the sidewalk where you can watch traffic drive past on Route 79. According to the menu, this was a favorite hamburger stop for both John Wayne and Roy Rogers on their way to and from the California desert.

Red's Donuts, Inc.

433 Alvarado St.   831-372-9761
Monterey, CA $

Monterey has dozens of linen-tablecloth restaurants, many of which are probably very good; but the first place we hit when we come to town is

Red's; and when we think of what's great to eat in the old seaside village, we don't think of rack of lamb or exotic seafood. We think of donuts— Red's donuts. Red's makes all kinds: raised and glazed, crumb-coated, plain and chocolate cake donuts, donuts frosted with maple or chocolate, and also big soft cinnamon rolls. The cake donuts are wonderful, with a crunch to their crust and an inside that is just sweet enough for a sugar glaze to complement with high style. And the chocolate cake donut is devil's-food-delightful.

We'll go anywhere to eat a good donut, but if it hadn't been for Roadfood correspondent Sadie Stein, we might never have known to taste the best thing Red's makes, which is *not* a donut. It is a maple bar, a.k.a. long john, with a thick blanket of maple frosting. We can describe it no better than Sadie did: "It's sweet, especially when you reach the frosting's thick epicenter, but unspeakably delish!"

Red's is a real old-fashioned donut shop, with a counter well situated for multiple cups of coffee and a morning of dunking and conversation. There is a newer branch in Seaside, but the original, which pastry-pro Sadie recommended as "a paradigm of its kind," is definitely the place with old-California charm.

Swan Oyster Depot

1517 Polk St.   415-673-1101
San Francisco, CA   L | $$

How thrilled we were back in the early 1980s to have the opportunity to present M.F.K. Fisher a copy of an earlier edition of this book. The first thing she did was to turn to the listings in California, look under "S," and tell us that she liked it! Her logic? We had included her beloved Swan Oyster Depot.

We, too, love the Swan Oyster Depot, although it can be nearly as frustrating as it is satisfying. Its problem is its charm: dining facilities consist of nothing more than a twenty-seat marble counter. But what fun it is to join the merry chitchat that never ends among the Sancimino family (proprietors since 1946) and their happy customers. Although the broad front window displays a wide array of sparkling local seafood to take home and cook, the eat-here menu is pretty much limited to raw or steamed fare: oysters on the half shell, cracked Dungeness crab, prawn or lobster salad, smoked trout and salmon, all accompanied by sourdough bread and washed down with Anchor Steam beer. About the only complicated cooking goes into the chowder, a buttery-creamy brew that is labeled Boston-style but is in fact—like everything else you can eat here—exemplary of the Pacific Northwest.

Wheel Inn

I-10	909-849-7012
Cabazon, CA	BLD | $

Open twenty-four hours, complemented by full-size, walk-in statues of a *Tyrannosaurus rex* and a brontosaur out back, with a dozen kinds of pie on *the front cover* of the menu, serving truck drivers, travelers, and kitsch connoisseurs, Wheel Inn is *the* Great American Truck Stop. It's hard to spot from the highway nowadays because it is partially hidden by a newer Burger King and a Denny's, but you can't miss those prehistoric creatures looming up into the sky out back. The dinos are in beautiful condition, their concrete toenails well "manicured," and they attract a lot of attention from tourists. The stairs into the brontosaur (through a door in the tail) lead to a gift shop with prehistoric-themed souvenirs; and there are additional gimcracks (toy rubber dinosaurs) for sale outside under its belly. The dinos were sculpted just after Wheel Inn opened as a counter and two tables in 1964.

It's a bigger place now, although not huge by truck-stop standards. In the mini-mart adjacent to the restaurant, travelers can buy candies, smokes, and sundries or have their photos taken in an instant-picture booth; and the knotty-pine walls of the café are arrayed with merchandise for sale: fancy cowboy-style belt buckles, novelty clocks, scenic handmade oil paintings (some on velvet). There is a short counter facing the pie case, and leatherette-upholstered booths are outfitted with Formica on which the wood-grain pattern has been worn out in places by decades of heavy plates and diners' elbows.

Pie is the specialty of the house; and Marie Kothera, the incongruously elegant Czech-accented hostess, proudly boasted that the pies are made according to recipes created by the lady who started the place. They are authentic truck-stop pies—not elegant or fancy, but satisfying in a big, sweet sort of way. We liked the banana cream filling; the apple pie is a sturdy classic; and fresh strawberry is made with real, firm berries.

Marie pointed into the kitchen pass-through to show her husband, Karel, hard at work. The two of them bought the truck stop back in

1992; and while they have kept its rugged roadside character, most of the food you will eat here is several notches higher than common gearjammer fare. Sing hallelujah, the turkey in the hot turkey sandwich is real meat from a roasted bird (not from a "turkey loaf"), and it is accompanied by mashed potatoes actually made from potatoes (not dehydrated potato flakes). French fries to accompany hamburgers or other sandwiches are cut here, served hot and salty, just oily enough to make perfect sense in this roadside setting.

The menu is wide-ranging, from homemade biscuits and sausage gravy or chicken-fried steak and eggs for breakfast to suppers of sirloin steak, prime rib au jus, and the "trucker's special" of three-fourths pound of ground beef topped with gravy. We enjoy the Dino burger, which is two quarter-pound patties on a whole-wheat sesame bun with tomato slices, lettuce, pickle, a small cup of Thousand Island dressing, and (optionally) raw or grilled slices of onion.

The beverage most customers prefer is coffee, which is served in a bottomless cup; but if you want a regional treat here at the edge of the Coachella Valley, order a date milk shake. It's supercharged with shreds of locally grown dates.

Oregon

Camp 18

Highway 26   503-755-1818
Elsie, OR   BLD | $$

A log cabin building the size of a train terminal, Camp 18 features a main room supported by what the management believes to be the largest known ridgepole in the United States: 25 tons and 5,000 board-feet of lumber. On the walls are massive lumbering saws and old photographs of lumberjacks at work; deep-cushioned couches surround a walk-in fireplace; even many of the customers look like outdoors types, dressed in jeans and flannel. The air smells of cut wood and flapjacks.

This is a theme restaurant, and the stage effects work. More important, the food delivers on the promise of the mise-en-scène. The kitchen's specialty is brawny Northwest cuisine, including family-style dinners of meat and potatoes or chicken and dumplings, big hamburgers and sandwiches for lunch, and proverbial lumberjack breakfasts.

You can order griddle cakes (here known as "flatcars") and blueberries, waffles ("corks") with slab ham and eggs, or four-egg omelets ("bunkhouse" style) served with chunky, well-oiled fried potatoes and big powdery biscuits with melting butter shoved inside. We especially enjoyed one breakfast of pan-fried razor clams, a regional specialty that is quite popular in lunch counters as well as deluxe restaurants. The clams were huge, crunchy, sweet, and relatively tender, accompanied by spuds, eggs, and biscuits. The Camp 18 cinnamon roll is ridiculously large, covering most of a normal-size dinner plate.

You will have no trouble spotting this place as you travel along Highway 26. It is surrounded for hundreds of yards by heavy tree-cutting equipment. It looks like it might be a lumber camp or, on closer inspection, a lumbering museum.

Cimmiyotti's

137 S. Main   541-276-4314

Pendleton, OR   D | $$

Cimmiyotti's has been Pendleton's favorite steak house since 1959. Dark and clubby, with red-flocked wallpaper and a long mirrored bar underneath crystal chandeliers, it is a civilized restaurant, but not snooty. It is deluxe in ways reminiscent of many years ago, when beefsteak was the undisputed king of the American dinner menu and Italian food with zesty red sauce was a little bit exotic. The affluent ambience is laced with heaps of local color, including pictures on the wall of famous chiefs of local tribes, rodeo champions, and one stern-looking mounted judge. Cimmiyotti's menu is bound in thick leather, hand-tooled by a nearby saddle maker. A bulletin board for customers' business cards features someone offering the services of a quarterhorse stud, a slaughterhouse that takes the worry out of dead animal disposal, and an enthusiastic plea to cattle ranchers to consider raising "the other red meat," ostrich.

Cimmiyotti's steaks are listed on the menu under a heading that reads, "From the Feed Lot." There are New York strips and tenderloins, filets mignon, chopped steaks and hamburgers, and teriyaki steaks. The specialty is ribeye, a beef-lover's cut with character that requires a good chew, as opposed to the plush, fork-tender steaks served in big-city steak houses. Naturally, potato is served with steak; ordered baked, it comes to the table accompanied by a three-bowl silver caddy holding chives, sour cream, and an immense globe of butter.

Curiosity demanded we try Cimmiyotti's Italian specialties, which are Americanized versions of Old Country food. Soft white spaghetti noodles are topped with oregano-flavored red sauce and shreds of Parmesan cheese. Lasagna is more complicated because it's got a bit of crunch (onions) and spice (sausage) and is made with three cheeses. Italian specialties—which also include cannelloni, manicotti, ravioli, and fettuccine Alfredo—come with glistening logs of gentle-flavored garlic bread.

Circle S Barbeque

210 S.E. 5th St.   541-276-9637
Pendleton, OR   BLD | $

The Circle S is an all-purpose, three-meal-a-day barbecue restaurant in eastern Oregon. And even the non-barbecued food is worth a whirl. We love the chicken-fried steak with gravy that is available at breakfast (also at lunch); pancakes are rib-sticking, and you can get German sausage as a breakfast meat alongside your hash browns and/or biscuits and gravy. At lunch, you can take your pick of hamburgers or buffalo burgers, as well as a full roster of hot meals and cold sandwiches.

Ah, but barbecue demands attention! Prepared in a cooker over apple and cherry wood, each kind of meat is flavored with the tang of smoke but still retains its own character. We especially like chicken, which glistens like polished mahogany, its skin as crisp as Peking duck, so fragile that you can hear it crackle when you ease a knife down through it, then watch the juices flow. The meat inside is moist and hugely flavorful. Barbecued beef isn't nearly as pretty, but the flat slices have a smoke flavor that is complemented by the dark red sauce that comes alongside. You can also get barbecued sausage, which is soft and porky, loaded with garlic that tends to overpower the taste of smoke. And there are spareribs, a royal mess to eat.

The Circle S is where we discovered red beer. "It's the best for hangovers," our waitress explained. "The guy that invented red beer wanted another drink but knew he ought to have tomato juice." Throughout much of the West, red beer is made by mixing beer and tomato juice (in varying ratios)—a sort of frontier Bloody Mary (but without the celery stalk). Our waitress said that she preferred to make her red beer with V-8. After four days at the Pendleton Round-Up some years ago, we developed a liking for the odd, salmon-colored beverage. It tastes rather healthful.

People drink red beer with breakfast, lunch, and dinner at the Circle S, which is a friendly town café loaded with western decor, including farrier's tools, vintage saddles, and antique farm implements. During the annual roundup in September, it is mobbed; every other time of year, it is merely very crowded.

Dan and Louis Oyster Bar

208 S.W. Ankeny St.	503-227-5906
Portland, OR	LD | $$

Warm milk, melted butter, and lots of briny oysters: this is Dan and Louis's oyster stew, the best dish in the house, and one of the unaffected seafood specialties of the Northwest. According to the menu, it was invented by Louis Wachsmuth long ago on a cold winter day. Its oysters are from the restaurant's own beds; and while they are not extraordinarily delicious on the half shell, they have just the right flavor to give this stew panache. It is bracing food, an unimprovable combination of tastes. We recommend ordering it with a double dose of oysters for extra marine snap; otherwise, it might seem too nursery-like.

Beyond stew, Dan and Louis sells plenty of raw oysters ("Eat 'em alive," says the menu), crab and shrimp cocktail with Thousand Island dressing or red sauce, pan-fried or deep-fried oysters, buttery stews of crab and shrimp, fish and chips, and a wonderfully dowdy "creamed crab" on toast in winter months.

The restaurant's decor is eye-popping: handsome wood-paneled walls arrayed floor to ceiling with an inexhaustible accumulation of nautical memorabilia.

Dory Cove Restaurant

5819 Logan Rd. (by Road's End Park)	541-994-5180
Lincoln City, OR	LD | $$

Dory Cove is mostly a seafood restaurant, with such dishes as the multi-fish Captain's Plate and a fried shrimp and scallop dinner topping the menu. The Dungeness crab salad is exemplary; and while we've always come for creamy-thick clam chowder followed by crisp-fried shellfish with toasted garlic bread on the side, we are tempted to try a broad range of items that have been added to the menu in recent years, including sautés of crab, scallops, or prawns (or any combination thereof) with vegetables in garlic butter and wine.

Many locals come to Dory Cove not for seafood but to eat meat. The hamburger is a beauty, available topped with cheese and/or bacon; and the steaks are the best for miles around.

For dessert, there's pie, of which nearly a dozen kinds are made every day, most of them available as a "mini pie," sized for two. The varieties include chiffons, meringues, creams, and a substantial sour cream raisin. They are big, gooey things, not elegant but mighty satisfying.

Fido's

Corner of S.W. Taylor St. and Park Ave.   503-740-9043
Portland, OR   LD | $

It was only recently that we recognized the elevated wiener-consciousness of Portland. Along with Otto's Sausage Kitchen (page 544), Fido's is why. This tiny street-corner trailer serves not only excellent all-beef franks, but also German wieners, garlicky kielbasas, andouilles, and red-hot Louisiana sausages. The muscular tube steaks are steamed, then grilled to crusty perfection and inserted in buttered, grilled potato rolls or bigger stadium rolls. The all-beef kosher franks have real snap to their casing, and the German sausage—available in a normal 10-inch size and also a foot-and-a-half version—fairly erupts with flavor.

You can have your frank topped with chili—meaty or vegetarian, with grilled onions, or with Oregon-made Tillamook Cheddar cheese, and on the side there's macaroni salad, German potato salad, and cole slaw. As for condiments, that's up to you. A vast table of mustards, ketchups, sauces, and relishes, plus salts and peppers, is available for customers to apply themselves.

Dining facilities consist of a few stools just outside the tiny trailer. If it's a pleasant day in Portland, you can feast standing on the sidewalk, and if it's raining, a small awning provides shelter for a handful of hot dog–eaters. Many cities have street-corner hot dog vendors, and we admit to having a soft spot for such casual facilities. But Fido's is extra special, partly for the goodness of its franks, but also because the place itself is so shipshape and eager to please. Proprietors David Richland and Mary Williams really want customers to savor their hot dogs . . . a wish that is fulfilled every day here in downtown Portland.

Fresco

2387 N.W. Thurman St.   503-243-3247
Portland, OR   BL | $

We found Fresco while on a mission to explore Oregon's hazelnut crop. Someone told us about the kitchen's hot ten-grain cereal, available with all sorts of sugars, milks, and yogurts as well as with hazelnuts and bananas. The latter combo is magnificent, the hazelnuts offering a toasty richness to the cereal.

What ensures Fresco's place on our Breakfast Honor Roll is waffles. They are baked in the old-style irons from pre-Belgian days, meaning they are thin and crunchy and have a small tread pattern that holds infinite droplets of syrup and plenty of melted butter. Listed on the menu as an "oat waffle," it has a bright sourdough tang and an earthy, satisfying flavor, and it remained crisp even under a pitcherful of syrup. We ordered only one, but the menu lists a stack of two ($7.95), and while ours came garnished with a few apple slivers, it is also possible to get one with a heap of fresh fruit, yogurt, and/or whipped cream.

All sorts of other breakfasts are available, familiar and fringe: steam-scrambled eggs, toasted bagels, a plate of salmon with all the fixin's, house-made granola, and the Forest Park Breakfast, which is toast, bran muffin, or scone served with a large smoothie and a cup of coffee. We returned a second day for one item titled "Complicated Potatoes." That's roasted redskins topped with vegetables and melted cheese.

Fuller's Coffee Shop

136 N.W. 9th Ave.   503-222-5608
Portland, OR   BL (closed Mon) | $

Off the tourist path and loved by locals, Fuller's is not only prime Portland; it is a taste of the sort of high-quality urban hash house now vanished from most American cities.

"This is a diner where they know how to fry bacon!" a veteran customer sitting at the counter declared. Yes, indeed. An order of bacon here is four medium-thick ribbons that are crisp but retain enough pliability so they don't break at first bite. And the hash browns are a short-order delight, fried so they are a mix of golden crust and soft, shreds of buttery potato. The pancakes are good, too, and the cinnamon roll, baked fresh each day, is yeasty and tender.

Our favorite thing at Fuller's is the bread. It's not artisan bread; it's not fancy at all. You get white or whole wheat. These slices are simple and perfect, especially when toasted and buttered and accompanying a big, well-rounded breakfast. Jelly and marmalade are set out in ramekins along the counter.

Lunch consists of such blue-plate specials as hot beef and gravy (on the good bread) with mashed potatoes and a corned beef sloppy joe. There is always interesting seafood: salmon steaks in season, batter-dipped fish and chips, fresh-fried oysters, and big, slightly scary (but easy to eat) egg-battered, fried razor clams with French fries and cole slaw.

Norma's Ocean Diner

20 N. Columbia St.   503-738-4331
Seaside, OR   LD | $$

We knew we were going to like Norma's as soon as we walked in and saw the chalkboard near the pass-through window to the kitchen. Here are listed all the fresh seafoods available along with a notation of where they came from: Oregon coast salmon, steamer clams and oysters from Willipa Bay, halibut from Alaska, and local petrale sole. Even the featured wine is Oregonian: Duck Pond Merlot.

The waitress congratulated us on our choice of petrale sole mid-April: "Oooo, it's in season right now," she said. And it was wonderful: delicate-flavored, buttery-rich, ocean-sweet. Nor could we resist Dungeness crab, which is available here in all sorts of ways. We chose the "Louis" presentation, which turned out to be about a dozen big, pearly hunks of white meat arrayed atop a pile of lettuce with all the proper garnishes, plus garlic toast made from fresh-baked bread, and a ramekin of excellent house-made Thousand Island dressing.

People at a nearby table were all eating fish and chips. The menu lists cod, salmon, halibut, and even albacore available as the fish part of the equation. We asked our dining-room neighbors how they liked it. Between bites, they were able to exclaim that it was the best fish and chips they had eaten anywhere, anytime.

Otis Café

Highway 18   541-994-2813

Otis, OR   BL | $

On the way to Lincoln City or Neskowin on the coast, look for the eat-shack with the big arrow on the roof pointing to its name: Otis Café. This car-friendly café is a fantastic stop for those of liberal appetite. As one Roadfood.com user wrote to us a while ago, "I always stop in Otis because the café packs a wallop. It has a few booths and a six-stool counter and a couple of tables, but go early and have breakfast with the fishermen and you won't have to wait for a table."

For sure, breakfast at dawn is the great meal of the day: eggs as you like them accompanied by hash browns blanketed with melted cheese. There are sourdough pancakes, cinnamon rolls the size of Oregon, and whole-wheat black molasses bread to accompany any meal.

As for lunch, we've sampled only a couple of sandwiches, both memorable: a two-fisted BLT made with flavorful slices of beefsteak tomato as well as an added layer of cheese, and a big, messy, juicy, fall-apart cheeseburger, served on a hefty bun with spicy mustard. For dessert: strawberry-rhubarb pie.

Otto's Sausage Kitchen

4138 S.E. Woodstock St.   503-771-6714

Portland, OR   L | $

The grandchildren of Otto Eichetopf, who opened this neighborhood meat market in 1927, maintain Otto's as a beacon of Old World sausage-making. Whether you come for an ordinary hot dog (which is far from ordinary) or extra-large sausages made from chicken or pork, you might just find yourself amazed, as we do, by how much better these fresh, homemade tube steaks taste than factory-made ones from the supermarket that we have learned to accept as normal.

There is nothing whiz-bang about the flavorings put into the bratwurst, the smoked sausages, the bangers, or the Swedish potato sausages; the beauty of the links, many of which are grilled al fresco until crisp-skinned, is that you taste the meat of which they are made. Spices are used to accent, not overwhelm, the primary ingredient. Served in ordinary hot dog buns with dill pickle relish, white onions, mustard, of course, and/or tangy sauerkraut, Otto's specialties come with a side of four-star potato salad . . . and a choice from among more than two dozen imported German beers and several dozen other beers from around the world and the Pacific Northwest.

Otto's appeal has a lot to do with its homey ambience and its setting on Woodstock Boulevard, a neighborhood of family-owned shops that make street-strolling one of Portland's pleasures.

The Oasis

85698 Highway 399   541-938-4776
Milton-Freewater, OR   BLD | $$

A short detour off the main road at the Washington State line leads to the Oasis, a sprawling roadhouse that seems to have expanded room by room over the last seven decades. It is ramshackle and rugged, a favorite destination for locals in search of meat and potatoes served with maximum cowboy atmosphere.

Sirloin steaks come branded with a neat field of crosshatch char marks on their surface. You will not mistake them for thirty-dollar prime steaks. These are cuts of beef with some chaw to them, available in all cuts and sizes. If you let the kitchen know you are up for a challenge, they will cook you a four-and-one-half-pound sirloin; if you eat it and all its trimmings in an hour, you get it free.

We like lunch at the Oasis, when we can get a hot beef sandwich made from slices of prime rib. The meat is piled atop slices of velvety white bread that seem able to absorb ten times their weight in gravy. The only problem with the sliced beef sandwich is the potatoes. Naturally, you want them mashed, preferably crater-shaped to hold extra gravy; but these mashed potatoes were pitifully powdery, no match for the meat. A better choice in spuds would be Oasis French fries, which are crusty gold with good potato flavor; and the best choice is hash browns, which are a heap of shreds and chunks of potato laced with onions. The hash browns are even more wonderful when juices from a nearby steak seep their way in.

Many customers who come from afar to dine at the Oasis make a grand night of the occasion by treating themselves to the most celebratory of all restaurant meals, surf and turf, which is such a house specialty that an entire section of the menu is devoted to its various permutations. Prime rib or sirloin are available with lobster tails, fried or sautéed prawns, scallops, or grilled oysters.

Breakfast at The Oasis is a roll-your-sleeves-up kind of meal, served all day with the exception of pancakes and biscuits, which are available only until 11 A.M. The biscuits are extraordinary, a single order consisting of three behemoths and a cascade of thick gravy. This is a meal of caloric content suited to the eater who plans to flex muscles all day.

Pacific Oyster

150 Oyster Dr.   503-377-2323
Bay City, OR   BLD (closed Sat) | $$

Just off 101, past piles of oyster shells and out a spit of pier into the water, there is an oyster processing plant where local mollusks are shelled, canned, and sent into the grocery food chain. One small part of this vast operation is devoted to a seafood market and sit-down deli/oyster bar where you can eat like a king at common man's prices.

It's as casual as can be: bare tables, menus listed on the wall, a waitstaff who will treat you like an old friend whether you like it or not. We love the range of available dishes, which includes all kinds of raw oysters—mediums, petites, or the alluring little Kumamotos—freshly opened and served on the half shell or in shot glasses for easy gulping. And of course, there is oyster stew, fried oysters, and even an oyster burger (four fried ones on a bun). Beyond oysters, you can get crab cakes, steamers by the pound, fish and chips, a cheesy crab melt sandwich on a croissant, shrimp or crab Louis, and fillets of salmon or halibut.

We were especially smitten by salmon sticks, which are, as the name suggests, skinny two-foot-long staffs of salmon smoked to salty-sweet deliciousness. The sticks are available in ordinary smoky flavor as well as mesquite, Cajun, and teriyaki. You gnaw on them like tender beef jerky.

Just to try another regional specialty, we ordered a grilled cheese sandwich, made with locally produced Tillamook Cheddar. Fabulous! Creamy, authoritative cheese melting out of generously buttered bread just slightly flattened and well-crisped from its tenure on the grill.

Reo's Ribs

17385 S.W. Tualatin Valley Hwy.   503-310-3600

Aloha, OR   LD | $$

Appetizing smoke signals emanate from huge cookers at the side of the front parking lot, where Reo's pit man uses a garden hose to spritz the exterior of the metal drums so they smoke all the more and infuse ribs and brisket with intense pit flavor.

Lured inside by the scent, we found spectacular barbecue: certainly the best ribs we've eaten west of Chicago, maybe the best ribs anywhere. They are big, muscular spare ribs, not the weenie-size baby backs that, by comparison, seem all too easy to eat. Meat does not fall from these bones. You tug it off with your teeth or sauce-drenched fingers. It is a pleasure to chew, radiating tidal waves of flavor from Reo's vibrant sauce.

Beyond ribs, Reo's is a bonanza of soul-food barbecue that reflects the proprietor's Southern roots. Side dishes include collard and mustard greens simmered with ham hocks, fried okra, red beans and rice, butter-sopped yams, and macaroni and cheese, plus big hunks of freshly made corn bread for the side and sweet-potato pie for dessert.

Sundays feature an all-you-can-eat barbecue buffet. Reo told us that he has some customers in the 800-to-900-pound range. "I'm scared when I see them come in," he said. "They eat rack after rack of ribs and pounds of brisket. But they leave some for others. Last week, one ate so much he crashed through a chair." In a strange way, we enjoyed hearing these stories of outrageous gluttony. By comparison, our eating habits are positively demure.

Bakeman's

122 Cherry St.   206-622-3375
Seattle, WA   L | $

Seattle has a booming restaurant scene, with new and exotic places opening all the time. Bakeman's is not new and is as non-exotic as can be, but
it happens to be one of the great urban Roadfood restaurants anywhere.

A working-class cafeteria with a menu that is pretty much limited to
soup and sandwiches, it is open only for lunch, Monday through Friday.
No reservations, no credit cards. You come to Bakeman's for turkey or
meat loaf on white or whole wheat: sandwich perfection. The bread is
homemade, stacked up at one end of the cafeteria line. It is not spectacular bread on its own, not like some elegant French baguette. It is bread
for sandwiches: tender slices that come to life when spread with mayo
and/or mustard and/or cranberry and/or shredded lettuce, then heaped
with turkey or slabs of meat loaf.

If meat loaf is your dish, we recommend it on whole wheat with catsup and shredded lettuce. The meat is tightly packed but tender, gently
spiced, and has a delicious aroma. As for turkey, get it any way you like,
because this is superb, *real,* carved-from-the-bird turkey with homey fla-

vor. The dark meat is lush; the white meat is moist and aromatic; either variety has an occasional piece of skin still attached, a nice reminder of just how real it is. The way we like it is, in the words of the countermen who hustle things along at breakneck pace, "white on white; M & M," which means white meat turkey on white bread with mustard and mayonnaise. You can also get it dressed with shredded lettuce and an order of cranberry relish. Turkey sandwiches get no better than this!

Bakeman's offers a couple of good soups each day, such as turkey noodle or beef vegetable plus a nice chili or, on one memorable occasion, Chinese eggflower—an egg drop variation. There are Waldorf and potato salads and such, but they aren't all that interesting. And dessert can be wonderful—carrot cake, cookies, or chocolate or lemon poppy seed cake, sliced like bread.

Beth's Café

7311 Aurora Ave. N   206-782-5588
Seattle, WA   always open | $

Not a restaurant for the faint of heart, Beth's serves gigantic portions of heavyweight breakfast in a truck-stop atmosphere of cigarette smoke and in-your-face Crayola art/graffiti on the walls. Because it is open round-the-clock, it is a *very* interesting place in the wee hours of the morning when people who haven't slept all night pile into booths and onto counter stools to coffee-up and chow down after doing whatever they've been doing.

The king of the menu is truly ridiculous—a dozen-egg omelet so immense it must be served on a pizza pan rather than a plate. Like its smaller brethren (there are six-eggers, and regular-size, too), it comes with crunchy/greasy hash browns and, if desired, bacon prepared the old-fashioned way, i.e., pressed flat on the grill as it cooks. Biscuits and gravy is another strapping plate of breakfast; and there are plenty of familiar entrees such as steak and eggs, pancakes, waffles, French toast, and what is known on the menu as a "mini-breakfast" of ham and eggs, potatoes, and toast—a meal most people would call normal.

Beth's big breakfasts are served all the time, but there is also a lunch menu of chili with raw onions, hamburgers with onion rings or French fries, and even salads.

Warning: There will be a long wait to eat at Beth's on Sunday morning.

The Crumpet Shop

1503 1st Ave.   206-682-1598

Seattle, WA   BL | $

Here is a great place to ready yourself for a day of grazing around Seattle's Pike Place Market. For a quarter century, The Crumpet Shop has been a First Avenue fixture known for crumpets, tea, and an al fresco atmosphere in earshot of the Market.

As you might guess, crumpets are the specialty of the house, a specialty we've come across nowhere else in our travels around America. As made here, a crumpet is vaguely like an English muffin, except it is made from a batter that is poured on a grill. The result is a thick round of bread that is chewy, rich-flavored, and begs to be heaped with melting butter and jelly or marmalade.

The Crumpet Shop serves crumpets all day along, for they are suitable fare at breakfast and lunch, or as an afternoon snack. You can get them simply buttered, or with a choice from among nearly two dozen different sorts of toppings, including honey, Nutella, local jams, and pesto-colored eggs with ham. On the side, have a cup of cappuccino or, better yet, imported tea. If crumpets are not your cup of tea, The Crumpet Shop also bakes terrific loaves of bread, including a rugged groat bread that is an apt foundation for a sandwich.

If you are visiting Seattle, consider buying edible or potable souvenirs at The Crumpet Shop. Its shelves are filled with exotic teas from around the world as well as honeys and preserves, oatmeals, grains, and cereals from the Northwest and the British Isles. Crumpets are available, too, already cooked: sold by the six-pack, ready to take home, heat, and eat.

Emmett Watson's Oyster Bar

1916 Pike Pl., Suite 16   206-622-7721

Seattle, WA   LD | $$

Oyster lovers, take note of this pint-size café just across the street from the Pike Place Market in a back street nook inside the Soames-Dunn Building. It's a laid-back treasure known to bivalve-and-beer cognoscenti, where the ambience is as much fun as the oysters. There is a sunny, flower-adorned courtyard behind the building for warm-weather dining at rickety little tables, and an indoor area with booths protected from the weather.

Few people come to Emmett Watson's eat a serious meal; the point is to linger over many beers, and many dozens of freshly opened Quilcines, Shoalwater Bays, Minterbrooks, or Canterburies on the half shell. For bigger appetites there are platters of fish and chips, smoked salmon with sweet and sour mustard, smoked trout with homemade dill mayonnaise, even Hangtown fry omelets in the morning, most accompanied by good French bread and butter. When there is a chill in the air, the dish we like best is one of the house soups: clam and salmon, or shrimp soup Orleans, a spicy gumbo made with tomatoes, garlic, and loads of small shrimp. Utensils are plastic, plates are paper, but the flavors of the food, and the smell and sound of the market just outside and upwind, are impeccably authentic.

14 Carrot Café

2305 Eastlake Ave. E   206-324-1442
Seattle, WA   BLD | $

Ownership of the 14 Carrot Café has changed a few times since we first wrote about it back in the late 1970s, but its character (and menu) remains familiar and eater-friendly. If there is such a thing as a typical Seattle café, this is it: casual and comfortably disheveled, nutritionally enlightened, and perfumed inside and out by coffee. One new feature, for those who are in desperate need of a quick caffeine fix when there are no seats available inside (a likely situation on weekend mornings) is barista John Hornall's coffee cart on the sidewalk outside. Seattle's coffee cognoscenti consider the latte from this particular cart to be the city's best.

Although lunch is served every day, and it includes some excellent salads and soups as well as vegetarian plates and no-beef hamburgers, most fans of the 14 Carrot Café consider it a breakfast place. Omelets are big and beautiful, served with good hash browns and a choice of toast, English muffin, or streusel-topped coffee cake. The coffee cake itself is something to behold: a moist crumble-topped block, served with a sphere of butter as big as a Ping-Pong ball. Other notable breadstuffs include blueberry muffins and cinnamon rolls. The latter, described as "large and gooey" by our waiter, is a vast doughy spiral with clods of raisins and veins of dark sugar packed into its warm furrows. It, too, comes blobbed with a ball of melting butter.

If eggs aren't your dish, how about hotcakes, sourdough or regular, with sliced bananas, apple slivers, or blueberries, with bacon on the side or cooked into the cakes? You can order hot oats with soy milk, dates and cashews, homemade granola, sourdough French toast, or a grand version of French toast known as Tahitian toast, gilded with a thin layer of sesame butter.

Frank's Diner

1516 W. 2nd Ave.   509-747-8798
Spokane, WA   BLD | $

Frank's Diner is an amazing-looking place. Located in Seattle from 1931 to 1991, then trucked to its current location in Spokane, it really did start life as a railroad car. For the last several decades it has served as a hash house with a traditional counter providing a view of the short-order cook at work.

Handsome as it is, the *truly spectacular* sight at Frank's is its King of the Road omelet. Made from six eggs and accompanied by a more than ample pile of hash browns, plus toast, it enfolds Cheddar and Swiss cheese, ham, peppers, and sweet onions. If your appetite is a healthy one, but not quite immense enough to deal with a half-dozen eggs and a few pounds of filling, we suggest you consider Frank's Joe's Special. To serious West Coast eaters, the name "Joe," when used to describe any egg dish, is reminiscent of the San Francisco Italianate meal known as a "New Joe Special," for which eggs and ground beef are scrambled together, usually with peppers, onions, and cheese. Frank's Joe's Special is a mere three eggs with ground beef, spinach, and onion and flavored with Parmesan cheese. There are plenty of normal-size breakfasts, too, from hefty biscuits and gravy to eggs Benedict, and from silver-dollar pancakes to French toast made with cinnamon-swirl bread. The breakfast menu boasts that Frank's serves 12,000 eggs per month.

We were clued in to Frank's Diner by a Washington State tipster named Charlie, who told us that breakfast is the best meal to eat at Frank's; but we have to say that the lunch selection has never let us down. It includes, and we quote from the menu, "the best hot turkey sandwich ever," made from turkey roasted in Frank's kitchen, as well as a grilled meat loaf sandwich, chicken pot pie, and a large assortment of one-third-pound Vista Cruiser Burgers made with assorted combinations of cheese, dressings, bacon, and barbecue sauce.

Julia's of Wallingford

1714 N. 44th St.   206-633-1175
Seattle, WA   BLD | $

Julia's is an art gallery, a bakery (adjoining), a bare-table coffee shop, a sunny juice bar, a bustling lunchroom, and best of all, a breakfast place. The art on the walls is always changing, but not the menu. For years, this cozy café has offered a large and reliable choice of morning meals that range from fried eggs with potatoes and toast to vegetables sautéed in sesame oil and soy sauce, with fresh-squeezed juice and espresso on the side.

Vegetarian-friendly Julia's offers breakfast of scrambled tofu chunks with scallions and mushrooms as well as whole-wheat and sourdough pancakes. We love the big breakfast burrito and orange French toast so much that we don't even miss bacon or sausage on the side. At lunch or supper, meat-frowners can enjoy soba noodle salad or terrific Greek salad, vegan all-vegetable soup, tofu steak, or black bean cakes, as well as a variety of meatless pastas. And nearly everyone likes to start a big meal here with a plate of hummus, including pita bread for dipping, Greek olives, and sprouts.

It is not necessary to be a vegetarian to like Julia's, for this accommodating kitchen also cooks up all-beef hamburgers, fried fish, and grilled chicken with or without Caesar salad. And you *can* have bacon with your scrambled eggs! To drink, in addition to an array of juices, you can select from a list of Northwest wines and microbrew beers.

Warning: Weekend brunch is huge, and you will likely wait for a table.

Knapp's Family Restaurant

2707 N. Proctor   253-759-9009
Tacoma, WA   BLD | $

All kinds of people give us all kinds of suggestions of places to eat; but when one of the nation's great restaurateurs tells us where to go, we pay special attention. It was Hap Townes, who for many years ran an estimable cafeteria-style lunch room in Nashville, Tennessee, who tipped us off to Knapp's. "It's your kind of place," Hap said with assurance born of watching us eat many of his fine meals.

The setting of Knapp's in the Proctor district helps create an aura of small-town charm in the midst of big-city life. Walking in is like going back half a century. The dining room is patrolled by teams of waitresses who wait tables for a living—pros, who refill coffee and replace needed silverware with the grace of a four-star sommelier.

The menu is nostalgic, too. This is a place to have a platter of liver and onions or turkey with sage-flavored dressing and a pile of mashed potatoes with a ladle of gravy on top. Every Tuesday, Knapp's serves corned beef and cabbage, every Wednesday, roast pork loin. Begin your meal with a shrimp cocktail or an iceberg-lettuce salad topped with thick dressing, and top it off with homemade peach pie. It is an all-American experience, not necessarily for the fussy epicure, but a treasure for aficionados of square meals.

Maltby Café

8809 Maltby Rd.	425-483-3123
Snohomish, WA	BL | $

If ever we write a book called *Really Big Food*, the Maltby Café would be featured for breakfast. Its cinnamon roll is not so much a "roll" as it is a loaf—a massive circular coil of sweet pastry scattered with bits of walnut. It is served on a dinner plate, which it fits edge to edge, and it is at least a couple of good breakfasts unto itself.

You must get a cinnamon roll at the Maltby Café, but there are some other terrific meals, too; and while none are quite so flabbergastingly immense, all are satisfying in the extreme. The Maltby omelet, for example, is another plate-filler, loaded with ham, beef, peppers, and onions. Maltby oatmeal is served with melted butter running all over the top of the bowl; the French toast is double-thick; and—lest we forget—the strawberry jam on every table is homemade.

After breakfast, there is lunch, which looks good . . . although we must admit that cinnamon rolls and omelets have pretty much put lunch out of the question for us. The menu includes pasta plates, homemade soup, and a piled-high hot Reuben sandwich.

The Maltby Café is a most unusual place (a former school cafeteria) in an amazing little town of nostalgic mise-en-scènes that include strategically situated old farm machinery, a few windmills, and uncounted numbers of vintage gasoline station signs. Other than the café, the town has a few knickknack shops and a drive-thru espresso stand shaped like a big gulp cup.

Yankee Pot Roast

4400 E. 4th Plain Blvd.   360-694-0988
Vancouver, WA   BLD | $$

Yankee Pot Roast is a theme restaurant, the theme being Sunday supper at grandma's house. Several years ago we went to a same-named place down in Grants Pass, Oregon, and it had a similar look, with a setting that verges on oppressively grandmotherly, including thick shag rugs, Victorian advertisements and sentimental pictures on the walls, and waitresses in long frilly dresses and aprons.

No surprise: The featured attraction on the menu, the eponymous pot roast, is the best thing to eat. This is fine meat—fall-apart tender, moist and full-flavored. You can have it as dinner on a plate with good mashed potatoes and dark gravy with soft-cooked buttery carrots on the side or inside a big hero roll with au jus on the side. With the dinner— and with such other old-fashioned family suppers as meat loaf, chicken-fried steak, and pork chops—everyone gets a crusty-topped biscuit, still hot and served by spatula direct from the baking pan. To complement the steamy sweet biscuit, tables are set with ramekins of marmalade and strawberry jam.

The menu goes way beyond Sunday supper. Yankee Pot Roast serves a variety of chiliburgers, cheeseburgers, and baconburgers, even a halibut burger for the meat-frowner. For breakfast, you have your choice from among 101 different omelets. Like the pot roast dinners and just about everything else served in this oversize place, the omelets are immense. You won't leave this grandma's house hungry.

New England